BETWEEN
TWO WORLDS

BETWEEN TWO WORLDS

Policy, Press, and Public Opinion in Asian-American Relations

BY John Hohenberg

PUBLISHED FOR THE
Council on Foreign Relations

FREDERICK A. PRAEGER, *Publishers*
New York · Washington · London

FREDERICK A. PRAEGER, PUBLISHERS
111 Fourth Avenue, New York, N.Y. 10003, U.S.A.
77–79 Charlotte Street, London W. 1, England

Published in the United States of America in 1967
by Frederick A. Praeger, Inc., Publishers

Library of Congress Catalog Card Number: 66–21781

Printed in the United States of America

Another for Dorothy

Preface

THE POSSIBILITIES FOR better understanding between the peoples of Asia and the United States have been viewed with mixed emotions, ranging from impatience to despair. Differences in background, culture, appearance, and language; in history, philosophy, and ordinary customs have led many well-meaning persons on both continents to conclude that a genuine understanding, no matter how desirable, will be most difficult to achieve. The belligerence of the Chinese Communists, important though it is, represents but one factor in the equation of uneasy relationships.

The frustrations of the West, in this respect, may be summed up by the exasperation of an American journalist in New Delhi who observed recently, "What can we do? We lead, but they don't often follow." Or, as Finley Peter Dunne's Mr. Dooley remarked in an inspired moment on the results of Commodore Perry's mission to Japan more than a century ago: "Whin we rapped on the dure, we didn't go in, they come out." And, of course, "they" have been coming out ever since to take their proper place in the world.

Those in the United States who have scant hope of finding common ground with the peoples of Asian nations are likely to forget that despite our vaunted common heritage with Europe, we still have no Atlantic community after fifty years of global war and its diplomatic extensions. Moreover, for those others who believe Asians will be faithful only to their own and will band together against the white man and all his works, it can scarcely be said that the two most populous powers in Asia, India and Communist China, live in a happy relationship. The relations between India and Pakistan are scarcely inspiring. Nor does the strongest power in Asia, the Soviet Union, have much in common with the Chinese Communists despite their Marxist heritage; since the Treaty of Nerchinsk, which brought them into diplomatic relationship for the first time in 1689, they have been rivals far more often than they have been allies.

All over Asia, around the seas, mountains, rivers, and naked plains that mark the boundaries between independent nations and the Communist colossi, there is a longing, sometimes even a hunger, for more information about the United States.

Sometimes the feeling is based on the understandable curiosity of millions of underprivileged and often semiliterate people who are becoming conscious for the first time of a far-off country whose future is insensibly intermingled with that of their own. Sometimes it is stimulated by the yearning of some young person for wider horizons and greater opportunities than he sees at home. Sometimes it is the irritated reaction of an intellectual or a member of an opinion-forming elite in government who feels his country and his people are being ignored by the United States.

But in no case and at no level of public consciousness, except for the illiterates who are outside the public communications network of their own country, are the peoples of Asia indifferent to what is going on in the United States and to the intricate and little understood processes through which American public opinion is shaped. Friend, foe, and neutralist alike echo the familiar complaint: "We receive so little news about the United States and you receive so little news about us. How can we hope to understand each other better?"

It is a problem that was posed over and over again during my sabbatical leave from Columbia University in 1963, when my wife and I journeyed 12,000 miles through seven Asian countries. At odd times during our six months of wandering through thirty-five cities (I was a lecturer in the State Department's American Specialist program and spoke some 250 times before about 10,000 people), I discussed this apparent news gap with all kinds of people. Among them were Asian government officials, editors and publishers, college and university presidents, deans, professors, and students, American diplomats, United States Information Service personnel, foreign correspondents, and people approached at random on the streets.

No one had any clear notion of what could be attempted to stimulate a greater and more meaningful exchange of news, opinions, and ideas between the United States and Asian nations beyond what is now done. Knowledgeable authorities conceded that the wire services and the correspondents serving the media on both continents now send much more than can be used in most instances, that space in newspapers is not limitless, that time on both TV and radio must be measured in terms of

electronic interest, that both news and prestige weeklies in whatever
language cannot turn handsprings over Asian-American relations in
every issue.

For all that, there was fairly general agreement that the end result of
this expensive communication between the United States and Asia left
a great deal to be desired and that considerable improvement could be
made. Out of such necessarily disjointed fragments of many conversations and a fair amount of reading and thought, some suggestions
emerged for a more systematic study of the problem.

It was my good fortune to be invited by the Council on Foreign
Relations to conduct such an inquiry with the help of a distinguished
study group, headed by Philip Horton.

The basis of the inquiry was an assumption that the shaping of foreign policy in an open society could be critically affected by the work of
the foreign correspondent, his editor, and, indeed, the press and radio-
TV media as a whole. During the course of the study, it was found that
this assumption was eminently correct today, just as it had been at various other times during the two centuries of the foreign correspondent's
existence as an independent force.

In the tangled affairs of East, Southeast, and South Asia, in fact, the
interaction of journalism and diplomacy was even more marked than
elsewhere for many reasons, the most important being the involvement
of the United States in the Viet-Nam war. In Japan and India, no less
than in the United States, the influence of the press on the governmental process was so evident that it could not be disputed. One could not
brush aside, with an official denial, the work of the correspondents in
Saigon, even if some were young and overly emotional, when they told
the truth about the failure of the "strategic hamlet" program in South
Viet-Nam and the government of the United States failed at first to do
so. Nor could any official in Washington, Tokyo, or New Delhi afford
to overlook the considered views of such newspapers as the Washington
Post, Asahi, or the *Times* of India, to name only three. There were
many more in these and other countries that exercised a powerful influence on public opinion.

Despite the importance of the press in foreign policy, little attention
has been given it by students of international affairs. Furthermore, as
the study progressed, it became appallingly clear that the processes
through which the independent press operated and reached its judgments were even less understood by many a government policy-maker
than even the mysterious workings of the broad mass of public opinion
of which it is a part. Because of this lack of understanding, government
officials often chose either to shrug off the press as an overrated influ-

ence or to shut themselves off from inquiring foreign correspondents. Correspondents in Asia still chuckle over the American ambassador who refused to see two of their number, both representatives of outstanding newspapers, because—as he said in a verbal message—it was not in the interest of the government of the United States for him to speak to them.

The influence of the press in foreign affairs has grown immeasurably in this century. The United States alone has more correspondents abroad today than at any time in the past two decades; a greater number, certainly, than at any time in its history except during World War II. The rise of the news magazines and of television—potentially the greatest force of all—reinforced the power of the mass media. The performance of the press on both sides of the Pacific is likely, in the long run, to influence decisively the future of the democratic experiment in Japan, India, the Philippines, and elsewhere in Asia as well.

These were the compelling reasons for this study of the exchange of news, opinions, and ideas between the United States and the nations of East, Southeast, and South Asia. Because there were no guidelines or models to follow for this research, I was very much on my own.

Consequently, following my 1963 journey, my wife and I set out once more for Asia in the summer of 1964 and for four months traveled even farther than we had in the previous year. An examination of my two dozen thick notebooks shows that I interviewed more than 300 persons before returning to New York. Included were heads of foreign states and foreign ministers, some American ambassadors and ministers and their principal political and information officers, foreign correspondents, editors and bureau chiefs for American and other news media, heads of press institutes, university professors, and students. With the generous assistance of a number of correspondents for American news-gathering organizations and their editors, I was able to collect nearly 100 detailed questionnaires on the work of such reporters in Asia. In the United States, Japan, and Great Britain, a score of Asian correspondents with American experience filled out the same questionnaire or talked with me at length. I also interviewed British, French, and other foreign nationals who worked for non-American news-gathering media.

During my journey and after my return, I worked with my wife on a comparative content analysis of the leaders of the Asian and American press, a far too ambitious project for the resources at my command. But it helped my study.

During 1965 and 1966, I had some fruitful discussions with members of my study group and a great deal of help from its individual members, some of them old friends. In addition, I had assistance from every major independent news-gathering organization interested in the dissemination of news to and from Asia, from the Department of State and the United States Information Agency, and from members of the Washington press corps, both American and foreign.

This book is the result. Of course I assume full responsibility for its contents, absolving all others of blame, but I must confess that I could never have done it by myself. So many helped, and I feel deeply obligated, as a result. The process of this kind of authorship amounts to a considerable deflation of the ego.

A few words about the focus of the study. Originally, the title was "U.S.-Asian Communications." It was described then as an examination of the flow of news between the United States and the nations of Asia. It was a forbidding concept. Somehow, I kept thinking of the editor standing like Moses at Meribah, raising his rod (the reporter) and at the Lord's command smiting the rock (a news source), bringing forth a pure and sparkling stream of news that refreshed the multitude. Unfortunately, I knew of no editors who possessed so convenient an alliance with Divine Providence, so another and far more complicated image formed in my mind. It was a variation of an old children's game—a chain of people passing a spoken message one to the other, with each interpreting it to the other and giving it a different meaning or emphasis, so that at the end the input and the output were seldom identical. That seemed to me to be far more realistic, although the news scarcely flowed, and few could be refreshed by it.

What I am getting at is that aside from the technicalities of journalism, the exchange of news (which includes ideas and opinions) between the United States and Asia is a political act. There is, as a result, an unending struggle between the independent news media and the governments directly and indirectly concerned for the control of it, in some cases, and influence over it, in others. It has been so for the wellnigh 200 years of foreign correspondence as an independent force, responsible to its managers and its particular publics. Moreover, with the exception of spot events such as storms and wrecks, news does not materialize out of nowhere. Somebody acts to create it; in the realm of international affairs, that somebody, more often than not, is in government.

It follows that what seemed at the outset like a rather simple inquiry became enormously complicated as I proceeded with my research. And when I began to write, at last, I was beset with doubts as I always am—a reflex action, probably, after the many years of quick and self-assured composition for newspaper deadlines. At that point, I think I might have bogged down had it not been for the calm and hard-headed advice given to me by Henry M. Wriston at the outset of my work for the Council. In effect, he warned me against letting statistics, measurements, and conflicting claims dominate my work. "I want to know what you think," he said. "Don't be afraid to write your own opinion, regardless of all else, and don't worry about controversy." I have tried.

It gives me a great deal of pleasure, therefore, to acknowledge my debt to Henry Wriston. I also wish to thank Grayson Kirk, Joseph E. Johnson, and Caryl P. Haskins for their support, which helped me carry on a difficult and demanding work. To Philip E. Mosely, who first suggested this study while he was the Council's director of research, I express my gratitude for his many kindnesses. After his return to Columbia University to become Associate Dean of the School of International Affairs, W. Phillips Davison assumed the direction of my study with the help of David W. MacEachron, Director of Program. Both were invariably helpful and encouraging and made many excellent suggestions. To Rob Valkenier, the Council's editor, I also acknowledge a profound debt for his preparation of the manuscript for publication.

I could not have gone very far, however, without the assistance, individually and collectively, of the members of my Study Group. I profited immeasurably from their spirited discussions and from the many contributions they made to my efforts during our meetings and afterward. Its members were: Philip Horton, chairman, Peter Black, Robert Blum, Hugh N. Boyd, John K. Cooley, Louis G. Cowan, W. Phillips Davison, Tillman Durdin, Arthur J. Dommen, Vernon A. Eagle, Emanuel R. Freedman, George F. Gant, Teg C. Grondahl, Harold R. Isaacs, Joseph L. Jones, David W. MacEachron, Clifford B. Marshall, Norman D. Palmer, Herbert Passin, A. M. Rosenthal, Paul C. Sherbert, Watson S. Sims, Stanley Swinton, and Kenneth T. Young, Jr. Richard Halloran and Everett Kelsey were the *rapporteurs,* and Pang Woon-yiu came from Harvard, where he was a Nieman Fellow, to help at one session. I thank them all, and, in particular, Herbert Passin for his help with the section of this work that deals with Japan.

Juris Pirvics, the holder of three degrees from Columbia University and now a candidate for his Ph.D. in mechanical engineering there, shared in the content analysis of the English-language newspapers, American and others. Gyo Hani, of the Japan *Times,* and Kazumasa Iinuma, of the *Asahi Shimbun,* did the Japanese newspaper content analysis and the headline translations, respectively. Once again I acknowledge my debt to the Columbia Graduate School of Journalism and Dean Edward W. Barrett for their support of my work, and to Wade Doares, our Journalism Library chief, for his expert assistance. To J. Montgomery Curtis and Walter Everett, of the American Press Institute, who referred me to so many distinguished API alumni abroad with salutary results, I say thank you. It was a pleasure.

It is impossible here to name all the distinguished American Foreign Service Officers and other State Department officials, the foreign correspondents for American and foreign news-gathering organizations, and the editors and publishers at home and abroad who helped me with this work. In addition to my gratitude, I also express the hope that they will consider the result to be worth their effort.

Finally, Dorothy Lannuier Hohenberg, my favorite editor, researcher, and traveling companion, shared both pleasures and a lot of hard work during this experience, particularly in going over the manuscript and in the time-consuming analysis of newspaper content. It must have required all her cheerfulness and professional know-how to keep going through some of those interminable sessions with piles upon piles of newspapers. I express my deepest appreciation to her once again. What we called the "Asian study" was a high point for us both.

JOHN HOHENBERG

Columbia University
New York City

Contents

BETWEEN
TWO WORLDS

Introduction

THE 1960's HAVE been lean years for American foreign policy in Asia thus far. While there have been a few successes, the failures have been far more spectacular and therefore have drawn the largest headlines, the most air time, and the greatest editorial anguish. It has been an unhappy era for the Department of State, never a particular haven of joy, and a time of troubles for the White House.

In consequence, around the bristling arc of crisis from Korea to the Indian subcontinent, American diplomacy too often has been forced on the defensive—an irritating role for the many proud and capable officers in our foreign service. Most of them have hung on grimly, hoping for a turn of the tide. But in the process even the most patient of them now and then have sought an outlet for their pent-up frustrations. It is scarcely a surprise, therefore, that they have attempted more often than not to attach a share of the blame for the shortcomings of foreign policy to the most visible source of their torment, the press.

The correspondents of American news organizations in Asia and their editors have reacted in an understandable manner. Many of the correspondents either mistrust the "guidance" they are offered on American policies or don't even bother to ask for it. Some take a rather exaggerated and sometimes foolish pride in saying that they hardly depend on American embassies and are well able to fend for themselves. Their editors seem pleased with their independence, although that in itself is no guarantee of superior performance.

There are, of course, exceptions to this mutually critical stance. There are a few members of the American foreign service who have been able to retain the respect of the press for their work in Asia without forfeiting the confidence of their superiors, a feat of diplomacy in itself. There

3

are also a few correspondents whose work is so highly valued by the diplomatic corps that they are sought out as trustworthy purveyors of information and sound analysis.

Essentially, however, there has been no slackening in the historic conflict between the government and the independent press. As every correspondent knows, the diplomat almost always has an ingrained doubt about the necessity for revealing bad news to the public and risking a loss of support. And as every diplomat knows, the correspondent almost always is looking for a story, particularly one that has been suppressed, for a variety of motives, some not always creditable.

In its least selfish form, the basis for this continuing rivalry was set forth best by Dean Acheson on his next-to-last day in office as Secretary of State, in January, 1953. James Reston, of the New York *Times,* had come to see him to ask why they hadn't gotten along better, and Acheson said: "To some extent, your purposes and mine are the same, since both involve public information and education. But in other respects they are antithetic. The modern development of the old newspaper 'beat'—being first with the news—is to anticipate the news, to report what is *going to happen*. This aspect of your job can be disastrous to mine. For instance, if I am about to go abroad to persuade another foreign secretary to agree to something which I wish to discuss with him first in complete confidence, your job would be served by discovering and reporting my plan. But this would frustrate my purpose. So it is fair, and should be understood, that your job requires you to pry; and mine requires me to keep secret." [1]

Yet, it would be folly to dismiss the inherent dangers of such a relationship in an age when missiles can carry atomic destruction to millions of people within minutes. There is something greater at stake than the old distinction between the public's "right to know" and its "need to know." It is, quite bluntly, national survival. Never before in world history has there been such a compulsion to publicize the highest national values, to enlarge upon the might of American deterrent power, to "signal" the enemy by every means of communication, private and public.

It follows, therefore, that the mass media—the newspapers and news agencies, the news magazines and electronic communications—have entered upon a more sensitive relationship with the government. In a bitter outburst after the failure of the Bay of Pigs invasion of Cuba, James Reston argued that the "press was debased for the government's purpose," that both the Castro regime and its Soviet advisers knew from the first what was going on, and that "the American people were the only ones to be fooled."

"No doubt," he concluded, "the press does have to learn greater restraint than in the days when the United States was an isolated country, but the government has to do the same. For the truth that makes men free is very often the truth they do not like to hear and also the truth that the government does not like to see published, either." [2]

Whether the press practices more self-restraint or not, and there is no evidence of substance to show that editors believe such an effort to be necessary, it is scarcely possible that any move made by the American government can be kept a state secret for very long. For if the press has greater international responsibilities in this age, certainly the President of the United States and his Secretary of State also are involved in a widening aspect of foreign policy. They must do more than formulate it and find a consensus for it in the executive and legislative branches of the government. They must also sell their policies in the marketplace of public opinion here and abroad, with friend and foe and curious by-standers alike looking over their shoulders.

In a very real sense, this process represents the growth of what, for want of a better term, may be called public diplomacy—although the old-fashioned journalist will insist on identifying it merely as bigger news management. He may have a point. But the government meanwhile must continue to inform, prod, and persuade a bemused public if its foreign policies are to be understood and supported at home. It is an unlooked-for extension of Woodrow Wilson's "open covenants openly arrived at," a policy to which, incidentally, he never adhered. Even if he had, he could scarcely have contemplated the extent to which his successors would have to court public opinion. Nor could he have foreseen the grievous process of trial and error—and propaganda—that would be involved in such projections of foreign policy as President Eisenhower's in Korea, President Kennedy's in Cuba, and President Johnson's in Viet-Nam.

It is time, therefore, to inquire with sympathy and with care into the relationship between foreign correspondence and foreign policy, particularly as it exists in Asia. That, in brief, is the purpose of this book. In the twenty-five years since Pearl Harbor, the United States has waged war three times in Asia, at enormous costs. During the four-year Pacific campaigns of World War II, 41,000 Americans were killed; in the three years of the Korean conflict, another 33,000 died. In Viet-Nam, as well as in the rest of Southeast Asia, the end is not in sight. That in itself is sufficient reason to be concerned over the kind of knowledge we have of Asia, and the extent of Asian information about us.

There are, to be sure, as many Asias as there are peoples. In the pages that follow, their problems and aspirations are of paramount interest, their leaders of major consequence. But of equal importance are the American policy-makers, the diplomats, military strategists, propagandists, editors, publishers, radio-TV commentators, and foreign correspondents at home and abroad. Their skills, integrity, judgment, and responsibility determine with abruptness and finality what 190 million Americans are usually told about Asia, and they have an effect on what Asians are told about us. Among them are few heroes and no villains of whom I am aware, but far more men of wisdom and discernment than one would suppose—and not many fools.

The tensions, the rivalry, and some of the unflattering attitudes that separate them are facts of life, particularly in the rising conflicts over Asia, and must be faced. But these things will scarcely lead to the undoing of the republic, however distracting the continuing debate may be. If there is any saving grace in this disorderly communications array, it is in the contrast with the dismal Communist conformity that makes an automaton of a diplomat and a parrot of a journalist. It is utterly unnatural and an affront to people who are bound to have honest differences of opinion.

This work seeks no consensus. It is a study in argument and diversity, in the sometimes frightening cacophony of a democratic society. It is addressed to an international audience. It is about people of gallantry and conviction. It is told, I hope, with respect for their opinions, a decent restraint, and not too much solemnity—the curse of a mechanized age. It celebrates the patient and sometimes painful effort of men of good will to seek the truth. It is dedicated to the hope of a better understanding among peoples in a peaceful world.

I

The Spinning of the Web

1. "AMERICA, AMERICA . . ."

F ROM THE FARTHEST OUTPOSTS of battle at the end of World War II, the two thousand correspondents who had followed the American flag to victory saw the United States at the apex of its power. It was the leader of a triumphant confederation against the oppressors of mankind, the sole possessor of the atomic bomb, the forge of Vulcan that had created the mightiest military machine ever seen on earth. There was, indeed, cause for rejoicing "from sea to shining sea."

Having reported on the appalling wreckage that Allied arms had wrought in Germany and Italy during the conclusion of the European conflict, correspondents now strode through the atomic wasteland of Hiroshima and Nagasaki and the fire-bombed ruins of Tokyo. It was patent that the Axis aggressors would never rise again. To add to the sweetness of victory, there was a profound and moving tribute from a Japanese member of the surrender party who faced General Douglas MacArthur, the Supreme Commander, on the deck of the battleship "Missouri" in Tokyo Bay. In reporting to Emperor Hirohito on the painful proceedings that momentous September 2, 1945, Toshikazu Kase wrote:

Indeed, a distance inexpressible by numbers separates us—America from Japan. After all, we were not beaten on the battlefield by dint of superior arms. We were defeated in the spiritual contest by virtue of a nobler idea. The real issue was moral—beyond all the powers of algebra to compute.

The day will come when recorded time, age on age, will seem but a point in retrospect. However, happen what may in the future, this Big Day on the "Missouri" will stand out as one of the brightest dates in his-

7

tory, with General MacArthur as a shining obelisk in the desert of human endeavor that marks a timeless march onward toward an enduring peace.[1]

What could be better calculated to please the American people than the assurance of their moral righteousness, particularly from a leader of the enemy (who happened to be an alumnus of Amherst and Harvard and a diplomat with twenty years' service in the Japanese foreign office)? True, dangerous forces were still at large in the world. Not all the editorial voices were silent over the ominous presence of Soviet armies on the Elbe, casting a long shadow across Western Europe. Nor could all the paeans to victory still the fear of Communism as it was practiced in the Soviet Union and elsewhere—a fear produced in part by a quarter-century of public education in the right wing press. But these things were reduced to mere editorial murmurs at the time and quickly drowned out in the uproar of celebration over the end of the war.

The whole thrust of the liberal-minded American press was toward an effort to work with the Russians to build up the United Nations and thus banish the prospect of another war. Generous, ever hopeful America was enthusiastic about the United Nations, the great dream of the age. "The old faith in American isolation is deader than the proverbial dodo," the New York *Times* proclaimed.[2] In an oblique thrust at those who doubted the good faith of the Russians in any new international organization, the *Times* flared: "Once again, as twenty-five years ago, the United States must choose whether it wishes to cooperate with the rest of the world on the basis of compromises made in good faith and with the prospect of future betterment, or whether it proposes to insist 100 per cent on its own program even if the world goes to pot as a result."[3]

While Europe rallied to the American standard, something quite different began happening in Asia, from the Korean peninsula to the Indian subcontinent. As the American correspondents chased the flashy headlines of the moment, true to their training and the desires of their editors, a great upheaval spread slowly but inexorably across a space of seven million square miles where Japanese hammer blows had sprung the locks that had imprisoned the aspirations of one and a quarter billion people. There were few journalists who recorded it, and their work was very largely ignored in favor of sensational news.

And why not? Under the unwritten canons of American journalism, Frank Bartholomew of the United Press was doing his job brilliantly when he hurried to see the fallen Prime Minister of Japan, Hideki Tojo, on September 11, 1945, and reported the sensation that followed. Major Paul Kraus of the U.S. Counter-Intelligence Corps also had arrived at the Tojo home in the Tokyo suburb of Satagaya-ku and announced to an interpreter: "Tell him to open the door. Tell him to prepare for a trip to General MacArthur's headquarters in Yokohama." Just then there was a shot inside the house. Said Bartholomew to Kraus: "Your pigeon just shot himself."

When they broke down the door, they found the Japanese war lord slumped in a chair, his white shirt stained with blood and an American Air Force pistol on the floor nearby. Toichiro Takamatsu of the *Mainichi Shimbun* leaned over the wounded man and heard him mutter his compliance with the code of the samurai: "I am happy to die. I wanted to die by the sword . . . but the pistol will do . . . I assume responsibility for the war . . . banzai!" [4]

There was little wonder that the American press followed Tojo's recovery, his trial as a war criminal, and his eventual hanging as one of the great events of the postwar years. This was something the American people could understand and appreciate. It was, after all, difficult to tell concisely and yet in depth (the contradictory new formula for interpreting the news) some of the far more important things that were happening on the Asian mainland.

There were dark and ominous portents in China, where Mao Tse-tung's Communist forces were probing and skirmishing all over the northern provinces. General Chu Teh made it perfectly clear, in a declaration presented to the Allied governments on August 16, 1945, that the Communists claimed the right to a full share in the acceptance of the Japanese surrender and in the peace settlements as well. That same day, under pressure from Patrick J. Hurley, the special Presidential representative and U.S. Ambassador, Chiang Kai-shek was wiring a message to Yenan inviting Mao Tse-tung to meet him: "We have many international and internal problems awaiting settlement."

The American government was in fact so anxious for an accommodation between the Nationalists and the Communists that Hurley himself flew to Yenan and on August 28 brought Mao back to Chungking with him for a month of fruitless conferences and arrogant Communist demands. This was the beginning of a similar and even less successful effort at mediation which General George C. Marshall later undertook.[5]

But if the uncertain course of U.S. policy in China was confusing to the public at home, what was going on in Indochina made no sense at all. Certainly, very little attention was paid to an experienced Communist revolutionary, Nguyen Ai-Quoc, who on March 28, 1944, proclaimed a "Provisional Republican Government of Viet-Nam" in Liuchow, with the blessings of the Chinese government. Taking the name of Ho Chi Minh ("He Who Enlightens"), the daring chieftain volunteered to lead his guerrillas into Viet-Nam to fight the Japanese. He began rescuing American fliers who had been shot down over Indochina. He deluged his people with anti-Japanese (and probably anti-French) propaganda and received the support of the American "cloak and dagger" operation of that day, the Office of Strategic Services, which parachuted arms to him and courted him with a mission.[6] But while the war was on, the Vichy-controlled French administration had no similar encouragement, and President Roosevelt, according to his son, Elliott, felt at one time that an Indochina "liberated in main part by American arms and American troops should never simply be handed back to the French, to be milked by their imperialists as has been the case for decades."[7]

The American people, uncaring and uninformed, were also supremely unconcerned. As late as 1954, when Dien Bien Phu was tottering before the power of Ho Chi Minh's large and well-armed forces, President Eisenhower without hesitation confirmed the American position: "I cannot conceive of a greater tragedy for America than to get heavily involved now in an all-out war in any of those regions, particularly with large units."[8]

That, of course, was immediately after the Korean War, when any further armed move in Asia would have been thoroughly unpopular. For, like the Indochina situation, the gathering Korean crisis was all but ignored in the American press during its initial stages, except for a few pieces from excited U.N. correspondents that crept into a handful of newspapers on a dull day. The stage for that tragedy was set at the Potsdam conference when an effort was being made to find a dividing line in Korea so that the Americans could accept a Japanese surrender in the southern region while the Russians performed the same military mission in the northern region. Rear Admiral Matthias Gardner (USN) simply pointed to the 38th Parallel, which roughly bisects Korea at its waist, and asked, "Why not put it there?"[9] By the time American troops arrived in southern Korea on September 8, 1945, the Russians already had effectively sealed off the 9 million Koreans in the north from the 21 million of their fellow countrymen to the south. And in the northern capital of Pyongyang, a group of thirty-six Russian-trained Korean leaders already had taken over, headed by a guerrilla chieftain called Kim Sung Chu and his friend Nam Il. The former became Kim Il Sung, the first Premier of North Korea.[10]

At the other end of the Asian arc of crisis, in India, the American press was better informed, but not in a way that pleased the Indians. During the war, when Mohandas K. Gandhi was developing his nonviolent campaign to force the British out of India, the *Hindu* of Madras, one of the most influential newspapers, cried out against what it called "the gross ignorance of American opinion." It was the Wardha resolution of the Indian Congress Party early in 1942 that touched off a frenzied denunciation of Gandhi in the American press, which had an effect on influential American opinion. Britain was warned to leave India, under the terms of the Wardha resolution, or face the force of Indian resistance. The Washington *Post* found help for the Axis in the Wardha plan and saw the Congress as an "enemy of civilization and freedom" if it was adopted. The Washington *Star* questioned Gandhi's "intellectual honesty." The New York *Herald Tribune* called it a "stick-up" in gangster fashion. Consequently, when the British put Gandhi and Jawaharlal Nehru and their associates in jail, there was the most determined support for the action in the United States.[11] And if the American public was quick to forget, the Indian public was not.

It was clear to thoughtful and well-informed Americans at the conclusion of World War II that in Asia, no less than in Europe, the end of hostilities did not presage peace. There was need for all of America's strength and wisdom to deal with the manifold problems of a world in which the power of the atom had been loosed, and would not long remain an exclusive American possession. Yet, across the broad expanse of the nation there suddenly arose a deafening and utterly unreasoning demand: "Bring the boys back home!"

If ever there was a massive demonstration of the raw power of the public will in the United States, this was it. Congress was deluged with mail and personal appeals. The radio reverberated with them. The chant was taken up by a very large section of the press, although some newspapers were appalled, and one warned that "the present pell mell rush out of Europe and Asia, under Congressional pressure, is nothing less than a new retreat into isolation."[12]

But the pressure grew. It extended to the centers of American military might in Europe and Asia, where disorders threatened. The Under Secretary of War, Robert P. Patterson, had to go on a tour to quiet the troops—an extraordinary situation. Accordingly, General Marshall, as Chief of Staff, devised a point system under which discharge would be determined on the basis of length of service, combat duty, time overseas, and other factors. Although some, like General Matthew B. Ridgway, called it a "shameful demobilization,"[13] and many agreed with him, President Truman unhesitatingly put it into effect.

There was, indeed, a weakness in the government at home. A magnificent leader, Franklin D. Roosevelt, had died at Warm Springs, Ga., on April 12, 1945, when victory was in sight. The capable Truman, pitched into the seat of enormous power from the quiet of the Vice Presidency, had not yet shown his real mettle. The Democratic Party, in power since 1933, faced the Congressional elections of 1946 with apprehension, having seen the Labour Party in Great Britain unseat the mighty Winston Churchill in 1945 in the midst of the Potsdam conference.

Nine days after the surrender of Japan, President Truman assured a press conference on August 23, 1945, that the Army and Navy were doing everything possible to "bring the boys back home." On January 8, 1946, the President issued a statement showing that 4,750,000 out of 12,000,000 men had been released from the Army; almost 1,250,000 out of 3,500,000 from the Navy; 183,000 out of 486,000 from the Marines; and 74,000 out of 180,000 from the Coast Guard. By April 17, the Army discharges had reached nearly 7,000,000, which the President called "the most remarkable demobilization in the history of the world, or 'disintegration,' if you want to call it that."

"Our frenzied demobilization, in fact, grew out of our antagonism toward maintaining a large standing army," he wrote. "There was only one alternative, in my opinion, and that was a prepared soldier-citizenry. . . . I told the Cabinet that the time had come to initiate a new military policy. If we were to maintain leadership among other nations, we must continue to be strong in a military way." [14]

But by that time, the damage had been done. The stormy excesses of public opinion slowly abated. The press and radio returned to normal, and Congress proceeded to go on about its usual affairs. After sustaining 1,078,674 casualties, including 293,986 battle deaths in all theaters, and the loss of $350 billion in civilian and military property, the nation at last was seemingly at peace. [15] The years of savage preoccupation with foreign affairs melted away into memory, almost as if they had never been.

Pearl Harbor, Guadalcanal, the Coral Sea, Tarawa, and Iwo Jima, where the Marines raised the flag on Mount Suribachi, were hallowed, well-remembered names in the Pacific. But soon, many Americans couldn't identify Okinawa, Osaka, Kyushu, or Java and even had difficulty finding Singapore on a map. [16] The most expensive geography lesson in the world's history was over. Truly, the vast majority of Americans were interested only in "America, the Beautiful," and wished the world would stop bothering them. No nation had ever before stood at the very pinnacle of world power and made so light of it. Perhaps it was symbolic of the average American's indifference to foreign affairs that Senator Tom Connally, of Texas, the Chairman of the Senate Foreign Relations Committee, shook hands warmly with the representative of UNESCO in 1946, saying, "UNESCO, eh? Great little country you got back there. Great little country." [17]

If Great Britain, France, and the Netherlands had their doubts about the depth of our commitment in the Pacific, who could blame them? And if our South Korean, Japanese, and Filipino allies were nervous over whether we would actually keep our defense commitments, the reason for it was painfully clear. As for the Chinese Nationalists, they already knew how little they could depend on American arms to defend them against the rise of Communist power.

Mao Tse-tung, Ho Chi Minh, and Kim Il Sung had drawn the obvious conclusions from the destruction of American armed strength in the Pacific. Who else was there to stop them now? And a little-known professional revolutionary, Sukarno, who had spent nine years in Dutch prisons, knew the moment for his own bid for the freedom of Indonesia was near. ("Sukarno, Sukarno, who the hell is he?" asked a wire-service editor in 1948. "And whaddya mean he doesn't have a first name? Our readers won't understand that." A correspondent then named him Achmed.)[18]

But correspondents' pieces about such unfamiliar figures found few outlets. Whatever the correspondents' feelings, there seemed to be little concern about Asia on the foreign desks. The great preoccupation of American policy in the immediate postwar years was with Europe, with which most telegraph editors (there were and are few foreign or cable editors) had at least a slight acquaintance. After the failure of General Marshall's mission to bring Chiang Kai-shek and the Chinese Communists into agreement, exotic Asian datelines appeared less frequently in the mass-circulation American press. When they did, they preceded cute pieces about snake charmers, geishas, coolies, Mount Fuji, and a little brown man in a loincloth named Gandhi. Only a few powerful and well-equipped newspapers paid any attention to Asian affairs.

For the bulk of the mass media, the communications network through which the United States had learned of the progress of the Pacific war had been ripped apart with the coming of peace on Tokyo Bay. The some 2,000 correspondents had been disbanded; only a few had stayed on. Now, the network had to be rewoven. But, unhappily, neither the governments nor the press on either side of the Pacific made it a matter of the first priority.

2. RETURN TO JAPAN

From his headquarters in Tokyo's massive gray Dai Ichi building, with its soaring columns, General MacArthur commanded Japan soon after the surrender to "develop a free and responsible press" and thereby bring itself "abreast of modern progressive thought and action." [19] The progress toward this shimmering but distant goal was lamentably slow. To give the appropriate guidance to Japanese editors, the newly liberated press was tenderly smothered under a "prepublication censorship" which lasted until 1948 in its most severe form and eventually vanished in 1952 after the conclusion of the Japanese peace treaty.[20]

Having suffered the strictest government controls from the early 1930's at the hands of their own savage military, the editors were understandably patient under the milder and far less menacing MacArthur regime. But some of the American measures rankled. For a time immediately after the surrender, the editors were under the rather large and forceful thumb of Major Daniel Imboden, the head of the press section, Supreme Allied Commander, Pacific (SCAP), who lectured them incessantly on the beauties of objectivity. Major Imboden, himself a former small-town publisher (in San Luis Obispo, Calif.), knew what he wanted. He tolerated no nonsense about devious "informed sources" or "official circles." Every piece of news for the Japanese press had to be attributed by name and organization to a reputable source, as far as Major Imboden was concerned, or it didn't get in the paper.

Even if there had been no American censorship or journalism lessons from Major Imboden, the Japanese press would not have been able to revive immediately after the war. In 1940, the total number of daily newspapers in Japan had reached 1,200, and including weeklies, the number went as high as 7,700. Two years later, after the Pearl Harbor attack, the government reorganized the press in order to strengthen its control and meet the prevailing newspaper shortage. Because of mergers and suspensions, only 55 daily newspapers were left in the entire land. With the exception of Tokyo and Osaka, each prefecture had only one paper. The national and provincial dailies by war's end were putting out only two pages, and sometimes only one.[21]

Of course, it made for a sound financial position, particularly for the provincial dailies. But once the war was over, the big national dailies soon engaged in a massive competition that was as expensive as it was spectacular. As in the United States, the provincials, in the main, made the money while the big city newspapers had the circulation, the glory, and most of the headaches.

There was still another change under the friendly ministrations of the MacArthur proconsulship. Domei, the predominant Japanese news service before the war, went out of business. At its peak, it had had some 300 foreign correspondents, but about 250 of them were in China, and it was widely believed that many of the dispatches were intended less for publication than for Japanese military intelligence and the foreign office. Nevertheless, there were some sound and even distinguished professional journalists in Domei who turned up in the successor organization, Kyodo Tsushin, or Kyodo News Service, when it opened for business on November 1, 1945. Backed by almost all the surviving

Japanese newspapers except the Big Three—*Asahi, Mainichi,* and *Yomiuri*—Kyodo immediately completed exchange news agreements with all the global wire services. Although it was an independent organization, its biggest client was the Japan Broadcasting Corporation (N.H.K.), and it also benefited from generous subscriptions to its service taken by various government bureaus.

A financial service, Jiji Press, which later developed into a general news competitor, also was founded in 1945 as a cooperative agency. In addition to government subscriptions for its daily file, Jiji had some handsome contracts for public opinion polls and various specialized printing services—government pamphlets and the like. It handled, as well, a variety of commercial business in an effort to emulate Comtelburo, the successful financial service of the great British news agency, Reuters.[22] It was obvious from the beginning that the Japanese Government, particularly the Foreign Office, was anxious for Kyodo and Jiji to succeed. And SCAP headquarters at the Dai Ichi certainly had no objections.

Thus, while laboring with the aid of a benevolent government to establish the façade of a free press in Japan, the MacArthur regime also re-created in effect the most profitable news market in all of Asia and by far the most influential. For in Japan, to a greater extent than in any other nation, the newspapers were accounted a potent force in the molding of public opinion. It was more than a jest that the three greatest influences in Japan were Tokyo University, *Asahi,* and the intellectual magazine *Sekai.* To some, *Chuo Koron,* another intellectual journal, ranked with these.

General MacArthur himself took an interest in re-establishing the American wire services in Japan on basically their prewar position. Miles W. (Peg) Vaughn of the United Press (UP), Murlin Spencer of the Associated Press, (AP), and Howard Handleman of the International News Service (INS) had come into Tokyo with him and were trying to hook up with their old clients in the Far East. It wasn't easy. Reuters, with its dominant position in India and its base in Singapore, was then too powerful for American expansion in these areas; moreover, the British were moving into Tokyo as well. Therefore, the Americans and British were cagey about their rates. As for the French, the old Havas agency had not been able to survive the burden of service for the Vichy government and had been replaced by Agence France-Presse (AFP), a new organization.

This was scarcely the time for a romantic foreign correspondent with his old-fashioned postures, looking around for scoops, although a few such characters managed somehow to survive the war. It was a time for business people. The problem was not to get the news out of Asia, because there wasn't too much demand for it, but to bring it in and distribute it. One of the pleasant parts of the era was that any agency man could rent a grass hut, string up an aerial, take an old Army receiver out of his suitcase, and start signing up clients for two-year contracts.

It was a frenzied period. Some organizations conveniently allowed their officials to report for income tax purposes far lower salaries for their employees than they were actually receiving. Others, who found they were accumulating too many yen under the SCAP currency restrictions, had to find ways to exchange them for dollars on the black market. In places like Shanghai, where a runaway inflation was adding to the woes of bureau managers, there were strikes of local help. Walter Rundle, the Shanghai manager for United Press, found one day that his striking messengers not only wanted more pay but also insisted that he get rid of a local ghost. The obliging Rundle, bowing to local custom, settled the strike with a raise and the following item on his expense account: "Firecrackers for exorcising ghost, $20." [23]

In Tokyo, the only superstition was an overwhelming awe of General MacArthur and his headquarters in the Dai Ichi. Any sensible Japanese editor knew that SCAP was far more likely to favor an American wire service than its foreign competitors. Within a short time after the surrender, therefore, the Big Three were back firmly in their prewar associations—*Asahi* with the Associated Press, *Mainichi* with the United Press, and *Yomiuri* with International News Service, the Hearst agency.

The most friendly to the United States was *Yomiuri* (the "Town Crier"), primarily because of the admiration of its owner, Matsutaro Shoriki, for William Randolph Hearst, Sr. The two newspaper barons had exchanged gifts before the war, Hearst having sent Shoriki some bison and the Japanese having bestowed suits of ancient Japanese armor on the squire of San Simeon. Shoriki fancied himself the "Hearst of the Orient" and had had his biography written by one of the stars of the Hearst service, Bob Considine.

Actually, the smiling and talkative Japanese publisher was far more successful than Hearst. He took over an almost moribund, fifty-year-old newspaper in 1924 after it had been weighted down by debts arising from the great earthquake of the previous year.[24] He had no knowledge of journalism then, having been chief of detectives in Tokyo and the son-in-law of the police chief. But with considerable persuasion, he was able to obtain financing and built the paper into a worthy rival for *Asahi* and *Mainichi,* each of the three having daily circulations of more than 4 million.

Shoriki liked the Hearst service and never quibbled about his bills.

By the time the Japanese peace treaty was signed and the probation period for the Japanese press was over, he was paying $5,000 a month for a package consisting of International News Service, International News Pictures, and some comics from King Features Service. Although he ran "Blondie" in *Yomiuri* before the war, he dropped it afterward but kept paying for it because he didn't want it in the opposition press. In the same manner, during the 1950's, he is reputed to have paid the New York *Herald Tribune* $2,000 a month for its service, with minimal use at best and usually no use at all.

It wasn't long before the price of the Hearst service to *Yomiuri* doubled. From that base, the relatively modest INS file with extras began grossing about $250,000 a year from Japan and Korea alone—a thumping return for what the Hearst agency had to offer and what it paid its people in the Far East. Using INS as a measure for the level of return in the agency field, there was good reason to believe that at that time each of the giants—the AP, UP, and Reuters—was grossing twice as much in Japan as its next smaller competitor. As for AFP, the probabilities were that it had to settle for about half of the INS total in this highly competitive field. Kyodo News Service was not a factor at that time, since it bought from all, except AFP, for stiff fees and put out no foreign service of its own.

As for personnel and the volume of foreign service in the mid-1950's, INS's position was approximately the same—midway between the low of the French agency and the highs of the great English-language agencies. It was able to build up a staff of thirty-five employees, including eight to ten people who served as reporters, rewrite men, and editors, to keep its Tokyo office going on a twenty-four-hour basis. It brought in a radioteletype file of more than 25,000 words a day from San Francisco for distribution in the Far East. There were small INS bureaus in Manila, Taipei, and Hong Kong, the latter manned only by a "stringer." * During the Korean War, it had a five-man bureau to cover the fighting and paid all expenses with the $1,000 a month which it received from the Hapdong News Agency of Korea for permission to monitor the INS radiocast directly from San Francisco.

Yet, for all of Shoriki's good will for his old friend Hearst and despite INS's ability to show a profit in the Far East because of *Yomiuri*'s support, the news agency could not compete against the Americans, British, and French on a global basis. Its financial base in the United States was too slender and the Hearst papers, which were undergoing retrenchment, couldn't carry it any longer. On May 24, 1958, INS was sold to United Press and went out of business. Through the merger, it

* A "stringer is a part-time employee. Originally, he was paid by the inch for his string of newspaper clippings—hence the name.

became a mere word in the new title of the combined agency, United Press International (UPI). There was keen interest in what would happen next, for the seventy-one-year-old Shoriki now was to be matched against the ebullient Earnest Hoberecht, an Oklahoman in his forties who served as the UPI's vice president for Asia and was the most hard-nosed news salesman in that vast territory outside the Communist orbit.

In 1945, after landing in Tokyo with General MacArthur and Peg Vaughn, the UP bureau chief there, Hoberecht quickly showed his mettle. Within a short time, he replaced Vaughn and went on to become probably the highest-paid American news executive in Asia.[25] Since he worked on salary and commission, as did at least one other among his early competitors, it was difficult to say what this generally amounted to; but most estimates ranged between $36,000 and $45,000 a year until his resignation in 1966. Early in his postwar career, he also found time to write a novel, *Tokyo Romance,* which was translated into Japanese in 1947 and introduced as the work of a new American writer. "Sold over 300,000 copies in two months," the proud correspondent informed the Pulitzer Prize–winning novelist James A. Michener. "You might say a cultural hurricane hit Japan with the advent of Hoberecht on the literary scene." [26] Japan had never read anything quite like *Tokyo Romance* until a 1949 novel by Hoberecht was published, *Shears of Destiny.*

Hoberecht had other things of which he was proud, such as his part in founding that venerable journalistic institution, the Foreign Correspondents Club of Japan, and giving it a mythical address. Until it moved to more appropriate quarters in the 1960's, the club's location was officially recognized by the Japanese Post Office as 1 Shimbun (Newspaper) Alley, Hoberecht's invention.[27] For him, there were three great loves—General MacArthur, Oklahoma, and the United Press—and now he had to do battle with Matsutaro Shoriki to uphold the UPI. At stake was the $250,000 annual business of INS, which Hoberecht believed would now fall by right to him.

Shoriki was paying $120,000 a year to INS at the time of the merger for its various news and feature services, the other $130,000 being made up by the rest of the Japanese and Korean clients, such as the Kyodo and Hapdong News Services, big provincial papers like *Chubu Nippon Shimbun,* and the like. If the owner of *Yomiuri* managed to frustrate the merger arrangements, it was obvious that Hoberecht might have trouble enforcing the other INS contracts. *Yomiuri,* which used the AP and Agence France-Presse, had been carrying INS out of its owner's affection for Hearst. UPI apparently was quite another story, particularly because Shoriki's powerful competitor, *Mainichi* (Daily), also had that service, and it was available in Japanese translation through

Kyodo. Although the three biggest newspapers were not members of the Kyodo cooperative, they bought its foreign service.

For a few days, there was some skirmishing at long distance. Then Hoberecht called on Shoriki to see what could be done. According to a version of the proceedings that was current in Tokyo at the time, the publisher sat like a flint-faced samurai on two cushions that elevated him above his visitor. It took a bit of elevating to dwarf Hoberecht, who was six feet tall and husky, but at the moment he was sitting in a low Japanese chair.

Having established a superior posture, Shoriki formally refused to accept UPI service, called it a legal matter, and challenged Hoberecht to take the case to the Japanese courts. He had the UPI wires torn out of the *Yomiuri* newsroom to make his point, all of which cut Hoberecht to the quick. The threatened loss of a large sum of money was bad enough, but it seemed downright ignoble for a publisher to refuse UPI service in so cavalier a fashion.

Evidently Shoriki based his argument on the loss of the exclusive services of INS and allegations that the contract had been breached in other ways. As for the other INS clients, there was no concerted rush to Hoberecht's banner. If he succeeded in picking up any of the $250,000 in INS contracts, or obtaining adjustments, it was not widely advertised; but those things never are. It was generally believed by Japanese editors, however, that *Mainichi* had increased its payments to UPI to at least $15,000 a month to maintain the agency's exclusive service.

Shoriki did something more than assert his independence when he stood up to UPI. He served notice that the easy days for American news agencies in Japan were over.

3. EXODUS FROM CHINA

On a pleasant day in May, 1949, Stewart Alsop made his way through the stifling atmosphere of crowded Shanghai to the well-ordered, well-supplied precincts of the Shanghai Club. He was more a tourist than a war correspondent, for he had just come out to China for a quick trip to do some columns for the New York *Herald Tribune*. Yet, he had had more than a passing acquaintance with war, first as a volunteer with the British at the outset of World War II and later as an American paratrooper who had jumped into France to join the Maquis shortly after D-Day. And he knew that Shanghai was doomed.

The celebrated long bar at the Shanghai Club was no different, to be sure. And the gimlets were as good as ever. The diplomatic set still gave cocktail parties where a talented hostess could conjure up an air of gaiety and well-being. Outwardly, American status and influence in the city were just as great as they had been since the defeat of the Japanese and the restoration of Chiang Kai-shek. But on the rooftops outside, his soldiers now squatted over machine guns that were trained on his own people in the jammed streets. Except for American bills and the Chinese silver dollars, money had lost its value. The vast economic powerhouse that had kept this city of 7 million going was slowed down. Soon, the power would be cut off and the old, organized life would come to a halt, for Mao Tse-tung and his Communists were on the march from the north.

Alsop had written to the *Herald Tribune* that the old China hands were saying: "The Communists will ruin Shanghai and Shanghai will ruin the Communists." But he scarcely believed it. Any correspondent in China knew how utterly ruthless the Communists were. The hard-bitten soldiers and revolutionaries who had survived the long march to Yenan and consolidated their power in all north China had little more than contempt for the old Shanghai that was dying. They would be building a new city on the ruins of the old.

The succession of Communist victories in the north could scarcely have been a surprise to any American who had even a mild interest in what was going on in China. Even before the war's end in 1945, American correspondents were streaming into Yenan, the Communist stronghold, and making comparisons that embarrassed Chiang and his government. Chiang's press people called it "a flood of pro-Yenan publicity from Chungking correspondents," men who "with few exceptions had shown themselves to be staunch and sincere friends of China." [28] Among them were Theodore H. White, of *Time;* Brooks Atkinson, of the New York *Times;* Darrell Berrigan, of the United Press; and Clyde Farnsworth and Preston Grover, of the Associated Press.

Atkinson and White, who had had experience with Chungking's censorship, wrote their most critical pieces once they were outside the country. Berrigan, who did the same thing, and Harold Isaacs, of *Newsweek,* who among others didn't get to Yenan, were denied re-entry permits by Chiang's government. Isaacs had written what all correspondents knew to be the case—that Chiang's regime was much like a government-in-exile in its own country, and that soon "the Americans will at best find themselves backing a government with no real basis of power except American support." [29] The truth about China wasn't popular at a time when American money and arms were trying to shore up a government that had lost all basis of popular support.

Nor could there have been any doubt about Communist strength. Among the older newspaper correspondents, Tillman Durdin and Henry Lieberman, of the New York *Times;* A. T. Steele, of the New

York *Herald Tribune;* and George Weller of the Chicago *Daily News* knew Mao's capabilities perfectly well. Of the wire-service correspondents, Seymour Topping and John Roderick, of the AP, and Robert P. ("Pepper") Martin, of the UP, had firsthand knowledge of Communist preparedness. Roderick, in fact, had spent six months in Yenan after the end of World War II.

Chiang, however, unwisely chose to make a stand in Manchuria and persuaded the United States to help arm and transport some of his best divisions. They were overwhelmed, and some defected to the Communists as the war surged toward its climax in 1948. From November 7, 1948, until January 12, 1949, a million men fought along the Hwai River, in central China, in what was later accounted the climactic battle of the long war. The Nationalists lost a half million men—including their last remaining American-equipped divisons—to the People's Liberation Army in that debacle.[30] From then on, the end was in sight.

A curiously optimistic American government almost invariably had accused American foreign correspondents of dwelling on the gloomy side of wars in Asia. But surely, the correspondents in Shanghai that last May of Chiang's unhappy era had reason for their apprehension. The tourist among them, Alsop, sensed it even if he had covered none of the final battles. For on May 13, 1949, he wrote from Shanghai:

> This huge, rich, productive megalopolis, fourth largest in the world, is now to pass within the Soviet sphere. So is most if not all of a country with one-quarter of the world's population. No amount of rationalizing, no multiplication of complex excuses by the little men behind the desks in Washington can alter the hard, plain, unpleasant truth that this means a very great disaster for the United States and the whole non-Soviet world.[31]

No correspondent in that unhappy time could envision the possibility that a Communist China would be anything but a kind of junior partner for the Soviet Union. Or if they did, they obviously didn't have confidence enough to publish their suspicions.

Shanghai fell less than two weeks later—on May 25. Just before the end, the wily Chiang left secretly for Taiwan without notifying his officials in Canton of his plans. Soon afterward, Secretary of State Dean Acheson issued his statement that the American government would wait until "the dust settled" in Asia.[32] It was an epitaph.

From that day on, and for many years thereafter, no American foreign correspondent was permitted on mainland China to report on the most populous land on earth. It was as if the news media had been blindfolded in the United States, first by the actions of both their own government and the Chinese Communists, and later by the suspicion and stubbornness of the Chinese regime alone. Occasionally, a few favored ones might be admitted for a brief, conducted tour, but that was all. It was from the Indians that the American press first learned of the Chinese decision to enter the Korean War, a warning that General MacArthur ignored. And it was from the Chinese themselves that the extent of their support for the Viet-Cong guerrillas in South Viet-Nam became known. By that time, the British, French, and Canadians had journalists in Peking.

One of them, Mark Gayn, of the Toronto *Daily Star,* had a postscript to Alsop's picture of the last days of old Shanghai. In 1965, it had become a city of 10 million crowded into not much more space. "General poverty remains," he wrote, "but there are no beggars displaying their sores to passersby and no starving children with distended bellies. Labor laws keep the children out of the factories and mill hands work only eight hours six days a week. Prostitutes have been 're-educated' and instead of girlie shows, the Great World now serves operas of the sufferings and triumphs of the revolutionary heroes." [33]

Among American journalists, most of the old China hands had long departed from Hong Kong, the gilded capital of the outside "China watchers." As for the younger foreign correspondents, China was like another world to them. Nearly a generation of them, schooled in China studies mainly in the classroom, had no firsthand knowledge of the most powerful American foe in Asia.

4. THE RIVALS

Long after the Chinese Communist conquest of the mainland, an American official learned that there was a lively competition among the global wire services for the trade of the Chinese-language publications in Hong Kong, including those that were officially Communist, as well as the sympathizers. The representatives of Reuters and Agence France-Presse, who had correspondents in Peking and sold their service directly to official publications there, reported that the Chinese paid well —and promptly. Such trade, of course, was forbidden to Americans.

The official approached Earnest Hoberecht, of UPI, who happened to be in Hong Kong on a business trip. "Why," he demanded, "should you sell your service to Chinese Communist publications in Hong Kong?"

"It is a patriotic duty," Hoberecht said blandly. "It takes a lot of dollars away from the Chinese Communists."

Nevertheless, centers like Hong Kong, Taipei, Singapore, and Manila could scarcely have provided by themselves the kind of major news markets that would support broad agency coverage of Asia in return for news of the rest of the world. Only Japan possessed the mass circulation newspapers, electronic media, and wire services on which agencies could count with some degree of confidence for the future. As far as agency sales were concerned, Japan became the big bazaar.

From the very beginning of postwar Asian relationships with the United States, it was plain that the wire services would have to supply most of the interchange of news and its by-products. True, the Japanese correspondents went out to the United States, Europe, and Russia in large numbers, and even began to cover major centers in Asia in the 1960's, but they could seldom compete with the wires for fast service. Their work was primarily commentary—"We want things seen through Japanese eyes," a leading editor said. As for the American correspondents who came to Asia, they represented relatively few news-gathering organizations, except for the specials who converged on Saigon during peak periods of the Viet-Nam war. And those who were permanently based in Japan often found it necessary to do extensive traveling. As one news-magazine correspondent was told rather crudely by his editor before setting out on his Asian argosy, "Now remember, don't get carried away. Japan is a back-of-the-book story."

Despite their comparatively small number, some of the correspondents from the great newspapers of the United States were accorded a rather exalted status that was not always based on their ability as journalists. Others, particularly the younger wire-service correspondents, found that diplomats frequently tried to avoid them. As for *Time* and *Newsweek,* they were particular problems for the diplomatic community because they circulated in most Asian countries in far greater volume than any other American publication and had a thoughtful, if sometimes apprehensive, readership. In short, the specials (as the newspaper correspondents are known) were important, but the wire services provided the volume—and that is what counted for the mass media.

News for the United States was not always of first importance in the agency operation, however. News for Asian clients had equal priority, particularly if they were important clients. Some agencies also sold pictures, in addition to feature services. Others sold television news film. Still others handled special projects for various clients, as they developed. It could not be said of any wire-service man, except for those on duty in Saigon, that his entire work was devoted to reporting for the United States. Most of them had assorted chores; bureau managers usually had to sell their services and keep the clients and visiting editors and publishers happy.

It was, all in all, a different kind of foreign correspondence, because the world was different. In the early nineteenth century, it had been possible in small-town America to begin publishing a newspaper with a few thousand dollars, a shirttail full of type, a little local gossip, and some letters written by travelers abroad. In the automated world of the 1960's, particularly in the United States, very large sums were required to found any newspaper or magazine, and the Federal Communications Commission had to approve all new radio or television stations.

If a news agency, a newspaper, news magazine, or electronic medium intended to maintain a foreign staff and still preserve its independence, it had to be certain that the extra expense could in some manner be justified. The most inflexible law of journalism in an open society was that a losing newspaper first forfeited its entire independence, economic and editorial, then its self-respect, and finally its subscribers. And sometimes, all three went together.

Of all the American media in the foreign field, only *Time* and *Newsweek* could be said to have made a consistent profit on their foreign operations in the 1960's, primarily because their international editions attracted a great deal of advertising support. But it was also true that they were able to engage competent correspondents by paying them reasonably well, although not all of the reporters were able to put up with the news-mangling that can sometimes result from group writing and group editing.

The New York *Times*, like its few newspaper rivals in the United States, pushed syndication of its foreign correspondents' work to cut down expenses. The American television networks, with a few hardworking correspondents in Asia, made so much money that they could afford foreign coverage as sheer promotion, if nothing else, and sometimes it was only that. As for the wire services, they were pleased if they could break even and keep the complaints from editors at a minimum. Few were satisfied with their foreign coverage, particularly in Asia.

The UPI was aggressive in pushing sales in Asia. It had to be, as an organization operating on the proceeds of direct sales of its services to clients in the United States and abroad. By the best Japanese estimates, UPI grossed more than a half-million dollars a year from the sale of its news service in Japan alone, its chief clients being *Mainichi* and the Kyodo News Agency. It also sold news pictures in a flourishing Japanese market, hired camera crews to supply television coverage for UPI Newsfilms, Inc., and handled various special projects. In a year without an extraordinary war expenditure, such as 1964, the UPI's Japanese income was believed to be sufficient to meet all its Asian expenses. However, two years later, the expanded Viet-Nam war coverage was sharply raising costs for all the news media involved.

Under normal circumstances, certainly, the Asian Division was no burden to UPI, the Asian coverage being only a small part of the agency's expenditures of $44,898,000 in 1964, a fairly normal year. Its total editorial staff of 51, including 18 Americans, covered everything from Tokyo to Karachi. There were about twice as many others to handle pictures, communications, business, and television work. Two years later, with the expanded Vietnamese war, the UPI's global cost had risen to $46,000,000.[34]

UPI had an efficient base in Tokyo. Most of the news of Asia cleared through the Tokyo Bureau for San Francisco and New York, while news of America and the rest of the world was received over the same route to the Japanese capital. Manila also received the incoming news, combined it with the Tokyo file from Japan, and then beamed the finished product to all UPI bureaus in Asia from two transmitters operated under a franchise from the Philippine government.

Improvements in communications actually were more costly to all the global wire services than increases in their Asian personnel. The newly opened telephone cable circuits in the Pacific in 1965 offered secure communications to the agencies for the first time but cost twice as much as the radioteletype, which was subject to interruption because of atmospheric disturbances. Moreover, twenty-four-hour-a-day radioteletype circuits had to be maintained from Saigon by the American agencies at the height of the war coverage. With Reuters leading the way in the use of the cable communications, the Americans felt themselves under increasing competitive pressure to follow.

Like the UPI, the AP built its flourishing news and picture service in Asia on a firm base in Japan. As a cooperative agency, the largest in the world, the AP had the membership support of 1,226 American daily newspapers and 2,828 American broadcasters, as well as 4,515 foreign subscribers in 103 nations and territories in 1966. The UPI had 1,191 newspaper and 2,796 broadcast subscribers in the United States in 1965, and in the following year it reported its total global subscribers as 6,267.[35]

Overseas, the AP sold its news and picture service but offered no TV newsfilm. Its projected annual expenditures for 1966 were put at $50,250,000, of which foreign news was estimated at $7,750,000.[36] The UPI, with a smaller figure for total costs, put its foreign coverage at about the same total. But whereas the agency people were on a five-day, forty-hour week, with a scale of fairly substantial minimum wages in the United States, no such conditions existed abroad except in London. In Asia, generally, the work week was six—and sometimes seven—days, and for the average employee the wage structure was considerably lower than in the United States.

Much of the AP's rebuilding in Asia was conducted under the supervision of Robert Eunson, a World War II and Korean War correspondent. As the successor to two earlier Tokyo bureau chiefs, Murlin Spencer and Russell Brines, Eunson expanded the AP's influence considerably between 1950 and 1956. He returned again in 1963 for two years, taking over from John Randolph, who had won a Silver Star as a Korean War correspondent for helping evacuate wounded soldiers under fire. Japanese editors estimated during the latter period that AP was grossing about $1 million a year in Japan, including about $325,000 in picture fees.

By 1965, when Eunson was summoned to New York to be an assistant general manager, the AP was in a stronger position in the Far East than ever before. Its clients included the leading Japanese newspaper, *Asahi Shimbun,* and fourteen others; the Kyodo News Service, and assorted radio-TV stations. In Asia, its staff was about the same size as the UPI's for a normal period—fifty-two editorial people, including eighteen Americans, and about twice as many in other departments. Like its competitors, the AP expanded its Saigon staff for war coverage in 1965-66.

Under the spur of war news, the Far East dominated general foreign coverage in those years. Both the brief India-Pakistan fighting in 1965 and the Viet-Nam conflict in 1965-66 filled the columns of American newspapers. A check of six leading American newspapers in the spring of 1966 showed that close to half the foreign news they ran was from Saigon. As for the AP, on some days during the same period, the news from Asia filled more than 50 per cent of its foreign report for its American members. However, editors and correspondents alike agreed that once the fighting ended, Asian coverage was likely to go back to its relatively modest share of the foreign news budget as evidenced by the findings of a 1964 survey.[37]

Reuters, the British cooperative, wholly owned by British, Australian, and New Zealand newspapers, kept pace nearly everywhere in Asia with the American agencies and in some places outdid them. David Chipp, who was Reuters' Asian manager, ran an operation that differed in many ways from those of his American rivals. He, too, had come into management from a long career as a foreign correspondent; as his major achievement, he had opened the first Reuters bureau in Peking in 1956 and had remained there for two trying but colorful years. Since Reuters does not report British domestic news for domestic distribution (that is the task of the British domestic cooperative Press Association), virtually all Reuters funds were for its foreign service. As of December 1, 1963, the British agency's trading revenue from all sources was $8,836,220 (£3,155,793) and its expenditures for the gathering of news were $8,707,454 (£3,109,805), which left about $75,000 as the year's carry-over profit after taxes. For the next two years, it was estimated that the revenues and costs were 8 to 10 per cent higher.[38]

However, Reuters' success as a global news agency depended, in large part, on its prosperous commercial service, Comtelburo, founded in 1869 and purchased by the parent agency in 1944. Comtelburo swiftly developed into the largest economic agency in the world, but its principal clients were not the press and radio; rather, it aimed its service deliberately at traders, bankers, brokers, industrialists, and governments in all parts of the world. It could and did file a 4,000-word report daily on economic developments in Asia, and at the same time it boasted that it could flash the price of cocoa in New York to Ceylon in 45 seconds.

It was difficult, therefore, to arrive at any accurate estimate of the Reuters' gross in Japan. Aside from the yield of the Comtelburo and its special contract with the Japanese financial service Jiji Press, Reuters sold its news to a number of newspapers, the chief clients being *Asahi* and the Kyodo News Service. Japanese editors estimated that the British agency could realize $500,000 from its news sales alone; because its expenses were lower than the American agencies, its net yield probably was equal to their best and, in a good year, even exceeded it.

Reuters had several advantages over the Americans, the most important being its early use of the new telephone cables. Chipp, a relaxed and smiling bachelor in his forties, pointed out with some satisfaction that Walton Cole, the late general manager of Reuters, had decided that the agency would link its fate to the new Commonwealth cable. The cable policy was followed with steadfastness, for it guaranteed secure communications. Accordingly, two communications routes to the Far East were set up, one from London across Canada and the Pacific to Tokyo for direct communication with Japan, and the other from London to Sydney, Australia, a safe base, from which news was forwarded to Singapore and Hong Kong and returned over the same circuits.

Necessarily, Reuters was able to negotiate for a reduction, perhaps as much as 20 per cent, in the monthly cable costs, according to reports in Tokyo. But even more important, the General Post Office in London for years had decreed that the agency could be considered a common communications carrier; therefore, *Asahi* and the Kyodo News Agency each paid $2,000 a month to Reuters for transmitting their file from London to Tokyo.[39] This was a comparatively small sum, but both American agencies raised a fuss about it because the Federal Communications Commission refused to let them do the same thing, holding that they could not be common communications carriers. Even if the FCC had given permission, it was not advisable for them to try it. There had been instances when newspaper copy, notably for the New York

Times and the *Christian Science Monitor,* had been carried on American agency circuits in an emergency, but this was rare. Most American editors preferred to deal with news agencies, not communications channels.

Reuters had a far more powerful advantage over the Americans—access to the Indian market through its alliance with the Press Trust of India, the Indian news agency. Up to the fall of 1966, UPI could not sell news in India because of a law that such transactions had to be made through an Indian-owned agency; however, the indefatigable Earnie Hoberecht was able to sell about $3,000 a month in news pictures to Indian newspapers. Frozen out of Pakistan, he also turned to selling pictures there. As for the AP, it had a tie-up with a new Indian news agency, United News of India, but realized comparatively little from it. With the exception of a dribble of copy from Agence France-Presse to the Press Trust of India, Reuters was the major source of supply for news of the United States and Great Britain to Indian newspapers and those in Pakistan, as well. In addition, it had outlets in the United States to about 100 newspapers, including some of the largest and most powerful.

For David Chipp and his forty-six editorial employees in the Asian bureaus he supervised, there was an increasing amount of satisfaction in the Reuters position. It was actively seeking to use more Asian journalists; its chief diplomatic correspondent in London in the mid-1960's was Monhin Ali, a Pakistani, and its Southeast Asian manager at Singapore was Jimmy Hahn, a Korean. It did not then sell news pictures, and it had the most powerful television tie-up of any of the agencies, being linked with the British Commonwealth film group, Viznews. Reuters was top-flight competition for the Americans everywhere in Asia.

As for Agence France-Presse, both its situation and its problems were completely different from those of its competitors. Although it had no American outlets (it had tried the New York *Times* without success), AFP nevertheless had an influence on the position of the United States in the Far East. The French ran a stripped-down service for Asia, specializing in hard news that was brief and written in basic English so that it could be easily translated by the Japanese, Koreans, Indonesians, Chinese, Thai, Burmese, and others. Because it was highly condensed, the English-language service from Washington sometimes would arrive first in Tokyo and other Asian centers. It was cabled to Paris, then sent by radioteletype casts to Asian points. And the service that arrived first, and was easiest to translate, often would get the break in the Japanese press, as well as others.

Agence France-Presse had a hard time of it at the beginning, since it was a replacement for the familiar Havas. In Tokyo, its chief representative was Leon Prou, a former teacher of French who had come to Japan in 1941 and remained there under surveillance throughout the war. When he was given a chance to sell AFP service in 1946, he tried Kyodo but all that the Japanese agency wanted was about three hundred words a day of French news. Prou then began selling his service directly to the Japanese papers at a price lower than his English-language competitors. He had no trouble obtaining contracts with the Japanese Big Three and a number of others. By 1965, most Japanese editors who were familiar with the AFP contract system estimated that its gross in Japan was probably about $150,000 annually. But its service was used; moreover, the same basic strategy worked elsewhere in Asia. In the Philippines, for instance, when the Manila *Times* dropped UPI, it took on AFP.

The French agency was able to do these things with its foreign service because it had a sound financial base in support from the French government, its principal client, which subscribed to its service for many different branches of the administration.[40] It had been created by law as an independent corporation, but under Article 13 of the 1957 statute, it was decreed that a covenant between the State and AFP would determine the number of subscriptions and the rate which the government would pay.[41] This, of course, was the only practical way in which a French news agency could operate, since it had only 120 French newspapers as clients. Unlike Havas, which sold advertising as well as news and thereby influenced a large section of the French press, AFP put a sound financial floor under its operations through its government subscriptions. In the 1965 budget for information, issued by the office of the prime minister, the total subscriptions listed for 1964 were NF 36,326,784, or more than $7.5 million. An increase of NF 2,362,344 (about $475,000) was budgeted for 1965.[42] On the assumption that AFP's total expense budget ranged from $12 million to $13 million it may be seen that the French government's contribution was substantial.

Despite that contribution and despite the charges by opposition newspapers and even some French correspondents in Washington that AFP was being turned into a Gaullist propaganda service, some Asian editors preferred to use it on a controversial story involving American policies. It was also true that while AFP had a very small staff, some of its correspondents were first-rate. As a general rule, it was less used than the English-language services in Asia, but now and then, it would take the play.

It was clear that the foreign news agencies would be the principal reliance of the Japanese press for fast service on overseas news for some time to come. Most editors conceded it. And yet, the Kyodo News Agency for 1965 had a total expense budget for news of $8 million, which put it up with the leaders. Kyodo in 1964 supplied its domestic and foreign news service to 93 newspapers and 33 radio and television stations. It put out AP, UPI, and Reuters in Japanese translations, thereby saving time for newspapers that took some of these services directly in English. Thus, a paper like *Mainichi,* which took UPI directly, also received AP and Reuters in translation through Kyodo.

Some 65 newspapers received Kyodo through a unique Kanji (basic Japanese script) teletype system, which printed about 187 characters a minute through electrical impulses that moved a wheel with 2,402 characters on it. The rest used facsimile transmission. Kyodo generally issued about 20,000 words a day in foreign news, using about 20 per cent each of AP and Reuters, 15 per cent of UPI, and the remainder from its own correspondents (it had twenty overseas in the mid-1960's) or other news agencies, including the Communists.

One of Kyodo's accomplishments was the construction of a large monitoring station at Noda City, 60 miles northeast of Tokyo, where Tass, the New China News Agency (Hsinhua), and other Communist agencies from North Viet-Nam and North Korea were copied 24 hours a day. AP and UPI were among the agencies that bought Kyodo's NCNA service on a 24-hour-a-day basis.

Kyodo's revenue was derived in the mid-1960's from a 12 per cent assessment of the monthly circulation subscriptions of its 81 member newspapers and, to a much lesser extent, the sales of its service to Japanese government bureaus and others. Eventually, it planned to sell its service abroad. To that end, it began an efficient English-language service, which it offered in Asia and Europe. But with only 2 hours a day of transmission, Kyodo could scarcely compete.[43]

It may fairly be said that the major news agencies operating in Asia— the two Americans, British, French, Japanese, and Indian—were annually investing more than $30 million a year in the gathering and dissemination of all foreign news. But except for war news, a comparatively small part of it generally dealt with the problems of Asia. As one agency editor said rather wearily, "I can place only two stories consistently in the American press. One is about the Viet-Nam war and the other is about Red China. The rest is a gamble."

Compared with the $227 million propaganda investment of the American government alone in 1965 for foreign information and exchange programs,[44] world news as gathered by independent wire services was demonstrably a cheaper commodity. The Russians, of course, spent much more on their propaganda, with which their so-called news operations were combined. In such circumstances, it was difficult for the often inexperienced government officials in Asian countries to believe that the global news agencies were as disinterested as they professed to be; or, if they were, that their governments could not bring pressure to bear on them. Even to relatively sophisticated Asians, the notion of news agencies as independent forces was as unfamiliar a concept as the democratic systems under which they operated. Actually, the agencies' competition for sales in Asia may have hurt them over the long run more than it helped them.

5. STORM OVER SOUTHEAST ASIA

When the first few American correspondents stopped off briefly in Southeast Asia after World War II, they were only faintly aware of the strange new war that was going on all about them. Those who paid attention to it could scarcely have foreseen the length, the tenacity, and the expansion of what seemed then to be an unequal contest between poorly armed natives and a France reborn. With few exceptions, their coverage was minimal if, indeed, they filed anything at all. Nor could they be blamed. If there was seemingly any area more remote from American interests than Southeast Asia, it was probably someplace in Africa like the Congo.

The Francophiles among the Americans who visited Indochina for the first time in 1946 were charmed by the leisurely ways of Saigon. It seemed to them very much like an old French provincial city with its steeples and weathered buildings, set down along gracious, tree-lined streets and quiet, open squares. The tiny Vietnamese girls, so fragile and lovely, drifted along in their close-fitting silken sheaths worn over a tight pajama-like costume. The young men in their white shirts and darker slacks were all smiles to strangers and appeared to be ever so obliging.

"It was possible in those days," wrote Robert Shaplen, of the *New Yorker* magazine, a Saigon visitor in 1946, "to arrange an appointment on the outskirts of town with a Viet Minh agent and his girl courier, take a 'cyclo'—a sort of bicycle taxi—to the rendezvous, discuss elementary Marxism and guerrilla tactics . . . and return in time to have tea on the veranda of the old Continental Hotel and watch the afternoon shoppers strolling through a French Impressionist sun-speckled haze." [45]

There had been no American correspondents in Southeast Asia during World War II, with the exception of those like Relman Morin, of the AP, who was captured in Saigon after Pearl Harbor and interned there for a time. To him, there was nothing lyrical about Viet-Nam—just a "succession of long days, hot and damp in the tropics." [46] Others, like Richard Tregaskis, who came in after World War II, called it a "miserable little country" and thought of Saigon as a collection of "gambling joints and opium dives." [47] If correspondents' attitudes meant anything, and usually they did, the readers of the *New Yorker* and of some of the newspapers in the United States could not have believed that they were being told about the same country.

A new phase of the Vietnamese struggle had begun in 1946 soon after the arrival of a new French high commissioner, Admiral Thierry d'Argenlieu, of whom it was said that his was "the most brilliant mind of the twelfth century." [48] With an obtuseness often found in the military in Viet-Nam, the Admiral brushed aside the formal French recognition of Ho Chi Minh's Republic of Viet-Nam on March 6, 1946, and granted his own recognition to the southern portion as the "Republic of Cochin China" on May 30. When the French started mopping up in the south, Ho's Viet-Minh struck back. Bit by bit, the thin cloak of peace that had sheltered the green and fertile land was ripped to shreds. And at last, on November 23, 1946, the French heavy cruiser "Suffren" opened fire on an unruly but unarmed mob in Haiphong, causing 6,000 deaths. Ho's answer was a rising in Hanoi and a general attack on all French garrisons on December 19, marking the first major blow of the war against the French.

Until 1949, a French army of 100,000 men tried without avail to clear and hold the country, using classical World War II methods and old but serviceable equipment. But with the triumph of the Chinese Communists and their arrival at the borders of North Viet-Nam, Ho's forces found a sanctuary into which they could withdraw at will. There, General Vo Nguyen Giap, the master strategist of the Viet-Minh, began training a superb army and at the same time kept the guerrilla forces going to harass the French. It was the end of French offensive pretensions; from then on, their battle in Viet-Nam became an effort to hold what they had. It was a losing struggle. [49]

The United States had more important concerns. The Marshall Plan and the North Atlantic Treaty Alliance were laying the basis for Europe's revival. And in Asia, on June 25, 1950, the North Koreans struck southward across the 38th Parallel and the United States quickly found itself involved in a major war. A total of 270 correspondents, most of them Americans, flocked to General MacArthur's headquarters at the height of the war. As a result, there was precious little attention for the slim beginnings of American assistance to the French in Viet-Nam in 1950—a small U.S. Military Assistance Advisory Group (MAAG) which arrived in July and a $23.5 million fund for the 1951-52 fiscal year. [50]

There were some in the United States, and a few correspondents abroad, who doubted the correctness of the American course and spoke out against it. In 1951, a young Congressman from Massachusetts, John F. Kennedy, stopped off in Saigon while on a round-the-world trip with his brother Robert and his sister Pat. The AP correspondent, Seymour Topping, met Representative Kennedy at the airport and later briefed him at his own request. The Congressman wanted the real story of what was going on, and he didn't hesitate to accept it from the young correspondent, then as now an acute observer with few illusions. Thereafter, for this and other reasons, Kennedy was critical both of the French and of American policy in Indochina while he was in the Congress.[51]

The war ground on hopelessly under one of France's most illustrious military figures, General Jean de Lattre de Tassigny, known because of his regal manner as *le roi Jean*. But he failed, and in July, 1953, General Henri Navarre took command, accompanied by an encouraging prediction from no less a figure than Secretary of State John Foster Dulles. He credited Navarre with a plan that would "break the organized body of Communist aggression" by 1955.[52] It was an extreme manifestation of what George F. Kennan has called "that curious trait of the American political personality which causes it to appear reprehensible to voice anything less then unlimited optimism about the fortunes of another government one has adopted as a friend and protege." [53] Though Kennan referred to American support of the Kerensky regime in Russia in 1917, as recommended by Elihu Root, his remark applied equally to Dulles' appraisal of the French on the eve of their great defeat.

At Christmas time, 1953, Joseph Alsop, writing in the New York *Herald Tribune,* was not at all convinced that either Dulles or the French were right. He had just come to Paris after a month in Indochina, and he feared that a disaster impended. But, as he put it, "The State Department had virtually commanded our embassy in Saigon to emphasize the positive in all its reports. Hence the normally capable staff of the Paris embassy had been grossly misled about the gravity of the situation by reports from Saigon that were much too optimistic; and the embassy staff in turn misled the resident American correspondents."

Alsop was determined not to be misled. In an interview with Georges Bidault, who was then the Foreign Minister, the correspondent understood him to say that France would have to yield Indochina in a short time unless the United States joined in the war. It was, patently, a "signal" for Washington transmitted through the amiable agency of a willing reporter, a not uncommon procedure in the cold war, or in the hot ones. But when Washington reacted negatively to the interview, Bidault denied the whole business and blamed it on Alsop's bad French. Until the French collapsed in Indochina a short time later, it made a fine story for Alsop's journalistic opposition.[54]

With the end of the Korean War, some of the more realistic American editors began surveying Indochina and measuring the extent of the American commitment. Dien Bien Phu, a fortress on the Laos-Viet-Nam border in the north, was creeping into the headlines as the probable scene of a set-piece battle in which the eternal optimists predicted that the French would mow down the Viet-Minh and force them to sue for peace. Even then, however, the United States knew that the French garrison was in dire straits. Allen Dulles, chief of the Central Intelligence Agency, had reported as early as January 14, 1954, that the 11,000 French troops at Dien Bien Phu were down to six days' supply of rations and more would have to be airlifted.

When General Navarre's proposal for Dien Bien Phu had first been laid before President Eisenhower, he had warned a French diplomat: "You *cannot* do this!"

"This will bring the enemy into the open," had been the cool reply. "We cannot find them in the jungle, and this will draw them out where we can then win."

"The French know military history," Eisenhower had said. "They are smart enough to know the outcome of becoming firmly entrenched and then besieged in an exposed position with poor means of supply and reinforcements."

That, of course, did not come out at the time. What did emanate from most American sources was the usual rosy optimism despite all evidence to the contrary. Just about the only basis for it, apparently, was a hopeful estimate by Lieutenant General John W. ("Iron Mike") O'Daniel, the head of the U.S. MAAG mission in Saigon.[55] But to all feelers for American armed intervention, the Senate now turned a deaf ear. John F. Kennedy, then Senator from Massachusetts, blamed the French plight on their "unreasonable" demands on Ho Chi Minh in 1946. Senator Alexander Wiley, the Wisconsin Republican, warned, "If war comes under this administration, it could well be the end of the Republican Party." And Senator Lyndon B. Johnson refused to send American soldiers to Indochina "on a blood-letting spree to perpetuate colonialism and white man's exploitation in Asia."[56]

All this discussion presupposed that the correspondents in Asia and perhaps the more alert and well-informed members of the American public were aware of the Indochina war. As early as 1952, the United States had been paying for one-third to one-half of the cost of it,[57] and by 1954 had invested more than a billion dollars. But in March, 1954, when the Chicago *Daily News* ordered its Pulitzer Prize-winning correspondent, Keyes Beech, into Viet-Nam to cover the final phase of the battle at Dien Bien Phu, he wrote:

"Where the hell was Dien Bien Phu, anyway? Somewhere in Indochina, I know. But that war down there had been going on for eight years. Why make such a fuss about it now? From all I'd heard, it was a pretty crummy war." [58]

Six weeks before the end, the French were still issuing optimistic statements to the world and breathing imprecations against any correspondent who dared to intimate that they were not precisely telling the truth. At that time, Fernand Moulier, of Agence France-Presse, was told in Paris by one of the highest French military officials that all hope was gone for Dien Bien Phu and that the French cause in Indochina was hopeless. He put out the story on Indochina, which drew frantic denials from the Quai d'Orsay; fortunately, his source stood by him. [59]

It was in this atmosphere that the Far Eastern conference began at Geneva on April 27, 1954. Two days later, President Eisenhower told his news conference in Washington that there was no plausible reason for the United States to intervene in Indochina. The French, whose forces at Dien Bien Phu had dwindled to fewer than 10,000, were confronted by 40,000 Viet-Minh, who dominated the hills around them and poured in a merciless artillery fire. On May 7, Dien Bien Phu fell. The French empire in Asia came to an end. And the St. Louis *Post-Dispatch* published a cartoon by D. R. Fitzpatrick showing Uncle Sam, gun in hand, standing before a morass labeled "French mistakes in Indochina." [60] The over-all caption was: "How would another mistake help?" It won the Pulitzer Prize for cartooning that year. But otherwise, the disaster in Indochina had little impact in the United States.

The negotiations at Geneva dragged on, but they were given little attention in the press of the United States, with only few exceptions. Eventually, on July 21, 1954, an accord was signed which divided Viet-Nam along the 17th Parallel, giving 22 provinces with 13 million population to the Communist North and leaving 39 provinces with 12 million population in control of the South. Laos and Cambodia were confirmed as independent states. The United States did not sign the Geneva agreements but consented to abide by them.

Both sides agreed that no new troops or weapons and no new military bases would be introduced in either North or South Viet-Nam, that French troops would quit North Viet-Nam, and that elections would be held to determine the country's future. Almost before the ink was dry on the agreement, however, it was violated. Instead of giving up the guerrilla war in the South, the Viet-Minh merely stowed their weapons and communications and prepared to renew the conflict at a signal from Ho Chi Minh in the capital city of Hanoi. But by then, most of the correspondents had drifted away from Saigon. There was no news in the place. As for North Viet-Nam, it was closed to American journalists.

Ngo Dinh Diem, a mandarin who had served in 1933 as Minister of the Interior under French rule, now came home after many years in monasteries in the United States and Belgium and accepted the premiership of South Viet-Nam from the French. Nominally, he was requested to form a government by the figurehead Emperor, Bao-Dai, who soon vanished from the scene for the more sympathetic Riviera. Some hint of the effect the new premier would have on journalists was included in a report to *Time* magazine by its Saigon correspondent in 1955, John Mecklin: "Said a prominent American journalist after his first interview, 'Sort of a screwball, isn't he? His eyes don't even focus.' A senior American official calls him a 'stubborn little gink.' . . . For lack of any alternative, we are stuck with a marginal man." [61]

Marginal man or not, Diem took over. With the Ngo Dinh Nhus, his brother and sister-in-law, he established a family dictatorship. Using threats, bribes, and swift military action, he put one after another of his enemies out of the way. He placed himself at the head of the nation's 2 million Catholics. As for the more numerous Buddhists, he feared them and maneuvered to curb their power. He talked interminably, hatched plots and counterplots, and looked at everybody outside his immediate circle with the deepest suspicion.

In 1956, the year heralded for the promised elections, nothing happened. And in the North, Ho Chi Minh took notice that he had acquired a strong-willed rival. Even more important, he saw that the French had retired and that the United States had quietly filled the vacuum, maintaining the 685 "advisers" set under the 1954 agreements. Had it not been for American help, Diem could never have resettled the nearly 900,000 refugees who poured in from the north. He was also the beneficiary of massive American aid, a flood of dollars that could have been turned into an efficient land redistribution program—a real blow at Communism. But Diem preferred to put the money into his army and other projects, including the much debated program of fortified villages, later called the "strategic hamlet" program.

By 1957, village leaders in South Viet-Nam's Delta region were being murdered with appalling regularity, and the people were being deluged with persuasive Communist propaganda. It was the first sign that Ho was reactivating his forces, now known as the Viet-Cong. By 1959, having perfected a system for supplying them along jungle trails through Laos, he was ready, and the Viet-Cong insurrection began. At almost the same time, the Communist-supported Pathet Lao opened an offensive in neighboring Laos. Even so, the world learned of it mainly from news-agency reporters and a few correspondents from the great American, British, and French newspapers. Indochina still was not a dominating reality for either the American press or the public.

But for John F. Kennedy, when he became President in 1961, the Communist gains in Indochina were no less alarming than those in Cuba. A whole new American team came to Saigon, headed by a courteous, easygoing Virginian, Ambassador Frederick E. Nolting, Jr., and a four-star general, Paul D. Harkins, who took command of the new Military Assistance Command, Viet-Nam (MACV). In late 1961 President Kennedy sent his personal representative, General Maxwell D. Taylor, to Viet-Nam to recommend some way of halting the Viet-Cong. With that, the United States was not only committed to Diem, the "marginal man"; it embraced him as a veritable Sir Galahad whose every move deserved support.

The Kennedy Administration was so fearful of being accused of violating the Geneva accords that it went to fantastic lengths to conceal the arrival of ships, troops, helicopters, and matériel. In early 1962, for example, while it was claimed that the limit of 685 had not been exceeded, there were closer to 4,000 military personnel in South Viet-Nam in American uniform. It took a correspondent's protesting news story to persuade the American government that it was no sin to award an American soldier a Purple Heart for wounds suffered in combat. And it took other correspondents' stories of the failure of the Diem "strategic hamlet" program—the fortification of villages—to cause some soul-searching at the embassy. This was the beginning of a war which was waged against the American correspondents, and two or three others, with seemingly greater enthusiasm sometimes than the life-or-death struggle against the Viet-Cong.

François Sully, of *Newsweek*, a French national, was ordered out of Viet-Nam for offending Mme. Nhu with his reporting. Jim Robinson, of N.B.C., also was banished. It took a stiff protest by Ambassador Nolting himself to keep the outraged Diem from expelling Homer Bigart, of the New York *Times*. No correspondent could feel safe with Diem's spies and Nhu's hatchet men around. All correspondents knew that far from being mere observers at this fantastic Asian war, they were being forced into the role of participants.[62]

John Mecklin, who had come back to Saigon in 1962 as the embassy's public-affairs officer, wrote:

In its dealings with newsmen, the U.S. Mission . . . was often wrong about the facts, in a situation of utmost importance to the U.S. national interest in support of a controversial policy that was costing the lives of U.S. servicemen. Even if conditions had otherwise been normal, this was

incompatible with the inquisitive, skeptical nature of American journalism, and trouble would have been inevitable. Unhappily, conditions
were not otherwise normal.[63]

Even in its early stages, this "press conflict" took much more time
and effort at the embassy and at Diem's headquarters than even the
correspondents conceived possible. At one stage in 1961, Diem hired a
professional public-relations consultant from the United States at a reported $100,000 fee, but he speedily retired in a cloud of suspicion and
intrigue.[64] At another, an American government press "specialist" was
brought to Saigon to "straighten out" the correspondents, always an
interesting exercise. He proceeded to do so by issuing a list of "available" and presumably agreeable girls. His professed object was to halt
the correspondents' trips into the field for information, which was seldom available in Saigon. He wanted to "keep them happy in Saigon"
and "take their minds off the war." [65] He didn't last long. Another celebrated contribution to the art of government public relations was made
by Admiral Harry D. Felt, who snapped at the too-inquisitive Malcolm
W. Browne, of the AP, in Saigon during a news conference: "Look
here, boy! You'd better get on the team!" [66] While his words were not
as exalted as Nelson's at Trafalgar, they, too, have become a part of
history.

What was wrong? Primarily, it was a resumption of the basic conflict
between government and press in an exaggerated form. In 1961-63 a
hard-pressed American government wanted its public to believe that a
badly planned war was going well, and a handful of correspondents
were determined to report what was really happening. While both sides
acted as if their involvement were new and extraordinary, the roots of
their differences lay deep in American history. General George Washington, in a letter to the Continental Congress in May, 1777, complained: "It is much to be wished that our printers were more discreet
in many of their publications. We see in almost every paper . . . accounts transmitted to the enemy of an injurious nature." And General
William Tecumseh Sherman, in the Civil War, exclaimed upon being
told that three correspondents had been killed by an exploding shell,
"Good! Now we shall have news of hell before breakfast!" [67] Such hostility had been accepted for nearly two hundred years by the independent journalist as an occupational hazard, and the wiser ones had made
due allowance for it.

In Saigon, however, there was no one either at the embassy or in the
press corps who had any patience with the long view. At best, the embassy people at the highest levels were patronizing, and the press was
frigidly polite. At worst, the officials made vigorous efforts to punish

the most independent correspondents, invoking at one point the prestige of the White House itself; as for the correspondents, the more volatile ones made angry threats or kicked up childish scenes when they felt themselves slighted. Some of the individual personality conflicts were almost incredible in their intensity, and the reporters were by no means blameless.

The peculiarity of the Diem regime was an added complication. On the testimony of officials and correspondents who were in Saigon at the time and who have been interviewed separately since, there is no doubt whatever that Diem and his brother Nhu were able to obtain the embassy's acceptance for false claims of battle successes and false figures on the progress of the "strategic hamlet" program. Since this documentation was forwarded regularly to Washington, it is no wonder that the government was incredulous when the correspondents persistently reported that the war was being lost. If high officials were sent to Saigon, they usually saw only the people who were convinced in the first instance that Diem and Nhu were telling the truth. It would have been a rare American "adviser" in the field who could have challenged the views of an ambassador or a four-star general in the presence of a visiting dignitary from Washington. But the "advisers" could and did confide their frustrations, their doubts, their fears, and their truthful information to the correspondents on the pledge that they would be protected. Since some of these sources were affiliated with the Central Intelligence Agency, the basis of their trust in their own organization in Viet-Nam could not have been very strong.[68]

President Kennedy intervened in the growing government-press conflict on April 29, 1963, when he summoned John Mecklin, the embassy's public-affairs officer, from Saigon. The President asked him: "Why are we having so much trouble with the reporters out there?"

Mecklin was completely frank. Short of winning the war, he said, the only way to maintain a credible position was to abandon the Saigon embassy's policy of issuing excessively optimistic statements, halt complaints over unfavorable publicity, and take the correspondents into the government's confidence. He was aware, of course, that the sensitive Diem and the Nhus would be horrified by any policy that did not credit them with overwhelming the Communists and winning all doubters to their side. The embassy, therefore, could not by itself work with the correspondents on a more realistic basis; the change, if any, would have to come from Washington.

The President was skeptical, but a cable was sent soon afterward from the State Department to the Saigon embassy, advising "cooperation with U.S. correspondents." [69] At that juncture, the Buddhists were provoked beyond endurance by a short-sighted and repressive regime.

All thought of a new era of sweetness and light with the correspondents had to be abandoned because they were caught up in the struggle by the very nature of their duties. And, as usual, the Diem regime compounded the crisis by falsifying the reasons for it, then looked to the Americans, as usual, to support its outrageous version of events.

The seemingly inconsequential issue of the right of Buddhists to fly their flags in Hué on May 8, 1963, the 2,527th anniversary of the birth of the Buddha, touched off the chain of events that led directly to disaster. Thich Tri Quang, a powerful young Buddhist leader, so resented the government's refusal to permit the flag display (the Catholics had been so favored) that he organized a throng of several thousand of his coreligionists and led them to the Hué radio station. The Hué military commander moved in troops and armored cars with fatal results. The Buddhists charged that the troops opened fire, killing some, and crushed others under the armored cars. Eight died on the spot, and others died later. The Diem regime immediately put out a story that a Viet-Cong agent had thrown a grenade, but nobody believed it, least of all the correspondents. Long afterward, a court of inquiry sentenced the troop commander of that day to life imprisonment, but by that time it was too late to appease the Buddhists. Mass demonstrations erupted in Saigon and Hué, growing in fervor with every refusal of the Diem government to make amends.

Then, on June 11, 1963, Malcolm W. Browne, who had been the chief of the AP bureau in Saigon since 1961, hurried to an early morning rendezvous with several Buddhists in response to their urgent summons. Within a short time, he was taken to one of the most important intersections in Saigon, and there he saw the Venerable Thich Quang Duc, a seventy-three-year-old monk, burn himself to death before a wailing crowd of other Buddhist monks and nuns. Browne made the pictures of that shocking protest against the excesses of the Diem regime, which overnight won world sympathy for the Buddhists.[70]

Everything about the Buddhists in Viet-Nam was controversial, and the sympathy for Diem's cause among the more conservative Catholic elements in the United States compounded the difficulties of the correspondents. To a dedicated anti-Communist, it became almost an insult to mention casually that Buddhists were in the majority in South Viet-Nam. Mme. Nhu, for instance, contended that only 15 per cent of the people in her country were Buddhists; however, the Vietnamese Embassy in Washington had a brochure that put the figure at 90 per cent. The correspondents settled for about 5 million practicing Buddhists, the rest being ancestor-worshipers.[71]

As the Buddhist demonstrations mounted, the correspondents' lives became more harried. Most permanent correspondents had had far more than their share of exposure to danger outside Saigon. Now, Saigon itself became dangerous. On July 7, 1963, Vietnamese secret police beat up Peter Arnett, of the AP, while he was covering a Buddhist demonstration, and his colleague, Malcolm Browne, was hit with a brick that smashed his camera.

It became still another issue between the correspondents and the embassy. President Kennedy sent Robert Manning, Assistant Secretary of State for Public Affairs, to investigate the press problem. Meanwhile, the two correspondents were accused of having attacked the secret police. Eight of their press colleagues charged the embassy with failure to take strong enough action, but eventually Manning was able to calm Diem and his people, and the charges were dropped.

Coincidentally, the correspondents learned that Henry Cabot Lodge would soon replace Ambassador Nolting. The Kennedy Administration had finally wearied of the highhanded treatment of the Buddhists by the Diem regime and the close support it had been invariably accorded by the embassy.

Two days before Lodge's arrival, Diem and Nhu faced him with another major problem by ordering a nationwide crackdown on the Buddhists, topped by a raid on the Xa Loi Pagoda in Saigon. It was carried out with ruthless violence and amid such secrecy that John Richardson, the CIA director in Saigon, said he had known nothing of the plans. However, Nicholas Turner, of Reuters, had filed a story some days before, saying that Nhu was planning such a cleanup. And on the night of the raid, a number of correspondents witnessed the Xa Loi attack. Yet, Ambassador Nolting still clung to Diem and Nhu. He told an interviewer there had been no "persecution" of the Buddhists in Viet-Nam.[72] When Lodge arrived on August 22, Nolting had departed, but two Buddhist leaders had taken refuge at the American aid mission's offices.

Almost the first thing the new Ambassador did was to look up the correspondents and establish decent relations with them, although he never undertook to give them much information. Within a few days, it was clear that the United States no longer intended to cover up for Diem. While the Kennedy Administration thus changed its position and even permitted the Voice of America to threaten that U.S. aid to Viet-Nam would be reduced unless the regime made amends for the Buddhist raids, the correspondents came under attack from a new direction. On September 20, 1963, in a piece dictated in the office, *Time* magazine accused the Saigon press corps of "helping to compound the very confusion that it should be untangling for its readers at home," of pooling its "convictions, information, misinformation and grievances," and of distorting the news. Worse still, *Time* charged that many of the correspondents "seem reluctant to give splash treatment to anything that smacks of military victory in the ugly war against the Communists, since this would take the sheen off the theory that the infection of the Buddhist troubles in Saigon is demoralizing the government troops, and weakens the argument that defeat is inevitable so long as Diem is in power." [73]

Charles Mohr, *Time*'s Southeast Asia bureau chief, resigned in protest and promptly was engaged by the New York *Times*. Ambassador Lodge didn't see it *Time*'s way, defending the correspondents as "appealing, brave, tremendously hard-working." Denis Warner, an Australian, agreed: "Not since the first month of the Korean War have I seen so many American correspondents in Asia working so hard and so honestly under such appalling conditions." Just about the only ones who sided with *Time* were Joseph Alsop, who thought the war was being won, and Marguerite Higgins, who was quoted by Mohr as having said, "Reporters here would like to see us lose the war to prove they're right." *Time* ended the argument by conceding the reporters had been right in reporting the deterioration of the Diem government.[74]

It was unpleasant for the young correspondents to be charged with distorting the news and worse. But on October 22, 1963, one of them— David Halberstam of the New York *Times*—was deemed objectionable enough to be singled out for special attention by the President of the United States. The incident occurred when Arthur Ochs Sulzberger, the new publisher of the New York *Times,* paid a courtesy call at the White House and was asked by President Kennedy if he had been thinking of transferring Halberstam. The correspondent, the President suggested, was "too involved." Sulzberger politely replied that the *Times* was satisfied with Halberstam's work.[75] Nevertheless, the correspondent was brought back to the United States some weeks later, was assigned to Poland (and later expelled for reporting that displeased the regime), and then attached to the Paris bureau.

The correspondents did not create problems for American policy in Southeast Asia, but they certainly magnified the ones that already existed. While they were regularly accused of giving aid and comfort to the enemy, this is a self-serving charge that has often been made by governments that are injudicious enough to claim mythical victories and otherwise delude public opinion. On the basic point of accuracy in reporting that the war was then being lost, which is what the furor was all about, the correspondents were right and the ponderous official machinery of the U.S. Government was wrong. It was for this that Browne and Halberstam shared the 1964 Pulitzer Prize for international reporting.

Their work, and that of the few other regulars, constituted almost the entire American press effort at that stage of the Viet-Nam war. Except for the news agencies, a few great newspapers, the news magazines, and the television chains, the American media did not regularly assign correspondents to cover the conflict. Even some of these were erratic. The unpalatable truth is that the job of covering the Viet-Nam war in 1963 was done by a mere handful of regulars, many of them young and inexperienced, who worked seven days a week and all hours of the day and night, a majority in the $6,500-to-$8,500-a-year bracket. (Some earned even less.) As late as the summer of 1964, there were fewer than a score of American correspondents regularly assigned to Saigon. The Department of Defense brought in others on junkets from Washington at a cost of about $1,000 per correspondent for travel, paid for out of a $50,000 departmental fund, in an effort to get what one official called a "less biased view." [76]

While it can scarcely be said of the correspondents that they overthrew the Diem regime, they did bring about a more realistic appraisal of the Viet-Nam war. They also helped change the U.S. Government's attitude toward the Diem regime. But after the regime's overthrow on November 1-2, 1963, by a military junta that had the implicit support of the United States, there was no perceptible change in the conduct of the war for more than a year. The American Presidential campaign slowed things up.

Ambassador Lodge, during his relatively brief first term in Saigon, held the line and ran the embassy with the astuteness of a seasoned professional diplomat who had the respect, if not the affection, of the press and the resident American staff. General Harkins and the CIA director, Richardson, were replaced. The total of American servicemen in Viet-Nam slowly climbed from an admitted 12,000 on January 26, 1963, to 15,000 in the summer of 1964, while American expenditures were stepped up, the press reported, to a rate of $1.5 million a day.

The official posture of determined optimism was not attempted again until General Maxwell D. Taylor's term as American Ambassador in Saigon. But even he gave up the pretense long before Lodge replaced him in 1965. By that time, the war had escalated, and at least two hundred correspondents were in South Viet-Nam, many of them Americans. Once more, it had taken a war to expand the network of communications between the United States and Asia.

6. THE LESSONS OF TWENTY YEARS

From the peace of Tokyo Bay to the bombing of North Viet-Nam, the American public did not often manifest interest in Asia except during Presidential election years or when Communist pressures drew American armed forces into battle. Then, a great cry would arise: "Why are secrets being kept from the American people? Why weren't the American people told that this was going on?" It was ironic that the very editorialists who were the first to protest represented newspapers that had been the most indifferent to the vital necessity for publishing significant news of Asia and engaging correspondents who had some knowledge of this vast and critical area.

The few correspondents who were permanently assigned to a post in Asia did their best to handle what was, under the circumstances, an almost impossible job. They reported the principal events. Their work was available to the mass media as a whole, either through the news agencies or the newspaper syndicates. But except for wars, comparatively little of it was published outside the handful of newspapers and news magazines that specialized in international affairs or the scholarly journals. Now and then, there would be a glamorous documentary on television, but it was generally confined to a subject like Hong Kong or India's teeming millions, complete with elephant boys and snake charmers.

Powerful forces began to reshape Asia in those twenty years. The most populous nations on earth shook off decades of colonial servitude. India, Pakistan, and Indonesia became free nations. China, under Communist rule, developed into one of the great powers, with an atomic capability of its own. Japan, shattered in 1945, reconstructed the mightiest industrial empire in Asia within less than two decades and challenged the trading potential of the West. For all that, the American public showed little interest. Indifference, apathy, and sometimes even hostility were the reward of most of those who sought to overcome the inertia of the mass mind.

It became evident to the few who were seriously concerned with a dangerous lapse in the coverage of Asia that only a decision at the top level could induce a newspaper to publish news of such nations as India or Japan on a regular basis. Most editors were altogether too willing to accept the results of public-opinion polls that the American public cared little for foreign news in general and Asian news in particular. They accepted, without question, what the *Times* of London called the "country bumpkin" theory of the public to justify "an unavowed censorship which, at its most oppressive, can produce conditions of news starvation, or acute malinformation, hardly less pitiable than those witnessed under totalitarian control." [77]

There is no doubt that such an "unavowed censorship" did exist in a very large part of the American press in the mid-1960's. It was precisely this unwillingness to publish news of Asia that constituted the principal reason for the lamentable state of public ignorance of the background of some of the major issues confronting the United States, such as the crises over Kashmir and Viet-Nam.

One of the phenomena of the day was the extent to which American journalists outside the main centers of population subscribed to such newspapers as the New York *Times* and the *Christian Science Monitor* "to find out what's going on in the world," as one editor put it. Any publisher could determine very easily the adequacy with which his newspaper informed his public by merely asking his staff how many of them had to buy out-of-town newspapers for national and international news. The argument that a paper would go broke if it printed a sufficient budget of such news simply didn't make sense, in view of the demonstrable need for such information by citizens who thought of themselves as responsible people. Nor was the "country bumpkin" theory an adequate excuse, either.

Aside from this basic flaw in the American machinery for public communication, which was a compound of under-representation of correspondents in much of Asia and the refusal of many editors to print even a part of what was available about countries outside the war zones, the relatively indifferent relationships between government and press in a number of key areas sometimes made it difficult to get at the real news. Facts, as such, were readily available in much of Asia, either from American sources or the Asian governments themselves. But the meaning of the facts and their significance for American policy were not always easy to establish. It was here that lack of understanding between press and government led, at times, to more complications than were either necessary or desirable.

Walter Lippmann was rather optimistic, on the whole, about the breadth of this conflict and its eventual result, but others were not as sanguine as he was. Before the International Press Institute in London, in 1965, Lippmann defined his views as follows:

> I have in mind the conflict between, on the one hand, the public's right to know, or it may be the public's curiosity to know, and, on the other hand, the right and the need of the government to be able to deliberate confidentially before announcing a conclusion, and in certain circumstances, especially in its foreign relations, the government's right to a measure of secrecy and dispatch.
>
> The conflict is, I am inclined to believe, perennial in the sense that there is no abstract principle which resolves it. The right of the press to know and the right of the responsible authority to withhold must coexist. In my country, we have a continual tension between public officials and reporters about the disclosure of coming events, what is going to be an-

nounced, what policy is going to be adopted, who is going to be appointed, what will be said to a foreign government. There is also a conflict about what has happened, and why it has happened, and who was responsible for it happening.

The tension is between vigilant, ingenious and suspicious reporters who haunt and pursue public officials, causing these officials never to be allowed to forget that they are withholding information at their peril, at the risk of being scalped in the newspapers. It is not a neat or an elegant relationship, but a *modus vivendi* which works tolerably well, at least in time of peace. . . .[78]

There was another difficulty in maintaining a thin flow of news between the United States and the nations of Asia that were not involved in the various wars of containment waged against militant Communism in the Far East. This was the vastly oversimplified concept that the United States dominated the flow of news in both directions and that, as a result, most of the obstacles also could be found in the United States. To an extent, this was so, but it was not the whole story. Asian journalists in the United States were emerging from a period in which they were often dependent on American news media for everything they sent. And Asian editors were not backward about reproaching the news agencies to which they subscribed for playing "the American angle" when it was done to excess.

Yet, in broad outline, the prevailing assumption in the mid-1960's was, as one authority put it, "that the news flows from the highly developed to the less-developed countries. It flows from Europe and North America to the other continents. It flows from the United States and the Soviet Union to all other countries." [79] Accordingly, it was argued that the United States, Britain, France, and the Soviet Union dominated the news flow because the four independent global news agencies were located in the West and the Soviet Union's service, Tass, was the voice of the Communist world. However true this might have been in 1945, or even as late as 1950, it did not approach reality in all sections of Asia in 1966.

In some Asian nations, the global agencies' output was filtered through a national news-service apparatus, with a consequent loss of time, volume, emphasis, and, very often, meaning. Asian editors, too, had reached a point where they did not humbly accept what was sent to them by the agencies, their own or others. Those editors who could afford their own foreign correspondents—and in Japan and India these were increasing—insisted on an "Asian view" of every controversial story. Those who didn't have correspondents (and many who did) very often rewrote agency copy to present their own "angle." American agency people even complained that sometimes they read a doctored version of their dispatches under the by-line of an Asian correspondent in the United States, a deplorable practice that can still be spotted in some American newspapers, too. But certainly, the "American view" of the United States was not dominant in the independent press of Asian nations; in the controlled press, it was, of course, nonexistent.

As a source of dependable news, the Soviet Union sometimes was as suspect among neutralist Asian editors as the United States. It was perfectly obvious to a casual visitor to some important newspapers in Japan, Korea, India, and Pakistan that the New China News Agency (NCNA) file was often given more attention than that of Tass. This did not mean that Peking's brand of propaganda was preferred; it was simply realistic for Asian editors to keep a wary eye on the mouthpiece of their largest and most aggressive neighbor. Besides, Moscow's reaction to most news had been predictable for years. Curiously, some Asian editors also advanced the argument of professional competence to account for their preference of the NCNA service over that of Tass. They contended that former Chinese employees of Reuters and other global news agencies now working for NCNA had a better knowledge of the Far East than the Russians. Whether it was true or not, Tass generally had a rough time in much of Asia.

The effect of the news flow from the United States, therefore, was subject to a number of complicating factors and could not be measured by any simple rule or even a set of charts. There was also a multiplying factor in Asian nations plagued with a low literacy rate, such as India, where the content of a single newspaper or radio news period might be passed on by word of mouth to ten people or to an entire village. The probability of distortion, or even unintentional falsehoods, was very high in such a society.

There were also complicating factors in the flow of information about Asian nations to the United States, the worst of which was the increasing tendency of smaller countries to emulate Peking by expelling or barring correspondents of U.S. news-gathering organizations. Even in those nations where they were reasonably free to operate, the correspondents were forced to depend to some extent on the indigenous mass media, such as they were. While this was not a problem in South Viet-Nam or Laos, it was a factor of growing importance in Japan, India, the Philippines, and a few other places.

In such areas, the correspondent, whether he liked it or not, became a part of the mass information complex of the nation to which he was assigned. Whether he did his own reading and listening or, not knowing the language, had a local assistant do it for him, he became immersed in the affairs of a strange nation which, however fascinating, had little meaning for his home audience.

It was a rare correspondent who did not react—sometimes favorably, often irritably and even angrily—to such involvement and its complications. Many correspondents took the easy way out by constant travel away from their base to places where there was news of more interest to the American reader. A number of younger men who stayed in Asia for some length of time took Japanese brides, and a few married other Asian girls, but the proportion of such marriages was no more than might be expected of American correspondents in Europe. There were also isolated cases of correspondents who had so little sympathy for an Asian assignment that they came home at their own request or were relieved.

Yet, American editors were wary of engaging Asian correspondents despite the competence of a few of them. There was also a spreading conviction against permitting American correspondents to remain very long in any post, in Asia or elsewhere, for fear that he might lose his objectivity. Hence, it became fairly general practice to move American correspondents every three years—and sometimes earlier in Asian hardship posts. The days of the correspondent who acted as virtual proconsul for his country were almost over. This was one of the few areas where American journalistic and diplomatic practices coincided.

Twenty years after the peace of Tokyo Bay, the spinning of the communications web between the United States and Asia was far from complete. What went over it in either direction, or within Asia, was seldom satisfying to those editors and correspondents who were aware of the grievous shortcomings of the system of news exchanges. It was only when there was a war, such as the long conflict in Viet-Nam or the shorter one over Kashmir, that the trickle of news suddenly expanded to flood stage. President Johnson's visit to the Far East in 1966, for example, brought 1,000 correspondents to cover the Manila Conference. The normal complement was a half-dozen regulars.

Yet, public attitudes, journalistic practices, and government policies were not particularly favorable to radical changes. Despite the growing importance of the news flow between the United States and the nations of East, Southeast, and South Asia, the channels to the mass media remained narrow; in fact, except in wartime, they tended to constrict rather than expand.

II

At the Center of Power

1. THE NEWS MANAGERS

AN UNPLEASANT SURPRISE was in store for most of the Japanese, Indian, and the few other Asian correspondents who picked up some five pounds of American Sunday newspapers outside their front doors in Washington and New York on April 25, 1965. In various front-page stories, they read that a government source had done some rather serious talking about atomic weapons and the Viet-Nam war.

Manifestly, this story was of the utmost importance. But from past experience, they realized that one American news agency, perhaps both of them, already had moved the story to their home offices in Asia and "rockets" would soon be arriving. (A "rocket" is the term for a message from an editor about a lapse in coverage that requires an explanation.) Some, in fact, already had received these abrupt inquiries and needed only a confirming glance at the newspapers.

The explanation, in this case, was obvious. The story must have originated at another of those Washington background briefings for selected American correspondents. If any others from Europe or Asia had heard a rumor about the session, it could have come only from an American, and not many of them were notably generous about sharing "inside stuff." It helped a correspondent's prestige to be tapped for such a top-level briefing. Few were indiscreet enough to jeopardize their status by leaking, particularly to correspondents who could provide nothing useful in return.

Any foreign correspondent who had been left out of the party would have been disturbed, indeed, by the New York *Herald Tribune*'s report, which said: "Although it sees no need for them now or, it hopes, in the future, the Johnson administration has not ruled out the use of nuclear weapons if the Vietnam war worsens, it has been learned reliably." [1]

The New York *Times* was more reassuring, since its report led with President Johnson's determination to maintain his Viet-Nam policy. But inside, on the runover, the *Times*'s Tom Wicker dealt with the sticky subject in this manner:

> The officials . . . emphasize that it is "inconceivable" that nuclear weapons should be used in the present circumstances. They do not rule out the possibility that circumstances might arise in which nuclear weapons would have to be used. These circumstances are carefully not defined, and the officials note that the "gigantic step" of using even small tactical nuclear weapons would have to be weighed against the high cost of such action. [2]

These and other accounts, obviously of the same meeting, led to what Arthur Krock called a "world-wide flap" because of the "unmistakable marks . . . of high official authority for publication." Krock agreed in effect with one deduction that "in a veiled warning to Communist China, the Johnson administration is letting it be known that it intends to use nuclear weapons, if necessary, to maintain its position in Vietnam." [3]

If this was the intent, it could have served as a classic example of the use of news as a weapon of government. In its modern manifestation, this esoteric procedure had been resorted to during the Cuban missile crisis in 1962. Arthur Sylvester, the veteran Washington correspondent who was then Assistant Secretary of Defense for Public Affairs, had explained: "The generation of news by actions taken by government becomes one weapon in a strained situation." [4]

However, unlike the "eyeball to eyeball" confrontation with the Soviet Union in the Cuban crisis, the United States evidently had no desire in 1965 for any similar challenge to Communist China, even if Peking's atomic devices were only rudimentary. As is so often the case with high-level briefings for a few "trusties," the British term for favored correspondents, those who were excluded magnified the affair out of all proportion to its actual importance. In this familiar journalistic process, the Asians played a particular role because of their proximity to the scene of conflict.

The United States quickly climbed down. On the following day, Secretary of Defense Robert S. McNamara told a Pentagon news conference that he saw "no military requirement for nuclear weapons in Vietnam" in either the present or in the foreseeable future. "No useful purpose," he added, "can be served by speculation on remote contingencies." [5]

Doris Fleeson, a syndicated columnist, asked the Secretary: "How come it was done, then?" He replied, "I don't know that it *was* done."

Krock commented drily that McNamara apparently had been one of the few in Washington who did not know the source of the atomic reference. For the benefit of the mysterious source, termed "Mr. X," the columnist recalled how President Truman's reference to an atomic arsenal had brought Britain's Prime Minister Clement Attlee flying to Washington during the Korean War and how bitterly the Democrats had attacked the Republican Presidential nominee, Barry Goldwater, in 1964 for suggesting atomic defoliation as a method of attacking the Viet-Cong. "If only the Mr. X of the week-end dispatches had remembered what happened to Harry and Barry," Krock concluded. [6]

Even that did not end the venture into atomic diplomacy. President Johnson, at his April 27 news conference, pointedly reminded the correspondents that he alone could decide if nuclear weapons should be used. He added earnestly that in his seventeen months in office, no one in government had ever suggested an atomic attack in Viet-Nam. Although the foreign correspondents had had no access to the original session, they were welcome at both the McNamara and Johnson open conferences and recorded the assurances by both officials.

There was a postscript, as there often is, from some of those who had handled the now-famous Sunday morning news that wasn't news. Richard C. Wald, associate editor of the New York *Herald Tribune,* disclosed that the "Mr. X" of the high-level briefing was Secretary McNamara. From other sources, it became known that his remarks had been made at a dinner background meeting for about forty American bureau chiefs and columnists on Thursday, April 22, with all participants agreeing to use nothing before Sunday. However, the AP had put out an advance for Sunday papers, and the "rockets" had started flying.

Under the trade rules for background briefings, the press assures the subject anonymity if he permits publication of his material. The procedure is widely used in Washington and elsewhere. For the government, it is often a practical device for testing public sentiment, releasing trial balloons for the attention of the enemy and others, and keeping troublesome newsmen occupied. For the correspondents, it is a means of maintaining touch with high-level sources. Everybody is generally happy about such "backgrounders" except the ones who are left out. They are the hazard. When the "backgrounder" blows up, the "trusties" have nothing to show for their pains but scars. "It happened but it didn't happen," Wald commented. "The moral is . . . if no name is attached to the inside revelation, maybe an extra grain of salt is needed before it is swallowed." [7]

The incident was another in a long series that had called American credibility into question, particularly in Asia. News management, real or fancied, was an inevitable topic of discussion whenever editors met with American correspondents. The more sophisticated Asians, of course, accepted the problem of dealing with a powerful government as one of the hazards that face any foreign correspondent.

Basically there was nothing wrong with the volume of news from government sources in Washington. President Johnson contended quite correctly shortly after his election in 1964 that he was making more news available to press and public than his immediate predecessors. The difference was a matter of attitude—a centralization of all major news developments at the White House and a sensitivity to criticism that threatened for a time to overshadow the President's success with his domestic program.

To be sure, all Presidents have had their troubles with the press; in the mid-1960's, the heat was on Lyndon Baines Johnson primarily because he had ordered the American troop buildup in Viet-Nam and military intervention in the Dominican revolution. The American public backed him then. Private polls at the time of the escalation decision showed that 84 per cent of those interviewed favored "stepping up the war" in Viet-Nam to win, although most people necessarily were vague about what constituted victory. His support was much stronger then than was President Roosevelt's before Pearl Harbor, when the House of Representatives renewed the draft by only a single vote. President Johnson also had more Americans behind him than President Truman could count on in the Korean War. Yet, the opposition of the liberal press at home and the doubts of friendly governments and usually friendly newspapers abroad created a rather formidable problem. The President's popularity, in polls taken during the fall of 1966, plunged to a bare 50 per cent of the electorate.

What, then, did it take to deal with the American press—a necessary prerequisite to any effort to make a favorable impression in the foreign press? Eleanor Roosevelt once said: "There was a real dialogue between Franklin and the people. That dialogue seems to have disappeared from the government since he died." [8] Except for the very real sense of loss that welled up after President Kennedy's assassination and the flashes of good feeling at various times in the Eisenhower and Johnson administrations, the special relationship between Roosevelt and the press in advancing American foreign policy also disappeared.

If there was an exception to the generally tense relationships between

Presidents and the Washington press corps, it was in the Roosevelt era. He liked the correspondents and they usually enjoyed being with him. It was not an accident that his program of voluntary censorship during World War II worked out well, for he trusted the journalists who ran it; furthermore, he so thoroughly dominated the Page 1 headlines that he seldom had to stoop to crude efforts to intimidate or persuade. In a sense, it was his good fortune that so many publishers and editorial pages were hostile to him; he could scarcely have manipulated them if he had tried.

To a large extent, this essential empathy between the Presidency and the Washington press corps persisted throughout the Truman Administration, even after the outbreak of the Korean War. But insensibly, even though the United States was the sole possessor of the atomic bomb until the Russian conquest of the atom in 1949, the government began moving for greater control over the sources of the news. There was an inherent nervousness over security information, based on public resentment of Russian spying. In 1951, the government established unilateral control over various types of security information through President Truman's Executive Order 10-290, which the press opposed.[9]

With the intensification of Soviet atomic might and the coming of French and Chinese atomic development, even the combined resources of the United States and Great Britain—superior though they were—could not guarantee the nation's security from a sudden wanton stroke by an aggressor. It was, therefore, no mere whim that made Presidents Eisenhower and Kennedy so conscious of the violation of even the appearance of national security. On one occasion when it was impossible to conceal a large missile, and a West Coast newspaper took a photograph that it published on Page 1, Eisenhower was appalled. At another time, he violently objected to the publication of an aerial photograph of an important military installation, even though it had been included in various souvenir booklets for years. It was not a surprise, therefore, when he unhesitatingly went through with an effort to use a "cover story" for the shooting down of Francis Gary Power's U-2 spy plane over Russia and then quietly accepted blame for the falsehood when Soviet Premier Khrushchev exposed it.[10] Thus, the credibility of the Presidency, the most valuable news resource of the United States, was laid open to attack.

During the Eisenhower Administration, the "backgrounder," used by Secretary of State John Foster Dulles to "signal" the enemy, also brought embarrassing results. Dulles had always fancied himself a master at manipulating the press, an estimate with which few correspondents agreed. During the Quemoy-Matsu crisis of 1958, Dulles decided on an unusual move while he was with President Eisenhower in September at Newport, R.I. First, he held a regulation news conference as Secretary of State, in which he announced that the United States had not yet decided whether to defend the offshore islands from a Chinese Communist attack. Then, he invoked the background rule, presented himself as a "high U.S. official," and proceeded to warn Peking, in effect, that the Eisenhower Administration had decided to fight, if necessary. It was too much for his predecessor, Dean Acheson, who exposed the double-talk diplomacy and identified Dulles as the author as soon as the first "news" stories were published in Washington.[11]

Like President Eisenhower, President Kennedy was caught up in a vital concern over national security when he made his first moves in Cuba and Viet-Nam in 1961. It was his decision, primarily, to try to conceal the modest buildup of American military "advisers" in Viet-Nam. And following the disastrous failure of the Bay of Pigs invasion in Cuba, he took the blame and, with it, the responsibility for the issuance of so much false information in a vain effort to deceive Fidel Castro about what was going on in his own country. Once again, the credibility of the Presidency was injured.*

In the second Cuban crisis, in which Kennedy succeeded in forcing a withdrawal of Soviet offensive missiles from Cuban bases, he entered the showdown with foreboding. On the night before his nationwide telecast of October 22, 1962, when he had already determined to confront the Soviet Union with a blockade of the Cuban coast, he learned that news of the crisis had leaked to the Washington *Post* and the New York *Times.* Fearing that a tip-off would ruin his strategy, he sought to stop the news break. The *Post* published a fragmentary account that did his strategy no harm; the *Times,* upon his personal appeal, printed nothing.[12]

In the aftermath of the successful resolution of the second Cuban crisis, President Kennedy argued vainly for some means of self-regulation by the press in situations involving national security.[13] Arthur Sylvester stirred up another tempest by saying, "I think the inherent right of the government to lie to save itself when faced with nuclear disaster is basic." He later modified that but maintained, "The government does not have a right to lie to the people but it does have a right in facing an enemy to disseminate information that is not accurate and is intended to mislead the enemy." [14] The highest information officer in the Pentagon was never contradicted by any of his superiors in government.

* Clifton Daniel, managing editor of the New York *Times,* revealed on June 2, 1966, that President Kennedy had told a *Times* editor afterward: "If you had printed more about the operation, you would have saved us from a colossal mistake."

Yet, Sylvester also was outspoken in his assessment of the role of the press. "If there is not tension between newsmen and those in government, then we are really lost," he said. "As a correspondent, I always thought government officials were jerks if they answered all my questions. There will continue to be leaks." [15]

Where President Kennedy tried in vain to get the press to do things his way, always an unhappy gambit for any chief executive, President Johnson used his superior knowledge of the structure of government to close as many sources as he could and to control the remainder. On the testimony of Tom Wicker, chief of the New York *Times* Washington bureau, Johnson "succeeded beyond any President in the memory of Washington in centralizing the information of the government, at least of the White House, in his own hands."

That was probably the most efficient way of managing the news of government. Naturally, it exacerbated the President's relations with the press on a number of occasions. It made him angry at times and philosophical at others. Some correspondents shared his state of mind. Wicker wrote of Johnson: "He is as accessible and as talkative as a President can be; yet, no honest reporter ever leaves a news conference or an interview believing he has learned a single fact that the President did not want him to know to begin with." [16]

In such an extremity, the American correspondents in Washington necessarily had to break the way for the rest. All they could count on was their own skill and the oft-demonstrated truth that there is a limit to the power of any agency, even the Presidency, to dam up news indefinitely. If the people had had to choose between the positions of the President and the press, moreover, there is little doubt that they would have supported the President. Despite all the campaigning that newspaper organizations had done for their concept of freedom of information, the public had never seemed even mildly interested. In short, the press simply did not have the popular following of the Presidency; nor was the public under the illusion that the Washington correspondents were paragons of virtue and righteousness.

The American press was well aware of the problem. But short of conditions that made the imposition of censorship inevitable, no editor of standing was willing to compromise on an issue that had meant life or death for free societies in the past. A moderate and reasonable statement on the basic issue by Price Day, editor in chief of the Baltimore *Sun,* gained considerable support:

> The press has a responsibility not to reveal security information that would damage the nation in its vital interests—a responsibility to understand that a world struggle is not a four-alarm fire. The government for

its part has a responsibility to keep the press informed so that the public will understand the logic of great decisions, when they come, and a duty above all to refrain from misleading the press and so the public.[17]

The predictable, self-serving Communist attitudes in Asia did less damage to the American position than the American government's own policies and some of the reportorial excesses. There was, in any case, a relative decline of the willingness to accept American strategy pronouncements at face value. Thus, after the opening of the B-52 bombing flights from Guam that did so much to harass the Viet-Cong guerrillas, James Reston was scornful of American claims that were not backed up by a body count of enemy dead. Accordingly, he wrote, "It raised doubts about the Administration's credibility and judgment just when these very qualities were being questioned in the public press." [18]

Such words had not been written by responsible American correspondents in the darkest days of World War II. If Asian editors who had survived all the repressions of dictatorial governments now watched and wondered at what was going on in the center of power of the "free world," who could blame them? No one had to give them lessons in news management. From the time of the publication of the first Chinese court circular, it had been their heritage for more than a thousand years.

2. THE VIEW FROM FOGGY BOTTOM

It was just an ordinary day at the Department of State, which means that the White House hadn't been on the phone too often that morning, and American troops hadn't landed anywhere within twenty-four hours. The Indonesians had gone on a rampage against American property. The Viet-Nam war was going badly. The Chinese Communists were angrier than usual, but the Russians were comparatively quiet. And a gun-running airplane of American registry had been seized at Malta.

Robert J. McCloskey, the efficient Director of the Office of News of the Bureau of Public Affairs, briskly entered a fair-sized conference room on the ground floor of the great gray building on Foggy Bottom, perhaps an appropriate name for a foreign ministry but one that had been attached to the area long before the arrival of the diplomats. He faced fifty reporters, including eight Japanese and an Indian, for his regular noon briefing.

Not many major correspondents from the Washington press corps had bothered to come that day because it seemed to be fairly calm. But it paid to be careful. Near McCloskey at a long table was the acknowledged foreign minister of the press corps, John Hightower, the diplomatic correspondent of the AP.

McCloskey, a tense, thin-faced man with brownish hair, deeply sunken eyes, and a broad, firm mouth, began the proceedings with an abrupt announcement: "I have nothing to report." But he didn't move and nobody expected him to do so. It was the beginning of a rather tiresome game of trying to guess what questions he was prepared to answer, a journalistic charade that is practiced with various refinements from Washington and London to New Delhi and even Tokyo.

As the reporters were aware, one of McCloskey's men usually came in at 6 A.M. to scan the newspapers, monitor the radio, and dream up questions which the reporters might be likely to ask at the noon briefing. These dummy questions then were sent to the various regional bureaus involved (the Far Eastern bureau, for instance, generally met at 9:15 A.M.) so that each could decide on its "morning line" and add other questions, plus suggested answers. At 11:30 A.M., McCloskey conferred with the public affairs representatives of the various bureaus, received their product, and prepared appropriate written or oral statements.

Naturally, he cleared some things with his superiors. On that particular day, however, there hadn't been much news affecting the higher echelons at State, the Department of Defense, or even the always demanding White House. As McCloskey awaited the reporters' questions, therefore, he had little to conceal. However, his clientele knew he wouldn't offer information in certain areas unless they happened to ask him about them. It was their problem to hit on a likely news subject; sometimes they didn't, but more often they did.

This particular session was thoroughly unproductive. But, as one of the Japanese explained later, McCloskey's briefing is one of the few places in Washington where they can see American government spokesmen regularly without an appointment and watch a particular "line" being developed.

The Asians could and did ask for appointments with various officials at State and other departments, but most of the correspondents believed the results were indifferent except when the American government wanted something special. Even then, at least one official confessed that he preferred to call in the representatives of the AP and UPI who covered Far Eastern affairs and give them the news. He explained, "They're geared to move the news to Asia quickly."

Now and then, of course, an Asian was called from on high and given an exclusive interview. During the Cyprus crisis, an Indian journalist was so favored by Under Secretary of State George Ball, but he made light of his experience later. "The Americans just wanted to get their view of the Cyprus crisis in my paper," he said modestly. "I suppose they think I'm read by our government."

Few Japanese had this exalted experience. The older correspondents, for the most part, had difficulty with the English language that was exceeded in severity only by the bafflement of a very large proportion of the American correspondents in Tokyo who tried to communicate in Japanese. Some of the younger Japanese correspondents in Washington, however, were thoroughly equipped to compete with the Americans on their own terms, but they couldn't easily break down ancient barriers. In the first place, as juniors, they had to defer to the older men in their own bureau in accordance with Japanese custom. In the second, they quickly learned that most American officials seemed to mistrust them on linguistic grounds, or perhaps for other reasons that were even deeper seated.

"In the beginning," a competent young Japanese correspondent said, "I wanted to go at it in the American way and get my own news. But I soon found that I couldn't. It is," and he hesitated, "a little difficult to find sources in Washington."

His explanation was involved, but it made sense. In part, the correspondent felt that he was obliged to work in the well-established Japanese manner—to read American newspapers, magazines, and specialized publications; listen to the radio; watch television; scan the wire services; and then write an article heavily weighted with political comment for Japanese consumption. It was, more or less, journalism in the European style, with Japanese complications. But in addition, the correspondent felt that there was a tendency in Washington to deal with the news corps in a descending order of importance.

"At the top," he said, "there is the inner circle, the important correspondents and commentators of the principal American media. After that, the rest of the Americans come before anybody else. Then, there are a few British and Europeans who might be given special consideration, and after them come the Europeans as a whole. We Asians are at the bottom of the list, and I sometimes think, mistakenly perhaps, that we Japanese come last of all."

Although *Esquire* magazine is not an authority on the Washington press corps, it did confirm Asian suspicions in general and Japanese feelings in particular by giving prominence in one issue to a two-page diagram listing the correspondents by status. It generally followed the outline sketched by the young Japanese correspondent, giving such correspondents as those of the York, Pa., *Gazette and Daily* and the Watertown, N.Y., *Daily Times* more prominence than all except a few of the foreign correspondents. As for the Asians, there were two Indians and, as *Esquire* put it, "many Japanese, names uncertain." [19]

"I don't blame you Americans for favoring your own," the Japanese correspondent concluded. "Everybody else does it. I suppose we Japanese are among the worst offenders. And that's what makes it so troublesome. Nobody is going to make changes unilaterally. If I only had a chance, I would cover everything I could on the spot. But under the circumstances, all I can do is read papers and go to the State Department's noon briefing."

There were others of the younger generation of Japanese correspondents who felt just as he did. They were sophisticated people, highly literate in English and often in one other language in addition to their own. They were well aware of the main political, social, and economic trends in the United States, having been educated at Japanese, British, or American universities.

But they all felt perilously shut in by the peculiar circumstances of their calling in Washington. It seemed almost like a holiday to them when they received notice in time to attend a Presidential news conference or were able to participate in a "backgrounder" held by Secretary Rusk or some other government official of the first rank. Very often, even if it meant nothing to them, a few would attend the daily briefings at the White House just to see President Johnson's press secretary in action.

Some of the more knowing Asians insisted that they were able to find out, often through friendly fellow correspondents, what went on at some of the "backgrounders" from which they were barred. One former correspondent, who had been assigned to the United Nations, remarked with a smile that he had paid an American correspondent for just such services. But mostly, the Japanese depended on the radio and the wire services for spot news and dug through the newspapers for the bulk of their factual material.

Their editors did not object. As one of the leading foreign editors in Tokyo told me when I asked him about it, "I don't care where my men get their raw material. Let them read the first-ranking American newspapers and use the factual data. I myself found that as good a way as any. But I do insist that whatever they write must be for Japanese eyes." It was his justification for the extensive use of what is known as "the Japanese angle."

The Indians, the Pakistanis, the Chinese Nationalists, and even the Koreans were generally not as inhibited as the Japanese, but all freely confessed that they had their difficulties in Washington. It was, of course, a comparative matter. Three members of a fairly large corps of

Japanese correspondents in London agreed that they found even greater restrictions in the British capital. One of them, whose English was excellent, remarked that at least there was the noon briefing at the State Department; in London, he complained, there was no accommodation. He had been told that he could write a letter to a British official requesting an appointment for an interview and had politely refused. "They never tell me anything when I do go to see them," he said. "What good is it?" In Great Britain, therefore, the Japanese also rewrote the newspapers, a procedure of which the Foreign Office was well aware. "We try to see that our papers get things reasonably straight," one spokesman said, "and that takes care of everybody, except the Americans and Canadians."

All efforts at census-taking among correspondents are treacherous, and the apparently simple business of determining how many Asians actually were represented among the Washington press corps in the mid-1960's was no exception. Going merely by names on lists and eliminating duplication as far as possible, the *Editor & Publisher International Year Book*'s tabulation of foreign correspondents in Washington and New York in 1965 showed that there were 90 British, 79 West Germans, 63 French, 50 Japanese, 38 Canadians, a scattering of other Europeans, 13 Indians, and a scattering of other Asians.[20]

A more realistic tabulation, obtained informally, gave the average number of Asian correspondents who had covered the Department of State annually for the years 1960-65 as follows: Japan, 27; Korea, 5; India, 4; Formosa, 2; and 1 each for the Philippines, Indonesia, South Viet-Nam, Pakistan, and Ceylon. Three countries, Malaysia, Thailand, and Burma, were without accredited representation. The average number of British correspondents for the same period was 20—fewer than for Japan.[21]

In addition, the U. S. Mission to the United Nations offered a list of accredited Asian correspondents at the world organization that included 14 Japanese, 6 Indians, 2 Chinese Nationalists, 1 Korean, and 1 Indonesian. By comparison, there were 14 accredited British correspondents at the United Nations.[22] Just as the Asians in Washington centered their work at the State Department, their colleagues in New York generally could be found either at the U.N. press rooms in the Secretariat Building or at the Foreign Correspondents' Center nearby, which had been created by the State Department to meet criticism that foreign correspondents were treated like "second-class citizens." Although the Center was an advance, it was not the entire answer to the problem, particularly for the Asians. They still believed that they were receiving "second-class" treatment; when the closing of the Center was threatened in 1966, it only confirmed their suspicions.

While the Asians may not have been willing to believe it, the State Department's press services represented a decided improvement over the past. During the first Roosevelt Administration, almost all news emanating from the Department had been handled by Michael J. McDermott, whose grandiose title was Chief of the Division of Current Information; actually, his operation was called the "McDermott office," and he had less than a half-dozen people to help him.[23] Up to the beginning of World War II, when the entire Department still had less than a thousand people, McDermott was the prime news source. Between 1938 and 1943, the Department tripled in size and then doubled again in the following three years; meanwhile, McDermott carried on with the notable assistance of Lincoln White, a former AP correspondent. At the war's end, the Office of Assistant Secretary of State for Public Affairs was created, the logical successor to the Office of War Information.[24] But its first three occupants—Archibald MacLeish, William Benton, and George Allen—dealt mainly with nongovernmental organizations and were not concerned with supplying news to the mass media. The McDermott-White team still handled the news, with precious little assistance from anybody.

Finally, in 1950, Secretary of State Dean Acheson decided it was time to make the news operation something more than a mere appendage of the larger public affairs operation. He appointed Edward W. Barrett, former editorial director of *Newsweek,* as Assistant Secretary of State for Public Affairs, and gave him direction of news policy. It was the beginning of a significant expansion in the size and importance of the Public Affairs Bureau. In the mid-1960's, with the State Department's strength at more than 42,000 employees and its budget exceeding $400 million, the Public Affairs Bureau consisted of 150 employees and had a budget of $2,220,800.[25] In a quarter-century, the Bureau's personnel more than doubled, and its budget increased tenfold.[26] But fewer than a dozen officials were authorized to handle news for the mass media.

McDermott was packed off to genteel retirement as Ambassador to the Dominican Republic soon after World War II, but the good-natured, easygoing White continued for years afterward to exert an individual influence on the news even though his policy-making function withered. The importance of McDermott and White was that they considered themselves newsmen rather than government public relations people; more often than not, they chose to act as "honest brokers" between their friends, the correspondents, and their employers, the responsible officials of the State Department. They were on the telephone day and night answering queries or talking to newsmen singly and in groups at the Department. It was a matter of pride with White, in particular, that either he was able to tell correspondents the truth, or he said nothing at all. Sometimes he even offered friendly, informal, and not strictly authorized "guidance" on touchy stories handled by correspondents whom he trusted.

The method had worked for many years in the better city halls and even the governors' offices of the land. To some extent, it had also been practiced by the various White House press secretaries. But with the coming of a different philosophy toward the news in the higher reaches of government, beginning at the Pentagon, the system of direct news transmission to the correspondents changed. The unfortunate White was caught in the middle during the U-2 incident. With complete sincerity, he told correspondents on May 6, 1960, "There was absolutely no—N-O, no—deliberate attempt to violate Soviet air space. There never has been." Twenty-nine hours later, crestfallen and shaken because he had unknowingly been led into issuing an untrue statement, he faced the reporters again and read from a piece of paper that "a flight over Soviet territory was probably undertaken by an unarmed civilian U-2 plane." [27]

It was the end of an era in the State Department's public relations. Not long afterward, White turned, with honors, to other responsibilities in the Department. The Office of News and its ten full-time people became less important than it had been. Instead, under the enormous pressures of government, the policy-making Assistant Secretary of State for Public Affairs developed into the top news-dispenser for the Department. It was he who now inherited the round-the-clock telephone calls from the correspondents, the informal news conferences in his office, the harried demands of editors for assistance, and all the other trappings of the old McDermott operation. The policy features of the office and its administration, which should have been primary matters, often had to be handled between the demands of the news. And when there was a "world-wide flap," everything but the news had to be put aside.

The theory that the most important news official in the State Department could delegate news handling to the lower echelons did not work out in practice. American correspondents of the first rank necessarily wanted to get their information from an office as close as possible to the Secretary's. The Public Affairs Bureau was it, but despite McCloskey's competence, few correspondents were content even to stop at the Office of the News. It was the nature of the journalist to try to go as high as he could for his information. For this reason, President Johnson and Secretary Rusk instituted a system of policy briefings for foreign as well as American correspondents, but such sessions could not be held very often.

With some 1,200 American correspondents in Washington, and perhaps 400 or 500 of them involved in one way or another with the daily news chores, it was inevitable that the news operation at State would be swamped. A routine news conference by the Secretary of State brought out 200 to 250 correspondents. On even an average day 50 or 60 of them were making the rounds in the Department. Often, despite all manner of good intentions, no one had the time to take care of foreign correspondents, European or Asian, unless they knew how to shift for themselves. This was no argument that would convince a Congressional committee, traditionally full of mistrust for both the Department and its press operation; understaffing, therefore, continued to be chronic at State. Funds were continually unavailable for the bold plans for expansion that had been formulated in the McDermott-White era.

The more things changed, the more they were the same. In the Bureau, there were major improvements in the policy plans and guidance staff and in the coordination of headquarters with overseas information programs. The offices devoted to public services and media services, too, had been modernized. A more efficient system had been devised to deal with the growing number of nongovernmental organizations interested in American foreign policy and even to send occasional task forces of speakers into the field. But the news operation was still cramped and starved for lack of funds.

Had it not been for Robert J. Manning, James L. Greenfield, and Dixon Donnelley, who successively headed the Public Affairs Bureau during the Kennedy and Johnson administrations, the complicated diplomatic and news machines might not have meshed as well as they did. Manning, a former UP bureau chief at the United Nations and London bureau chief for *Time* magazine, served from 1962 to 1964, when he resigned to become managing editor of the *Atlantic Monthly*. He was succeeded in the Assistant Secretary's office by his deputy, Greenfield, a former *Time* correspondent in Japan, Korea, and India, with broad experience in Asian affairs. If anybody could have improved the Department's news operations to and from Asia, Greenfield had the best chance. He had the knowledge, the inclination, and the interest. But he had no more luck with Congress than his predecessors; on February 12, 1966, for personal reasons, he resigned and was replaced by the Treasury Department public relations man, Donnelley.

Whatever the successes and failings of the State Department's public relations effort, they were not sufficient to induce Congress to appropriate more funds for the news operation. But the Defense Department, with more than $50 billion in appropriations, generally did well in the same area, although its news problems were often linked with those at State and the White House. Assistant Secretary of Defense for Public Affairs Arthur Sylvester estimated that in public information work at the Pentagon alone he had 127 officers and civilians at his own office and 150 each in the Army, Navy, and Air Force.[28] There were probably several times that many in the Defense Department and the individual services who worked on public information elsewhere in the United States and abroad and in other branches of the information field. Theoretically, there was a Congressional fund limitation on Defense Department public information work, but it was so narrowly defined for the benefit of the budget people that it had no practical effect.

There was growing criticism, too, of the United States Information Agency (USIA), known overseas as the United States Information Service (USIS), and its radio branch, the Voice of America. Edward R. Murrow had been its respected director in the last years of his life and his successor, Carl Rowan, had achieved success in an eleven-year campaign to admit its people to full status in the U. S. Foreign Service. With a staff of 11,975 people and a budget of $172 million in 1965, it was expected to act as the nation's propaganda agency overseas, but it was being attacked on various grounds for ineffectiveness.[29]

In the spring of 1965, Henry Loomis, chief of the Voice of America, resigned with a warning to his staff against acting as a mere agency of praise for the government. "We must by our very stance communicate . . . the fact that diversity is preferable to uniformity," he said in an emotional farewell. "To sweep under the rug what we don't like, what does not serve our tactical purpose, is a sign of weakness. To acknowledge the existence of forces and views in disagreement with the policy makers, to take them specially into account in the formation of our output . . . is good, persuasive propaganda. We must show that the United States gains strength, not weakness, from diversity." [30]

Before the reaction of Loomis's blast had died down, Ernest Wiener, public-relations officer at the U. S. Embassy in Moscow, cabled a private message to the State Department which somehow leaked out, as such things have a way of doing in Washington. He, too, criticized the Voice of America. "In almost every case," he wrote, "news citings and comments seemed too obviously selected to bolster the official government position; correspondingly, there was a notable lack of hard news from either the Caribbean area or Southeast Asia—and this precisely when hard news [of the Dominican intervention and South Viet-Nam] was wanted by the Russians." [31]

While the White House and the USIA both denied pressure on the Voice of America to slant the news by omitting criticism of the policies of the Johnson Administration in Asia and Latin America, the editorial cannonading against the Voice and USIA continued. After four and a half years in government, during which he occupied more high offices than any other Negro, Rowan resigned to become a columnist for the Chicago *Daily News* and, incidentally, to double his salary. "My conviction," he said, "is that few men should put in more than four years in government at a stretch. With rare exceptions, it isn't good for the man and it's not good for the government." [32]

President Johnson appointed Leonard H. Marks, a Washington lawyer and a close friend, as the new USIA director and brought a Texas newspaperman, Robert Wood Akers, out of retirement to become his assistant. As the new director of the Voice of America, he named John Chancellor, the White House correspondent of N.B.C., calling him "a man whose voice and whose face and whose mind is known to this country and to most of the entire world."

Chancellor went into his difficult post with the understanding that he would be free to tell the world "the good as well as the bad" in order to present a truthful report of the United States. He also took a pay cut to embark on his new responsibilities. Propaganda, he maintained, was a "two-way word." He explained: "Of course we want to project American policy. But we also have to admit our own problems. If we try to brush something under the rug and Radio Moscow is covering it in their broadcasts, then we lose our audience. Our main weapon is our freedom to make our own mistakes and solve our own problems, out in the open. We can't be Buddha-like." [33]

There was little doubt that the Voice and USIA had been hurt by the attack on their credibility and that it would take time to repair the damage. It made the task of the State Department even more complex in seeking to build up support for the administration's foreign policy.

Now and then, help came from unexpected places. For example, N.B.C. devoted three and a half hours to a detailed examination of American foreign policy since World War II, canceling an evening's regular television schedule on September 7, 1965; and it engaged in exhaustive "live" telecasts of the Senate Foreign Relations Committee hearings on the Viet-Nam war during the following winter. It was in protest against the decision of its rival, C.B.S., to show a re-run of a little comedy program, "I Love Lucy," instead of following N.B.C.'s example, that Fred W. Friendly resigned as president of the C.B.S. News Division on February 15, 1966. He said, quite correctly, that business and entertainment were paramount in TV. The immediate result helped focus public attention on Secretary of State Rusk's seven hours of testimony before the Senate group three days later, thus shoring up a shaky administration position. For the long term, it raised questions of policy for the use of TV, the most powerful of all the mass media.[34]

Such were the events that gave the news from Washington so peculiar a flavor in the latter part of the decade. If the Asian correspondents felt puzzled and inadequate to the task of reporting what was going on at the seat of American policy-making, they had a lot of company.

3. THROUGH ASIAN EYES [35]

"I have encountered no discrimination in the United States," the Indian correspondent wrote, "but I have become conscious of the color of my skin. Two incidents linger in my mind. One was my first day in a small American town. It was early morning, and I went out to have breakfast. I entered a drugstore and took a corner table, finding it vacant. Suddenly a little girl next to my table said, 'Look, Mamma. He is black.' Her mother immediately came down on her. 'You shouldn't say that. You shouldn't say that.'

"I was half frozen in my seat, wondering what had happened to me after flying 12,000 miles. Although facing them, I avoided the looks of the little girl and the mother for five minutes. But when I did look at them, the girl was still looking at me with wonder. But her mother smiled at me, apologetically perhaps, until I left. Of course, after having my breakfast.

"One evening more recently, I was going back to my apartment in upper Manhattan in the Broadway subway, but I could hardly miss the looks I did not know how I had attracted, rushing, as I was in a great hurry. I didn't know the reason until I read the next morning in the *Times,* with a sketch of a person purported to have committed rape in Brooklyn. The only resemblance was possibly in height and in skin—light black.

"I recall these as incidents that I did not feel were discriminatory, but they reflected the sensitivity of either the people, or me, or both."

The Indian correspondent was one of a score of Asian journalists whom I interviewed in New York, Washington, and London in 1964 and 1965. Many more, principally in Tokyo and New Delhi, had worked in Washington and other foreign capitals, and they also contributed their experiences. Out of these comments I tried to piece together some notion of what it is like to work in the United States as an Asian correspondent, in contrast with other nations, and whether their experiences had any bearing on their reporting. I had, further, the inestimable assistance of a panel of ten permanent correspondents in Washington and New York, each of whom represented a major Asian newspaper or news agency in 1965. Seven were Japanese and three were Indians, all of whom answered a detailed questionnaire which I also submitted to more American correspondents in Asia.

Like the Indian correspondent who became conscious of the color of his skin, a Japanese who went to Birmingham to cover the racial crisis in Alabama related that he "had a strange feeling." He explained, without rancor, that nobody harmed him but that he felt "creepy" about Birmingham. "And so I took most of my news from the National Association for the Advancement of Colored People," he concluded.

But it wasn't very easy otherwise to link attitudes directly with the handling of the news. Another Japanese related how he had applied for an apartment in a nice section of Washington and had been told that the building unfortunately was "fully rented." The correspondent permitted himself a slight smile as he concluded, "But they still kept advertising their apartments." It was the only case of outright discrimination that was reported, although still another Indian said, "I wasn't discriminated against as an Indian, but occasionally I was mistaken for a Negro in Alabama and Mississippi."

All but one of the Asian correspondents' panel concluded that the United States is a friendly country; all but one found it expensive, and three thought it very expensive. Six reported that they were asked regularly to visit in American homes, one was seldom asked out, and three made no reply. Eight said they would want to return to the United States as correspondents if given their own choice; one gave a conditional reply; and one did not answer.

The correspondents in the panel averaged 41 years of age, the oldest being 55 and the youngest 34, and they had been journalists an average of 15.5 years. They had been in the United States an average of 2.3 years; the longest 6 years, and the most recent arrival, 6 months. Since the average time they had spent overseas was 3.7 years, it appeared that the American assignment was the first one abroad for most of them. With three exceptions, their English was good; three of the Japanese also spoke German, one French, and another Chinese. The Indians, by coincidence, all spoke Urdu; one also knew Telugu, another Hindi, and a third French. All had their bachelor's degrees and four had their master's. One was a former Nieman Fellow at Harvard, another had a master's degree in political science from Columbia, and a third had a bachelor's degree from London University.

There was no uniformity in the length or frequency of their dispatches because of the difference in their assignments, but most of them filed the equivalent of 500 to 700 words a day, and three reported that their monthly file cost averaged $1,500 each. (*Asahi* at the time had a two-way leased line by Pacific telephone cable on a twenty-four-hour-a-day basis which cost about $10,000 a month; it was the ultimate in sheer communications luxury.)

Six of the correspondents estimated that with cable tolls excluded, it cost their employers an average of $13,250 to maintain them in the United States for a year. That was less than one-third what it cost to maintain the average American newspaper correspondent in Asia annually, cable tolls excluded. The Asian with the highest cost reported a total expense of $20,000, while the lowest reported $9,500. When foreign editors in Tokyo were asked the same question, their figures tallied roughly with the correspondents' estimates; the highest was $20,000 to $25,000 per correspondent, and the lowest $12,000.

One of the correspondents analyzed his costs as follows: His salary is $1,000 a month, but living in Washington is quite expensive, and American taxes are higher than he would pay at home. Moreover, he had to pay his family's moving expenses to Washington, and he has been given no assistance in meeting his rent of $150 a month. (The Asians in New York and Washington reported rents of $120 to $180 a month.) Despite all that, he estimates that he usually has about $500 a month to take care of his family and his own costs. Since he is in a bureau, he doesn't have to worry about office expenses, and he is on an expense account when he is sent out of town.

Within a year, all ten correspondents in the panel traveled, but not all saw much of the United States. One was in South Bend, Ind.; Akron, Ohio; Detroit; and some towns in Arizona and New Mexico. Five others traveled to California and back. One was in Canada twice, three were in Europe. It was probable that only a few had any extensive firsthand knowledge of what the United States was like outside New York, Chicago, Washington, and Los Angeles.

All were reasonably well-informed about the United States before arriving to work as correspondents, and they said they had had few misconceptions. Most of them had gained their impressions from their studies, through books, newspapers, visits with American journalists and, occasionally, the movies.

All but one of the correspondents reported little difficulty in obtaining news in the United States. They were polite, with one exception, about the assistance which they received from the U.S. Government. The exception: "It is rather poor. They don't give us any notice, which they do to American newspapermen, of irregular briefings on U.S. policies given by officials." Another agreed that the arrangements for regular background briefings were inadequate. The most typical answer was: "I do appreciate the fact that they are very willing to assist us and are spending much money and manpower for that purpose. However, I think there is much room for improvement."

On the issue of official American credibility, the panel members were kinder than the American correspondents in Asia. Nearly all agreed that news from official U.S. sources was "believable most of the time," although one said it was "believable factually."

One correspondent reported that "bureaucracy" separated him from his sources. Another complained of the State Department's "more important briefings exclusively for the American and West European correspondents." A third observed: "It is true with any country that newspapermen of that country are in a much more advantageous position than foreigners." Their choice of subjects may, of course, have had something to do with their attitudes. All but two noted that they were interested primarily in analysis, for which they are more likely to be dependent on background briefings or published reports based on such exercises.

Although a majority of the panel members believed that the American media were inclined to be favorable to their own countries, the often skimpy coverage did not please them. One Japanese said he thought of American coverage of Japan as "impartial" rather than "favorable." Another didn't care for the note of "paternalistic generosity" in the American press toward Japan. An Indian, overlooking the scanty volume of news about his country, expressed the opinion that the American press was fair, but the electronic media "project certain aspects of India grotesquely." Only two out of ten spoke of the American media's coverage of their countries as satisfactory, one thought it was poor, and the rest called the performance "fair." Many American correspondents in Asia took a more critical view of the work of their own media.

The Asians were somewhat more forthright in their assessment of the weak points in American coverage of their countries and the reasons for such lapses. The Indians were critical of "insufficient volume and irregular reporting due to a preoccupation with Europe," a decrease in the number of American correspondents in India, and some rather appalling distortions in the reporting of political, economic, and social conditions. This, of course, was a reference to the usual old-fashioned feature stories about a Kiplingesque India, peopled exclusively by exotic little brown men, snake charmers, dancing girls, and elephant boys.

The Japanese criticized what one called "the persistent image of an outdated 'exotic' Japan which concentrated on stories about Fujiyama and geisha." They concluded that the American correspondents, for the most part, overemphasized what they conceived to be the traditional aspects of Japanese life. The most forceful comments were from the younger correspondents, one of whom said: "I believe the time has come for American journalists to discover the diversity in so-called 'Asian affairs.' Surely, with the ever-expanding news coverage in the

Far East, they can afford to evade dangerous generalization, untrained confusion, trite expressions based on exoticism—in a word, the observations of a foreign tourist. In this aspect, I see a bright future in the appearance of a new breed of 'Asian hands'—not the old 'China hands' or the 'Pacific war hands.' "

All the panelists were united on one professional point, which gave them pleasure. Nearly everything they sent from the United States was used. Most of them said that the volume of their news and analysis was restricted only by the cost of filing and the comparatively small size of their newspapers. But certainly, almost anything about the United States was printed and avidly read, particularly when it was written by the paper's own correspondent in the United States.

One of the most influential correspondents in Washington, and one of the least known to Americans, was Mitsugu Nakamura, the chief of the four-man bureau of *Asahi Shimbun.* As the first representative of Japan's leading newspaper, Nakamura exerted his influence primarily through the selection, editing, and writing of American news for *Asahi,* and the emphasis that was to be placed on it. He was no Walter Lippmann, for the individual columnist is not yet a part of Japanese journalism, and as late as the mid-1960's, both editors and staff were deeply mistrustful of what they called the "American star system." Yet, what came out of Nakamura's bureau in Washington on issues affecting the relations of the United States with Asia probably had a more profound effect on Japanese opinion than any "American star."

Nakamura had been a journalist for nearly twenty years. He was born in 1921, near Kobe and educated in Peking University and the Osaka School of Languages. His Chinese is fluent, while his English is clear and grammatical although he has an accent. Like most Japanese of his age, he fought in World War II; his battlefield was China, where he served for two and a half years as a first lieutenant. In 1946, he was one of the fortunate few who were invited to join the staff of *Asahi* and became a reporter at Nara. Five years later, he was promoted to the Osaka office and went on to cover the Korean War and the conclusion of the truce talks at Panmunjom. From 1953 to 1957, he was in the Washington bureau of *Asahi* and for seven years thereafter he was the assistant foreign editor in Tokyo. He returned to Washington as bureau chief in 1964.

At his office in the National Press Building, Nakamura made no secret of his deep concern over the course of U.S. policies in Southeast Asia and the deepening war commitment in Viet-Nam in the summer of 1965. A small, earnest man with an almost judicial air about him, he expressed in effect the view not only of his own newspaper but also of the overwhelming majority of the Japanese press. He could not see the

reasonableness of any policy other than the opening of immediate negotiations to end the fighting. It was clear that this was the theme of his
correspondence. As he pointed out, the Japanese press was more like the
European than the American concept, being full of comment and heavily political. He wasn't entirely sure that this was a good thing, but it
was the way things were in Japanese journalism.

While *Asahi* probably spent around $400,000 a year for wire services,
Nakamura's bureau usually provided the bulk of the news out of
Washington on any political issue affecting American policies in Asia.
He had the best facilities in his own office—the services of the AP, Reuters, and the New York *Times*. From these and from the Washington
and New York papers, he and his staff obtained the greatest part of
their material, but what they wrote was their own. Qualified American
sources, even for *Asahi,* were hard to find in Washington, although
Nakamura remarked, with a slight smile, that he did have one or two.

The *Asahi* operation was more expensive but otherwise fairly typical
of those of its principal rivals, *Mainichi Shimbun* and *Yomiuri Shimbun,* each of which had bureaus of comparable size in the National
Press Building. Kyodo and Jiji Press were there, too, with small agency
offices, but they didn't pretend to compete with either the Japanese correspondents or the American agencies. But N.H.K., the Japan Broadcasting Corporation, did an aggressive job of covering the United States
from time to time with TV documentaries that were frank, effective,
and pictorially powerful, particularly on the race issue. A score of Japanese media, in all, maintained bureaus in either New York or Washington, and some had offices in both places. There were also a few stringers
in Chicago, the Pacific Northwest, and Hollywood.

Among the newer correspondents, two were representative of what
might be expected from Japanese journalism in the years to come. One
was Hiroshi Ishihara of *Yomiuri Shimbun,* a former Nieman Fellow at
Harvard, and the other was Yuzo Hatano of *Mainichi Shimbun,* a
former Fulbright Fellow at Columbia who obtained his master's degree
there in political science. Both were in their mid-thirties, spoke excellent
English, and were to be found all over Washington on assignment.
Ishihara came to Washington in 1962 from the foreign news desk in
Tokyo. His biggest assignment in the United States was the coverage of
the assassination of President Kennedy and the subsequent murder of
Lee Harvey Oswald in Dallas. Hatano's journalistic career closely par-
alleled that of his colleague. He was born in 1930 in Kyoto Prefecture
and was graduated from Tokyo University in 1953. Because of the excellence of his English, he escaped the local news-bureau indoctrination
upon joining the staff of *Mainichi* and was assigned to the English desk
for a year. During the next four years, he worked on the foreign desk.

From 1957 to 1958, he was at Columbia on his Fulbright and returned thereafter to the foreign desk in Tokyo. He came back to the United States in August, 1964, in the middle of the Tonkin Gulf crisis, an exciting beginner for any newcomer.

While Ishihara and Hatano were members in good standing of the "Japanese phalanx," they had the aggressive temperament of the better American and European correspondents and did not seem content merely to read the American newspapers or watch the agency teletypes. It seemed self-evident, with the inevitable development of an independent Japanese foreign policy, that Japanese journalism as well would manifest a far more independent spirit.

The Indian correspondents, although small in number, were as independent and aggressive as any foreign journalists in Washington. One of them was appalled when a senior American diplomat asked, in a kindly and patronizing manner, if the *Indian Express* was government-owned. It was and is, of course, the largest Indian newspaper. Most of the Indian correspondents found such ignorance fairly typical outside the narrow circle at the State and Defense departments that dealt with them and their work. As for the Pakistanis, always ready to complain at any suspicion of favoritism for the Indians, there were only two correspondents in Washington, and they could do little or nothing, with their strictly government-controlled press.

There was influence out of proportion to their number in the work of such Indian correspondents as T. V. Parasuram, of the *Indian Express,* and his colleague at the United Nations, P. R. Reddi; H. R. Vohra, of the *Times* of India; Ajit Bhattacharjea, of the *Hindustan Times;* Easawar Sagar, of the *Hindu* of Madras; and Chakravarti Raghavan, of the Press Trust of India. Reuters was their competition out of Washington, and then only on spot news developments. As for the AP and AFP, neither was as easily available for Indian editors, and UPI couldn't circulate at all. The Indian specials' reports from Washington were major sources of news of the United States in India's English-language press.

Perhaps the most energetic of the group was Parasuram, a dark, fast-moving native of Kerala with a ready wit and a bright, engaging smile. His first names were impossible for Western tongues—Tattamangulam Viswanathaiyer, the names respectively of his birthplace and his father. He was born in 1923, went to high school in Chittur, and later won two gold medals for speed stenography at the Lakshmi Tutorial Institute in Bombay.

In 1939, he became a reporter-stenographer for the National Planning Commission, of which Jawaharlal Nehru was then chairman. Later, he worked for Reuters in Bombay and its subsidiary, the old Associated

Press of India (no connection with the Associated Press of New York). In 1942, he became a deputy bureau chief for the Indian AP and called attention to himself by taking Roosevelt's and Churchill's wartime speeches directly from the radio and distributing them to fifteen newspapers in and near Hyderabad, his headquarters.

From 1945 until 1958, he covered the Indian Parliament; in 1949, he shifted the Press Trust of India (PTI) when it was formed to replace the Indian AP. Then in 1958–59, when he won a Nieman Fellowship, came his first American experience, a year's study at Harvard. There followed three years in New York as the PTI's correspondent at the United Nations and, in 1962, the coveted post of Washington correspondent for the *Indian Express,* of which Frank Moraes had become editor.

It was from such correspondents that the Indian public, from the elite groups in government and the business people to the growing middle and lower-middle classes, learned of events in the United States from their English-language newspapers. There is no doubt that the correspondents' influence spread far beyond these groups, for most of the press groups in India also published large and powerful vernacular newspapers. These together were the principal means of disseminating intelligence on foreign affairs to the Indian public, for All India Radio in the mid-1960's was extremely casual about its news broadcasts.

Clearly, the Asian correspondents in the United States exercised considerable influence in the Japanese and Indian press. While relatively few Americans recognized the importance of their role and even fewer knew their names, what they wrote of events in Washington often had a marked effect on their papers' editorial policies and their readers' opinions.

As professional journalists, they accepted gracefully the limitations that inevitably surrounded any correspondent who works outside his country. For example, they understood that there was a "gentlemen's agreement" that foreigners would not ask questions at certain types of news conferences—if, indeed, they were even invited. There was, in any event, little basis for the belief among some American correspondents that the Asians were decisively influenced by their ingrained views of the United States and the American way of life. As for the common prejudice among American correspondents against the supposed journalistic inferiority of all Asians, that was perhaps the most shocking myth of all. Some of the Asians were better educated and had a better background for their work than a number of Americans and Europeans at work in Washington; a few, indeed, could have held a Washington correspondent's job for a first-rate American paper. The number of those who fitted the old stereotype was dwindling.

What they saw, and what they reported, had growing influence at home. In the United States, however, where their work should have merited serious attention, it was frequently overlooked and even ignored. Somehow, it was considered exotic that an Asian newspaper should have a Washington correspondent; even sensible editors sometimes were inclined to be lighthearted about it when they came across a Japanese who spoke imperfect English. Inevitably, they would learn that times had changed.

4. AMERICAN MEDLEY

Horst Faas, a Pulitzer Prize–winning AP photographer, joined a South Vietnamese army contingent bound for a major attack on the Viet-Cong in Binh-Duong province early in the spring of 1965. He noted that the troops were on edge and soon learned that helicopters were about to squirt nonlethal "nausea gas" on the enemy. There had been rumors for some time that such a gas was being used by American and Vietnamese forces, but this was the first time that any journalist had been able to confirm it. Although the attack was called off, Faas had a story and hustled back to Saigon to report to his chief, Malcolm Browne, and to Peter Arnett, a staff correspondent. Much has been made of the fact that Faas is German-born and Arnett is a New Zealander, but that was beside the point. Browne, an American, was in charge, and he knew a story when he saw one.

"U.S. and Vietnamese military forces are experimenting with nonlethal gas warfare in South Vietnam," wrote Arnett at the beginning of a dispatch that girdled the globe on AP's circuits on March 22, 1965. It created a major problem of policy for the United States, for everybody from the British to the Communists overlooked the use of the word "nonlethal." While it might be expected that Peking would accuse the United States of being peopled with "fascist cannibals," and Hanoi would wail over "barbarity," it remained for the leftist British *New Statesman* to write: "The Americans, like Hitler and Mussolini in Spain, are treating the hapless inhabitants of Vietnam as a living laboratory in which to test their new weapons." And the British Foreign Secretary, Michael Stewart, forgot himself sufficiently in Washington to demand that his American hosts "display what your Declaration of Independence called 'a decent respect for the opinions of mankind.'"

The official American governmental machinery, which is seldom able to react well in a crisis of this kind, performed in a predictable manner. The White House issued an announcement that President Johnson hadn't known the gas was being used, which, next to a denial of a palpable truth, is just about the worst thing any government can say of its leader. Johnson himself did a much better job when he decided to do things in his own common-sense manner. First, he called upon Secretary McNamara to demonstrate that these nonlethal gases were common riot-control weapons which had been used by many nations in many places for well-nigh a half-century. Next, he stepped aside for Secretary Rusk, who summoned a news conference on short notice and announced, "We are not embarking on gas warfare in Vietnam." Rusk also pointed out that such things as tear gas and a gas that causes diarrhea, which had been given limited and ineffective use in Viet-Nam, were not prohibited under the 1925 Geneva Protocol. They were, he insisted, "minimum agents," and were actually more humane than shooting down Viet-Cong in circumstances where they used innocent villagers as human shields.

But neither the righteous American opposition nor the British, who had often used such gases themselves, was in any mood to listen to reason at that point. As for the Communists, they had a field day with propaganda that summoned up visions of poison gas drifting over all of Viet-Nam and killing millions of people. The United States forbade further use of the nonlethal gases in South Viet-Nam, thus depriving the South Vietnamese as well as the Americans of a perfectly legitimate weapon to be used to empty tunnels 30 and 40 feet underground of Viet-Cong without harming the villagers they had taken along with them as innocent hostages. Later in the year, when an American Marine battalion commander used such nonlethal tear gas in Viet-Nam to clear a cave and tunnel system, instead of blowing it up or burning it out and killing foemen and innocents alike, the New York *Times* and others came to his defense when he was hauled up for investigation. The *Times* said, "Nonlethal riot-control gases can be far more humane and will cause far fewer casualties than many of the weapons now being used in Vietnam." [36] The use of tear gas was authorized in South Viet-Nam soon afterward without any fuss.

Such an extreme example of reactions to the news from Asia did not occur often. Generally, the handful of wire-service reporters assigned to Asian news in Washington had to generate their own news for the Far Eastern radio-teletype channels and cables. Every morning, their first task was to read the file of news that was circulating from the Far East and scan the important specials in the newspapers. If there was a demonstration in Manila or a riot in Djakarta, it was their business to draw Washington comment and bounce back a follow-up story. The Washington dateline was important in the Far East, and reaction stories kept moving under it.

This was the routine. It was seldom exciting or dramatic. But in some ways it was more important than the single reaction to a big news break. The New York–to–Tokyo circuits had to be supplied with copy, and not all of it could be fresh. This was the way the news day often began. Later, the government often generated something better. But if the Far Eastern reporters had waited for a daily sensation, the file would have run out.

The wire-service reporters in the more remote bureaus in Asia worked in much the same way. In Djakarta, for example, the problem was to find enough material to fill a thirty-minute radiocast twice a day—usually about 2,000 words each. If the regular news sources had nothing to offer, then a species of dialogue also had to be begun with Washington, Tokyo, the United Nations, Peking, or other news centers for pieces on reaction to news elsewhere. However often correspondents in far places were told by their headquarters that the radiocasts did not have to be filled if there was no news, it was difficult for them to refrain from filing something. The net result was that the various radiocasts poured wordage into a center like Tokyo or Singapore. The news quotas were filled. What wasn't of sufficient importance to go on the Tokyo–New York or Singapore–Sydney–London channels was circulated in Asia.

Naturally, it was possible for experienced journalists with a thorough knowledge of the Far East to make something more out of the routine than a mere string of items to take up teletype time and space. In the AP's four-man State Department bureau in Washington, there was such a seasoned correspondent—Spencer Davis, a quiet and dignified veteran in his fifties who had been covering the Far Eastern and South Asian sections of the Department for a dozen years, and the Asian embassies as well. Davis had the background and the know-how for his post: born in Los Angeles in 1910; a graduate of Stanford; reporter for the Los Angeles *Record,* Honolulu *Advertiser,* and INS for a decade; AP war correspondent in the Pacific with 17 landings from the Solomons to Tokyo; correspondent in North China, Manchuria, and Manila; and San Francisco bureau editor handling cables during the Korean War. He had been at the State Department since 1954.

Davis worked with John Hightower, the AP's diplomatic correspondent; Lewis Gulick, another veteran; and Endre Marton, the brave Hungarian correspondent who had covered the Soviet army's repression of the 1956 Budapest uprising almost to its tragic end. Their office was crowded in a small space at one end of the State Department's inadequate press room, but they seldom could be seen working at their typewriters. The place was a hall of echoes, with correspondents so cramped in tiny glassed-in cubicles that they preferred to work almost anywhere else.

Loud-voiced, swaggering types did not fit in such surroundings. When the AP men were ready to file, they telephoned their Washington bureau and dictated softly and rapidly to save time. The dictationist funneled the news to the proper desk in the AP's Washington bureau, which was staffed by more than a hundred editors and newsmen. From there, it went on the wire to New York and, if required, to the nation, the Tokyo teletype channel, and the rest of the world.

Hightower set the pace for his group. At fifty-five, he was the dean of the diplomatic correspondents—tall, slim, handsome, and gray, with the deliberation of a market analyst and the bearing of an ambassador. He had covered eight Secretaries of State, and more than one of them had asked his advice from time to time. There was reason for his prominence and his prestige: He had been a journalist for more than thirty years and a diplomatic correspondent since 1943.

"Since the government also has an interest in an informed citizenry," he once wrote, "it is sometimes said that this turn of events has made partners of officials and newsmen. If every citizen may have the impulse to be his own Secretary of State, then the man who, like Dean Rusk, actually has the job must at least seek a popular consensus on major issues. But secrecy is a convenience for officials conducting foreign affairs even when it is not a necessity, whereas secrecy is anathema to the newsman. The real interests of journalists and policymakers generate a love-hate relationship. What the two groups must accept is that both are necessary to the functioning of a democracy." [37]

Hightower was a realist. He expected government officials to act the part and not to tell everything they knew. Moreover, he was not as much concerned with what was "true" as he was with trying to describe American foreign policy, its aims, and its implications. The ultimate truth represented by these things was, he believed, more in the province of the philosopher than the reporter. Being a realist, he accepted nothing he heard in the State Department at face value. And as a journalist, he never of his own accord kept a story off the wire because of its actual or fancied effect on American vital interests.

Such policies would have been endorsed by most members of the Washington press corps. Stewart Hensley, the diplomatic correspondent of UPI, was even more an individualist in his work at the State Department. He made it an article of faith never to demand access to news by invoking the sacred precepts of freedom of the press, one of the oldest dodges in the profession. It was, Hensley thought, irrelevant in most cases and self-defeating in others. He had his people operate without demanding anything, and they generally managed to do very well.

The UPI operation in Washington was much like that of the AP, except that a number of different correspondents had handled the Asian assignment. LeRoy Hansen, a forty-three-year-old correspondent with eleven years' service in Korea and Tokyo, had been Davis's competition for three years in Washington before going on in 1965 to the Los Angeles bureau of *U.S. News &World Report*. He had liked the Far East and had married a Japanese wife. Upon being transferred to Washington, he had used his background to good advantage in his Asian coverage.

Hansen found that Asian embassies deluged him with material, often sending it by special messenger, in the hope that some of it would be channeled back to their newspapers. In this, they were seldom any different from the American ambassadors who schemed to get their views into the New York *Times*. Because of Hansen's special knowledge of Japan, he also was frequently interviewed by Japanese correspondents—a practice that most Americans disliked and tried politely to discourage. Like Spencer Davis, he was adept at generating news, but he didn't like to be asked to give it away to his Japanese competition. Marlyn E. Aycock, his successor, had no previous experience in the Far East.

Stewart Hensley had a routine that differed from that of some of the other diplomatic correspondents, because UPI required him to travel with the President, Secretary of State, or some other leading figure of government at least 25 per cent of his time. But in the small UPI office, at the other end of the State Department's press room from the AP quarters, he ran his shop in much the same manner as Hightower when there was no travel assignment. He was a veteran correspondent with an easy, good-humored manner and a vast fund of diplomatic experience. Born in 1913 in Saguache, Colo., he had learned Spanish as a child and was fluent in it. After receiving his journalism degree from the University of Missouri in 1934, he began work at $10 a week on weekly papers in Nevada, Texas, and New Mexico. He turned up in Washington in 1941 with the Foreign Broadcast Intelligence Service, then under the Federal Communications Commission. In 1944, UPI engaged him and sent him to India. For thirteen years thereafter, he was in and out of the Far East and on the UPI foreign desk in Washington and New York, at the United Nations and on tour with the leading political figures of the time. In 1958, he became the UPI's diplomatic correspondent, but his routine did not change too much. He covered every major international conference abroad, in addition to his work at the State Department, and often shared the responsibilities for Presidential news coverage with Merriman Smith, the UPI's White House correspondent.

The Reuters and Agence France-Presse chiefs in Washington, John ("Pat") Heffernan and Jean LaGrange, both of whom had served in the United States for two decades, had backgrounds that were just as impressive as their American diplomatic counterparts. Both had begun their American service at that superb training ground for both diplomats and diplomatic correspondents, the United Nations. Both had gone on to enlarged responsibilities in Washington. And both now struggled, unsuccessfully, for treatment on the same level as the American agencies. Just about the only place where they had a fairly equal opportunity was at the State Department, but they naturally could not muster the manpower of the Americans. Yet, their rivalry for the play in the Asian papers was stiff and effective.

Necessarily, the effectiveness of the diplomatic correspondents in Washington was only as great as the efficiency of the organizations for which they worked. Each of the wire services saw to it that their Washington copy was moved to headquarters for world-wide distribution as rapidly as possible. Particularly in the Far East, where translations were often required, the agency story that was first in was generally the first one used. Newspaper translators in Tokyo, Seoul, and Taipei weren't impressed with soaring leads or fancy writing. The quicker the story could be moved, and the simpler its language, the more chance there was that it would get in the paper.

Of the agencies, the AP had the most elaborate setup. Its staff of foreign correspondents operated under its Foreign Service for the benefit of its American clients. Its World Service transmitted a general news report all over the globe. After several weeks of experience with this joint operation at the AP's New York headquarters in Rockefeller Center, Jun Kusano, of Tokyo's *Sankei Shimbun,* wrote these impressions for a Japanese magazine:

"There are no deadlines. There is no pause. News keeps flowing constantly for 24 hours. Every minute is a deadline, therefore everybody is hustling and bustling in a way which made me suspect their sanity. If an editor leaves the desk to wash his hands another editor has to cover the desk." [38]

From fifty-seven bureaus outside the United States, a staff of foreign correspondents, including seventy Americans, filed about 100,000 words daily to the Foreign Service desk. There a basic staff of fifteen men, under Ben Bassett, the AP's foreign editor for thirty-five years, worked in shifts around the clock to supervise coverage and select and edit the product for the United States.

At the same time, the World Desk was filing to more than a hundred countries from a collection of regional news outside the United States, with which it combined portions of the American and general foreign news report. News for Asia radiated in two directions by radioteletype channel, one spanning the Pacific to Tokyo with an automatic relay at

Manila to strengthen the signal, and the other across the Atlantic to the Middle East, Africa, and South Asia with a booster relay at Tangier. This same report was carried by cable to London for European relay. For Latin America, there was a separate operation to handle a Spanish-language service.

Stan Swinton, a forty-five-year-old former war correspondent who had spent a part of his boyhood in Java and the Philippines, headed the world operation as an AP assistant general manager. The World Service selected from the "A" and "B" main general news wires from the United States; the State, Regional, and Local wires; the Sports wire; the Business News wire; a United Nations wire when needed; and all the cable and radioteletype channels from overseas. Since AP domestic teletypes ran around the clock at 60 words a minute on the main circuits, each producing 85,000 words an hour, and some of the overseas circuits operated at 66 words a minute, the total file would have been astronomical if it had all been put together.

It wasn't. The main domestic wires were split into three cycles—one for afternoon papers, one for morning papers, and the overnight for the first editions of the next afternoon. Thus, the output of the two main general news wires for an afternoon newspaper in New York City came to about 50,000 or 60,000 words a day. It was a healthy but manageable file.[39]

The foreign report was, of course, a part of it. Depending on the nature of the day's news, it could run anywhere from 15,000 to 20,000 words. While American participation in the Viet-Nam war was increasing, the Asian report sometimes totaled half the foreign file. But without a war, Asian news often constituted no more than 10 per cent of the foreign total.[40] Although the incoming channel from Tokyo ran continually, the outgoing file from the World Desk was limited in 1965 to eighteen hours a day for a total of 64,000 words. Unlike domestic practice, there was no arrangement for cycles of news in the Far East. In accordance with the desires of editors in Asia, the news was told only once and often was arranged chronologically.

The system which UPI had built up over forty years under the direction of Joseph L. Jones, its general foreign manager and vice president, was equally extensive but differently organized. Jones had worked for the UP since 1921, three years before his graduation from the Columbia School of Journalism, and from 1924 until his retirement in 1965 had dominated the service's expansion. The chief difference was in techniques, all the incoming and outgoing file being concentrated in a single organization at UPI's New York headquarters in the Daily News building. The system was continued by his successor, LeRoy Keller.

Reuters, in its refurbished building on London's Fleet Street, worked on a decentralized basis as an organization devoted entirely to the gathering and dissemination of foreign news. While both AP and UPI had many foreign nationals among their bureau chiefs, editors, and foreign correspondents, Reuters probably had a greater percentage of foreigners in its employ. This was a deliberate decision, based on the theory of an entire series of national and regional desks, arranged very much like a small foreign office. Agence France-Presse tried to do the same thing in Paris, but on a necessarily smaller scale.

Even though the wire services were the prime wholesalers of foreign news, particularly for the Far East, they did not by any means have things their own way. The growth of the newspaper syndicates in the United States gave them added competition. More diplomatic correspondents, foreign correspondents, domestic political writers, and columnists were available than ever before. Although the syndicates concentrated on the domestic field, some of the outstanding newspapers of Europe and Asia eagerly sought their services. It was an added bit of prestige, and the information was useful.

The New York Times News Service, founded in 1917, ranked third in size among the news agencies in the United States, with 180 clients in 1966, surpassed only by AP and UPI. Its domestic wire reached 93 newspapers in the United States and 6 in Canada. Its international circuit, which was opened in 1963, serviced 72 newspapers and newspaper groups in Europe, Asia, Canada, Australia, and Hawaii (the fiftieth state is technically on the international band). *Asahi,* the Manila *Times,* and the *Times* of India were among its Asian clients, each of whom received 20,000 words a day.

But the New York *Times* also had stiff competition. The combined Washington Post–Los Angeles Times service, established in October, 1962, had become a major challenger within four years, accumulating 130 subscribers, 60 of them abroad. The even younger Copley News Service had also made a good start, particularly in Latin America. The Chicago Daily News Service, founded in 1898 and once the leader in the field, still had 78 clients in the United States in 1966. The Chicago *Tribune,* the Scripps-Howard Newspaper Alliance, and the North American Newspaper Alliance all maintained syndication for their foreign output, as did smaller organizations.[41]

To the American syndicate array, a discerning student of Asian affairs added, of necessity, the correspondents of the London *Observer,* the *Times* of London, the London *Daily Telegraph,* and occasionally some of the correspondents of *Le Monde* and *Figaro* in Paris, all of whom appeared in the Asian press from time to time. The British syndication, however, was by no means the competition to Reuters that the American operation was to AP and UPI.

Some of the individual American newspapers and newspaper groups that supported correspondents in Asia were able to compete on equal terms with the syndicated correspondents and the wire services in their own circulation areas. The foremost of these were the *Christian Science Monitor* and the Baltimore *Sun*. The Washington *Evening Star*, Chicago *Tribune*, Kansas City *Star*, Minneapolis *Star-Tribune*, San Francisco *Chronicle*, Seattle *Times*, and the Gannett and Knight Newspaper Groups were among those who manifested interest in Asian developments outside the Viet-Nam war.

The news magazines, too, contributed to the coverage of Asia. Of the weeklies, Time-Life assigned an increasingly large staff of correspondents and photographers, once the Viet-Nam war escalated. *Newsweek*, too, expanded to cover the war. While *U.S. News & World Report* had only a few correspondents, they spanned an enormous amount of territory. The business press—the *Wall Street Journal*, the McGraw-Hill business magazines, and the Fairchild organization—all maintained correspondents in key centers of Asia.

As for the electronic media, they made the most of the relatively few first-ranking correspondents they had in Asia until they were obliged to expand because of the Viet-Nam war. After a record profit in 1964 of $415.6 million before taxes, an increase of 21 per cent over the previous year, television might have been expected to do a better job on Asian affairs without the stimulus of war and, to some extent, there was an improvement. N.B.C., for example, gave Asian coverage a good share of the $1.5 to $1.8 million it spent annually for foreign news coverage, including newsfilm, out of its $30-million annual news expenditure. C.B.S. lagged behind the N.B.C. effort, particularly in Asia. A.B.C. was a distant third, hitting the high spots when it could.[42] But for 1965 and 1966, all were competing hotly for sensational war footage out of Viet-Nam because the public demonstrably was interested. Belatedly, the networks recognized that this was "television's first war."

Despite its seeming complexity, it was primarily an American news medley that emanated from the power centers of Asia up to the time of the escalation of the Viet-Nam war. Its volume, before and after, often was deafening in Washington and New York, where the news was concentrated. But with the exception of battle pictures, over TV, the intelligence from Asia became increasingly thin as it radiated outward from the center. And in large parts of the United States, there was so little amplification from the media, except for an occasional news-magazine cover story, that it could scarcely be heard at all until there was a crisis.

5. THE INFLUENCE OF THE NEW YORK *TIMES*

Most correspondents in Saigon openly speculated in the summer of 1964 that Tchepone, then a Communist staging area in Laos, would be bombed with American help. Nothing came of it at the time. But on December 11, 1964, the same story cropped up in the New York *Times* under the by-line of Hanson Baldwin, its military editor for more than 20 years. It was complete with a one-column map and menacing arrows pointing at Tchepone.

To be fair, Baldwin had something more going for him than mere gossip. Following President Johnson's election in November, Ambassador Maxwell D. Taylor had come to Washington on one of his frequent visits and discussed the broadening of American participation in the Vietnamese war, including air attacks on Communist supply bases. "The staging area, supply depot and distribution point of Tchepone and other Communist supply routes in Laos will probably be the first targets if a limited air interdiction campaign is undertaken shortly," Baldwin wrote.[43]

Within a short time, a high government official protested to the *Times* that Baldwin had revealed a military target and that the U.S. command in Saigon had been obliged to shift its goal and its strategy. Yet, American plans involving Tchepone had been virtually in the public domain for five months, whether the knowledge was based on shrewd guesswork or a military indiscretion. The difference, in the main, was that correspondents' gossip in Saigon could be ignored, but the story by Baldwin in the *Times* could not. Although the entire network called the Ho Chi Minh Trail eventually was bombed, the attacks in Laos were overshadowed when the United States undertook its North Viet-Nam bombing attack, which Baldwin also had anticipated. If he interfered with American military planning, which is doubtful, there was no evidence of it.[44]

Baldwin was one of the great correspondents who had made the *Times* a power in the United States. When he published an exhaustive survey intended to show that American armed forces were spread too thin because of the Viet-Nam war, none other than Secretary McNamara had to try to rebut him at a Pentagon news conference. But within a few days, the Los Angeles *Times* revealed the existence of a confidential Senate report showing that four domestic-based Army divisions were below combat-ready status; this time the Pentagon admitted it, although McNamara kept insisting nothing was seriously wrong.[45]

Unhappily, such exploits were not as frequent in the pages of the New York *Times* as they had been. The ranks of the great correspondents were thinning. True, the *Times* still published more foreign news than any other American paper, but the volume had declined; in the *Times*'s "go-go" campaign for circulation, it gave an inordinate amount of space to the trivia of women's pages, from "reporting" in the Cholly Knickerbocker manner to huge picture spreads of the jet set. Such articles as "The Bride Wore Pants" would receive more news and picture space than a solid news report from Japan. If there were new hair-dos, they rated nearly half a page; when the new Paris fashions came out, nothing less than a dozen columns of pictures would do. Except for the old restrained Page 1 on a dull day, it was no longer the "good gray *Times*," and something precious had passed from American journalism.

Yet, the *Times* was able to maintain its prestige. Despite the development of the Washington *Post* and Los Angeles *Times* foreign services, the growth of rivals in Baltimore, Boston, St. Louis, and Chicago, and the increasing efforts of both the television and news-weekly correspondents, the old champion in New York still had enough left to stand off most of the competition. As a critic once wrote: "The fact that it [the *Times*] is a blatantly public medium—seen simultaneously by bureaucrats, members of Congress, foreign ambassadors and agents, lobbyists and citizenry at large—thrusts events into the open, often to the consternation of the principals." [46] If the *Times* did not have all the brilliant reporting of foreign affairs in its greatest days, it still retained the courage of its convictions. This, basically, was the reason why it continued to hold the respect of its readers, although some would have welcomed more news and less froth in its pages.

Arthur Hays Sulzberger, son-in-law of Adolph S. Ochs, had guided the growth of the *Times* with the frequent admonition to his editors, "Remember, when you are selling a newspaper, you are selling a habit." They had made it a habit for 722,705 readers on week-days and 1,432,-000 on Sundays, a week-day gain over a decade of nearly 175,000 and a Sunday increase of more than 200,000.[47] And this at a time when all other newspapers in New York except the tabloid *Daily News* were losing readers and money in the media wars with television, radio, and the news magazines. Hearst's *Daily Mirror,* a fun-loving sheet with nearly a million circulation, had died suddenly. The once great *Herald Tribune* also had been obliged to cease publication following a long strike that kept it off the streets after its merger with the afternoon *World-Telegram* and *Journal-American.*

It was often said that no quality newspaper in the United States had ever developed such a mass circulation as the *Times;* taking the figures alone at face value, it was true. But what the growth did to the quality of the paper was another matter entirely. By no means everything in the *Times* now would have met Adolph S. Ochs's definition: "All the news that's fit to print." Moreover, in the face of growing competition and rising costs, the advertising kept making its inroads on news space. The *Times* was no longer the first news medium in the nation in terms of volume. The Los Angeles *Times* was rated first in 1965 with the publication of 40,316,468 lines of news and feature content; the Miami *Herald* was second, with 33,466,743 lines; and the New York *Times* was third, with 27,194,114.[48]

Through good management and a certain number of justifiable economies, plus the fatal weakness of the rival *Herald Tribune,* the *Times* continued to be a profitable newspaper. Its consolidated net income in 1965 was $5,131,301, equal to $11.26 a common share, despite a twenty-four-day newspaper strike in October. Of the total, $1,169,889 was earned by the *Times*'s interest in the Spruce Falls Power and Paper Co., Ltd., but the rest came from advertising and circulation revenue, both of which were at new highs. It was an operation that would have been viewed with respect by any business executive, commanding, as it did, consolidated revenues of $140,546,000 in 1965 and prospects for even greater earnings in the succeeding year.[49]

While any system for calculating the cost of a foreign service depends on variables that make comparisons difficult, it is probable that the *Times*'s foreign coverage in the 1960's easily attained the level of $4 million annually. With forty-five foreign correspondents on the staff, and most of them serving at permanent posts abroad for terms of two to three years, the annual average cost for each correspondent, excluding communications charges, was estimated at $50,000 to $55,000. This included salaries, travel, office rent and expense; cost of local secretarial, reportorial, and translating assistance; and allowances for housing, educational benefits for children, cost-of-living differential, and fringe benefits. In some posts, notably Moscow, costs were higher; a rival organization, the Los Angeles *Times,* budgeted the cost of maintaining a single correspondent in Moscow at $85,000 a year. In most Asian assignments, excluding Tokyo and Saigon, the costs were lower than average, in the opinion of some of the *Times*'s own correspondents.

The correspondents' expense of about $2 million was the basic cost. To it was added the maintenance of the *Times*'s own communications operation in New York City, nonstaff and part-time correspondents, the cost of cable and radio messages and of the other communications services, such as the AP, for which the monthly charge amounted to $30,000 alone for standard and special services. By contrast, the AP's most important paper in Asia, *Asahi,* was believed to be paying around $17,000 a month. Without doubt, the extra expense involved in the coverage of the enlarged Viet-Nam war boosted the cost of the total foreign operation.

The news space into which this product had to be fitted was less than it had been a decade before. Not even the *Times* could afford to run a wide open paper every day with rising expenses in every area of operation. The *Times*'s news hole in 1965, including everything except advertising, was set at a quota of 195 columns, with texts extra; but it was exceeded when news was heavy. Normally, the foreign news quota in the main news section was about 20 columns daily, but when political or sports news claimed primary attention or an astronaut was in orbit, it was less. However, it seldom went below a minimum of 16 columns —two full pages of type.

In quantity of foreign news published daily, therefore, the *Times* could still claim national leadership, and it remained the standard against which its rivals were measured. But there was no doubt that the standard had been lowered. In 1953 the International Press Institute had reported that the *Times* had carried a daily average of 32 columns of foreign news a day.[50] Allowing for all conceivable differences in measurement, evaluation, and other criteria, the gap between an average of 32 columns in 1953 and 16 to 20 columns only a little more than a decade later indicated a drop in the volume of daily publication of foreign news. The *Times*'s own correspondents, as may be expected, were the first to notice it and the first to complain. What spared the newspaper's reputation was the routine performance in reporting foreign affairs of the bulk of the American press, with only a few exceptions.

The slimmed-down space for foreign affairs, which was in such striking contrast with the lavishness of space given to sports, pictures, amusements, women's and social news, led to tighter stories for *Times* foreign correspondents. While the newspaper had the services of the AP, UPI, Reuters, the *Times* of London, and others, these generally were used as backstops and limited to a column or two a day. Thus, *Times* correspondents in Asia had to contend with the general run of news, and their space allotment varied with the fortunes of the Viet-Nam war and the activities of Communist China, plus an occasional explosion over Kashmir or Indonesia. Over a considerable period in 1965-66, with a stepped-up war situation in Viet-Nam, the *Times* ran an average of from three to five columns a day of news from Asia. Had there been no war, it would, of course, have been less.

In common with the rest of the American press, the *Times* had not paid major attention to Asia from the end of the Korean War until the early 1960's. Then, Turner Catledge, the *Times*'s executive editor, made his first tour to the Far East and decided on a modest expansion in Asian coverage. In place of one correspondent in Tokyo to handle Japan and Korea, two were assigned. A Southeast Asia service was created, with a staff correspondent each in Hong Kong, Saigon, and Kuala Lumpur and stringers in Djakarta, Manila, Taipei, and Bangkok. The theory was that the staffers would be in constant motion. There was a *Times* man in New Delhi and another in Karachi, which was more than any other American newspaper provided for the Indian subcontinent. As for coverage of Communist China, in addition to Reuters service from Peking, the main effort was in Hong Kong. Seymour Topping, who was to become foreign editor of the *Times* late in 1966, was in charge there.

This was the standard for American newspapers in the coverage of Asia. Until the Viet-Nam war reached larger proportions, that was the way it remained. But in Washington, there was no tendency on the part of government to lower its guard. The "good gray *Times*" had passed into history. But its successor, the "go-go" *Times,* also carried a healthy punch.

6. PRESS AND GOVERNMENT: A DIALOGUE

On the morning of September 2, 1965, the New York *Daily News* presented its 2 million readers with this summation of American undercover activity in the Far East, set in large type across the top of Page 1:

>*CIA's 007 Goofs in Singapore*
>3-MILLION BRIBE
>OFFER FLOPS

The *News,* in common with the rest of the press of the United States and the world at large, proceeded to relate an almost incredible story of a CIA operative who, unlike the fictional 007 of British intelligence, James Bond, did the wrong thing at the wrong time and was caught at it. The tale was so fantastic that the New York *Times* carried the initial account of it from Singapore on Page 5 on August 31. But as the U.S. Government compounded the original error by going into its usual routine of issuing a denial, and then being forced to retract it, the affair was built up into another instance of an American diplomatic blooper.

Prime Minister Lee Kuan Yew, the forty-two-year-old Cambridge-educated chief executive of Singapore, made the disclosure in a press conference on August 30, just three weeks after his largely Chinese city of nearly 2 million people had been forced out of the Federation of

Malaysia. His motives were not clear, but the effect was to heighten the impression that he was veering toward nonalignment by attacking the United States and at the same time trying to placate a hostile Indonesia and a critical Communist China. He stoutly maintained that his regime was still non-Communist, opposing the Communist elements that were so strong in his orphaned city.

All these factors should have created a state of alertness in the governmental agencies in Washington concerned with such things when the details of the Lee interview became known. The burden of the Prime Minister's remarks were that he would not turn to the United States for help if Britain withdrew from its powerful naval and air base in Singapore. He argued that Americans, unlike the British, did not possess the "depth and judgment or wisdom which comes out of an accumulation of knowledge of human beings and human situations over a long period of time."

As an instance of American ineptitude, he told of an American CIA agent who was arrested in 1960 in what was described as "an apparent attempt to bribe and subvert Singapore intelligence authorities." He went on to say, according to the original account of the interview, that he had told the American government, "All right, we keep quiet. You take this man away, $100 million to the Singapore government for economic development. Through an intermediary, they offered me and my party $10 million. I mean, the insult! I told them, you can keep it."

James D. Bell, the U.S. Ambassador to Malaysia, promptly issued a denial. Robert J. McCloskey, the State Department's spokesman, solemnly announced in Washington: "First, we are surprised at these statements attributed to Prime Minister Lee. With respect to allegations of a CIA involvement, we deny that allegation."

In Singapore, Lee reacted angrily. He received reporters in his office on September 1, took out files marked "top secret," and produced a letter from Secretary Rusk which he pressed into the face of an American correspondent. "The Americans stupidly deny the undeniable," he flared.

The letter, dated April 15, 1961, read:

Dear Mr. Prime Minister:
   I am deeply distressed to learn that certain officials of the United States government have been found by your government to have been engaged in improper activities in Singapore. I want you to know I regret very much that this unfortunate incident had occurred to mar friendly relations that exist between our two governments.
   The new administration takes a very serious view of this matter and in fact is reviewing activities of these officials for disciplinary action.

Prime Minister Lee also had some tape recordings in the case which he threatened to play for the diversion of the assembled press, saying, "If the Americans go on denying, I will have to disclose further details, which may sound like James Bond and Goldfinger, only not as good, but putrid and grotesque enough. It will do them no good and our future relations no good . . . If they continue to repeat the denial, I will have to disclose who the intermediary was and very high circles would be greatly embarrassed."

The Prime Minister's secretary then gave the press a different version of the case, saying that the United States had offered Lee $3.3 million for his personal and political use to conceal the arrest of the CIA agent who had been caught trying to bribe Singapore intelligence officials. Instead, Lee was reputed to have asked for $33 million in formal economic-development aid for Singapore. The incident occurred in 1960, just before the Kennedy administration took office.

After appropriate consultations, the embarrassed McCloskey reappeared before reporters and reversed himself. "Those who were consulted yesterday," he said, "were not fully aware of the background of the incident, which occurred four and a half years ago." For their own background, the reporters were informed that the CIA had issued a routine denial of its activities, which is its standard operating procedure; that Secretary Rusk had not been consulted; and that "new officials" in the department hadn't bothered to look up the files. In any event, the case was now marked "closed." [51] A call on Prime Minister Lee by Ambassador Bell in Singapore served to draw the curtain of charity over the rest of the incident but left unanswered for the time being some urgent questions of public policy that had been raised.

Six months later, the New York *Times* retold the Singapore tale at great length on Page 1 under a three-column headline: "CIA: Maker of Policy or Tool?" This opening article in a series of five discussing the role of the CIA contended that what really happened in Singapore in 1960 was as follows:

A CIA agent flew from Tokyo to Singapore, joined a colleague there in a hotel room on a recruiting mission, plugged in a lie detector to test the reliability of a third person, a potential spy, and blew out all the lights. All were discovered and jailed. An effort was made to buy their freedom from Singapore authorities, but the price was too high. In any event, the CIA denied trying to bribe anybody, and eventually its agents were freed.

There was no attempt to explain away the Rusk apology, however, or the subsequent embarrassment of the American government.[52] But the *Times*'s articles argued that there were adequate checks on the CIA despite the disclosures of ineptitude in Singapore and elsewhere.

The notion that CIA agents could clothe their operations in secrecy indefinitely was a delusion that was commonly shared in Washington, but not at all in most parts of Asia where their operations were a favorite subject of gossip among foreign correspondents. The CIA was evidently aware of this, for instructions went out from time to time that its agents were not to talk with certain journalists. One American correspondent in Asia told how a CIA man, who was forbidden to talk with him, tried to arrange to meet him outside the country to which both were assigned with the objective of trading information. One of the most poisonous things one correspondent could say about another—and some did it repeatedly—was that the CIA had been able to "plant" a story in his paper by using him.

Necessarily, the CIA was at an obvious disadvantage. It could not talk about its triumphs, although its defeats often became a matter of public record. There was little public understanding of its operations, leading Allen Dulles to observe, "It is hardly reasonable to expect proper understanding and support for intelligence work in this country if it is only the insiders, a few people within the executive and legislative branches, who know anything whatever about the CIA." [53]

The CIA's enemies, of course, saw to it that its activities were well advertised—both the real and fancied operations. President Sukarno, of Indonesia, Prince Norodom Sihanouk of Cambodia, and General Ne Win of Burma all had charged that the CIA had sought to overthrow their regimes at one time or another. David Wise of the New York Herald Tribune and Thomas B. Ross of the Chicago Sun-Times, in their book about the CIA, The Invisible Government, agreed with Sukarno, in effect, by relating the story of an American CIA agent who flew air missions in support of an Indonesian rebel group in 1958. [54]

It was scarcely a new problem in government. On the basis of his two years' service as ambassador to India, John Kenneth Galbraith made some trenchant observations on the usual practices of governmental secrecy. "The first difficulty," he maintained, "is the surviving conviction that diplomacy is a privileged occupation into which the press and the public should not really be allowed to obtrude. . . . Fear is also a factor and the feeling that the press, like Congress, exists largely to louse up foreign policy."

Galbraith proceeded on the theory, not generally accepted in the State Department and positively scorned by most of the military and the entire CIA, that anybody with a decent record in various encounters with the press should be allowed to commit a few errors. "The man who seeks to avoid all error, all misinterpretation, will say nothing and do the worst job. He will live, as do a surprising number of our officials, in a mentally crippling fear of his own tongue." [55]

I remember a young embassy press officer in Asia discussing the application of what might be called Galbraith's "Law of Calculated Risk." "If you are going to work with the press," he said, "you have to get as close as you can to the line of unauthorized disclosure if you are after the truth, or any part of it. Now and then, you may even go over the line and get into trouble, but that's the risk you take. If you don't live dangerously, you're not worth a hoot as a press officer and nobody will talk to you."

It was not a point of view that was calculated to win the confidence of those government officials who are devoted to the notion that the trickery of general intelligence practice is worth trying on the press. During a lecture at the Air War College some years ago, I was asked by an aggressive colonel: "Why *shouldn't* we issue false information and have the press print it to fool the enemy, just the way they do with us?"

There was no mass public following for the less savory practices of the CIA or for those military zealots who favored planting deceptive information in the press. The ignominious experiences of the Bay of Pigs fiasco and the acceptance of bad information in South Viet-Nam, added to the U-2 and Singapore incidents, could not help but make an impression upon even the habitual cynics in government. Moreover, so eminent an authority as Senator J. W. Fulbright publicly protested when a full-time CIA analyst, George A. Carver, Jr., was not identified as such when he wrote on the Viet-Nam conflict in the distinguished quarterly *Foreign Affairs*.

In sum, the usefulness of independent press inquiry, together with healthy criticism of the press itself for not going far enough, was thoroughly upheld even by those in government who often tried to use the press. As the New York *Times* concluded its critique of the CIA:

Is there some point at which meeting fire with fire, force with force, subversion with subversion, crime with crime, becomes so prevalent and accepted that there no longer remains any distinction of honor and pride between grim and implacable adversaries? These questions are a proper and necessary concern for the people of the United States. . . . The New York *Times* study of the CIA suggests that it is not an invisible government but the real government of the United States upon which the responsibility must lie whenever the agency may be found "out of control." [57]

Essentially, no one in government could openly advocate a policy of less militant inquiry and criticism by the press. There was no William Tecumseh Sherman around to curse the inquiring reporter for his nosiness and denounce him as follows: "We don't want the truth told about things here—that's what we *don't* want! Truth, eh? No, sir! We don't want the enemy any better informed than he is!" [58]

The closest anybody came to that iniquitous but thoroughly honest declaration—and it wasn't really very close—was during Ambassador Taylor's term of service in Saigon. During Taylor's visit to Washington on December 1, 1964, a reporter heard Secretary McNamara protest to President Johnson as the three of them approached a group of correspondents: "It would be impossible for Max [Taylor] to talk to these people without leaving the impression that the situation is going to hell." [59] Ambassador Taylor, on that occasion, was not interviewed.

The reason for official caution was best outlined by Carl Rowan when he said, while in the service of the State Department, "Far too few newsmen—or editors—are willing to weigh their stories against the national interest, especially if it means giving up a 'beat' and the opportunity to boast about it in a promotion ad." [60] In the same vein, Robert J. Manning argued when Assistant Secretary of State for Public Affairs: "The occasionally mindless devotion of the press to exposure for exposure's sake can put us at a disadvantage. This is especially so in the sensitive area where military and political considerations merge." [61] To this, Robert U. Brown, editor of *Editor & Publisher* magazine, commented in an editorial on government practices in South Viet-Nam, "How can our government expect to be believed around the world— how can USIA expect to be accepted as telling the truth—when we indulge in such subterfuge, coverup and half-truths even in one situation?" [62]

Sophisticated foreign correspondents in the United States were not particularly worried by all this. T. V. Parasuram, Washington correspondent of the *Indian Express,* saw some merit in the tension between press and government. He wrote: "To take a recent instance, the [American] wheat deal with the Soviet Union was not announced for ten days after the President had decided to go ahead with it. During this crucial period, the administration was able to judge whether it was politically safe to enter into it. The administration left the way open to proceed or retreat. News dispatches in some newspapers revealed the deal was firm. Other dispatches raised doubts." Recommending such procedures to the Indian government, Parasuram concluded: "Something is surely wrong with a system in which almost every major development comes to the public as a surprise. This ought not to happen in a democratic society. After all, the public are the masters. They have the right to accept or reject a policy not only after it has been framed by the government but during the process of formulation." [63]

James Reston, who was seldom tempted to play the reformer, was all for working with governments as they are, not as he would wish them to be. Once he advised some young reporters: "The public official is in a difficult position in the United States, particularly when he deals with foreign affairs. On the one hand, he is security conscious but must give his views to his opposite numbers abroad and to Congressional committees. He must also try to make the best of everything. The reporter, therefore, is advised to check with other governments as well as his own." [64]

Had all American news media been devoted to the principle of using significant foreign news in such volume as to make it understandable to a mass public, the argument over truth in the news from abroad might have attracted more public attention. As it was, all except a small but articulate segment of the public remained relatively unconcerned, and the press went on doing pretty much what it pleased.

In a nation with 1,751 daily newspapers totaling 60,357,563 circulation in 1965, with nearly $5 billion in annual advertising revenue, there was no doubt that sufficient foreign news was available either from the wire services or the syndicates.[65] By and large, it was usually a good report. But not many papers bothered with foreign material. A relatively low pattern of interest was shown in a check on what happened to twenty-two foreign stories offered to twenty-nine daily newspapers, with circulations of 60,000 to 500,000, by a major wire service. Although news magazines generally have their greatest success in areas where newspapers concentrate on local news alone, this apparently had no effect on the pattern of use. Only one newspaper out of fourteen published all ten stories that were chosen for the study of morning papers. Among fifteen afternoon newspapers, no one newspaper used all twelve stories in the afternoon newspaper test, and no one story appeared in all of the papers. Yet, according to the test director, Earl J. Johnson, who was editor of United Press International at the time, all the stories were of the type that would have been used by news magazines.[66]

Half the morning papers in the test omitted a speech by Secretary Rusk explaining why the United States treats some Communist nations differently from others. The dispatch was sent at 5:54 P.M., EST, in ample time for most first editions. Roger Hilsman's resignation as the Assistant Secretary of State for Far Eastern Affairs was used by ten newspapers but omitted by four. It also was sent in good time. A Russian warning to the United States against going into North Viet-Nam, plus a demand for American troop withdrawals from South Viet-Nam, was used by only one newspaper and it was sent at 5:33 P.M., EST. This was not a matter of the mere omission of a UPI story on these subjects. The AP stories were also left out.[67] Since TV coverage is necessarily sketchy and radio reporting even more so, the results of the test indicated that large areas of the United States probably were without sustained day-to-day access to knowledge of international events.

It was often said in the 1960's that increased coverage of foreign affairs and a better quality of foreign correspondence generally would come in due time, granted that there was sufficient public demand for improvement. But who could measure the demand when the supply was often severely restricted? The offering of news was not like the offering of food, or shelter; yet, it was no less a basic necessity. The heedless often laughed and remarked that what people didn't know wouldn't hurt them. But it was clear enough from the reaction to the Viet-Nam war that lack of news did hurt people—and it hurt their government even more.

One could fairly blame the government for unnecessarily withholding foreign news or issuing incomplete or inaccurate foreign news on occasion; there was sufficient documentation for such charges. But the amount of foreign news that was mangled or blocked by government machinery was demonstrably much smaller than the flow of wire-service and syndicate copy from abroad that was shut off by newspaper editors in most of the nation's communities. Thus, there were two sides to the problem of presenting a reasonable amount of foreign news to the American public, particularly from Asia, and neither could be considered separately. When the framers of the Constitution decreed freedom to print the news as an inalienable right of benefit to the American people, they had scarcely been able to foresee that freedom not to print the news would be a source of major concern to some of their countrymen at a future time. But it was. And the time was now.

III

The Restless Japanese

1. IMAGES AND REALITIES

TWENTY YEARS AFTER the peace of Tokyo Bay, the relatively few American correspondents whose newspapers were seriously interested in such things noted that the United States had entered a new era in its relations with Japan. Having changed status successively from a defeated foe to a dependent and latterly to a hesitant partner in some of the uncertain ventures of the United States into Asian affairs, the Japanese were beginning cautiously to seek a more independent policy in the latter part of the 1960's.

Eisaku Sato had said as much during his first visit to Washington as Japan's premier, using the homely phrasing: "Friendship should not be permitted to interfere with a person's decision when it has any bearing on his course of action in public life." [1] It was a tentative departure from the "low posture" that had caused Japan to speak softly and avoid controversy as often as possible in world affairs for almost two decades. Until then, Japanese diplomacy seemingly had been overshadowed by such lesser figures as Prince Norodom Sihanouk, leader of 6 million Cambodians, and the disheartening parade of premiers in South Viet-Nam.

The United States had not discouraged Premier Sato. To the masters of American statecraft, hard pressed in Southeast Asia, the injection of Japan as a new factor in the complex Asian rivalries was at once an opportunity and a challenge in the development of U.S. foreign policy. As one shrewd observer noted: "Rivalries among Japan, China and Russia are older than Marxist ideology." [2]

However restless the Japanese may have been and no matter how much they were tempted to assert themselves, they walked quietly.

95

They were pleased with their economic progress and in no mood to support the building of another military machine. One military disaster had been enough for the generation that was still in power. Consequently, the Japanese saw no particular point in hastening a confrontation with either of their giant Communist neighbors; nor, for that matter, was there much advantage in cutting loose from the protection provided by American military strength. It was clearly in Japanese self-interest to make commitments slowly and then only with great care.

A new epoch was opening for this ancient and beautiful land. There was a growing ferment in its traditional society which had been opened to Western influences in 1853 under the guns of Commodore Matthew Calbraith Perry's "black ships" in Tokyo Bay. With the approaching centennial of the Meiji Restoration of 1868, that vast revolution again stirred the imagination of young Japan. For the rising generation, bringing their nation abreast of modernity was a far more powerful stimulant than the shame over the lost Pacific war, the fierce resentment toward the militarists who had caused it, and the genuine gratitude for the moderation of the American occupation as well as the MacArthur reforms. Few traces of the old Occupation psychology now remained. Japan, a giant in Asia, was on its feet again.

What did the future hold? No one could be certain. Within Japanese society there was a great deal of pulling and hauling between the rejuvenated zaibatsu, who wanted a land where business could do pretty much as it wished; the intellectuals, who had fuzzy and impractical notions about a Marxist Japan; and a growing middle-class trend toward some kind of an Asian "welfare state." A radical historian, Shigeki Toyama, put the problem as follows:

> We are forever saying that "Asia is one" and that "Japan is a member of the Asian community," but in reality we do not fully believe in these statements. Even between two Oriental countries such as China and India there are qualitative differences which arise from their different historical traditions. These differences point up the fact that the statement so often used by the Japanese that "Asia is one" is actually no more than an empty slogan. . . . If we Japanese are ever going to understand Asia and the rest of the world, it is necessary that we first make an effort to clarify in our own minds Japan's position in Asia and formulate *for ourselves* the tasks which that position dictates.[3]

The nature of Japan's position in Asia was definite enough; what to do about it, however, was something else again. Dai Nippon had thrust itself above all its neighbors despite the setback of a lost war and a ravaged economy. For all the aggressiveness of the Communist Chinese, they had almost insuperable problems at home in providing for a population of 750 million that was bogged down, for the most part, in a primitive economy. India, bereft of the strong leadership of Jawaharlal Nehru, was being rent by the pull of provincialism, conflict with Pakistan, and the constant problems of hunger and disease. The upheaval of war had reduced most of Southeast Asia to near impotence, while in Indonesia the colossal ego of Sukarno and his terrifying incompetence in government had reduced to penury a prosperous and productive nation. In Pakistan, a land divided against itself at birth, only the exigencies of military rule and American aid had staved off disaster. Around the Asian crescent, an essential stability and growth seemed to be displayed more by such smaller nations as Thailand, the Philippines, the Republic of Korea, and Formosa under Chinese Nationalist rule, all of them beneficiaries of massive American aid.

The prevalent American hope for Japan, as expressed by A. M. Rosenthal, in the New York *Times,* was to look to the Japanese as "the industrial cement for a wall of economic achievement running through the threatened Asian nations in Communist China's path." [4] But not even the Gaimusho, the Japanese Foreign Office, was quick to jump at the prospect of participating in the construction of a new Chinese Wall as a means of containing the spread of Communism in Asia. Even among those Asians who were fearful and perhaps terrified of the Communist Chinese threat, there was no enthusiasm for Japan as a prospective ally. The victims of Japan's Greater East Asian Co-Prosperity Sphere —among them Filipinos, Koreans, Formosans, and the peoples of Southeast Asia—could not be expected to hail the new Japan as a deliverer. It was as if the peoples of Central Europe had been asked once more to depend upon their German neighbors.

Conscious of being the cynosure of the peoples of the Pacific, Japan moved slowly ahead with an acute understanding of the anxieties, suspicions, and even latent hostility among many of its fellow Asians. After fourteen years of negotiations, the Japanese, on December 21, 1965, entered into full diplomatic relations with the Republic of Korea —a land they had held in thrall for forty years. They had already offered to the Koreans $800 million in loans, credits, and grants. [5] They also matched a $200 million American pledge for the Asian Development Bank. [6] Loans flowed out to India and Pakistan. Large-scale reparations were paid to the Filipinos and Indonesians, among others. These funds and additional foreign aid placed Japan fifth in giving aid to other nations after the United States, Great Britain, France, and West Germany. [7]

As for the Communist lands, Japan did not neglect them. Despite long-standing differences with the Soviet Union, relations became normal, trade missions were exchanged, and each country readily admitted correspondents accredited by the other. It was far more difficult to reach even a tentative understanding with the Chinese Communists, for the matter of diplomatic relations was complicated by a thumping reparations problem, as well as many others. The Chinese foreign minister, Marshal Chen Yi, pointedly alluded to this tender subject when he warned a Tokyo radio representative: "The Chinese people have a right to ask for reparations." [8] However, Peking took a long first step toward a more normal relationship with Japan by agreeing to an exchange of trade offices and correspondents. [9] It was pleasing to both the businesslike Japanese right and the Marxist left, and amounted to so little that no more than the usual amount of anguish could be detected in Washington.

The horizon for Dai Nippon was bright. Now it had become a nation of more than 96 million, concentrated in an area about the size of California. In terms of arable land, the population density was approximately twenty times as great as that of the United States. Nevertheless, Japan had been able to exceed all nations in the Western world in terms of economic growth over a decade. From 1952 on, it averaged more than 9 per cent annually, up to 1965. As for the per capita national income, it was estimated at $600 for 1965, more than three times what it had been in 1953. [10]

The Japanese became the largest shipbuilders in the world, the second largest chemical-fiber manufacturers, and the third largest steelmakers and cotton-yarn producers. In electronic equipment and automobile production they were also near the top. And while they were fourth among the world's exporting nations, they had yet to return to their prewar export sales levels. [11] In less than two decades, Japan had risen from the ruins of war and defeat to become the fifth largest industrial power in the world. [12]

But in 1965, the booming economy overheated. The growth rate dived to less than 3 per cent because of what was called a recession in the midst of an expanding economy. Despite affluence and high living among the middle and upper classes in the cities, the people as a whole began to feel the pinch of rising prices. The government statistics bureau showed that although the average monthly income of Japanese households rose 7.3 per cent in 1965, actual real income dropped 0.3 per cent because of rising consumer prices. In February, 1966, the consumer price index for all cities (with 1960 as 100) hit 138.5, while average disposable income per family after taxes was about $177 a month. Price supports, food discount days, and higher tariffs for farmers began to be talked about, but the abiding concern in Japan was over the inflationary trend. For 1966, despite all negative factors, the government was hoping for a recovery to a 7 per cent rate of growth. [13]

Little of this was apparent at first to the newest young American correspondent who would leave his trans-Pacific jet at Haneda Airport with Ruth Benedict's *The Chrysanthemum and the Sword* and Edwin O. Reischauer's *The United States and Japan* in his flight bag. To his eyes, Japan was a roaring Western land somehow peopled by Orientals. Even such veterans as Arthur Koestler cheered the readers of *Life* magazine by reporting that Japan was "moving away from the Asian mainland in every domain, from foreign trade to life and letters." He even concluded with an appropriate jingle, composed for the occasion:

> If East is East and West is West,
> Where will Japan come to rest?
> In the restless West.[14]

A distinguished Japanese editor, who concentrated more on geography than sentiment, was not so sanguine. He meditated silently over the situation of Japan and the West, then placed a cigarette next to a large lacquered bowl on his tea table. The cigarette was Japan, the bowl China. The West was far away from both.

"We can't get away from China," he said. "We are here and the security of our society depends in large part on the attitude of the Communist powers. What happens out here is not really going to be determined alone by the behavior of the United States, right or wrong. Our problem is that we have to live right here alongside Communist China.

"As an immediate guarantee of our security, we must rely on the United States. The doubt in our minds arises over exactly how long we can expect American forces to stay in Asia. When the time comes for us to face up to the problem of a confrontation with Communist society, will American forces still be here to defend us and will they really go into action to save us? This is the doubt which we really have and I am sure it is mirrored in our publications. So although we believe our relationship with the United States is indispensable now, what shall we do in thirty to fifty years? Can we perhaps count on a stronger United Nations, acting as an organ of collective security, to keep us from being pulled back into the Asian Orbit?"

He shrugged, picked up his cigarette and lighted it, his face impassive. "I don't know. It is just a faint hope." [15]

The old slogan, "Asia is one," still had an almost paralyzing effect on this supple and sophisticated Japanese mind. And yet, he knew—far more than many others—how great was the pull of the United States in attracting Japan to the West.

As the leading customer for American exports after Canada, and a leading exporter to the American market, Japan was very largely dependent on the good health of the American economy. Moreover, about 70 per cent of Japan's borrowed long-term capital came from American sources. As one authority put it, "When the American economy has the snuffles, Japan already has acute pneumonia." [16]

In the matter of national defense, the Japanese were influenced to an extent by the steady drop in the American military commitment in their country, from 260,000 troops in 1952 to 36,000, who maintained 150 installations in 1966. Some did not realize how quickly entire divisions could be flown in from the United States. But in view of the American difficulties in Southeast Asia, even this would not have been a source of great assurance.

There were those, of course, who talked and wrote with knowing cynicism about the possibility of a Japanese military buildup under the stimulus of the United States. Some in the American military advocated it as a way of lessening the American commitment in Asia. But the war renunciation clause of the Japanese Constitution was still an article of faith with a public that remembered the utter desolation of 1945. Nevertheless many powerful elements in Japan were in favor of repeal, and some even talked about building a Japanese atomic bomb.

Japan was committed to self-defense and a species of mutual assistance under American treaty agreements. For 1966, the Japanese Ground Self-Defense Force was set at 210,000 men, 30,000 of them reserves. The Air Self-Defense Force's strength in the same year was put at about 1,200 aircraft, including F-104J's, and about 40,000 men. As for the 1966 Maritime Self-Defense Force, it was limited to about 200 ships totaling 140,000 tons, handled by more than 35,000 men. [17]

It was not a strong force by modern standards. It was not equipped with offensive weapons, either long-range rockets or bombers. Beside the 600,000-man army of the Republic of Korea, with its modern American equipment, the Japanese force was puny and it had no capacity to get off the home islands and move in elsewhere. That, too, would take years to change, and no such policy decision appeared at all imminent in Tokyo. Japan, in any event, was unlikely to help fight U.S. battles on the Asian mainland with armed forces, however much economic or fringe assistance might be offered.

There was, finally, the dread touchstone of modern times, atomic energy. Japan, like India, had the capability and the scientists and even greater plant and materials for the manufacture of atomic energy for military purposes, but not the will. It would have taken a political catastrophe to have changed this situation. For any doubters, it should have been sufficient to visit Hiroshima. Each year, thousands of Japanese came to the rebuilt city to stand grimly before the shattered Atomic Dome near ground zero and walk in tears through the museum of atomic horror, a memorial of that tragic August 6, 1945, when the first atomic bomb carried retribution for Pearl Harbor. For these people, atomic destruction was a shattering reality.

That was the reason for the national concern over the atomic reactors at Tokai-mura and the devotion of Japan's distinguished atomic researchers to the medical and industrial uses of atomic energy.[18] For the Pacific-war generation of Japanese, any suspicion of action to develop the military uses of atomic energy was a political issue of the first magnitude, and their government fully realized it.

American political, economic, and military influence, therefore, was still very great two decades after the end of World War II, but it had its limitations. By contrast with other nations in Asia and Europe that had benefited from American aid, the American investment in Japan in money terms had been moderate. The bill totaled about $2.6 billion in foreign assistance and $1.3 in military aid, the latter sum being almost one-third of what the Japanese themselves had invested in their reconstituted Self-Defense Force.[19] Seldom before in history had a conqueror so conducted himself in lifting up a defeated enemy; what would come of it in the end, of course, only the Japanese themselves knew, and they had not finally made up their minds.

An American in Tokyo could delude himself quite easily over the extent of American social influence. In the heart of the greatest city in the world, with 11 million people jammed together, he might well feel that Japan was Westernized, even crudely Americanized. Here was the same traffic congestion, furious construction, blatant advertising, and rush-hour subway crowding that also overawed the countryman visiting New York. Along the fashionable shopping streets in the Marunouchi district and in the great department stores of the Ginza area, there were the same lavish displays of quality apparel and luxury goods that could be found in Paris, London, and New York.

In addition, there were great new speedways in the California style which were flung across the housetops, a fascinating steel and concrete spider's web. A gleaming new monorail connected Haneda Airport with the city proper. The youngsters strolled along the streets to school, transistor radios blaring. And from the TV sets that were displayed on every side, one could hear such brisk little advertising jingles as:

Saatto-sawayaka-Koka Kora
Koka Kora o nomooyo!

The scenery was Japanese but the script for the advertising commercial was familiar. It was a picnic for Japanese boys and girls, who were drinking from the little pinch bottle that had become a characteristic of American civilization abroad. The refrain, in translation, was familiar, too: "How refreshing Coca Cola is—let's drink Coca Cola."[20]

The American might be deluded, too, by the frequency with which American English cropped up in Japanese conversation, modified appropriately to take care of the familiar Japanese difficulty with the letter "l." For the Japanese, Oxford English simply wasn't "with it." They asked for *gasorin*, not petrol, for their automobiles and took an *erebēta*, not a lift, in a department store, which they called a *depāto*. Naturally, the American influence was the most marked in the Japanese national game, *bēsu-bōru*, in which the umpire called *bōru* and *autoraiki* on the batter and ruled the runner *sēfu* or *auto* at the plate.[21] In the new and modern palaces that served as hotels in Tokyo and the other great cities of Japan, many of the 250,000 tourists each year found themselves surrounded by a fusion of Japanese and American decor and American methods, although the cooking frequently was in the British tradition.

By night, with a riot of neon color flaring over the Ginza, the Akasaka Strip, and a half-dozen other centers of mass gaiety, the American often had a larger selection of night spots to choose from than he had at home. If sex was an American national obsession, Japan made an industry of it. There were chorus lines and mass strip-tease performances in some of the music halls, nude acts in other spots, and friendly Japanese hostesses who dressed like movie starlets in many of the 50,000 bars, for those who wanted them. In lusty display and in humor, the spirit was more typical of Berlin than the more sophisticated precincts of Paris or New York.

For a stage performance of *My Fair Lady* in Japanese or of *Hello, Dolly!* by touring Americans, crowds lined up a whole night in advance; Shakespeare, Chekhov, and Tennessee Williams, too, could be seen on the Japanese stage. The American movies drew far greater crowds, of course, to the big houses. And in the coffee shops and the night clubs, the Frug and the Watusi were performed with abandon by Japanese who seemed to play as hard as they worked. They adopted anything in the West that attracted them, from bikinis to sports cars, from tight slacks and blue jeans to the slick black leather of the motorcycle maniacs.

Yet, beneath it all, the Japanese retained their own identity with a tenacity that no foreign intrusion could shake. The heritage of family solidarity, reverence for tradition, and obedience to authority continued to exert a strong influence, particularly among the older generation. Younger people, however, were slowly beginning to break away. For example, in the labor force of 45 million almost 100 per cent literate and to a large extent highly skilled, the pressure for better living standards was strong. In the mid-1960's, wages already had reached a standard comparable to that of Italy, but the Japanese were far from satisfied.

The growth of the union movement was an indicator of change. Nearly 50,000 unions were molded into the pattern of the Soyho, the General Council of Trade Unions of Japan, and the Zenro, the Japanese Trade Union Congress, with almost 10 million members together. [22] By American standards, their conduct was mild—nothing like the wild outbreaks that had been led by Japanese Communists during the Occupation and immediately thereafter. But the potential still existed. The Japanese labor movement had more strength than was apparent on the surface, despite the belief of some American labor leaders that Japanese unions lacked essential drive.

The frequency with which modern ideas penetrated Japanese society was scarcely a sign, however, that traditional values were being discarded. Many a modern Japanese family changed to traditional costume within the family circle. House numbers and street signs in the Western manner were infrequently seen. Modern sewage disposal systems existed in relatively few places; even in Tokyo in 1966, there was no central sewage system.

To many Japanese, the foreigner was often viewed with misgivings if not mistrust; a greater point seemed to be made of that in Japan than in other advanced industrial nations. For instance, an outwardly modern young Japanese mother, seeing a foreigner in a crowded train, would discipline her children by warning them, "Be careful, or the foreigner will laugh at you." To be sure, there was a Japanese following for the unclad dancers at Akasaka, but many thousands also turned out for the traditional Bon Odori ceremonial dances. The older Japanese still liked their traditional dramatic forms, No and Kabuki, despite the growth of a following for modern Western drama. In sports, aside from the ever popular ritual of baseball, Japanese TV popularized the enormous *Sumo* wrestlers and their ceremonial combat. The office worker did his job efficiently; yet, in many places at a given signal daily, he rose and indulged in mass calesthenics. On a holiday, the mass ascent of Mount Fuji or pilgrimages to the temples of ancient Kyoto were still popular among Japanese of all ages.

Even in the countryside, modern and old Japan existed side by side in many places. A beautiful new split double-lane highway rolled across the far green hills, which farmers often continued to till by hand. Forests of TV antennas sprouted from the rooftops of the humblest fishing villages. A 125-mile-an-hour train roared along the trestled roadbed of the new Tokaido line between Osaka and Tokyo, sometimes passing hideous new concrete apartment houses that were built beside rice paddies. True, there were some tractors on the hilly farmlands, and modern fertilizing and cultivating practices were firmly installed on the average Japanese farm, but the farmer still accepted machinery with great reserve. Fishing was a modern industry, with big new fishing boats, but the old Japanese cockle-shell fishing craft had not yet vanished from coastal waters. From the volcanic black of the beaches into the shadows of the vast green mountain forests, this was a Japan that did not easily change and continued to cling to its heritage.

There were others besides Americans who recognized the influence of their own cultures on Japanese society. A British diplomat, weaving through left-moving traffic to the Japanese Foreign Office, often would be pleased to meet bright young Japanese diplomats who had been sent to Oxford or Cambridge, among other great foreign universities. A German, sauntering through Meiji Park, could hear choral groups diligently practicing some of his favorite lieder; among the older generation of Japanese, some spoke German with greater facility than English, which still was poorly taught in Japan. A Frenchman would have approved of many of the young Japanese in the great universities on two counts: in literature, they admired Sartre and Camus; in politics, they were attracted to "Charles le Grand." (Often, at the height of an argument, a youthful Japanese would exclaim passionately, "Why can't we, too, have a De Gaulle?")

There was balm for the Communists in Japan, too, even if they could find little evidence of favor for their beliefs in this largely traditional society. If there was no great demand for the works of Mikhail Sholokhov, Vladimir Dudintsev, and Ilya Ehrenburg, the mighty nineteenth-century Russians—Tolstoy, Chekhov, and Dostoyevsky—still were widely read in Japan. As for the Chinese, whatever their politics, they could see on every side the overwhelming debt that Japanese culture owed to their own civilization.

Despite all the manifold foreign influences, none could say that the Japanese identity was in danger of becoming submerged, now or in the future. The measured gavotte of Japanese politics, so full of hints and signs and movements that meant little to any but the Japanese themselves, was the best evidence of that. For in the long reign of the Liberal Democratic Party (LDP), from the rebirth of Japan as a nation after World War II, there had been a succession of complicated inner shifts of power, but in no case until the mid-1960's had these involved a swing from a conservative, middle-of-the-road pattern.

Then, several things happened. The Japanese Socialist Party (JSP), which had been plodding along in the wake of the triumphant Liberal Democrats, began to show some political acumen. It made considerable progress by playing on the public's fear of being dragged into a war because of the LDP's support of the American policy in Viet-Nam. The JSP had maintained and sometimes increased its strength at each national election, as it was measured in the popular vote, primarily because it had a fast hold on the intellectuals, the leftist labor unions, and the Zengakuren, the National Federation of Students' Self-Government Associations, which was now badly split. Now, the JSP appeared ready to move.

An even more important development in Japanese politics was the rise of a nativist party, the Komeito, or Clean Government Party. Founded by the fast-growing Buddhist group known as Soka Gakkai, or Value Creation Society, the Komeito at one bound outstripped the fading Japanese Communist Party, which at best was never able to get more than 4 per cent of the Japanese national vote from 1951 on and which in 1966 was split.

With twenty representatives in the Upper House of the Diet (Parliament) in 1965, Komeito was a recognized political power. On the basis of Soka Gakkai's estimated membership of 15 million, it had a potential for growth, with a platform calling for the abolition of income taxes for low-paid workers, peace, disarmament, an end to nuclear weapons, and an independent foreign policy. In the mid-1960's, it already was the third force in Japanese politics, with 15 per cent of the popular vote in the 1965 Upper House elections as against 23 per cent for the Socialists and more than 50 per cent for the LDP. It outranked the mildly leftist Democratic Socialists as well as the Communists.

As a result of a bribery and vote-buying scandal that caused the arrest of 17 members of the LDP in the Tokyo Metropolitan Assembly, the Socialists for the first time snatched leadership away from the LDP in the ensuing 1965 election by 45 to 38, but here the powerful Buddhists really showed their strength by electing their 23 candidates and attaining the balance of power. Promptly, the Komeito united with the Socialists to jam a resolution through the Tokyo Assembly, demanding that the U.S. troops leave South Viet-Nam, and that the Japanese government bar the use of American bases on Okinawa for attacks on Viet-Nam. Worse still, a public-opinion poll by *Asahi Shimbun* showed that the LDP had dropped to 37 per cent in its popularity rating, a loss of 10 points in 10 months.[23]

Komeito was important in another way. It gave the right wing a home and a chance to be dissociated from the terrorists. A police census showed there were 170 neo-fascist groups in 1964. Their members had been blamed for an abortive attack on Hayato Ikeda while he was premier, the burning of the home of Ichiro Kono while he was construction minister, an assault on a Communist leader, Sanzo Nosaka, and the assassination of the Socialist leader Inejiro Asanuma. The stabbing of American Ambassador Reischauer, however, had been blamed on an insane youth without political affiliation.[24]

It was a complicated political pattern, from the composition of the LDP in the middle to the anti-American Socialists on the left and the politico-religious Komeito on the right. It was endlessly discussed in the Japanese press but rarely outside Japan, except when an election was held or an important cabinet change was made. Then it was written about in the United States in terms of whether Americans were winning or losing. Most of the correspondents understood what was going on, or had a knowledgeable Japanese explain it to them. However, the country's politics, like its society, was too complicated for the understanding of most editors abroad. The end result, in a large part of the world press, including the American, was an uneasy silence on some of the most important facets of Japanese life.

On his first day in Japan, a reporter once wrote:

> There is some charm unutterable in the morning air, a cool with the coolness of Japanese spring and wind-waves from the snowy cone of Fuji . . . The street vistas, as seen above the dancing white mushroom-shaped hat of my sandaled runner, have an allurement of which I fancy that I could never weary. Elfish everything seems; for everything as well as everybody is small, and queer, and mysterious: the little houses under their blue roofs, the little shopfronts hung with blue, and the smiling little people in their blue costumes . . . The stranger finds himself thinking of fairyland.[25]

The place was Yokohama, the date April 4, 1890. The author was a former reporter for the Cincinnati *Enquirer*, Lafcadio Hearn. Then, as now, it was so much more pleasant to illustrate the images of Japan with pretty word-pictures rather than to grapple with the hard realities. The images, after all, were easy to note and simple to understand, even if they were somewhat misleading.

2. THE JAPANESE PRESS

Despite the growth of television at one end of the spectrum of Japanese mass opinion and of the intellectual magazines at the other, the great daily newspapers remained an important means of reaching the

Japanese citizen in the mid-1960's. On the basis of their massive circulations, the leading newspapers were also often accepted as a strong indicator of the public will on a variety of government policies, including foreign affairs. It was in the latter area that the press was deemed to have a particular significance in Japan, although here as elsewhere the readership of foreign news lagged behind news of more immediate concern to the average family.

As one of the leading Japanese editors put it:

One of the main roles of the press in foreign affairs is to inform those who lead the country and who mold public opinion, although it is certainly true today that the mass of the people play a more important role in policy-making than they once did. In Japan, public opinion is formed by the opinions of leading people—the politicians and intellectuals and the rest. But when public opinion seems to have crystallized, as on relations with Communist China or the war in Southeast Asia, then the newspapers may well act as amplifiers of public opinion.[26]

It was an observable phenomenon in Japan that press and public opinion sometimes fed on each other, thus attaining a "rolling consensus" on some issues, such as the riots over the mutual security treaty in 1960. It was also true, despite the press's avowedly critical attitude toward government, a posture that was popular with the public, that many newspapers nevertheless maintained close liaison with the government. Generally, editors believed that this could be done without sacrificing a newspaper's integrity or compromising its independence.

What often happened was that leading editors would be invited to meet informally with government leaders and asked to support certain policies. On domestic affairs, many editors often offered only partial support or refused altogether to help the government; on foreign affairs, there was less likelihood of a fight after the kickback from the mutual security treaty riots. Contact was also maintained through the various Japanese reporters' clubs, one of which was attached to each ministry and some to large businesses and other sources. However, no major matter was put to editors and publishers through this channel, or it would have become common property. Reporters are paid to get news, not to conceal it, and this is as true in Japan as it is everywhere else outside the Communist orbit. While the press in no known instance reverted to its ignominious role as a weak and hapless echo of the Japanese military regime before World War II, it permitted its representatives to give information to the government and sometimes to trade information, a procedure not at all unknown in the Western world, including the United States.

An effort to create favorable public opinion in Japan for a visit of an American atomic submarine to a Japanese port was an illustration of such an effort. When the issue developed, the U.S. Department of State hit on the notion of taking a group of Japanese correspondents for a demonstration trip on an atomic submarine off Guam. The specified purpose was to show that everything was so well-controlled, in capable American hands, that no Japanese had to fear an inadvertent atomic explosion. The Defense Department was persuaded to offer the invitation. The Japanese press responded with a complete lack of the atomic jitters which had been shaking the intellectuals.

Off Guam, all sensitive areas on the submarine used for the invitation cruise were put out of bounds, so that the superpatriots in the United States could not charge wholesale treachery. The guests had the thrill of a novel experience and wrote at length about it for their respective journals. However, the visit of the nuclear submarine to Japan still aroused protests, even though it had no atomic bombs aboard.

There was another unlooked for result of the trip. Once the Japanese journalists had returned to Tokyo, some of them complained that they were kept busy for days thereafter at informal briefing sessions for appropriate Japanese governmental agencies. Despite all Japan's fuss about maintaining a humble attitude in foreign affairs, the celebrated "low posture" policy, it was no Uriah Heep among nations. Whenever information affecting the national interest was available, the government seldom bothered to conceal its concern.

It follows that what the press published on foreign affairs in Japan could, and often did, become intertwined with the formulation and execution of foreign policy. No less than in the United States, the government watched the press as a test of public opinion.

If the government meanwhile was able to persuade a recalcitrant newspaper to be more patient and understanding of some of its foreign policies, so much the better.

It could not, however, afford either to underrate or disregard the influence of the press. Without doubt, the Japanese newspapers constituted the strongest and most powerful independent engine of publicity in Asia, and one of the greatest in the world. In many respects, they rivaled the American, British, and Russian press systems; in a few ways, notably in scientific advances, they excelled all three.

The total daily circulation of the 276 newspapers, including the 5 national dailies, was 28 million if morning and evening editions of the same newspaper were counted as a unit in the Japanese manner. If the morning and evening editions had been counted separately in the American style, the figure would have been 41 million. With 22 million households in Japan, each subscribed to 1.26 copies of newspapers on the average, a very high figure.[27]

The national giants—*Asahi Shimbun, Mainichi Shimbun, Yomiuri Shimbun, Sankei Shimbun,* and the financial daily, *Nihon Keizai*—were circulated all over Japan from multiple printing plants and editorial offices. Together they accounted for 52 per cent of the total circulation,[28] with provincial and chain newspapers taking the remaining 48 per cent. The largest and most prestigious, *Asahi Shimbun,* published in five cities by facsimile transmission from Tokyo to separate printing plants, had 6,500 employees, 56 domestic bureaus, 231 domestic correspondents, 22 foreign correspondents, and 13 aircraft.[29]

All this had developed in a little more than a century of newspaper publication in Japan. There were no newspapers in the accepted sense to record Commodore Perry's historic visit to Tokyo Bay. In fact, the only correspondent aboard the "black ships" was Bayard Taylor, of the New York *Tribune,* who had been put into a uniform. "The Japanese officials," he wrote, "were treated in such a polite and friendly manner as to win their good will, while not a single point to which we attached any importance was yielded." [30] In later years, Taylor evidently attached little importance to his pioneering journalistic role in the opening of Japan to the West; except for the record of his journey, it occupied a skimpy part of his collected work.

A Japanese victim of a shipwreck, picked up off the coast of Japan by an American vessel and taken to the United States, eventually proved to be of far more importance than the journalist-poet who became the laureate of the "Gilded Age." He called himself Joseph Heco and he was recognized, long after his death, as the father of Japanese journalism. There are many colorful stories about him in the sketches and monographs dealing with early Japanese newspaper work. One of his associates contended that he had been a member of the Perry expedition.[31] Other records made him the only Japanese to shake the hand of Abraham Lincoln. It is reasonably certain that he was born some time in the 1830's in Hyogo Prefecture to a farming family. By the time he returned to Japan with Townsend Harris in 1856 to become the interpreter at the Yokohama Consulate, he had been educated by American well-wishers, converted to Christianity, and made an American citizen.[32] On March 1, 1864, he published the first independently owned newspaper in Japan, a twelve-page sheet called *Shimbunshi* ("News") which consisted mainly of translations of the American press. Almost immediately, he incurred the displeasure of the Tokugawa Shogunate, which, like other repressive regimes, had an almost hysterical fear of any unregulated publication. After ten issues, *Shimbunshi* suspended publication.[33] Heco returned to the United States to await an improvement in the Japanese climate. When he came back to Japan, eventually, he had had his fill of journalism and the persecution that accompanied it.

Two official bulletins, the *Batavia Shimbun* and the *Kaigai Shimbun,* had preceded his newspaper. A number of others followed, including some in English. Perhaps the outstanding foreign journalist of the period, J. R. Black, the British publisher of several newspapers, wrote:

> Hardly any editor has escaped punishment at one time or another by imprisonment for a longer or a shorter period; or fines of a greater or less amount. The very persecution . . . has seemed to strengthen the growth and importance of the press; and it has found employment for thousands of samurai of all ranks. It is remarkable that the compositors of all the Japanese newspapers in Tokyo, and I fancy elsewhere, are samurai.[34]

Genichiro Fukichi, one of the most illustrious of early Japanese journalists, also had his share of abuse. He fiercely opposed the Tokugawa regime and fought for the restoration of power to the young Emperor, Mutsuhito, who took the name of Meiji (Enlightened Rule). "We cannot be satisfied," he wrote in his newspaper, *Koko Shimbun,* "unless . . . sovereign rights are restored to the Emperor in fact as well as in name." He was imprisoned, charged with inciting to revolution; but unhappily, his sacrifice was in vain, for the enlightened Meiji regime retained the stiff censorship and punishment provisions of the Press Code of which Black had complained. No newspaper could be circulated without the government's approval. No newspaper had the right to criticize the government with impunity. No newspaper, in fact, could be certain of what it could and could not publish. In Japan, as in the West, crusading editors had a heavy burden to carry. No matter how liberal-minded the regime might be politically, it was often just as wary as the foggiest conservative of the power of an independent, unrestricted press.[35]

Nevertheless, there was progress of a sort. While many upstart newspapers perished, others hopefully took their places. The leaders prudently became organs of various branches of government. In this fashion, editors learned through a process of trial and error, still used in many parts of Asia, how far they could go in criticizing the regime. It took a thick skin and a stout heart to put out a daily newspaper under such circumstances. It took daring, as well, to campaign for the so-called People's Rights movement, as many early Japanese newspapers did.

The first newspaper that approximated the modern Japanese press in appearance and style was the Tokyo *Nichi Nichi,* founded in 1872; once Genichiro Fukichi was restored to favor, he became the editor and at least a pro-forma supporter of the government. He had his say as the first writer of signed editorials in the Japanese press, a practice that had few followers then, or now, and took part vigorously in the public debates on the important questions of the day.[36]

Another who pioneered in the development of Japanese journalism was Yukichi Fukuzawa, Japan's "Great Enlightener," and the founder of what later became one of the great private universities in the nation, Keio. In his *Jiji Shimpo,* which he established in 1882 in the belief that Japan needed an independent quality newspaper like the *Times* of London, he tried to elevate the tone of the Japanese press and to popularize Western art, literature, and science.[37] Quite contrary to this peaceful, liberal-minded journal, Ichiro Tokutomi founded the nationalistic *Kokumin Shimbun* in 1890. Because of his attacks on the government for not advancing Japan's interests as vigorously as he wished, Tokutomi suffered disciplinary punishment fourteen times in *Kokumin's* first six years of publication; once, his newspaper was suspended for 138 days. But with the coming of the Sino-Japanese War of 1894-95, he basked in public favor. His original subscription list of 2,000 increased tenfold.[38]

In this initial period of Japanese journalism, most of the themes that would animate its newspapers in succeeding generations became evident, as did the manifold forms of government repression. While *Nichi Nichi, Jiji Shimpo,* and *Kokumin Shimbun* eventually were absorbed in an expanding field, their contemporaries and their successors did not have an easier time. This was true, among others, of the leaders of the Japanese press today—*Yomiuri Shimbun,* founded in 1873; *Asahi Shimbun,* founded in 1879; and *Mainichi Shimbun,* founded in 1883.

Asahi, because of its prominence, often had a more difficult time than some of its competitors. Two spirited young men, Ryuhei Murayama and Riichi Ueno, founded in Osaka what was to become Japan's greatest newspaper. Their first day's circulation, on January 25, 1879, was only 2,500 copies. But within six years, the paper's brightness and originality had attracted 30,000 subscribers, the largest circulation in Japan at the time. During that period it was suspended once for three weeks for reasons that the government never made clear. Shortly after *Asahi* had extended its operations from Osaka to Tokyo by buying up the *Mesamashi Shimbun* and renaming it the Tokyo *Asahi Shimbun,* the government cracked down again in 1891 with a week's suspension. The ebullient Murayama was so pleased when it was lifted that he engaged all the horsecars on Tokyo's transportation system for a day and gave the public free rides. That was promotion that put the Western newspaper barons to shame.

Asahi never wanted to let a rival get a head start on the news. When the new Meiji Constitution was promulgated on February 11, 1889, a great event in the history of Japan, Murayama stunned his opposition by sending the entire text by telegraph from Tokyo to Osaka—10,730 characters that were transmitted between 11.25 A.M. and 4:00 P.M. During the Russo-Japanese War, *Asahi* sent 26 reporters to the mainland and hired a ship which was inconsiderately sunk by the Russians off Port Arthur.[39]

Mainichi, however, took top honors for enterprise, despite *Asahi's* lavish expenditure of funds. A *Mainichi* reporter, working as a coolie, was attached to the 11th Division of the Japanese Army and got through to Tokyo first with the news of the victory at the battle of Nanshan. *Mainichi* also showed a sharper sense of communications, instructing its reporters to use the Chinese telegraph system when necessary to get around delays in the field.[40]

The importance to journalism of the Russo-Japanese War rested on something more than the battle enterprise of either *Asahi, Mainichi,* or their rivals. The Japanese Army, determined to protect itself from the prying eyes of a small battalion of foreign correspondents, invented the modern military censor and his allies, the wide detour, delay en route, and breakdown in press communications. Throughout the course of the war, the foreigners were effectively blocked; they saw no more than the Japanese wanted them to see, and they were permitted, at the proper time, to join in the press chorus that hailed every Japanese victory. The Japanese press, necessarily, was the prime beneficiary, for while the foreigners were treated with the utmost courtesy and given everything they wanted except news, the Japanese reporters cleaned up. No wonder *Asahi* and *Mainichi* between them put out more than 500 war extra editions! [41]

Following the peace conference at Portsmouth, N.H., almost the entire Japanese press, under the leadership of *Asahi,* joined in condemning the government for terms that were deemed unsatisfactory. Primarily, the Japanese at home were disturbed because their delegation had failed to hold out for a huge indemnity from Russia. In the most striking instance up to that time of the "rolling reaction" between press and public in Japan, riots in the main cities coincided with rising editorial attacks. *Kokumin Shimbun,* the only paper favoring the government, was attacked by a mob on September 5, 1905. Eventually, the Katsura cabinet had to invoke a three-month censorship. *Asahi* was suspended for 35 days.

An editor wrote in despair: "The *Asahi Shimbun* of September 1, 1905 was put together from sentences of tears and letters of blood." But Murayama, now the president, refused to give in. "Our firm," he said, "may well collapse under government pressure, but we must stick to our opinions." The Katsura cabinet resigned on January 7, 1906, and the first Saionji cabinet eventually restored a more satisfactory relationship between government and press, but only for a short period.[42] The riots had shown what could happen when press and public both were aligned against a government policy. The lesson was not lost on those who were to come to power in later years.

Despite increasing pressure from the government, *Asahi* tried to maintain its independence. It was the first to learn of the Twenty-One Demands against China, through which Japan served notice in 1915 of its intentions on the Asian mainland. When the news was published, *Asahi* first was suppressed, then was forced to deny its own story. Later, it repeated the correct story and again was suppressed. During the rice riots of 1918, the government feared *Asahi* had given too much information, and it was suspended again, this time for twenty days. Murayama was beaten up, he temporarily retired from his position of authority, and *Asahi* had to apologize and promise to support the government.[43]

The era was growing very dark for the independent newspaper in Japan. "There is a well-known maxim to the effect that 'the pen is mightier than the sword,' " wrote the newspaper's historian, "but when there is a clash between writers and militarists, the sword usually prevails. Even though the pen may win in the long run, it is likely to be a costly victory."

And so it was. From 1925 on, despite initial newspaper resistance, press restrictions became increasingly severe. No matter could be discussed in print which could be construed as "undermining the existing governmental and economic system." The press was warned repeatedly against printing certain kinds of news.[44] The power of the military was rising, and the arrogance of the younger officers knew no bounds. On May 15, 1932, a group of officers assassinated Premier Ki Inukai. Four years later, on February 26, 1936, a former premier, Makoto Saito, and some prominent associates were assassinated in an attempted military uprising. The *Asahi* plant at the same time was raided by soldiers and badly damaged, a sure sign of the importance which its enemies attached to the newspaper.

It was the beginning of the end. If ever the free press had had a chance to contest the rising might of the military, it was now gone. The time for protest and for rallying the public had been over for years. *Asahi* and a few others had tried to take a stand, but they had been almost alone. In 1937, when the Japanese military machine moved against China after the Marco Polo Bridge incident outside Peking, no newspaper dared protest.

The military cause was now holy. It could not be criticized. And if there had been hope of deterrence from abroad, that was fleeting. In the United States, there was a flareup of interest when President Roosevelt called for "quarantining the aggressor," but he didn't name the aggressor. Soon enough, it became clear that the Americans wouldn't intervene because they had neither the power to do anything in the Far East nor the interest to take extreme measures to develop it.

The Japanese government became a captive of the military and the press turned into a mere appendage of the government. The members of the Berlin-Rome-Tokyo axis began consulting. From then until the attack on Pearl Harbor, it was just a question of time. The Japanese press, like the public, was swept along with irresistible momentum on the crest of the war tide.

"Under the militarists," wrote one commentator, "newspapermen lost much of their self-esteem and most of their initiative. They were treated with disdain by pompous government officials. Their way of getting a 'news' story about the government was to await a formal handout or, infrequently, to decide among themselves what to print in the 'public interest.' " [45]

After the war, it wasn't easy to shake loose from the torpor that had descended on the press and made of it a voiceless, mindless automaton. For the relatively few remaining newspapers and their staffs, the years of the Occupation were hard years, a time for the regaining of lost confidence, lost self-respect, lost ability to think and act independently. With the first small grant of freedom, the press was so poorly oriented to its responsibilities that it often published rumors as news and innuendo as fact. As a result, inevitably, censorship was applied once more, this time by the American authorities. [46]

The painfully familiar restraints appeared again, this time in new guise. Channeled information, stage-managed news conferences, and a veritable blizzard of official handouts came from General MacArthur's headquarters. It was a "free press"—but in name only. The Japanese well understood that the Americans were "training" them and "re-educating" them in all the journalistic virtues, beginning with factual accuracy. All things considered, they accepted all this fussy supervision with surprisingly good grace, probably because they knew that there would be an end to it soon enough.

When that time came, in 1951, with the conclusion of the peace treaty, the Japanese newspapers were so limited in size and resources that it was a struggle to stay alive. Their first great effort was to expand, but it was a long and difficult process in a land that needed a great many other things ahead of larger newspapers. Consequently, their newfound independence meant little at first. They seemed, to some, to be interested primarily in turning a profit and showed little sense of social responsibility.

And then, on March 15, 1954, a fishing boat called the "Lucky Dragon" ("Fukuryu Maru") returned home to the port of Yaizu, on Honshu, with a crew of twenty-three sick and frightened men. They had had a long voyage from their fishing grounds around Bikini Atoll, more than 2,000 miles east of Japan. But it was not weariness alone that bothered them. They had seen a flash in the sky, as bright as a thousand suns, and heard an ominous rumbling far worse than thunder, on March 1. Then, an ashen material had rained from the sky upon them. They had been burned about their hands and arms, their necks and faces. Some of them had noticed their hair falling out.[47]

There was no local newspaper in Yaizu, but a district reporter for *Yomiuri*, Mitsuyoshi Abe, heard about the strange story a short time after the "Lucky Dragon's" arrival. He tipped off his office, then went after everybody he could find who knew anything about the story. A reporter who had been sent from Tokyo helped him interview some of the patients taken from the fishing boat to the local hospital.

On the morning of March 16, *Yomiuri* broke the story: "Japanese Fishermen Encountered Atomic Bomb Test at Bikini: 23 Men Suffering from Atomic Disease."[48] It was the first indication that the Pacific atomic test by the United States had involved a new kind of bomb. All the Japanese papers went for the story with a vengeance, making it almost a second Hiroshima. By contrast, the New York *Times* on March 17 ran a Page 1 story under the headline: "Japan Gets Radioactive Fish." And Lindesay Parrott, the *Times*'s Tokyo correspondent, commented: "The case of the Bikini fishermen has become Japan's newest political football."

The Japanese press piled on detail day after day—the results of scientific examinations, reports on the condition of the patients, political arguments, and interviews, interviews, interviews. If ever a thorough job was done by an independent press that was aching for a story worthy of its efforts, this was it. On March 24, the issue was placed before President Eisenhower at his news conference. In the fashion of the day, the reporter's question was phrased exactly as uttered, but the President's reply was put in the third person:

Q. Some anti-American newspapers in Japan and other countries have seized upon these cases of radioactive poisoning to make some very strong anti-American propaganda. I wonder if you would care to give us some statement of policy of the government toward the rest of the world in these tests.

A. It was quite clear that this time something must have happened which we had never experienced before, and must have surprised and astonished the scientists. And very properly, the United States had to take precautions that had never occurred to them before. Now, in the meantime, he knew nothing of the details of this case. It was one of the things that Admiral [Lewis L.] Strauss [chairman of the Atomic Energy Commission] was looking up, but it had been reported to him that reports were far more serious than actual results justified.

The American Embassy in Tokyo and the Atomic Energy Commission then tried to soothe Japanese fears by issuing statements arguing that there was "negligible hazard, if any" in the consumption of fish caught outside the test area and "some hazard" for "a short time" in the immediate test area. Both might have saved themselves the trouble. Several leading Japanese scientists immediately reported that the radioactivity from fish caught in the area was "certainly not negligible." The market for fish in Japan declined precipitously, as did the prices.[49]

Eventually, the storm passed. All but one of the fishermen recovered and the lone fatality was variously blamed on radiation sickness and infectious hepatitis brought on by blood transfusions. The United States paid $2 million in damages, which the Japanese government distributed in part to the fishing industry to compensate for its losses and in part to the crewmen of the "Lucky Dragon," who received an average of about $5,000 each.[50] The voluntary settlement, a considerable sum for a Japanese fisherman, salved the American conscience even if it did not serve materially to quiet anti-American feelings that had been stirred up by the atomic testing.

Mitsuyoshi Abe, of *Yomiuri Shimbun,* had done far more than break an exclusive story. Through his alert reporting, he had given his own newspaper and others a chance to demonstrate that the Japanese press was once more an independent force which deserved the world's attention and respect. As for the high policies that were involved in his disclosure, these were far beyond the ken of a district reporter in the fishing port of Yaizu. It had been his job to get the news to his office. What happened afterward was history.

3. THE "BROKEN DIALOGUE"

Long after the Mutual Security Treaty riots of 1960 in Tokyo, Sannosuke Matsumoto, a Japanese political scientist, assessed the damage to Japanese-American relations and concluded: "Quite apart from how one wishes to evaluate . . . the 1960 affair, it was an epoch-making event for Japan which has left in its wake a number of unsolved political and intellectual problems." [51]

One of the foremost of these was the basic matter of communication between Americans and the large and influential body of Japanese intellectuals, many of whom occupied important and sometimes commanding positions in education, the arts, journalism, labor, and left-wing political organizations. While he was the American Ambassador in Tokyo, Edwin O. Reischauer tried to persuade this group, with its dominant Marxist orientation, to give a fair hearing to American policies, ideas, and social and cultural movements. He asked them to reconsider their own position in the light of changes in circumstances both in the United States and Japan. He sought to stimulate discussions between American and Japanese intellectuals in an effort to resume what he called the "broken dialogue" between them. It was his confident thesis that there was no deep and irreversible anti-Americanism in Japan.[52]

He made good progress for a time. But after three years, a Japanese view of his campaign, while friendly, was scarcely glowing. Yoshihiko Seki, a professor at Tokyo Metropolitan University, wrote: "In the interval since the 1960 riots, Japanese left wing intellectuals have mellowed considerably, but a 'broken dialogue' between them and Western intellectuals still exists." The business community in Tokyo grumbled, in fact, that the Ambassador was spending too much time worrying about the intellectuals and not enough about its affairs.

Seki's view of his Japanese associates was somewhat more caustic than Reischauer's. He pointed out that in the United States, Great Britain, and India, among others, the positions of the intellectuals who enter politics do not often differ greatly from those of their governments. "But in Japan," he went on, "the similarity is between the views of the man in the street and the views of the government, while views expressed in Japanese intellectual magazines seldom coincide with either." [53]

There was still another aspect of the "broken dialogue" which was not a part of Reischauer's original definition. That was the tendency in Washington to show irritation at Japanese press opposition to major American policies, such as the bombing of North Viet-Nam. American officials sometimes would rush in where the sympathetic Japanese Government itself feared to call its press to task. Necessarily, as an ambassador, there was little Reischauer could do when such snarls developed except to explain matters away as best he could.

One of the most vexing of these incidents occurred a little less than five years after the Mutual Security Treaty riots. On April 7, 1965, the U.S. Senate Foreign Relations Committee was told in executive session that at an unspecified time Communists had infiltrated two of Japan's largest and most renowned newspapers. The credentials of the witnesses were impeccable. One was George W. Ball, Under Secretary of State, and the other was Douglas MacArthur II, an Assistant Secretary of State who had been Ambassador to Japan at the time of the riots.

Technically, the hearing was on the Foreign Assistance Program; but in Washington, discussion of foreign aid can be made a platform for almost anything. On that particular day, Ball and MacArthur were asked by the committee about the persistent criticism of American policies in the Viet-Nam war by nearly the entire Japanese press. In the record, as it was later made public, Ball was quoted as saying that "*Mainichi* . . . has on its staff quite a number of Communists . . . and has taken a critical attitude." After an observation by the committee chairman that *Asahi* also had been critical, MacArthur was quoted as follows: "They are both infiltrated. *Asahi* had over 200 members of the Communist Party on the editorial staff . . ." [54]

Although the news made little impression in the United States and wasn't even carried in most newspapers, it created a sensation in Japan. Ambassador Reischauer's statement, issued to the Japanese press, was read on April 29 by Robert J. McCloskey at his news conference in the State Department in Washington. It was a masterpiece of noncommunication on the main issue:

> The vigor with which communication media report on and scrutinize public policies and action is the best protection of democracy. We welcome the candid appraisal of our policies by the great independent media of other free nations. The Japanese press is no exception. It has the responsibility to speak out clearly and forthrightly on the great issues that concern men everywhere. Even when it disagrees with or criticizes United States policy, we admire its professionalism and enterprise, welcome its independence and forthrightness and respect its political integrity.

This colloquy followed between McCloskey and a reporter:

> Q. Well, the statements by Ball and MacArthur then still stand, that the Japanese two largest newspapers are infiltrated by Communists? Is that correct? There is no revision of that testimony?
> A. There is no revision of that testimony. [55]

On the following day, McCloskey, again acting as the State Department's spokesman, corrected an "unfortunate misunderstanding" regarding the Ball-MacArthur testimony. He said:

During that testimony, both Under Secretary Ball and Assistant Secretary MacArthur indicated that certain Japanese newspapers had a number of Communists on their staffs. Unfortunately, their testimony as published did not clearly reveal the fact that they were referring to a situation that prevailed some years ago when Assistant Secretary MacArthur was Ambassador to Japan. Furthermore, the published version of Mr. MacArthur's testimony was somewhat garbled in that he did not state that one of the Japanese newspapers had "over 200 members of the Communist Party on the editorial staff." It is not the view of any responsible United States government official that the major Japanese newspapers today offer slanted news or are Communist dominated. . . . We value Japanese views concerning United States policies and accept differences in opinion by the Japanese press as a result of honest differences in information and judgment.[56]

Ball himself completed the round of official reassurances on May 1 in an interview with Kenkichi Konishi, *Mainichi*'s bureau chief in Washington, by pointing out that neither he nor MacArthur had meant to make a public statement. He emphasized that he had referred to what he called "the situation some years ago" and expressed his regrets.[57]

The incident was important because it illustrated the sensitivity of Japanese-American relations. It was also a reflection of the crisis through which Japan had passed in 1960. To some extent, the effect was still felt by a very large section of the Japanese intellectual community—the people of spirit and ideas who were disaffected and disenchanted with the way Japan was developing. As Yoshihiko Seki put it:

Though Japan now has a democratic constitution, this does not mean that democracy is the guiding principle of her society. Only one facet of democracy seems to be understood; that is the right of opposition. In pre-war Japan, intellectuals opposed the autocratic form of government, but their opposition was weak. Post-war Japanese intellectuals have reflected on what happened before the war and have become anti-administration. They oppose the established social order, to use a Marxist term. Many even believe that it is the moral responsibility of the intellectual to stand opposed and to be critical of the domestic and foreign policies of the government.[58]

In the mid-1960's, the spirit of opposition in the Japanese press and even some of the intellectual magazines varied with the times, sometimes mild, sometimes vehement. Is the early years of the Occupation, it tended to be violent, particularly in the struggle over control of the press. The Communists, many of whom had just been released from prison, were then at the height of their power. They enjoyed the favor of some of the Occupation officials for a short time and also were popular with a considerable section of the Japanese public because of their prewar opposition to the rise of Japanese militarism. To some, they even appeared to be martyrs to their beliefs.

While the Japanese Communist Party claimed a membership of 500,-000 in 1948, SCAP put the figure at about 16,000.[59] But these disciplined, devoted, and well-organized cadres were able to turn much of Japanese journalism into turmoil. Burrowing within the Shimbun Roren, the Japan Federation of Newspaper Workers' Unions, they soon acquired positions of power in some of the most respected newspapers. The Occupation authorities, in their drive to democratize the press, had given the Communists their opportunity by purging some of the leading editors and obliging publishers to sell the controlling interest in their newspapers, very often to their employees. So powerful a figure as Matsutaro Shoriki actually lost control of his newspaper, *Yomiuri Shimbun*, to a union dominated by the far left but regained his authority after a sharp struggle in June, 1946.[60] Three years later, in order to prevent a similar takeover of the Kyodo News Agency, the Occupation authorities had to order it to discharge a number of Communists.[61]

The struggle for press control thus was waged on three different levels. The American military wanted to break the power of the prewar ownership by admitting the employees to a new role as shareholders. The principle, on the whole, was accepted although it did not result in the kind of "cooperative ownership" that had been expected by some Americans. At the same time, the American authorities wanted to build up the power of independent unions as a counterweight to management. After the Communist threat had been controlled, this, too, became possible, but it did not develop very rapidly. Finally, the Americans wanted to be certain that a reconstituted Japanese government would not again be able to dominate the press at some future time. For as long as the Occupation lasted, they could guarantee that; afterward, it depended largely on the strength and determination of the newspapers themselves.

Side by side with the newspaper struggle, an ideological contest for the loyalty of the Japanese intellectuals developed in their magazines, both the monthlies and the newer weeklies. The most representative was *Chuo Koron,* established in 1886, which had more than 100,000 circulation and considerable prestige. The smaller but often more influential *Sekai,* under the editorship of Genzaburo Yoshino, had particular acceptance among the more leftist intellectuals because its publisher, the Iwanami Publishing Company, was one of the largest and most important in Japan and in the 1950's was termed the "fountainhead of Marxist publications in Japan." [62] Even after the appearance later of such influential magazines as the weekly *Asahi Janaru,* with 600,000 circulation, and the monthly *Bungei Shunju,* with 700,000, *Sekai* retained a special influence in the intellectual community, although in the 1960's its circulation fell. [63]

There was a strong pull toward the Soviet Union among those intellectuals who styled themselves progressives. They called the peace treaty with the United States a violation of the spirit of the "no war" article of the Japanese Constitution because it provided for American forces on Japanese soil and did not contemplate a simultaneous peace treaty with the Soviet Union. They denied the Communist responsibility for the Korean War, holding it immaterial that the North Koreans invaded South Korea. Once the peace treaty with the United States was signed, *Sekai,* in May, 1952, devoted an issue to disarmament and called for the termination of the Mutual Security Treaty with the United States. [64] It was the beginning of a drive to win Japan to neutralism.

At this point, the anti-American campaign began to build up in intensity. Impressed by the fury of their own feelings, many of the progressives were deluded into the belief that they were carrying the Japanese public along with them. The storm of press criticism over successive issues involving the United States was one source of encouragement. The other was the increasing willingness of workers and students to take to the streets in mass demonstrations that made up in noise for what they lacked in political force.

Unable to block either the peace treaty or the mutual security pact, both of which came into effect in 1952 with U.S. Senate ratification, the Japanese opposition centered its efforts on almost any handy issue, old or new. It attacked the peace treaty's sanction of American control over the Bonin and Ryukyu Island groups, including Okinawa. It protested the continued presence of American troops in Japan as a defense against outside attack and internal disturbances, the key to the mutual defense arrangements. It condemned the McCarran-Walter Immigration and Nationality Act, passed in 1952 over President Truman's veto, which gave Japan an immigration quota of 185, compared with 65,000 for Great Britain.

Despite American action to compensate the "Lucky Dragon's" crew for illnesses caused by fallout from atomic testing in 1954, the Japanese left made it a *cause célèbre*. They also used the fatal shooting of a Japanese woman scrap-metal collector by an American soldier, William S. Girard, to attack the six-year-old Status of Forces Agreement in 1957. The Japanese didn't like it because it was too limited; some Americans, suddenly realizing that American boys were being tried by foreign courts, called it a blow to the flag. Although Girard was sentenced to three years in prison by a Japanese court, which suspended sentence, it did not stop the agitation in either country.

Now, the demand for revision of the Mutual Security Treaty began in earnest in Japan. The Communists, progressives, neutralists, and ultranationalists all wanted to do away with it altogether, a position which was enthusiastically backed by the *Peking Review*, with a warning that Japan was "approaching the brink of an inevitable crisis." Nobusuke Kishi, the Japanese Premier, who had initiated negotiations on revision with the United States, was excoriated in the *People's Daily* of Peking as a "grim imperialist visage which is no different from that of Hideki Tojo." [65]

From 1956 on, after Nikita Khrushchev's denunciation of Stalin's long and brutal tyranny in the Soviet Union, the most radical wing of Japan's intellectuals had been turning increasingly toward China. As the agitation against the Mutual Security Treaty revision mounted, and tension over the Taiwan Straits increased between the United States and Peking, the Japanese left raised the fear that their country might be dragged into war against China. *Sekai*, in particular, condemned the proposal for treaty revision.[66]

The first mass demonstration against the negotiations, on November 27, 1959, brought 12,000 members of the Zengakuren student group and others into the Diet compound. The Socialist Party and Soyho, the largest labor federation, had joined in sponsorship of a new organization, the People's Council Against Revision of the Security Treaty, in which the Communist Party role was limited to that of an observer. Despite everything the People's Council could do, however, the negotiations were successfully concluded. When Premier Kishi flew to Washington at the beginning of 1960 to sign the treaty, 700 Zengakuren students rioted at Haneda Airport. But after the White House ceremony on January 19, 1960, at which Premier Kishi and President Eisenhower signed the pact, a curious and unreal calm descended on Tokyo. The opposition was considering its next move.

Actually, the revised treaty was a considerable improvement over the original pact. It limited to ten years the commitment of American forces to be based in Japan and pledged that the Japanese Government would be consulted on their deployment. It also strongly committed the United States to the defense of Japan.[67] To give the agreement an added fillip, President Eisenhower agreed to visit Japan and invited Crown Prince Akihito to the White House.

In retrospect, the Japanese public at large remained singularly unimpressed by the opposition arguments that the treaty would make Japan a party to the cold war, that it was ineffectual because it gave Japan no right of veto over the deployment of atomic weapons within her borders, and was downright objectionable because it failed to return the Ryukyus and the Bonins to Japan. However, as the Diet debated the treaty's provisions throughout the winter, both the intellectuals and the press became ever more deeply committed to the opposition.

One of the links between the newspapers and the organized protest group was the Japan Congress of Journalists (JCJ), an affiliate of the Communist-dominated International Organization of Journalists with headquarters in Prague. While there were Communists in the JCJ, it was scarcely possible to so characterize all members of the organization. And the influence of the JCJ was difficult to measure.

The JCJ fought the ratification of the treaty and sought to persuade all its members to join in the campaign. It was not an admirable position for a newspaper organization to take in a land that had known very little real freedom of the press. In 1960, it issued a trumpet call to its members: "Let us answer the expectations of the masses on June 4 with our news stories! Let newspapers carry the voice of the people who are giving support to the strike!" The latter was a reference to a general strike that had been planned by the organized protest groups.

The JCJ's membership at the time was estimated at 1,600, more than three-quarters of them in the Tokyo area. With twice the number of JCJ members as its two main rivals combined, *Asahi* was closely watched on all sides as the struggle developed. "It is understandable," an American observer wrote drily, "that on the *Asahi* a number of editors and reporters often found factual coverage inadequate." [68]

To many who were in Japan at the time, the riots of May 19 and June 15, 1960, were landmarks in Japanese modern history comparable to the assassinations of February 26, 1936, and the peace of August 15, 1945. The part that both the intellectuals and the press played in them has been studied extensively without shaking the conclusion that both let their emotions sway them into adopting extreme and basically untenable positions. No doubt, the shock of the U-2 incident, the disclosure that U-2 planes had also been flying from Japan, and Premier Kishi's handling of the treaty all contributed to the disorders. But fundamentally, it was the determination of the Japanese left to force the issue that strained Japanese-American relations and severely damaged American prestige in Asia.

There was provocation from Premier Kishi to begin with. On May 19, he unexpectedly called up the treaty revision bill for a vote. When the Socialists staged a sit-in strike to block a plenary session, police dragged them out. Both the treaty and a fifty-day extension of the Diet session were then approved.

It was a story that shocked the press, which in general had not been on the government's side in any case. *Asahi,* in particular, was vehement. In its news account, it told how the Diet "fell into the most evil conditions," and went on: "The public's expectations were completely betrayed. 'Serious debate' proved to be a lie." It added, with a flourish of indignation, "The Diet showed for the first time what its wretched condition was going to be in the future." [69]

That, however, was just the beginning of a campaign of incitement, in which both the daily press and the intellectual magazines joined. Demands for Kishi's resignation mounted. Street demonstrations increased, with an occasional caution in the press against violence. But the editorials and the news stories continued to drum away at the weakening government. At length, when Soyho's general strike on June 4 produced no lasting result, the first cautionary attitude began to appear in *Mainichi* and *Yomiuri.* On June 10, when demonstrators penned Presidential Press Secretary James C. Hagerty in his automobile at Haneda Airport in a riotous attack, some of the more sensible editors saw that things had gone too far. But by that time it was too late to halt the mob. At the climax, on June 15, thousands of rioting students broke into the Diet grounds, burned police trucks, and finally were driven back by police using tear gas. In the melee, a woman student was trampled to death, and about 400 persons were hospitalized. It ended the patience of the press.

Premier Kishi on June 17 notified President Eisenhower that his safety in Japan could not be guaranteed, thus causing cancellation of the Presidential visit which had been scheduled to begin two days later. The Emperor signed the Mutual Security Treaty on June 21, and the U.S. Senate ratified it the following day. Kishi's cabinet fell; it was succeeded by another LDP government, headed by Hayato Ikeda. But the left wing, for all its excesses, had failed. While the right wing had participated in the fighting, it did not share the principal responsibility for the disorders. The bitter truth for the intellectuals was that while they had taken to the streets, the public, for the most part, had stayed home.[70]

It was not a performance of which the Japanese press was proud. *Asahi,* turning on the left after the June 15 riots, called them a "bloody disaster" and added: "It was that way in Germany just before the Nazis emerged." *Yomiuri* asked sadly: "Is the Japanese nation so slovenly that it can be shaken by the fists of a few young military officers or even students?" [71] Yoshihiko Seki summed up as follows:

> The 1960 riots against revision of the mutual security agreement caused great confusion in intellectual magazines and newspapers. Before and during the riots, magazines and the press actually stimulated and sup-

ported riotous demonstrations and accused the Kishi government of undemocratic conduct.

After the riots failed, however, these publications, and particularly the press, criticized themselves on the extent to which they had attacked the government and forced the resignation of Prime Minister Kishi. Disillusionment set in after the failure of the riots and after ratification of the revised agreement.

Splits began to occur even among left wing writers who contribute to the intellectual magazines. There was increased opposition to the editorial policy of *Sekai* which advocates neutrality for Japan, socialism, peaceful coexistence on Khrushchev's terms and complete disarmament . . . *Sekai* and *Chuo Koron* have noticeably altered their editorial policies. Their anti-administration and anti-American sentiment has been moderated and there has been a decrease in the number of articles on international politics written by doctrinaire left wing authors.[72]

Ikutaro Shimizu, professor of sociology at Gakushuin University in Tokyo, one of the intellectuals who took to the streets at the height of the rioting, changed his views completely. His choice of *Chuo Koron* for a statement of his changed position made it doubly significant. For Americans, what he had to say was almost painfully obvious. But for Japanese intellectuals, who had set such store by a Marxist Japan, it was a shock.

What Shimizu did was to declare the Marxist view of history relevant only for the England of Karl Marx's time. He contended that it fulfilled none of today's requirements. "The modernization of the United States, Russia, Japan and Germany was not accomplished in order to prove the correctness of Marxism," he wrote. Turning to the Sino-Soviet split, he argued that it foretold the collapse of Marxism. He ridiculed the Japanese intellectuals who still took Marxism seriously by comparing them with the European and American intellectuals who were left floundering by the Hitler-Stalin pact. Finally, he called for a "new view of history" to replace Marxism: a concept of modernization that he found spelled out in the works of economists such as Jan Tinbergen, W.W. Rostow, Gunnar Myrdal, and others. He had kind words in particular for Rostow's theory of economic growth. If Japan's modernization is to proceed with benefit to Japanese society, he concluded, it must be on the basis of a "view that is faithful to the dynamics of Japanese history, its energy, wisdom, evil and tragedy."[73]

Gradually, other changes came. Some of *Asahi*'s top executives at the time of the riots quietly turned up in other, less responsible posts. Divisions deepened in the Zengakuren student movement, causing it to assume less importance in the estimation of a majority of the serious-minded university students. "Today's *ango* [postriot] generation is less keen about such harsh political matters," one observer wrote. "Times have changed, and a handful of students—an age group long famed for its poverty—now even drive their own cars to campus." [74] Even the Gensuikyo, the peace movement, split apart under the pressures of pro-Soviet and pro-Chinese rivalry among Japanese radicals to control its destinies.

It was easy, of course, to overestimate the importance of these things. A perfectly well-intentioned intellectual, Yuzuru Okada, chairman of the sociology department at Tokyo Kyoiku University, wrote in triumph: "Today we are witnessing the collapse of Marxist domination over the intellectual . . . [He] is no longer able to assume that the socialist revolution in Japan is an absolute certainty or that such a revolution would bring absolute good." [75] Had this been true of the body of Japanese intellectuals, there would have been no concern in the United States over a "broken dialogue" with them.

Sannosuke Matsumoto probably was somewhat closer to reality when he pointed out, in a survey of the Japanese intellectual position, that some intellectuals feared that broader cooperative Japanese-American relationships illustrated "a growing tendency for Japan to become more closely tied to America." He wrote:

> The general apprehension some Japanese have over the way in which Japanese-American relations have developed since 1960 is reflected in their negative attitude toward bi-national conferences sponsored by the two governments on scientific and technological cooperation and cultural and educational affairs. Some of them have even been suspicious about the intent of grants being made by private foundations to academic circles in Japan. [76]

Yet, during the relatively short era of good feeling that followed the failure of the Mutual Security Treaty riots, more vigorous spirits recognized that there were mossbacks among Japanese intellectuals as there are in any educational group—liberals whose thinking remains firmly postured against the evils of another day. While the Japanese press remained critical of many American policies, it moderated its customary suspicion of everything American. Even the intellectual magazines seemed to soften up; on several occasions, *Chuo Koron* let Ambassador Reischauer into its pages. Only in education did the Marxist's influence maintain such power that one despairing critic wrote: "It is impossible for Japanese students to develop a pro-Western point of view." However, as the Japan Teachers Union appeared to weaken its hold on its members, Yasumasa Oshima, a professor at Tokyo Kyoiku University, wrote: "It appears that the teaching world has finally entered a period of armistice." [77]

Just when it seemed as if the period of the "broken dialogue" might be ending, the escalation of the Viet-Nam war revived the anti-Americanism of intellectuals in Japan. *Sekai* published an appeal by ninety-two prominent Japanese intellectuals on April 20, 1965, blaming the United States for broadening the conflict and expressing fear that Communist China would be drawn in. Correspondents of the Japanese daily press in South Viet-Nam also were almost uniformly hostile to the American position.

The situation grew so bad that William P. Bundy, Assistant Secretary of State for Far Eastern Affairs, charged that many Japanese "seriously misunderstand" the policy of the United States in Viet-Nam. To this, Akira Sono, a spokesman for the Japanese Foreign Ministry, replied with a reassuring statement that "not all newspapers reflect public opinion" in Japan. The unfortunate Sono was immediately battered by the Japanese press and had to issue still another statement, arguing that even if a majority of the Japanese people opposed the Viet-Nam war, that did not necessarily mean they were anti-American.

Ambassador Reischauer also entered the fray, summoning a news conference and vigorously assailing the Japanese press for what he called an "unbalanced" presentation of the Viet-Nam war. He accused some Japanese correspondents of accepting the "propaganda handouts of a police state" in Hanoi and "swallowing them whole," while playing down the American justification for the Viet-Nam war. There was some evidence that the Japanese press was sobered by Reischauer's assault, for it was apparently more willing to accept criticism from a respected foreigner than from one of its own. But as for the "broken dialogue" between the intellectuals of Japan and the United States, it was far from being mended.[78] The task of bridging the gap was assumed in 1966 by Reischauer's successor, Ambassador U. Alexis Johnson.

4. JAPAN'S AMERICA

The American viewer who flipped on a Japanese television set in the mid-1960's found himself in a familiar world. The voice was the voice of Japan, and so were the faces, but in many a program the hand was the hand of America. Entertainment was flung at the viewer with lavishness, furious action, and the usual interruptions for commercials in the American manner on the commercial networks. There were also the same half-measures toward the fulfillment of the public purposes of television—education, culture, and the news. The quiz shows were mostly copies of old models from the Madison Avenue "think factories," the song-and-dance routines smacked of Hollywood. Even the overacted Japanese soap opera was reminiscent; however, the old American cowboy movies were completely authentic except for the dubbed-in Japanese dialogue.

The net result was bluntly put by Tsuneji Hibino, president of Dentsu Advertising Ltd., sixth largest advertising firm in the world: "To be honest, it seems to me that Japan's commercial telecasters are engrossed in making money." [79] That was no great sin, as far as Matsutaro Shoriki was concerned. The publisher of *Yomiuri,* who also had pioneered as the board chairman of the Nippon Television Network Corp. (N.T.V.), once remarked to an interviewer: "I make ten times as much money in television, with four times less help, as I do on my newspaper. But my newspaper has the influence!" [80] In defense of the commercialization of television on the fiercely contending private networks, he exclaimed, "Look at television sets and other electric appliances. What do you think was the factor that enabled manufacturers to lower their costs?" [81] He referred, obviously, to TV advertising's ability to boost sales.

For both the Japanese equivalent of the B.B.C., the Japanese Broadcasting Corporation (N.H.K.), and its commercial rivals in the mid-1960's, the average television programming time was 16 hours a day. Of all television programs, 56.8 per cent were on film and 27.2 per cent live. Most of the films were of American origin—Westerns, thrillers, and action dramas. In a single week, five key stations in Tokyo, including N.H.K., telecast 130 films, 96 of them imported. The four most popular foreign imports, and their viewer ratings, were: "Laramie" (43.2); "Rawhide" (40); "Disneyland" (30); and "Father Knows Best" (28).

A survey showed that Japanese television consisted of 58.1 per cent entertainment, 15.8 per cent news, 14.3 per cent cultural programs, and 6.7 per cent education, with a scattering for other categories. [82] It was an imbalance that so deeply concerned the government that the Ministry of Posts and Telecommunications, in charge of licensing television stations, warned that educational programs should account for up to 30 per cent of the total. It was generally regarded as a blow at the "vast wasteland" of Japanese television, and it did have some effect, but not much.

N.H.K., as a publicly owned network that carries no advertising and is financed by fees from each set-owner, tried to set a higher standard. Among its programs were serials on news reporters, a plain Osaka citizen, a domestic comedy about a retired university professor and his family, and a socko comedy show by the Funny Trio. There were quiz shows, too, including "What's My Secret?," "It's Me" (a guessing game to find which of three persons is the *real* one), "Charades," and "Gesture Game." But the program with the highest rating, 81 per cent, was the annual "Year-End Grand Musical Parade," a two-hour New Year's Eve show.[83]

Twelve years after television's modest beginning in Japan on February 1, 1953, with only 866 viewers, there were 13,960,000 subscribers (licensed television sets), covering 67.6 per cent of the nation's households. (And like American television, Japanese television had a firm hold on an enormous public.) There were 131 radio stations and 121 television stations run by 46 companies. It is worth noting that five channels in the Tokyo area were assigned to commercial television companies with heavy newspaper backing.

As in the United States, television was cutting heavily into the newspaper advertising dollar in Japan. Of total advertising expenditures of $830 million in Japan in 1963, 37.6 per cent went to newspapers and 30.1 per cent to television, with magazines, radio, outdoor, and other advertising sharing the remainder.[84] In many respects, therefore, the Japanese and American television experiences were similar and almost equally discouraging to those who sought some better use for this most pervasive and powerful of all mass communications media. What both needed more than anything else was serious, honest, and unrestrained criticism by experts who knew something of television's problems. Unfortunately, such knowledgeable critics were in short supply in the United States and, with perhaps one or two exceptions, they did not exist in Japan.

If the Japanese television viewer gave any thought at all to the form and derivation of many of his entertainment programs, he would have recognized much the same crazy, mixed-up America that was familiar to him in the movies—an unreal never-never land where irresponsibility was king, and anything could be justified if it amused people. For the short run, television culture was probably as damaging to the United States as any commercial movie produced by Hollywood. For the long run, the stunningly great potential still remained.

There was a small proportion of serious Japanese television, other than news, which tried to give viewers some notion of how real Americans lived and worked and tried to solve their daily problems. Television documentaries were made in America and shown in Japan, particularly by N.H.K., but, like American television, these efforts were diffuse and few in number. The American South and desegregation were favorite subjects. One team, with USIS aid, did a series on American students. As for American documentaries on Japan, the market for them was very small.[85]

Aside from the documentaries and other special programs, television and radio were scarcely considered the best sources of news of the United States in Japan. Their total news time was not very great, and their emphasis necessarily was on domestic events except when war, catastrophes, or other sensations from abroad intruded on normal news patterns. As in the United States, Japanese television was capable of a magnificent performance in news coverage when it had national attention. But its average showing scarcely satisfied its own people.

Generally, the B.B.C. news programs were held out to the Japanese radio-TV media as examples of technical excellence, truthfulness, and broad impartiality, but no knowledgeable Japanese professional contended that that standard was approached. For instance, at the time of Ambassador Reischauer's stabbing on March 24, 1964, Radio Japan (the Japanese equivalent of the Voice of America) announced in an overseas newscast that he had been "injured." An indignant Japanese newsman was credited with having changed that equivocation to "stabbed by a deranged youth."

Of all the Japanese electronic services, Radio Japan probably broadcast more news than any other. A week's test of its coverage for the period June 15-21, 1964, showed that it had broadcast 172 items of foreign news, of which 14 per cent were sent by N.H.K. correspondents and the rest by wire services. Of this total, amounting to 24.5 items daily, only about 17 per cent originated in the United States.[86] Necessarily, domestic services could scarcely be expected to do as well as Radio Japan; even so, overseas listeners apparently were unimpressed with the Japanese service, for it was reputed to have only about 1 million listeners.[87] The Voice of America, whatever its failings, and the Armed Forces' Far East Network (F.E.N.) had more acceptance in Asia.

There were a few commentators on Japanese television who devoted a part of their time to a discussion of problems involving Japan and the United States. One of the most popular, according to Japanese ratings, was the N.H.K. team of Ryugen Hosokawa, a commentator for seven years, and Ritoku Obama, former head of the financial newspaper *Nihon Keizai*. Generally, their views balanced, in line with their position as commentators on the publicly owned network. Hosokawa, for example, was inclined to be critical of the American position in Southeast Asia, while Obama at one time applauded the strength of American policy there.[88]

The development of Japanese television illustrated the enormous advance that had been made in the techniques of electronic communication between the United States and Japan. At the time of the Washington naval disarmament conference of 1921, for example, communications between Washington and Tokyo were so poor that the facilities of the U.S. Navy had to be pressed into emergency service, with embarrassing results. Because of a transmission jam at Guam, some of the Japanese correspondents' messages to their home offices were delayed from four to six days.[89]

In the 1960's, the last obstacles that separated Japanese media from the rest of the world were overcome. On November 23, 1963, the first trans-Pacific television broadcast by communications satellite brought Japan news of President Kennedy's assassination.[90] On June 19, 1964, the new submarine trans-Pacific telephone cable between Japan and Hawaii was opened, linking Japan with the United States and the rest of the world. The Japanese international telecommunications firm, Kokusai Denshin Denwa (KDD), was able to provide telex, telephone, and other services to more than eighty countries.[91] During the Olympic Games of 1964, the Syncon 3 television satellite made possible the direct transmission of "live" television coverage from the Olympic Stadium, but it wasn't generally used in the United States because of cost, lack of viewer interest, and interference with prime evening time entertainment.[92]

Despite the marvels of electronic development and the very real need for some kind of stimulus to a public dialogue between Japan and the United States, it was perfectly apparent that the project had a low priority in both countries. In the broadcast media, there was no disposition to affront a public conditioned to such shows as the "Beverly Hillbillies" and the "Funny Trio" by introducing the theme of Japanese-American relations. It would have required the determination and the genius of an Edward R. Murrow to change such a situation, but his kind was exceedingly rare. Whatever impression the Japanese gained of the United States through television was fragmentary and generally unflattering. In the United States, of course, the American public's impression of Japan through television probably was close to zero, with the rare exception of a documentary film now and then. In a world living in the shadow of atomic destruction, fun and games were more important than the feeblest gesture toward the growth of a firmer world understanding. In any event, very little could be expected from a medium that had only eyes and ears and no backbone.

At first glance, the English-language press in Tokyo, largest and most active in any non-English-speaking city in the world, offered the best opportunity for bridging the information gap between Japan and the United States. The display of American news and opinion and the consideration given to the American point of view were comforting to the visitor whose Japanese was limited to a badly pronounced greeting and a few words memorized from a menu. But the circulations of even the oldest of these newspapers were small—Japan *Times* (founded in

1897), 48,083; *Asahi Evening News* (1954), 45,934; *Yomiuri* (1955), 31,909; *Mainichi Daily News* (1922), 28,304; and the specialized trade paper *Shipping and Trade News,* 12,000.[93]

Together, they totaled only 166,200 daily, about 1 per cent of the combined morning and evening circulation of *Asahi Shimbun, Mainichi Shimbun,* and *Yomiuri Shimbun.* At best, fewer than half were Japanese readers—the businessman, the intellectual, and the student who subscribed regularly. Generally, the handling of the news in the English-language offshoots of the Big Three showed little resemblance to what appeared in the parent newspapers. In the independent Japan *Times,* which was reputed from time to time to represent the views of the Japanese Foreign Office in its editorial columns, the American invariably found that U.S. foreign policy was treated with respect and the discussion was well-informed and moderate in tone.

For all that, there was considerable evidence to show that the Japanese English-language press did not have the undivided attention of the foreign community. American publications competed successfully with them, probably increasing to some extent their substantial operating losses; if any made a profit, it could not have been very large. By comparison, there was both influence and affluence in the pages of *Time's* Far East Edition, *Life* International, *Newsweek's* Far East edition and the *Reader's Digest. Stars and Stripes,* the American military newspaper, issued a daily Pacific edition in Tokyo for distribution throughout the Far East that exceeded in sheer volume anything the Japanese could offer in American news and features as well as presentation. The *Army–Navy–Air Force Times,* specialized independent publications, also were widely read by American military personnel. For the American community, the New York *Times* Sunday supplements were a must when they arrived, several days after publication date. And *Asia* magazine, a cooperative venture of Asian newspapers, put out an interesting weekly newspaper supplement.[94]

The Time-Life operation in Asia was an example of what the Japanese were up against in competing for the attention either of the Americans abroad or of Asians interested in the United States. They were without doubt the most successful and the most profitable of any of the American publications published for sale in Asia. Whatever their editorial shortcomings, they carried conviction to their Asian readership and presented a view of the United States that was widely accepted. Among less sophisticated readers, they were even credited at times with reflecting official American policy, something which embassies and Time-Life people both hastened to deny.

Of the total circulation of 459,785 for *Time's* English-language international editions at the beginning of 1965, the Far East edition's 24,314 was the smallest. (Others: Atlantic, 253,115; Latin American, 92,275; South Pacific, 90,081.) In Japan alone, *Time*'s sale was 9,746 weekly, with another 10,027 distributed generally among the U.S. military in the Far East.[95] There were generally five or six pages of foreign news each week, and up to ten when there was a foreign cover story. As for international advertising acceptance, the scope of the operation and the extent of the profit may be gauged by its foreign staff, with forty-two correspondents listed in the Time-Life News Service, nine in Asia, at a total cost of $3 million annually, about a quarter of it in Asia. *Newsweek*, which also ran a profitable international operation, gave similar space to foreign news but had a generally smaller circulation abroad and got by with a smaller staff, a list of twenty-two correspondents including five in Asia.[96] *Newsweek*'s foreign news service cost about $1.5 million annually.

Against this kind of competition, the weaknesses of the Japanese English-language press became fairly obvious to informed readers. While all had improved professionally over the years, cutting down on Japanized English phrasing in stories and headlines, there was little of the flavor of Japan in them. They were given over to wire-service reports from abroad, columnists on almost every conceivable subject, and social chit-chat; only the Japan *Times* in the mid-1960's made even an effort to cover the news of Japan with the realism of the great Japanese-language press. Except for its authoritative shipping information, the big feature of the *Shipping and Trade News* was a Page 4 girlie pin-up in the old-time French postcard tradition. When an outraged editor (American) finally sickened of the routine and demanded that a choice be made between his services and continuation of the Page 4 feature, the management unhesitatingly picked the pin-up.

The truth of the matter was that the English-language newspapers of Japan, with the exception of the Japan *Times*, were the poor relations of the Japanese press. They received neither the financial support nor the promotion that was lavished on a Japanese-language newspaper, even in the provinces. Young Japanese journalists who had studied in the United States or in Great Britain often were placed on an English-language newspaper on their return to Tokyo for a year or two until they were considered to be sufficiently Japanized again. Such service was looked upon as penace, except for the few who preferred working in less hectic surroundings.[97]

The Japan *Times*, therefore, was a beacon of change. Shintaro Fukushima, its publisher and the manager of the Kyodo Agency, wanted his newspaper to be something more than a mere receptacle for English-language advertising. As the leader of Japan's delegation to the U.N. General Assembly, he often spoke warmly of the need for a stronger world organization although he had few illusions about the United Nations itself. As for the United States, he tried as best he could to give an honest account of American affairs in his newspaper, struggling against the handicaps of limited space and few special correspondents. A small, dark, eloquent man with a handsome and earnest face, he conveyed that special sense of involvement which is the hallmark of the superior journalist.

"So many Japanese judge the United States only by its politics and its big cities," he once said, "and so little is known here of all the other phases of American life. It is almost as if the United States were an unknown country. The movies and television give a very false impression." [98] The English-language press in Japan, as a whole, was too small to counter that impression among the Japanese public.

The great Japanese language press was obviously the principal hope among the mass communications media for a proper understanding of the United States and its position in the Far East. A great deal depended, therefore, on how well the Japanese newspapers had learned the stern lesson of preserving their independence, and how effectively their editors were able to resist pressures of all kinds.

Outwardly, at least, the leaders of the Japanese press gave an impression of financial security, the first requirement of an independent newspaper. They published a lot of advertising and were accustomed to enter into large-scale promotional campaigns. Many of the exhibitions of foreign art were sponsored by newspapers. So were scientific inquiries, voyages of exploration, medical offices, and sports contests galore. The press was a major patron of music. It sought to develop the arts of the writer. It brought distinguished foreign visitors to Japanese cities. It was, in effect, the Japanese equivalent of the beneficent private American foundations.

Yomiuri, the most aggressive of all the newspapers, owned a championship baseball team, the Yomiuri Giants, long before C.B.S. bought the New York Yankees. *Yomiuri* also built what it liked to call the Japanese equivalent of Disneyland, named Yomiuriland. *Asahi* brought the "Venus de Milo" to Tokyo. *Mainichi* had a large baby clinic, a beauty parlor, and other such personal benefits for its subscribers. In a single year, one newspaper alone was calculated to have sponsored 137 promotional affairs to help increase its prestige and, even more important, its circulation. [99]

Yet, in Tokyo, it was generally understood that most of the great newspapers owed their prosperity less to their daily publications than to such by-products as their interests in television, radio, book publishing, magazines, and other diversified activities. They were chronically in need of capital for expansion and it was not as readily obtainable as it was for newspapers of stature in the United States.

One reason for this financial stringency was the organization of the Japanese press, which, as with all Japanese business, had to rely for its capital either on funds invested by its management and staff or on loans secured mainly from banking organizations. Of the 76 joint-stock newspaper companies that were members of the Japan Newspaper Publishers and Editors Association, 60 per cent were supported by shares more than half of which were owned within the company. Of the five national newspapers, all the shares of three were held entirely within the company.[100]

Theoretically, this kind of financing, sanctioned by statute, guaranteed the press against domination by special interests. Actually, it did not prevail against occasional intervention by influential stockholders, as some of the public and private battles over newspapers demonstrated. It also placed a burden on many investors who worked for newspapers, since they were in theory a main source for the needed increases in capital. What actually happened, of course, was that most of the larger newspapers had to depend on banking institutions for their financing in periods of expansion.

The leader, *Asahi Shimbun,* went through a management fight that attracted international attention. In the long struggle, some of the chief executives of the news and business departments lined up against the continued domination of its editorial and business policies by the proprietor, Nagataki Murayama. Before the contest ended with the retirement of Murayama from control, it had gone through the courts and involved the good offices of some of the members of the Cabinet.

The affair shed some light on the manner in which the greatest newspaper in Japan was managed, and how it arrived at some of its policy decisions. Murayama, at seventy years of age, owned 40.5 per cent of the voting stock, and one of his associates, Sei-ichi Ueno, owned 20 per cent, while the remainder was held in small blocks by present and former *Asahi* employees. Teruhiko Kimura, the managing editor, represented dissident members of the board of directors and also the *Asahi* employee stockholders in the fight against Murayama, whom he characterized as a "weak" executive.

As the battle developed in 1964, it became apparent that the real issue was Mrs. Murayama, the fabulous Fujiku, daughter of the founder of *Asahi,* who had long been accustomed to having her own way. When she married, her husband, in accordance with Japanese custom, took the family name and replaced her father as publisher and president of *Asahi.* But over the years, Mrs. Murayama was accused of improprieties such as demanding that her editors kill a story about an accused jewel smuggler and ordering that *Asahi*'s expedition in the Antarctic rescue some dogs even at the cost of Japanese lives. Of course, the editors refused both times.

With Kimura out campaigning for proxies among stockholders, his post as managing editor was filled by the capable and energetic Tomoo Hirooka, who had been managing editor at the time of the 1960 riots. After several years during which he ran *Asahi*'s western editions from Fukuoka, he came back to power with a blast at the Murayamas. He termed the sixty-seven-year-old Mrs. Murayama "reckless" and charged that both she and her husband had interfered in editorial affairs. To all this, both the Murayamas gave firm denials. "I have expressed my opinion or given advice, but we (my wife and I) have never forced the editors to do anything," he said.[101] It was an Oriental version of some of the calamitous rows that shook the *Times* of London during the Northcliffe years.

The showdown came at a general meeting of *Asahi*'s stockholders on November 17, 1964. The much-courted Sei-ichi Ueno, second largest stockholder, sided with the newspaper's executives, and Murayama resigned, with 56.3 per cent of the stockholders against him. With Ueno, he was listed thereafter on the managing staff of the newspaper as co-owner. The president, however, was Masaichi Midoro, a veteran journalist, and the redoubtable Hirooka was listed directly below him as representative executive director. The American-educated Isami Suzukawa, who had been foreign editor, was made managing editor.[102]

The new management of *Asahi* was highly professional in character and seriously impressed with its responsibility as the leader of the Japanese press. If it was critical of the American position in Southeast Asia and sought more contacts with Communist China, it was at the same time devoted to maintaining a friendly and mutually profitable arrangement with the United States. Once, Suzukawa tried to persuade Chester Bowles to "take the long view" by accepting a theoretically neutralized South Viet-Nam and then waiting patiently until the Vietnamese threw out the Communists. Bowles replied, "We can't wait."

Suzukawa, born in Japan in 1911, had gone to the United States when he was twelve and had close friendships with many Americans. He was graduated from the University of California in 1935 and Tokyo University in 1937. His English was as perfect as his Japanese, and he had an accurate and detailed knowledge of the United States as a New York and Washington correspondent from 1951 to 1956.

As *Asahi*'s foreign editor from 1956 on, he made it a practice to talk with his younger correspondents before they went to either the United States or the Soviet Union for the first time. Generally, he found that they looked forward to the Russian assignment as a visit to a land of equal opportunity and well-nigh idyllic conditions. As for the United States, it was his observation that before their first visit, many correspondents looked upon it in exaggerated terms as a capitalistic nation of great wealth, where there was oppression and even persecution of the Negro minority. But when the correspondents returned to Japan and reported to Suzukawa, it amused him to note how often their views had taken an entirely opposite turn. He found none who liked working in Russia; most of them thought the life was hard. A number of those whose duties took them to Washington, however, came back with greater respect for the United States than they had had before their assignment.

Regardless of the change in personal attitudes of correspondents and the effort that *Asahi*'s editors made to present what they hoped would be a balanced account of American events and policies, it was patent that the net result was critical of the United States. *Asahi*'s attitude necessarily created problems for American diplomacy that could not be easily overcome. Fair, well-tempered, moderate criticism could scarcely be met with stump speeches from Washington or references to the political characteristics of some staff members in the past.

At the time of the passage of the Civil Rights Bill of 1964, *Asahi* gave prominence to the articles of its correspondents in Washington, even though the measure was difficult for most Japanese readers to understand. It was, as Suzukawa said, an important story and deserved important treatment. He wanted to show, through *Asahi*'s reportage, that the United States had made progress toward an eventual solution of its greatest social problem. One of his associates commented at the time: "I wish we Japanese could make as good a beginning on breaking down discrimination against the Koreans in our country."

This was the manner in which *Asahi* fulfilled its role as the strongest voice in the Japanese press. Much the same attitude was found among the top editorial managers of *Yomiuri*, the same type of experienced professionals who dominated the work of *Asahi*. Minoru Okuhata, the foreign editor, was also critical of the American position in Southeast Asia; yet, he managed to find space in a generally tight newspaper for the work of his Washington correspondents, with their sometimes more balanced views of American policy. He was one of a number of Japanese editors who had begun using a non-American wire service, Reuters in his case, to report on sensitive American news, the theory being that readers thereby would have a more balanced account. But by and large, *Yomiuri* maintained its owner's long reputation for friendship with the United States.

Somewhat different tendencies began to develop in *Mainichi* in the mid-1960's. Minoru Omori, the aggressive and hard-driving foreign editor, made a stir with his insistence on a "Japanese interpretation" of American news and his frequent demands both in Tokyo and in Washington for "explanations" of American policy in South Viet-Nam. At one time he ran a series on American participation in the Viet-Nam war by Neil Sheehan, then a reporter for UPI. That was followed immediately by a series from North Viet-Nam by the Australian Communist writer Wilfred Burchett, who was incorrectly identified as a former *Christian Science Monitor* correspondent. Omori's response was that he had no proof of Burchett's membership in the Communist Party, and that Burchett had sold a few articles to the *Monitor* at one time.

Another of Omori's exploits occurred in South Korea, after President Chung Hee Park had put down a student uprising. The *Mainichi* foreign editor produced a story alleging that the Korean Army was on low food rations and on the verge of revolt, which was patently untrue.

During Ambassador Reischauer's attack on the Japanese press for biased reporting of the Viet-Nam war in 1965, Omori was one of the targets, although he also had many other critics. The *Mainichi* foreign editor had gone to Hanoi and produced some violently anti-American reportage. Perhaps the worst instance was his assumption that a North Vietnamese propaganda film "proved" that U.S. aircraft had bombed a leprosarium.

Although the Japanese press had been quiet up to this point about Omori's leading role in stirring up anti-American feeling, he had made himself vulnerable to those in *Mainichi* who rightly or wrongly thought him guilty of sensationalism and exaggeration for the sake of potential circulation increases. *Mainichi* no longer supported his kind of reporting of the Viet-Nam war. On January 21, 1966, at a board of directors meeting in Tokyo, he therefore submitted his resignation, and it was accepted.[103]

The storm over the Viet-Nam war did not abate notably in Japan, however. The leading Japanese newspapers left no doubt that they were against the American position in Southeast Asia and in favor of increased Japanese relationships with Communist China. However, they did not sway their government from its firm alliance with the United States. Nor were they able to carry a substantial part of the Japanese public with them, as had happened at the time of the Mutual Security Treaty riots. A public-opinion poll taken by the Japanese Cabinet Secretariat in the spring of 1966 indicated that 50 per cent of those questioned—a veritable cross-section of Japanese life—favored continued Japanese alignment with anti-Communist forces. It was a seven-point increase over a similar poll taken in 1964. Of the remainder of those who gave a definite answer, 25 per cent favored a neutralist Japan, a 3 per cent drop in two years, and only 1 per cent said that Japan should join the Communist bloc. On this basis, the government began discussions looking to the eventual renewal of the Mutual Security Treaty with the United States.[104]

The influence of the newspapers could scarcely be disregarded, however, and their power over public opinion could not be discounted. They were the greatest single communications medium between the government and the people. Yet, to Western eyes, their appearance was uniformly unimpressive. In physical appearance, the three leaders— *Asahi, Mainichi,* and *Yomiuri*—were very much alike. Their pages were crowded to suffocation with type and pictures of postage-stamp size. The notion of make-up and graphic display, so expert in anything put out for foreign eyes, was well-nigh abandoned by the Japanese-language press. Everything was jammed together in bits and pieces, forcing the reader to do at least as much work as some of the junior editors to unscramble the news. The Japanese magazines, by contrast, were thoroughly modern.

Unlike the thick American newspapers, which sometimes weighed six pounds or more on a Sunday, the Japanese press was relatively small in size but it managed to run plenty of news. The Big Three usually published sixteen pages in the morning and ten to twelve pages at night. (The provincial press ran to ten or twelve pages, and the English-language press usually put out eight pages, with the exception of the Japan *Times,* which published ten to twelve.)

The average proportion of news to advertising space was 63 to 37 per cent respectively, according to a survey of the Japan Newspaper Publishers and Editors Association (NSK), and the space allotted to foreign news amounted to 7 per cent of total news space on the average. Consequently, in a sixteen-page paper, foreign news could be expected to occupy from one-half to three-quarters of a page—or the equivalent of four to six American full-size columns. That was generally more than the average American daily gave to foreign news. As for news of the United States, the space assignment necessarily varied, but even at a quiet time the American reportage often reached 20 to 25 per cent of the total given over to foreign news.

Advertising revenue, primarily from Japanese sources, accounted for 50.2 per cent of all newspapers' total income while sales of newspapers brought in the remaining 49.8 per cent. Since 90 per cent of the Japanese press was sold by subscription, there was no reason for headline journalism, and little of it appeared, even in the more sensational section of the press.

Even though the foreign-news space allotment may have seemed generous by American standards, it really wasn't very large. The same NSK survey—a space analysis of three national dailies, one chain newspaper, and six local newspapers—showed that on the average, city desk news (local) received 15 per cent of the total news space; culture and the arts, 15 per cent; economic, 9 per cent; political, 7 per cent; international, 7 per cent; and sports, 6 per cent.[105] However, the readers devoted less time to their papers than they did to television. The largest proportion of readers (45 per cent) read papers daily for only thirty minutes to one hour.[106] At that, it was better than the usual survey of American press reading time, which ran thirty to forty-five minutes.

While it was evident that the Japanese national newspapers tried, within their natural limitations, to provide a decent selection of American news for their readers, and did more than either their mass media rivals or their American counterparts on the average, the flow of American news to the Japanese people was not very large. A column or two a day in a Japanese mass circulation newspaper, scanned quickly by busy readers, provided them more often than not with analysis rather than fact. Most Japanese editors at home wanted a better type of foreign correspondence from their staffs in Washington, but they also knew of the handicaps of language, poor techniques, and usually inaccessible sources.

A former Japanese foreign minister, Masayoshi Ohira, whose first knowledge of the United States came from the maps he copied from his geography book as a schoolboy, summed up the dominant impression of his fellow citizens as follows:

The United States is regarded as Japan's closest ally, but even so the United States is not well enough known. The image of the United States in Japan is far from satisfactory.

This, incidentally, makes those in charge of foreign policy uneasy because of the superficial nature of the image. It is necessary for us to have more news of the United States and to develop a greater capacity to absorb it so that the Japanese people will have a more accurate image of the United States.

It is true, of course, that the United States is better known in Japan than most countries. But it is also true that only the cities of the United States are really known—such cities as Washington, New York, Los Angeles and San Francisco—while very little of the life of the people of the United States is known. I think it would be well if we in Japan knew more about the average American's home life, of rural life, of the workaday world of the factories, of the schools and churches. All these should be better known in Japan.[107]

Ohira might have made the same general observation about the average American's knowledge of Japan. In each country, the areas of mutual ignorance of the other were painfully large, and the capacity and the will to absorb more information were pitifully small. The Americans and the Japanese were alike in another respect twenty years after the end of World War II. They were perpetually perplexed by unflattering world opinion of their own countries and preoccupied with the improvement of their national image. It was not without reason that a Japanese cartoonist sketched a Japanese reporter challenging the "Venus de Milo" on her arrival in Tokyo with the stock question for all visitors: "How you like Japan?"

5. AMERICAN CORRESPONDENTS IN JAPAN

A sampling of routine news items in the spring of 1965 showed that Japan had attracted attention in the United States for the following reasons:

A strike closed public bathhouses in Tokyo, leading to the revelation that men and women there bathed together. As one unnamed enthusiast put it: "When everybody is naked, camaraderie just naturally follows." [108]

Japanese farmers were using plastic greenhouses to increase crops but wouldn't share such know-how with other nations. To quote one farmer: Taiwan would "start competing with their cheap labor and ruin markets for us." [109]

Japan's second largest brokerage house was helped out of a financial squeeze by the government, which also persuaded Tokyo newspapers to suppress the story for a month. [110]

Japanese fishermen increased their catch of sockeye salmon to such an extent that American fishermen organized an automobile sticker campaign: "Save our fish. Boycott Japan." And Japanese auto-makers pushed a cheap compact car in the United States to rival the Volkswagen. [111]

Expense-account living, including a guided tour of the Ginza, became an integral part of the story of how to succeed in Japan. [112]

Such intelligence was a part of the routine coverage of Japan by American news magazines. It was what made Japan known to some news-magazine correspondents as a "back of the book" story—coverage that wasn't often of sufficient importance to rate a good play up forward with the big world news. Nor were the news magazines alone in their evaluation of Japan as a general source of news. The nature of the output was such that American news organizations usually stationed their top correspondents in Tokyo only as a base for a roving or specialized assignment and covered Japan with younger or less experienced men. There was no disguising the rating of Tokyo as a news center of secondary value behind such world capitals as Washington, London, Moscow, Peking, Paris, and Saigon. Tokyo was important mainly as a principal collection and distribution point for news in Asia and not intrinsically for its news-making potential.

With the exception of the Mutual Security Treaty riots of 1960, the magnificent conduct of the Olympic Games in Tokyo in 1964 had been the biggest single Japanese story in a decade. On a sustaining basis, the Japanese industrial miracle was the subject of the greatest attention. The correspondents assigned to Japanese business and financial news did a first-rate job for the American news media as a whole. The financial reporting services and the wire services poured a steady stream of daily information into the United States that could have been used by any newspaper with the slightest interest in the subject. In accuracy, detail, and depth of reporting, there was little to criticize in this specialized field. In fact, so much of the activity of the news weeklies and the specials was devoted to business and finance that it was probably overcovered in some respects.

A number of magazines and newspapers customarily devoted generous space to special sections on Japan, and sometimes entire issues were given over to Japanese life. These, of course, were financed in part by Japanese advertising, or advertising placed by American corporations doing business in Japan, so that they became profitable ventures. The New York *Times*'s annual review of business in Asia and *Life* International's special issue on Japan were illustrations of this kind of interest. The Japanese themselves helped matters along by boosting their advertising in the United States, one example being a twelve-page special section entitled "Japan . . . A Progressive Partner," in the New York *Times* in the summer of 1965.[113]

There was one other major subject of Japanese news—earthquakes. It was one of the peculiarities of the editorial mind, regardless of nationality, that a Japanese earthquake was news that meant more than far greater disasters elsewhere in Asia. A typical instance was the comparative play given to the Niigata earthquake of June 16, 1964, in which 23 persons were killed, and a wind storm in West Pakistan on June 14–15, which brought death to 250 persons. The New York *Times* displayed the Japanese quake under a four-column picture on Page 1 and gave four inches on Page 3 to the Pakistan disaster. The *Times* of India displayed the Niigata story on Page 1 and published the Pakistan story next day in brief form. The *Straits Times* of Kuala Lumpur did the same thing. The Manila *Times,* after giving Page 1 display to the Japanese quake, ran the Pakistan story on Page 3 on the following day.

It was a remarkable demonstration of the unanimity of news judgments in the United States and Asia. If it meant anything at all, it was that earthquakes fascinated editors and windstorms didn't; also, that the wire services, in addition to providing most of the global news, were influential in evaluating it.

Once the weightier matters were disposed of, it became a problem for correspondents to fill the dull stretches between news breaks with material that would titillate the editorial mind in the United States. Even the greenest hand soon realized that it was no longer good form to develop a tired feature about cherry blossoms, sukiyaki, geishas, paper lanterns, or Mount Fuji. But few worked for editors who had ever seen Japan or knew much about it; consequently, the exotic feature story in exaggerated form was still a part of the staple fare of journalism in the United States. The "back of the book" feature of the news magazines therefore cropped up elsewhere in all its familiar and meretricious forms—the funny little people who do and say outlandish things, the makers of cheap merchandise who undersell or outproduce their American rivals by unfair means, the copycats who can imitate anything but are seldom original. The journalists had a heavy responsibility to share with W. S. Gilbert's Pooh-Bah, Wallace Irwin's Japanese Schoolboy, and J. P. Marquand's Mr. Moto. Not even a desperate and bloody war had disposed of such outdated imagery. There was a new Japan at the crossroads of the western Pacific, and it wasn't precisely a "Teahouse of the August Moon." But most of the gatekeepers of American journalism didn't want to bother with that problem.

Influential Japanese recognized their position quickly enough. They scarcely had to be told that there was a lack of interest in their country among American, British, and European mass media, which in turn had an effect on the Asian media that were consciously or unconsciously influenced by the leaders of the West. The Public Information and Cultural Affairs Bureau of the Japanese Foreign Office couldn't help noticing that most senior American correspondents may have been based in Tokyo or stopped off there, but usually wrote about almost any other place.

Manifestly, the 206 names listed as active regular members of the Foreign Correspondents' Club of Japan seemed to offer evidence that the coverage of Japan was somewhat better than the Foreign Office's gloomy conclusions indicated. However, forty-nine of the members were Japanese employed by Japanese news media in Tokyo, a revenue-producing measure that was also countenanced by the Overseas Press Club of New York.

Of the sixty-three listed as correspondents for American news media, twenty-three worked for the wire services, eight for financial and economic news organizations, seven each for news magazines and broadcasting companies, five for magazines as free-lancers, and two as photographers. The American newspapers represented by correspondents permanently assigned from the home offices were limited to the New York *Times* (2), Chicago *Daily News,* Chicago *Tribune, Wall Street Journal, Christian Science Monitor,* Los Angeles *Times,* Washington *Post,* and the Copley News Service (San Diego *Union-Tribune* and others). The San Francisco *Chronicle,* New York *Daily News,* and Seattle *Times* representatives were stringers.

No other nation approached the United States in the size and variety of its correspondents' corps. The British had a respectable Reuters-Comtelburo staff and correspondents from the *Times* of London, London *Daily Telegraph,* London *Express and Evening News,* and the B.B.C. The Russians had six representatives for *Pravda, Izvestia,* Tass, the Novosti News Service, and Moscow Radio and Television. For France, there were representatives of Agence France-Presse, *Figaro,* and *Paris-Match.* For West Germany, correspondents covered for the Deutsche Press Agentur, *Frankfurter Allgemeine Zeitung,* and one or two others. A scattering from Korea, India, Formosa, Sweden, and a few freelancers completed the roster.[114] The Chinese Communists were a later addition.

The acknowledged leader of the American correspondents in Tokyo, when he was in residence, was Keyes Beech of the Chicago *Daily News,* who had gone to neither high school nor college but had nevertheless become a Nieman Fellow at Harvard and won a Pulitzer Prize. At fifty-two years of age, he had survived the rigors of combat correspondence on the varied battlefields of three wars and the lesser but no less authentic hazards of eighteen years as a correspondent in the Far East. Such a record, in the best journalistic fiction, could have belonged only to a hearty giant of a man with an imposing manner and a booming voice of command, but the *real* Keyes Beech was a mild, balding little newspaperman with a gentle manner and kindly blue eyes. He spoke no language other than English and had no special training except as a reporter, but, like Ernie Pyle, he managed to hold his own.

Once, during his third war when he was painfully hauling himself through the muddy and guerrilla-infested Delta country of South Viet-Nam, a condescending young captain of the U.S. Marines had said to him, "Mr. Beech, aren't you getting a little old for this sort of thing?" Mr. Beech indignantly picked up the challenge and plastered the taunt on Page 1 of the Chicago *Daily News* as the theme of a report detailing his movements and adventures: from Viet-Nam to Vientiane in Laos for a week, then under forced draft to Honolulu to cover a top-level Pacific conference, and from there with equal urgency to report on a riot against the government in Seoul.[115] It was a fair example of how a correspondent of Beech's stature operated from his base in Tokyo.

The other oldtimers based in Tokyo traveled as much as Beech did, and sometimes more. In the final year of his quarter-century of service in Asia, Robert P. Martin, of *U.S. News & World Report,* was in Southeast Asia as much as he was in Japan; at fifty-one years of age, he was one of the last of the old China hands of pre–World War II days, a graduate of the Columbia Graduate School of Journalism, a former Nieman Fellow at Harvard, and a respected journalist in the Far East. Robert Eunson, AP's general executive for the Far East, and Earnest Hoberecht, while he was UPI vice president for Asia, were both constantly on the move, but mostly they were selling their services and working with clients. Robert Trumbull, the fifty-three-year-old New York *Times* bureau chief, who had been covering Asia—"the prickly heat beat," as he called it—for more than half his years, was back in Tokyo for the second time after serving in every major *Times* bureau in Asia.

The champion travelers, however, were the television correspondents, because there were so few of them and their assignment was so vast. John Rich, the forty-six-year-old N.B.C. correspondent in Tokyo, traveled twice around the world in a twelve-month period and put in at least 50,000 miles in addition in his general Asian coverage. Peter Kalischer, the fifty-year-old C.B.S. correspondent, like Rich a veteran of three wars, was in Saigon more than he was in Tokyo during 1965, and was rewarded with the Paris location in 1966. Taking a random check on his travels for the first six months of 1964, he found that he had been in New York, Okinawa, Taipei, Saigon, back to New York for a special show and an Overseas Press Club prize, then to Seoul, Saigon, New Delhi, back to Seoul again, and in Tokyo. In all, he was at his base forty-two days during the six-month period. Some of the news-magazine correspondents were active, too, but not in that class.

Necessarily, such correspondents had a practical knowledge of Asian affairs and an accumulation of sources that made them invaluable as journalists. While all except Beech and Kalischer were college graduates, their academic training had contributed sketchily if at all to their work as Asian specialists. With the exception of Rich, who learned Japanese while he was in the Marines in World War II, and Martin, who knew Chinese, none of them pretended to be linguists; like Homer Bigart, the greatest of the surviving war correspondents, they got along perfectly well in English wherever they went. This was the old breed —a tough, devoted, hard-headed, unsentimental crew that could stand up unflinchingly against the wrath of a general or a prime minister, go into the field unhesitatingly under enemy fire, or quietly and quite privately feed and bathe ragged refugee children.

The younger men were of different backgrounds. Bernard Krisher, of *Newsweek,* was thirty-two years of age, a graduate of Queens College in New York City and a Ford Fellow in international reporting at Columbia, fluent in French and German and above average in Japanese by training and by grace of his good-natured Japanese wife. He was a former New York *World-Telegram & Sun* reporter who had thoroughly prepared himself for the assignment he sought in Japan. Richard Halloran, the bureau chief for *Business Week* who later shifted to the Washington *Post* as a specialist on Japan, had his bachelor's degree from Dartmouth, his master's from Michigan, and his advanced training from Columbia, where he had been a Ford Fellow in international reporting. At thirty-four years of age, he, like Krisher, was committed to a developing specialty in Asian affairs and had some knowledge of both Chinese and Japanese. Sam Jameson, of the Chicago *Tribune,* a twenty-seven-year-old graduate of the Medill School of Journalism at Northwestern, had begun studying Japanese in the army and continued as a correspondent. Robert Liu of the AP, a twenty-six-year-old Chinese-born graduate of San Francisco City College, could thank his Chinese father and his Russian mother for his fluency in English, Chinese, and Russian and his knowledge of Asia, as well. Kim Willenson and Dan Southerland, both twenty-eight-year-old UPI staff members and both from the Columbia Graduate School of Journalism, also had sought service in the Far East. Willenson, with a bachelor's degree from Wisconsin, had been a Pulitzer Traveling Fellow at Columbia. Southerland, with a bachelor's degree from North Carolina and a master's in Far Eastern studies from Harvard, had studied Japanese, Chinese, and Russian; later, he was assigned to Saigon.

The new group, well aware of the lower status of Asian reportage in the scale of values of American journalism and of numerous other difficulties, nevertheless had chosen to work in Asia and had been fortunate enough or persistent enough to find a way to begin. Most of the old-timers had come to Asia as soldiers or war correspondents; many, after marrying Oriental wives, had elected to remain. This was less true of the new breed, which had been so largely prepared in the college classroom; on the job, however, the younger men were developing the same tough resilience and resourcefulness that had been so characteristic of their elders. That was what it took to survive in a difficult and ever demanding profession in which hard news was still sought on a competitive basis.

Between the veterans and the youngsters was a competent group of professionals who had been obliged to resort to on-the-job training to develop the necessary background and skills, when travel assignments did not interfere. Some of these men were editors or bureau chiefs who directed the work of correspondents; others were executives or bureau chiefs who had come to the Far East by choice to serve as correspondents for two or three years.

Robert Crabbe, one of the UPI's Tokyo editors, had taught himself Japanese at thirty-nine because he had found it so necessary in his work. Emerson Chapin of the New York *Times,* turned up in Tokyo at forty-three years of age after a decade as a *Times* editor and began studying Japanese during his three years of service. James McC. Truitt, a former vice president of the Washington *Post,* came to *Newsweek* in Tokyo as bureau chief, also at forty-three years of age, and felt himself almost cut off because of his ignorance of Japanese, a deficiency he set about remedying. Lee Griggs traveled so much during his two-year Tokyo assignment as *Time*'s bureau chief that he didn't bother with Japanese.

There was one other major group within the American news organization in Tokyo—the local Japanese and the Nisei who were described by one appreciative bureau manager as "my eyes and ears." Less honest executives, some of whom knew no Japanese and made no effort to learn, treated this vital group like a part of the battered office furniture and scarcely deserved the loyalty that they received from them. Actually, any wire-service organization in Tokyo would have been lost without such experts who read the Kyodo teleprinter, which transmitted in the Japanese script known as Kanji; monitored N.H.K. television and radio; read the Japanese newspapers; and talked with Japanese officials.

That was where much Japanese news came from, although American correspondents did manage to dig up a fund of news on their own. But the wire services in particular had neither the time nor the personnel to cover all the news firsthand, except when it was of major importance to the United States or a special feature such as a Hiroshima atomic anniversary. What the wire services did was to select from the Japanese exchange services, rewrite, and edit; when they could, they would try to dig up a fresh angle but almost always this involved detaching a man from a desk where he was needed. Few Japanese sources, even in the mid-1960's, took kindly to telephone reporting and usually lost what little proficiency they had in English if they were called for information. Not even a Japanese reporter could break down that prejudice.

For the AP, Ken Ishii, a thirty-year-old Japanese graduate of the University of California, was typical of the local newsmen who held responsible posts. Wes Gallagher, the general manager in New York, was so impressed with the need for maintaining a corps of such editor-correspondents that he insisted on a special training program for them. The first to be sent to New York in this new effort to break the language barrier was Mark Kuramitsu, a thirty-six-year-old Tokyo-born graduate of Waseda University, who had begun work for the AP as a copy boy in 1953 and developed into a wire-filer, writer, and editor. Others followed.

The UP office was no less dependent on its locals, like Leslie Nakashima and Ted Shimizu, who could do everything an American correspondent could do and still go places where the average American wasn't welcome. But there were no training programs for them at the UPI; if they made headway, it was because they were superior journalists.

In almost every other American news-gathering office in Tokyo, and the British and French as well, some dependable Japanese journalist—and in some cases, a pretty and talented Japanese girl secretary—served as a channel between the correspondent and Japanese society. In the Reuters bureau, a capable and charming Japanese girl was the news editor. Perhaps the dean of the group was the New York *Times*'s Jun Ofusa, who was fifty-six years old and, with the exception of the war period, had been in his post for thirty-four years.

Because of the almost universal tendency of American news-gathering organizations to rotate their correspondents after periods of service of up to three years, it appeared certain that the locals would remain an integral part of American news-gathering abroad—in Japan and elsewhere. It scarcely paid a newspaper or wire service to devote years to the training of a specialist under such circumstances. With few exceptions, they depended on the locals, or the correspondents trained themselves. Even for the *Times* of London, the old days of the resident correspondent of ambassadorial prestige were over. The risk of involvement was considered too great; moreover, the locals were a lot cheaper.

The AP, which maintained the largest and best-trained corps of locals in Asia, staffed its Tokyo office with seven American editors and reporters and sixteen Japanese on the editorial side. Of the total of ninety employees, some of them part-timers, two-thirds were Japanese, dominating the administrative, traffic, and photo services as well as editorial. The assistant chief of bureau, Shin Higashi, operated with equal facility in Japanese or English, as did the fifty-year-old night editor, Kay Kanemitsu Tateishi, a graduate of UCLA. One of the top reporters, René-Georges Inegaki, was fluent in English, Japanese, German, and French.

The best locals were paid up to $700 a month, but not many were in that bracket. As Japanese citizens, all signed articles of employment with the AP, which were registered with the Japanese Government. These articles included provisions for salary, job security, medical care, and pensions. Generally the pay was approximately the scale maintained by *Asahi Shimbun*.[116]

The AP set the standard among American news-gathering organizations for the treatment of Japanese nationals and other local correspondents. However, it was not unusual for some other organizations to pay as little as $25 a month for locals outside Japan on as important an assignment as Vientiane. For many reasons, foreign nationals in Asia found it desirable to work for American organizations and competed for such jobs whenever they were available. The supply far outran the demand, but it was also true that first-rate people always were exceedingly few. The average local could scarcely be trusted to write a story for the wire because his English usually wasn't good enough, either in Japan or elsewhere.

On the crucial problem of whether a local correspondent, or editor, could be trusted to serve an American news-gathering organization impartially and withstand pressures that were brought by his own government, there was a considerable difference of opinion both in Asia and the United States. In Japan in the mid-1960's, few American executives were worried, because Japanese-American relations were good at the government level. Robert Eunson was able to say with firmness and conviction: "We are never concerned about the loyalty of our local people to the AP. We trust them implicitly." Others were not so outspoken in Japan; elsewhere, particularly in areas of conflict, the locals were in a tight spot and could not be expected to do anything more than file straight factual material. Even that sometimes took on the appearance of a heroic feat when the facts reflected on the government of a reigning Asian dictator.

For Americans, too, there were difficulties as well as a kind of detachable glamour in the business of being a foreign correspondent in Tokyo. The biggest problem was job satisfaction—the day-by-day task of scanning the news for something that could be developed into a story for a particular medium in the United States. The by-lines were neither as frequent nor as prestigious on pieces sent from Tokyo as they were from Saigon or even Danang. And when a correspondent couldn't see himself in print with fair regularity, he felt he wasn't much good to anybody, least of all to himself.

In Tokyo, one of the most expensive cities in the world, the problem of pay and the sheer expense of living inevitably arose to haunt most of the American editors and correspondents. A newsman with two degrees could be hired by a wire service for as little as $4,800 a year, less than the going rate for beginners on some of the larger American newspapers. In one case, a bureau chief even boasted that he had been able to "hire" a highly qualified beginner for nothing. Generally, a correspondent with a year's experience could expect to receive from $5,500 to $6,500 a year; those with somewhat more experience received $7,000 to $8,000, and an experienced wire-service editor could earn $9,650. Correspondents for some of the major newspapers and news magazines earned from $10,000 to $12,000, the highest bracket for wire-service people under the level of bureau chief. A few outstanding correspondents earned up to $16,000, with bureau chiefs handling major responsibilities making $18,000 to $20,000 and the stars of press and television somewhat more. But most correspondents were paid less than $10,000, and the average was probably around $8,000 to $9,000. The situation was such that an American with broad knowledge of the field, asked what could be done to improve the level of correspondence, snapped: "Pay them!" [117]

The swashbuckling era of foreign correspondence had long ended; for that matter, so had the usefulness of the occasionally brilliant but permanently alcoholic correspondent. The men who reported from Tokyo for American news media were generally no more flamboyant than the secretary of a Rotary Club, and they probably didn't live as well.

Most of the American correspondents in Tokyo had families, and enjoyed their homes but seldom had time for them. They worked six days a week at all hours and sometimes came in on the seventh day, too. Most of them had to worry about finding a school for their children, placating distraught wives who couldn't cope with Tokyo's marketing and social customs, and finding doctors to handle family illnesses. If they had cars, the mere matter of locating a parking space was an international issue. All correspondents were easy marks for avaricious Tokyo landlords, who charged anywhere from $300 to $500 for a house and as much as $700 to $1,000 for an office, depending on the location and elegance of the quarters. The costs of travel over Asia's enormous distances and the monthly file, which could run as much as $1,500 for a large newspaper, made the maintenance of a correspondent a luxury.

Without doubt, the language barrier was the greatest difficulty for Americans in Japan. On general principles, most of them groused about the Japanese reporters' clubs, which kept foreigners out of all regular contact with government offices except, occasionally, the Foreign Ministry. Actually, the situation was no worse for Americans in Tokyo than it was for Japanese in Washington; by training and inclination, the Americans were in a better situation because they were accustomed to using their legs and scrambling for their news.

As for the Americans' relationships with their embassy, there were few complaints. Many a correspondent, in fact, put aside ingrained suspicions of the Department of State while Reischauer was Ambassador.

There was even a certain amount of pride in the usually dissatisfied ranks of the journalists over Professor Reischauer's learning, his unabashed enthusiasm for his work, and his much envied ability to converse in Japanese as easily as he did in English. When he returned to duty on July 3, 1964, after a slow four-month recovery from his near-fatal stabbing, every American journalist who could do so made it a point to attend the homecoming press conference. No one expected news because the Ambassador, customarily, was better at lecturing on Japanese history. But after the senior Japanese reporter expressed his colleagues' shame over the attack and their gratification over the Ambassador's safe return, Reischauer addressed them in Japanese and then did his own translating. A veteran correspondent, one of the hardest-shelled of the Americans, fairly beamed. "Great, isn't he?" the correspondent murmured, then recollected himself and frowned.

There was, of course, no pressing need for any correspondent to consult the embassy. In the Reischauer regime, his USIS chieftains devoted most of their time to the Japanese press and worried about the neglect of the Americans. They needn't have been concerned. As one American phrased it, "I hate to say so, but those guys at the embassy do a good job for us when we need them. I'm happy to say that we don't need them too often."

For the press, at least, Reischauer was a model Ambassador. Coming from an academic atmosphere, he conducted himself as openly with the press as he would have in a Harvard classroom. Necessarily, there were many questions he could not answer, and he trusted correspondents to realize it; by and large, they did. But when there was a lunch or a press conference or a special occasion at which the correspondents would be present, he made an occasion of it. He gave his guests pleasure and made them want to come back. More than one correspondent confessed, a little abashed, that he had arranged for a luncheon with Reischauer just to hear him talk about Japan and the Japanese, and not to pick up some inside story.

Reischauer was an exception, however. To most others in the American foreign service, so obvious in their mistrust and open dislike of the press, nearly all American correspondents reacted predictably. They generally applied the rule laid down by Keyes Beech at a conference between correspondents and American government officials who wanted to know how to improve their relations with the press. In a glorious Freudian slip, when asked what he would do to ease the press's habitually tense relations with the government, Beech exclaimed: "Let's have more mutual mistrust!"

6. COVERING JAPAN: A SURVEY [118]

The average correspondent for American news-gathering organizations in Tokyo in the summer of 1964 was an American, 41.6 years old, married, had children, had been on the job less than 5 years, and traveled at every opportunity. His dispatches averaged around 600 to 700 words, if he filed daily, and his costs were around $1,000 a month for communications alone. He spoke Japanese poorly if at all, had a rather critical attitude toward the Japanese, and cost his employer more than $25,000 a year, exclusive of filing charges.

This is the profile of the average foreign correspondent in Tokyo who reported news for the United States, as it emerged from a questionnaire to which 34 journalists responded. They were a well-educated group, with 30 baccalaureates, including 7 with master's degrees and 1 with 2 master's. Among them were 2 Nieman Fellows from Harvard, 2 Ford International Fellows from Columbia, a Council on Foreign Relations Fellow, and a Pulitzer Traveling Fellow. They had attended 24 colleges and universities.

Twenty of the correspondents knew no Japanese, and 11 were able to speak it with varying degrees of proficiency, but only the 3 Japanese were bilingual. Three of the correspondents knew a little Russian, 4 could speak Chinese (1 was Chinese-born), 12 had a basic knowledge of French, 4 could speak German, and 4 Spanish. Five conceded that they knew no language except English.

For 13 of the correspondents, Japan was their first experience abroad. Ten had been in service, based in Tokyo, for only a year or less; 9 others, 1 to 3 years; 3, with 3 to 10 years; and 5 for more than 10 years.

By their own estimates, which generally checked with those of their employers, they were an expensive group to support. For all expenses exclusive of filing charges (salary, travel, office expense, office help, cost of living bonuses, fringe benefits), 5 estimated costs at $50,000–$55,000 annually; 4, $30,000–$50,000; 2, $15,000–$30,000; 3, $10,000–$15,000; 3, $5,000–$10,000; and 2 at $5,000. Of the 19, the top costs were for television, news-magazine, and newspaper bureau chiefs, whose office costs and travel expenses were high; the lowest were for individual-newspaper or wire-service newsmen. While 15 did not respond, there is no reason to believe that they would have substantially changed either the top or the bottom figures.

The travel record was a fairly accurate index of the amount of time the correspondents were able to spend in Tokyo. Only 11 of the 34 did not travel outside Japan within a 12-month period. Of the rest, 10 traveled more than 50,000 miles (some more than 100,000 miles), the others less. Under such circumstances, it would have been difficult to maintain any kind of continuity in the reporting of news of Japan, except for the wire services, a newspaper such as the New York *Times* or Washington *Post,* and the news magazines.

Nearly all the American correspondents in Japan were baffled by their inability to penetrate the closed circle of Japanese society. Even those with Japanese wives, or ex-wives, remarked on how difficult it was for a foreigner to go beneath the surface of Japanese life. One veteran remarked philosophically, "I had a Japanese wife for 13 years and even that did not break down the barriers of Japanese society for me."

If there was a sense of professional discrimination, it centered entirely about the Japanese press clubs, but no American complained that he couldn't cover the news because of it. In fact, after a successful two-year campaign was waged by John Randolph to break down the Foreign Office press club barrier against Americans while he was the AP's general executive in Asia, he was not able to persuade many Americans to attend Foreign Office news conferences. Much of the opposition to the Japanese press clubs, therefore, was identical with the opposition of the Japanese correspondents in Washington to high-level briefings for selected Americans.

The discrimination against Americans and other foreigners in such commercial areas as rents and prices was also no worse than Japanese experiences in the United States. Both, probably, were better off than most foreigners who had to live in France in the mid-1960's. One knowledgeable correspondent in Japan explained it this way: "The discrimination works both ways. Foreigners generally get favored treatment in public transportation from other travelers; in shops, stores, restaurants and such places, they usually get special attention. There is discrimination in obtaining rooms at some Japanese-style inns because they often don't want to cope with foreigners. Foreigners may also be overcharged by landlords, carpenters, plumbers and other service people." Another correspondent agreed: "A foreigner gets a break sometimes because he is a foreigner. I figure we come out even in the long run."

One of the younger correspondents stated his complaint in this manner:

There is general discrimination against *gaijin* [foreigners] in Japan. This is most evident in social affairs where many Japanese resent your being with a Japanese girl. The Japanese are a tight society and rarely admit outsiders to their homes, private clubs or bars. In neighborhood communities, you are usually shut out, as is your wife, whether she is white or Japanese. If she is Japanese, she will usually be slighted and ignored by other Japanese housewives. Children are even more cruel and uninhibited in their attitudes and behavior toward mixed blood or white children.

An older correspondent was more patient. "I have occasionally been turned away from a place of entertainment, as from certain accommodations," he said. "This may not have been discrimination in the usual sense, but a Japanese inability to assimilate foreigners into various compartments of their closed society. On the whole, their hospitality and service counterbalance discrimination."

While the minority of correspondents who felt injured had valid reasons for their attitudes, it was probably true that some of these reactions may have stemmed from an exaggerated notion of what Japan and the Japanese were like—images that were acquired long before their first visit to the country. Eleven of the correspondents in the panel derived their main impressions of the Japanese from the manner in which they fought in World War II and the use that American propaganda made of it. Nine others came to Japan expecting to find a dynamic, industrial nation of expanding power and resources and were not disappointed. Four had the child's image of a quaint land of cherry blossoms, geisha, and matchbox houses. Two admitted to confused, empty minds, and eight had no observations to make.

Most of these images stemmed from wartime service, movies, or romantic books. The more realistic views of Japan were acquired in university classrooms, on the whole, and from a systematic study of modern textbooks and the few newspapers that devoted some space to Japanese affairs. Of those correspondents in the panel who gave frank answers to questions about the images they carried around with them before they reached Japan, fourteen said their impressions were not valid, ten found that they saw just about what they expected, and two had a mixture of satisfaction and disappointment.

But, as a summation, most of the thirty-four correspondents in the panel were satisfied with their assignment. Twenty said that they would return, if given their own choice, and two others said they probably would want to do so. Only eight were so disappointed that they didn't want to come back, and four made no reply.

Despite the academic and professional accomplishments of the American correspondents' corps in Tokyo, which approached the level of American contingents in most other world capitals, it did not have comparable standing among either influential Japanese or Americans in Japan. Primarily, this was a reflection of the inadequacy of the coverage of Japan in the American mass media and growing dissatisfaction with the tendency of correspondents to use Tokyo merely as a base. Yet, at the American embassy and in private groups such as foundations and religious organizations, there was also a tendency to criticize the competence of the correspondents as a group.

Such critical observations had the weakness of all generalities, but they had to be taken into account. One American foundation executive of wide experience charged that the American correspondents were "too ingrown," shared each others' opinions too much, and stayed too close to the Foreign Correspondents' Club when they were in Tokyo. A Japanese in a somewhat comparable position made almost the same criticism; moreover, he struck out at the correspondents' most vulnerable point—their general lack of proficiency in Japanese. "Not many of them do their homework," he said, "and not many of them see much of Japan outside Tokyo."

There was even more dissatisfaction with much of the Japanese correspondence from Washington. "They sit in the office in Washington too much and do not use their legs enough," one distinguished Japanese remarked. "They rewrite too much from the American newspapers and magazines and do not go to see for themselves. They are not doing as well as they should." An American with an intimate knowledge of Japanese journalism doubted that a majority of the Japanse correspondents in Washington were well informed, did not like their practice of group movement and group thinking, and had the impression that they sometimes were given orders to write the same story that appeared on a wire-service budget, but with a "Japanese slant." To a limited extent, any group of foreign correspondents has faced similar general criticism in difficult situations, and some of it undoubtedly has been valid.

In the reporting of Japanese-American affairs in Washington and Tokyo, however, this was not the whole answer in the mid-1960's. Some of the more reflective American correspondents did not really believe that they were doing a first-rate job on the whole, although they were understandably reluctant to criticize the entire corps. But critics within the profession saw the wire services, the heart of international coverage, tied down by lack of staff, lack of time, and lack of interest in Japanese news in the United States. It was also perfectly obvious to any competent observer that the wire services were locked into a routine. It was an event when a senior man was detached from his desk for all of four days to prepare an in-depth account of the anniversary of the atomic destruction of Hiroshima. It was a virtual declaration of journalistic independence when a correspondent in some distant spot failed to file his usual thirty-minute cast to Tokyo because he was away in the countryside, digging for a story.

For all correspondents working for American media, whether they were wire-service newsmen or specials, the interpretive pieces too often had to be tossed off between spot news assignments without adequate preparation or sufficient time to consult knowledgeable sources and think things through. It was the historic complaint of the journalist, of course, that he never had time to do much thinking about his work. But in Japan, it was particularly true.

Wire-service people were conscious of criticism that they were too wedded to the "American angle." Despite evidence produced in New York that the American agencies were international in character and staff and in the presentation of their news report, not many of the Americans in the field believed it. "But we *are* working for an American agency," one veteran said, with an eloquent shrug of his shoulders, "and when we write for the United States we *must* be conscious of the angle that American editors want. Otherwise, we lose the play to the opposition and go out of business. What do they want us to do? Pretend that we're writing for Patagonia?"

If the American special had any particular grievance, it was based on a feeling of inadequacy induced by the system under which he worked. The younger and more sensitive correspondents had a kind of suppressed envy for the few British who wandered around Asia and wrote pretty much as they pleased, without regard for dynamic opening paragraphs or slashing disclosures. "I sometimes think the British, on the whole, are more able writers than we are," one of the Americans said. "They are given the freedom to make a story out of almost anything, but we must be full of significance at all costs."

The news-magazine correspondents, who seriously covered Japan and often dispatched several thousand words of copy to New York, only to have it rewritten into a short piece, felt this professional inadequacy more than the newspaper or wire-service staffs. To those who had special competence as writers, it was both annoying and constricting to be rewritten week after week in New York, except for an occasional cover story. The usual anonymity of the news-magazine format, too, was difficult for some to bear. Despite salary levels and working conditions that were above most newspaper services, the news magazines frequently lost first-rate correspondents.

The few television correspondents, working in a new form that was free of hard-crusted old journalistic patterns, were much happier than the others and much more active. They were often like the spoiled brats of a family accustomed to prodigal and sometimes witless expenditures of money. Correspondents and their camera crews were accustomed to race anywhere in Asia upon little or no notice. The New York office sometimes suggested an assignment, but generally the coverage was left to the men on the spot. If there was grousing over what was used, or not used, it didn't last long because there was always another assignment, another plane to board, another sequence of action to film and talk about. It made ninety seconds on a national television news show seem more important than a Presidential news conference.

Television might amuse and distract both its people and its audience, but it did not essentially change the flow of the news between Japan and the United States. A hard-headed news executive of experience, viewing the panorama of journalism from Tokyo, concluded matter-of-factly, "I detect in all American news media a disinterest in the political and economic facts of life in Japan as opposed, say, even to a country like Holland." And the hard-working American correspondent in Tokyo, baffled and frustrated and sometimes a little angry, threw the burden of his complaint back on editors in the United States. "I spend my time supervising and rewriting for wire service consumption in Japan," he said. "I don't do foreign correspondence in the usual sense except periodically, when I will write long dispatches on economic or political subjects for American newspapers. But there doesn't appear to be demand for such from many papers."

There matters rested. Very little, in reality was being done to bring about any perceptible improvement in the mid-1960's, either in the coverage of Japan for the United States, or of the United States for Japan. Between the correspondents, their editors, and the public, there was a stalemate. The language barrier loomed large for both sides. While the Russian correspondents in Tokyo spoke Japanese, and some knew Chinese as well, few of the Americans and Japanese could come close to matching them. It was the difference between a totalitarian government, using its vast resources to train its people in the service of the state, and the far more limited capabilities of the independent news organizations that served an indifferent mass public in an open society without recourse to government assistance. In this seemingly unequal struggle, the stakes were very high. For all his handicaps and all his faults, no one knew it better than the American foreign correspondent. He was the man in the middle.

7. THE EMERGING PATTERN

When the bone-tingling Pacific winter descends on Japan, hordes of Japanese school children crowd into the libraries and reading rooms of the United States Information Service. They need a good place to study and they want to keep warm. From Sapporo to Fukuoka, the phenomenon is a familiar one each year to American officials who do not quite know what to make of it. It is their function to offer the most favorable impressions of the United States to the Japanese. To this end, they stock their libraries with many thousands of books and the latest magazines and newspapers of all kinds. They arrange for exhibits, art shows, concerts, lectures on cultural topics, and motion-picture showings.

But with Japanese children taking up all available places in the libraries late in the afternoon and early evening, doing their homework, what chance is there for an American propagandist to reach a more discerning Japanese public? Or is the warmth of the library a greater attraction than all the propaganda offerings? Is it possible that a few of the children, in such proximity to American culture, may become interested in it, and that others may absorb it by osmosis?

These were some of the questions that troubled the USIS people as they went about their unnoticed and often unrewarding routine in the more remote cities of Japan in the mid-1960's. To most of them, the very notion of clearing the children from the warm reading rooms was repugnant; in consequence, the children stayed, often blissfully ignorant of the propaganda activity that went on about them in fits and starts. They were by all odds the quietest, the most respectful, and the most faithful visitors to American establishments in Japan.

This was what made it so difficult for officials in Washington to reply when Congressional committees bore down on them for categorical proof that the American investment in USIS was paying off. How could a USIS man in Sendai testify that he had made an impression on his Japanese public with a touring art exhibit or a wandering lecturer who came his way? What results could be noted in a report to Tokyo following a tea at the USIS office in Kanazawa for Japanese university women? What tabulation was there of the impression that had been made in Takamatsu of a display of the salient features of the Civil Rights Bill of 1964, or the Gemini astronauts' flights?

The American investment in USIS was greater for Japan than for any other nation in Asia except India. While living in Tokyo was comfortable for policy-making officials and some of their more fortunate associates, there were instances in which life was grim in the smaller cities where the USIS man and his wife frequently were the only American officials in town. Between the USIS people and the missionaries, a minimal contact was maintained with the Japanese public; at that level, all the airy theories in Tokyo tended to disappear, and the reality of trying to communicate in a cultural vacuum remained.

It was sheer folly to expect an organization of this fundamental character to exert any recognizable influence on the powerful and highly centralized communications media of Japan. The provision of still photos and canned articles, which might have been suitable for country weeklies, was scarcely appropriate for submission to the large national and provincial dailies in Japan. Now and then, a canned piece might slip into print, just as a taped USIS program might be used on a Japanese station. Japanese journalists were even paid at one period to make tapes of their views, suitable for distribution by USIS to radio stations. But the end result of such crude and often misdirected propaganda was dubious.

It did not take long for Ambassador Reischauer to decide that dealings with the Japanese press, television, radio, and magazines would be handled at the top level in his office, and that USIS in Tokyo would be given the less demanding assignment of working with the American press. There were several advantages to this arrangement. Reischauer, Minister Fahs, and Nat Thayer, then the embassy's press officer, all were fluent in Japanese while most Americans in USIS were not. Thayer, an articulate Foreign Service career officer, knew most of the key people on the Japanese newspapers and had their respect because he knew their language. Whatever differences there were in ideas between Japanese and Americans under this arrangement, the language barrier at least was surmounted.

What the American press did and said, therefore, was usually of less moment at the embassy than the reactions of the Japanese press. Its temperature was checked daily on such issues as American commercial relationships with Japan, the Japanese pressure for closer relations with Communist China, and the Japanese reaction to the stepped-up American participation in the Viet-Nam war. All these were indicative of the delicacy of Japanese-American relations. When Japan Air Lines won the right to fly around the world through New York City, it was hailed by the Japanese press as a major victory for 1966.

Yet, the business community, the intellectuals, and the press all harped continually on the need for a better relationship between Japan and Communist China, but for different reasons. The business and industrial interests were anxious for an expansion of their old markets in mainland China. For ideological reasons, the still-dedicated Marxists among the intellectuals also argued for a resumption of close Japanese ties with China. Some talked feelingly of a "guilt" complex for the wrongs that militarist Japan had done to China. However, it was easily observable that those in Japan who should have felt guilty about China did not, and those who did usually had no reason for their state of mind.

The Japanese press, with only a few exceptions, ably represented the desires of both the business community and the intellectuals on the China question. At the management level, where relationships with business and industry were bound to be close and sympathetic, there was a natural urge to project the views of this dominant segment of Japanese postwar society. At the staff level, where so many reporters and writers were admittedly in greater harmony with the Japanese Socialist Party than they were with the ruling Liberal Democratic Party, the Chinese story could be handled with a gratifying amount of emotion and enthusiasm.

The unresolved part of the equation, as far as the observing American diplomat or correspondent was concerned, was the response of the Japanese public to this pro-Chinese propaganda drive at almost all levels of mass communication. Despite the fervent editorials, there was evidence that the Japanese people had not by any means overcome their feeling that the Chinese were troublesome and unpredictable. While a militaristic Japanese government had trumpeted its victories in China for almost a decade before World War II, the average Japanese knew only that the war in China had brought misery, hardship, and death to many a home in his islands. After the final defeat of 1945, the Japanese public's view of China was hardly enthusiastic; nor did the Chinese Communist victory bring about dancing in the streets in Japanese cities. There were not many average Japanese citizens who would have agreed of their own free will with those who told the world confidently, "Japan knows how to deal with China." History didn't support such a claim.

The pro-China feeling of some intellectuals nevertheless flourished despite student apathy toward Chinese subjects, all of them exceedingly difficult. More students registered for courses in American literature in the universities than for any other foreign cultural subject, although American writers still did not have the prestige of the French and the nineteenth century Russians in Japan. Tough courses in Chinese culture and the Chinese language, however, drew comparatively few students. Chinese books did not sell very well on the Japanese market. Nor was there any rush to read up on China in the libraries.

The outburst of Japanese solicitude for Communist China, as it appeared in the Japanese press, had all the symptoms of a carefully promoted campaign conducted by specialized groups to serve their own political and economic interests. Of these, the Marxist intellectuals were dominant in expressing their feelings despite their failure to carry the public with them in 1960. The far more powerful business community was notably discreet, but then it had good reason to be. With the growth of economic difficulties in Japanese industry and an increase in American financial safeguards to halt the outflow of gold from the United States, there were more immediate issues to tackle than the search for new treasures at the end of the Chinese Communist rainbow. While Japanese business missions continued to visit Peking, members of the Japanese cabinet came to Washington to discuss trade.

For if there was a "broken dialogue" between Japanese intellectuals and the West, the Japanese businessman could scarcely be expected to take the lead in breaking through the communications block. He was as devious and secretive as ever. While he had learned the value of advertising to market his wares, he still regarded public relations as one of the black arts. The thriving public-relations firms of the United States flocked to Japan and signed up large corporations, headed by the many Mitsui interests, but even they had their troubles in persuading the Japanese to talk for publication.

The Nissan Automobile Company, which had high hopes of breaking into the American market, wouldn't permit the representative of an American news magazine and his photographer to tour its factories. Honda, which manufactures one-third of the world's motorcycles and sells more than 70 per cent of the motorcycles that are purchased in the United States, took days to produce an out-of-date report on its sales for an inquiring reporter. An N.B.C. crew that went to a large shipbuilding yard to take film virtually had to be cleared for security. At the Yawata Steel Company, the largest in Japan, the local Japanese reporters' club had to be consulted before a foreign correspondent could be admitted to do a story. During a tour of a synthetic fiber plant, foreign correspondents were forbidden to take pictures and refused information on production figures.

Summing up the corporate Japanese introduction to public relations, the *Wall Street Journal* said:

Their nervous aversion to public notice probably harkens back to the early 1930's when industry was controlled by the military preparing for war against China. . . .
Rather than help, publicity might well hurt. A newspaper story could, for example, draw tax investigators. A man's competitors, too, might learn more than he'd like them to know. And there's always the danger some sharp-eyed reader overseas might spot a patent infringement in a photo.[119]

Such a frame of mind was not conducive to leadership in a campaign with troublesome ideological overtones in Japan. The strongly anti-Communist business community, accordingly, seldom showed its hand publicly in the discussion of Communist Chinese trade. Yet, an important segment of industry quietly made common cause with the Marxists on this issue through the mid-1960's, and the Japanese press obliged them both.

During a period of increasing American participation in the war against Peking's ally Ho Chi Minh, the American Government understandably was not impressed by the pro-Chinese campaign in Japan. The Johnson Administration was in no mood to go out of its way to appease Japanese sentiment as it was reflected in the national press. Moreover, the opposition in the great Japanese newspapers to the American military effort in Viet-Nam was not calculated to win many new friends for Japan, either in Washington or among the American correspondents in Tokyo.

The revival of anti-Americanism in the press campaign in Japan produced few immediate results aside from a certain amount of image-twisting. After the sobering-up period following the 1960 riots, there was a tendency even among Japanese who were friendly to the United States to look upon America as a well-meaning but vacillating power with wobbly and impractical policies in Asia. The Marxist intellectuals argued that the United States would not remain in Asia indefinitely, and the Japanese sooner or later would have to face up to treating with Communist China. But as the Viet-Nam war escalated, and the United States showed its determination to stand by its commitments, the enraged Japanese minority began depicting America as a ruthless, racist, military power.

Neither the vacillating nor the ruthless image of the United States was drawn with much conviction. Intelligent Japanese were troubled by the war in Southeast Asia, just as many Americans were, but they weren't carried along by the artificial Marxist torrent. Between Communist China and the United States, they saw only one choice. Although Japan's trade with Communist China was passing the half-billion-dollar mark annually, Tokyo was showing increasing interest in improving relations with the Soviet Union. And the Japanese Communist Party, shaken by the Red Guard outbreaks in Peking in 1966, wobbled toward Moscow in a swing of the ideological pendulum.

Once again, as in 1960, the Japanese left had misread both the American character and American intentions and departed from the mainstream of Japanese opinion. However much they distorted the image and the purposes of the United States, they could not fundamentally change American policy in Asia. The keystone of this policy was the Japanese-American alliance, as both Communist China and the Soviet Union fully realized. A few months after the 1960 riots, Reischauer showed what the probable consequences of a weakening of Japanese-American ties would be when he wrote:

A Japanese repudiation of its alliance with the United States might stir up a momentary pro-American reaction in such strongly anti-Japanese and firmly pro-American countries as South Korea, Taiwan and the Philippines . . . But even in these countries, to say nothing of the less committed areas, the long-range reactions would undoubtedly be most unfavorable to the United States. Neutralism, if not open pro-Communism, would be shown to be the obvious "wave of the future," and a scramble to get on the Communist bandwagon would probably soon follow.

At the same time, American defense potentialities would be drastically reduced throughout East Asia. This might not be true in the field of nuclear weapons . . . but it certainly would hold for limited wars with conventional weapons, which seem to be the more present danger in the Far East. It would probably be folly to attempt to stem a second attack from North Korea on South Korea if the United States lacked the backing, not so much of its bases in Japan, as of the great industrial facilities available in Japanese ports and cities. Bases in Okinawa, Formosa and the Philippines offer no real substitute for the latter. Thus, an unfriendly Japan or even a strictly neutralist Japan might well mean the inevitable withdrawal of the American defense line to the mid-Pacific—with all the vast political consequences this would entail for the whole of East Asia.[120]

Reischauer correctly predicted that the events of 1960 justified no such pessimistic outlook. Despite the leftist campaigning against the United States in Japan, the prognosis still held good six years later.

Nevertheless, the Japanese press pursued its erratic course. Communist China and North Viet-Nam, on the whole, received more favorable treatment in many Japanese newspapers than did the United States. Not even the first explosions of atomic devices by Communist China, and the likelihood of others, served to change the balance to any great extent, although some *pro forma* protests were made to Peking. However emotional the Japanese may have been about Communist China, Peking showed no emotion whatever about its relations with Japan. It warned that in case of an atomic war, the Japanese would have to "bear the brunt" of a "nuclear holocaust."[121]

To justify their position, some Japanese editors righteously compared their opposition to the Viet-Nam war with that of the New York *Times*. But they could hardly contend that their news columns, day in and day out, gave balanced coverage of the conflict. While the Japanese press often displayed the ability to do good work, equal to the best anywhere, Japanese journalists sometimes were frank enough to concede that there was no newspaper in Japan that could be ranked consistently with the world's quality newspapers.[122] And that, of course, was the nub of the difficulty of reporting on the United States in Japan. Too often, the Japanese press, for all its good qualities, permitted its policies to influence its news judgments. There was substance to Ambassador Reischauer's complaint of "unbalanced" coverage, and he could with some justice have extended it beyond the Viet-Nam war.

While some prejudice may have existed in the American press against Japan, it was not a real factor in the reporting of Japan to the

United States. On the excuse of public disinterest in Japan, a majority of the press and television in the United States either covered Japanese news minimally or ignored it altogether.

That attitude, while difficult for American foreign correspondents in Tokyo to justify, nevertheless relieved them of the often thankless job of trying to give Japan the coverage it deserved in the American press. True, there were big splurges on Japan from time to time in leading newspapers and magazines as well as television documentaries, but the day-to-day reporting was lamentably thin for long stretches. Thus, whether one blamed some of the prejudiced editors in Japan or some of the bored editors in the United States, the outcome was more or less the same, as far as the publics of both nations were concerned. The coverage was inadequate both ways.

If there was any hope for a change, it rested on the young Japanese and American journalists who came to their first posts in the United States and Japan, respectively, without the preconceived notions of their elders. To an even greater extent, it also depended on the development of larger publics in both the United States and Japan who were willing to learn something more than mere superficialities about each other. The Japanese children who crowded into the USIS libraries each winter to do their homework in warmth and comfort therefore represented a hope for the future as truly as did the American children who were taught to think of the new Japan as a neighbor and ally, rather than a potential enemy.

IV

Along the Asian Perimeter

1. THE "INITIAL RELIANCE"

IN THE LONG and tangled relationship between journalism and diplomacy, there is a special place for those purposeful public acts in either profession that turned out, by accident or design, to be the harbingers of war. The most celebrated in the modern era is the speech that has been incontinently blamed for touching off the Korean War. At the time it was delivered by Secretary of State Dean Acheson, before the National Press Club in Washington on January 12, 1950, it was thought to be exceedingly dull. But with the remarkable gift of hindsight, opposition orators and unsympathetic journalists have almost succeeded in making of it another Ems Telegram, Bismarck's trick that drew France into the disastrous Franco-Prussian War, or another Hearst message to Frederic Remington in Cuba on the eve of war in 1898: "Please remain. You furnish the pictures, and I'll furnish the war." [1]

Had General Douglas MacArthur drawn the perimeter of American defenses in the Far East that day, as he did in fact on an earlier occasion, little would have been made of it. The Joint Chiefs of Staff had made the basic decisions, excluding both Korea and Formosa. But because the speaker was Acheson and because Senator Joseph R. McCarthy's reign of terror against those suspected of being "soft on Communism" was then at its height, a great many consequences flowed from an otherwise unspectacular address.

Acheson's retracing of the defense perimeter, endorsed by the Joint Chiefs of Staff, ran "along the Aleutians to Japan and then . . . to the Ryukyus [and] from the Ryukyus to the Philippine Islands . . ." When the North Korean Communists, with Russian help, struck southward across the 38th Parallel on June 25, 1950, it was recalled quickly enough that Acheson also had said in January: "So far as the military security of other areas in the Pacific is concerned, it must be clear that no person can guarantee these areas against military attack. But it must also be clear that such a guarantee is hardly sensible or necessary within the realm of practical relationship."

There it was! An outright invitation, the opposition press charged, to a Communist attack on the weakened Republic of Korea, a Communist target since 1945. In vain did Acheson's defenders point out that he had made no new policy of any kind and that, in fact, a key part of his January 12 statement on the subject had been omitted. He went on that day with this explicit declaration of intent:

> Should such an attack occur—one hesitates to say where such an armed attack should come from—the initial reliance must be on the people attacked to resist it and then upon the commitments of the entire civilized world under the Charter of the United Nations, which so far has not proved a weak reed to lean on by any people who are determined to protect their independence against outside aggression.[2]

But unhappily, in both journalism and its more deliberate parent, history, there are those who will see only what they want to see and quote only what will support their particular assumptions. Instead of being hailed as a seer who foretold the armed intervention of the United Nations, Acheson was forced to occupy a prominent place in McCarthy's gallery of the damned. Under the circumstances, there were only wry grimaces at the Department of State when a private poll, taken at the time, showed that 24 per cent of the Americans who responded had never heard of Acheson.[3]

Yet almost everywhere in Asia it was as true in the mid-1960's, as it had been in 1950, that the "initial reliance" of the United States had to be on "the people attacked"; but that part of Acheson's speech was forgotten in the United States. The French in Viet-Nam, fighting a losing war against an enemy that had won over a large part of the populace, learned to their cost that they could not go it alone. They needed the native peoples they had once despised. Subsequently, despite the superior resources and armed might of the United States, the very notion of maintaining military bases in the Far East in the midst of a hostile people became a nightmare for American commanders.

Could Japan, at the heart of the U.S. position in the Far East, be defended against the wishes of the Japanese? Could the surrounding defenses in South Korea and the "big island" chain from Japan south to the Philippines and Formosa be maintained against a disaffected people? The answers were self-evident to both American diplomats and military leaders.

To the arts of diplomacy, the workings of foreign aid, and the program of usis, the American armed forces therefore added a community relations program which, as it was developed in the Far East, became an effort to draw closer to the peoples who were the "initial reliance" of the United States. Members of the U.S. Air Force, for example, helped with the re-education of a Korean "Slicky Boy," as the juvenile delinquents were known there, and flew a fifteen-year-old Korean girl to Texas for a delicate heart operation. In Japan, airmen at Misawa Air Base provided funds for eye operations for Japanese who could not afford them. In the Philippines, at Tarlac, they built a Youth Civic Center. In Okinawa, during a water shortage, they turned tank trucks and water from the Naha Air Base reservoir over to the surrounding community. And on Formosa, the Tainan base helped support special clinics for the area.[4]

In the light of the nation's generosity with foreign aid and these and many other acts of individual kindness and friendship, it was difficult for many Americans to understand why there was rioting in Seoul, disaffection in Naha, grumbling in Taipei, and even criticism of the United States in that special ward of American democracy, the Republic of the Philippines. Because of the relatively few American correspondents in the area and the disinterest of most American editors in the sketchy news report that was available, little except bad news usually got through. Consequently, when signs of anti-Americanism cropped up in this perimeter of American defenses in the Pacific, it was as much of a shock to an unprepared American public as was the defacing of the American flag in Panama.

To the American public, these were countries or territories that were known primarily because the United States maintained military bases there. The effect of the American military presence, it was popularly assumed, was beneficial; therefore, the peoples concerned should have been properly grateful that they were being protected. Any other attitude drew wrathful editorial condemnation in the United States and cries for an end to all foreign aid because it was wasted on "ingrates." They scarcely understood, any more than did the admirable organizers of ancient Roman Asia, the "invincible repugnance of the Oriental" to any semblance of foreign mastery.[5]

No Asian of independent mind could take kindly to the American notion that he was a latter-day species of Benedict Arnold because he followed the precepts of American democracy by speaking his mind to his benefactors. It may well be imagined what thoughts this American posture of outrage aroused among Koreans who remembered their 300,-

ooo casualties in the battles of 1950-53, the Okinawans who lived under American military rule, the Filipinos who felt so deeply that the price of their loyalty to the United States had been neglect, and the Formosans who knew all too well that they were ruled by the Chinese Nationalists by grace of the United States.

The problem was put in this fashion by Pyong Choon Hahm, a member of the faculty of Seoul's Yonsei University:

> If I were an American taxpayer, I would regret the necessity of paying for the defense of the free world and contributing to the economic development of underdeveloped countries; I would no doubt be resentful that the United States is the country bearing the chief burden. What I wish to point out is that in terms of economic necessity the Koreans feel the strain with greater urgency.
>
> Some years ago, former President Eisenhower reportedly justified United States military aid to Korea by explaining that to maintain one U.S. soldier in Korea would cost the United States $3,000 a year, but to maintain a Korean soldier cost only $600 a year. In other words, it was cheaper to have Korean soldiers defend the common defense line than to have American soldiers do it. We are willing and proud to render satisfactory service in defense of our common frontier cheaply. But how cheaply are we expected to do so? Is it a mendicant mentality to expect $600 from the United States? How hard a bargain will the Americans drive? [6]

How hard, indeed?

In varying forms, this was the question that was asked increasingly along the perimeter in the Far East. The increasing tensions of the war in Viet-Nam and the growing belligerence of Communist China did not make it any easier for the United States to answer. Despite their dependence on the power and good will of the United States, whether by choice or by necessity, the Koreans, the Okinawans, the Filipinos, and the Formosans no longer felt obliged to accept humbly what Washington offered. Like the Japanese, they were charting an independent course as best they could.

Had this state of mind been understood in the United States, there would have been less agonizing over the lack of affection in Asia for an ever-bountiful and open-handed America. But if scanty intelligence of these wards of the United States was available in the American mass media, even less was known of the United States by their peoples.

2. KOREA: THE FORGOTTEN FRONT

"Not since the bloody student riots of 1960 brought down autocratic old Syngman Rhee had South Korea seen anything like it," said *Newsweek*'s report of the Seoul riots of June, 1964. No correspondent had seen anything like it, either, for the piece was a minor classic of news-mangling. Somewhere between the stringer in Seoul and the immutable coldness of print, fact became fancy, and even the major parties were reversed.

Newsweek had 30,000 students at the Seoul riots, whereas *Time* estimated 12,000, and the wire services and the Korean papers settled for 15,000. *Newsweek* closed down the papers, although they never missed an issue. It linked what it called "the major opposition party, the Democratic Republican Party," to the riots, although the DRP actually was not the opposition at all but the party supporting President Chung Hee Park.

"And, in fact," *Newsweek* went on, "the Democratic Republican executive council did make use of the riots to demand that Park 'step down peacefully . . . and hold new Presidential and parliamentary elections in an honest way.' " It wasn't a fact at all, for the opposition Civil Rule Party made the demand, not the President's own party.[7]

After digesting this intelligence, a Korean journalist told the visiting Floyd G. Arpan, a professor at the University of Indiana's School of Journalism, "Maybe you had better return to New York and help train *Newsweek* correspondents on the simple fundamentals of accurate reporting."[8] Though untypical of *Newsweek*'s foreign report, the piece did serve as an unfortunate illustration of how wrong an otherwise responsible news-gathering organization could be about a small Asian country that many called the "Forgotten Front."

There were others among the American news media that had their troubles trying to explain an unfamiliar but important land to a largely indifferent American audience. In a thirty-minute C.B.S. documentary in 1963, the usually painstaking Peter Kalischer did not appear to have given South Korea a particularly balanced treatment. Marie A. Nagorski, the wife of a veteran USIS officer in Seoul, wrote to him in reproach:

The picture you presented was correct—of poverty, hardships, lack of resources, great American involvement without visible results. But the most dominant note in your presentation was a thoroughly negative attitude toward the achievements of South Korea, leaving the viewers with a sense of complete hopelessness that nothing has been done and nothing will be done, but we have to stay here nevertheless.

This is the point on which those of us who live and work here have to disagree most strongly. One of the most rewarding experiences for us who have to work with Koreans in various fields is the feeling of respect for their incessant efforts, for their fighting spirit not only on the field of battle but in their hard daily lives. There is no apathy in this country . . .[9]

Charles Collingwood, replying for C.B.S., wrote that the film had been edited in New York by people with far less knowledge of Korea than Kalischer, but defended his viewpoint as follows: "People so far away from the scene as the American television viewing public are not apt to notice fine points of interpretation. I suspect that the main residue left by the program was the feeling that both we and the Koreans face terribly difficult problems in the area, problems which are not susceptible of a short-term solution, but on which some progress is being made . . ."[10]

It is, of course, one of the staples of journalism to take the grim view, particularly on foreign policy. The correspondent thereby has a better chance of being right, for as Gunnar Myrdal has observed, "The most obvious evidence of frailty in foreign policies is that they so often fail."[11] Walter Lippmann thus explained the reasoning of the journalist who is called upon to make a judgment: "I know from my newspaper experience how risky it is to be optimistic and I know that the prudent man who wishes to play it safe will always lean to Cassandra, never to Pollyanna. For if Cassandra is right, which I am sorry to say is all too frequently, the man becomes without any trouble at all a true prophet. If, on the other hand, Cassandra is wrong, everybody is too well pleased to remember what he said . . ."[12]

Contrary to the lightly stated, but nevertheless very real, journalistic failing that bad news often tends to drive out good news, Emerson Chapin, of the New York *Times*, wrote as follows of South Korea's prospects:

After an agonizingly slow start, South Korea, always predominantly agricultural, has moved to the stage where some experts believe it ready for an "economic takeoff." If the still precarious political stability can be maintained, the outlook is hopeful.

Just three days ago the nation entered a new era by signing agreements normalizing diplomatic relations with an old enemy, Japan, and providing an inflow of $800 million of grants and credits in the next ten years. This aid, coupled with Japanese technical assistance and industrial investment, is expected to spur industrial development significantly. The five-year plan inaugurated in 1961 by President Park's military government,

modified after an impractically overambitious start, is now yielding practical results.

Industry is growing at the rate of 10 to 12 per cent annually and the
over-all economic growth rate has reached the high level of 6.8 per cent
in the last two years. . . . Inflation, which rose almost out of control for
several years, has been held well below the 10 per cent level in the last
year and the dangerous "inflation psychology" is being dispelled.[13]

It was, truly, more hopeful than the world had been led to expect.
Although the young republic still had to support a standing army of
600,000 men on an annual per capita income of $100 and spend 32 per
cent of its national budget to defend a truce line against its divided
countrymen and Communist China, there were rewards in sight for all
its sacrifices. There was satisfaction, too, for the United States after the
expenditure of $5.3 billion in aid of all kinds since 1953, including direct
grants of $2.8 billion, for a land the size of the state of Indiana.[14]

This country of 28 million would never be "The Land of the Morning Calm" except in its ancient name, Chosun. By the accident of geography, it had been a corridor for conquest for much of its 4,000 years of
history. Mongols, Japanese, and Manchus by turn had stormed its cities
and devastated its rugged countryside until, at last, its people had regained the land and for 250 years sealed it from the world as the "Her-
mit Kingdom." The United States had played a part in reopening Korea in the nineteenth century, but the Japanese influence had been far
greater; in 1905, after the Russo-Japanese War, it had become a Japanese colony for four decades. But the rebirth of freedom in 1945 and the
re-attainment of the status of a free nation in 1948 had brought only
new problems and a bloody and ruthless war with the Korean Communists in the North.

It was this war, and the continued American occupation afterward,
that gave Korea such an unflattering image in the United States. Americans, dissatisfied with a limited war and a limited peace that produced
160,000 American casualties, including nearly 60,000 dead, tended to
blame much of their unhappiness on their Korean allies. As late as the
mid-1960's, prospective visitors to Korea were warned by the well-
meaning military to guard their possessions against Korean thievery,
stay inside at night, have as few dealings as possible with the Korean
people, and leave the women and children home. Whatever the American government tried to do to change this distressing and distorted image, it wasn't very effective; for many of the military and even some of
the diplomatic personnel, an assignment to Korea was depicted as a
misfortune. It wasn't true.

American civilians in Seoul lived far better than they did in most of

Japan, India, and Southeast Asia, and visitors found that they were safer on the streets of Seoul than they were in New York City. The Park government, with the exception of its times of trial with student rioters, maintained order and gave its people reasonable protection. Food was usually plentiful. When a rice shortage developed just before harvest time, it was generally anticipated by imports from the United States or Japan. Stores were well stocked with goods and, in Seoul, great new buildings were beginning to rise in testimony to its status as a thriving capital city with a population of 3 million.

It was probably necessary to give Americans something more than they had elsewhere to bring them to Korea and keep them reasonably content for their tour of service. In any event, the diplomatic community was sheltered in a "compound civilization" of American homes no different from any well-to-do suburb of New York or Chicago. But the stockades were guarded day and night by armed Korean troops; while Americans were passed in automatically, almost all Koreans were carefully checked. Such precautions might have been necessary in a hostile land, but the Americans still clung to them in the mid-1960's, regardless of Korean opinion. It was the way things were when 55,000 American troops remained on Korean soil, with planes, tanks, armored cars, and all the other essentials of war.

At the Demilitarized Zone (DMZ) near Panmunjom, the Americans still were on the alert after a dozen years of the Long Truce in the war that never really ended. Infiltrators still slipped over the 38th Parallel at night and melted into the countryside to carry out their espionage missions in South Korea. Consequently, not knowing which Korean was the enemy and realizing from long and painful experience that not even a uniform was a guarantee of friendliness, American guards seized any Korean found in the area without authority. While this did not prevent busloads of Koreans from touring the DMZ under escort, it did create a cleavage between the American soldier and the people near the area whom he was protecting.

The daily propaganda drama in the shack that served as a meeting place for American and North Korean representatives also perpetuated the feeling that nothing in Korea really had been settled. Both sides were deliberately rude and insulting to each other, a state of mind which it was to the advantage of the Communists to continue. Even though the session was usually over in a few minutes, since it consisted merely of exchanging bits of routine information noted on documents, any tourists in the DMZ flocked to the windows of the shack to see the show—the U.N. flag on one side and the North Korean flag on the other.

President Park had had fair warning through the overthrow of the aged Korean strong man, Syngman Rhee, that his people would not forever be docile and tractable citizens of a police state, however great their danger. Rhee had rigged the 1960 elections and condoned bribery, ballot-box-stuffing, and widespread intimidation of voters. When a protesting student was slain by a police bullet, the youth of the nation had taken to the streets on April 19, 1960. Before the revolution was over, 183 Koreans had been slain and more than 6,000 injured, but Rhee had been overthrown.[15] Nine months later, on May 16, 1961, Park had come to power as a major general at the head of a military junta that had toppled the indecisive Premier Chang Myun (John M. Chang). Park had promised civilian rule, put through a new constitution, and, to the astonishment of his enemies, had run for president as a civilian and won in late 1963 by a plurality of 150,000 votes out of 11 million cast. He also swept into office a National Assembly in which he controlled 110 of the 175 votes.[16]

Yet, in the years that followed, President Park's tight control, his censorship of the press, and his remarkable improvement of Korea's economic situation did not save him from more severe tests. Under the prodding of the United States, the Koreans were being pushed into a resumption of relations with Japan at a faster rate than some of them wanted to go. Park's opposition, working on the suspicions of the students, made political capital out of it. And in a land where 60 per cent of the population were under twenty-five years of age, and 100,000 of them were students in thirty-two colleges and universities in the Seoul area, that meant trouble. It broke in the late spring of 1964 with another outburst of student rioting, followed by Park's declaration of martial law on June 3. This time, there was no shooting of students; moreover, the leader of the negotiations with Japan, Kim Chong Pil, conveniently discovered that he would be welcome at a Harvard seminar on Asia and departed for a time. The universities were closed, thus depriving the demonstrators of a meeting place. In this manner, Park rode out the storm.[17]

In retrospect, the solemn-faced Korean leader, who was forty-seven years old at the time, conceded that part of the trouble was the undue secrecy with which the Japanese-Korean talks had been surrounded by his government. It was a rare admission for any Asian ruler, but particularly for one with such dictatorial power. Summing up the causes of the 1964 uprising, he said they included a "tendency to resort to demonstrations as a means to settle problems . . . various social conditions that resulted from revolutions occurring in rapid succession . . . shortcomings in government in public relations efforts to enlighten the people concerning the Korea-Japan talks and impatience among the people about efforts the government was making as it was entering a period of vigorous activity after establishing civil rule." [18]

The gap in communications with his own people wasn't entirely Park's fault. During the years of Japanese rule, accompanied by the strictest control of the press, the Korean people learned to disseminate information primarily by word of mouth and therefore to put little trust in what their rulers said. After the 1964 riots, a member of the Ministry of Public Information in Seoul, Ki Uk Hahn, demonstrated that newspapers still ranked third, below personal conversation and radio, as a means of disseminating information. A government-sponsored survey showed that 30 per cent of those polled said their news came primarily from other people, 26 per cent from radio, 23 per cent from newspapers, and the remainder weren't interested in informing themselves. This was generally confirmed by American findings of a similar nature.

Hahn's survey also found that the better-educated groups subscribed to one or more newspapers, but only 55.7 per cent believed what they read, and 21.7 per cent believed but half of what they read. As for the publication of foreign news, he estimated that 3.9 per cent of the news space in Korean newspapers on the average was devoted to international affairs, as compared with 5.1 per cent in 1962.[19]

Kyu-whan Kim, the associate managing editor of the *Orient Press,* shed some light on the reasons for the public's skepticism of its press. Referring to the nine-month period under Premier Chang, when the newspapers were free of restraint, he wrote:

Korean journalism, which had plodded along the long and tortuous path that leads to freedom of the press, began to act, as soon as that freedom was won, as if it was determined to prove that it was not worthy of it. This was an historical irony, but there was a reason for it. It stemmed primarily from the backwardness of Korean society. Therefore, Korean journalistic circles should not be held solely responsible for it, for Korean journalism was only one of the many areas of Korean culture that followed the same pattern.

It was a pattern which, as far as the newspapers were concerned, meant resistance to authority, political leadership of the people, and a kind of primitive newspaper operation in which the press was an auxiliary of some other industry. As Kim warned: "Newspapers subjugated to other industries will find it impossible to criticize the holding companies or the government uprightly, as they will be directly influenced by their own criticism. And if such an unhealthy triangular relationship persists, such papers will eventually become discredited among their readers and they will perish." [20]

The press in the mid-1960's was centered in Seoul. Despite a government claim of 95 per cent literacy among South Koreans (it was probably closer to 85 per cent by any standard other than the mere recognition of the twenty-four letters of the *hangul* alphabet), the newspaper circulations at most were estimated at 1.7 million daily, or 6.9 copies for each 100 people.[21] Four newspapers in Seoul alone accounted for 1 million of the total—*Dong-A Ilbo*, 350,000; *Hankook Ilbo*, 250,000; *Chosen Ilbo*, 200,000; and *Sanup Kyongie Shinmun*, 200,000.[22] Both English-language newspapers, the *Korean Republic* and the *Korea Times*, were tied to the government, so that Americans usually depended on the Pacific edition of the *Stars and Stripes* for news of the United States.

Key Young Chang, a large and vigorous businessman who founded both the *Hankook Ilbo* and the *Korea Times*, was an exception to the general tendency of the Korean press to oppose the government when it was able to do so. He operated with a dozen telephones on his desk and would tell visitors boisterously, "I want two more—a direct line to the White House and a direct line to the Kremlin." Although he wasn't able to swing that, he did move into the Park government as a deputy prime minister and economic planner who temporarily divested himself of his newspaper properties and proceeded to support the law against his former colleagues.

At the beginning of 1966, the annual censorship report of the AP summed up Korea's press problems as follows: "Officially, South Korea has no censorship except under martial law, but Korean newsmen must observe self-imposed censorship under legislation penalizing articles considered helpful to Communism." Dispatches of foreign correspondents remained uncensored.[23]

The government's domination of radio broadcasting through its Korean Broadcasting System and ownership of most of the important transmitters narrowed the selection of news for the owners of approximately 900,000 sets. Members of the elite groups said they generally listened for an hour a day to radio, and most of those tuned in for about fifteen minutes a day either to the Voice of America or to the Armed Forces' Korean Network (F.E.N.).[24] Television was in the development stage, mainly because of the small number of sets that were available and the cost involved.

As for the introduction of foreign news into Korea, it was conducted entirely through Korean-owned companies that were subject to government regulation. The Donghwa News Agency, which provided AP and Reuters service, was the largest and most influential, with the UPI outlet, *Orient Press,* as its main rival. The Hapdong Agency offered Agence France-Presse and the Deutsche Press Agentur. However, in view of the complicated process of selecting, editing, and translating the items and then offering them for use in the limited space allotted by the Korean press to foreign news, not very much of the original file of any of the foreign agencies came through to the newspaper-reading public.

The spreading of the news was graphically illustrated by a survey of the 1960 revolution, a major event in South Korea's history, which showed that 42 per cent of the respondents first learned of the uprising by word of mouth, 40 per cent by radio, and only 17 per cent from the press. Of the total, 36 per cent heard of the revolt on the day it happened, 32 per cent the following day, and 24 per cent two to three days later.[25]

On the basis of such a reaction for a great domestic news event, it could scarcely be expected that much would be known about events in the United States by the average Korean and only a little more by those Koreans who considered themselves better informed. In fact, keeping abreast of the news was even a problem for the American Embassy in Seoul, which as late as the beginning of 1966 had no direct wire-service teletypes because there was no budgetary provision for the relatively small expense. State Department informative messages were generally hours behind AP and UPI, so that the ambassador himself would often hear of important developments first through Koreans. The embassy learned of the Kennedy assassination in 1963 from a *Hankook Ilbo* reporter, who telephoned with an AP bulletin.

For the run of the news, the Americans in the embassy and the armed forces picked up bits and pieces from the Korean press, the American wire services at second hand, and the armed forces radio. They read the Pacific *Stars and Stripes* and the Japanese English-language newspapers that were flown in from Tokyo daily, sometimes arriving ahead of the State Department's own news report. On a longer term basis, they could read the international editions of *Time* and *Newsweek* (*Time* sold 2,508 copies in Korea weekly and *Newsweek* somewhat less) and, of course, the New York *Times* whenever it arrived.

The image of the United States in Korea, therefore, was primarily the one projected by the Americans stationed in the country. For fear of arousing an adverse reaction, it was the embassy's policy to operate quietly; as one high official put it, "to keep the American presence muted." That was about as successful as silencing a giant at a circus to keep him from attracting attention.

Even at the height of the rioting against the Park government, however, there was little semblance of anti-Americanism among the people. This did not mean that there was no criticism of the United States. On the contrary, the embassy generally had all it could do to handle the criticism of leading Koreans in and out of government and the discontent of the intellectuals as it was spelled out in such periodicals as *Sasanggye* ("World of Thought") and *Saebyok* ("Aurora"). Those Koreans who were most interested in industrial development didn't believe that the United States was doing enough to help. To this, the embassy usually responded that the United States was doing all it could, and that Koreans needed more practical planning and, above all, more patience. The Korean intellectuals, preoccupied by a search for national identity and a realistic policy for achieving reunion with the 9 million Koreans in the Communist North, sometimes feared that the United States was doing too much and thereby making people dependent on a foreign power. To such quixotic views, the embassy people often replied with fervor that the United States would welcome joyfully the day when Koreans became self-sustaining.

While these attitudes were often evident in the endless political discussions in the Korean press, they did not seem too prevalent among a people preoccupied with their daily effort to scrape a living in the cities, the narrow valleys, and the towering hillsides. It was evident to foreign correspondents who ventured outside Seoul that the average Korean didn't worry too much about the resumption of relations with Japan if it tended to improve his lot.[26] The cry of opposition politicians that the United States had pushed Korea into the arms of Japan did not make a great impression in the countryside, regardless of how much disorder it caused in Seoul.

Partly, this could be attributed to indifference to political attitudes in Seoul; partly, also, to a basic lack of communication. But a curious mixture of beliefs about the meaning of democratic government was also involved. One study project showed that more than two-thirds of students and others questioned in Seoul believed that the authority of a democratic government comes from the people; however, of the rural sample that responded to the same question, 42 per cent said they believed that under a basic principle of democracy, "the government decides what is best." Moreover, only one-third of the rural respondents held that the people were the ultimate authority in a democratic government.[27]

Hyo-chai Lee, professor of sociology at Ewha Women's University, concluded that the pressure of economic problems and low living standards seemed to overshadow concern with democratic ideals. He warned, "As long as the economic problems are not solved and the people's economic needs are not satisfactorily met, there is always the danger of totalitarian forces taking over the government." [28]

There were few places in Asia where the revolution of rising expectations dominated the public mind to a greater extent than it did in South Korea, where it meant more to many than freedom of the press. At a seminar in American studies, Chi Ho Lew, a political reporter for *Hankook Ilbo,* remarked:

> I believe as long as the emerging nations and policy makers consider the freedom of the press as an idealistic good concept, it has a danger to aggravate already unstable conditions. I do not mean that the concept of the freedom of the press is inhibiting economic progress. What I do mean is that this concept should be realistically appraised and the needs of the emerging nations considered realistically.[29]

At the rates fixed by the government in 1964 for Korean journalists, the lack of enthusiasm for a press conducted in the Western tradition was understandable. Reporters received the equivalent of $24 a month as beginners and $40 a month at the end of two years. An experienced journalist could hope to earn $68 to $76 a month.[30] At that, the rates for journalists were said to be better than those of a number of government officials, which was one explanation for the continuing preoccupation with charges of corruption.

In view of the prevalent attitudes and beliefs, and the political and economic conditions that helped give rise to them, it is no wonder that thoughtful American editors were concerned because the permanent correspondents who represented almost all foreign news organizations in South Korea in the mid-1960's were Korean nationals. This was no reflection on the Koreans. It would have been difficult to find better-qualified correspondents in Seoul than the wire-service locals, all fluent in English, and the handful of locals who served the American staff men who flew in now and then from Japan.

Had the coverage of Korea been as little subject to pressure as coverage of Sweden or the Netherlands, there would have been no problem about the use of locals as heads of bureaus. But the government in Seoul could play rough at times and officials could use pressure tactics, with or without the knowledge of their superiors. One of the locals was threatened with vague disciplinary measures during the coverage of the 1964 riots. Government agents regularly inquired into their sources. All of them had to be careful of whatever they wrote. They knew, of course, that the American embassy would be able to do very little for them if they did happen to get into trouble. In fact, most of them felt that they were not given the same treatment as the visiting American correspondents by either the embassy or the military headquarters, which was obviously true.

The position of the locals was made still more difficult by the unfamiliarity of their government with the way American news organizations worked. For instance, one local told with some amusement how he had been approached and promised anything he wished in return for a publicity splurge on President Park in the American press. He had to explain, without giving offense, that the Americans didn't operate in the same way that a section of the Asian press did. Other locals told of subtle methods of intimidation practiced by government agents, who warned the locals' friends or their families after stories unfavorable to Korea had appeared in the United States. Many in government evidently could not believe that the local man would not have a hand in the editorial position adopted by a great newspaper on some Korean issue.

There were many things that locals could do, of course, which were beyond the powers of any American, no matter how well versed he might have been in Korean affairs. They were in a far better position to evaluate honestly the extent to which the Korean press encouraged student riots, something the government implicitly believed. But they couldn't write much about it, except in veiled terms. There was also very little about the probity and trustworthiness of government officials that they did not know; however, once again, it was scarcely a subject for which it was worth while to risk a career.

The Korean journalists were proud of the trust that was reposed in them. From 1962 on, they had a monopoly on the day-to-day coverage for foreign news organizations, with only one or two exceptions. Most of them were well paid by Korean standards (one first-rate correspondent received $66 a month). Several insisted that they had suffered no interference of any kind, but they were the exceptions. All of them realized that they could expect the Americans to come flying from Tokyo for any major story. They also knew that the American embassy had sought without success to convince AP and UPI that American correspondents should be stationed in Seoul on a full-time basis. But, like Reuters and Agence France-Presse, the American agencies relied on locals as a matter of practical operation. It was manifestly impossible to cover every important point on the globe without the generous use of local correspondents.

Even those American editors and diplomats who had the most doubts about this practice could not change matters perceptibly. The wire services, in particular, stoutly protested their faith in the locals and their readiness to send in American correspondents at short notice whenever they were needed. As a result, a kind of accommodation was reached. With or without instructions, locals in Seoul generally confined themselves to verifiable factual material and were cautious about interpretation. Their American editors accepted the consequences, knowing that a critical report by a local could not be expected.

At best, the spreading use of local correspondents in Seoul and elsewhere in Asia and the sale of wire services to various Asian governments produced a growing amount of "down-the-middle" reporting—give both sides and stay out of trouble. As one wire-service director for Asia conceded with becoming frankness, "It is a ticklish thing to sell services to governments, and everybody is aware of it because all wire agencies have clients among governments." It was no less ticklish to place a formidable burden on local correspondents when they could be made subject to pressure by their governments.

For those who had faith in the local correspondents' ability to withstand undue influence, there was a modicum of encouragement in the attitude of a tough old Korean editor. Asked how he could resist his government on a key issue, he smiled grimly and said, "The Japanese were here for 40 years and they put me in jail three times because they didn't like what I published. I have learned how far I can go with any dictator." [31]

Syngman Rhee, the old Korean patriot who died in exile at the age of ninety, would have understood such an attitude. Because of the people who carried on indomitably in that spirit, Korea was once more a land of promise. The conclusion of the Japan–South Korea Treaty and its ratification by the National Assembly in Seoul and the Japanese Diet at the end of 1965 was a landmark of progress. Depite an opposition boycott and a certain amount of student rioting, the Park government surmounted the test. [32]

American and Japanese capital increased in South Korea. The Europeans also were encouraged to invest. An efficient textile industry flourished, turning out well-made clothes. The Korea Electric Co., a state monopoly, had a surplus of power. Three large cement plants were turning out road and building materials. More fertilizer plants were opening up. The government was encouraging the production of everything from nylon to the mining of silver and gold in cooperation with foreign enterprise.

In the southern port city of Pusan, now a metropolis of 1.4 million, foreign shipping was being attracted, and the Korean fishing industry was showing sturdy growth. And at nearby Ulsan, visualized as a "Pittsburgh" of the future, the new Korea Oil Company refinery was turning out close to 35,000 barrels of oil a day. Five new plants were being built there, and a steel mill and iron foundry were in the planning stage. In 1965, exports rose to a record $170 million a year, and

South Korea was ready for an economic takeoff.[33] It was a pity that so little of this story was known to Americans who were then preoccupied with the defense of still another Asian nation torn apart by Communist attacks. For if the war in South Viet-Nam was the challenge to the United States, the hard-won truce in South Korea was the hope.

3. OKINAWA: THE BILLION-DOLLAR BASE

The Japanese press flocked to interview a new U.S. High Commissioner for Okinawa when he reached Tokyo in the summer of 1964. The official, Lieutenant General Albert Watson, II, former commanding general in Berlin, was prepared for cross-examination, for the Japanese were determined to seek "reversion"—the return of Okinawa and the rest of the Ryukyu Islands to Japanese rule. What he scarcely expected was to be questioned about the views of an American reporter, Rafael Steinberg, special correspondent of the Washington *Post,* who had done a critical series of articles on Okinawa that spring.

For anybody who was concerned with Okinawa in either the American or Japanese governments at that particular time, the Steinberg series was required reading.[34] It was highly opinionated. It was controversial. In some respects, it was even sensational. It struck so hard at the autocratic quality of American military rule by General Watson's predecessor, Lieutenant General Paul W. Caraway, that some of his friends suspected the whole business had been a put-up job inspired by the State Department. It wasn't. The responsible official who had sent Steinberg to his destination was Alfred Friendly, then the managing editor of the Washington *Post*. If anything, the reaction to the series at State was even more unhappy than at the Pentagon.

Steinberg, a 1950 Harvard graduate with a decade of service in the Far East for INS, *Newsweek,* the *Saturday Evening Post,* and others, had made an issue out of Okinawa. He wasn't alone. Others had written about the island's troubles, but not with the kind of exposure that Steinberg's pieces received in the nation's capital. Even one of the constantly orbiting television correspondents in the Far East had touched down at Okinawa and inquired breathlessly, so the story went, "How can we show that Okinawa is becoming another Panama?"

The subject was sensitive to begin with. As Robert Eunson, of the AP pointed out, the billion-dollar installation on Okinawa was "believed to be Uncle Sam's most important nuclear weapons base in the Far East, 15 minutes as the new jets fly from China." [35] Steinberg wrote more delicately, explaining that Okinawa was vital "because the Army,

Air Force and Navy can freely deploy here, or to here, whatever weapons and forces they may need in any emergency without any government's permission." [36]

The point was crucial. For if Okinawa won home rule and if eventually it reverted to Japan, then the United States would no longer be able to keep nuclear weapons there or use the area as a troop staging area for the Viet-Nam war without the agreement of the Japanese. By invoking the United States–Japan Mutual Security Treaty, the Japanese would have a voice in the military uses of Okinawa and Japanese public opinion would certainly see that it was heard.

Okinawa therefore presented its new High Commissioner with a difficult set of alternatives. If he measurably weakened the American military authority on the island, he endangered the effectiveness of the U.S. armed forces in the Far East. If he continually interfered with the attainment of a greater measure of autonomy by the Okinawans, he increased the hostility of the populace and also raised an even greater threat to the success of his mission. General Watson therefore had to be something more than an efficient military governor and a first-rate administrator, the outstanding qualities of his predecessor, General Caraway. He had to be a diplomat, as well. In consequence, he listened carefully to the Japanese in Tokyo and their amplification of the Steinberg charges before proceeding to his new assignment.

The lines of conflict had been drawn long before his arrival. Okinawa and the sixty-three other islands of the Ryukyu chain, with a total population of about 1 million, came under American military rule in 1945 with the end of the Pacific war, an arrangement that was confirmed by the Japanese peace treaty. The 67-mile-long island, about one-quarter the size of Rhode Island, was turned into an armed camp, albeit a beneficent one. Its 758,000 people, subordinated to the requirements of the 100,000 or so American troops normally stationed at the bases there, keenly felt their separation from their homeland, despite the boom conditions that came with the American occupation.

It was a situation made to order for agitators. In addition to the patriots who drummed on the theme of reunion with Japan, there also were leftists who were not at all sorry when overheated partisans lay down on the runways of Okinawa bases to keep American aircraft from landing. That happened in 1955, but the Okinawa courts sensibly handled the cases with a minimum of fuss. For those Japanese who remembered a time when Okinawans had been discriminated against in the home islands to almost as great an extent as the Koreans, the end to nationalist sentiment in the Ryukyus must have been a surprise—and a relief. A separatist movement in Okinawa, under pre-1941 conditions in the Ryukyus, could have been a lively possibility; however, now that some

Americans were covertly attempting to stimulate it, the Ryukyuans simply weren't interested. To the native population, seemingly, everything depended on whose hands bore aloft the banner of dissent from the established order. Now, without question, the Japanese were favored.

The Kennedy Administration recognized that there was a problem in Okinawa—which at least represented an advance over its predecessors. After a study by a special Presidential commission and a visit to the island by Attorney General Robert F. Kennedy, the hopes of the Ryukyans rose. On March 19, 1962, President Kennedy inaugurated a new policy with the symbolic statement: "I recognize the Ryukyus to be a part of the Japanese homeland." He also authorized increased American economic aid and called for the opening of negotiations with Japan to boost Japanese assistance to the Ryukyus as well. What the Ryukyuans and the Japanese both tended to overlook, however, was his emphasis on the "military imperative," as he called it, for continued American rule of the Ryukyus.

The net result, as it turned out, was a shattering disappointment to those on Okinawa who had visualized full autonomy and a speed-up in reversion to Japan. Worse than that, General Caraway, who had an almost fatal predisposition to use unfortunate phrasing, called autonomy for the Ryukyus a "myth." He also publicly branded the Okinawans as irresponsible, charged that they wouldn't accept authority, and that in consequence he would give them none.

While recognizing the military necessity that made the needs of the armed forces paramount on Okinawa, the indignant Steinberg wrote in his Washington *Post* series:

Democracy in the Ryukyus is a sham . . . and the people resent it . . . Although the 32,000 jobs the bases provide, armed forces construction and off-base spending by troops have brought a considerable measure of prosperity to the islands, many Okinawans believe that they would have been better off sharing Japan's phenomenal economic growth without the base income, although they admit that any sudden shutting of the bases now would cause serious economic dislocation.[37]

This was his principal finding. He justified it by using the complaints of the Okinawan leaders at considerable length, thus amplifying their distant voices through the agency of one of the most influential newspapers of America. The High Commissioner's tendency to act as the sole authority on the island in all matters, including some far outside the military province, had been the subject of other unfavorable comments for some time. It was no secret that the State Department, in the interests of maintaining good relationships with Japan, had been trying discreetly to interest the Pentagon in giving the Okinawan authorities and legislature more power in nonsecurity matters. Here, without doubt, Steinberg was on firm ground.

But like so many passionate crusaders in journalism, he unnecessarily weakened his case by describing what he called "luxury living" by the military on Okinawa and making much of the clubs, swimming pools, and other facilities, often built out of nonappropriated funds to ease the monotony of military life. Such devices cost the taxpayers little or nothing and served to cut down the civilian-incident rate (fighting with local civilians in bars and elsewhere) and to raise the re-enlistment rate. As for "luxury living," this was an unjustifiable reference mainly to the well-stocked PX's selling at low prices, without which many a large military family simply could not make both ends meet. However, the military had long since come to recognize that the few pleasant features of their monotonous peacetime existence invariably provoked any correspondent who was looking for a story. These were low blows.

But in remarking on the rising tension between white and Negro GI's in their off-the-base hours, Steinberg once again was on firm ground. Emerson Chapin, of the New York *Times,* two months before, had pointed out that the Old Koza section of Koza City, second largest urban area in Okinawa, had become "a racially segregated area frequented almost entirely by United States Negro servicemen in civilian clothes." [38] It was not a tolerable situation, which both correspondents were well justified in discussing at length, since the military was paying so little attention to it.

Perhaps the most controversial part of the Steinberg series, in the opinion of the government agencies concerned, was his evaluation of what he called a "feud" between the Defense Department and the State Department over Okinawa. It appalled the top administrators of both. As is so often the case in government, any official in Washington or at the American embassy in Tokyo who was asked to discuss the matter hastily denied that any differences existed. That was manifestly untrue. In the development of foreign policy at the highest government levels, it is not only necessary but desirable that departmental representatives speak their minds when they have differing objectives. Any correspondent of knowledge and sophistication knew that such differences inevitably existed and disregarded the denials.

Steinberg's reporting charged more than that. He wrote: "So bitter is the feud between State Department and the military over the question of Okinawa that the High Commissioner . . . withholds important information from the U.S. Embassy in Tokyo, and Embassy officials have been known to exaggerate grossly reports of the military's autocratic rule." [39]

How true was it? Obviously, the military wouldn't say, but Howard McClellan, president of the American Chamber of Commerce on Okinawa, made this comment even before the publication of the Steinberg series: "Sometimes, it seems the United States State Department is working for the Japanese." [40] Certainly, there was bitterness among the Americans on Okinawa and some of it affected intergovernmental relations. But other correspondents scarcely characterized the situation as a "bitter . . . feud."

American officials frequently argued, before and after the Steinberg series, that the Okinawans' desire for reversion was a figment of the journalistic imagination. Yet, other able correspondents who visited Okinawa found little evidence to document the official position. Norman Sklarewitz, of the *Wall Street Journal,* and Robert Eunson, of the AP, both spoke with Okinawans through interpreters and found that a majority of those questioned favored reversion. [41]

"The Associated Press talked to at least a dozen responsible Ryukyuan persons, young and old," Eunson wrote. "Every one of them favored 'reversion' but stipulated, 'When the time comes.' It was granted that certain Ryukyuans had done better under the Americans than they would have under the Japanese. This small minority would oppose reversion." [42]

Okinawa, in this manner, became a classic example of the tensions between government and the press that inevitably affect the making of foreign policy and its execution. A complicating factor here was the rigidity of the military administration and the anxiety of the State Department to do something to appease the growing restiveness of the populace and of the Japanese press and government. It should not be assumed that the Okinawans had as little means of communication as, for example, the Koreans. On the island were no fewer than fifteen daily newspapers, with a total daily circulation of 281,000, an average of 34.8 copies for each 100 people; two privately owned and commercially operated radio stations and a powerful Voice of America transmitter; two privately owned and commercially operated television stations; and a U.S. Air Force television station at Kadena Air Base. With the exception of the American government operations and the small Okinawa *Morning Star,* everything was in Japanese and such pieces as Steinberg's therefore were widely circulated and discussed. AP, UPI, and Kyodo brought news into Okinawa and took it out. [43]

Within a short time after the Steinberg series, the Okinawan discontent reached a critical point. On June 10, 1964, the Ryukyu Legislature approved a resolution calling for the assent of the American military government to expanded self-government on Okinawa. The legislators complained that General Caraway had interfered in such nonmilitary matters as control over the sale of sleeping pills, establishment of a public water works in Miyako Island, assessment of taxes on mackerel pike, and enforcement of stricter controls on travel to the mainland. Seisaku Ohta, the chief executive of the Ryukyu Islands by American appointment, resigned, as did his deputy and other administrators. The Japan *Times* reported the Okinawan government was "on the verge of paralysis."

The newspaper went on: "The widespread discontent of the people threatens to flare up into an anti-U.S. base campaign. The Japanese Communist Party, closing ranks with the Okinawa People's Party, is already moving to stir up such a movement both in Japan and in Okinawa." [44] The *Mainichi Daily News* warned also against an anti-American campaign that could "flare throughout this island group." [45] And George F. Kennan, who happened to be in Japan at the time, took up the cudgels for the State Department against the military, saying, "All one could ask is that the American military authorities bear in mind that the fate of the Okinawans is something to which Japanese opinion is extremely sensitive." [46]

With such advice dinning in his ears from Japanese and American sources, each for different reasons, General Watson within a year moved to consolidate the power of the conservative forces on Okinawa. Despite a demonstration by 5,000 leftists, the Okinawa legislature proceeded in the fall with the nomination of a new chief executive in Naha, Seiho Matsuoka, a sixty-eight-year-old American-educated businessman, who was quickly accepted by the High Commissioner. He served by appointment until March 16, 1966, when the same legislature elected him to become the chief executive of the Ryukyus for a three-year term. Upon his inauguration a week later, he said:

"The United States administrators should be just a small advisory body instead of running our government for us. But from the American point of view, I can see how it is desirable to keep civil and military jurisdiction in the same hands." [47]

Okinawa also became involved in continuing Japanese agitation for the return of the Kurile Islands from Russian sovereignty. The Russians had agreed to return the Habomai and Shikotan groups off northern Hokkaido, but only upon the conclusion of a Japanese peace treaty and nullification of the Mutual Security Treaty with the United States. When the Chinese Communists joined Japan in demanding the return to Tokyo's rule of the Kunashiri and Eterofu Islands in the Kuriles,

Moscow grimly proposed to consider it when the United States gave up Okinawa.

The expanding war in Viet-Nam put an end to such unrealistic talk. Okinawa became the main American logistical base for operations in Viet-Nam. More than 350,000 types of items were stocked in its great warehouses. In the Machinato service area alone, 5,000 Okinawans worked with 4,000 American soldiers to keep the war supplies moving. By sea and air, the material flowed out to Quinhon, Nhatrang, Vungtau, Camranh Bay, and Saigon. In a single month in 1966, for example, 167,000 tons of war matériel were dispatched from Okinawa by sea in heavily loaded trailers that were rolled on and rolled off the transports. In the same month, 6 million pounds of high-priority military items were flown from the big Naha base to Viet-Nam. Without Okinawa, clearly, the United States would have been hard-pressed to supply its growing forces in the Southeast Asia zone of combat.

The Japanese Socialists and the Communists felt that it was to their advantage to keep a continual storm brewing over this strategic use of Okinawa. When American B-52 bombers used the base upon returning from one of their many raids in Viet-Nam, the Socialists made a major issue of it. The result was that the raiding B-52's were thenceforth denied the use of Okinawa. However, when Premier Sato flew in from Tokyo on a three-day visit soon afterward, he made it clear that early reversion of the Ryukyus to Japan was out of the question. The only concession he made to leftist demonstrators was to cancel an inspection of American military bases. He pledged increased Japanese aid for the islands, which scarcely satisfied the champions of reversion.

The indirect election of Matsuoka as the Ryukyuan chief executive was the only major concession made by General Watson, despite the increasing protests. In doing so, he did not really yield any authority to a civilian regime, however. While the threat of a major confrontation between the United States and the Communist world hung over Asia, it was unlikely that the American position would change.[48]

More demonstrations were probable and even firmer American counter-measures were likely in a war situation. It was not a time when autonomy for Okinawa could be realistically considered. However, that did not invalidate some of the findings of Steinberg and his fellow correspondents; nor did it settle the interdepartmental differences between Americans and the arguments of the American business community against the State Department. Except for friendly gestures toward eventual autonomy and a more sympathetic administrative posture, there was little that Americans could promise either to the Okinawans or the Japanese. The settlement of the future of Okinawa, like the future of many another controversial area in Asia, awaited the coming of a generation that was more likely to be able to achieve a genuine peace in the Pacific.

4. THE CHANGING PHILIPPINES

A bronze Pulitzer Prize plaque—the only one outside the United States—decorates the entrance to the home of the Philippines *Herald*. It memorializes the achievements of the most distinguished of its former editors in the days of American sovereignty, Carlos P. Romulo, who in 1941 returned from an Asian tour with a prediction that Japan was on the verge of a Pacific war that it would lose and that Asian peoples, in the process, would rid themselves of Western imperialism. For the series of articles in which he elaborated on his findings, General Romulo won the Pulitzer award for foreign correspondence in 1942.

The plaque is something more than a memento.[49] It is a graphic reminder of the Philippines of another day—the era of the "little brown brother" of the United States. Today, awkward and somewhat angular as he strikes a new nationalistic pose, the Filipino is searching for identity with his fellow Asians no less anxiously than the Japanese, the Koreans, the Malaysians, the Indians, and all their neighbors. Particularly in Manila, because of the long history of alliance and friendship between the Philippines and the United States, the Filipino intellectual is made to feel almost guilty because of the slenderness of his Asian association. In his mind's eye, he sees a new kind of magic arising from what he speaks of vaguely as an Asian community of interest. Yet, all the while, he knows perfectly well that he cannot shed overnight an intellectual commitment shaped by four centuries of Western association.

Certainly, to the Filipino, there is an importance in being Asian. It means that he is no longer the "little brown brother"—the term used by anti-American columnists to characterize the views of their opponents —but has grown up. He feels that he must make an effort to treat with the United States now on equal terms, or face the jeers of his fellow Asians. Even Romulo, the sturdy American comrade-in-arms of other days, the last man off Corregidor, the first Asian president of the U.N. General Assembly, has felt the force of the change.

Almost a quarter of a century after his Pulitzer Prize journey, he returned to his alma mater, the University of the Philippines, as its president. "The Western reporter who writes of the Filipinos as the most Westernized of Asians utters a half truth," he said. "The reporter has accurately described his clothes, but he has subsumed, under a wrong category, the memories and manners and even prejudices of his subject. He has mistaken an aspect of appearance for total truth." [50]

Despite the Filipino's liking for American clothes, music, dancing, and movies, his proficiency and sometimes even his genius in the use of old-fashioned oratorical English, there was no doubt whatever that his attitudes were changing. That was to be expected. What was confusing to those in the United States who thought of the Philippines as an Asian extension of America was the growth of a different kind of influence among a reckless and irresponsible Filipino minority of varying political attachments. At one extreme were the unbridled nationalists, including some of the columnists of the Filipino press who received extraordinary license to write anti-American commentaries. At the other were the tattered remnants of the underground Communist Party, outlawed since 1957, and its surviving front groups, which operated among students, labor, and farm organizations. In between were a variety of malcontents whose loyalties were blurred.

Together, these disparate elements often created dismay among the government leaders and the substantial Filipino majority which valued its ties to the United States. For when the propagandists made common cause, they could produce an impression of rampant anti-Americanism that was plastered across the press of the United States. It was still true, unfortunately, that conflict generally was of greater news value than good will and any fly-by-night anti-American agitator abroad knew how easily he could take advantage of the American press by exploiting this weakness.

In one such adventure, a little-known Filipino and groups calling themselves Patriotic Youth and an Association of Free Labor Unions burned a cardboard "Uncle Sam" outside the American Embassy in Manila in 1965. It was a sensation, attracting a crowd of 5,000. The demonstrators held signs such as "Go Home Whites," "Death To U.S. Imperialism," and "Yankee Go Home." They carried coffins to symbolize the Filipinos who had been shot and killed as looters by American and Filipino security police since 1952 at Clark Air Base and the Subic Bay Naval Station, both American installations. [51]

There was ground for Filipino concern over the fatal shooting of two Filipino trespassers, which had touched off this and other demonstrations. But the presence of armed guards at every large business building and apartment house in Manila and the patrolling of the Manila Hotel at night by private guards with rifles showed that there was a problem which affected Filipinos and Americans alike. It could scarcely be solved by a storm of outrage in the Filipino press, which only helped provoke riots at home and somewhat less than sympathetic press comment in the United States.

After one such Filipino demonstration during Indonesia's flirtation with Communist China, *U.S. News & World Report* carried a headline: "WHY FILIPINOS TURN AGAINST U.S." Nor was the opening of its article on the subject much more restrained:

> Dig for the real story behind the latest anti-American outbreak here in the Philippines and the role of Indonesia's President Sukarno soon becomes evident.
>
> Filipino firebrands sparked a mass protest late in December demanding that the U.S. give up its military bases in the Philippines.
>
> But it was Indonesian money, poured into some sectors of the Philippine press, that created the wave of anti-Americanism which culminated in the big demonstration at Angeles, near Clark Air Base, a U.S. installation . . .

It was only in the body of the article that the alarmed American reader learned the anti-American Filipinos were a "noisy minority" and that the bases were in no danger. "Most Filipinos," the article pointed out, "are intensely anti-Communist and have a deep fear of Red China. They know they are in no position to shoulder the burden of their own defense. Then, too, U.S. military spending is the fifth biggest 'industry' in the Philippines . . ." [52]

Despite the exaggerated headline, the presence of a certain amount of anti-American feeling, the influence of the press in promoting it, and the contributing role of corruption were not figments of the imagination.

The press was important in shaping public opinion in the Philippines. Diosdado Macapagal, while president, kept abreast of what the Filipino press was saying about him by reading cabled extracts sent at considerable expense whenever he was away on a trip. The American embassy, too, went on reading and worrying even though it deplored what it called the excesses of some of the newspapers in their discussions of Filipino-American relations. As for corruption, that was no special Filipino press problem, as was pointed out by Macario T. Vicencio, of the Manila *Times,* the president of the National Association of Philippine Journalists, and secretary general of the Asia Press Organization. In a general discussion of the extent to which an Asian press could be considered free, he wrote:

> The Asian journalist is generally underpaid and overworked. This increases his vulnerability to corruption, and the seekers of power quite naturally try to manipulate this potent source of influence.
>
> In the Philippines, where newspapers command large audiences, politi-

cians and businessmen on the make avidly court the reporter, the columnist and the editor. Charges of press corruption have often been aired, most seriously by the Administration itself during the recent Stonehill scandal. In this particular case, the journalists' organization challenged the accusers to produce evidence—which they failed to do. But we of the Philippines press would be foolishly idealistic if we believed that all of us can equally resist these blandishments at all times.[53]

Regardless of motivation, the strength of the Indonesian campaign in a portion of the Philippine press led the conservative Manila *Bulletin* at one stage to chide "some segments of the press friendly to the Indonesians, some government officials antagonistic to the U.S., and others openly active in promoting closer relationships with Indonesia . . ." The editorial went on:

President Macapagal has cited time and again the imperatives of regional cooperation in efforts mutually beneficial, without impairment of special ties of affection and consideration that bind the American and Filipino peoples.

If there have been deviations from these norms, as in the case of some government officials who have aroused suspicions of their motivations for according preferential treatment to Indonesians while treating Americans like strangers and intruders, such could not have been compliance with superior orders. . . . Let us not, while seeking new friends, ditch old ones. That would be tragic in its short-sightedness.[54]

To these and other appeals, J. V. Cruz, a columnist of the Manila *Times,* retorted with a protest against "the unceasing campaign to cow and intimidate Filipinos saying anything favorable about Indonesia and the Indonesians." He accounted the number of Filipino admirers of the United States as "awesome" and their pro-Indonesian opponents as few, and concluded:

It may yet be some time before most Filipinos can view the Indonesians, who are their fellow Malays and Asians, through Filipino eyes rather than through American or British or Australian or Dutch-colored glasses. And so tales of an Indonesian lobby, gleefully fanned by all the Westerners who hate Sukarno's guts and by America's little brown brothers, to whom his fierce nationalism and intense patriotism is a standing insult, will persist.

Yes, Virginia, there is an Indonesian lobby. And you don't have to look far for it—it exists right there in your colonial mentality.[55]

The journalistic infighting reached such a low point that Cruz attacked Mauro Mendez, Secretary of Foreign Affairs at the time, and also one of the most distinguished of Filipino journalists, as "Field Marshal von Mendez" for suggesting Philippine aid for the United States in Viet-Nam. To this, Nestor Mata, columnist of the pro-American Philippines *Herald*, responded with some equally pointed criticism of "fanatical anti-American nationalists in our midst" and an observation that the Foreign Secretary "is tickled pink by references to his being a 'Field Marshal' by some joker." [56]

The Filipino press exercised its undoubted freedom, certainly, but the evidence did not indicate a similar devotion to the tenets of public responsibility at all times. Caught in the middle of such an immoderate situation, President Macapagal told the National Press Club in Manila that he preferred a "licentious press to a bridled one." To which Macario Vicencio added bluntly: "Where the press allows itself to be manipulated in the service of foreign interests or a privileged class, it will not find defenders among its audience." [57]

Despite its influence with Philippine policy-makers and its sometimes unsettling effect on Philippine-American relations, the press actually did not penetrate very deeply into a nation of 30 million spread over a 7,000-island archipelago with a total land area slightly larger than that of Arizona. The 22 daily newspapers, most of them in Manila, had a total circulation of only a little more than 500,000, or less than 2 copies for each 100 people by UNESCO standards. Of these, six English-language newspapers in Manila accounted for 329,000 and a single newspaper, the Manila *Times*, had almost as much circulation (156,791) as its four principal rivals put together. The four Chinese-, two Tagalog-, and one Spanish-language paper in Manila had relatively little influence by comparison.

As in Korea, word of mouth and radio transmission both accounted for a greater part of the news-communication process in the Philippines than did the press. There were 120 radio transmitters and 600,000 receivers concentrated mostly on the eleven main islands of the archipelago and five television transmitters, mostly press-owned, with 150,000 receivers. The U.S. armed forces had their own radio-TV systems, and the Voice of America ran a Philippine transmitter, too.[58]

Joaquin P. ("Chino") Roces, editor and publisher of the Manila *Times* and associated papers, was the dominant force in Filipino journalism in the 1960's. He had many ties with the United States, but he could be one of the sharpest critics of American policy and of his own government's actions as well.[59] On the *Times* he permitted free expression for the views of both pro- and anti-American columnists, arguing that he wanted his newspaper to be independent and to represent all prevailing opinions. His success, particularly with the elite group that ran the nation, indicated there was considerable support for his position. It was generally believed in Manila that his newspapers alone were able to pay their own way.

The Philippines *Herald,* second largest newspaper, with 42,000 circulation, was part of the widespread Soriano industrial empire founded by Andres Soriano, Sr., an American citizen and Filipino war hero who died in the United States in 1964.[60] His son, Andres, Jr., and P. K. Macker, an American journalist who served as general manager, made the *Herald* the firmest supporter of the United States in the Philippines. The Manila *Chronicle,* the third largest newspaper, with 41,000 circulation, was owned by the Lopez sugar interests and run by Oscar Lopez, its thirty-four-year-old publisher with a master's degree from Harvard, who could take a waspish view of American political and economic positions. Colonel Hans Menzi, another industrialist who had become a Filipino, ran the only other paper with influence, the Manila *Bulletin,* which had 34,000 circulation.

The state of Philippine journalism and its comparative lack of progress with a mass public caused these publishers and their principal associates to found the Philippine Press Institute (PPI) in 1965 to undertake needed reforms. With Carlos P. Romulo as the chairman of the board and Juan L. Mercado, of the Manila *Evening News,* as the director, the PPI's objective was to improve the status of journalism as a profession and win greater respect for it in the society. Nobody connected with the organization had any illusions about the size of the task. As one publisher remarked frankly, in discussing the major problem of ridding the press of corrupt influences, "I hope something can be done, but it may already be too late to institute the kind of reforms that are needed." [61]

Among the Filipinos there were first-rate journalists, some of whom held advanced degrees from American universities. They had proved themselves, not only as editors and managers, but as foreign correspondents for American, British, and French news agencies, newspapers, and magazines. There was no question here of lack of ability. What both the publishers and the journalists really were talking about, when they worried about the basic honesty of some of their colleagues, was the insecurity of the newspaper business—as a business—in the Philippines. There wasn't much encouragement for the average Filipino journalist to be interested in the "elevation of standards," always a vague term, when the going rates for a good professional on a Filipino newspaper were the equivalent of $125 to $200 a month, and a stringer for a major American news organization was given only $25 or $50 a month for his services.

There were many reasons why the Filipino press was having a difficult time, but the most obvious one was the earning power of the average Filipino, which did not exceed $150 a year. As P. K. Macker pointed out, that put even a cheap commodity such as a newspaper outside the reach of the average Filipino. He also blamed substandard literacy (although at 75 per cent, the Philippines rated high in Asia), lack of a cheap newsprint supply, and the rivalry of radio and television with the press.

By contrast with the press, the future of the electronic media was bright. "These two media, requiring less formal education to enjoy and appreciate, will undoubtedly make the most highly accelerated gains in audience," Macker said, speaking as the manager of three TV stations. "This is particularly true with the advent of transistor-powered radios and television sets, making the availability of hydroelectric power to operate them unnecessary." [62] However, Filipino journalists generally were contemptuous of the quality of the news programs that were offered on television and saw little hope for a change. Radio reached more people in more languages.

As was the case elsewhere, television was an amusement and advertising medium and demonstrated little sense of public responsibility. The most popular programs came from the United States—"Suspense Theatre," "The Defenders," "Twilight Zone," "The Walt Disney Show," "Perry Mason," and, of course, the old movies, particularly the old World War II shows. American comedy and the "America-I-love-you" material were not for Filipino audiences. They were even beginning to weary of Westerns, and they were dead set against repeat shows.[63]

Despite all its handicaps, the Philippine press vigorously exercised its function as a watchdog of the public's business. Ramon Mabutas, in the Philippines Herald, ran a series on "How To Stop Congress Cheating," in which he condemned the "smuggling, railroading and irregular passage of laws" and general malpractice of the legislative function.[64] Maximo V. Soliven, in the Manila Times, told how the sale of contraband American cigarettes was carried on openly at the customhouse, and how customs agents, some earning less than the equivalent of $40 a month, were driving new American cars, including a Cadillac.[65] Despite his ownership of the Manila Evening News and his other associations with the press that were continuing sources of embarrassment, all the newspapers jumped on the affairs of Harry Stonehill, the ex-GI from Chicago who became a Filipino millionaire and was deported because of his tax dealings.

The Philippines press did a great deal of editorial writing about its Asian identity; but, aside from the Viet-Nam war and the ever-present problem of Communist China, it published comparatively little news of other Asian countries. It used generous amounts of news of the United States, particularly of the personalities in politics and entertainment who were known to Filipinos, and all the familiar American features and comics from "Peanuts" to "Mutt and Jeff." But for a cosmopolitan press, it leaned heavily on the social activities of a comparatively small group of influential upper-strata Filipinos of a rather tightly knit establishment. In make-up and pictorial presentation, the newspapers would have been accepted without hesitation in any medium-sized American city.

The volatile nature of the press and the multiplicity of its problems reflected to a large extent the transitional era through which the Philippines was passing in the 1960's. As the beneficiary of $1.8 billion in American foreign aid from 1949 through 1963, the young nation was still too dependent on the United States to suit its leaders. By a treaty concluded a year after the Philippines became independent on July 4, 1946, the United States had ninety-nine-year leases on fifteen army bases and naval "operating areas" in the new nation. But the United States also assumed the responsibility for defending the islands against outside attack; even the most nationalistic of Filipinos recognized their essential weakness militarily. It was with the help of American arms that President Ramon Magsaysay was able in 1954 to crush the Communist-led Hukbalahap rebellion, which had been in progress since 1945. And in 1965, when the Huk threat was reviving in sections of western Luzon, American support again was necessary as Filipino troops faced the difficult prospect of hunting down 10,000 armed terrorists who were using Viet-Cong tactics in the Pampanga villages.[66]

The Magsaysay administration tried hard to lift the Philippines out of a rut. One of its achievements was the Laurel-Langley economic agreement, signed in Washington in 1954 and put into effect two years later. It was intended to point the new republic toward economic independence and stimulate its economic growth, but it achieved only minimal gains and did not solve the main problem—stagnation of trade. While the United States remained the chief trading partner of the islands, their American imports declined from 70 per cent of the total in 1956 to 41 per cent in 1964. Moreover, while Filipino foreign trade increased 51 per cent in those eight years from $893 million to $1,345 million, the U.S. share of the total declined from 64 per cent to 23 per cent. Japanese trade for that period, however, increased from 9 per cent to 21 per cent, or $303 million.[67]

Where the United States retained its trade advantage was in the consumption of 70 per cent of the Filipino sugar output, an average annually of 1.2 million tons, which compensated for the loss of Cuban sugar. Moreover, American business almost exclusively consumed the Filipino output of such products as cordage, cocoanut oil, plywood, and filler tobacco and stimulated such new industries as electrical goods, home appliances, drugs, foodstuffs, and construction materials. Bernardino Ronquillo, a financial specialist, warned: "Although it has been the policy of all administrations [in the Philippines] to attract foreign, especially American, capital, there has lately been fear that too heavy an inflow of such funds will make it difficult for Filipinos to compete with the experienced and financially powerful American corporations." [68] The road to economic independence was long and hard. It would take more than devaluation of the peso, a land-reform law, and good will for the Philippines to earn prosperity.

The Philippines changed in other ways. Its leaders, unwilling to celebrate their independence on the American Independence Day, changed it to June 12, the date when the islands declared their independence of Spain in 1898. Dewey Boulevard vanished from the maps of Manila, although the doughty old Admiral could scarcely be expunged from Filipino history. While 75 per cent of Filipinos retained their Roman Catholic faith, a heritage of Spanish rule from the sixteenth to the end of the nineteenth century, only about 500,000 persons still were able to speak Spanish. As for English, after less than a half-century of American sovereignty, 60 per cent of the people did not understand it. Moreover, referring to the 50,000 students graduated annually from Filipino colleges and universities, one educator said, "It would not be an exaggeration to say that more than 50 per cent of our bachelor's degree holders cannot write a brief paragraph of coherent and grammatically correct English." There was factual support for his view. In English tests at 1,500 public and private high schools in the Philippines in 1962, the national median score was only 39 per cent.[69]

The government, in a major effort to stimulate interest in a common language other than English, backed Pilipino, which is based on Tagalog, and made it a required course in the schools. However, there was no perceptible evidence that Visayan, the language of the central islands, or Ilocano, which is spoken in northern Luzon, or seven other tongues of regional importance were being discarded in favor of Pilipino. The study of English alone suffered.

Carlos P. Romulo, who became Minister of Education in the Marcos cabinet, had a somewhat different approach to the cultural heritage of the Filipino. "So much of the life of modern culture has been preoccupied with responding to America," he said. ". . . The truth is that the so-called Americanization that . . . we, Asians, talk so much about consists, actually, in the impact of American culture on our private sensibilities and our societies. And the vivid suggestions of this culture are to be perceived with greater immediacy in American literature." [70]

Yet, so great was the resistance by some Filipinos to the continued growth of cultural ties with the United States that a grant agreement between the U.S. Government and the Philippines-American Cultural Foundation had to be dropped in 1964. The grant would have assured the development of plans to support, maintain, and operate a cultural center. William E. Stevenson, the American Ambassador at the time, charged subsequently that some of the foundation's trustees sought "to eliminate from it everything American except, of course, the three million pesos provided by the United States government." To this, a trustee replied, "What we wanted to eliminate was not 'everything American' but everything government which, as it happened, turned out to be entirely American government." [71]

The Filipinos ran into trouble also during their continual search for accommodation with their more powerful neighbors. The concept of Maphilindo—the association of Malaysia, the Philippines, and Indonesia —was one that appealed particularly to Manila. But Sukarno, at the height of his power, made a veritable joke of it. To sustain him in the style to which he was accustomed, he needed more than Manila or Kuala Lumpur could offer; consequently, he was more interested in Peking. Yet, on one occasion, the pro-American Philippines *Herald* came across a UPI story on which it based this alarming headline during the Macapagal regime: "DM HINTS SHIFT AWAY FROM U.S." President Macapagal angrily denied it, and events bore him out.[72] There were more such reports, however, during the period of intensive Filipino courtship of Djakarta. But eventually, Sukarno refused to give up his small war on Malaysia, Filipino mediation efforts collapsed, and the slumping economy at home forced President Macapagal back into closer dependence on the United States.

The American public, which in the absence of a flow of news to the contrary had assumed that all was well in the Philippines, was mildly surprised by Macapagal's defeat in the 1965 elections. The underlying reasons for it were given with dismaying candor by his successor, Ferdinand Edralin Marcos, who cried out in Manila's palm-fringed Luneta Park:

> The Filipino has lost his soul and his courage! Our people have come to a point of despair. We have ceased to value order. Justice and security are as myths. Our government is gripped in the iron hand of venality, its treasury is barren, its resources are wasted, its civil service is slothful and indifferent, its armed forces demoralized and its councils sterile. . . . Not one hero alone do I ask from you, but many—nay all.

Now the foreign journalists began describing the ills of the Philippines with gusto. It was said that the Filipino government was spending

$1.5 million a day and taking in only $1 million, that graft and smuggling of an unspecified nature were depriving the government of nearly $125 million a year in revenues, that not enough rice and other food was being produced to feed the people, and that industrial progress was sluggish. This reporting of woe after the fact, typically, did not take into account some of the more hopeful signs, including a rise in exports during 1965 and a favorable response to the new official rate of 3.90 to $1 for the peso. Consequently, Marcos and his program both appeared to be widely misunderstood at the time of his accession to power.

For example, immediately after his election, most American correspondents filed pieces predicting that the new president would take a somewhat more independent line with the United States than had Macapagal. Yet, almost the first thing Marcos did in office was to demand that 2,000 Filipino troops, mostly from the engineering corps, be sent to help the United States in South Viet-Nam, and that combat forces be dispatched later. When Vice President Hubert H. Humphrey came to the Philippines on the second of two visits in 1966, he found the government more committed to its American alliance than ever before.

As a great Filipino war hero who fought as a guerrilla officer in World War II, won twenty-two American and Filipino medals, was wounded five times and captured by the Japanese, Marcos could be expected to press for a stronger Philippine defense force. But he scarcely believed it possible for the Filipinos to dispense with the primary American responsibility for defending the island republic; nor could he give up the $25 million a year the Americans were spending in support of the Philippine armed forces.

Whatever was expected of him as the leader of the Conservative Party in the light of his record as the president of the Philippine Senate, Marcos adhered to his country's treaty commitments at the outset of his regime. He gave the rampant nationalists and the small hard-core anti-American group no comfort.

Almost his first move was to obtain more American military assistance and intensify joint U.S.–Philippine defense arrangements to halt Indonesian infiltration of Mindanao and other southern islands.[73] Despite Manila's technical claim to Malaysian North Borneo (Sabah), the new president also moved to restore Philippine ties with Malaysia. Diplomatically, he assured the military regime in Djakarta, which had wrenched Indonesia from its alliance with Peking, of the good will of the Philippines, but he realistically remained on guard against his huge and restless neighbor to the south. Maphilindo was still only a dream.

As for Communist China, the anti-Communist Filipinos did not have to be reminded of Peking's power. In fact, the presence of a substantial minority of Chinese in the Philippines was a source of constant concern because of the ties of some of their leaders with Peking. Because the Chinese owned 30 per cent of all the retail enterprises in the Philippines, the Retail Trade Nationalization Act was aimed primarily at them at the beginning. Once the law took effect in 1964, it limited retailing, and other direct selling to consumers, to corporations that were 100 per cent Filipino or American. However, it soon became evident that corporations which were only partly American in ownership would be vitally affected unless the Philippine Congress passed an exemption statute. It turned out that a law aimed at the Chinese actually had a more immediate effect on the Americans.

As early as May, 1964, the *Journal* of the American Chamber of Commerce of the Philippines recognized the danger and said editorially: "The drive behind nationalization legislation during the past decade and more is the natural desire of the Filipinos to play a dominant part in the conduct of the industry and trade of the country—when it is not merely the aim, as, no doubt, it is of a few, to enrich themselves by stealing from others."

The author of these lines was the editor of the *Journal*, A. V. H. Hartendorp, a seventy-one-year-old American journalist and teacher who had lived in the Philippines for more than a half century, a former editor of the Manila *Times* and an adviser to two Philippine presidents. Accused of "acts inimical to the interests of the Filipino people," he was called before the Philippine Deportation Board to defend himself against removal proceedings as an undesirable alien. It was a case that attracted international attention because of Hartendorp's prominence in Filipino public affairs, his standing in the American community, and his history as a survivor of a Japanese prison in the Philippines in World War II.

Benito Legarda, Jr., wrote to the Manila *Bulletin:* "Is Philippine democracy such a weak, fragile thing that it cannot tolerate . . . frank criticism from its best friends?" And the *Herald* commented editorially:

If Mr. Hartendorp has unwittingly gone against the grain of some officials, it was perhaps only because he had, more than the others, expressed himself in pointed and unmistakable terms on a subject that undoubtedly seriously affects the interests of the American community here. Surely, now, a country that deservedly prides itself in having a free press cannot, without appearing illogical and selfish, deny the enjoyment of the same right to others in its premises, albeit those others may be foreigners.[74]

The Philippine Deportation Board ruled in Hartendorp's favor, saying that he had written with "keen observation of the various facets of the nationalization move in this country during the past decade or so." [75] The editor took his vindication in stride, but the incident was nevertheless one that deeply disturbed the American community. It demonstrated once again the sensitivity of ultranationalists in Asia and the lengths to which they would go to try to suppress those who opposed them.

All these varying reflections of change in the Philippines brought new problems to the U.S. Embassy in Manila, which, for want of a diversified group of American correspondents reporting on Philippine affairs, had a somewhat greater incentive than most posts to keep information flowing steadily to the United States. There was in no sense a feeling at the embassy that the government should perform a news-transmission function. The AP and UPI both had decent bureaus in Manila, but most of their daily report circulated in Asia and comparatively little was used in the United States as a rule. Aside from the agencies, not one American newspaper or news magazine had a resident staff correspondent in Manila who devoted his full time to its service. It was fairly obvious, as a result, that any background briefing on American-Philippine relations for the American press had a better chance of publication if it was done in Washington. Whether the embassy planned it that way or not, and usually it didn't, that was one of the consequences of the news coverage of Asia as it existed in the 1960's.

Under Ambassador Stevenson and his successor, William McCormick Blair, Jr., the Embassy in Manila was one of the largest maintained by the United States anywhere in the world, with more than six hundred on its roster. Primarily, that was because the Philippines had always represented friendly territory on which such important operations as printing, broadcasting to Asia, and other activities could be based. It was also a first-rate centralized collection point for the study, evaluation, and transmission of intelligence to Washington. However, some of its senior people were scarcely impressed with the results.

Everything was supposed to clear through the embassy, with the ambassador in firm command of all agencies. But in the Philippines, as in most other American posts in Asia, the heads of the military and economic missions did not necessarily see things in exactly the same way as the ambassador and his political and economic advisers did. Sometimes there were differences of consequence at even the ambassadorial level, with some of his advisers arguing for different courses of action. And as every correspondent knew, it was often possible to find separate points of view on policy matters among the representatives abroad of the Army, Navy, and Air Force. As for the USIS, it was frequently more sinned against than sinning because some of its outranked officials had trouble finding out what was going on within their own government.

At one period in the 1960's, these natural rivalries seemed to get out of hand at the embassy despite every effort that was made by the ambassador. "Too many agencies were spreading different stories and reporting differently to Washington," one senior official said, in recounting his troubles. "It got to a point where the different agencies ran their own shops, made their own reports, and thoroughly confused the Filipinos. Theoretically, everything had to be coordinated with the embassy, but in practice it didn't operate that way."

In addition to the embassy itself, which often also forwarded the messages of the Central Intelligence Agency, direct reports to Washington went from the Agency for International Development, the Joint United States Military Assistance Group (JUSMAG), and other component agencies of the embassy. Thus, USIS, theoretically an agency separate from the State Department but actually under the direct control of the ambassador, reported through State to its own chief at the USIA. And the separate military services each filed to their own headquarters at the Pentagon. It would therefore have taxed the capacity of the speediest and most knowledgeable wire-service editor to coordinate this tremendous flow of information daily; in practice, it could be done with an effort on only one or two outstanding issues. As one official observed, "We build chaos into our government reporting system and we call it coordination." He concluded, from long experience with government reporting, that if more officials practiced clarity and conciseness, cable bills could be cut by one-third or more, and Washington would be better advised.

Another senior official mourned that some of the embassy's reports, particularly on Indonesia, either were overlooked or disregarded.[76] Such diplomats deeply felt the strain of American intragovernmental rivalries in Asia generally and their separation from the center of decision-making. Thus, if any advantage was taken of the opportunity to provide Washington with dependable background material on Philippine-American relations which could be of incidental use for press briefings in the nation's capital, little evidence of it was seen by the embassy people in Manila. Most interpretive reporting therefore was left to the few correspondents, plus the visitors who called now and then.

The Manila Overseas Press Club was a friendly organization, well staffed and efficiently run, but it was primarily for the Philippine press. Not too many others were usually around, except when curiosity, boredom, or an infrequent crisis brought them from Tokyo or Hong Kong. Generally, neither the resident correspondents nor the Filipinos themselves were concerned over the thinness of foreign news representation or the amount of attention the nation attracted in the United States. One of the firmest friends of the United States in the Philippines, Mauro Mendez, summed it up this way while he was Foreign Secretary in the Macapagal regime: "All we ask is that American editors and correspondents take a realistic view of the Philippines as they exist today—an independent nation in a key position in Asia—and not a colony of the United States. That part of Filipino development is over and old colonial attitudes are out of date." [77]

The AP dominated the foreign news field in the Philippines. It served twelve of the thirteen important daily newspapers in Manila—five of the six English-language dailies, all four Chinese, two Tagalog, and the single Spanish paper. It also had some electronic outlets, but many stations merely rebroadcast Voice of America news instead of paying for an independent service. To handle both incoming and outgoing reports, the AP had a staff of six—four Filipinos and two Americans, one the bureau chief. UPI, with a staff of almost the same size and composition, served the Philippines *Herald,* Manila *Bulletin,* and three Chinese papers. Reuters, with a Filipino staff of three, distributed no general news but sold Comtelburo service. Agence France-Presse, with five Filipinos on its staff, served the Manila *Times* and the Manila *Chronicle.* One Manila publisher said that Antara, the Indonesian agency, Kyodo of Japan, and the Deutsche Press Agentur all were being offered to his newspaper for nothing, and that he was "under pressure" to buy Agence France-Presse for "almost nothing." [78] There was also a small domestic Philippine news service, but its entire budget was less than $18,000.

Of the other resident correspondents, the most active was the Manila *Times* columnist Maximo V. Soliven, a graduate of the Ateneo de Manila and the holder of a master's degree from Fordham University in New York, who was a correspondent for the New York *Times* and *Newsweek. Time* magazine was represented by another Filipino journalist, Bernardo de Leon, and the *Christian Science Monitor* received occasional pieces from David Sternberg, an AID official. A variety of stringers did a little work for some other news organizations.

Albert Ravenholt, a former UP correspondent in China during World War II, was the only resident American correspondent other than the two American agency bureau chiefs and their principal assistants. Like Henry Hartzenbusch, the AP's bureau chief who subsequently moved on to Tokyo, Ravenholt could speak Chinese and had some familiarity with China and Southeast Asia. In his work for the Chicago *Daily News* and the American Universities Field Staff (AUFS), he traveled widely and wrote on a variety of subjects.

The most important and original part of his reportage was for the AUFS, founded in 1951. He was part of a group of correspondents who reported from specific areas for AUFS, and also lectured at some of the universities that supported it. In Asia, the staff included Lawrence Olson in Japan, Willard Hanna in Singapore, and Louis Dupree in Afghanistan. Their work had the virtue of analyzing at some length, and in a scholarly manner, the problem areas in underdeveloped lands that appealed to an academic audience. It was, on the whole, an interesting experiment in foreign correspondence although it could not compete with the major news media and did not try.[79]

Despite the diligence of the few resident foreign correspondents, the thin news flow continued to plague American relations with the island republic. The slightest indication of a move in Washington that would affect Manila was jumped on by the Philippine press, often with a distorting effect. But in the Philippines, there had to be what amounted to a political upheaval to catch the attention of the American public for more than a fleeting moment.

There was good reason for the Philippine-American Assembly, a gathering of business, educational, and political leaders of both nations, to conclude at Davao in 1966 that communications was a major source of discord in the relations of the two nations. In its final report, it warned that misconceptions based on inadequate communications and differences in approach "often erode mutual trust." One lamentable result, the report went on, was that Philippine-American relationships had become "so burdened with slogans and clichés that mutual understanding [was] frequently inhibited." [80]

It was a sign of a new relationship between the Philippines and the United States when leaders of both could agree that they simply didn't know enough about each other. The unobtrusive movement of the American wire services to set up more of their centralized Asian operations in Manila, the exchange of visits by Presidents Marcos and Johnson, and the Manila Conference of 1966 were welcome notes of progress.

5. THE VOICES OF TAIWAN *

It is an American military axiom that Taiwan can best be defended outside the confines of the island. President Eisenhower expressed it as follows for the benefit of the Chinese Communists in a news conference

* Taiwan, the Chinese name of the island, is used here. Successive American administrations have all used the Portuguese name, Formosa, which means "beautiful."

on August 17, 1954: "Any invasion of Formosa would have to run over the Seventh Fleet." [81]

Politically, too, it is axiomatic that the best place to defend the Chinese Nationalists and try to influence the United States in their favor is not in Taiwan, but in Washington. With good reason, President Truman struck out at "those members of the Senate who have sometimes been called the 'China First' block" when he was rebutting senseless charges that Secretary of State Acheson somehow helped bring about a Communist victory in China.[82] President Eisenhower, and not Chiang Kai-shek, determined the course of events in the 1954 crisis over Taiwan although, as Richard Rovere pointed out in the *New Yorker,* the Chinese Nationalists had support from Senator William F. Knowland, of California, various members of the Joint Chiefs of Staff, and—some of the time—Secretary of State Dulles.[83] In the 1960 Presidential campaign debates over the fate of the offshore islands of Quemoy and Matsu, the advance bases of the Chinese Nationalists, the American public listened with fascination to Vice President Nixon and Senator John F. Kennedy, but gave scarcely a thought to the views of the aged Chiang Kai-shek.

With 46 per cent of the American population under twenty-five years of age and 51 per cent under thirty,[84] the reasons for the historic involvement of the United States with Chiang Kai-shek and his government were becoming increasingly remote to the American public in the mid-1960's. In a survey for the Council on Foreign Relations of a representative sample of 1,501 Americans, the University of Michigan Research Center found that only 72 per cent knew that mainland China was under Communist rule and 40 per cent of those "informed" respondents could not think of the name, the leader, or the location of the "other Chinese" (Nationalist) government.

"If we assume that all of those who are not aware of the existence of a Communist government also do not know about the Nationalist government," the report said, "then only 43 per cent of the total sample can be classified as knowing about the Nationalists." [85]

It was thus made evident that there were practical reasons for the journalistic axiom, paralleling military and political practice, that the fortunes—or misfortunes—of the Chinese Nationalists were more easily followed from outside Taiwan than inside. While the result was a mere trickle of largely pro-Nationalist news from the island, this was somewhat less of an evasion of journalistic responsibility than it seemed to be at first glance. There was a law of diminishing returns in the aggressive coverage of any dictatorship from inside its borders, and the less important it became, the less justification there was for permanently assigning a correspondent who could do a better job on the subject elsewhere.

Of all American news organizations, only the Associated Press had consistently staffed Taiwan with a non-Chinese resident correspondent from the time of Chiang Kai-shek's overthrow on the mainland in 1949. The correspondent was a British subject, Spencer Moosa, who followed Chiang to Taiwan in December, 1949, from Chengtu by way of Hong Kong and took up his long death watch on January 2, 1950. No correspondent knew more about Chiang Kai-shek and his government than Moosa and, for understandable reasons, none was more factual. In a dictatorship, no matter how repressive, it is the first duty of a wire-service correspondent in particular to stay on the job and cover the news, not to get himself thrown out of the country. Moosa's history as a journalist was bound up with his life in China. He had been born in Shanghai in 1905. For 13 years, from 1926 on, he was a subeditor, and later chief editor for Reuters in Shanghai. Upon joining the AP in 1939, he followed the war from a variety of posts, and from 1941 to 1946 he was based at Chungking.

When the Japanese surrendered, Moosa returned to Shanghai and worked as a correspondent in North China until the fall of the Chiang Kai-shek regime. In Taipei, from then on, he was a familiar figure—tall, severe-looking, and rather taciturn in disposition, always inclined to keep his own counsel, frequently ahead on any important news break in Chinese Nationalist affairs that originated on Taiwan. No other AP correspondent had remained so long in such an Asian backwater.

The rival agency, UPI, had a succession of correspondents, among them some competent young Americans who were anxious for the experience if nothing else. One such was Ken Gale, who served at Taipei for two years until he departed in 1964, at the age of twenty-seven, to become a Ford Fellow in International Reporting at Columbia University. There wasn't much future for Americans as correspondents in Taiwan under prevailing conditions, and there was none at all for the local Chinese.

The AP, in a rather bland summation of this state of journalistic affairs, reported in one of its annual roundups of world censorship: "Censorship is not applied to outgoing dispatches or newspapers on the Chinese Nationalist island of Formosa, but newspapers observe certain recognized taboos, such as avoiding criticism of what is called the supreme goal of national policy—recovery of the mainland. Nationalist China remains barred from the International Press Institute for alleged lack of freedom of the press." In publishing this passage, the New York *Times* changed the final sentence to "on the ground of a lack of freedom of the press." [86]

James Shen, director of the Government Information Office in Taiwan, argued despite the IPI position that his press was "free" although it was subject to government registration and bound by a Publication Law. Among the law's provisions were some capable of wide interpretation such as the following: "No publication shall contain any item that (1) commits or instigates others to commit sedition or treason; (2) commits or instigates others to commit offenses of interference with the lawful exercise of public functions or with voting, or offenses against public order . . ." [87]

What this amounted to, of course, was self-censorship in which sole responsibility was thrust on the correspondent. For those who may have thought otherwise, the case of Albert Yuan (Yuan Chin-tao), a Chinese national in charge of the Taipei bureau of Agence France-Presse, was a stern reminder of what could happen to correspondents under a dictatorship. He was arrested May 28, 1963, by the Taiwan Garrison Command, accused of "secretly collecting important military information, thus seriously undermining national security" and "under heavy suspicion of espionage." Following indictment on a charge of sedition, the forty-seven-year-old correspondent was sentenced to fifteen years in prison. All efforts made in his behalf by Agence France-Presse were without avail. His accusers held that he was a member of an "intelligence organization of international Communism and worked for it for regular pay." [88]

It was possible to describe from Taipei the patriotic annual "Double Ten" military display celebrating the birth of the Chinese Republic on October 10, 1911. One could also write at length about economic affairs, for Taiwan was proud of its new-found prosperity, and even the restive Taiwanese saw that progress was being made although they were scarcely a contented lot. Interviews with Chiang could be arranged for distinguished visitors such as the Hearst team (William Randolph Hearst, Jr., and associates), as well as other selected foreign correspondents. But if there was speculation on the succession, on the declining membership of the National Assembly (no election had been held since 1949), or on the proposal to have "two Chinas" in the United Nations, that had to be filed from abroad.

Any news of importance that bore on American relations with Taiwan was announced in Washington. Such an event was the end of economic foreign aid for Taiwan in 1965, after the expenditure of $1.5 billion in American economic assistance, plus $2.5 billion in military aid, which was continued to insure the readiness of Chiang's 600,000-man army. The result was hailed in the United States as proof that Taiwan at last had been made self-supporting, with industrial production up 300 per cent since 1951, agricultural production up 70 per cent as a result of a successful land-reform program, exports almost tripled, imports almost doubled, and industrial plants increased from 10,000 to 25,000 in number.[89] The Chinese Nationalists Government was anything but happy about being cut from the foreign-aid roll of the United States, but it had to accept the verdict.

In Asia, Chiang still had a limited amount of leverage that he tried to use, but it was not impressive. Alarmed by the drive in Japan for closer trade relations with Communist China, he had his government kick up a fuss about it. There were demonstrations. A rock was thrown through the Japan Air Lines office windows in Taipei. But in the end, he didn't break off relations with Japan and was mollified, on the whole, by a visit from the Japanese elder statesman and former premier, Shigeru Yoshida.[90] Except for such matters, the details of Taiwan's diplomacy, internal politics, and economics circulated on the Asian wires of the news agencies and seldom popped up in the pages of the American press.

When there was an unfavorable development, such as the defection of the seventy-four-year-old General Li Tsung-jen from his enforced American exile to Peking, the Taiwan press published the news as a short item on inside pages. Yet, General Li had been an acting president of Nationalist China, despite his later break with Chiang and his expulsion from the Kuomintang in 1952. As one high-ranking Kuomintang official explained, "We are purposely playing this one down. Why help the Chinese Communists with the propaganda barrage that is sure to follow?" [91] It was further testimony, if any were needed, to the closeness with which the press on Taiwan followed the desires of its government. Nor did foreign correspondents in Taipei make much out of the Li story beyond reporting the bare reaction.

The mass communications network on Taiwan was large for a population of 11 million with a 70 per cent literacy rate. But the 2 million Chinese were avid newspaper readers and the 9 million Taiwanese favored local radio programs in their own dialects. Together, the rulers and the ruled were served a careful mix of news and opinion under government scrutiny. In an island the size of Maryland and Delaware, 240 miles long and 60 to 90 miles wide, national security was the first consideration, and the slightest suspicion of Communist influence was cause for alarm.

There were 31 daily newspapers on Taiwan with a total daily circulation of 720,000, an average of 6.5 copies for each 100 people. There were 19 newspapers in Taipei, and the most important, the *Central Daily News* and the China *Daily News,* were owned by the Kuomintang Party and spoke for the government. The most vigorous of the independently owned newspapers, the *United Daily News,* was popularly supposed to have a larger circulation. All were served by the government-supported Central News Agency, which had exchanged agreements with most of the independent global wire services.

The journalists with American training played a special role both in the government and in the press. Among them were nearly a score from the University of Missouri School of Journalism and about half as many from Columbia, some from the wartime school at Chungking and others from the Graduate School of Journalism. They could be found in the Foreign Ministry, the Information Office, the newspapers, and in key positions abroad in the service of their government.

One of the best, Nancy Yu Huang, ran the English-language China Post, which she and her husband had begun without government help and built into an efficient newspaper with a circulation of 15,000. It was the only one with an offset press, and one of the few in Asia to pioneer in new methods of printing.[92]

Nancy Yu's achievement was an indication that there was more flexibility in the intricate relationship of press and government on Taiwan than was evident on the surface. Of course, no serious public disagreement with the national defense policies of the regime was possible. It was also true that there was no tradition of rebelliousness in Chinese journalism, as there had been for forty years in Korea. Yet, in the limited sense in which the journalist could deal with local issues, he could and sometimes did represent public opinion. He was one of the few sources of appeal against corruption.

While the Chinese dominated the government, not all the Taiwanese elected to local offices were hostages to the Kuomintang. In fifty years of Japanese rule, they had learned how to survive and gain concessions from the dominant forces which they could not control. They did not forget the repressions of the early years of Chinese rule, although the improvement of economic conditions on the island had eased their lot. In addition to the native dialects of Fukien and Kwangtung Provinces, from which their forebears had migrated over 300 years ago, nearly all adult Taiwanese spoke Japanese, and their children learned Mandarin, the official Chinese language, at school. Their word-of-mouth communication was their chief reliance, although even that wasn't safe from the secret police.

Among the younger generation on Taiwan, restlessness and dissatisfaction cropped up from time to time among both Chinese and Taiwanese. There were some Chinese who, despite their loyalty to their government, had severe doubts about the future and could talk of going to the mainland to live under a regime more repressive than their own. There were others who didn't like what was going on about them, as was the case with a university student who startled a meeting for a foreign visitor with a demand for a crusade against political corruption. The young Taiwanese displayed an even greater resentment against the old order, when they dared to speak about it, but there was precious little they could do to change it.[93]

With the exception of the Voice of America and the American Armed Forces Network, all 156 transmitters on the island were supervised by the Ministry of Communications. The most important ones were run by the Broadcasting Corporation of China under government contract. The two features worth special attention were the broadcasts to the Chinese mainland, which served a propaganda purpose, and the native dialect programs for the Taiwanese, which furnished an outlet for their cultural aspirations.

However, neither press nor radio on Taiwan did as much damage to the Chinese Nationalist cause abroad as did a usually less controversial aspect of mass communications, book publishing. While foreign intellectuals had little sympathy for Chiang Kai-shek's regime, the activities of the book pirates of Taiwan served as an additional stimulus to critical opinion. The American book-publishing industry in particular was outraged.

Within a short time after the publication of any American best seller in fiction or nonfiction, or a representative work of importance in any scholarly field, it was reproduced for sale on the crowded bookstalls of downtown Taipei at a fraction of its original price. One of the pirate organizations, Literature House of Taiwan, issued a thick catalogue advertising the work of Hemingway, O'Hara, Michener, Gunther, Wouk, and many another American for a little more than $1 each, with standard works of literature of the past at even less. Moreover, the low advertised price was discounted by 10 or 15 per cent during recurring price wars.

As a nonsignatory to the World Copyright Convention, along with the Soviet Union and others, the Taiwan regime followed Communist tactics in the wholesale unauthorized reproduction of thousands of books, in all branches of learning, from art to zoology.[94] To the repeated protests of the American embassy, Mme. Chiang Kai-shek is reputed to have said, "Our students are too poor to buy books at the prices set by foreign publishers." Finally, the government did agree to try to stop the shipment of pirated books from Taiwan to other countries where they were eagerly purchased, but no one could say that the widespread book smuggling had been effectively halted.

For those who looked to the American Embassy at Taipei for a frank assessment of the Chinese Nationalist Government and its difficulties in world affairs, there was bound to be disappointment. For both political officers and the USIS, all considerations were secondary to the importance of retaining Taiwan because of its strategic position between the Philippines and Okinawa. It was, in the opinion of the American Government, a "symbol of hope" to the Chinese mainland.

While the Taiwan regime was not notable for its enthusiasm for the United States, and while it suspected the State Department of secretly favoring a "two Chinas" policy, the American Embassy endeavored to leave no doubt of its own steadfastness. In its relations with Chiang's government, the Taiwanese, and even the book pirates, it tried very hard to give no public offense.[95]

One of the consequences of the lack of dependable information in Taiwan was that an exaggerated amount of importance was given to some sources outside Taiwan, notably the group around the exiled Dr. Thomas Liao and other Taiwanese intellectuals in Japan who fled from their homeland and in 1955 organized a "Provisional Government of the Republic of Formosa in Tokyo." It was this group which agitated for a U.N. trusteeship for Taiwan or some form of independence, neither of them very practical measures at the time.[96]

The lack of forthrightness on the part of both the Taiwan and American governments also cost the former a great deal of the credit to which it was rightfully entitled for a major Asian land-reform program. Like Japan, Taiwan should have been a widely respected example of what could be done by a determined government to wipe out centuries of land-holding abuse. Through assurance of tenure for tenant farmers and the sharp reduction of rent, plus the forced sale of land by absentee landlords at fixed government prices, owner-operated land in Taiwan rose from 60 to 85 per cent and in Japan from 54 to 92 per cent.

Wolf Ladejinsky, an agricultural expert formerly in the service of the U.S. Department of Agriculture, wrote:

> Just as Soviet Russia was the progenitor of the Communist type of reform, Japan and Taiwan are the progenitors of non-Communist reforms in Asia. Japan, the leader, and Taiwan, the follower and innovator, provided between them all the pertinent elements of leadership, content, and implementation which made for a successful reform.
>
> In Taiwan as in Japan, reforms were not designed to satisfy the claims of both contending parties: the tenant was to gain at the expense of the landlord.[97]

After the abysmal failure on the mainland of China, the Nationalist regime thus had been able to prove to the world that it could make land reform work for the benefit of the people of Taiwan and that it could put a war-paralyzed economy back into an impressively efficient and self-sustaining operation. Yet, when it came to demonstrating a superior form of technical assistance for the agriculture of the newly emerging nations of Africa, Taiwan won the interest of many of these underdeveloped lands but not their political support, as measured by their votes in the U.N. General Assembly on the admission of Communist China.[98]

It was apparent that Nationalist China, despite its praiseworthy economic development and its achievement of a $120 per capita income, one of the highest in the Far East, could not create a favorable climate for itself. The voices of Taiwan inspired neither trust nor belief in many places throughout the world. Because the spreading power of Communist China was too great to be overcome, except by the United States, Taiwan waited on the outcome of the Viet-Nam war, the test of American strength and resolution in Asia. The old war cry, "Return to the Mainland!" became just a hollow echo, believed in by few, even on Taiwan itself.

The old leader, Chiang Kai-shek, was the representative of a bygone era. In the spring of 1966, when he was re-elected to a fourth term as president of the Chinese Nationalist regime, it was made known that he had arranged for an orderly succession if he failed to complete his six-year term. Chiang was then seventy-eight years old and was reported to have complained of a failing memory, although his health was good. While a preponderance of the military and police powers on Taiwan reposed in his eldest son, the fifty-six-year-old General Chiang Ching-kuo, the Minister of Defense, the old dictator seemed to depend more on his sixty-one-year-old Premier, C. K. Yen, who became Vice President and theoretical heir apparent. But no one on Taiwan doubted that Chiang Ching-kuo was the stronger of the two.[99]

The issue for Taiwan now was sheer survival in a changing world. Although the island was attracting foreign capital and even tourists, the diplomatic corps accredited to Chiang's government shrank to eighteen missions. And half of these were headed by chargés d'affaires rather than ambassadors or ministers. From the high drama of the Taiwan Strait bombardment of 1958 and the Quemoy-Matsu crisis of 1960, Taiwan relapsed into a relatively minor position in the world's news. Few correspondents visited it. For, by the latter part of the 1960's, the belief was general that its fate would be settled elsewhere.

6. THE HALF-FORMED IMAGE

Thousands of Americans traveled along the Asian perimeter in the 1960's, most of them nervously aware of the international tensions that existed all about them. Many were business people or retired professionals, teachers in particular, with a great curiosity and a limited time to tour the vastness of the Orient. They did not generally fit the old concept of the American tourist, for it took a certain amount of intellectual stimulus to plan such a trip and the constitution of a road-show acrobat to survive it.

American travelers in the Orient swarmed from their jets at Tokyo's Haneda Airport, or hustled from the cruise ships, to dart through Japan in a few days—ancient Kyoto, the Hakone lakes around Mount Fuji, and the ultramodern hotels, stores, and night clubs of Tokyo. Some of the more venturesome—more than 33,000 in 1965 alone—took a side trip to Korea to visit Seoul, the cease-fire zone, and the multi-million-dollar tourist playground known as Walker Hill. But by far the most popular second stop was Hong Kong with its bargains, some of them largely mythical. One could see the tired but determined travelers tramp from airplanes or cruise ships at ungodly hours into the magnificence of the Grand Hotel in Taipei, a painted red-and-gold pleasure palace. They also overwhelmed the old but comfortable Manila Hotel in Manila, where armed guards patrolled the dreamlike patio and swimming pool. The bravest dropped in on jam-packed Saigon, even in the midst of a war, while others trooped through the Angkor Wat of Cambodia or the temples of Thailand and India.

Now and then, the tourist was likely to come across an Asian street demonstration, complete with paid students, red banners, and "Yankee Go Home" posters. He could be confused, perhaps, by what looked like the New York *Times* for April 2, 1962, proclaiming, "The unification of Korea is an international question which should be decided by the exercise of the free will of the Korean people, not by U.S. imperialists." He did not know, of course, that Communist propagandists had put out phony copies of two- or three-score American, European, and Asian publications with such misleading material.[100]

Occasionally, the wandering American in Asia had an even more unsettling experience—a chance discussion with an Asian intellectual who challenged him to explain the treatment of the Negro in the United States. Race was an issue almost everywhere in Asia. Unless the tourist happened to be a veteran traveler, he could not reflect philosophically that Asians, too, have their prejudices of race, caste, and tribe and their problems of color. For example, the Japan *Times* once observed, "Japanese stubbornly refuse to admit that they are as racially prejudiced against Koreans as well as other races. Perhaps Oriental peoples are so color-conscious that mutual prejudice among the yellow groups cannot be accepted consciously as racial bias." To this, Tarzie Vittachi added the following out of long experience as a journalist in Asia:

Many of us South Asians—Indians, Pakistanis, and Ceylonese—who violently resent color discrimination when we are the victims or whenever we read about racism in the Southern States of America, South Africa, England or Rhodesia, are ourselves not free from prejudice. . . . There are many Asians who think nothing of exploiting the slightest shade of color difference between themselves and the Negroes to avoid being discriminated against.[101]

The net result of the usual American journey to Asia, therefore, was likely to consist of a few troublesome and half-formed images of the outer fringe of an immense continent—impressions that aroused a vague discontent and even testiness, plus a sense of frustration. Some, with an awakened interest in the lands they had skimmed over by plane or skirted by ship, may have watched their daily newspaper or their favorite television news program for some intelligence of the Asian perimeter or the heartland itself. Except for war news, however, there was little to satisfy them as a rule; insensibly, their temporary interest in Asian affairs was submerged in the pressures of the more immediate problems of daily life. A few may have reached out for help from the libraries, but for the majority, the Oriental argosy diminished to a small pile of travel documents, phrase books, snapshots, and bargains that could often have been purchased more cheaply at home.

It was therefore too much to expect, as some optimists did, that a looked-for increase in travel to Asia during the next decade would bring about a greater mutual understanding between Americans and the peoples of the Asian perimeter. Such things didn't happen as a result of the wartime experiences of whole armies of Americans in the Far East. Moreover, it was not without significance that after many years of often discouraging experiences in France, despite its historic ties with the United States, the Americans finally began taking themselves and their dollars elsewhere in the 1960's. In the less developed and less sophisticated Asian countries, where the links to the United States were ephemeral by comparison, tourism was just as likely to remain an industry instead of an arm of American foreign policy. The promotion of better relationships between Asians and Americans was, after all, a function of government and of specialists who were trained in such matters.

As for the correspondents who served American news organizations in Asia, there was little hope for improvement in the coverage of the perimeter. Most of those who skimmed by were little more than tourists themselves, subject to the same vague and irritating half-formed images. During the escalation period of the Viet-Nam war, more American correspondents began dropping off occasionally in Okinawa and

Manila, but generally something exciting had to be in prospect to bring them there. Because of the greater space and time that was taken up by news from Saigon and other Asian war centers and the announcements from Washington affecting them, it was to be expected that correspondingly less attention could be paid at that time to news of the Asian lands of less immediate importance to the United States.

As the ranks of veteran correspondents in Asia began thinning out, and newer and younger faces began to appear, a new kind of correspondent emerged along the outer fringe of Asia where American interests were concentrated. To the old-timers in the State Department in Washington, he was known disparagingly as the tourist correspondent. On the record, he was young, well-educated, decently motivated, and perhaps even trained in Asian affairs to a certain extent. It is also true that he had more sources, a heritage usually handed down to him by his predecessors, and his travel was a part of his work. But except for surface impressions, which he could turn into an interesting story if he had the ability to write, it was scarcely possible for him to absorb a whole new set of complicated relationships within a short time, any more than it was for a well-educated tourist. This kind of thing took time. The Orient would not be rushed.

The young and inexperienced tourist correspondent, skirting the ramparts of Asia, was likely to bring little more understanding to his readers than the tourists themselves could gain by dogging his footsteps. Such insights did not grow merely by travel, the sniffing of the air in far places, and the hasty exchange of views with busy officials, American or foreign. Without something better to offer, the press was not in a particularly good position to deliver well-considered reports to a majority of the nation on the mutual problems confronting the United States and the peoples of the Asian perimeter.

The half-formed image of the lands from Korea to Taiwan was a residue of the consistent failure over almost a generation to create a body of informed American public opinion on Asia. The responsibility for such neglect was widespread. The press was by no means solely to blame, and the press could not, through its own efforts, create a suitable climate for change.

V

In Red China's Shadow

1. OUTSIDE THE BAMBOO CURTAIN

WHEN AN AMERICAN correspondent based in Hong Kong drove to the Red Chinese border in the mid-1960's, it was little more than an exercise in sheer frustration. He couldn't go across, having no visa. Nor was the border itself a particularly good place to look for refugees who were fleeing for their lives. They could be found in disheartening numbers elsewhere; often, in their despair, they were willing to tell almost any kind of story their involuntary hosts wanted to hear.

Regardless of the paucity of news at the border on most occasions, there was a rather morbid fascination about it for the newer correspondents. Their knowledge of the land was based solely on what they had learned from books, professors, classroom discussions in the United States, and the few old-time correspondents who remained in the area. Going to the border, consequently, took on the aspect of a ceremonial rite. It was the thing to do.

The trip itself was a pleasant hour's excursion along the well-kept Tai Po Road, which winds from the Kowloon Peninsula through the rugged hills of the New Territories. For any one viewing the green farmlands, grazing pastures, and duck ponds of this beautiful and prosperous enclave, it was hard to believe that the most menacing and aggressive power in Asia lay over the next rise. In spite of that, the outing was no more venturesome than a New Yorker's Sunday drive to Long Island or Westchester and far less burdened with traffic. As the highway approached the bridge at the border village of Lo Wu, a wooden barrier diverted the motorist to an abrupt rise and an overlook from which the Shumchum River could be seen half merged with the distant mists that spread from the mountainsides. The river was the border.

If the correspondent cared to do so, he could view the outer fringes of Communist China through a telescope at the Lok Ma Chau Police Station nearby. Perhaps he would see life stirring in the village of Shumchum across the bridge from Lo Wu, or passengers from the Kowloon train leaving the Lo Wu terminal to board the Chinese train for Canton on the other side of the border. Now and then, he might catch the glint of the sun on the rifle of a Communist border guard. Otherwise, nothing.

When the correspondent turned aside, he would more often than not see a group of natives from the nearby walled village of Kam Tin perched hopefully near the overlook, inviting tourists to take their pictures for a few coins. They were members of the Teng clan, shepherded by an ancient and courtly Chinese with a pointed beard, huge straw hat, and a beguiling manner. The correspondent, for lack of anything else to do, would succumb, as a rule, and snap a few pictures. It was good for an illustrated mailer or a travel piece on a dull day and there was nothing better in sight. So it happened that the old man of the border received more prominence in some American newspapers than, say, the governor of Hong Kong.[1]

There were other anomalies that grew out of the mutual suspension of reportage between the United States and Communist China for the better part of a generation. Edgar Snow, the old Chicago *Daily News* and *Saturday Evening Post* correspondent who had made himself Mao Tse-tung's biographer in *Red Star Over China,* became the source of a steady flow of pronouncements on China's policy, including some unkind thoughts about the United States from Mao himself. At one point, Mao assured Snow that Red China wouldn't fight in the Viet-Nam war unless attacked first by the United States.[2]

In addition to the selected correspondent, the Chinese Communists for their own reasons now and then admitted a few correspondents for American news organizations. Mostly, they were citizens of British Commonwealth countries, and they recounted ingenuously how they had tricked the Peking government into admitting them by posing as noncorrespondents. The pose sometimes showed in their work, unhappily, in spite of all the ballyhoo that was launched in the American press to hail each of these scarcely earth-shaking exploits.

As an example of the kind of coverage that was offered to the American press generally through syndicates, American or others, there was a six-article series by a Canadian free-lancer, Michael Cope, who obtained a tourist visa after five years of effort but had little more to show for two weeks of travel than could have been learned in Hong Kong. He had had no previous knowledge of China and therefore was in a difficult position in so short a time and under tight surveillance to evaluate progress, or lack of it, under the Communist regime.[3]

A series by Mark Gayn, an editorial writer for the Toronto *Daily Star,* also a Canadian citizen, was more informative, because the author was less a tourist and more a reporter who had a basic familiarity with prewar China. But as he conceded after two months of incessant travel, the memory becomes "a disjointed record of things seen and heard," and what emerges is "one man's Chinese kaleidoscope." Nevertheless, despite the necessarily restricted reporting he was able to do during so short a guided tour, he projected the most dramatic and sweeping conclusions.

"Chairman Mao and his companions," he wrote, "have given China more than an able and uncorrupted government, national cohesion and a sense of pride. There is a remarkable moral crusade afoot in China with almost religious vows of poverty, integrity, chastity and self-sacrifice. Education, and physical fitness, have become national obsessions. The whole country seemingly comes to a halt at 10 each morning while its people, in factory yards, streets and parks, do their daily calisthenics."

There were, Gayn conceded, a great many drawbacks in this "most regimented of states" with its constant barrage of anti-American propaganda. Its worst feature, in his opinion, was the self-delusion about the outside world among its leadership, which made Red China's future course in world affairs a towering uncertainty.[4]

It remained for a thirty-five-year-old Australian woman, married to an American citizen, to provide her newspaper, the San Francisco *Examiner,* and nine others in the Hearst chain with a staff-written account of a 22-day, 4,000-mile tourist excursion in Red China. Once again the reporter, Lisa Allen Hobbs, related how she had fooled Peking into granting her a visa as a tourist, but she would have done better if she had read up on her assignment before departing. In her first piece, she reported that Red China spends an inordinate amount of time on anti-American propaganda, of which she had previously been "unaware." There were no startling new insights in her reportage, nor could any have been expected under the circumstances.[5]

Having read such accounts, the new correspondent, standing on the overlook above the Shumchum River, could scarcely be blamed for wondering why he had devoted so many years to preparing himself for his assignment. In Hong Kong and in Tokyo, there were other Americans like him, some with many years of experience in Chinese affairs, who also were waiting without much hope for the lifting of restrictions. In all, there were about fifty correspondents with varying degrees of expertise whose passports had in effect been prevalidated by the State Department for travel to mainland China whenever they could get a visa from Peking; many had tried and none had succeeded.

Following a conference with Secretary of State Rusk, Stanford Smith, general manager of the American Newspaper Publishers Association, had informed his members: "We are now confident that any bona fide news reporter who can get permission of the Chinese Communists to enter Red China will be given immediate passport approval by the State Department." [6] After nearly a decade, the State Department had finally modified Secretary of State Dulles' view that "United States foreign policy inevitably involves the acceptance of certain restraints by the American people," correspondents included. [7] The State Department's refusal to let a selected group of American correspondents visit Peking in 1956 at the invitation of the Communist government had precipitated the argument. Dulles had held that American relations with Peking could not improve until American prisoners from the Korean War had been released. On that ground, he had also turned down a Chinese Communist plan for an exchange of journalists.

In 1960, however, the American Government revived the journalistic exchange plan, but Peking no longer was interested. Edgar Snow said Chou En-lai had told him there would be no concessions "unless the United States would agree to mutual rejection of the use of force in the settlement of Sino-American disputes and simultaneously recognize, in principle, the sovereignty of China over the Taiwan territories." [8]

In effect, the Chinese attitude, Peking's support of North Viet-Nam, and the growth of American participation in the war against Hanoi effectively disposed of the possibility of a large-scale exchange of correspondents. Undoubtedly, selected correspondents might still be admitted to mainland China from time to time; although there was no doubt about their integrity, it was nevertheless a hard truth of both journalism and diplomacy that a government had a better chance of projecting a favorable image of itself by selecting its visitors than by letting everybody in.

In the mid-1960's therefore, Peking permitted few Western resident correspondents to operate in the city and on occasion to travel in the countryside under the most careful supervision. The principal ones represented Reuters, Agence France-Presse, and the Toronto *Globe & Mail*. There was no censorship in the old-fashioned sense, but the correspondents knew quite well that anything they did or wrote that was unacceptable to the regime would bring about their expulsion. Moreover, for the two agency men an additional consideration, although not a very compelling one, was the continued sale of their agencies' respective services to the Peking government. They could file as much as they wished, at a high rate, and they could telephone Hong Kong and Tokyo. When the regime wanted to impress the West particularly, as was the case with the atomic blasts of the mid-1960's, the Western correspondents were found to be useful. Specialists such as Robert Guillain, the Far Eastern editor of *Le Monde*, also were invited. Since few if any resident or visiting correspondents from the West spoke Chinese, the "guidance" provided by interpreters often served as an effective communications block between the correspondent and his subject. The nine Japanese correspondents in Peking were often treated with more liberality.

Despite London's continuous diplomatic relations with Peking from 1950 on, British correspondents had no special privileges and were not wildly enthusiastic about the work there. One said after completing his assignment that he had had a feeling of claustrophobia during his service in Peking; he wondered why he was spied upon so incessantly, since any Caucasian stood out in the Chinese capital. Moreover, there were times when utter boredom overcame him. Yet, for all that, he maintained that it was a distinct advantage merely to be in a country in which a quarter of the world's peoples were concentrated; if little other than government pronouncements could be filed, it still mattered greatly to have correspondents abroad who had first-hand knowledge of Communist China.

Those who served in Peking had varying reactions. Reuters had begun with David Chipp, who served from 1956 to 1958 and ultimately became the agency's Asian director. He was followed by others, all save one at two-year intervals, who lived in a Reuters house in Peking and didn't seem to mind their isolation. An Agence France-Presse correspondent in Peking, Jacques Marcuse, finished his two-and-a-half-year stint with a series of articles and a book in which he demonstrated the wideness of the separation between the ordinary Chinese and the foreigner. It was his impression that an estimated 3 million executions by sentence of the "People's Courts" in 1951 for "counterrevolutionary activities" had created a wave of fear that inhibited contact with foreigners long afterward. He pointed out that servants, clerical help, shopkeepers, officials, and others who deal with foreigners daily must have special permission from the government, without exception. [9]

Since the regular American correspondents in Hong Kong could not cross the border, they had to consider how to handle their assignments in such a way as to satisfy their editors at home. As Marvin Kalb, of C.B.S. explained it:

Unfortunately, editors back in New York have thus far failed to realize that Hong Kong is a gold mine of information about China, and is easily the best substitute for on-the-spot reporting. They consider Hong Kong a convenient place for changing underwear between planes for Saigon, Djakarta or Vientiane or leaving wives and children while the reporters themselves go racing around the jungles of Kuching or the Plaine des Jarres.[10]

The New York *Times,* the Los Angeles *Times* and Washington *Post,* the *Christian Science Monitor,* and one or two others based their detailed coverage of Communist China in Hong Kong, but for the wire services everything centered in Tokyo. In fact, the wire-service bureau chiefs were so busy with clients in Hong Kong that they seldom had a chance to be correspondents in the proper sense of the term unless they were called away to Saigon, Vientiane, or Djakarta. The agencies could save time, and probably money as well, by handling any major news break out of Red China from Tokyo.

Hsinhua, or the New China News Agency (NCNA), the Peking government's primary news resource, was monitored for sixteen hours a day by the Kyodo agency in Japan and brought into Tokyo's major foreign news agency offices in English by teletype. Another important outlet, Radio Peking, usually slower than NCNA, was monitored by Radio Press, a private monitoring service, and made available in Tokyo in the same manner. Radio Press also monitored other Communist sources such as the North Korean and North Viet-Nam radios. Finally, the Japanese Foreign Office and embassies with good contacts inside Communist China sometimes put out information of significance. There was always the perennial favorite of the foreign correspondent, the returning traveler, but in Asia he had pretty much worn out his credibility.

For a short time the American agencies experimented with Asian correspondents in Peking, but it didn't work out. D. R. Mankekar, a first-rate correspondent and later the managing editor of the largest newspaper in India, the *Indian Express,* served briefly as a UPI correspondent in the Chinese capital. Although he was frequently ahead on the news and wrote in a colorful style acceptable to most American editors, few newspapers in the United States used his material. It was clear that American correspondents were preferred, and if they couldn't write from Peking then they would be used from almost any point outside. To the average editor, it didn't make a great deal of difference whether his material on Red China was datelined Hong Kong or Tokyo. They were both in Asia, weren't they?

The AP in 1966 still kept its principal Chinese expert, John Roderick, in Tokyo. He was a vigorous and knowledgeable journalist, fifty-one years old, with thirty years of service, twenty of them overseas, and he had been in Tokyo for six years. With such other old China hands as

Seymour Topping, Tillman Durdin, Pat Morin, and A. T. Steele, he had worked in China, knew Chinese and Japanese, and had a firm grasp of the complicated politics of Asia. Of all the veterans, he alone was involved daily in the specialty for which he had trained himself.

Roderick's task was far more difficult than that of an academic Sinologist, who could take months to arrive at a conclusion, or even the work of a newspaper special who handled news out of Red China routinely in Tokyo or Hong Kong. By watching the NCNA wire and Radio Press and digesting whatever came from the AP bureau in Hong Kong, the AP's Sinologist had to do daily literary detective work on Peking's intentions and file at once. Under the circumstances, it is remarkable that his score for accuracy was so high. Although UPI also had competent people, there was no one either in Tokyo or Hong Kong with Roderick's background in Chinese affairs. He was, therefore, the main source of daily intelligence on Red China for the American press; what he wrote, in a very real sense, affected public opinion.

It should not be imagined that because of the complications of the Sino-Soviet quarrel there was any lack of press interest in the story. On the contrary, any pronouncement made on the subject by either Peking or Moscow was news that had to be quickly and correctly interpreted and filed without delay to the United States. As Roderick explained, "After a while, even the most suspicious editor in the United States began to believe that the split between the Soviet Union and Communist China was genuine instead of being a gigantic Trojan Horse. As a result, an enormous amount of material on Red China began appearing in the American press. Next to Viet-Nam and Laos, it was the big foreign story out of Asia."

Roderick could never be sure of editors' reactions. Once, he wrote a routine backgrounder on Mao Tse-tung, pointing out the Chinese leader's advancing age and various signs of his ill health. It was used by 78 per cent of the AP newspapers in the United States. Another time, he wrote a straight historical piece, explaining how the Communists had been able to triumph over Chiang Kai-shek despite huge American aid to the Nationalists. An editor sent back a clipping marked for Roderick's attention with the scrawl: "What are you, a lefty?" Fortunately, the dissenter was in the minority.

One of the things that did bother Roderick was his separation from the editors and their own separation from the public on so important and complicated a subject as the understanding of Red China. He said:

By and large, it would be better if news out of Red China did not have to be "sold" through the bulletin, the news lead and the other essential techniques of the news agency file. There is always a danger that this can produce over-stressed, over-dramatized news which is likely to mislead less informed people. I myself prefer the AP newsfeatures approach, in which a subject can be treated with some care in 1,000 to 1,200 words. Our shorter Spotlight program also uses such material. But when you have to try to tell a complicated story about the Sino-Soviet split in 400 words, that creates trouble for the writer and the editor very often. We know it and we try to guard against it.

There is another difficulty. It is not every story out of Red China that can be supported with factual documentation, direct quotes and the kind of material most editors expect in straight news. The interpretation of news out of Red China can be very tricky. There are too many complicated forces acting on Peking to permit any easy interpretation of events . . .[11]

Those like Roderick who specialized in Chinese affairs, whether they worked in Tokyo, Hong Kong, or even London, were also haunted by the old-fashioned American editor's suspicion of anything that had to do with research. Somehow, the old anti-intellectualism that clung to a considerable segment of the American press still cropped up from time to time. Editors of such newspapers could scarcely appreciate the need for a library of material on Communist China, such as the AP maintained in Tokyo, and the vital need for collecting materials daily and adding to it. Nor were they sympathetic to the enormous amount of reading that Roderick and other specialists had to do merely to keep themselves abreast of events. To that particular type of editorial mind, it was almost as if the news had a special life of its own which caused it to materialize at a given instant on a teletype machine. The hard, unrewarding duty of delving through piles of documents and pushing through the weary clichés of Communist writing were scarcely envisioned as a part of a reporter's work. He should, the old-time editors maintained, confine himself to going out and "digging"—although where a reporter could "dig" in Tokyo, other than in documents, no one could say.

There was a great deal of opportunity in Hong Kong for the independent investigator of Communist Chinese affairs, but it took an enormous amount of time. As in Tokyo, a great deal of work with documents was involved. That, primarily, was why so few news-gathering organizations were willing to permit correspondents to invest effort in developing their knowledge of Communist China. The wire services were doing well enough out of Tokyo, so the reasoning went; Hong Kong was secondary, and much of the news there wasn't particularly timely anyway. With the exception of a mere handful of American newspapers and news magazines, therefore, the American correspondent in Hong Kong who wanted to work on news of Communist China had to develop his own background on his own time. The bridge at Lo Wu was only an hour away, but it would take years before many American correspondents were able to cross it. For them, the Bamboo Curtain was no mere phrase but an unlovely reality.

2. THE HONG KONG BEAT

A few of the paladins among the American foreign correspondents in Hong Kong lived in handsome $500-a-month apartments overlooking Repulse Bay in the mid-1960's. It was a fashionable part of the island, facing out to the sea, and it was favored also by the more affluent Americans in diplomacy and the elite among the CIA. Others in the American correspondents' corps had to make do with more modest abodes in the city itself, overlooking crowded streets, and picked up what they could by free-lancing to eke out their small and uncertain incomes. These were the extremes among the correspondents on the Hong Kong beat, one of the most romantic—and vexing—in all Asia.

Because Americans, British, Chinese Communists, Chinese Nationalists, and many others of less prominence all were jammed together in the tiny British Crown Colony, the gateway to Red China, it served as a center for many interesting activities that were not often publicized. Such things made the British nervous for fear that the Chinese Communists would find out about them; actually, it was perfectly clear that Peking had both the people and the opportunity to know in detail of any activity in Hong Kong. The place was honeycombed with Communist agents, not to mention any number of others.

One particularly naïve correspondent, who wrote at the outset of his stay about the recognized and unrecognized sources of information in Hong Kong, was unceremoniously boycotted for months by almost all of them. It wasn't the thing to do. The journalist never knew from one day to the next whether his information might come from Chinese millionaires or prosperous American businessmen, diplomats or military experts of a number of nationalities, hotel men or busy shopkeepers, or some among the hordes of Chinese refugees, spies, tourists, sailors, anonymous tipsters, barkeepers, and pleasure girls. Among such a motley crew, if a man looked long enough, he could find support for almost any kind of a tale he wished to put out.

There was, as a result, a special emphasis on caution and responsibility for the correspondent in Hong Kong—and for the editor at home who passed on the news from such a varied collection of sources. True, any correspondent worthy of his salt would stoutly maintain that he dealt only with the very best sources; some, perhaps, did. But no one who had ever worked in Hong Kong could fail to note the many influences that could be brought to bear on a correspondent, whether or not he realized it. The place wasn't exactly a Sunday school. The record contained cases of first-rate men who were persuaded by one device or another to put out sensational stories that didn't stand up under examination, but who still believed that they were right and their disapproving editors wrong.

The problem of the journalist, in effect, was the problem of Hong Kong itself. Its nucleus was, of course, the shining 35-square-mile island with its array of dazzling white buildings rising almost to Victoria Peak —an island of incredible wealth and grinding poverty placed in a lazy blue and sun-dappled sea. Opposite it lay the Kowloon Peninsula, where tourists frantically sought bargains in the shops and markets and expected to have well-fitting clothes made overnight, and beyond that the New Territories—a total area of 398 square miles into which 3.7 million people were thrust. More than 99 per cent were Chinese, 1.2 million of them having fled from Red China to live in hillside shack colonies, filthy boats on the mudflats of Aberdeen, or the relatively few new tenements the British government had provided. Of the 50,000 non-Chinese, 33,000 were British Commonwealth subjects, and the rest included a few thousand Americans, Portuguese, and others. To add to the problems of the squeezed-in population in one sense, and to help with their support in another, more than 33,000 tourists annually moved in and out of Hong Kong and spent upward of $25 million.

Since the British had snatched Hong Kong back from the Japanese after World War II, it had become the second largest market for British goods after the United States. The United States, however, had remained Hong Kong's best customer, purchasing in 1964 alone $217 million in garments, textiles, plastic flowers, and other items, all certified not to have originated on the Chinese mainland. But Red China was the biggest gainer of all, having received almost $500 million in foreign exchange from Hong Kong during the same year—nearly 60 per cent of the total earned by Peking in business dealings with the non-Communist world. At the current rate of expansion, it was estimated that Peking would earn $700 million a year in 1966.

The American economic embargo against Red China seemed to have little effect on Hong Kong's economic growth as either an industrial or banking center. Red China did not seem to be reeling under this commercial blow; in breaking down its 1964 sales to Hong Kong, Peking's profit from garments, textiles, food, and other items amounted to $310 million, and $200 million more flowed in from "invisible earnings" of banks, commercial interests, and remittances from Overseas Chinese to relatives on the mainland. Everybody was happy except the American tourist who unwittingly bought a bit of Chinese jade in Hong Kong and had it taken away from him by a scornful American customs officer. Embargo or no embargo, it was business as usual at Hong Kong, and the correspondents for business publications dutifully reported it in statistical detail. The Crown Colony became the sixth largest customer of the United States in the Far East.

The argument was advanced that Hong Kong in British hands was worth far more to Communist China than it was as merely another bit of territory dominated by Peking, with which the United States would have no dealings whatever. The earnings of the free port were counted on to salve whatever propaganda wounds the Chinese Communists might have sustained from taunts by the Soviet Union over their dealings with the capitalists. Moreover, wasn't it true that Red China supplied Hong Kong with much of its food and even its emergency supplies of drinking water during the always critical water shortages that plagued the colony? All these things made for an air of assurance in Hong Kong, but underneath there was a discernible nervousness. Despite the British genius for dissembling, it was scarcely possible to disguise the sensitive position of the colony as hostage to an uncertain fortune.

Of the eighty banks in Hong Kong, fourteen were Communist-owned or controlled. When two non-Communist banks failed in 1965 because of unwise speculation, deposits in the Communist banks rose. Even though the canny Chinese still waged a "battle of the flags" on the "Double Ten" anniversary and usually displayed more Nationalist than Communist banners, having one eye on the British regime's reaction, it was evident that more of them were trusting the Communist banks with their money. Nor did the principles of Marxism-Leninism, as interpreted by Mao, stop the banks from offering as high as 7 per cent interest on savings or investing in private insurance companies and private corporations, building shopping centers, and collecting rents.

The Chinese Communists were known in the mid-1960's to operate at least thirty-one retail shops, and were building two large department stores as well. Like the capitalist Chinese, the Communist businessmen in Hong Kong cut their profit margins to achieve a sales volume and attract more tourist money. They even sold to the Chinese Nationalists on Taiwan, particularly building up trade in such items as Chinese native medicines, which could be obtained from no other source. [12]

The British colonial administration watched these business developments with a beneficent eye. The unspoken rule seemed to be, "What's good for trade is good for Hong Kong." But there was a great deal more government vigilance where the press was concerned. It was exercised through the Government Information Office (GIO) and a system of press licensing which included a fee of 25,000 Hong Kong dollars (about $4,400) for each publication. The fee was not of great importance, but the implied threat of a license withdrawal made an impression on even the boldest and least responsible editors. Few of the press arguments with the British came to public notice, except when they reached a critical stage.

Nigel Watt, chief of the GIO in the mid-1960's ran his office with briskness and efficiency. He gathered and issued all Hong Kong news for the local media, and he did not permit reporters to question other departments. All queries had to be addressed to his office. Although he did not interfere with foreign correspondents, he did try to keep up with what they were doing and complaints to home offices were not unknown.

The Americans seemed not to mind the activities of the GIO, but British Commonwealth nationals who served as foreign correspondents had a different view. There was much talk by some of them about "press freedom," and "unwarranted activity" by the colonial government. The same kind of talk was heard among the non-Communist Chinese press. But all conceded that the British colonial administration was in a difficult spot. While it had to maintain the outward trappings of a free press, acting under certain undefined restraints, it also could not afford to condone any widespread anti-Communist campaigning on its territory.

All foreign propaganda activity in Hong Kong was therefore conducted in low key; in fact, those British organizations which were involved in such work did not publicize it. The theory was that if undue attention was not called to it, the Chinese Communists would not feel it necessary to make a public protest. Hong Kong offered the unusual spectacle of unacknowledged publications by both the U.S. and British governments of materials dealing with events inside Communist China. On some, the Americans made no secret of their interest, using the address of the U.S. Consulate in Hong Kong, 26 Garden Road, as the place of publication. On others, the material was issued without attribution.

The most important source material in Hong Kong on Communist China was a voluminous official translation service issued daily by the U.S. Consulate, the "Survey of the China Mainland Press." It ran to as much as thirty-five to fifty pages of single-spaced mimeographed sheets each day. There were other official services covering the China mainland magazines and provincial radio stations, as well as a number of interpretations and commentaries. One of the unacknowledged services was an important commentary, "Current Scene."

The British equivalent of the major American translation service was the "China News Summary," issued daily by the colonial regime's Regional Information Office, at 52 Robinson Road. This was the Hong Kong branch of the British Information Services, and acted in liaison with the local Government Information Service. For correspondents, the British translation had the virtue of compactness, greater selectivity, and often more useful information; the Americans, typically, put everything they could find into the hopper. In such unacknowledged British services as "The Interpreter" and "The Asian Analyst," the correspondents frequently found more meaningful material than they did in the much larger and less selective American outpouring.

The private services disliked calling attention to themselves; nevertheless, such excellent organizations as the Union Research Service, supported in part by an American foundation, and the China News Analysis, issued by Father Ladislas Ladany, a Hungarian Roman Catholic priest, were justly celebrated for their work and eagerly read.

In the mid-1960's it was a status symbol among American academics to be called to Hong Kong by one agency or another. The more furtive they were about their work, the greater status they achieved among the more impressionable correspondents. Much of the skulking around was neither seemly nor necessary under the circumstances. Visiting American scholars were received at the American-supported University Service Center and often given generous help. Organizations such as the Asia Foundation also were active in Hong Kong, but showed both discretion and wisdom in their public posture without resorting to pretentious mystery. The refugee organizations, including those supported by the American government and by various religious groups, did much to relieve human suffering but received precious little credit for it because of their self-imposed restrictions. Refugee interviews, in any event, had lost their popularity among most journalists because so many contradictory and unverifiable claims were made about what was going on inside Red China.

In view of Hong Kong's importance, the U.S. Government with good reason gave its consulate the status of one of the more important embassies in Asia and placed a seasoned diplomat in charge. E. E. Rice, the Consul General since 1964, had been a member of the State Department's Policy Planning Staff. He had the average diplomat's generally unfavorable impression of the press, but he displayed a thoroughly journalistic attitude as the editor of the world's largest news service on Communist Chinese affairs. His first instinct was to reach for the blue pencil and make it less notable for its bulk; however, only an editor of long experience could have made vital changes in the system without weakening the whole structure. Rice kept things going.

The translation service on Wanchai Road, in which thirty-five Chinese were employed, was under the direction of the political section of the consulate, with seven Foreign Service officers actively engaged with the result in whole or in part. It was classified as intelligence work, although most of it represented a completely open operation. The USIS in Hong Kong operated separately, originating what was called "outgoing propaganda," based to some extent on the translation service. In USIS, too, there were both acknowledged and unacknowledged materials, one of the latter being the widely read China News Service, for which some resident journalists did piecework. Also, the consulate's political and economic officers generally were respected by the more knowledgeable American correspondents for their willingness to talk for background.

Despite the extent of the American reporting machinery and the experience of the political officers who directed it, there were some obvious drawbacks. The most serious was the basic matter of diplomatic rotation, which was so poorly scheduled in Hong Kong that virtually all knowledgeable officials were removed in the mid-1960's and an entirely new team came in with scanty knowledge of what was going on. It also seemed strange that so few Americans in key spots in the consulate understood more than a smattering of Chinese, either Mandarin, Cantonese, or any of the lesser-used tongues, and even fewer could make sense out of a Chinese newspaper. Even among the American correspondents, there were some who didn't need a translator to read a Chinese newspaper.

The English-language newspapers in Hong Kong were, of course, a boon to both diplomats and correspondents. The largest was the British-owned *South China Morning Post,* with 18,000 circulation, and its evening and Sunday editions, all published by the quiet and retiring T. G. N. Pearce, an important figure in the British community. The smaller Hong Kong *Tiger Standard,* with 10,000 circulation, was patterned after an American newspaper and carried all the standard American features, from comics to baseball and movie news. Both reflected the dominant interests of their readers in the detailed coverage of shipping and financial news.

The *Tiger Standard* was important primarily because it was the English-language publication of the dominant Sin Poh newspaper group, consisting of three large and influential Chinese dailies and the Sing Tao *Weekly.* The publisher, Miss Aw Sian (Sally Aw), was a respected conservative with strong American and Chinese Nationalist ties, a diligent alumna of the American Press Institute, and an active participant in the affairs of the International Press Institute. She was the daughter of Aw Boon Haw, whose colorful Tiger Balm Gardens, named after his patent medicine, had become a veritable Chinese Disneyland for the children of Hong Kong. After comparatively few years as a journalist, his daughter was successful enough with her newspapers to build an impressive new home for them. She owned the largest newspaper in Hong Kong, the Sing Tao *Wan Pao* ("Star Island Evening Post"), with 125,000 circulation. Her *Express,* a morning newspaper, had 58,000 circulation.

Another important conservative Chinese newspaper operation was the *Kung Sheung* ("Industrial and Commercial Daily"), with a morning edition of 56,000 and an evening edition of 20,000. It, too, had ties to the American and the Chinese Nationalist communities, one of its most active officials being Robert Ho, the secretary, an alumnus of the Columbia Graduate School of Journalism. Of the forty Chinese-language newspapers that were important enough to classify, two were official Communist organs, one was an official Kuomintang (KMT) paper, fifteen were pro-KMT, six were pro-Communist, and seventeen called themselves independent, although some were little more than mosquito sheets (papers of mysterious origin and short life). The conservative press, as might be expected, had the advertising and the affluent readership.

The Communist organs, *Ta Kung Pao* ("Impartial Daily") and *Wen Wei Pao* ("Literary Concourse Daily"), both were relatively small, with circulations of slightly more than 10,000 each. As branches of parent newspapers on the mainland, they were closely watched for swings in the Chinese Communist line.* It was widely believed that their instructions were transmitted through the New China News Agency by way of the regional Chinese Communist Party headquarters at Canton. NCNA maintained one of its largest establishments outside the Chinese homeland in Hong Kong, but it barred unfriendly foreigners from its premises and did not often permit its agents to mingle with the other journalists. One of the few places where Westerners might see a Chinese Communist editor or reporter was at an Agence France-Presse party.

Among the refugees, in commerce, in industry, and through the press and radio, the contest for the loyalties of the Chinese in Hong Kong went on in low key. Although there were no demonstrations or raised fists or threatening red banners in the streets of the colony, this did not mean that the Chinese Communists were any less determined. They simply did not want to upset their capacity for earning foreign exchange while they went about their propaganda work. The Peking

* The Peking edition of *Ta Kung Pao* ended its sixty years of publication during the 1966 purge and was reissued as *Chien Chin Pao* (*March Forward News*).

Radio, the words of the *Jenmin Jih Pao* (*People's Daily* of Peking) and of *Hung Chi* (*Red Flag*) had many ready outlets in Hong Kong. Among the 600,000 copies sold daily by the Chinese press alone, it was calculated that the Communists had at least 120,000 among the pro-Communist papers, plus the two official Communist organs. All the effective devices of Communist propaganda on the Chinese mainland, from group dramatics and group reading to the *tatzepao* (posters), had ready acceptance, although their use was necessarily more restricted in the colony.

The Chinese border, so forbidding to unwanted American foreign correspondents, was far less a problem to the ordinary Chinese. Citizens from the mainland with relatives in Hong Kong could and did visit the Crown Colony and take back with them such things as food, medicine, and other essentials. It was not as easy for Chinese in Hong Kong or other Overseas Chinese to visit relatives in the homeland, but some did so with regularity and returned without incident. It made for good feeling among Chinese—a sense of belonging, the friendly grasp of identity with the homeland. If it outraged the unfriendly foreign correspondents at the same time, that also suited Peking's purposes. The Chinese Communists were well aware of the importance of the press, but they also realized it was least useful to them when they could not exert control over it.[13]

3. THE CHINA-WATCHERS

The tricky business of watching China from Hong Kong and reporting on developments to the American mass media became increasingly important in the 1960's. However, relatively few correspondents could be considered full-time China specialists, and not many of these were as well qualified as their academic counterparts. China-watching took time, effort, a great deal of money, and solid support from the few mass media at home that were interested in an essentially irritating and often dismal subject.

For the correspondent who came to Hong Kong for the first time to report on China, the paper work was a shock. The New China News Agency daily report, which came from Peking in the early morning hours, averaged sixty pages a day and constituted the basic source of information. The voluminous material from American, British, Nationalist Chinese, and other official and unofficial sources had to be scanned. Yet, there was seldom much of a startling nature in this mountain of paper and teletype copy. Days might go by without the discovery of anything worth digging out and examining for publication.

No one could blame the established correspondents for varying the monotony by seeking action elsewhere. Some periodically made the rounds of Southeast Asian capitals. Others went back to their old calling as war correspondents in South Viet-Nam. Nor could there be real ground for complaint against the television correspondents who roved the area in search of film footage and dramatic stories that would interest American viewers. TV documentaries on China, like newsmagazine cover stories on the same subject, were inclined to repeat themselves, because China, under Mao Tse-tung, changed slowly, and essentially the same themes were sounded day in and day out from Peking.

Takashi Oka, of the *Christian Science Monitor,* a Harvard-trained American of Japanese birth who acquired a reputation as a China specialist while in Hong Kong, expressed the frustration of a sensitive correspondent in this manner:

> I'd like to know China as a Chinese does, but it is very difficult to do.
> . . . Here in Hong Kong, I have just not felt free about contacting Chinese and talking to them. . . . If I myself had been born and raised in China, or if I could have identified myself with it during the Sino-Japanese War or during World War II, if I could have been in Chungking when it was being bombed or with the Communists at Yenan or the Nationalists in the Southwest, it might have been different.

It was in this mood that he left Hong Kong for a two-year study assignment in Southeast Asia under the auspices of the Institute of Current World Affairs. Upon his arrival in Saigon, he wrote: "This is a controversial country, too, but it is smaller and more manageable. One can get to know the people, one can argue with them. One can visit them in their homes. . . ." [14]

Nor was Oka the only specialist who grew restless while watching China from a distance. Robert S. Elegant, after almost a decade of China-watching for *Newsweek* in Hong Kong, welcomed a shift to Bonn and Moscow; in 1966, after being away three years, he returned to Hong Kong for the Washington *Post.* Seymour Topping, the New York *Times's* chief correspondent in Southeast Asia, varied his Hong Kong reporting on Communist China with frequent trips to areas where the news was breaking, until he was called to New York as the *Times* foreign editor in 1966. The news-magazine bureau chiefs, Frank McCulloch, of *Time,* and Robert K. McCabe, of *Newsweek,* also roamed the area, with Frank McCulloch of *Time* frequently working more in South Viet-Nam than he did at his Hong Kong base. *Time* had its own China specialist, Loren Fessler, who stayed on the job and wrote almost exclusively about the news from behind the Bamboo Curtain.

As for the American wire services in Hong Kong, each had an American in charge of a small staff of Chinese and bothered very little with the story of Communist China except as a backstop for Tokyo. Occasionally, a specialist such as Roy Essoyan, of the AP, born and brought up in the Orient, was assigned to Hong Kong. But more often than not, the American wire-service bureau chiefs in Hong Kong were mainly salesmen and competent technicians.

The British differed little from the American routine except that their numbers were fewer and their concern over Communist China less intense because they had direct access to Peking. The dean of correspondents in Hong Kong, Richard Hughes, a much-respected Australian, held court now and then at the Hong Kong Hilton, but generally he was all over Southeast Asia as correspondent for the London *Sunday Times* and the *Economist*. The same was true of Frank Robertson, of the London *Daily Telegraph*; Denis Warner, a correspondent for Australian newspapers and *The Reporter* magazine; and Jeff Thursby, of the London *Sunday Express*. Ian McCrone, the brawny New Zealander who ran the Reuters bureau in Hong Kong, was the backstop for China news for the British correspondents.

What it came down to, in reality, was that Hong Kong, for Reuters and for the Americans to a lesser extent, was the main center for a large volume of business and financial news of Asia. From the standpoint of Reuters Comtelburo and such American agencies as the McGraw-Hill News Service, there was a lot more dollars-and-cents value in the dull daily financial statistics out of Hong Kong than the often obtuse analyses of Communist Chinese affairs by specialists in international affairs.

Next to the Americans and the British, the Japanese journalists were the most numerous in Hong Kong. Most of the major Japanese newspapers and the two agencies, Kyodo and Jiji, had representatives there. Agence France-Presse maintained a small bureau, but did nothing special with it. The West Germans, Chinese Nationalists, Indians, and a few others also had correspondents in the Crown Colony. But the unappetizing truth was that the China story took more time, money, and effort than most editors cared to spare, particularly in the United States, except when there was sensational news to report. The few China specialists who stayed on the job, therefore, were likely to become bitter and disillusioned men, if they were not already.

Hong Kong was far better known to the journalists who flocked to

Saigon and the war as a place for a lively stopover on the way to South Viet-Nam and even livelier recreation on the way back. China-watching was only an incidental consideration to those who moved quickly in and out of the Crown Colony. They were not the kind of reporters who had much use for working with documents when there was any prospect of action in their general vicinity. Not many documents could produce eight-column headlines or ten minutes of prime time on network television in the United States, even during the Red Guard rampage inside China in 1966.[15]

An analysis of a list of correspondents made available at the American consulate in a typical year, 1964, bore out the comparative thinness of the group permanently assigned to Hong Kong. Out of a total of 56, 28 were Americans; but 16 of these were usually in Viet-Nam or elsewhere in Southeast Asia, 3 were stringers and only 9 were left to make an effort to keep in touch with Chinese affairs. There were only 2 from the news magazines, and only 7 from newspapers. Of other nationalities in Hong Kong, there were 12 British, 8 Japanese, 4 Germans, and 1 each from France, Nationalist China, India, and Indonesia.[16]

Very few of the correspondents were happy about the flow of news from Hong Kong either to the United States or from the chief American news centers. One correspondent wrote:

The dominant feature here is the presence of Red China and the fact that United States power and influence is the only thing that keeps Peking from establishing a hegemony in the area greater than at any time in Chinese history.

Now that Europe has recovered stability, I consider the Far East as the most important problem in United States foreign policy. It is fascinating and a real challenge. I'm appalled that United States newspapers and wire services don't give it more emphasis by assigning men of the caliber we have in Europe and in Washington.

Another correspondent observed:

Almost all coverage of the United States in Southeast Asia comes from wire services. Few media in these countries have correspondents based in the United States although occasionally editors from here visit the United States on study tours. Otherwise, they rely on wire services, USIS handouts and the syndicates . . .

Not enough United States newspapers, magazines and other news-gathering organizations have correspondents based in Hong Kong. But like their Asian counterparts, these American publications that do have correspondents here invariably deal with Asia in blacks and whites. The greys and intangibles in this region rarely show through in the United States coverage . . .

There was self-criticism and soul-searching, too. A correspondent wrote:

On China, at least at the outset, I tried to be as fair as possible, and in some respects I feel I did better stories while I was still in the States—researched them more carefully, for instance, than after I came here. I was genuinely touched when a Chinese friend in the United States . . . told me he liked my articles because I did not automatically consider everything Chinese as bad.

But I must confess that since those early years, my attitude toward China—both Chinas—has been extremely ambivalent. I try not to hurt the pride of any Chinese—Communist or Nationalist—in being Chinese. But I have written many articles . . . which have been page 1 but which I considered trashy and of not even ephemeral value . . .

In Hong Kong, as elsewhere in Asia, however, it was often evident that those who least required such critical evaluation of their own work were the first to worry over it, and those who needed it most seldom made an effort to improve. If the home office didn't want more than the bare routine of Chinese news coverage out of Hong Kong, the policy was not challenged except by the most resolute and experienced correspondents. And if headlines blossomed elsewhere, then the heart of the China story was left to the wire services and a mere handful of important publications. The story of the journalist in Hong Kong, during the mid-1960's at least, was with few exceptions one of neglected opportunities and little-used resources.[17]

4. THE PROPAGANDA WAR

When Jacques Marcuse left Peking after two and a half years, by "mutual disagreement," he was understandably discouraged over the status of the Western journalist in Red China. To a greater extent than any articulate Western correspondent who had tried to tell the story of the Russian revolution forty years before, he felt himself to be a pawn in a ruthless propaganda war. He was, he said, merely a "cloakroom ticket" that was necessary to the Peking regime so that it could maintain an office for the New China News Agency in Paris.

In addition to his work for Agence France-Presse, Marcuse had also written occasionally for the New York *Times* and the London *Sunday*

Times. Needless to say, despite the requirements of precensorship by the correspondent himself, his views had not always been complimentary. Once, at the outset of his stay in Peking, he had been accused of "slandering the Chinese people," but the charges had not been pressed. At the end, he said of himself and his few Western colleagues who could see Peking's "Forbidden City" from afar but were not allowed to enter it: "We're completely ignored, with no contact except at official functions. No briefings, no press conferences, no interviews—just handouts. There are no good stories floating around Peking. We work on what we get, usually in the dead of night." But the special correspondents who arrived for a visit received welcomes fit for minor potentates from the emerging African states. As Marcuse phrased it, "You are taken in hand, shepherded around, shown sights and politely ushered out—with an impression of a country that doesn't exist." [18]

An aggressive, powerful, and self-confident China used the few Western correspondents in Peking in whatever way it wished and tried to influence others with its vast propaganda machine in every Asian center from Tokyo and Hong Kong to New Delhi and beyond. Peking's propaganda war was necessarily based on the control of its 750 million people. The regime used endless demonstrations in the cities and in the countryside to project its manifold purposes, both declared and real. The Chinese Communists had taken the most energetic steps at the very outset of their rule to regulate newspapers, news agencies, broadcasting stations, and other news media. The directives that were issued from Peking in March, 1950, called in effect for the mass media to serve the needs of the state and to advance the cause of the Communist revolution. To quote Mao Tse-tung's list of five major functions, the press was "to organize, to stimulate or encourage, to agitate, to criticize and to propel." [19]

Every device was employed to magnify the influence of the press, including the use of thousands of part-time correspondents (for the New China News Agency alone, there were 70,000 in China), collective reading and study groups in the towns and villages, and the radio transmission of important articles in leading papers. Yet, in a country which was only 50 percent literate at best and probably a good deal less in many sections, the press alone could not do the propaganda job set by the government. There were only 392 daily newspapers, with a total of 12 million daily copies, to cover a great nation, and the principal organ of government, the *Jenmin Jih Pao,* was listed at 800,000 daily circulation.[20]

It was for this reason that Peking built up the use of radio, with 233 transmitters, nearly 7 million receivers, and 8,800 wired radio systems for collective listening groups.[21] It was contended that each people's commune had its own reception service. This caused Robert Guillain to observe, "The head of a good Chinese citizen today functions like a sort of radio receiving set. Somewhere in Peking buzzes the great transmitting station which broadcasts the right thought and the words to be repeated. Millions of heads faithfully pick them up, and millions of mouths repeat them like loud-speakers." [22]

Dr. Sripati Chandrasekhar, an Indian scholar, was even more impressed with the pervasiveness of the Chinese radio propaganda. He heard it blaring "in the bus, in the train, in the trolley, the sleepers, and dining cars, on street corners, in villages, towns and cities—just about everywhere." He told of seeing a loudspeaker in a treetop in a backward village and mused, "You can escape the sun and the moon but you cannot escape the radio and the loudspeaker . . . A few times on trains I had to feign illness so I could pull out the plug under the loudspeaker to enjoy a few hours of quiet. The citizen does not have a minute of silence in which to rest his mind or reflect on his new life." [23]

As if this were not enough, there were tens of thousands of *tatzepao,* which were put up everywhere to convey crude propaganda messages. Most effective of all was the Chinese system of incessant meetings, in which no participant could escape voicing his views; if he balked, he was drawn out by an "activist" with threats. Movies, traveling shows, and the beginnings of a television system all were made to play a part.

Mark Gayn wrote:

Mainland China is seemingly involved in a perpetual demonstration. It is a rare day that people aren't called out to march in protest against something or other, to shout defiance, to listen to words of hate and anger.

The man produced by this is militant, intense, humorless. He is taught to accept exaggeration as normal, to use barnyard language, to see the complex panorama of world events in only two colors, white and black. How can an individual do otherwise when President Johnson is customarily called "gangster" and "bandit," Britain is described as "pimp," and the authoritative *Jenmin Jih Pao* employs four-letter words? To a much greater degree than in the Soviet Union of the 1920s, personal lives in China are subordinated to the needs of the state and the Communist Party.[24]

The journalist from time to time produced more sympathetic images of Communist China—a nation devoted to such higher virtues as cleanliness, honesty, and the education of the young; a land that was impoverished, but virtuous and moral beyond human belief, being even more rigidly puritanical than most modern revolutionary states; a harsh police-dominated regime which had, nevertheless, banished prostitution and crime in Shanghai and made it a nine o'clock city. These were surface manifestations that were pointed out to the correspondent, if he happened to be too dull to notice. But the West seldom heard of such things as the Chinese Communist narcotics traffic, because information of that kind was very difficult to get, even in an open society. Nor was there much in print on the other ills that afflict mankind, including Chinese, such as the bribery of police, the miscarriage of justice in the courts, the breakup of the family, the rise of juvenile delinquency, and the favoritism shown to those who were valued by the regime. These things, Peking indignantly contended, did not exist in the land, but there was room for doubt even if proof could not be produced. The great purge of 1966 testified eloquently to the strains inside China.

During the time of the "hundred flowers" era in 1957, when Mao Tse-tung temporarily permitted the Chinese to criticize their regime, there was such an outpouring of resentment that the government speedily put the lid on again and punished the dissenters. But enough was seen and heard to indicate that the problem of food shortages had not been solved, that a substantial body of intellectuals was outraged by Communist "thought control" patterns, that the Chinese genius for trade had been bottled up by ruthless socialization, and that the peasantry had been desolated by the communes. The failure of the "Great Leap Forward" policy in the following year had added to the disillusionment over the economic methods of the Chinese Communist state. While there was no organized opposition to it, the Chinese Nationalists having been so thoroughly discredited on the mainland, some specialists believed Peking's support at home was by no means as great as it pretended.[25]

For the Western correspondent outside its borders, therefore, Red China presented a constant problem. The propaganda images, all of which had some basis in reality, were not easy to combat because they were so widespread. They were propagated by a program of foreign broadcasting that was among the most extensive in the world, by attractively printed magazines and brochures in foreign languages, and by a parade of distinguished members of the government to friendly nations near and far. The Communists abroad who had gone over to Mao Tse-tung were among the most fanatical in their support of the new China and its ways.

Even to those who were not well disposed toward Peking, the notion gained ground that the Chinese Communists were in absolute control of the land. Consequently, when refugees by the tens of thousands began pouring across the Chinese mainland's borders in the spring of 1962, the correspondents had difficulty persuading their editors in New York and elsewhere that the exodus was real and vital. For those who believed in Peking's reports of progress toward universal education, it was a letdown to learn that Loren Fessler, of *Time,* had spent two days interviewing Chinese refugees in the Portuguese colony of Macao before he found one who was literate.[26] Red China was neither as potent as its friends believed nor as weak as its enemies contended. Because it was the largest state in the world, with a population that had neither enough food nor enough education, it also had the greatest variety of problems, and none could be solved overnight.

Bit by bit, the correspondents found that there was a degree of meaning—a kind of code—to the public posture of the Peking government. The constant warnings to the United States, which ran into the hundreds in the mid-1960's, came so frequently that they no longer were news; the same was true of all except the most violent street demonstrations. But when there was an editorial in the *Jenmin Jih Pao,* written by the editorial department and so labeled, it was regarded as a serious statement of government policy. Almost as meaningful was an editorial in the same publication written by an "observer." The commentary that ran through the newspaper sometimes carried clues to future events, as well, for those who had the background to make their own interpretation. Other pieces of the "code" were carried in statements issued in the name of the government, articles in the ideological publication *Hung Chi,* the once respected independent newspaper, *Ta Kung Pao (Impartial Daily),* and the English-language *Peking Review.*

For all his effort, there was a limit to what the journalist could do. In the great power struggle that was waged in 1966, he had to pass along what he learned from the Chinese mass media and guess at the significance of the news. It was apparent that Chairman Mao Tse-tung's favorite, Defense Minister Lin Piao, was being built up as a future master of China. But if he was No. 2 to the seventy-two-year-old Mao, such figures as Premier Chou En-lai and two newcomers to power, Tao Chu and Chen Po-ta, still bore close scrutiny. The once important Mayor of Peking, Peng Chen, and the armed forces Chief of Staff, General Lo Jui-ching, both had fallen, and the head of state, Liu Shao-chi, was just a figurehead. But as to the inner meaning of all these moves, there could only be the sheerest speculation.[27]

Another limited contribution which a number of correspondents made to the journalistic literature on Communist China was the continuous examination of its borders. Richard Dudman, of the St. Louis *Post-Dispatch,* who made several such tours, returned from one with a denunciation of widely held beliefs and expectations about Red China in the United States, among them that starvation was widespread, internal revolt was possible, and that the Chinese people would return to their traditional friendship with the United States if they could. Such thinking, Dudman wrote, was "false, a compound of exaggeration, wishful thinking, misinformation and ignorance about what is going on in the biggest country in the world." [28]

The *Wall Street Journal* had two of its correspondents make a detailed examination of the Chinese-Russian frontier in central Asia, to the extent that they were able to do so. One, Ray Vicker, wrote from Alma Ata that shots had been exchanged across the border and that Soviet guards had captured Chinese infiltrators. Along great stretches of the frontier, he reported, the Chinese had fortified and mined a belt 200 miles deep. [29] Norman Sklarewitz, after viewing some of the contested lands along the Amur River, wrote of Russian machine-gun emplacements, barbed-wire installations, and air fields crammed with the latest model Soviet jet fighters. In the spring of 1966, Peter Grose reported from Moscow in the New York *Times* that large movements of Soviet troops were taking place in Mongolia as part of a show of strength against the Chinese. All signs pointed to continued tension along the Chinese-Russian frontier. [30]

It remained for specialists like Takashi Oka to put together a meaningful report on the economy of Communist China that could be understood by the daily newspaper reader. He wrote in 1964:

After three years of desperate floundering, Communist China's economy is moving forward again. It is a slow, difficult uphill climb. And it is a solitary one—for this time there is no Soviet helping hand. . . . Peking must spend its meager hoard of foreign exchange to buy wheat from Canada, Australia and other Western countries. . . . Nevertheless, it seems to have enough additional purchasing power to attract scores of businessmen from Western Europe and Japan.

This assessment was given dramatic verification in 1966 by the agreement of a West German consortium to build a $150-million steelworks in China, which eventually would require the assistance of literally hundreds of Western European companies. It was only belatedly that the United States announced its opposition. [31]

As for estimates of Communist China's military strength, most of the authorities who testified before the Senate Foreign Relations Committee in 1966 expressed the belief that the People's Liberation Army was fundamentally weak. Brigadier General Samuel B. Griffith II, USMC (Ret.), called China a "paper tiger" and argued it was likely to remain one for ten years despite its boasting. He based his judgment on what he believed to be Peking's inability to equip its 2.5-million-man army for action beyond peripheral areas. [32]

Yet, General Griffith and other commentators tended to agree with Hanson Baldwin that while China could not successfully challenge the United States, it could and did present a very real threat to American allies in Asia.[33] Another specialist, Donald S. Zagoria, of Columbia University, called Communist China weak compared with the world's other great powers, but conceded it was an "imposing power in Asia." He summed up: "For all its weaknesses, a messianic, Communist China, armed with nuclear weapons and determined to assume what it regards as its rightful place in the world, will certainly preoccupy American policymakers throughout the latter decades of the twentieth century, largely because of its strength in Asia." [34]

The effort to counteract the Chinese propaganda emphasis on its vast manpower, which was thus undertaken by individual analysts, had a parallel in the public discussion that surrounded the explosion of China's first atomic device. Here, the U.S. Government determined to take the edge off a momentous scientific and political achievement by giving advance notice of it. Secretary of State Rusk himself issued a public statement predicting the nuclear blast in the Sinkiang desert, which took place on October 16, 1964.

When the news was announced by the Foreign Ministry in Peking and spread by the New China News Agency and the Peking Radio, it was carried to the rest of the world quickly by the Western wire services out of Tokyo. The relatively small size of the first device and the lack of any means of swift, certain delivery of a nuclear blow outside Chinese Communist territory both were emphasized in most accounts. Japanese atomic scientists, who were in a position to know a good deal about the test, lent their prestige to pointing out these limiting features.

Nevertheless, there was exultation in Peking over what the Communist regime called "a powerful blow at the United States imperialist policy of nuclear monopoly and nuclear blackmail." [35] The reaction elsewhere in Asia wasn't as favorable as Red China might have expected for the first non-Western atomic blast. There had been time to prepare, to think things through. In Japan, there was a protest march by leftist students before the Chinese Communist trade mission office in Tokyo. In India, the split in the Indian Communist Party was deepened when its publication, New Age, proclaimed, "The Chinese leadership has filled its cup of chauvinistic power mania to the full. The explosion of its dirty bomb affords the latest and most perilous proof of its militaristic power mania." [36]

When the second Chinese atomic test came on May 14, 1965, it was preceded by a routine announcement from Robert J. McCloskey, the State Department's spokesman in Washington. Chinese atomic capability, like the weapons shortages that plagued its army, had already been placed in perspective. It did not have to be overstressed. In Japan, *Mainichi* burst out with an editorial, "However little radioactive dust falls over Japan, we are fed up with it. What the Japanese people really seek is an immediate halt to all nuclear tests for the sake of mankind." [37] But China would not participate in any nuclear-test ban, however limited, and refused otherwise to accept any check on its ability to develop the most powerful of all modern weapons.

It was the opening of a new and dangerous phase in the atomic era. For Peking did offer to discuss the prohibition and destruction of nuclear weapons, a favorite device to tickle the leadership of underdeveloped lands, but refused meanwhile to do anything constructive. Moreover, Peking's propaganda boasted of "world-wide acclaim" and took no notice of world-wide criticism. "Within a week," Professor Ralph L. Powell wrote, "Peking was casually referring to its 'nuclear weapons,' as if one test made it a full-fledged atomic power. This trend reached preposterous proportions in late December [1964] when Radio Peking declared that China had refrained from taking nuclear arms 'to the doorsteps' of the United States when Washington sent Polaris submarines to the Far East." [38]

Nowhere, however, did diligent research and continuity in the reporting of Communist affairs establish its value to a greater extent than in the successive stages of the great Communist schism. To the average newspaper reader in the United States, brought up on a steady diet of editorials proclaiming the unity of Communism as a world force, the break came as a great surprise; for a long time, some editors even refused to recognize it and had their doubts about correspondents who accepted it as a fact. By and large, American opinion had been unprepared for such an event, although there surely was no great secrecy attached to China's history as a great Asian power, the innate feeling of cultural and political superiority among Chinese people, and the early struggle of the Chinese Communist Party for survival without much help from the Soviet Union. The Sino-Soviet alliance of 1950 and the Korean War, of course, did much to give currency to the belief of the vast majority of the American public, and the press as well, that the two Communist giants would never be separated.

Yet, beneath the surface, all was not well. Harrison Salisbury often said that while he was a New York *Times* correspondent in Moscow in the early 1950's, he was conscious of veiled differences between China and the Soviet Union but had no way of pinning them down. In retrospect, it is probable that the Chinese were not at all satisfied with the arrangement under which they did the fighting in the Korean War and the Soviet Union did the supplying while also gaining major economic advantages in Asia. Certainly, Peking lost no time after the Korean War in obliging the Russians to agree in 1954 to the restoration of Port Arthur to China and the dissolution of joint Sino-Soviet stock companies. When Nikita S. Khrushchev ushered in the "de-Stalinization" era in 1956 at the Twentieth Congress of the CPSU, the time came for a change. Peking did not like the new line, and it did not like "Titoism," the slightly independent policy of President Josip Broz (Tito) of Yugoslavia. Through its championship of the Communist regime in tiny Albania, its sole ally in Europe, Red China pressed its differences with Moscow.

The Chinese "hard line" probably began in 1957. It was then that the first pressures were observed for an "Asia for the Asians," and it was seen that the Chinese could not be kept in line. There were some in the West who scoffed at the whole business as a "family quarrel." To this Edward Crankshaw responded, "If the Sino-Soviet quarrel is a family quarrel, then so was the Thirty Years' War." [39] Added to the ideological split were such practical differences as Russia's refusal to give China nuclear arms or help develop a Chinese nuclear capability, Russia's failure to give full support in the campaign against Taiwan, and the deep division over the Chinese campaign for greater Soviet backing in its Asian adventures.

At the Twenty-second Congress of the CPSU in Moscow on October 20, 1961, when the doctrine of "Wars of National Liberation" was approved, Chou En-lai scornfully thrust aside Premier Khrushchev's attack on the Albanian Communist Party. He said:

> We hold that if a dispute or difference unfortunately arises between fraternal countries, it should be resolved patiently in the spirit of proletarian internationalism and on the principles of equality and unanimity through consultations. Any public, one-sided censure of any fraternal party does not help unity and is not helpful in resolving problems. To lay bare a dispute between fraternal parties or fraternal countries openly in the face of the enemy cannot be regarded as a serious Marxist-Leninist attitude. [40]

These were fighting words within the Communist hierarchy. Yet, to the American reader, they represented but a small Communist squabble about a tiny country, Albania; few took the affair seriously. Even when Chou En-lai suddenly went home soon afterward, there was no way to gauge the seriousness of the split, either for correspondents with a general background or for specialists. Merle Fainsod, of Harvard University, recognized that there was a struggle for ascendancy between Khrushchev and Mao, but he thought its reverberations "will probably be contained within the Soviet Union itself." [41] Philip E. Mosely wisely remarked on "a wide-open field for speculation . . . for the future." [42]

In the wake of the Cuban crisis, when Khrushchev backed down on his policy of offensive rocket installations in the confrontation with the United States, both the specialists and the correspondents saw a deeper meaning in Peking's criticism of the Soviet failure. John Hightower, the diplomatic correspondent of the AP, wrote of the growing strain between the Communist giants over Cuba, over their leadership struggle, and over the Chinese border invasion of India. He raised the possibility of a "hidden crisis" between Peking and Moscow, saying, "An open split between them would change the political map of the world." [43]

From the fall of 1962, neither the correspondents nor the specialists had much doubt of what was going on, although there was still a great deal of skepticism in large areas of the American press. At length, the Chinese met the issue head-on. In a letter to Moscow on June 14, 1963, the central committee of the Chinese Communist Party attacked Khrushchev as an "adventurer" for putting his 40-odd missiles into Cuba in 1962 and then called him a "coward" for withdrawing them. The letter told him it was "sheer illusion" that he could hope to bring about a "world without weapons, without armed forces, without wars," as he put it, as long as "the system of imperialism and the exploitation of man by man still exists." To this, the Central Committee of the CPSU retorted on July 14, 1963, that it had a "well-justified suspicion" that "this is no longer a class approach in the struggle for the abolition of capitalism but for some entirely different aims." The Russians asked, "If both the exploiters and the exploited are buried under the ruins of the old world, who will build the 'bright future'?" [44]

In this manner, the split in world Communism, with all its portents, was confirmed. Within three years it had widened to such an extent that the Chinese rejected an invitation to attend the Twenty-third Congress of the CPSU, charging Moscow with working "hand in glove with the United States in a whole series of dirty deals inside and outside the United Nations." It was, the Chinese declared, a part of a "vain attempt to establish a Holy Alliance against China," and to "sell out the struggle of the Vietnamese people against United States aggression." [45]

These were the materials that made the daily pile of documents in Hong Kong—the English translations from Chinese sources—such difficult and important reading. They also led a scholarly correspondent to despair that he could ever disentangle himself sufficiently from the reporting of this violent propaganda war to see something of the people and the action behind it.

But if the Chinese Communist position was to be understood, the reporting and analysis of propaganda from Peking was the touchstone. From it, such an expert as George F. Kennan developed a sophisticated position which he urged upon Washington—a new policy through which the Chinese would be voted into the United Nations and recognized by the United States. This in itself was enough to revive the debate on American policy toward Peking. Another participant, Roger Hilsman, former Assistant Secretary of State for Far Eastern Affairs, was against recognition but urged the lifting of all American restrictions on trade and travel in Communist China. Despite his hard line against Peking, Secretary of State Rusk was willing enough to experiment with a limited group of scientists, other scholars, and journalists who wanted visas to get into Communist China. But there was no encouragement from Peking; if there was any prospect of an immediate benefit for the United States in the Sino-Soviet split, Washington couldn't find it.[46]

In addition to the recording of propaganda positions and the stimulation of national debate in the United States, the detailed reporting of the Communist Chinese output had one other result. The Peking propagandists were the first to report that the United States was sending bombers on raids in Laos. The Washington *Post* rebuked the administration, saying, "The country has come to a sad pass when it must turn to Communist China's New China News Agency for reports on covert military operations being conducted by the United States." [47] It was the ultimate triumph for a propaganda agency when it could publicize such a reproach to the American government from one of the greatest of American newspapers.

But if propaganda gained Communist China some victories, it also brought crushing defeats, as well. Castro's Cuba was one of the first to desert Peking. Another setback was the failure of the much-publicized "Second Bandung Conference," so named after the Afro-Asian conference of 1955 in Indonesia, to meet as scheduled in Algiers on June 26, 1965. On the eve of the projected meeting, which Communist China had hoped to use as a forum for rallying Asians against the United States, a revolution deposed the Algerian president, Ahmed Ben Bella, who had been just as vigorous in his support of the Chinese Communist cause as he had been of that of the Soviet Union. Subsequent street riots discouraged the delegates from meeting even though Chou En-lai, in Cairo, tried his best to save the conference.[48] It was put off, and Chinese pressure was much resented. Peking now faced a formidable struggle to seize control of the hearts and minds of the Afro-Asians. For the myth of Afro-Asian unity, like that of Communist solidarity, had turned out to be a fragile propaganda shell.

The propaganda war went on, nevertheless. On a short-term basis, the Chinese Communists harried the British in Hong Kong and inconvenienced the United States by protesting against the visits of American troops from South Viet-Nam to Hong Kong for rest and recreation. When the total reached 2,000 a month, there was a temporary suspension of the American troop movements in the late summer of 1965. Peking warned the British that Hong Kong had become a "base of operations for United States forces of aggression in Vietnam." But the American Seventh Fleet continued to use the port for "liberty visits" for its men, and soon ways were found by the soldiers and Marines to share in the pleasures of the one-time citadel of the South China Sea, as well as other rest centers from Tokyo to Bangkok.

On a long-term basis, the Chinese Communists took a more formidable and less flexible stance. Defense Minister Lin Piao signed his name to a major statement of Maoist policy on the twentieth anniversary of Japan's surrender in 1965, calling for "people's wars" in Asia, Africa, and Latin America to destroy the American "colossus" in the guerrilla manner, "piece by piece." It was a detailed analysis of the Maoist doctrine of world revolution by the control of the farmers and peasants, rather than the familiar Soviet program for the "dictatorship of the proletariat" through the formation of workers' cadres in the cities. Marshal Lin assailed Moscow as the center of a heretical philosophy opposed to "people's wars" and implied that henceforth Peking was the only true center for the Communist faithful.

The 50,000-word propaganda blockbuster was calculated to reinforce the struggle of the North Vietnamese and the Viet-Cong in their war against their southern countrymen and the United States, but it drew only the jeering response from Saigon that Peking was "prepared to fight to the last Vietnamese." Nor were the ferocious Chinese warnings to India somewhat later much more productive for Peking. When the Indians refused to evacuate certain border posts within three days, the Chinese extended their ultimatum by two days and then announced— much to New Delhi's surprise—that the Indians had complied. But nowhere was the Chinese policy of blackmailing its neighbors given a worse rebuff than in the "guided democracy" of one of its best friends, Sukarno's Indonesia.

It was at this stage, quite by chance, that the Senate Foreign Relations Committee entered on a public education campaign of its own in Washington to give the American people a broader view of China. Academic witnesses opened an attack on what some called the frozen position of the United States toward Peking. Others argued that China had so many troubles of its own, economic and military, that it could not be the kind of threat to the United States that was portrayed by Secretary of State Rusk. The upshot was a declaration by Vice President Humphrey, on the N.B.C. "Meet the Press" program, that he believed American policy on China should be one of "containment without necessarily isolation"—a phrase picked up from one of the academic witnesses, Professor A. Doak Barnett of Columbia. Nobody was really sure what that meant, least of all Peking, which proceeded to call Humphrey's vague offer of friendship "the kiss of Judas." [49]

Thus, whether China was covered from a Washington hearing room, from Peking by Reuters and AFP, or from Hong Kong by American correspondents, the net result almost invariably reflected a certain amount of confusion between the beliefs of the bold new thinkers, who wanted China in the United Nations with American recognition, and those who held to the old propaganda values that had dominated American public opinion for so many years. Yet, history would not wait. The 47-47 tie vote on Peking's admission in the 1965 General Assembly (with 20 abstentions) pointed to the shape of things to come in the United Nations. The question really was not whether the United States could keep Peking out, but whether Taiwan could be kept in.

This was an urgent reason for the offensive of the old liberals in Washington to try to change American policy. The fear of a new Chinese military venture was another. But unhappily, the issue was never clearly drawn. For example, the press became an incidental target in the inquiry (as often happens) rather than a mere medium of record. Professor David Nelson Rowe, of Yale, testifying before the Senate committee, accused the New York *Times* of "distortions of propagandistic journalism" for publishing a scholarly petition advocating a soft line toward Peking while not publishing another that called for a hard line.[50] Such incidents were scarcely calculated to change the opinion of the average American citizen that his government should walk warily in the view of Communist China while the war was on in Viet-Nam.

5. OVERTURN IN INDONESIA

Indonesian demonstrators roughed up John Hughes, of the *Christian Science Monitor*, late in 1964 after they had sacked the cultural center of the USIS in Djakarta. Some less aggressive bystanders saved him, one of them pleading with the mob, "How do you know this man is an American? He might be a Russian. Even if he is an American, there are good and bad Americans."

Hughes, a British-born American citizen, didn't bother to debate the matter. As a veteran foreign correspondent and a former Nieman Fellow at Harvard, he had learned to take such things in stride. But after he had returned to Hong Kong, his base, he brooded over the anti-American course the Sukarno government had taken. Neither he nor any other correspondent doubted at that time that a break between Indonesia and the United States was near.[51]

In less than a year he was back in Djakarta, where he and other correspondents reported the Communist-inspired coup that failed on September 30–October 1, 1965. The Indonesian Army's fear and resentment over the assassination of its chief of staff, General Achmad Yani, and five other leading generals burst all bounds. Even President Sukarno's efforts to spare the Communists were ruthlessly brushed aside by the new military dictator, General Suharto. Within a few months, the Indonesian Communist Party, third largest in the world, with a reputed membership of 2.5 million, was torn apart, its leaders slain, imprisoned, or in hiding. Estimates of the number of members killed ranged from 100,000 to 400,000. Its firmest supporter, Foreign Minister Subandrio, was jailed under death sentence, and Sukarno himself was reduced to a figurehead.

This was one of the biggest stories of the year but it caught the world press entirely by surprise. For with the exception of Communist China, no large nation in the world was covered more skimpily than Indonesia from the beginning of Sukarno's "Confrontasi" policy in 1964 to the early spring of 1966. At the time of John Hughes's frightening experience in Djakarta in 1964, only two Americans had been there day by day for any length of time. They were Neil Sheehan, who had covered the Viet-Nam war for UPI and at twenty-seven years of age had been hired by the New York *Times,* and Roberta ("Bobbi") Roth, then twenty-three years of age and a Barnard graduate, who had become UPI bureau chief in Djakarta because she happened to be on the spot when her predecessor, Ray Herndon, was expelled. The only other permanent representative of an American news organization in Indonesia then was Tony Yared, a forty-year-old Lebanese, employed by the AP. All had Indonesian help, for locals were indispensable in Djakarta, the city of a thousand rumors.

Correspondents such as Hughes, Seth S. King of the New York *Times,* and Bernard Krisher of *Newsweek* visited Indonesia from time to time. Many others were barred by some whim of Sukarno or his immediate entourage. Thus, the burden of day-to-day coverage was carried by the Americans, their colleagues for Reuters and Agence France-Presse, and a few correspondents of less importance. The Russians of Tass, the Indonesians of the Antara Agency, and the Chinese of the New China News Agency outnumbered the Westerners. In fact, the Chinese were the most powerful of all the correspondents' groups and easily dominated Antara and the local press.

At the time when Communists and pro-Communists were plotting to seize control of the army in a sudden coup, this was the extent of the news machinery on which the world press had to depend for whatever intelligence it could get of Indonesia, the fifth most populous nation in the world with more than 105 million people. It was a land in economic chaos, despite its great wealth in oil, rubber, tin, and other natural resources in its 3,000 islands, stretching across 3,000 miles of the Indian and Pacific oceans. Although its farmlands were rich, it was prey to chronic food shortages that plagued its people; even when the rice crop was good, as in 1965, the price skyrocketed, going from 320 rupiahs a liter in December, 1964, to 1,600 rupiahs less than a year later. But worse was to come, for the rupiah collapsed altogether in early 1966, going to 40,000 to the dollar. When a new rupiah was then established at 10 to the dollar, it quickly dropped to more than 100 to the dollar.[52]

Djakarta itself, a city of 3.5 million, was bleak and slumridden, with not a sign of a major effort to attack a monumental housing problem. The shiny new eighteen-story Hotel Indonesia, built by Intercontinental for an almost nonexistent tourist trade, and the ruin of the British Embassy, burned out by demonstrators in September, 1962, stood side by side as the symbols of hope and the ultimate result of Sukarno's foreign policy.

The fruit of that policy was war. With Sukarno's announced decision to destroy the Federation of Malaysia, created September 16, 1963, out of Malaya and three former British colonies—Singapore, Sarawak, and Sabah (North Borneo)—much of Indonesia's resources had been bent to that purpose. It had the support of the Indonesian Communist Party. It also engaged the efforts of the Indonesian Army of 270,000 with its estimated $1 billion in Russian arms.

Sukarno, a master in the devious ways of Southeast Asian political maneuvers, played one off against the other in his Malaysian confrontation and sought thereby to maintain his precarious balance as Indonesia's dictator. But it was a piecemeal fight—a series of commando attacks on the Malay peninsula by tiny parties of Indonesians that were generally picked off by the vigilant defenders before they could do much harm. Quite unexpectedly, when Singapore was wrenched out of the Malaysian Federation on August 9, 1965, because of Malay mistrust of growing indigenous Chinese power in the great port city, Sukarno temporarily won an advantage. He accepted the Malaysian split with Singapore as a personal victory and proceeded to step up his campaign in Kalimantan (Borneo) to try to pry loose Sarawak and Sabah, as well.

To the outer world, Sukarno at sixty-four seemed to have reached the height of his power. He elevated himself from the Bung ("Brother") of his people to their Bapak Presiden ("Father President"). His concept of "guided democracy" became a holy faith, apparently impossible to challenge. His vision of the New Emerging Forces (NEFOS) doing successful battle with the Old Established Forces (OLDEFOS) was accepted as the Indonesian gospel. He gloried in the building of a magnificent highway outside Djakarta, starting nowhere and ending nowhere, and such splendid public works as a new sports stadium for the NEFOS and the skeleton of a new international building complex for the same group to rival the United Nations. When his attention was called to Indonesia's weak and faltering industries and the nation's mounting economic problems, he brushed them aside. Economics, he told an interviewer, made his head ache. "I am Indonesia," he said.[53]

Despite his history of violence, ruthlessness, and double dealing, the Indonesian dictator liked to think of himself as a charming, polished man of the world with a special appeal for women. He had had three wives. Once, in a characteristically erratic change of mood, he even relaxed his ban on *Time* magazine to permit a girl correspondent to tour the country. He welcomed Bernard Krisher and Bernard Kalb, correspondents whom he liked, and consigned those he did not like to wait outside Indonesia's borders. With such a figure to write about, it is scant wonder that Sukarno's foibles and his amorous adventures became notorious in the world press, and particularly the American press.

Otherwise sensible American diplomats, noting the growth of Sukarno's anti-American feeling, assigned a share of a blame for it to the American newspapers and news magazines. However, the pitifully small group of Americans in the island dictatorship could scarcely spread these tales, since it was their business to remain in Djakarta for as long as they could. As for the rest, it was no sensational journalist, but a scholarly observer, Willard A. Hanna, who wrote the toughest assessment of Indonesia under Sukarno. It was not published in any sensational sheet, moreover, but in the American Universities Field Staff Reports:

The Republic of Indonesia, by practice of Sukarno's "Guided Democracy" and "Guided Economy," has worked itself into a political and economic state which amounts to neo-anarchy. The government has deteriorated into an ineffectual dictatorship, while the military, the Communists, and the palace politicians stalemate each other in the contest to determine who will inherit Sukarno's authority.

The economy has been wrecked beyond the ability of even a good government to put it together again in less than a decade. The currency is virtually worthless; consumption so far outdistances production that massive foreign aid serves mainly as a relief program; and manipulation, rather than development, has become a way of life. . . . Sukarno is beset by domestic problems that are irresolvable because he has rejected the devices of rationality.

Bemused by a sense of manifest destiny, he is driven to assert his own authority and Indonesia's throughout Southeast Asia. He is quite aware that relaxation of eternal crisis will lead to a violent recurrence of the domestic. Indonesian confrontation of Malaysia is the consequence.[54]

It was in connection with the Malaysian attack that Sukarno's anti-American drive took its most dangerous turn in the summer of 1964. After having spent $1 billion in American foreign aid, he swung for the headlines—and perhaps the favor of new sources of assistance elsewhere—by proclaiming before the long-time U.S. Ambassador, Howard P. Jones: "To hell with your aid!"

The Indonesian crowds, whom he swayed with ease at that time, acclaimed his demagogic appeal to their sense of independence from foreign masters. It meant something more than the end of an average annual $50-million American aid program to Indonesia and the closing of five wrecked USIS libraries. It was a sharp turn from the United States, which in 1949 had supported Indonesia before the United Nations in its war for independence against the Dutch. In 1965, when Sukarno belatedly realized that his Malaysian enemy had been elected to the Security Council, he took Indonesia out of the United Nations in a fit of personal pique.

No correspondent could shape the headlines for Sukarno. He created them quite deliberately by his own actions. The extent to which Indonesia made approaches to Red China was realized somewhat belatedly, in fact, in the Western press. The new relationship had been going on for some time before the Chinese foreign minister, Marshal Chen Yi, visited Djakarta in December, 1964, to seal a pledge of financial assistance for Indonesia. John Hughes wrote in the *Christian Science Monitor:* "With Communist China to the north and a Communist Indonesia to the south—between them controlling the two most powerful military establishments in Asia—Southeast Asia would be caught in a relentless Communist pincer movement. Clearly, Indonesia is not to be lightly dismissed." [55]

So great was Sukarno's vanity that he even rattled nonexistent nuclear weapons. An initial announcement that Indonesia's first atomic device might be produced in 1965 was greeted with derision in the West. Not at all discouraged, Sukarno then declared Indonesia would have an atomic bomb "in the near future," and tried to make a deal with China to explode one on his territory.[56] In his latter days, the Indonesian dictator had an almost Mussolini-like capacity for generating bad publicity outside his own country. But within his own borders, until his fall, he received the homage that would have been given to the most powerful of monarchs.

In addition to his efforts to play off the Indonesian Army and the Indonesian Communist Party against each other, Sukarno's absolute control of the Indonesian mass media helped to bulwark his regime. In the spring of 1965, when his Malaysian campaign seemed to be going well, he went before the Indonesian Journalists Association and announced that he was closing down all anti-Communist newspapers and periodicals in the country. "In a revolution," he said, "there should be no press freedom. Only a press supporting the revolution should be allowed to exist, those of the press hostile to the revolution must be eliminated."

The dictator thereupon purged nearly fifty newspapers by causing the Information Ministry to withdraw from them their licenses to publish. Next, the Journalists Association, under the leadership of a Communist editor, expelled thirty-two members and thereby barred them from working in their profession. Their crime had been to associate with an anti-Communist movement that had taken Sukarno's name, hoping it would be spared because it was "Sukarnoist." It wasn't.

The number of Djakarta dailies was reduced from some thirty to eleven, of which six were Communist. Of the five non-Communist papers, one was the semi-official Indonesian *Herald,* organ of the Foreign Office; another was an army-controlled paper; and the rest were organs of the Muslim parties.[57] Antara, the sole source for foreign news, continued under the influence of the New China News Agency and spread Peking's line, which evidently was then pleasing to Sukarno.

For any who might have thought of protesting, the example of Mochtar Lubis was a powerful deterrent. Lubis, the editor of the Indonesian *Raya,* had been thrown into jail on December 21, 1956, after publishing an exposé of government corruption by a "rapacious bureaucracy." He had never been brought to trial, but on April 29, 1961, had suddenly been freed. When he seized the opportunity to attend a meeting of the International Press Institute in Tel Aviv, where he denounced Sukarno, he forfeited his freedom once again. Upon his return to Djakarta, he was arrested and penned up once more. At forty-three years of age, he had been in prison for nine years despite an international campaign for his release.

Although its status was debased, the Indonesian press had not always been servile. From 1950 to 1957, it had been considered by the IPI to be "one of the most vigorous, ambitious, febrile and controversial groups of daily newspapers produced in any country." In 1958, when Lubis had won the first Ramon Magsaysay Award in Journalism, he had sent this message to the Magsaysay Committee, in Manila:

In our own time, the task of serving the people must become an increasing and vigilant confrontation with the facts of our time. Today in Asia, we may find leaders who yesterday were quite willing to die for democracy and human freedom, but are now easily beginning to say that in order to achieve freedom from want, it is excusable to do away with the freedom of expression, which is another way of saying that democracy and human freedom may be thrown away for the sake of filling the stomachs of the masses . . . We maintain that rice alone is not enough and that it is not by rice alone that we can promote and enrich human values.[58]

Sukarno did not have to pay attention to Mochtar Lubis. He controlled the Indonesian radio as well as the single television channel in Indonesia, which had an estimated 350,000 viewers, and did what he liked with the electronic media as well as with the press. Even on TV, at odd moments, there would be a sign warning the audience to beware of subversives. Most of the radio and TV news of foreign affairs, like other dispatches from abroad, came by way of Peking.[59]

While the dictator could not control the foreign correspondents, he was able to shut off nearly all of their Indonesian sources. For in Djakarta, as elsewhere in Southeast Asia, there were no recognized channels through which to follow the news. The correspondent could not go to a designated official for a statement of policy, a factual account of what happened yesterday or what was planned for today or tomorrow, or statistical material and other standard news fare. Such factual news, as well as files, libraries, and source books, simply did not exist in Indonesia. Even if it did, there were few trained officials who could issue such material and properly interpret it.

In Djakarta, by default, the news was handled by Sukarno, by Foreign Minister Subandrio, or by his press spokesman, Ganis Harsono, the second deputy foreign minister. It was seldom that anybody else was deputized to speak for the government. Had it not been for the American, British, Indian, and Australian embassies, the correspondents would have had little insight into the workings of the regime. As it turned out, not even the embassies knew much of what was going on in Indonesia.

To add to the troubles of the few foreign correspondents, their communications with the outside world were seldom dependable. News often moved with exasperating slowness, not only because of the dilatory processes of the Indonesian Government but also because of frequent difficulties with atmospherics. President Johnson's speech of August 4, 1964, calling for a "limited and fitting" response by the American Seventh Fleet to an attack on the U.S.S. "Maddox" in Tonkin Gulf, circulated in Djakarta at 2 P.M. on August 5 by USIS motorcycle carriers.

The wire services, which usually were first with big news, had atmospheric trouble that day, and USIS circulated the initial reports. However, four hours after the bulletins had been distributed, a check of guests at a USIS party showed that nine out of ten persons still did not know that anything unusual had happened.[60] As one correspondent said resignedly, "Indonesia is at the end of the line."

Like the Chinese Communists, the Indonesian government permitted the correspondents to file and telephone abroad. The AP's censorship report said tactfully, "Indonesia's Foreign Ministry Press Section maintained a close watch on stories about the country printed abroad, but there was no direct censorship. Unfavorable accounts sometimes led to action against the correspondent, ranging from a warning to expulsion." [61] These diplomatic phrases could not convey the insulting manner in which Ganis Harsono was accustomed to lecture correspondents, particularly Americans, on their duties to Indonesia; nor, for that matter, could they even hint at the state of mind of the correspondents whose work took them to Indonesia. It was regarded as one of the least desirable assignments in Asia.

The government, not content with harassing and discouraging the few foreign correspondents in Djakarta, also piled on the expense for their news organizations. It cost 45 cents a word for press-rate transmission to London and $1 a word for a straight message. The twice-a-day Morsecasts (a 30-minute transmission sent by Morse code) used by the wire services from Djakarta to points like Singapore and Hong Kong were cheaper, but not by much. In a city where accurate information was difficult to obtain, and even transportation was sometimes a major problem, the mere act of filing was a tribute to journalistic skill and determination. Some correspondents were glad to get away from Djakarta after two months, feeling that their judgments had been warped, and their news sense distorted. Others, like Bernard Kalb, maintained a long-distance love affair with the Indonesian people and never tired of talking of their experiences.

This separation from familiar standards and public reactions was, perhaps, the greatest difficulty for the Western correspondents to bear. To most of them, the meekness of the people outside Djakarta was beyond all belief. As Seth S. King wrote in the New York *Times:* "The capacity of the Indonesian people to tolerate hunger, inconvenience and their government's bungling and corruption seems limitless . . ." [62]

It was understandable, against such a background, that the correspondents in Djakarta should have given the world a picture of a resolutely anti-American Indonesia which in the summer of 1965 was at the point of concluding an arrangement with Communist China in return for Chinese atomic protection. The phrase "Peking-Djakarta Axis" was already current in the world press. Sukarno helped matters along when Marshall Green, a career Foreign Service official, presented his credentials on July 26, 1965, as the new American ambassador in Djakarta, succeeding Howard P. Jones. The dictator told him candidly that American-Indonesian relations had reached their lowest level. To emphasize the point, the new Ambassador was made the object of a violent demonstration by 2,000 Indonesians as he returned to his official residence. "Go home, Green!" they chanted, and they held aloft posters that read: "Get out or we'll kick you out." For emphasis, the American Consulate in Medan, Sumatra, was stoned by another mob and plastered with "Go home, Green!" signs.[63]

Time magazine reported that the Indonesian Communist Party "dominates the streets and, through the streets, President Sukarno." The *Christian Science Monitor* worried that the Communist Party might "attempt a coup should President Sukarno be removed for any reason from the political scene." And the New York *Times* quoted a Western diplomat in Djakarta on a probable break in American-Indonesian relations: "There is really nothing the Americans can do. It's just like the tide coming in." [64]

Sukarno and those closest to him had succeeded in creating an atmosphere of doom, much like the wave of despair that Moscow cast over the West long before the Communist takeover of Czechoslovakia in 1948 became a reality. The Indonesian Communist Party was pictured as a well-nigh irresistible force by many a commentator. Its leader, Dipa Nusantara Aidit, and his chief aides, Mohammed H. Lukman and Njoto, the chief theoretician, were dissected in columns of type in the most important newspapers in the Western world. The thin, black-haired Aidit, a Sumatran of Arab descent, was called the strongest power in the land next to Sukarno and frequently was said to have swayed the Bung himself. The Communist chieftain's main source of strength was, of course, his party; however, he also depended on most of the 2.5 milllion Overseas Chinese in Indonesia whether or not they were Communists. The poorer ones mostly belonged to the party, but the wealthiest, whether they liked Peking or not, were obliged in devious ways to help finance the Aidit forces.

General Abdul Haris Nasution, the Minister of Defense and Security, was given little chance of maintaining power against the Communists despite his control of the army. A part of it was said to be heavily infiltrated with Communists and the air force was held to be pro-Communist. Moreover, rumors spread throughout Djakarta that there was rivalry between General Nasution and the chief of staff, General Yani.

Thus, on the eve of the uprising by the leftist forces, few questioned the likelihood that Indonesia would fall to the Peking-oriented Communists. In fact, amid growing reports of Sukarno's physical infirmities, there was a suspicion that the change might come suddenly. The AP even sent in an extra man, just for protection against the unexpected. Yet, when the crisis occurred, the course of events was so chaotic that weeks elapsed before the whole story could be put together.

The Communist high command left Djakarta before the uprising began on October 1 to avoid blame for the murder of the six generals. But General Nasution escaped by scrambling over a back wall. General Suharto, commander of the elite Strategic Reserve, at once flung his troops against the rebel Palace Guard and two dissident Army battalions. Within hours, he was master of Djakarta.

Despite every effort the wily Sukarno made to spare his Communist allies, the army's wrath could not be contained. A story spread that Sukarno had been willing to sell out his country to Peking in return for the power and prestige of exploding a borrowed Chinese atomic bomb on his territory. It inflamed the Indonesian street mobs. Suharto, the new army chief of staff by Nasution's appointment, joined forces with the resurgent Muslims and drove the Communists from every position of power they occupied. From an estimated 100,000, the toll of the Communists was reported to have gone as high as 400,000.

Peking's embassy, under mob attack, became the No. 1 target in Djakarta. The Indonesian Communist leaders were hunted down and most of them were killed; the survivors were cast into prison. The army did not neglect to seize the Antara agency, purging it of Communists, and later the Indonesian press as well. It was almost a clean sweep.

Although the United States was no longer the prime foe in Indonesia, its immediate benefits were small. Sukarno, retaining his posts as president and premier for the time being, expelled the few remaining American reporters in a fit of pique. The army let him do it. Next, in a final gamble to stay on top, he fired General Nasution from his cabinet. That was his fatal error. For now the students took to the streets in support of the army, and the end was soon in sight. On March 11, 1966, faced with the inevitability of an army takeover, he yielded the last shreds of his authority to a triumvirate consisting of General Suharto, Adam Malik as foreign minister, and the Sultan of Jogjakarta as the minister for economics.

General Nasution returned in triumph to the revised cabinet. Subandrio, so long the chief ally of Peking's strategists in the foreign office, was dismissed to make way for Malik, a founder of the Antara agency and a former ambassador to Moscow. The Chinese Ambassador suddenly departed on "home leave," taking his staff with him. In a frenzy of fear, the Chinese residents of Djakarta tried to show their loyalty to Indonesia by rioting repeatedly outside the Peking embassy. The New China News Agency was closed, its 40-odd staffers expelled.

To the embattled generals who had been at the center of these dramatic changes, there must have been a certain amount of grim humor in the lyric dispatches of the few returning American correspondents who wrote of a "children's crusade" that had toppled Peking's bid for power over Indonesia. Now the correspondents had many stories to write about. Mochtar Lubis at last was released from jail, along with many other political prisoners. The Indonesian press, timidly at first, began to reassert its independence, but nobody could say for how long. The United States made modest gestures intended to relieve the desperate need of Indonesians for food and other necessities of life. And Foreign Minister Malik, shuttling between Bangkok, Rangoon, Manila, and Djakarta, ended the "Crush Malaysia" campaign and acted to restore normal relationships with Kuala Lumpur and the Philippines. Indonesia now resumed its participation in the United Nations, following a visit by Malik.[65]

If events in Indonesia had any meaning at all for Americans, it was that they could take nothing for granted in most of Asia. The few correspondents in Djakarta, caught between the comparative indifference of most American editors and the lack of dependable sources in Indonesia, had not been able to divine the course of events. Moreover, while Howard P. Jones was trying to hold the line at the American embassy and maintain an area for manuever, he was given an unsympathetic press at home. Thus, it was the Indonesians themselves who first shed light on the massacre of Communist leaders and the violent swing against Peking. If there was any intrepid reporting of this overturn by foreign correspondents during the most critical days, it had to be done for the most part by listening to the Djakarta radio. The result was to place a disproportionate responsibility for news from Indonesia on government sources in Djakarta, Singapore, Kuala Lumpur, and Washington.

6. THE DOMINOES

During the final stage of the French collapse at Dien Bien Phu in 1954, President Eisenhower drew his famous analogy between Southeast Asian countries and a row of falling dominoes. At his press conference of April 7, he dealt as follows with Communist strategy: "You have a row of dominoes set up and you knock over the first one and what will happen to the last one is the certainty that it will go over very quickly. So you have the beginning of a disintegration that would have the most profound influences."

If the Communists were able to knock over Indochina, he warned, the next to go might be Burma, Thailand, Malaya, and Indonesia. These, in turn, could topple into the American "big island" defense chain from Japan to the Philippines and even threaten Australia and New Zealand, he concluded. He counted the toll in terms of territory, the loss of vital raw materials, and the tens of millions of people who would fall under Communist sway.

The Joint Chiefs of Staff and the Pentagon were depicted at the time as "unhappy" about the President's enunciation of the "domino theory." [66] Eleven years later, with the United States committing its own large forces to the battle against the Communists in Viet-Nam and the British fighting to save a disintegrating Malaysia under Indonesian attack, Crosby Noyes wrote in the Washington *Star*, "The domino theory is a good deal less popular in administration circles today than it once was." Any clever American diplomat could open up a number of options to counter the notion that disaster could have a chain reaction in Asia. And yet, the unpleasant Eisenhower analogy could not be exorcised. It remained a part of the language.

"It is time to face up to the fact that we are engaged in a continuing process of containing or at least limiting the thrust of Communist China which threatens all of Southeast Asia," Noyes wrote. "To pretend that this thrust does not exist, or that it does not represent a threat to vital American interests, or that it can be limited by diplomacy, could well turn defeat into disaster." [67]

In Malaysia, so deeply involved at the time in its own struggle against Indonesia and so conscious that its fate was linked with Viet-Nam's, the sense of crisis was greater than anywhere else in Southeast Asia outside Saigon. As one Malaysian leader expressed it, "If Vietnam goes, Thailand will be next and Malaysia will go after that . . ."

Nobody was soft-pedaling the "domino theory" in the former center of British colonialism in Southeast Asia. The ejection of Singapore from the Federation of Malaysia was only a foretaste of things to come, for few then saw hope of retaining in the union the other former British colonies, Sabah and Sarawak, for very long. In Malaysia, consequently, there was a certain amount of impatience toward the American policy of patience in Indonesia. Ronald Stead, who had represented the *Christian Science Monitor* in Singapore for twenty years, remarked sadly, "The United States has gotten nothing for its policy but recrimination." [68] The Malaysians had become downright indignant over the U.S. proposal for a payment of 2.5 per cent interest on a defense loan, to be repaid in five to seven years. The offer had been rejected.[69]

During the events leading up to the separation of Singapore, American diplomats in Kuala Lumpur continued to give assurance that the United States—after hesitation—had "come down on the side of Malaysia." Much was made of the visit of Malaysia's Prime Minister, Tunku ("Prince") Abdul Rahman, to the United States. But at the same time, there were small things that rankled, such as the tendency of the Malaysian press to publish pictures of race riots in Harlem, but not of communal riots in Singapore. It also puzzled Americans that Malaysian institutions refused to recognize many American graduate degrees, including some in medicine. There were similar annoyances in other fields, particularly the press, where the strict Press Licensing Act and the Internal Security Act both were the basis for unfavorable comment.

In a situation in which both the United States and Great Britain were involved in Asian crises, they were far from fighting side by side in the mid-1960's. To those Americans who gave any degree of thought to it, Malaysia's cause was "the other war," in which the British Navy and 60,000 British troops were involved. Among American journalists, the story was told of a prominent news executive who hadn't realized there was a country called Malaysia until he had reached Singapore.

Although Malaysia made little impression on American public opinion, it had a limited but favorable press in the United States—all things considered—up to the time that Singapore was suddenly and unceremoniously ejected. Willard A. Hanna, in a report for the American Universities Field Staff, called it a "remarkable success story." [70] Robert Trumbull, of the New York *Times*, pointed out that "no other former colonial country in Asia has done so well," despite a twelve-year war it fought against bands of Communist guerrillas that did not end until 1960.[71] Robert K. McCabe, in *Newsweek,* wrote admiringly of the struggle of 10 million Malaysians (including, of course, the 2 million in Singapore) against 105 million Indonesians. Citing Malaysia's leadership in the production of tin and natural rubber, he compared its $309 per capita income, second largest in Asia after Japan's, with Indonesia's $85; the prosperity of modern Singapore and Kuala Lumpur with the backwardness and near chaos of Djakarta.

"In Kuala Lumpur," he wrote, "there is none of the feeling of being constantly watched that haunts a journalist in Djakarta. Malaysian officials talk freely, openly discussing the faults and virtues of their country without the nervous over-the-shoulder glance which punctuates this sort of conversation in Djakarta." [72]

Alas for Malaysia! All the nice things that correspondents wrote about the gallant little nation and the nasty things they reported about the big bully, Indonesia, meant very little once the break with Singapore occurred.

There had been high hopes when Malaysia was formed in 1963 that it would be a multiracial democracy of wealth and power, a beacon of modernity, an example for the troubled millions of Southeast Asia. Malaya, Sabah, and Sarawak all clustered about Singapore, the hub, a green and gracious city of 2 million, with the fifth largest port in the world. It was a place of magnificent homes, new hotels, spreading shopping centers, and wide and busy streets. There was a tendency to overlook the slum areas seething with discontent, the racial animosity between the dominant Chinese within the confines of the island and the glowering Malays. Optimists said everything was going to be wonderful. But the American wire services and the New York *Times* prudently moved their offices to Kuala Lumpur, the small but impressive Malaysian capital of 300,000 population, nestled in tropical splendor beside its magnificent Moorish-style government buildings and stretched far out into the Malayan hills.

It was a nation that needed many years of peace to resolve its manifold problems; yet, peace was as far off within its borders as it was without. All the efforts to sit on bad publicity about the racial tensions between Malay and Chinese were of no avail. Nor was there much sense to the pretense that all was well within Singapore because the Communist Party was outlawed, for its strength was as great a threat to Malaysia from the inside as Sukarno's "Confrontasi" campaign was from outside.

The fierce rioting in Singapore during July 21–25, 1964, between Chinese and Malays was the beginning of the end. Before order could be restored and the fanatical mobs on both sides dispersed, 24 persons had been killed, 460 others were injured, and 2,000 were jailed.

Had the correspondents realized it, they might have been forewarned. For some time before the riots, the extreme nationalist Malay press had been campaigning against the Chinese and their shrewd and resourceful leader, Lee Kuan Yew, Prime Minister of Singapore. But few correspondents except Dennis Bloodworth, of the London *Observer,* had learned of it or, if they knew, had taken the proper journalistic precautions. All the correspondents had long realized, of course, that the Malays feared Chinese political as well as economic ascendency in Malaysia. The Chinese had a 76 per cent majority in Singapore itself, and sufficient strength elsewhere to outnumber the Malays.*

---

* The ratio between Chinese and Malays in Malaysia was almost as much an issue as the number of Buddhists and Catholics in Viet-Nam. Journalists differed

Not much of this detail got into the world press. Besides the wire services, the main source of intelligence about Malaysia, resident correspondents were maintained only by the New York *Times, Christian Science Monitor,* London *Observer,* and, sometimes, the London *Daily Telegraph.* While the Americans often remained in Kuala Lumpur, Reuters, Agence France-Presse, and the British specials clung to Singapore, although it wasn't considered a good listening post any more. The American television tourists didn't show up for weeks at a stretch. The news magazines and some of the British and American papers had stringers. A few Indians, Japanese, and Australians would show up at irregular intervals, but that was about it before the storm broke.

The Reuters chief for Southeast Asia at the time, John Joseph Hahn —Jimmy Hahn to friend and foe alike—was a key man in the coverage of Malaysia and Singapore because of the British agency's dominant position. He was extraordinary—a small, brisk thirty-four-year-old Korean, Chinese-born and educated in Shanghai by French Catholic priests. In 1949, after the Chinese Communist victory on the mainland, he had gone to Hong Kong as a penniless refugee. As first, he had worked in a bank as a clerk; later, he had found a small night job in the Reuters bureau and combined the two posts to help support his parents and six brothers. When the time came to make a choice between the bank and Reuters, he decided without question on Reuters and had the good fortune to be trained by David Chipp, then the Southeast Asian manager. After Chipp became head of Reuters' Asian services, Hahn succeeded him.

The plucky little Korean inherited the large brick Reuters residence in Singapore, plus gardens and a car with chauffeur, but he had little time to enjoy life with his family. He was often all over Southeast Asia, directing seventy hours of transmission daily.

The smaller AP bureau in Kuala Lumpur at the time of the riots was a base of operations for Southeast Asia. Ordinarily, the news out of Malaysia was light. The two Americans and a few locals in Kuala Lumpur had a fairly easy time of it, except when they were traveling. There was, in addition, a talented and energetic thirty-four-year-old Filipino, Tony Escoda, with eleven years' experience as a journalist, degrees from Yale and the Columbia Graduate School of Journalism, and a Pulitzer Traveling Fellowship. He had been a bureau chief in Bangkok and was soon to take charge of the Manila bureau.

---

widely. The AP said that the 4.2 million Chinese in Malaysia plus those in Singapore outnumbered the Malays. Willard A. Hanna, by including Indonesians and other related racial groups with Malays, gave them 41.5 per cent and the Chinese 38 per cent. The 1961 census gave "indigenous" 46.2 per cent and Chinese 42.2 per cent.[73]

The UPI bureau in Kuala Lumpur was even smaller, consisting of Pat Killen, a thirty-five-year-old graduate of Colorado College, and a few locals. But he also had the unenviable task of fighting Reuters as well as the AP for news and sales. Agence France-Presse had an Indian, M. K. Menon, as its chief in Singapore, but he made no sales in Malaysia at the time and did a minimum amount of filing. In the Far East, AFP's strong point was Tokyo, with some sales in the Philippines, and a little in Hong Kong, Indonesia, Cambodia, and one or two other places.

The Singapore riot coverage was a good example of how the news machinery worked. When the fighting began on the birthday of the Prophet Mohammed, July 21, 1964, the AP sent in Tony Escoda by special night plane from Kuala Lumpur, a two-hour journey. He had no curfew pass and, soon after his arrival, was warned away from the Chinese quarter by police with the observation, "You look too much like a Malay."

That was the least of Escoda's problems. He was in a struggle against a Reuters task force on its home grounds. Because of the curfew, he couldn't walk the fifty yards across the street from the small AP office in Singapore to the Cable & Wireless Office, but had to file to Kuala Lumpur and have his messages relayed back to Singapore for transmission to Tokyo. Better arrangements were made subsequently.

Jimmy Hahn was away in Bangkok when the rioting began and took the first plane back to Singapore. Most of the specials who came piling in from Hong Kong and elsewhere headed for the Reuters office, which they used as a base. Hahn, therefore, soon found himself being called upon for information by correspondents of client newspapers who didn't know where to concentrate their attention. He used his government sources to good advantage. The AP had much of its information on casualties from government sources in Kuala Lumpur. As for UPI, the outnumbered Killen kept up as best he could.

There is no particular evidence to show that Hahn, Escoda, and Menon did better work on the riots because they were Asians. In fact, Hahn and Escoda were at a disadvantage, in some parts of Singapore, because of their appearance. It was in the handling of the story that both excelled, for they took care not to make wild guesses at the probably origin of the riots and made every effort to maintain a certain amount of restraint in describing the fighting between the Malays and the Chinese.

Time magazine, by contrast, produced a colorful account in which a Chinese policeman asked a procession of Muslim Malays to close their ranks so as not to obstruct traffic, was knocked flat by five Malays, who in turn were set upon by Chinese gangsters. In the excitement,

Time made the British territory of Brunei in Borneo a part of Malaysia. "Armored cars carrying cops and troops whispered through Singapore's old colonial arcades over streets covered by a snowfall of broken glass," *Time* reported.[74]

The AP took it easy: "No one is certain yet what touched it off. According to one version, five Malay youths attacked a policeman when he ordered stragglers back into the parade. Another account has it that a spectator threw a bottle at the marchers. Whatever it was, recalled a European eyewitness, 'It was almost like a signal.' "[75]

The riots also demonstrated the extent to which the government was able to exercise control over what was published in the Malaysian press when it chose to do so. Of the thirty-six daily newspapers with more than 500,000 circulation which were published in English, Chinese, Tamil, Malay, and Punjabi, the prosperous English-language *Straits Times* was the leader, with a combined circulation of 240,000 in Singapore and Kuala Lumpur, 23,000 more for its afternoon *Malay Mail,* and nearly 200,000 for its *Sunday Times* and *Sunday Mail.*[76] It was, without doubt, one of the most prosperous publishing houses in the Far East, with 1,500 employees, about 250 in editorial alone. The average reporter earned the American equivalent of $100 to $150 a month, and the average editor up to $200 a month.

Like all its Malaysian competitors, however, the *Straits Times* was able to publish only as long as the government maintained its license. And like the rest of the Malay press, the *Times* was extremely careful in its coverage of the riots and did not identify the participants as Malays and Chinese until the government permitted it. Moreover, many of the details in the foreign press were not published in Malaysia. Radio and television, being government-controlled, were equally circumspect.

One of the government officials primarily concerned with the affair conceded later that the press had been "very careful." He explained bluntly, "They were careful because they knew what would happen if they were not. We would have closed them down." The same official told of "calling some of the foreign correspondents on the carpet" for what they wrote.[77] It was only to be expected in a land at war.

Almost anything that had to do with the Overseas Chinese was a sensitive matter for the press, whether or not there were warnings from the government. In a land with an average of 50 per cent literacy, it was the Chinese who were better educated and better off financially on the whole, and they also controlled a substantial amount of advertising. They were more numerous in Malaysia than in any other country of Southeast Asia and formed a larger percentage of the population. There were more than 2.5 million each in Thailand and Indonesia, nearly 1 million in South Viet-Nam, 320,000 in Burma, 400,000 each in the Philippines and

Cambodia, and much smaller numbers elsewhere.[78] With the exception of Indonesia, the Chinese had greater influence in Malaysia than anywhere else.

It was a complicated situation for American foreign correspondents to explain, and few bothered to try before it became necessary to do so. On the one hand, Peking was known to use a substantial number of Overseas Chinese as a source of subversion in Malaysia and elsewhere in Asia. On the other, the Prime Minister of Singapore, Lee Kuan Yew, and his Chinese followers seemed to be at constant war with the Communists in his city and the Malay "Ultras" as well.[79]

Considering the array of forces against him, the pugnacious Lee, great-grandson of an emigrant Chinese peasant, had shown himself to be a brilliant politician. The British, mindful of his Cambridge education, called him "Harry" Lee and tried briefly and unsuccessfully to make a pet of him. Lee made his People's Action Party (PAP) with its socialist orientation the dominant political force in Singapore. He had repeatedly defeated the opposition Barisan Sosialis, which was pro-Communist, pro-Indonesian, and anti-Malaysian. Had he not challenged the Alliance Party, which was dominant in Malaysia outside Singapore, perhaps the crisis might have been staved off for a time. But for better or worse, Lee made the decision and his people in Singapore backed him.

The Alliance Party was composed of the United Malay National Organization (UMNO), the Malayan Chinese Association, and the Malayan Indian Congress. Of these, the UMNO and its fanatical Secretary General, Syed Ja'afar bin Albar, became Lee's principal enemies. It was Syed Albar who led the attack on Lee as a Malaysian "enemy" who wrongfully called him pro-Communist and demanded his arrest, who stirred up the hatreds of the Malays within Singapore. Lee had not only to hold off the Malay politicians, but also at the same time fight the Communists at Nanyang University, in the labor unions, and in the Barisan Sosialis.[80]

The Communist problem also troubled the Federation's Prime Minister, the Tunku, and his tough deputy, Tun Abdul Razak. At one time before the beginning of Sukarno's campaign against Malaysia, the Tunku estimated that there were 50,000 pro-Communist subversives at large in his country. With the commitment of British power in defense of Malaysia after the Indonesian "Confrontasi" began, it became a nation in a virtual stage of siege. Had Syed Albar and the fanatical Malay Ultras been kept quiet by the Tunku and Tun Razak, some kind of arrangement with Lee in Singapore might have been possible. But after the 1964 rioting, it seemed foreordained that Singapore was too big and too troublesome to remain in Malaysia.

Yet, Lee wanted very much to keep his island state in the Federation. Until the Singapore radio announced the change, effective at 12:01 A.M. on August 9, 1965, the success of the Malay ultranationalists in forcing the ejection of their Chinese-dominated chief city had been a carefully guarded secret. Later that day, Lee went before television cameras in his office and told how Singapore had been forced out because of the Tunku's supposed fear of another explosion between the Chinese and the Malays. But Singapore's practical Chinese business community had another reaction. Anticipating more trade from Communist China and Indonesia, they developed a bullish trend on their own stock exchange. Lee, however, maintained an anti-Communist posture while taking the precaution of inviting a Soviet trade mission to show he hadn't gone over to the Peking side.

For the time being, it was clear that the British intended to hang on to their bases and their Far East military headquarters in Singapore for as long as they could. Because an abrupt British withdrawal would have been a blow to the city's economy, Lee raised no objection but cautioned the British to use their strength for defense purposes only.[81]

Malaysia remained aligned with the West, although it now had to guard against the possibility, as the Tunku put it, of Singapore becoming "another Cuba." Singapore technically became nonaligned, but it was just as dependent as ever upon trade with its Malayan hinterland in the absence of any immediate decision by Indonesia to renew old trade ties. Thus, although separated, the two main parts of the Federation continued along parallel courses, but each was weaker than before.

At the most critical moment for Malaysia, in the fall of 1965, the abortive Communist-supported uprising began in Indonesia and was crushed, with the Army taking power. For the time being, the Indonesians had all they could do to maintain order in their own country without troubling their neighbors; the Malaysians' fear of being caught in a giant nutcracker between China and Indonesia was at least temporarily allayed. The fall of Sukarno and the end of his war policy gave Kuala Lumpur the respite it needed and solved some of Singapore's immediate problems.

The events in Indonesia had a decided effect elsewhere in Southeast Asia as well. The position of Thailand, with South Viet-Nam the most dedicated of American allies in the area, was strengthened. The Thais, unlike the Vietnamese, had an established and unified national state. The foreign aid of $320 million from the United States had been put to good use, as had the generous trade built up with Japan. The national resolution of Thailand showed in the constant increase of rice, rubber, and teak shipments for export, and the upsurge in other export products in apparently successful efforts to cut an annual trade imbalance.

National income was up. The tourist traffic was booming, going from 55,000 visitors in 1958 to 220,000 in 1964. The ancient kingdom, in its modern military guise, was thriving.[82]

Thailand had changed from a backward musical-comedy kingdom, in the eyes of the West, to a prosperous and progressive modern country fairly bursting with enterprise. Had the regime relaxed its ban on the famous Rodgers and Hammerstein musical *The King and I,* the Thais might have been amused to see for themselves what their image was in the United States. In any event, Bangkok, a bustling capital of 2.5 million people, was as much a showcase of the new Asia as was Tokyo. It had modern streets and modern buildings, air-conditioned hotels, shiny automobiles, and brand-new taxis with unused meters (Thai drivers still loved to bargain).

Thailand had jumped from the most primitive means of communication squarely into the center of the electronic era. The government-controlled radio and television exercised a major influence on 30 million Thais, with a 70 per cent literacy rate. The twenty-odd radio transmitters and two television stations, had the largest audience among the mass media, with 163,000 radio receivers and almost the same number of TV receivers. Next came such Thai newspapers as *Phim Thai* and *Thai Rath,* with circulations of about 30,000 each, and such Chinese-language dailies as *Hsking Hsien,* with 37,000, and the *Sing Sian,* with 20,000. Together, the Thai press had less than 300,000 circulation, 1 per cent of the population. For the English-speaking colony in Bangkok, there was a Thomson newspaper, the Bangkok *Post,* which was as solidly British as its erstwhile competition, the Bangkok *World,* had been whimsically American.[83]

In the mid-1960's, despite all these signs of affluence and well-being, Thailand was very much on its guard. It was evident that the Thai forces of 100,000 would be no match for Communist guerrilla incursions either from Laos or the Chinese border. Early in 1965, Marshal Chen Yi, the Chinese foreign minister, had warned of things to come: "We may have a guerrilla war going in Thailand." The threat was real. There was a Thailand Patriotic Front and, behind the Bamboo Curtain, a "Voice of the Thai People" broadcasting a call for insurrection. The discredited Chin Peng, Chinese leader of the Malay Communist guerrilla war, was reported active again on the Thai-Malay border.

Thailand had outlawed its Communist Party in 1958, but there was pro-Communist activity among 30,000 so-called "refugees" from North Viet-Nam who lived in northeast Thailand, and guerrilla camps had been found there. Moreover, Laotians continually crossed the border; there were many more Laotians in Thailand than in Laos.[84] And the more than 2.5 million Overseas Chinese were a contributory cause of unrest. It was a far different Thailand—this threatened land of South-east Asia covering an area as large as Kansas, Iowa, and Missouri—from the vague American image of a dreamy Asian country whose young King Bhumipol played jazz with Benny Goodman and whose beautiful Queen Sirikit graced the fashionable European salons.

The Southeast Asia Treaty Organization, for which the Thais had built in new Bangkok headquarters, was no longer a major hope for their defense. Pakistan and France, charter members in 1954, were no longer interested. Great Britain had other troubles. Australia, New Zealand, and the Philippines were in no position to give much help to a threatened ally. Essentially, then, for its security Thailand was as de-pendent as South Viet-Nam on the United States.

The Thais had swung back and forth in their attitude about the United States in the period following World War II, depending on their national interest. Now, they were pro-American, but they wanted some show of determination that the United States would do more for them than use their bases. To touring correspondents in Bangkok, For-eign Minister Thanat Khoman talked in tough terms of safeguarding his country from being sacrificed for foreign advantage. He was, he said, conducting an independent foreign policy.

What news was there in the United States of this little Asian ally? In 1964, the headlines went to a disclosure by Thanom Kittikachorn, the new premier, that his predecessor, the late Field Marshal Sarit Tha-narat, had amassed a fortune estimated at $140 million. The old dicta-tor, who had seized power in a bloodless coup in 1957 and started Thailand on the road to modernity, died on December 8, 1963. The Thai press, which for the first time in five years had been permitted to express opinions, almost immediately began hinting at scandals to come, although the editors were warned not to print anything "prejudi-cial to peace and public order." Nevertheless, the Thanarat scandal mounted.

In 1965, there was pleasanter news from Thailand, but it was made in the United States. An eighteen-year-old, Miss Apasra Hongsakula (35-22-35), became Miss Universe in the annual Miami Beach beauty pag-eant. The American public was solemnly informed that the former Miss Thailand had once been nicknamed Pook ("Fatty"), and that her first words upon winning were, "I hope my Queen is happy." If the wire services were to be trusted, Thailand was delirious.[85] But of the serious aspects of Thailand's difficult situation in the darkening crisis of Southeast Asia, the American public heard little.

Unhappily, there wasn't much demand for news of Thailand, even among its neighbors. Apart from the wire services, there were lament-ably few correspondents in residence, although in some ways Bangkok was as good a listening post as Hong Kong. Certainly, the Chinese Communists found it so; without doubt, among the Overseas Chinese in Thailand, Peking's sources of information were excellent. The problem of corruption among the poorly paid journalists of Thailand complicated matters, as the editors of some of Thailand's newspapers were well aware. There was good reason for the keen interest which Prince Wan Waithayakon, Thailand's senior statesman and a former president of the U.N. General Assembly, took in the establishment of a Thai journalism foundation to try to lift the standards of Thai journalism. But, as was the case in the Philippines, what the average journalist in Thailand needed first was a living wage.

Bangkok was a city where indigent journalists seemed to congregate. Both the foreigners and the Thais took on stringing jobs for almost anybody who would want them, usually at ridiculously low rates of pay. There seemed to be little thought among the news organizations that hired them over the reliability of the kind of help they were getting. What the organizations wanted was "protection," as the journalistic practice puts it, and if some received first-rate "protection," it was an accident. Necessarily, such correspondents were not likely to attract much attention to Thailand with their work.

There was a time, just before the American decision to escalate the Viet-Nam War, when such journalists did a great deal of speculation over the likelihood that Thailand might be made the southern bastion of American power in Asia if South Viet-Nam fell.[86] This kind of "think piece" had a two-way effect. It spread uncertainty in the United States, and it also served to make the Thais themselves more fearful. Obviously, whatever appeared in the American press about Thailand was echoed in the press of Bangkok after a time. Eventually, the theme was taken up by the most responsible journalists and abandoned only after it became clear that the United States had no intention of letting the Viet-Cong achieve a military victory in South Viet-Nam.

With more than 30,000 American troops in Thailand in 1966, and big American bombers flying daily from supposedly secret new Thai bases to attack North Viet-Nam, Bangkok suddenly became important in the American press. The wire services strengthened their bureaus, and some of the better newspapers assigned first-rate correspondents to the capital. It took a major turn in the Viet-Nam war to make Thailand of sufficient importance to win recognition in the American mass media. President Johnson's 1966 visit helped with the transition.

In Burma, another of the theoretical dominoes, the press also served as a barometer of change. Its foremost editor, Edward Michael Law Yone, lost both his freedom and his newspaper, the influential English language weekly, the *Nation* of Rangoon, soon after General Ne Win assumed dictatorial power. Law Yone had been a dedicated anti-Communist, warning President Sukarno as early as 1958 against "flirting with the Communists." [87] Six years later, the *Nation* was no more and Law Yone was "in protective custody." No American correspondents were permitted inside Burma, except on twenty-four hour visas, and there was no opportunity for independent inquiry. American economic aid no longer was wanted. Burma faced the cruel necessity of placating Communist China across their 1,000-mile common border.

Burma's most distinguished diplomat, U Thant, Secretary General of the United Nations, tried to make a virtue out of this course of conduct. He held up his native land as an example of what could have been done in Viet-Nam, arguing that Burma had stopped Communism without the loss of an American life or "the expenditure of one American dollar in military assistance." He contended that the American people had not been told the "true facts" about this state of affairs. If Burma had accepted American or other outside help against the Communists, he said, "Either the country would be divided into two parts or the whole country would have become Communist long ago." [88]

This was still another Asian formula for meeting the Chinese Communist threat. Seemingly, General Ne Win was enthusiastic about it. Law Yone would not have been so enthusiastic, for he was one of 1,300 political prisoners who were the victims of Ne Win's policies. They included some of the outstanding leaders of the nation, such as former Premier U Nu. Ironically, the *Nation* before its demise had made a point of emphasizing U Nu's advice to the International Press Institute to "spread the ideals of democracy and propagate its virtues." [89] Although he was freed in 1966, he talked no more of democracy.

This land of 23 million people, thrust together in an uncertain union in an area the size of Texas, was now a dictatorship in the increasingly familiar Asian mold. Its strength was its tremendous rice production, the largest in the world, and the underpopulation of its bountiful countryside. Its weakness was its proximity to an aggressive Communist China and the feuding of the disparate groups within the Burmese Union, including the Shans and the Karens, who fought the dominant Burmans, and the pro-Peking and pro-Moscow Communists. The Burmese Army of 70,000 had its hands full keeping order among some 10,000 dissidents, split into small groups.

From the time of its independence in 1948, after more than a century and a quarter of British rule, Burma had struggled to maintain the trappings of a parliamentary democracy. Between 1958 and 1960, General Ne Win, then the dour chief of staff, had seized power; unaccountably, he had made the mistake of permitting a free election in 1960, and his old chief, the easygoing U Nu, had won. Two years later, the redoubtable general again had overthrown him and seized power, enforcing Burma's peculiar brand of state socialism at the same time.

After having accepted $89 million in American foreign aid from the end of World War II, Burma now dispensed with nearly all American assistance.[90] The Fulbright educational program was suspended. The Ford and Asia foundations were sent packing. Even a highway from Rangoon to Mandalay, which was being planned with American financial and technical assistance, was abandoned. In the words of a Burmese writer, "The Revolutionary Government has now evolved a new order of priorities for economic development. In this, the highway project no longer occupies the same prominence in the allocation of Burmese resources as originally contemplated. The Government has therefore requested the United States Government to cease its assistance to this project . . ."[91] However, some $85 million in credits from Communist China were accepted.

To Americans brought up on the imagery of Kipling's "Road to Mandalay," the Irrawaddy, and the heroics of the Burma Road of World War II, this new Burma was something they did not understand. And in Rangoon, there was precious little in the way of news resources that would have helped dissipate the confusion. For independent journalism in Burma had gone the way of all other freedoms under General Ne Win.

That, indeed, was the significance of the story of Edward Michael Law Yone. While Burma had still been devoted to the principles of self-government, Law Yone had been the leader of a lusty, brawling press that at one time included as many as thirty-two free-swinging dailies. He was a past president of the Burma Journalists Association and the Foreign Correspondents Association, and a winner of the Magsaysay Journalism Award in 1959. He had not hesitated to expose corruption in the Burmese government. And in 1956, when there had been unacknowledged incursions of Chinese troops in northern Burma, he had called attention to them.

In 1961, when U Nu's government was tottering and the press was restricted in its right of publication, Law Yone led a movement among twenty-six newspapers to urge the government to abandon its repressive measures. On November 6, 1962, to protest against the regime's position, the newspapers ran blank space in the section reserved for editorial comment. Premier U Nu reconsidered, but before anything of substance could be accomplished, he was removed during General Ne Win's second military coup, and parliament was dissolved.

Law Yone remained at liberty for less than a year; at 2 A.M. on August 8, 1963, he was arrested for "hindering the implementation of internal peace." On May 18, 1964, his newspaper closed by court order after being accused of failing to pay taxes. Several other independent editors and their newspapers received similar treatment. There was only one voice in Burma and that was Ne Win's.[92]

"Burma maintained its ban on stationing of Western newsmen in the country," the AP reported at the beginning of 1965. "Local newspapers were fed from a single government-controlled source. Stories filed by foreign correspondents visiting Burma were scrutinized carefully but not censored."

Since no Western correspondent could remain more than twenty-four hours on a transit visa, the lack of formal censorship was purely academic. The representatives of Tass and the New China News Agency, the most powerful foreign journalists in the country, would scarcely have concerned themselves with a Burmese censor in any case. The Indians had to watch their step. The rest were stringers, all Burmese under the control of their government, who technically represented some American and British news organizations. Agence France-Presse maintained a Frenchman as a correspondent in Rangoon for as long as possible.

Ne Win stubbornly kept his defenses up as much as he could against Chinese Communist influence. When he took over the banks, he included two that were run by Peking. In nationalizing all trade, he ousted some of the Chinese shopkeepers among the 320,000 Overseas Chinese in Burma, as well as the long-suffering Indians. Probably the Chinese were mainly anti-Communist. He tried to enforce his ban on the Communist Party but that was almost hopeless, with the Peking-backed White Flag Communists openly battling the Moscow-supported United Workers' Party and the Red Flag Communists.

An American in Burma wrote at an early stage in Ne Win's crackdown on the press:

It is very frustrating. There is only one man who says anything and that is Ne Win. The lower government officials live in deadly fear of saying the wrong thing and getting into trouble, which means that they say nothing. On most news stories, there is a government release and that is the news. The government radio station has an "officer on special duty" who checks the news stories and makes sure nothing goes on the air that shouldn't. It is not too pleasant a situation since Ne Win is xenophobic, especially toward Westerners.[93]

But new times were coming to Burma as well as to its neighbors in Southeast Asia. General Ne Win received a New York *Times* correspondent in the summer of 1966 and was hailed on page 1 as a "Cromwellian military chief of state." While he conceded that Burma's economy was faltering, more attention was paid to his feat in keeping his country out of Peking's clutches. To balance a visit to Peking and the Soviet Union, he was enthusiastically welcomed in Washington late in 1966 by President Johnson as an indomitable neutralist. Ne Win was treated throughout as a very special person. As one diplomat put it, "If he were to embrace the West, he would have a Chinese guerrilla war on his hands in twenty-four hours." [94]

Cambodia was an even more difficult problem for the West. Prince Norodom Sihanouk, the forty-three-year-old ruler of 6 million Cambodians, was in a seemingly advantageous position in the Southeast Asian wars of the mid-1960's. His largely undeveloped country, a remnant of the ancient Khmer Empire, was peaceful and prosperous while its former associates in French Indochina, Viet-Nam, and Laos were torn apart by an ever widening conflict. He could see his old enemy, Thailand, braced behind a shield of American military and economic aid for a guerrilla assault by Communist China from the north. He had no love for the Vietnamese, either, but he did not fear them now. The North, aided by Peking, was supporting the Viet Cong guerrillas and absorbing a fearful daily punishment by American bombers. The South, reinforced by enlarged American armies, was suffering from a combination of civil war, Communist incursions from the North, and American combat operations.

Sihanouk had but one aim—to keep out of war. Accordingly, he proclaimed himself a neutralist, but it was clear that he had decided the Americans would lose in Southeast Asia. Despite $366 million in American military and economic aid that had been showered on a country the size of Kansas from 1954 on, the determined ruler dispensed with further American economic and military assistance on November 20, 1963, charging the United States with intervening in Cambodian affairs. Promptly, he sent missions off to Peking and Moscow to bring back funds and matériel for his 28,000-man army. Within less than a month, he recalled his ambassador from Washington because of "press insults" but did not finally break relations.

Sihanouk, like Sukarno, had been having trouble with the Western press in general and the American press in particular. Some correspondents treated him as if he had been a musical-comedy character; to them, the Cambodian ruler replied in kind. Others insulted his ever sensitive feelings. Among American correspondents, it became a mark of distinction to have been thrown out of Cambodia for some petty reason—one of the least significant being the description of Sihanouk as "mercurial." For some obscure reason, he didn't like that particular word. Soon, having few correspondents he could discipline, he took to writing long letters to American and other Western publications that criticized his ties with the Communists and attacked both his good sense and his good faith.

Sihanouk wasn't set against all Americans and all criticism. When Keyes Beech, of the Chicago *Daily News,* came to Phnom Penh late in 1964 and wrote that the Prince was "a madman but a genius," the reaction was gratifying. "I don't mind being a madman as long as I am a genius," Sihanouk said. It was evident that he also was pleased by the remark of a disgruntled American, "He may not be good for us but he's good for Cambodia." [95]

From time to time, the Prince permitted various American correspondents to enter his domain, with the result that *Newsweek* announced in its issue of April 5, 1965, "One of the least understood nations in troubled Southeast Asia is the Kingdom of Cambodia. The nation's proud, mercurial ruler, Prince Norodom Sihanouk, has contributed to this lack of understanding by barring most Western newsmen. But recently *Newsweek*'s Bernard Krisher was granted a month's visa to visit the kingdom."

What followed was mainly a mood-and-atmosphere piece by Krisher, a competent correspondent who reported at length on everything he saw and heard and left nothing out. Most news-magazine correspondents do this as a matter of practice, because they assume that their material will be rewritten in New York, and they never know how much, if anything, will be published. In the case of Krisher's piece, however, *Newsweek* chose not to rewrite but to publish the original work at length. It included the following passage:

> The Prince is revered by his six million people. Even though he has formally renounced his throne for the role of Chief of State, he is respectfully called "Monseigneur" (a French title for princes and clerics), and he refers to his nation as *royaume* (kingdom). Still there is an undercurrent of criticism leveled by young intellectuals at Sihanouk's private life and at his mother who is said to be money-mad and reportedly runs a number of concessions in town plus a string of bordellos at the edge of the city. Almost everyone who can afford it from the Prince on down has one or several concubines, which is one reason why the royal family is so large and why there are so many Cambodian princes.[96]

At just about the time the article appeared, Sihanouk was under Communist China's pressure to withdraw from a conference to guarantee Cambodia's neutrality, which he himself had proposed. To add to his perplexity, President Johnson let it be known through the State Department that he would be willing to attend such a conference. It was then regarded widely in the Western world as a possible entering wedge for a much-desired settlement with Communist China and the Soviet Union of the future of all of Southeast Asia, including Viet-Nam. The Chinese Communists, however, were so confident of forcing the United States out of Southeast Asia that they were by no means ready for a settlement.

It took the Prince three weeks to decide what to do. When he did, the following from UPI foreshadowed his final decision:

PHNOM PENH, Cambodia, April 26—A mob of 20,000 Cambodian students attacked the United States Embassy today, hurling rocks, ink bottles and other missiles at the building and ripping down the American flag . . .

Authorities said the Cambodian demonstration was set off by United States policy in Vietnam and by a "slanderous" article in the April 5 issue of *Newsweek* magazine . . . Among the anti-United States slogans shouted were . . . "No more Anglo-Saxon journalists in Cambodia." [97]

On May 1, Sihanouk decided against his proposed nine-power conference, which meanwhile had attracted the support of Great Britain, the Soviet Union, and, among the press leaders, the New York *Times*. Two days later he announced Cambodia was breaking diplomatic relations with the United States. He blamed an alleged Vietnamese air attack on two Cambodian border villages and the *Newsweek* article.[98] *Newsweek* contented itself by announcing its full confidence in the reporting of Krisher and publishing one of the many letters of protest it had received from Sihanouk. The protest said in part:

It is frightful to think that such cowardly accusations, based on "is said" or a "reportedly"—in other words, on nothing—could be leveled against an elderly woman in fragile health, who lives withdrawn from public life and who devotes herself solely to social works.

My mother and I, like many wealthy people, own certain commercial enterprises acquired from our family. The income we obtain from them helps us to live and to cope with our numerous obligations without having to impose burdensome levies on the state, and without obliging us to accept "gifts" in the manner of certain foreign leaders well known to the United States.

But to describe our family as "owners of bordellos" exceeds all tolerable limits—and even all likelihood, since prostitution is forbidden and severely punished in Cambodia . . .[99]

If it was any balm to *Newsweek* and Krisher, the New York *Times* loftily ignored the article as an evident pretext seized upon by Sihanouk and concluded editorially:

Prince Sihanouk's decision to sever diplomatic ties with the United States stems from his conviction that he can avoid complete vassalage to Communist China by paying occasional political tribute . . . Unfortunately, this policy is increasingly making Cambodia a pawn of Peking. Nowhere is this more evident than in Prince Sihanouk's twists and turns on the project for a new Geneva conference . . ." [100]

Sihanouk came back against the New York *Times,* as well, vigorously denying that he was a Peking puppet, and drew still more editorial fire.[101] But by that time, Major Edward H. White, II, of the U. S. Air Force had floated in space for twenty minutes outside the *Gemini 4* spacecraft, and the American public had forgotten all about Sihanouk, if in fact it had ever paid much attention to him.

But as far as American policy-makers and diplomats were concerned, that was another matter entirely. Just as some resented the journalistic attention to Sukarno's sex life (publicity which he seemed to enjoy), they also felt that the press's treatment of Sihanouk had complicated American problems in Cambodia. To the foreign correspondents, it seemed rather ridiculous that a diplomat with any sense whatever could believe that a different press treatment of such dictators as Sukarno and Sihanouk would make them more amenable to Washington's approaches. Yet, such beliefs were held, and at least one responsible diplomat in Southeast Asia consciously tried to persuade correspondents not to be so mean to the rulers of Indonesia and Cambodia.[102]

True to his French training, Sihanouk had the French intellectual's ingrained dislike of the United States and managed to show it on particular occasions. American correspondents who had followed him around Asia and in the United States were familiar with his moods, his high-pitched voice, and his tendency to burst into a squeaky denunciation of any American act that displeased him. They knew, too, that it was difficult to deal with him at Phnom Penh on a day-to-day basis because he much preferred to work with the correspondent of Agence France-Presse and even the correspondent of Reuters. American wire-service correspondents said that, at one time, an AFP man was a part of the Prince's inner councils, and accordingly managed to file an important story long before the Chief of State decided to make it known to the rest of the press. It is probable that Sihanouk's press relations might have improved a little if he had not discriminated so pointedly against the Americans. Certainly, he couldn't have made matters worse than they were when he seemed to rejoice publicly over the assassination of President Kennedy.[103]

Sihanouk's perennially youthful appearance and his high spirits often made visitors to Cambodia think of him as a newcomer to power and responsibility. Actually, he had had much experience. On April 26, 1941, ten months after the fall of France, he had become the King of Cambodia, at nineteen years of age, during the Japanese occupation of Indochina. After the war, when the French returned, he created a parliamentary government and drafted a constitution for Cambodia, but the country was ready for neither. Neither were the French. But after a long and patient campaign, enormously assisted by the French defeat in Viet-Nam, he won independence for Cambodia on November 8, 1953, in advance of the 1954 conference at Geneva that ended French rule in all of Indochina. Subsequently, when opposition arose to the kind of authoritarian government he sought to give his country, he abdicated in favor of his father on March 2, 1955. Five years later, upon his father's death, he resumed his reign, this time as Chief of State, not as King.

Sihanouk's decision to turn aside American assistance and turn out the American press, so far as possible, were the acts of a mature and clever ruler. His immediate calculation was to Cambodia's benefit. France and Communist China rushed in to take up the slack in Cambodia's economy after the break with the United States on economic matters. To replace about $30 million annually in American economic and military aid, France granted the small nation $32.6 million in gifts, loans, and suppliers' credits; the Chinese came through with about $10 million more, and the Soviet Union gave unspecified help. A number of Communist bloc nations made individual gifts of various kinds, for there was joy over the new apparent acquisition. American imports to Cambodia dropped 71 per cent in the first half of 1964, but Prince Sihanouk had more than $95 million in foreign-exchange reserves in his treasury at the beginning of 1965.[104]

The Prince took the position at the time that Cambodia eventually would be gobbled up by Communism but, meanwhile, he sought to make the transition as pleasant for himself and his people as possible. "When the inevitable moment comes," he wrote piously, "I want my country to meet its fate with the least possible loss of life and destruction." However, the would-be martyr to Communism let out a howl of rage late in 1965 when the Soviet Union abruptly canceled arrangements for his visit to Moscow. Earlier, having thoughtfully observed the effect of the widening American war in neighboring Viet-Nam, he received an American reporter and sent up signals that he might now be willing to resume relations with Washington if he received satisfactory guarantees of security.[105] In Cambodia, self-preservation was the first law of statesmanship; in practicing it, Prince Sihanouk displayed the greatest agility.

Willard A. Hanna once observed that there are two images of Siha-nouk:

The Cambodian stereotype, that is, of *"le père de l'indépendance,"* and the Western stereotype of the mercurial Marxist playboy-prince-politician . . . almost everybody knows about iced champagne at 10 A.M. in the throne room. And almost nobody, whether he relies on *Paris-Match* or the New York *Times,* is at all likely to forget that the Prince is a musician— to be indelicate about it, a saxophonist. Prince Sihanouk, in brief, con-denses into his compact, convex person contradictions enough to make it almost equally plausible to call him, as various people do, Samdech Saha-chivin (Prince Companion, or Prince Comrade), Snooks, Monseigneur, Son Altesse Royale, or a second Sukarno.[106]

This kind of reporting, done for American universities in the main, would have barred any number of American foreign correspondents from Phnom Penh. The only way the literate Cambodians had of knowing that such estimates appeared abroad was when the half-dozen or so newspapers in Phnom Penh (with a total circulation of less than 30,000 daily), the national Agence Khmère de Presse (AKP), the gov-ernment radio, or Monseigneur himself denounced an American or British correspondent. The French, however, occupied a privileged po-sition in Cambodia as the principal suppliers of foreign news and as a source of influence in the two French-language newspapers of the coun-try.

In Cambodia, as well as in Laos and Viet-Nam, the inevitable conse-quences of government efforts to repress information was that literate people regarded both their newspapers and their radio with mistrust, if not contempt. As an acute observer, Jacques Champagne, has written: "Foreign and domestic facts, information, news, rumors, comment and propaganda in their most detailed form seem to travel, arrive, spread and return to their original source faster by word of mouth in these countries than even by Telstar anywhere else in the world." [107]

This was particularly true in Laos. As Keyes Beech said in a moment of depression, "Laos is a good story until you get there." Or, as a British correspondent put it, "Covering Laos is like being in the eye of a hurri-cane." An Australian, Martin Stewart Fox, representing UPI, vowed after six months that he believed but one-tenth of what he heard and triple-checked even that, especially when it came from a Lao source.

There was, in short, one war in the headlines and quite another in the middle of a confused, harassed, landlocked nation of less than 2 million people, where nearly everything was difficult to understand. To the new correspondent who arrived hopefully at the Hotel Constellation in Vientiane, an indifferent hostelry that served as an informal press center, it was a topsy-turvy world.

In this primitive land, slightly smaller than Oregon, there were so many exaggerations and so few sources of reliable information that mere rumors often were given credibility, straggling groups of soldiers became formal military units of formidable power, and desultory Asian skirmishes were described as pitched battles. Western-style combat reporting, with its emphasis on front lines and offensives, strategic retreats, and other mass movements of the military, was ill adapted to this kind of conflict. In Laotian terms, war simply wasn't conducted that way.

Laos was a nation without railroads, with no decent highways and uncertain air transportation at best. Its population was largely illiterate, its climate discouraging. Typically, most maps of Laos showed a heavy black line, numbered 13, indicating the route of a supposed major highway that linked Vientiane, the administrative capital, with Luang Prabang, the royal capital of King Savang Vatthana; however, it was just 165 miles of little more than a dirt track that became impassable in the rainy season. The United States planned eventually to build an all-weather two-lane road there as a military necessity, but everything in Laos moved slowly.[108]

When Laotians gathered in a crowd, it was usually at the market place to haggle for food in terms of a debased currency. Oden Meeker, a visitor, found that to many in the country "a sense of Lao nationality is hazy or non-existent," and that some "have never heard of Vientiane or Luang Prabang." [109] To this Jacques Champagne added: "There is total freedom of the press. But there are no press and no journalists, because there are no readers. The radio plays the part of the press." It was his belief that the Laotians on the whole were little involved in the war, except when it hit them directly. "There is," he wrote, "no need either to stir, or to repress, what is practically a non-existent public opinion." [110]

This was the land to which the United States had committed its military power as a defense against a Communist takeover, already effective in more than half the country, and some $500 million in military and economic aid. From 1954 until 1963, $328.4 million had been allotted for economic assistance, and up to June 30, 1962, when the figures became classified, military aid had amounted to $128.5 million.[111] In 1965, military aid was still high, and economic aid was running at the rate of $50 million annually. It was far more than Laos could absorb.[112]

Despite this enormous American effort, the American public usually received a sour report on Laos. Robert Trumbull, of the New York *Times,* was expressing a view held generally by most responsible American correspondents when he wrote:

> Laos represents one of the most inglorious chapters in United States diplomatic history. Washington poured half a billion dollars into this artificially created country, with little if any lasting benefit to the Laotians and a completely negative result to the United States. Americans equipped and paid an army that would not fight, spent tens of millions of dollars on economic aid that served little purpose but to enrich corrupt Laotian officials and a few sharp merchants, and misjudged the political and military situation at almost every step. If ever we deserved to lose, it was in Laos.[113]

A Time-Life correspondent in Southeast Asia, Eric Pace, writing in *Foreign Affairs,* concurred that Laos was essentially unstable. Two years after the fourteen-nation Geneva conference of 1962 guaranteed the neutrality and independence of Laos, Pace wrote, "The events of the past two years have left the situation there [Laos] as complex and explosive as before. . . . In the same period, when the United States was busy shoring up South Vietnam, the Laotian situation had come unstuck." [114]

To the American public as a whole, Laos was therefore presented as a disagreeable blur on the map of Asia in which the United States had been entangled without much hope of emerging with honor, let alone victory. It was, to begin with, a complicated position that could be explained decently in a 4,000-word article in *Foreign Affairs,* but not in the average 400- or 500-word wire-service dispatch that came out of Vientiane and was the main reliance of the American press. This was a serious limitation of daily journalism, and it could not be overcome. The correspondent had to assume, often wrongfully, that his editors knew the background and that a certain number of readers could make sense out of the new developments without too much explanation.

There were few more complicated situations in all Asia, a continent with which the American public is not notably familiar. Laos had been recognized by France as an independent sovereign state in 1949, and by the United States and the Communist powers in 1954 under the Geneva agreements that sealed France's defeat in Indochina. But almost before the ink was dry on their signatures, the Communist side had turned loose their Pathet Lao force of 20,000 troops to war on the right-wing and neutralist groups in Laos. That, in turn, had led to the 1962 Geneva accords, which also were violated.

After numerous coups and attempted coups, in which more civilians than soldiers were usually killed, there was still an uneasy, three-way stalemate in the mid-1960's: Prince Souvanna Phouma, the so-called neutralist Premier, and his military commander, General Kong Le, were in control of a force of about 8,000 soldiers who maneuvered between Vientiane and the western edge of the Plain of Jars. Once bitterly anti-American, Souvanna Phouma was now held in office primarily by the use of American air power against his Communist enemies. Kong Le had a little of everything—Russian, Indonesian, and American equipment.

Linked to the Premier in an uncertain alliance was the Royal Laotian Army of about 50,000 American-equipped troops. This was the military arm of the so-called right wing, which itself had split as a result of an attempted coup early in 1965 that forced General Phoumi Nosavan, the one-time rightist "strong man," to flee across the Thai border.

The Pathet Lao, reinforced by a substantial number of North Viet-Nam Army units, numbering perhaps as many as 15,000 troops, were ranged against the neutralist and right-wing government forces. It was against this enemy that American air power was concentrated in the northern part of Laos. For the time being, the Pathet Lao was contained; but, in guerrilla warfare, containment was often meaningless.

There was no doubt that both the United States and the Communists now had linked the war in Laos with the war in Viet-Nam. The infiltrators from the north, who plugged the ranks of the Viet Cong, had been accustomed for years to come through Laos along the network known as the Ho Chi Minh Trail. But when Secretary of State Rusk announced that units of the 325th North Viet-Nam Division were in Laos,[115] it became evident that Hanoi had reached a new stage in its war in Southeast Asia. Just as the U.S. Air Force dominated the air, Hanoi and Peking seemed intent on controlling the ground warfare outside the zones firmly occupied by the American and South Vietnamese armies. In Laos, the most responsible correspondents estimated that the Pathet Lao, under the leadership of Prince Souphanouvong, Souvanna Phouma's half-brother, controlled and adminstered up to two-thirds of the country.[116] Had it not been for American air power, the entire position would have eroded.

From Vientiane, it was obvious that this story could scarcely be told accurately. If the correspondents listened to Laotian sources, they had to discount what they heard because of the Lao weakness for exaggeration. The American embassy and its military attaché, together with the British embassy and its military attaché, were often relied on for an analysis; the trouble, of course, was that neither embassy could be sure of its facts without the most extensive on-the-ground reporting. As for correspondents' travel, it had to be by air, and there wasn't much space available on American aircraft. They were needed for more important purposes.

These difficulties, plus the not inconsiderable effort that it took merely to keep working and stay well in Vientiane, contributed to the thorough dislike which nearly all American correspondents expressed of the Laotian assignment. In the spring of 1964, when American planes first began flying combat missions over Laos, correspondents' cables were being held up as much as thirty-six hours in Vientiane. When the first two American aircraft were shot down, the news was announced first from Washington by the Pentagon—an infuriating tactic to the reporters in the field but one which was to the advantage of the American government.

There were, generally, three types of correspondents in Vientiane for Western news organizations. The least numerous but most important were the permanent staff correspondents, men of experience and reliability; at one time, only the AP had such a correspondent in Vientiane. Next were the stringers, who came in from almost everywhere, hoping to catch on with either the U.S. aid mission or an American news organization. This was how Martin Stewart Fox started with UPI, proving himself in Vientiane before being assigned permanently to Saigon. At about the same time, Thomas ("Tammy") Arbuckle caught on for Reuters in Vientiane on the basis of a little work for the Bangkok World, while nineteen-year-old Simon Dring, with no previous experience, filed for several American and British news organizations. Arbuckle, relatively inexperienced at twenty-five, had some of his string correspondence published under his byline in the New York Times. As one stringer put it with a broad grin, "There are no experts on Laos." [117]

When something of major importance happened in Laos, the specials would come piling into Vientiane from almost anywhere in Asia. Louis Rukeyser, of the Baltimore Sun, arrived in Vientiane on one occasion from New Delhi and had to turn around at once to cover Nehru's death. At another time, Emerson Chapin of the New York Times arrived from Tokyo and had to go back to Seoul because a student riot had broken out there. Laos could scarcely be considered a triumph of American journalism.

During the spring crisis in 1964, when a number of specials were in Vientiane, there was a Lao censor who could not read English, and some correspondents who could not speak French. If the censor could not read the copy, he would not stamp it; if the copy was unstamped, it could not be sent. Often, even at crucial periods, the censor would simply let the copy pile up; once, he took a weekend off and nothing left Vientiane for forty-eight hours. Except for those sharp-witted correspondents who had themselves transported across the Mekong to file daily from Thailand, the foreign journalists in Vientiane were unhappy. All of them received messages from home at one time or another demanding an explanation for their unaccustomed silence.

These professional considerations necessarily led to bad feeling between the correspondents and the Lao government. On a Sunday when Premier Souvanna Phouma decided to hold a press conference, a hardpressed correspondent made a fervent plea on behalf of the corps of correspondents to let press messages go through without delay. The obliging Souvanna Phouma announced, after a brief conference with an aide, "C'est fait." But the only result was that a 1,500-word message to the New York *Times,* based on an exclusive interview with the American ambassador at the time, Leonard Unger, was held up for thirty-six hours. At a cost of 20 cents a word press rate, and 50 cents urgent, such delays were both expensive and disconcerting.

An AP correspondent wrote an open letter condemning the Lao censorship. Other correspondents began putting their copy on the Bangkok plane. The rest simply gave up and went home. Frequently, to make certain an important story got out, it had to be double-filed—that is, one copy was given to the censor in Vientiane and another went out by one of the slower but more certain routes. In time, as the activity in Laos receded, the coverage from Vientiane was left largely to stringers, who received anywhere from $25 to $150 a month.[118]

For the United States, in any event, Laos held far less interest in the spring of 1966 than the rising tempo of the war in Viet-Nam, and its probable consequences. To the well-informed in Washington, that conflict suggested two different conclusions. As James Reston reported in the New York *Times:*

> It suggests to one group that only a victory for the United States in Vietnam will halt the drift of most of these [Asian] countries toward an accommodation with Communist China. It suggests to another group that even the present American adventure in Vietnam, designed from the start to halt the spread of Communist influence, is not yet having that effect but, on the contrary, is merely demonstrating that Communist guerrillas can fight effectively against the air, naval and ground power of the United States.[119]

South Viet-Nam was far from an ideal American battleground with its marshy delta region, its jungles, and its mountain fastnesses all infested with guerrillas and regulars supplied and reinforced from Hanoi and supported by Peking. It was not a place where armored forces, heavy artillery, and rocket bases were of much immediate value. Nor could it be said that the war had been undertaken with the massive support of the people of that troubled land.

But for better or worse, the American commitment to battle had been made, and all the protests in the United States could not undo it. If victory in the sense of unconditional surrender was impossible for American arms in a war fought on such terms, the prospect of a military defeat inspired by the forces under Peking's leadership was just as unacceptable to American public opinion.

Viet-Nam was the test. The future of much of Asia, in a very large sense, depended greatly on the outcome.

VI

The War in Viet-Nam

1. THE PRESIDENT AS NEWSMAKER

MANY ARE STILL alive who can remember America gaily marching to war in 1917 as if it were a Cecil B. DeMille movie—flags flying, bands playing, crowds chanting "Over There," and hordes of superpatriots attacking people with German-sounding names. It became unpopular to listen to Beethoven, almost a crime to hear a Wagner opera; most of the Berlins and Hamburgs of the land became Liberties and Freedoms. And it took many months before an ill-equipped and poorly trained army began taking part in the trench warfare in France.

All that seems like a part of another age today; yet, it was only a little less than fifty years ago. The very manner of declaring war had a kind of pageantry about it. Just before President Woodrow Wilson went before Congress with his war message, he was in a somber mood. Turning to his chief supporter in the American press, Frank I. Cobb, the editor of the New York *World,* he said, "Once lead this people into war and they'll forget there ever was such a thing as tolerance. To fight you must be brutal and ruthless, and the spirit of ruthless brutality will enter into the very fiber of our national life." [1]

But quickly, he set aside the doubts of the historian and became the great war leader. With idealistic fervor and evangelical zeal, he thrilled a nation that did not know the meaning of war with his declaration of war aims before Congress, "The world must be made safe for democracy. Its peace must be planted upon the tested foundations of political liberty." [2] Those brave words were to go ringing down through the years—so magnificent in concept, so unattainable in an imperfect world. The only tears that were shed four days later when Congress formally declared war on April 6, 1917, came from Representative Jeannette Rankin, of Montana, a Republican and a pacifist. For to an exalted and adventurous America, this was a righteous war against a hated tyranny. A week later, the Committee on Public Information, headed by the liberal George Creel, was created by Presidential proclamation to manipulate public opinion and keep the press in line.

During the war, it didn't have much opposition. It was so successful that in 1918 the *Nation* complained, "During the past two years, we have seen what is practically an official control of the press, not merely by Messrs. Burleson and Gregory [of the Post Office Department and the Department of Justice], but by the logic of events and the patriotic desire of the press to support the government." [3]

None of this was in evidence nearly a half-century later when another Democratic President committed the United States to an enlarged war in Viet-Nam. The pageantry, the extravagant rhetoric, and the exuberant mood of the Wilson era were quite remote from the new America. Lyndon Baines Johnson did not go to Congress but instead addressed the nation through the improvised platform of a news conference attended by 200 journalists who assembled in the East Room of the White House on July 28, 1965.

Standing before a television camera and a teleprompting device, the President told the nation: "This is a different kind of war. There are no marching armies or solemn declarations. Some citizens of South Viet-Nam, at times with understandable grievances, have joined in the attack on their own government. But we must not let this mask the central fact that this is really war." [4]

Neither Presidents Eisenhower nor Kennedy had been as forthright in defining the American role in the conflict. Nor had Congress been asked for a declaration of war. The most that Congress had been asked to do was to pass a resolution in August, 1964, supporting the Presidential initiative in ordering the U.S. Navy to punish North Vietnamese gunboats for attacks on American warships. That it had done, overwhelmingly supporting "the determination of the President to take all necessary measures to repel any armed attack against the forces of the United States and to prevent further aggression" in Southeast Asia.

This was, truly, a "different kind of war." It was, first of all, an unpopular war. Next, it marked a change in American policy, with the Soviet Union being depicted by some as a potential mediator rather than an enemy, and Communist China being singled out as the real foe because of its all-out support of North Viet-Nam. Finally, the United States was committed to a land war of indefinite size and duration on the Asian mainland, with President Johnson warning that the goal of Peking and Hanoi was "to conquer the South, to defeat American

power and to extend the Asiatic dominion of Communism." In a kind
of Johnsonian adaptation of the domino theory, he argued, "If we are
driven from the field in Viet-Nam, then no nation can ever again have
the same confidence in American promise or in American protection.
. . . We did not choose to be the guardians at the gate but there is no
one else." [5]

Because of the strength of the opposition at home and abroad,
the Johnson Administration had to resort to all the pressures of government, as well as the arts of politics and public persuasion, to maintain
support for its policy of escalation. The doubling of draft quotas and
the ordering of 50,000 additional American troops to Viet-Nam in mid-
1965 were coupled with a futile appeal to the United Nations to find a
way of restoring peace. The end of a thirty-seven-day halt in the American bombing of North Viet-Nam on January 31, 1966, a pause undertaken to prove Washington's willingness to negotiate, coincided with
still another fruitless effort in the United Nations to bring Hanoi to the
conference table.

A highly publicized conference between President Johnson and Vietnamese leaders in Honolulu in February, 1966, and a swing around
friendly Far East nations by Vice President Hubert H. Humphrey preceded the next major escalation of American strength in March, when
30,000 more troops were ordered to Viet-Nam. With the American
forces in Viet-Nam approaching 300,000, well-founded reports in Saigon
and Washington indicated that the figure could go to 400,000 by the end
of 1966 and 600,000 in 1967. The Manila Conference, at the end of 1966,
gave the foe the strongest kind of signal of American determination.[6]

But the enemy did not intend to give in easily. There was little doubt
that both Peking and Hanoi closely followed the activities of the political opposition in the United States, the New Left in leading American
universities, and the sympathy of newly emerging nations in Asia and
Africa. It was fashionable for American intellectuals, at "teach-ins," to
depict the power of the United States being frustrated by a handful of
little brown men in black pajamas. Yet, the most casual study of the
war without a front showed that the enemy was formidable, indeed,
when he could fight the war on his own terms.

The number of pro-Communist troops estimated by American intelligence sources to be in South Viet-Nam in the summer of 1966 was
280,000, more than double the total of a year earlier. Besides the Viet
Cong guerrillas, these fighters included numerous well-disciplined
North Vietnamese regiments, totalling more than 110,000 men of an
army of 400,000. It was clear that a force that could increase its strength
despite an estimated 34,000 dead and 11,000 captured in 1965, was more
than a match for the South Vietnamese Army of 550,000, which still

had much to learn about tactics and combat operations. The American forces, totalling more than 300,000 in September, 1966, supported by nearly 50,000 South Koreans, 4,500 Australians, and others, alone stood between the South Vietnamese regime and defeat.

If the prosecution of the war turned into more and more of an American responsibility, it became equally important to find a meaningful role which the shaky South Vietnamese Government could play in its own land. At the Honolulu conference of February, 1966, Premier Nguyen Cao Ky proclaimed his goal: pacification. The trouble was that the Saigon regime firmly held so little of the countryside that there wasn't much to try to pacify at the outset. Moreover, it was decided initially to apply pacification tactics—more food, supplies, a better life for the peasants—to only about one-third of the hamlets under government influence. It was the best that could be attempted. The cruel facts were that, after years of warfare, the Viet Cong controlled 20 per cent of the country to such an extent that the government could not even think of "pacifying" such areas; in addition, an even larger area was so bitterly contested that no rural improvement was possible. Even the most optimistic official American estimates had to concede that the Saigon government had the allegiance of less than half its 14 million people.* After a brief visit, James Reston concluded that except for American bases on the seacoast, Saigon and other cities, "this country is terrorized if not controlled by the Viet Cong and even Saigon is riddled with guerrillas." In early 1966, the situation had not markedly changed; for despite massive American bombing of North Viet-Nam and much-publicized "sweeps" against the Viet Cong in South Viet-Nam, the enemy appeared to be stronger and more defiant than ever.[7]

Premier Ky sounded a new note for a Vietnamese general: "We are dedicated to the eradication of social injustice among our people. We must bring about a true social revolution." To those who doubted a whole nation could be rebuilt while it was at war, President Johnson snapped: "They belong to a group that has always been blind to experience and deaf to hope."[8] Nevertheless, it took more than rhetoric to change a primitive land.

Despite the strength of the President's leadership and the ingrained hostility to Communism in the United States, the "spirit of ruthless brutality" was slow to rise across the nation. It was a war that found most average Americans without passion, without much conviction, and without great hope that any lasting victory worthy of the name could be achieved. Only a few draft-age Americans and the intellectual sympathizers of the New Left lashed themselves into a frenzy; from the

---

* In 1966, it was estimated that 30 million people lived in the two Viet-Nams, 16 million in the North.

Senate to the influential editorial rooms of the country, the critics of President Johnson's policy were, on the whole, rather temperate and extremely careful not to advocate withdrawal in the face of a Communist enemy.

Every group had reasons of its own for the state of public opinion. The public relations experts, to some degree, blamed public apathy on mistrust of government news-management policies and lack of adequate coverage by the mass media, neither very convincing. Some said people were basically not well informed; others, in earlier stages of the war, remarked that most Americans couldn't locate Viet-Nam on a map or account for the presence of American troops there.[9] However, after the Senate Foreign Relations Committee hearings on the conduct of the war at the outset of 1966, there was less basis for such observations.

In the running controversy between the President and the opposition press, the New York *Times* was the most persistent of the administration's critics on war policy. At one stage early in the escalation of the conflict, the President became so concerned about the *Times*'s attacks that he sent Vice President Humphrey and General Maxwell D. Taylor, at that time ambassador to Saigon, to see John B. Oakes, editorial-page editor of the *Times*.[10] *Time* magazine thought it had noted a subtle change in tone in the *Times,* but Oakes retorted that "we have . . . been critical of the deepening American involvement in the land war on the continent of Asia, and we still are." [11] Some months later, *Time* took out the brass knuckles by pointing out that the *Times*'s editorialists "have long argued" against a major U.S. commitment in Viet-Nam and adding, "Some readers feel that *Times* reporting and play of the news are colored by the same attitude." [12] After reading *Times* reports, frequently written by a correspondent under fire, there is no doubt that other readers felt this blow was unfair.

It is true that the *Times*'s policy permitted a wide range of opinion almost everywhere except in the editorial columns. Consequently, it was possible to read vehement arguments in favor of calling up the reserves and increasing the American commitment in Viet-Nam, signed by the paper's military editor, Hanson W. Baldwin, or devastating attacks on President Johnson's critics, written by Cyrus L. Sulzberger. But the *Times* could—and did—give generous news space to little-known personalities who conducted teach-ins and otherwise demonstrated against the Viet-Nam war.

Now and then, the *Times* also broke a news story that embarrassed the administration. One such was the secret testimony given by Henry Cabot Lodge before the Senate Foreign Relations Committee prior to his confirmation for reappointment as ambassador to South Viet-Nam. E. W. ("Ned") Kenworthy, a *Times* correspondent in Washington, reported Lodge had said that the United States "would keep forces in South Vietnam even if a South Vietnamese government requested their withdrawal." The attribution was merely to "a Senate source." [13]

Spokesmen for the White House and the State Department denied it, but the credibility of the government at that stage was low. The AP, UPI, and Washington *Star* all published accounts confirming the authenticity of the *Times's* story. President Johnson himself finally had to announce, after swearing in Lodge for his second tour of duty in South Viet-Nam on August 12, 1965, that both he and his Ambassador agreed the United States would not remain there "if its help were not wanted and requested." To this, Lodge finally added, in a comment to a reporter who asked him about the original story, "I didn't say that. I'll tell you that." [14] The *Times* said primly, "President Johnson has performed a useful service by personally scotching the report that the United States would keep its forces in South Vietnam even if their withdrawal was requested by the Saigon government." [15]

Walter Lippmann was also embroiled in the controversy over Viet-Nam. He defended the view that the United States could not be the "policeman of the world" and demanded, "How many Vietnams can the United States defend in Asia?" To which the New York *Herald Tribune* in one of its dying gasps replied, "When Mr. Lippmann asks how many Vietnams the United States can defend in Asia, perhaps the best reply is an indirect one. How many are there to be? And if we yield in the present confrontation, how much more difficult will be the next?" And the old internationalist Dean Acheson added grumpily, "The escapists, the new (though mostly old) isolationists are still with us." [16]

The anti-Administration news breaks were by no means confined to such critical newspapers as the New York *Times,* the Washington *Post,* and the St. Louis *Post-Dispatch*. One of the most damaging stories was broken by Willard Edwards, of the Chicago *Tribune,* who quoted a CIA report to show that the Viet-Nam war was going badly. The report, by Willard Matthias, of the CIA Board of National Estimates, said, "The guerrilla war in South Vietnam is in its fifth year and no end appears in sight. The Viet Cong in the South, dependent largely upon their own resources but under the direction and control of the Communist regime in the North, are pressing their offensive more vigorously than ever . . . There remains serious doubt that victory can be won, and the situation remains very fragile . . ." In order to disown the report, the State Department released the document and called it a "think piece" which did not represent the Administration's views. [17]

A number of correspondents in Washington, representing newspapers of varying position on the Viet-Nam war, disclosed almost at the same time that Senator Mike Mansfield, the Senate's majority leader, had read a three-page memorandum to the President expressing great doubt over the American intervention in Viet-Nam. The incident had occurred during the eight days of conferences before the President's decision not to declare a national emergency in 1965. Some versions had it that Mansfield's doubts had persuaded the President to back away from such precipitate action. In the furor that followed, the President blamed the leak of the Mansfield memorandum on Representative Gerald Ford, the Republican minority leader of the House, who had also been present and who later had held an off-the-record news conference with correspondents. Ford, not at all unhappy over his prominence in the news, maintained his innocence and was fortunate enough to have some of the correspondents defend him.[18]

Essentially, however, there was solid bipartisan support for the war in Washington. The Republican Congressional leaders differed from the President only on the degree to which the fight was being carried to North Viet-Nam. Their talk was tougher. The most respected of all Republicans in his generation, Dwight D. Eisenhower, agreed that "the Communists must be stopped in Viet-Nam." If there was a difference between him and President Johnson, it was over the extent of the pledge that had been made by the United States to help defend South Viet-Nam in 1954.

But here, too, no one could doubt that the Republicans were as interested as the Democrats in maintaining a free and non-Communist South Viet-Nam. To show that the United States was honoring a commitment made under a Republican President, President Johnson frequently cited a letter written by President Eisenhower in October, 1954, to Premier Ngo Dinh Diem of South Viet-Nam. President Eisenhower demurred mildly, saying that the United States had offered economic aid at the time, and not military programs. It was true that the military buildup had not begun in earnest until 1961, in the Kennedy Administration. But there could be no question about the intent of the United States in 1954, for Eisenhower wrote to Ngo Dinh Diem:

> We have been exploring ways and means to permit our aid to Viet-Nam to be more effective and to make a greater contribution to the welfare and stability of the Government of Viet-Nam. I am, accordingly, instructing the American Ambassador to Viet-Nam to examine with you in your capacity as Chief of Government how an intelligent program of American aid given directly to your Government can serve to assist Viet-Nam in its present hour of trial, provided that your Government is prepared to give assurances as to the standards of performance it would be able to maintain in the event such aid were supplied.

The purpose of this offer is to assist the Government of Viet-Nam in developing and maintaining a strong, viable state, capable of resisting attempted subversion or aggression through military means.[19]

Despite the outcry from his critics, the nation was well satisfied with President Johnson's performance in Viet-Nam for a considerable period. Following his record-breaking victory over Barry Goldwater in the Presidential campaign of 1964, the President's popularity soared to a 70 per cent verdict of approval for his policies in a Gallup poll in June, 1965. A Lou Harris poll, in the following month, found that 69 per cent of the respondents believed the Johnson performance to be between "good" and "excellent." It was particularly significant that his Viet-Nam policies were specifically endorsed by 65 per cent of those questioned, a five-point gain over a poll taken in March, before the big American troop movement to Viet-Nam began. This feeling that the American public wanted more vigorous action in Viet-Nam was confirmed by one of the most free-wheeling of pollsters, Samuel Lubell, who found in August, 1965, that nearly 75 per cent of those he questioned supported the President's decision to send more American troops into Asian combat.[20]

The New York *Times,* still sharply critical of the President, conducted its own check of public opinion by having reporters question people at random in eleven cities. The conclusion, reached immediately after the Presidential warning that the country was in a "real war," indicated that Americans generally supported President Johnson. *Time* magazine, in another check, came to the same conclusion.[21]

But that wasn't enough. As the fighting intensified and casualties mounted, efforts were made through polls to "demonstrate" what the public was for. A Harris poll on February 28, 1966, purported to show that the President's support had dropped to 49 per cent of the public that was asked to judge his conduct of the Viet-Nam war. On March 9, a Gallup poll held that 50 per cent of those questioned backed the President's conduct of the war, 33 per cent disapproved, and 17 per cent had no opinion. But only a few days later, a combined polling effort by seven social scientists at Stanford University and the National Opinion Research Center at the University of Chicago produced utter confusion. Out of 1,474 respondents chosen nationally, the high-level pollsters reported that 61 per cent approved the President's handling of the war, 52 per cent were willing to support a coalition South Vietnamese government that would include the Viet Cong, 88 per cent wanted direct talks with the Viet Cong, and 60 per cent preferred a major war if that were the only alternative to pulling out of Viet-Nam. It was a poll that had something for everybody—a poll to be remembered. It proved only that polls cannot be used to govern the United States.[22]

Despite these diversions, the President persevered in his massive effort to lead public opinion. Editors, citizens' groups, the Congress, and his immediate advisers were all on his White House agenda. Some columnists, like Ralph McGill of the Atlanta *Constitution,* William S. White, of United Features Syndicate, and Max Freedman of the Chicago Daily News Syndicate, were Presidential supporters, as were many in Congress. As for the President's foes, these included Senator J. W. Fulbright, Senator Wayne Morse, Walter Lippmann, the New York *Times,* the St. Louis *Post-Dispatch,* and a group generically identified as "the professors." The President worked on all of them, but sometimes he was in a black mood about the press in particular.

The President did not neglect his foreign critics. On one occasion, he conducted what amounted to a question-and-answer seminar for twenty-three Washington-based foreign correspondents from major world capitals, using Max Freedman's living room as a classroom. In such off-the-record sessions, the President would often speak with utter candor. He was once credited with having said, for example, that he could well understand why the Communists didn't want to negotiate in Viet-Nam when they thought they were winning.

In a typical press assessment of the President, *Newsweek* wrote: "He is a man of excesses and contradictions. He works too hard, gets too little sleep, attempts too much, is hurt too easily and is never satisfied. He is hypersensitive to criticism for two reasons. Personal criticism bruises the ego of any man in politics, and a Texas-size ego suffers Texas-size bruises. More important, Mr. Johnson is convinced that public criticism cuts into his support with the public and Congress and that enough criticism could cut his support to the point where he could not act." [23] It was a verdict with which most of the correspondents in Washington generally agreed, regardless of whether they liked or disliked the President.

Most American newspapers supported the President's Viet-Nam policy with some qualifications. His success in putting a monumental domestic program through Congress, headed by civil rights legislation and Medicare, was a factor in building up support for his foreign policy. To this, he added his own missionary efforts with the press. No President had ever courted the press with such ardor and persistence. The very notion of a virtual public relations campaign from the White House would have been repugnant to the most publicity-conscious of his predecessors from Theodore Roosevelt to John Fitzgerald Kennedy.

One of the President's critics, Ben H. Bagdikian, wrote:

The problem is that Lyndon Johnson appeals to reporters with all the dignity and power of his position as President and, when this does not produce the results he wants, he begins manipulating them and the news in ways that are not highly regarded even at the Press Club bar. He is trying to have it both ways. The weakness of many correspondents is that the President is too valuable a source in the competition for news to be ignored as a lesser PR man would be. But deeper than that is the conflict the President creates in many serious correspondents who respect the office of President and the man in it, but whose professional standards tell them that what is going on is common, ordinary press agentry.[24]

The President's efforts had a curious effect on those in his immediate entourage. Instead of emulating their chief in his press campaign, many of them seemed to be as scornful of newspaper criticism as he was concerned by it. McGeorge Bundy, the former Harvard dean who served at the time as special assistant to the President for National Security Affairs, told an interviewer that the press is probably not as important as it thinks it is.[25] A top Presidential official who was asked to make still another attempt to convert the New York *Times* made this response, "No, Mr. President, I won't go to the *Times*. I've got more important things to do right now, and besides, what in hell do you care what the *Times* says?"[26] The ever-pugnacious Arthur Sylvester, Assistant Secretary of Defense for Public Affairs, was quoted as having told American correspondents in Saigon at an off-the-record session on June 17, 1965, that "the press should be the handmaiden of government."[27] Of course, he denied it.

Even the usually mild George Ball, then Under Secretary of State, became a part of this pattern during the press briefing that preceded President Johnson's speech at Johns Hopkins University, in which he offered unconditional discussions on a Viet-Nam settlement. When Max Frankel, of the New York *Times,* asked why the government had waited so long to make public its aims in Viet-Nam, Ball remarked patronizingly that there had been no delay and the government's position had been the same. "It may," he added, "be a little clearer to you." John Scali, the American Broadcasting Company's diplomatic correspondent, retorted crushingly, "Since this has all been said before, would the Secretary please refresh the reporters' memories on the last time any one in government offered unconditional discussions on Viet-Nam?" There was no reply except laughter.[28]

All this could not help but complicate the job of the youthful and competent Presidential assistant Bill D. Moyers, who was then the White House press secretary and also the unofficial coordinator of the government's public relations efforts. James Reston wrote that Moyers had not been able to "establish confidence in the public and private statements made in the name of the President." To these and other critical remarks, Moyers fired back, "You [the press] often see things through a keyhole, you see only a small portion of what we in government see. Yours are errors of incompleteness." That was the spirit of Washington at the time, as typified by relations between press and government.[29]

Secretary of State Rusk had confidence in only a few correspondents, but saw them regularly. Secretary of Defense McNamara was even more selective. The main burden of conducting the intricate and immensely complicated task of stimulating and guiding public opinion was left to the President. That coincided with his own desires. If the country responded to his leadership, even reluctantly, it was in large part due to his unceasing efforts to convince the people by every means at his command. Even after his operation for the removal of his gall bladder late in 1965, and his enforced retirement to his Texas ranch to recuperate, he maintained his war leadership. In the fall of 1966, therefore, Lyndon Baines Johnson remained the single most powerful force in determining what the American people and the world should be told about events in Viet-Nam, and how the news should be broken to them.

2. THE ROLE OF THE U.S. EMBASSY

Few Americans are geared by background, training, or temperament to serve as proconsuls in the Far East and to preside over the application of fantastic amounts of military and economic power. Yet, because Douglas MacArthur was able to work a seeming miracle in Japan, the impossible has often been expected by a bemused public of other American and diplomatic representatives in critical posts in Asia. The greatest demands of all—and the most unreasonable—have been made of a succession of American ambassadors and generals who served in Saigon during much of the 1960's. Much of their trouble stemmed from the dismal situation in which they found themselves. But often they did not help their own cause very much.

Such was the case in the cheerless summer of 1964, when the excitement of a Presidential campaign was rising in the United States, and a reassuring appraisal of the war in Viet-Nam was spread before the people. As UPI reported from Washington on September 9, in common with others, "President Johnson said today that Maxwell D. Taylor, United States Ambassador to South Viet-Nam, has reported 'continued progress' in the war against the Communists there despite recent politi-

cal turmoil. . . . The President said Mr. Taylor gave Congressional
leaders a 'full and frank examination of the situation. . . .' "

Newsweek, in its own account, reported that General Taylor "fairly
oozed optimism," although the American correspondents in Saigon
turned up nothing to justify such a mood. It was typical of the long
confrontation between the American government and the American
press over events in South Viet-Nam, a basic problem that was at the
root of much of the public confusion over the course of the war.

Only six days later, after another of the numerous government up-
heavals in Saigon which took place while the Ambassador was spreading good cheer in Washington, the New York *Times* brushed aside the
phony optimism and exploded:

> Less than a year ago high officials were proclaiming that the war against
> the Vietcong could be won by 1965. If illusions of that extreme nature
> have now been dropped, it is still true that the information given to the
> American people only last week has already proved to be too optimistic—
> and its overoptimism was evident to well-informed observers even before
> the latest development. American soldiers are dying in South Viet-Nam
> daily. In return for willingly bearing these and other sacrifices, the Ameri-
> can people deserve to know all the facts, regardless of how grim they may
> be.[30]

General Taylor, who had helped design the underpinnings of American strategy in Viet-Nam, was the latest in a long line of distinguished
politicians, diplomats, and soldiers who had been betrayed by a policy
that sought to distract national attention from dismal failure by prema-
turely sounding the sweet chimes of victory. As early as the winter of
1962, Attorney General Robert F. Kennedy found during a visit to Saigon that the war wasn't going at all badly for "our" side and stressed
the pledge of his brother, the President, to stand by South Viet-Nam's
President Ngo Dinh Diem "until we win." Frederick E. Nolting, Jr.,
who was then the American Ambassador to Saigon, was trying to quiet
Diem's critics;[31] until his departure on August 15, 1963, he refused to
believe that anything was wrong and insisted, as he boarded the plane,
that the Vietnamese were conducting a "winning program." [32]

After the overthrow of the Diem regime that November and the
bloodless coup that brought General Nguyen Khanh to power on January 30, 1964, Secretary of State Rusk himself announced in Saigon that
the situation showed "steady improvement." [33] Secretary of Defense Mc-
Namara, during his frequent inspection visits at the time, was the most
determined of optimists. Even the hard-headed realist Henry Cabot
Lodge gave President Johnson an encouraging report at the end of his

first tour of duty as American Ambassador to Saigon on June 29, 1964.[34]

But coordinated optimism wasn't enough to convince the press. The correspondents in Saigon were reporting almost continual governmental chaos and setbacks in the field throughout this period. The Johnson Administration therefore decided at the Honolulu conference of June 1–2, 1964, to make the USIS a kind of superagency to see that the war was properly reported to the American people. This was, to put it mildly, stretching its original purpose: "to help achieve U.S. foreign policy objectives by influencing public attitudes in other nations and advising the President, his representatives abroad and the various departments and agencies on the implications of foreign opinion for present and contemplated United States policies, programs and official statements." It is true that USIS also was charged with encouraging "constructive support abroad for United States policy objectives" and striving "to unmask and counter hostile attempts to distort and frustrate the objectives of the United States." [35]

But this Honolulu conference was by no means as concerned with the foreign press as it was with the manner in which the American press was presenting the Viet-Nam war. Secretaries Rusk and McNamara, Ambassador Taylor, and others concurred that a significant shift had to be made in government information policy. For years, it had been considered routine at many American embassies for USIS personnel to handle both American and non-American journalists who sought "guidance" in one form or another; indeed, those few who wandered into USIS in Saigon had found more "guidance" than they desired.

It was now decided that a more vigorous program should be developed through USIS to assure that the "true story" of American efforts was reported in the United States and elsewhere. To that end, the conferees determined that this much-desired goal could best be attained by placing, under the direction of the Ambassador, a single government official in charge of all information from American sources in South Viet-Nam—political, military, and economic. This official was also given the duty of checking on the reliability of certain correspondents when it became necessary and publicizing information to refute and counteract "erroneous and misleading reports," their origin unspecified. He was told that he must develop "positive information," surely a most difficult assignment in a place like South Viet-Nam at that time.[36]

The official to whom this king-sized propaganda job was entrusted was Barry Zorthian, a stocky, determined, and hard-working career information specialist. He was then forty-four years old. His parents had brought him from Turkey, where he was born, to New Haven, Conn., when he was three years old. At Yale, he majored in international relations; upon his graduation in 1941, he was briefly a Vermont weekly newspaper editor, then served as an officer in the U.S. Marines in the Pacific during World War II. Afterward, he was successively a reporter on the New Haven *Register* and a news editor for C.B.S. until, in 1947, he joined the Voice of America in New York. While he rose to program manager for the Voice, he also studied law at night at New York University and in 1952 was awarded his LL.B. degree *cum laude*. For a decade thereafter, he worked for USIS in various parts of the world until he was brought from New Delhi, where he was deputy director for India, to Saigon early in 1964.

As Minister Counsellor and Public Affairs Officer at the American embassy, and later the director of the Joint U.S. Public Affairs Office (JUSPAO), Zorthian began expanding his staff to take care of all programs, both external and internal. Within two years, he had more than a hundred experienced government information officials and others working in his heavily guarded headquarters in the heart of Saigon, and almost as many military information and other specialists. A considerable part of his work, of necessity, was directed toward the Vietnamese themselves, seeking to convince them that they should take a greater part in the fighting in order to ensure their survival. One of his operatives remarked in the early days of the effort, "We're producing almost enough paper to sink this peninsula." It didn't seem to have much effect, taken by itself. Nor were his efforts to change the viewpoint of the American correspondents notably successful.

It was not an enviable spot for one of the outstanding men in USIS, as the correspondents were the first to concede. While some were sympathetic and quite willing to wait and see whether there was any advantage to them in the new program, they were not inclined to let down their guard. They realized that Zorthian had inherited a situation in which Vietnamese falsehoods had been deliberately spread to make a bad position look good; he could scarcely reverse such bad habits overnight and win the confidence of correspondents who basically mistrusted government-inspired information, whether it was issued from JUSPAO or USIS.

A visitor to Saigon, Claude Witze, senior editor of *Air Force–Space Digest* magazine, commented as follows on the new government position at the outset of Zorthian's campaign to win friends among the correspondents, if not to influence them:

A distressing amount of intellectual dishonesty is scattered through the record we have built up here in the 1960's . . . Whether there will be any improvement is highly dubious. The same officials are still giving the orders, and they now have put a single man in charge of dealing with the press in Saigon. The new and more unified effort to tell the story has as its real goal the correction of what is called erroneous information coming out of Saigon. The erroneous information, it is indicated, is critical of the South Vietnamese contribution and its willingness to fight. The same reports tend to ignore Vietcong terrorism, defections, and losses. None of these criticisms of the reporting out of Saigon acknowledges that early 1964 was studded with Vietcong successes . . ." [37]

Zorthian tried a number of new procedures to capture the attention of the rebellious press—more background briefing sessions with high officials, greater access to the Ambassador and others, a special helicopter set aside for correspondents, trips with the American commander, General William C. Westmoreland, and instant availability on his own part. Only an official with the physique of a New York Giants linebacker and the hide of a water buffalo would have attempted so strenuous a regimen, and some progress was achieved.

But presently, General Westmoreland's confidence was broken by a correspondent over a relatively trivial announcement. That discouraged the general for a time from participation in a program to make more news available. Other "backgrounders" failed to come off as scheduled; some backfired. Soon the philosophical Zorthian was saying that he was "expendable" but would hang on for as long as he could. Doggedly, he took to debating with the correspondents over some of the news breaks that showed the Americans and the South Vietnamese in a bad light, but he made scant headway.

On one occasion he asked a photographer why he took so many pictures of South Vietnamese atrocities, which were duly circulated to the world press, when it was of course impossible to get many pictures of the Viet Cong atrocities. The astonished photographer was flabbergasted. He exclaimed, "You think these pictures are bad? You should see the ones I didn't use!"

On another occasion, a correspondent reported that Ambassador Taylor and General Nguyen Khanh had had a violent argument. The embassy formally denied it through Zorthian's office. Ambassador Taylor himself went on a taped American television program to say that his relations with General Khanh, then the South Vietnamese premier, were excellent. But not long afterward, the correspondent was given private assurance that his story had been completely accurate, and that he could so inform his superiors.

When the first reports came from the South Vietnamese Army in the summer of 1964 that it had captured soldiers from organized units of the North Vietnamese Army infiltrating below the 17th Parallel, there were vociferous American denials. However, two American correspondents were permitted by the South Vietnamese to interview the prisoners and thereby established the truth of the story. Much to their amazement, the American authorities once again insisted that no North Vietnamese were operating in the South. Subsequently, Ambassador Taylor conceded privately that the South Vietnamese had, indeed, captured North Vietnamese soldiers but emphasized that there were "only three men." A year later, American authorities were contending that upward of 10,000 soldiers of the North Vietnamese Army were operating south of the 17th Parallel.

Newsweek assessed some three months of "positive" information as follows:

> In the nine months since the fall of Diem, harassment of reporters critical of South Vietnam policy has abated. Yet the truth of what is really happening in the Southeast Asian nation seems just as illusory . . . The State Department and the Pentagon, which have rarely let events disturb their sanguinity, insisted that newsmen tend to believe too much of what they hear in back alleys, and consequently misrepresent the tangled situation. "Those reporters in Saigon take a defeatist attitude," one Pentagon official said. Nevertheless, it was clear to any one within gunshot of Saigon that American policy and American interests were in serious trouble last week.[38]

One of the most reprehensible methods that was used by some government officials to discourage correspondents from reporting bad news was to warn them that they might bring on a "bigger war, maybe with Red China." The reasoning behind this peculiar philosophy was that criticism of the American war effort in South Viet-Nam was encouraging to the enemies of the United States; in addition, it served to give the foe the feeling that the American public was not behind its own government. The conclusion was that continued criticism might lead both Hanoi and Peking to what some government officials called a "dangerous miscalculation." It was just about as far-fetched a device for suppressing critics as had been devised in the long and miserable history of censorship.[39]

While the war itself was not going well in 1964, the power struggle among the South Vietnamese in Saigon was creating a condition of near anarchy. Having survived a coup in September, General Khanh temporarily stepped out as premier the following month in favor of a civilian, Tran Van Huong, and a new chief of state, Phan Khac Suu, an elder statesman. It brought about even worse disorders. Under the leadership of the enigmatic monk who had helped overthrow Diem and who was being increasingly identified with the Communists, Thich (Venerable) Tri Quang, the politically minded Buddhists began a series of disturbances which were intended to paralyze the new government.[40] They almost succeeded.

General Khanh, supported by his younger generals, used his leadership of the South Vietnamese Army on December 20 to place himself at the head of a newly formed Armed Forces Council and dissolved the High National Council, the underpinning of the civilian regime. In this obvious bid for power, Ambassador Taylor tried as best he could to save the civilian government. Three days later, General Khanh granted an exclusive interview to the New York *Herald Tribune*'s correspondent in Saigon, Beverly Deepe, in which he warned that if Ambassador Taylor "does not act more intelligently, the United State will lose Southeast Asia and we will lose our freedom." The Vietnamese leader angrily accused the Ambassador of "activities beyond imagination" in seeking the restoration of the civilian High National Council.[41]

Although the Johnson Administration had not intended to take a major role in the struggle, the publication of the Khanh interview disposed of the official contention that relations with the South Vietnamese military leader were good. Every correspondent in Saigon, and every official of both governments, knew that the relationship had been anything but good, and Miss Deepe's interview served to confirm it. Consequently, with the approval of President Johnson, the State Department issued a warning to General Khanh that American support was based on the continuation of a civilian government free of "improper interference" by the military. The statement fully supported Ambassador Taylor's position, but it settled nothing.[42]

Miss Deepe, who had been excluded from current background briefings by both Ambassador Taylor and General Westmoreland, learned of the details of one that was given by the Ambassador for eight selected American correspondents immediately after the blow-up with General Khanh. Since she wasn't bound by any agreement, she published his remarks in the New York *Herald Tribune,* none of them complimentary to General Khanh. The Ambassador was quoted as saying that the Vietnamese leader was the center of an anti-American group of generals, that some of them were first-class but others "are bordering on being nuts," and that they weren't doing well in the war against the Viet Cong.[43] The U.S. mission hinted at withholding aid but didn't really mean it. After a few days, the break was papered over. As for Miss Deepe, she had to bear up under cool treatment during the official Saigon Christmas parties. The Taylor "backgrounders" were quietly put on ice for the time being. It was the end of a long period of unjustified official optimism over the progress of the war.

3. THE BIG CHANGE

The deadly power game for control of the government of South Viet-Nam went on. Additional information about the war began emanating from American sources, none of it very detailed, but the more knowledgeable correspondents would not be distracted from the main issue in Saigon. They were right. On January 27, 1965, General Khanh again seized power, overthrowing the civilian Tran Van Huong regime during a one-day visit by Ambassador Taylor to Bangkok. One excited South Vietnamese officer told the correspondents, "Now it's Taylor or Khanh. One or the other has to go." But the embassy replied that Ambassador Taylor had no intention of resigning. The Buddhists were overjoyed, for they had considered the Ambassador their principal enemy.[44] Like most political alliances in South Viet-Nam, the accommodation between General Khanh and Thich Tri Quang didn't last very long. In a matter of days, the military leader was saying he would not tolerate dissension, regional or religious. And the Buddhist monk was saying, in reply, that General Khanh was a "bad man."[45]

Washington now no longer offered cheery optimism, bland reassurances, and patronizing tolerance for the views of a majority of the press that the war in South Viet-Nam was going badly. After his inauguration on January 20, 1965, President Johnson felt freed of his pre-election political restraints, and Ambassador Taylor, loyal soldier that he is, was relieved of much of the embarrassment of trying to make a deteriorating situation look promising. Yet, while a changing emphasis developed in American military and political policy in South Viet-Nam, the administration found that it was reaping the lean harvest of years of exaggerated claims, diplomatic denials, wriggling equivocations, and embarrassed silences. A skeptical world waited for the new line to emerge, while at home the President's critics began urging him to go to the conference table at a time when the war had been all but lost. It would have been the very worst time for him to do so.

Whenever the role of the press in South Viet-Nam was brought up for discussion with government officials, even seasoned and knowledgeable men grumbled that the newspapers and the correspondents were partly to blame for events in South Viet-Nam. Just how the press could have remedied a deteriorating situation as it existed at the end of January, 1965, no diplomat could say. But some responsible officials, talking privately, insisted that if some way could have been found for the press to "cooperate" in reporting all the failures in the Viet-Nam war, everything would have turned out much better. It seemed to be an unreasoning attitude, but there was no doubt that it was held in high places, and that both editors and their correspondents in Saigon were well aware of it.

On February 7, 1965, President Johnson announced the opening of attacks on North Viet-Nam by American land-based and carrier-based bombers—the long-awaited and much-feared escalation of the war. Despite the uproar at home and abroad, the American policy gathered force; at last, something was being done to strike back at the root of the guerrilla insurgency, to deny the enemy a "privileged sanctuary" north of the 17th Parallel. Almost overnight, the American government's preoccupation with the reporting of the war from Saigon was overshadowed by its concern over the editorial attacks on its position at home. The editors, the professors, and the "teach-ins"—the opening of what amounted to a national debate on the conduct of the war—gave both the correspondents and the hard-pressed JUSPAO staff in South Viet-Nam a welcome respite from almost continual criticism. The argument between them now became centered about the coverage of the war; in place of the handful of correspondents in Saigon, new arrivals from the United States, Great Britain, France, Japan, and India—plus the inevitable tourists who became ten-minute experts—sent the press corps total over 200.

This represented an opportunity as well as a challenge for Zorthian's organization. For the first time, it gave him the diversity of views among correspondents for which he had been hoping. Those who were veterans of the conflict between government and press in South Viet-Nam now were outnumbered by the newcomers. They cared less about news management than obtaining sufficient news to justify their continued presence in South Viet-Nam. One competent observer wrote as follows of the manner in which JUSPAO adjusted to the new situation:

Zorthian is by far the most intelligent of all officials to have tackled the press problems here. He has been aware from the start that the press is apt to leap on any issue likely to provide a peg for getting to the truth. By its nature, the press here [in Saigon], as elsewhere, is fairly combative—partly because of competition between the reporters themselves and partly because a reporter always wants to know more than what he is voluntarily told.

Rather than provide issues by withholding information, Zorthian has adopted a much more subtle and effective technique. He deluges the reporter with information, generally accurate in character. He holds a daily briefing for reporters in his office, which covers not only the daily doings of embassy officials, but backgrounds political and military developments fairly inclusively. A military communiqué is released at each briefing which covers a large part of the war developments. Press trips are laid on with increasing frequency. Separate backgrounders and briefings are scheduled night and day and these often are given by top-ranking Americans.

It sounds good, and it is. No organization can afford to miss these sessions because they are so inclusive. It is now possible for a reporter to do an adequate job (by the standards of his home office) covering Vietnam without ever setting foot outside USIS. There are a lot of reporters who confine themselves to just this. The Defense Department still is shipping in people at a heavy rate for 10-day tours of Vietnam, and this influx swells the regular assignment to Vietnam of newsmen.

For the vast majority of the newcomers to Vietnam, Zorthian is the major font of information. The building of a network of sources in Vietnam is a tricky and time-consuming business, and a newcomer is more or less forced to rely on Zorthian and his huge organization. With all the merits of Zorthianism, it is, none the less, a self-interested government deal. Ninety-nine per cent of the handout information it provides is accurate and useful. But inevitably, there are sometimes vital omissions and even distortions. I certainly don't blame Zorthian for these because they are the payoff of his way of doing business. He deserves the influence and control he wields. The fault lies with the reporters who have too great a tendency to rely on Zorthian for everything . . .[46]

The government effort was stepped up in Washington, too. A separate task force on South Viet-Nam, which was responsible for a number of policy matters, was also given the assignment of developing more information which could be made available to the mass media. The number of background briefings increased markedly. At no stage of the Viet-Nam war had the news flow been greater in Saigon and in Washington; both the front pages of the newspapers and the news programs of the television networks reflected it. The volume of news and government-inspired comment soon matched the criticism and even overshadowed it, except when there were particularly unfavorable developments in South Viet-Nam.

The American government had long since dropped the notion that optimistic talk would improve the situation, although one or another official would revert to type now and then. As editors and broadcasters were told at one of the more important briefing sessions in Washington during the spring of 1965, intensified military action was far more likely in Viet-Nam than peace talks for the immediate future. And in July, President Johnson warned the "situation will get worse before it gets better." While an effort was made to show that the United States was keeping all avenues open for diplomatic approaches to negotiations, the government's spokesmen continually stressed the refusal of both Peking and Hanoi at that stage to consider a peaceful settlement.[47] In this manner, much of the domestic criticism was rebutted and the critics disarmed, but only for a short time. For in the process, an offer of peace talks had actually been suppressed.

Had it not been for continual unrest in South Viet-Nam, the American war effort might have achieved more immediate respect. But the South Vietnamese could not be managed. President Johnson's plans for a grandiose Southeast Asian development scheme aroused more skepticism than interest among the South Vietnamese military leadership. Among the people themselves, so buffeted by the misfortunes of a generation of war and the inevitable weakness among their officials, some hopelessly corrupt, the war weariness was becoming more marked. An observant correspondent, Richard Critchfield, of the Washington *Evening Star,* found that American economic aid had created a prosperous middle and upper class but had done little to improve the lot of the peasants, who made up 80 per cent of the population.[48] The Communists made a certain amount of progress among the peasantry by stressing that all Saigon governments were, to some extent, the instruments of the rich and landed class. Yet, official optimists like George A. Carver, Jr., argued that a non-Communist revolution was in progress in South Viet-Nam which for the long term, if successful, represented a grave threat to the Communist North.[49]

It was apparent, however, that the revolution, if that was what was going on in Saigon, could wreck the country if it continued to race out of control and force continual change in the power group. Long before Ambassador Taylor ended his tour of duty in South Viet-Nam, his old adversary, General Khanh, was upset by his own erstwhile allies in the winter of 1965 and sent from the country in involuntary exile. Eventually, on June 12, another military government emerged to take over from the civilian regime of Premier Phan Huy Quat, which had served in the interim. It was the ninth government in the nineteen months that followed the downfall of Diem.

Air Vice Marshal Nguyen Cao Ky, the colorful thirty-four-year-old chief of the Air Force, emerged from the new military junta as its front man. Ambassador Taylor protested to the junta leader, Major General Nguyen Van Thieu, the former defense minister, that Marshal Ky was too inexperienced.[50] The Ambassador had no luck. On June 20, the flamboyant Air Force leader became the new premier, with General Van Thieu as chief of state.

Among Marshal Ky's first moves was the closing of the thirty-six daily newspapers published in Vietnamese, followed by the restoration of publication privileges to twenty-three of them. None of the newspapers had much of a following, the highest estimate of their circulation being 200,000, but a principle was at stake. As it was expressed by Barry Bingham, publisher of the Louisville *Times* and *Courier-Journal,* on behalf of the International Press Institute, "Authoritarian suppression of newspapers defeats the claim that your government is fighting to uphold free institutions." [51]

Unhappily, such terms as democracy, press freedom, religious liberty, and the like were only dimly understood in South Viet-Nam. Marshal Ky once told a British correspondent that he admired Hitler, and was astonished at the resultant flap. A Vietnamese government statement explained, "It goes without saying that Marshal Ky's admiration does not go to the Hitler dictator, warmonger and Nazi, but rather to the leader who, in the 1930's, by sheer energy and dynamism, was able to build the unity of Germany, a country then divided." [52]

Despite the awkward beginning, Ky hung on. He was, at first, built up in some sections of the American press as a "strong man." He never was that. In a country that had no sense of national identity and for a people who were more faithful to family and group than to an ill-defined state, Ky was merely a general who had been designated as front man for the military clique that had split up South Viet-Nam among themselves. There were nine other generals, in addition to Ky, who controlled the ten divisions of the army and, through them, the four corps areas of South Viet-Nam. Always ready for a chance to bring down a military-supported government, the crafty Buddhist leader, Thich Tri Quang, bided his time, knowing that Ky sooner or later would get into trouble.

It was mainly through an American miscalculation that the little airman's luck began to run out. With the growth of American armed strength, the approval of Ambassador Henry Cabot Lodge, and finally the enthusiastic Texas-type embrace of President Johnson himself at the 1966 Honolulu conference, Ky began to believe his press clippings. He had been jealous for some time of the Buddhist-supported war lord of the five northern provinces of South Viet-Nam, Lieutenant General Nguyen Chanh Thi, commander of the I Corps. And so, on March 10, 1966, he led the military junta in Saigon into a break with the Buddhists and the expulsion of General Thi from the regime.

At once, another of South Viet-Nam's interminable political crises began, and not even the promise of early elections served to quiet the Buddhists. It was considered remarkable that the voting for a national legislative body, held in September, 1966, drew a turnout of 4 million. Thus, the Ky Government hung on.

The difficulties in Saigon, coming on top of evidence that Hanoi and Peking were relentless in their pursuit of the war, was a grave setback for Ambassador Lodge as the American proconsul in Viet-

Nam. His role in the liquidation of the Diem regime during his first tour of duty in Saigon had made him feared in the land. John Mecklin had written of that turning point in the American involvement: "For application of the new policy, which was likely to be an unpleasant operation, President Kennedy had found exactly the right man. Ambassador Lodge proved to be an able executioner." [53]

However, from the beginning of his second experience in Saigon, he had been in the forefront of the supporters of Marshal Ky. The young airman had found the American envoy a sympathetic adviser and, after a dubious beginning, had turned increasingly to him for support. [54] The correspondents had recorded the change and marveled just a little. Most of them stood in awe of the Ambassador.

Lodge was not the kind of man who slapped the press on the back; once, he had remarked to Krishnamachari Balaraman, the U.N. correspondent of the *Hindu* of Madras, "You know, they call me a Boston Brahmin. It's so nice to meet a *real* Brahmin!" Consciously or not, that was his attitude. As the Senator from Massachusetts whose career in Congress had been ended by John Fitzgerald Kennedy, and later as the chief of the U.S. Mission to the United Nations, Lodge had often referred to his beginnings as a reporter for the New York *Herald Tribune*. But he had never been a great hand at fraternizing with his former colleagues. At the United Nations, he had aroused a considerable amount of grumbling in the press section by refusing to issue advance texts of his speeches, arguing quite correctly that it only helped the Russians to prepare an immediate rebuttal. Through such experiences, the correspondents had come to consider him "difficult."

However, after the press's conflict with Ambassador Nolting and General Harkins in South Viet-Nam, Lodge had appeared in Saigon as a welcome change in 1963. He had established himself almost immediately as an ambassador who would deal fairly with the correspondents, but grant few favors. Throughout the tense period of Diem's overthrow, he kept his own counsel; even afterward, it was almost as difficult for his colleagues at the embassy to find out what he was doing as it was for the press. [55] Yet, despite his reserved and well-nigh formidable manner, he had emerged from his trying experience with almost universal respect among both Americans and Vietnamese. It was, in effect, a fund of good will on which he was able to draw during his second term in Saigon.

Lodge's primary task was to find a way to restore South Viet-Nam to at least a semblance of stable rule, placate the Buddhists, reassure the Catholics, and stimulate the bogged-down economy of a nation that was close to being dismembered. General Taylor had relied to some extent on his deputy, U. Alexis Johnson, for such matters. But with Lodge's return Johnson was shifted back to his post in Washington as Under Secretary of State for Political Affairs. The way was open for a determined effort, under distinguished American civilian direction, to revive hope in South Viet-Nam.

One of Lodge's principal assistants was Charles Mann, the director of the U.S. Operations Mission in South Viet-Nam, as the country's branch of the Agency for International Development was known. In Mann, who had fourteen years' experience in Southeast Asia, including six years in South Viet-Nam, the embassy had a hard-headed, nononsense aid director who knew how difficult it was to administer the expenditure of $350 million a year in a small country. His predecessor, James S. Killen, Jr., who charged he had been "dismissed" at Lodge's insistence, had channeled much of these funds through the Vietnamese government rather than to retain such power in American hands for direct distribution. Mann recognized that widespread graft was possible without close supervision and argued that it could be eliminated. Even greater problems that confronted him included the rising inflation in South Viet-Nam, the necessity for importing rice to feed an impoverished people, and the probable growth of refugees from war zones from 600,000 to 1.5 million within a year. These things were not as dramatic as military action, but they were no less important in the successful conduct of the war, and they had been largely neglected in the news under Lodge's predecessors.

Another member of the new Lodge team, who also served to stimulate interest in the nonmilitary aspects of the conflict, was Edward G. Lansdale, a former agent of the CIA and a retired Air Force major general. For the record, he was identified as a "special assistant on pacification" who worked under the Ambassador's direction and had a team of eight to ten intelligence experts. The publication of a report that Secretary of Defense McNamara had opposed his appointment served, from the outset, to attract interest in what was, by news standards, a controversial appointment.

Lansdale was celebrated in Southeast Asia first as the leading adviser in the Philippines who had helped formulate the Magsaysay program for crushing the Communist-led Hukbalahap insurrection in the 1950's. But even more important, until his departure in 1956 he was credited with having supported the regime of Ngo Dinh Diem. He had been out of touch with South Viet-Nam for nine years, up to the time of his return, but he had continued to urge on the government a program for a "democratic revolution" in South Viet-Nam to counter the Communist revolution. It was his conviction that the first move was to create a stable South Vietnamese government, which was easier said than done. Next, he wanted to find, and presumably have a hand in selecting, new political leaders and to establish political parties capable of participating in free elections. He insisted that the military should "protect and help people," and that local aid programs should not be used to try to buy the loyalties of people but to reward them for showing the capacity to make improvements. "It would be a drastic change," he wrote, "for most United States officials to try to satisfy the hesitantly expressed desires of leaders and peoples of sovereign states for political advice with a higher content of American idealism in it." [56]

New times clearly were in store for the American mission in Saigon behind its protective barbed-wire entanglements.

4. BATTLEGROUND

After the battle of Chulai, the first major engagement between American forces and the Viet Cong on August 18–19, 1965, a weary young lieutenant in the Marines counted a 50 per cent casualty toll in his company and said, "I always thought the Viet Cong were a kind of scraggly bunch. They sure surprised me."

No doubt the surprise was mutual. For up to that point in the guerrilla war, the Viet Cong had seen few soldiers like a twenty-one-year-old Texan, Corporal Edward L. Vaughn, who stood up in an enemy cross-fire, killed an entire Viet Cong mortar crew with his machine gun, and then cut down seven other Viet Cong who ran to the rescue. "It was either stand up and get shot or stay on the ground and get shot anyway," he said.

The victory-starved American press made much of the engagement, although by World War II and Korean War standards, it was a relatively small encounter between 2,000 guerrillas and three Marine battalions in the hilly country bordering the central Vietnamese coast. There was a great deal of editorial speculation that this defeat in itself would cause Hanoi and Peking to sue for peace—an indication of how unrealistic the atmosphere was in a considerable part of the United States.

A much different military evaluation came from Brigadier General Frederick J. Karch, the assistant commander of the Third Marine Division, after the battle of Chulai. Referring to the Viet Cong, he told a correspondent, "I thought that once they ran up against our first team they wouldn't stand and fight. But they did. I made a miscalculation." [57]

Some of the veteran correspondents in Viet-Nam had feared that the Viet Cong, their methods, and their fanatical fighting ability would be underrated by the newly arrived American troops. Earlier that month, Malcolm W. Browne had written:

A lot of dedicated newsmen and women have tried during the last five years or so to make Vietnam come alive for the American people—to highlight the dangers, to explain how the war is fought, to present the issues, and so forth. As a whole, this effort has failed, I believe.

Some Americans, to be sure, have become very much interested in Vietnam and read everything on the subject they can get their hands on. They feel involved. But they would have in any case, regardless of what newsmen did here. . . .

Therefore, there is no particular art in involving these people. It is the writer who has grabbed the attention and understanding of the Kansas City milkman who has succeeded. And that is precisely where we have failed. The milkmen's sons are now coming to Vietnam in uniform in large numbers, and it is obvious that these boys have even less idea of what this is all about than did our troops in Korea. At least, Korea involved an enemy invasion and a front line.[58]

While there was an uncomfortable amount of truth in Browne's analysis, it could be argued that the press was scarcely a text for troop indoctrination; its presentation, of necessity, had to be much broader. All three military services over the years had developed large and expensive troop-information programs for this purpose. Yet, it was evident from the outset that these had encountered the same apathy among captive soldier audiences as the less expert presentations in World War II and the Korean War. Dedication came with commitment to battle. It had been that way in the other wars of this dark century. It was that way, too, in Viet-Nam.

Out of his own lengthy experience in South Viet-Nam, Charles Mohr commented in the New York *Times:*

As the number of Americans in South Vietnam has increased, the quotient of knowledge about the country has dropped. In previous years, almost all American troops were "advisers" and almost all were volunteers who developed a deep and almost touching interest in the country and a humbling knowledge that the intellectual baggage they brought with them was not adequate to the task.

Some of the non-volunteers among the newly arrived American combat troops are just as sensitive and committed but it is too much to expect that all could be.[59]

One of the features of the heightened American participation in the Viet-Nam conflict was the extent to which modern public-opinion polling techniques were being used to try to determine Vietnamese viewpoints. The American leadership had two major sources of concern about its South Vietnamese allies—first, that too much peace talk from Washington to please the academic-minded would undermine the already weakened will of the South Vietnamese to keep on fighting; and second, that the Viet Cong might be crippled by bombing attacks but still retain the loyalty of the people whose villages were destroyed in consequence.

American social scientists, assisted by excellent Vietnamese interpreters, learned that there was cause for such concern. After twenty years of war, and the necessity of placating and paying taxes to both sides, the average Vietnamese peasant was sick of the whole business. If he harbored the Viet Cong in his village, he was likely to find himself the target of American bombers; if he did not, he could expect to be dismembered by a savage Viet Cong patrol. For him, there was no place to hide.

Some of the sociological studies were undertaken because of the continuing disappointment of the American command that people in South Viet-Nam would not volunteer intelligence readily on where the Viet Cong were and when they were likely to strike. Whatever areas the government claimed by day outside Saigon in addition to the coastal areas occupied by Americans, the Viet Cong generally took over by night. It took a brave peasant, therefore, to forward intelligence to American or South Vietnamese forces. The wonder was that some already had done so and more were taking the chance. The Viet Cong policy of terrorism and of doubling taxes in areas they controlled had begun to cost them some support. Word even came to Saigon of isolated peasant groups protesting against the Viet Cong. Yet, as one correspondent noted, "The studies show that many people have no sense of loyalty or commitment to either side . . . but only a deep desire to get away from . . . danger." [60]

A few correspondents with special interests made their own studies of the countryside and came to other conclusions. One of the most colorful reports came from Arnold Beichman, an official of the AFL-CIO who also wrote as a free lance. During a visit to Saigon in the summer of 1964, he had contributed $250 to a strike of the Saigon Hotel and Restaurant Workers' Union against the correspondents' hostelry, the Hotel Caravelle.[61] He wrote:

Ambassador Taylor . . . has done little to support a group of men in South Vietnam about whom I can say from personal knowledge that they are devoted democrats, socialist-minded if you will, and as hostile to Communist totalitarianism as they once were to French colonialism.

I met many of these labor leaders in Dalat, Natrang and Danang, in towns and villages of the interior and on rubber plantations. In one town

I met peasants who had walked all night from their own little village 30 miles away to talk to my Vietnamese friends and me. They lived in an area that had been in Vietcong hands for five years. They paid taxes to the Vietcong, quartered their men and did their bidding—and fervently wished to be rid of them, for all the good reasons that peasants anywhere want to be rid of their landlord oppressors.[62]

As might be expected, there was no single point of view on anything among American correspondents in South Viet-Nam, any more than there was among any other group in the land that was closely identified with the conduct or observation of the war. The interpretations of correspondents of wide experience in the affairs of South Viet-Nam could vary according to the situation and the extent of their own involvement. Some, of course, were better than average, and there were, inevitably, others who were not too reliable. The strength of the first-rate correspondents based in Saigon lay in their independence and the willingness of their organizations, with few exceptions, to support them when their work led them into conflict with either the American or the South Vietnamese officials. Most of them had the will and the energy to work unlimited hours, the courage to go under fire wherever the news was breaking, and the curiosity to dig into any situation they did not understand. The weakness of the correspondents' corps as a whole was the extreme competitive urge that led some to seek sensation rather than responsible reportage.

Nearly all of them suffered from the frequently crippling ailment, endemic to journalism, that led the victim to conclude that whatever he wrote was gratefully received by a large and appreciative public and therefore never had to be repeated. Consequently, to the veteran correspondents, the somber realities of the difficult terrain in South Viet-Nam, its war-ravaged economy, and its long history of conflict had been told so many times that few bothered to enlarge on them. To the newcomer, therefore, the mere act of flying over the land was more revealing than many columns of newsprint. It was possible to learn more about the problems of the war by flying with General Westmoreland on one of his inspection trips than from any number of relatively dull and repetitious briefing sessions in Saigon.

Along the thousand miles of gently curving coast line from the Chinese border to the Gulf of Thailand, Viet-Nam was vulnerable to both sea and air power, which the United States possessed in such great abundance. Beyond the monsoon seasons, which varied in different parts of the country, there were no natural defenses against such attacks. But across the varied width of the land south of the 17th Parallel, ranging from 50 to 300 miles, the green expanse of watery rice paddies, the marsh-like terrain created by great river systems and the treacherous nature of the jungles and rugged uplands created many a trap for heavy and cumbersome modern armies. This was a country which favored the movement of small, lightly armed guerrilla forces. Moving rapidly along the densely populated coastal shelf, such a native army could melt away in a matter of minutes into villages and countryside. The heavily armed American soldier could not tell friend from foe until one of them produced a rifle and began shooting.

In Saigon, with its nearly 2 million people, and in the Chinese suburb of Cholon, with 600,000 Overseas Chinese, there was an artificial air of gaiety and separation from the war. But even in Saigon, guerrillas moved in and out and could have paralyzed all life in the city had they chosen to risk a force of any size. The crowded hotels and restaurants, the "little blue bullets," as the Renault taxis were known to some, and the hundreds of bars where Vietnamese hostesses entertained the GI's all presented merely an illusion of well-being. A few miles away, at places around the perimeter of the city, the guerrillas were in control and could choke off highway traffic at will in most places. That was what made the helicopter so necessary; for all parts of the country where larger and swifter aircraft could not move from Tan Son Nhut Airport outside Saigon, the choppers provided the only reasonably safe method of transportation.

From Tan Son Nhut south to the Mekong Delta at Can Tho, a sleepy provincial market town, a helicopter would skim along at tree-top height while leaving Saigon, then soar to 3,000 feet to discourage always hazardous sniper fire and more efficient Viet Cong antiaircraft weapons. Such a flight, followed by a river voyage on a South Vietnamese gunboat, soon demonstrated to a visiting correspondent that about half of the great Vietnamese rice bowl was controlled by the Viet Cong. While some roads were reasonably safe, American and South Vietnamese outposts in the Mekong Delta were in constant danger of being overrun, the principal exceptions being the various corps headquarters. Had it not been for the constant pounding of enemy positions by American bombers, few outposts could have turned back a determined attack.

Here and elsewhere, there had been a long and distressing history of South Vietnamese commanders who did not relish large-scale combat, who advertised their coming to give the Viet Cong a chance to escape without firing a shot, and who betrayed the trust of their troops by giving them no leadership worthy of the name. Brigadier General S. L. A. Marshall, one of the most distinguished of American military commentators, had written of this strategy of noninvolvement as early as 1962 in describing the activities at the time of the Vietnamese 22d Division. He wrote:

The 22d tries to avoid waste motion. There is no deep patrolling just on the chance of ambushing, or fighting meeting engagements with roving [Viet] Congs. Forces guide pretty much on the intelligence data. When the information points to a [Viet] Cong assembly anywhere in the neighborhood, a battalion or so is mounted in Shawnee helicopters [handled by U.S. crews] and flown to a spot marked "X" on the acetate [map]. Sometimes there is a blood payoff. Four times out of five at least, either the bird has flown or the information proves wrong.[63]

The most active correspondents in South Viet-Nam raised the issue of the South Vietnamese Army's dilatory tactics after the so-called Battle of Ap Bac, on January 3, 1963, a defeat which was officially billed as a victory. Lieutenant Colonel John Vann, one of the key American advisers at the time, told the reporters that the Viet Cong had escaped and a golden opportunity for a real government victory had been lost. "A miserable damn performance, just like it always is," he said. And Brigadier General Robert York replied when Neil Sheehan asked him what had happened, "What the hell's it look like happened, boy? They got away—that's what happened." [64]

True, in the rough villages, with their stockade-like protection in the manner of the old American West, there were a number of Vietnamese company and field-grade officers who honorably discharged their duties then and later. And in the outposts in the *montagnard* country, the mountain tribesmen proved their fighting ability when they were given competent leadership and adequate support. But the failures unfortunately received far more notice than the places that were strongly and ably defended, for the latter were seldom attacked. The Viet Cong knew which ones to hit, and which to avoid; for them, intelligence was no problem. Fear was their most potent ally. After dark, they still moved freely through much of the countryside.

It was only when American troops began landing on the Vietnamese coast in large numbers and American air power was exerted with telling effect that the balance in favor of the Viet Cong began to shift slowly and the South Vietnamese commanders began to show signs of greater willingness to fight in the Delta and elsewhere. It didn't happen with any degree of logic; war, for the most part, is scarcely an exercise of man's highest powers of reasoning. At Pleiku at 2 A.M. on Sunday, February 7, 1965, Viet Cong mortars opened up with devastating effect on a whole field full of American aircraft, killing 8 Americans, wounding 108 others, and destroying planes worth many millions of dollars. The only correspondent in the action was the celebrated ex-sergeant of World War II, Bill Mauldin, who had been visiting his son, a helicopter pilot, and who now wrote and drew vividly to describe this American defeat for his newspaper, the Chicago Sun-Times.[65]

There were more such setbacks. But the story of the siege of Duc Co, a beleaguered post in the Vietnamese highlands that held out for seventy days against enemy attacks, seemed to signalize a change for the better. There were only a dozen American special forces troops in Duc Co and 400 Bahnar mountain tribesmen who opposed the Viet Cong and a regiment or more of the North Vietnamese 325th Division. The post was important because it commanded Route 19, a key highway leading to the Cambodian border, a major supply route. In the past, it had been almost routine to expect that if the South Vietnamese sent a relief force down that highway, it would be ambushed and decimated. But this time, it didn't happen. American bombers held off the enemy while a South Vietnamese relief column fought its way into Duc Co on August 11, aided by a brigade of American troops.[66] Such an example was contagious. Less than two weeks later, another South Vietnamese column with American ground and air support burst through Route 14, long closed by the Viet Cong, to bring supplies to Kontum.[67] And in the Delta, the South Viet-Nam Army's IV Corps became a respected fighting unit.

The American military command in Saigon began issuing figures of a different nature, which were widely used despite continued skepticism by some of the old-line correspondents who remembered the kind of "numbers game" the Diem regime had played with the American embassy. Having lived through that era as a correspondent for Time, Charles Mohr wrote with considerable feeling in the New York Times of what he called a "continuing controversy" over the reliability of casualty and other military statistics. It was based, he explained, on "the methods used to count or estimate Vietcong casualties" and, in particular, on "the accuracy of South Vietnamese figures on Vietcong casualties." [68] But American credibility also was questioned. Denis Warner, an Australian correspondent, wrote in the Sydney Morning Herald that U.S. Army public relations "are the worst I have known in any war anywhere"; to which a compatriot, Pat Burgess, added in the Sydney Sun: "No one in Saigon believes the kill rate given by American briefing officers daily in their briefings to the press." [69]

Although the essence of the correspondents' charges was that bad news was being withheld from the American public, the casualty figures did not reflect it. The news was bad. In September, 1966, the Department of Defense said that more than 5,000 American servicemen had been killed in Viet-Nam since January 1, 1961; more than 10,000 had been wounded; and 161 were missing in action.[70] Moreover, the

South Vietnamese government admitted that about 96,000 men had deserted from its armed forces during 1965—far more than the 13,000 killed; 23,000 wounded; and 6,000 missing in action or captured.[71] While estimates of Viet Cong dead and captured for 1965 were 45,000, there was little doubt that some of these had been peasants caught in a crossfire.[72]

For the United States, the cost of the war was mounting; a supplemental appropriation of $13.1 billion for Fiscal Year 1966 was approved by Congress. For Fiscal Year 1967, as a beginning, $10.3 billion was requested in President Johnson's budget. Moreover, from 1954 to 1963, the United States had spent an estimated $2.4 billion in economic aid to South Viet-Nam, a figure that had settled at $350 million annually in succeeding years and was likely to double with the intensification of the drive to pacify more territory. The decision of the South Korean Government to increase its force in South Viet-Nam also made for sizable boosts in the total commitment.[73] All told, the 1966 cost was $2 billion a month for the U.S.

It was evident that for the duration of the war and for years to come, South Viet-Nam would be heavily dependent on the American economy. Its exports of natural rubber and other products paid for less than one-third of its imports; even worse, in its sharply reduced rice-growing areas, it could not raise sufficient rice to feed its own people and had to look to the United States to supply the deficiency.

Land redistribution, rent control, and the opening up of new farming areas, a program admirable in concept, ran into all kinds of wartime troubles, mainly because of Viet Cong terrorism as well as government fumbling in Saigon. Inflation sent prices soaring in the cities, with the price of rice going up nearly 50 per cent and that of shrimp almost doubling, so that the government had to act to keep staples within reach of the people. The Viet Cong tax collectors swarmed over much of the land, making their demands for doubled and tripled imposts at the point of a gun. It was one factor in their decline in some areas.[74]

Yet, because of the massive American influx, business in Saigon was booming. The U.S. Support Activities Headquarters alone was spending enormous sums annually to take care of housing for Americans within the city. Outside, the coastal bases were being enlarged, and new ones were being built from Phu Bai on the north to the great new deepwater port at Cam Ranh Bay on the south. Between were such major installations as Danang, Chu Lai, and Qui Nhon, all of them tributes to American engineering skill and the willingness of the nation to risk both its manpower and its wealth in a forbidding foreign land half-way around the earth.

Marshal Ky, no economist, was asked about the status of South Viet-

Nam's shaky currency, the piastre, which had fallen from 73 to $1, the official rate, to 150–180. "We are seeking a solution that retains the economic sovereignty of our country," he said. In a nation that had lost control of many of its towns and villages and which could use less than one-third of its 12,000 miles of highways and perhaps 100 miles of its 1,000 miles of railroads, both military security and economic sovereignty long since had vanished. Had it not been for the charter planes of the U.S. Operations Mission and the Air Viet-Nam carriers, plus the coastal vessels and the military supply columns that moved along the danger- ous highways, the extent of Viet Cong control would have been far greater than it was.[75] In any event, the National Liberation Front, the political arm of the Viet Cong, already was acting as if it were a sover- eign government, dispatching both diplomats and missions to friendly countries and putting out its own daily quota of anti-American propa- ganda by radio. Sometimes, it had unexpected and inadvertent assist- ance.

There never had been a time when the Vietnamese story had not been sensitive in the United States from 1954 on. Somehow, the things that happened in Viet-Nam seemed to take on an added intensity in the telling. And when the government's version differed from that of the newsman on the scene, there was nearly always trouble. A case in point was the burning of the village of Camne, near Danang, on August 4, 1965.

In an emotional broadcast that was read over C.B.S. and appropri- ately illustrated, Morley Safer, a C.B.S. correspondent, gave this descrip- tion:

> After surrounding the village and receiving one burst of automatic fire from an unidentified direction, the Marines poured in 3.5 rocket fire, 79 grenade launchers and heavy and light machine gun fire. The Marines then moved in, proceeding first with cigarette lighters, then with flame throwers, to burn down an estimated 150 dwellings. . . . I subsequently learned that a Marine platoon on the right flank wounded three women and killed one child in a rocket barrage. The day's operations netted about four prisoners—old men. Two Marines were wounded, both by their own fire, although this has been denied.[76]

The Secretary of the Navy, Paul H. Nitze, gave this account of the same incident:

> In this operation, 51 huts were burned, not 150 as reported by various media. It is important to know the background which caused these burn- ings.

The sweep of this heavily fortified village, which had been controlled by the Vietcong for some time, was conducted in a methodical manner. The houses were surrounded by trench lines, spider-type trap firing positions and connecting tunnels which led to houses throughout the village.

Many of the houses burned were as a result of small arms tracer, 3.5 rocket and grenade fire directed at houses from which hostile fire was being received. Others were burned incidentally as a result of flame-throwers, demolitions and grenades being used to neutralize the tunnels, bunkers and caves, either within the houses or in close proximity.

The company commander of the unit involved in this action has stated that one house was burned deliberately by application of a cigarette lighter. This was a house which covered a concrete basement which had a concrete tunnel outlet leading to a tunnel complex. In his opinion, this was a tactical installation rather than a peaceful dwelling. He approved the burning.

On the night of Aug. 8, Marines outside of Camne were again fired on by Vietcong in Camne. Marine Corps casualties were 21 wounded, two of which died of wounds.[77]

Safer was shifted elsewhere temporarily, but that departure did not resolve the problem of TV coverage. Major General Lewis W. Walt, commander of the Third Marine Amphibious Force, was deeply concerned over the prominence given to civilian deaths and the hut burnings, although he saw no easy way to avoid such incidents. It was made known, for example, that one Marine unit stationed near Danang had suffered 10 per cent casualties by sniper fire, mines, and booby traps without once being in an engagement with the Viet Cong. Under such circumstances, it required a tremendous amount of forbearance to respond to sniper fire from a village with gentle treatment of the inhabitants, medical help, and even gifts. Some Marine units tried to do it anyway. One Marine chaplain, Lieutenant Peter MacLean, at Danang, started a drive for Christmas toys to be sent from the United States.[78] That didn't help solve the basic problem of the correspondents, however, in reporting such adverse incidents; they usually knew in advance that they were headed for controversy, and they were seldom let off easily.

The reporting of incidents that were likely to affect relations between the United States and the Soviet Union also created difficulty from time to time. The Soviet Union's installation of missile sites near Hanoi, presumably operated by Soviet citizens, became big news in the United States in the summer of 1965. The news was even bigger after the U.S. Air Force reported a successful raid on the Soviet operation on July 27. However, a few days later, Peter Lisagor, of the Chicago *Daily News,* and Jack Anderson, a syndicated columnist whose work appeared in the Washington *Post,* reported from Washington that photographs had failed to support claims of extensive damage. Both correspondents said that the sites might have been decoys; one, quoting "military intelligence" as a source, said that dummy missiles might have been set up by the Chinese Communists to try to provoke an incident between the United States and the Soviet Union.[79] Whatever the reason, the correctness of the correspondents' story of the failure of the July 27 attack was made known belatedly a month later. But with it came a reassuring assumption by government officials that several more successful attacks had been made on the Soviet missile sites, although the raids had not been announced. It was also assumed that several Soviet citizens operating the antiaircraft installations had been either injured or killed. With that, both the State and Defense departments again temporarily closed down their information on the indirect hostilities against the Russians, although Soviet weapons were a growing threat in the North.[80] By that time, the long-debated Soviet consular treaty had been set aside in Congress, a casualty of the undercover conflict. In November, much of the secrecy surrounding attacks on missile sites was dissipated when a determined assault was opened on them.

It was to be expected that the military would threaten censorship on a broad scale as a result of these and other conflicts with the press over the disclosure of sensitive information. The announcement that the United States was studying this possibility came from General Earle G. Wheeler, Chairman of the Joint Chiefs of Staff, during a television interview over the A.B.C. network from Washington. The military had been complaining about correspondents who were accused of announcing the departure of military aircraft from Danang or other bases long before the completion of their mission. Now, General Wheeler seized upon dispatches by UPI and C.B.S. which told of the departure of American troops for the relief of Duc Co before their mission was completed. The UPI dispatch had been killed after being sent.

While the Defense Department conceded that neither dispatch had done any damage, the officials directly concerned insisted that they had violated the agreement of correspondents to withhold such information. "I feel that we must find the means to make sure that this kind of thing doesn't happen again," General Wheeler said. He called the situation "unsatisfactory" and blamed "some young men, relatively inexperienced men, in the field." However, he conceded that "invariably when known people—that is, men and women who have made their mark in the news profession—go out there . . . the reporting is of a very high caliber." [81]

The reporting restrictions referred to by General Wheeler had been issued by agreement between the United States and South Vietnamese governments on July 15, 1965. As a result, casualty reports and unit identifications no longer were issued on a daily basis or related to specific actions. American and South Vietnamese casualties were described officially only as light, moderate, or heavy. No troop movements were to be given until it was determined that the information was in the enemy's possession.

While correspondents were said to have agreed to observe the restrictions on a voluntary basis, General Wheeler was dissatisfied after less than a month of trial. It was, on a smaller scale, a repetition of the censorship argument during the Korean War after General MacArthur had made each correspondent responsible for policing himself and not "giving aid and comfort to the enemy." But since the military and journalistic definitions of what constituted such aid rarely were in harmony, censorship had been the eventual outcome in Korea. It was no great surprise, therefore, that it was also contemplated in South Viet-Nam.

The correspondents and their editors, however, did not accept the prospect meekly. Edwin Q. White, chief of the AP bureau in Saigon, wrote:

> Some correspondents here say they see nothing wrong with the new ground rules, but others see them as another deliberate effort to present a more favorable view of the war. . . . Among those genuinely concerned over the new rules are some veteran field correspondents who feel the change in reporting casualties is highly significant because of the nature of the war in Viet-Nam. They point out that the accurate indication of how the war is going is reflected in the number of casualties. . . . By refusing to disclose casualties in specific actions, this school feels, government officials are seeking to color the way the war is reported.[82]

Among the older correspondents, particularly the hardy few of World War II vintage who were still active in South Viet-Nam, there was considerably less disposition to question the government's point of view. Having been through experiences that were far more trying, they complained less than their younger competitors. They had more confidence and more assurance, qualities that often come with experience. Consequently, they did not feel that somebody was trying to fool them every time there was an announcement of an air raid or a small engagement. They reserved their energies for issues that really challenged their independence as correspondents or involved the life and death of the troops they often accompanied on missions.

Charles Arnot, of A.B.C., was such a correspondent—a veteran of Guadalcanal in 1942. What amounted to voluntary censorship in South

Viet-Nam didn't particularly disturb him. "This is only common sense," he said. "It's only when our side suffers a big defeat—in these cases [Vietnamese] government forces, not U.S. forces—that we have difficulty digging out the facts. And even that situation, once pretty grim, has improved." [83] Hal Boyle, an AP columnist who won a Pulitzer Prize for his World War II reporting, also had no complaints after a ten-week tour of duty in South Viet-Nam. But he also had no illusions. "In a military and political situation as full of dubiety as this is," he said, "it is hard to know whether or not we are getting the full truth. . . . American reporters have been reasonably honest in reporting this war, but they are not optimistic about it." [84]

There was a tendency in the American press to refer to South Viet-Nam as "another Korea" because both wars were against the spread of Communism in Asia. However, there were important differences. The Vietnamese terrain, 30 per cent larger than Korea's mountainous countryside, presented even greater obstacles to the movement of troops and matériel. The Vietnamese enemy, unlike the foe in Korea, could not easily be located; he was everywhere. The Vietnamese people, decidedly unlike the Koreans, had little feeling of national identity and even less loyalty to a central government.

The most striking difference was in the nature of the opposing forces. In Korea, the conflict had been a United Nations war, fought under American leadership against a Communist aggressor. At its height, 400,000 American troops had been in action, fighting side by side with 460,000 South Koreans and 60,000 troops from fifteen other nations. Against them were North Korean and Chinese forces totaling more than 1 million troops. In South Viet-Nam, the United Nations was sitting on the sidelines.[85]

There was one other major difference. Few Americans went into Viet-Nam either as soldiers or correspondents with anything but the healthiest respect for the qualities of the enemy as a fighting man. The disposition to consider the Asian as a kind of subhuman, to be described as a "gook" or even less flattering and thoroughly unprintable terms, had quietly been buried with the Korean War. The GI's who arrived in Viet-Nam often referred to the enemy as "Charlie," and by those who used Army nomenclature, "Victor Charlie" or "VC," for Viet Cong. Sometimes, he was even "ol' Charlie." [86] It was with good reason that Ambassador Taylor warned his old outfit, the 101st Airborne, upon its arrival in Viet-Nam, "The Vietcong is an enemy who is shrewd, well-trained and with the guile of the American Indian during his best days." [87] The jungle war meant mean, savage fighting, usually without quarter.

For those who sought an easy peace, Ho Chi Minh and his chief strategist, General Vo Nguyen Giap, had only scorn and defiance. They were not men who would soon admit defeat. It had taken a long time to persuade them to come to the conference table in Geneva in 1954, and then they had paraded in as victors beside their allies, the Chinese Communists and the Soviet Union. In 1962, their return to Geneva had turned out to be merely a strategic pause, for they had honored none of their agreements. Despite the modest extent of American war aims listed in a twenty-seven-page booklet "Why Vietnam" and the suggestions of Secretary of State Rusk for a return to the principles of the 1954 Geneva accords, the enemy was no more likely to yield what he believed to be a dominant position in 1966 than he had been in the past.

For one thing, there was reason to believe that Hanoi was convinced it could hang on for a long war. For another, the best available information in the fall of 1966 was that divided councils had made agreement on any other course doubtful in North Viet-Nam. Under the aged Ho, three groups appeared to have emerged in Hanoi that clung together in an alliance against the South Vietnamese and the United States. The first of these was led by Premier Pham Van Dong, which was accounted to be pro-Soviet; the second, a pro-Peking faction headed by Truong Chinh, the National Assembly president; and the third and probably dominant group, the party apparatus headed by Le Duan, the First Secretary of the Lao Dong (Communist) Party. The appearance of the fifty-eight-year-old Le Duan in Moscow at the head of the North Vietnamese delegation to the Twenty-third Congress of the CPSU seemed to support the theory that he had become the man to be reckoned with.

The peace demonstrations in the United States, which received generous space from sympathetic newspapers, meanwhile gave renewed hope to the enemy. When 20,000 demonstrators massed in Washington on November 27, 1965, and tolerated a display of North Vietnamese flags in their midst, the Communists were jubilant. Nguyen Huu Tho, president of South Viet-Nam's Liberation Front, the Viet Cong's political arm, congratulated the Americans in the National Coordinating Committee to End the War in Vietnam. The Chinese Communist Party in Peking announced that the peace movement "would sweep the whole country and finally reduce the United States imperialist system to ashes."

Seymour Topping, then Hong Kong correspondent of the New York *Times,* which devoted the better part of two pages to the display of news about the demonstration, cabled:

The Communist leaders evidently believe that American public opinion may exercise a decisive influence in persuading the Johnson administration to retreat on the Vietnam issue. The shaping of American public opinion, therefore, is of prime importance. This may explain the costly frontal assault tactics recently adopted by the Vietcong and infiltrating North Vietnamese troops. The principal motive may be to inflict maximum casualties in American troops so as to excite anxiety in the United States and lend momentum to the anti-Vietnam war movement.[88]

To those Americans who had lived through the rise of Hitler and through World War II, it was a sobering demonstration of how little the new aspirants for world domination knew about the American people.

5. THE VIET-NAM CORRESPONDENTS

A correspondent for an American television network received the following message from New York in Saigon after a previously secret air base nearby had been opened to accredited newsmen:

WANT COVERAGE OF AIR BASE WHICH NOW BEING OPEN TO NEWSMEN. WANT SCENES AMERICAN PILOTS, GENERAL ACTIVITIES AROUND BASE, SHOTS OF BASE, EVEN AERIALS IF POSSIBLE, TYPES OF AIRCRAFT U-2 ETC., JETS TAKING OFF AND LANDING, GOOD CUTAWAYS, CLOSEUPS OF PILOTS WHO STATIONED AT BASE AND WHO HAVE BEEN CONDUCTING SECRET FLIGHTS. ITEM: WANT COVERAGE OF CAMPS WHERE SPECIAL PARATROOP COMMANDO UNITS BEING TRAINED, EFFORT GET FOOTAGE OF GROUP MAKING ACTUAL JUMP OVER VIETCONG HELD GROUND. . . .[89]

Needless to say, the network did not receive exclusive shots of the U-2 and its pilots, plus views of the base from which flights had been conducted. Aside from irresponsible orders to commit major violations of security, the message also showed how far removed some of the editors in New York were from the realities of the Viet-Nam war. Nor did this apply to just a few television men, anxious to get colorful war footage and beat the opposition at all costs. There were correspondents in the other news media who could produce messages from home suggesting equally impossible assignments.

Every part of the American communications complex had its own particular problems in maintaining a smooth working relationship between the correspondent in the combat area and the editor at headquarters. For wire-service people, the hazards were the pressure of competition and the mechanics of rewriting copy far from the scene of action. For newspaper specials, except for those whose reputations gave them

close rapport with their editors, there was always the unenviable prospect of a message from home saying that the opposition had a better
story, or at least a different one. The news-magazine correspondents
had long since become resigned to cabling thousands of words to the
office and finding that only a small part of the file was used. As for the
"trained seal," the visiting syndicated columnist who became a ten-
minute expert on Viet-Nam, almost any extravagance of thought or expression was permitted and spread through scores of American newspapers.

One experienced correspondent wrote from Saigon:

A correspondent coming in from the states who must work on his own is
up against fantastic odds in information gathering, communications and
every other aspect of existence here. His only hope of survival against such
competition is to join the USIS gang. That is, unless he has editors back
home with vision enough to say, "To hell with the inclusive story. Leave
that to others. What we want is your own probing, even if it is only a very
small aspect of the big picture." But this attitude is very, very rare.

An editor who has invested a substantial sum in sending someone to
Vietnam expects "results." If the story of the day is about some complicated coup or counter-coup, or if it is about the latest bombing of North
Vietnam, that is what the editor wants to hear about in his man's copy,
even if his man knows nothing about these subjects other than what he
gleans from USIS. And that is why you see an appalling likeness in much
of the copy coming from here.[90]

The more thoughtful American editors, and some of the publishers
as well, began going to South Viet-Nam to see for themselves what this
new kind of war was all about. For many, it was an awakening to the
realities of the American involvement in Southeast Asia; whether they
were hawks or doves, none could fail to be impressed by the experience.
Nor could they easily become indifferent again to the manner in which
the news of the war was being presented in their newspapers. Fortunately, such visits were not confined to those editors whose organizations could afford to maintain correpondents at the scene of action.
There were a number of others like Jim Fain, the editor of the Dayton,
Ohio, *Daily News,* and Bill Hosokawa, the associate editor of the Denver *Post,* who made the long trip from home and turned themselves
into correspondents for a brief period. Ben Bassett, the foreign news editor of the AP, also found it expedient to get away from his desk in New
York to study the conduct of the war and the operation of his Saigon
bureau, the largest and most elaborate of all. "The question for newspapermen," he said afterward, "is whether we have the guts to continue

to tell the truth insofar as it can be determined. The pressure will grow with our involvement." [91]

The coverage grew, too. The widening American commitment in Viet-Nam changed the entire nature of the presentation of the war to the American public. While the size of the correspondents' corps increased perceptibly, it was artificially inflated still more by swarms of tourists, curiosity-seekers, vacationing journalists, amateur commentators, youngsters out of college, and others who were able to wangle a letter of accreditation from a careless news organization. For the hardworking Vietnamese nationals who served American organizations, it became a fantastic industry; their services, naturally, were in great demand as reporters, translators, photographers, tipsters, and tour guides. The accreditation lists became a jumble of familiar names diluted by television technicians, still and motion-picture photographers, all manner of magazine people looking for an angle, and stringers by the dozen.

From the center of a continuing news story that had too often been neglected, Saigon blossomed into a prestige assignment. The old pros came back to the wars for a limited time to take another well-merited bow on the world stage. Walter Cronkite, at forty-eight years of age, lost his aplomb while describing the dive-bombing attack on enemy targets in Viet-Nam from a seat next to the bomber pilot and thrilled an American television audience. James Reston, who was eight years older, soared over enemy positions in the Mekong Delta in a helicopter during another American onslaught and wrote of his mission for the readers of the New York *Times*. The retreads of other wars—Hal Boyle, of the AP; Phil Newsom, of UPI; Jim Lucas, of the Scripps-Howard Newspaper Alliance; Keyes Beech, of the Chicago *Daily News;* and Jack Foisie, of the Los Angeles *Times,* hustled around the countryside in competition with the youngsters. A new generation of war correspondents came in, too; among them, Takashi Oka, of the *Christian Science Monitor;* Richard Dudman, of the St. Louis *Post-Dispatch;* and Johnny Apple, the chief of the New York *Times* Bureau in 1966.

Soon enough, the same old journalistic pattern that had been developed in other wars began to emerge in the coverage of this new conflict which was so difficult for people to understand. Out of the wire-service teletypes three times a day, there came the daily roundup—a catch-all of military announcements, claims, counterclaims, and odds and ends that too often added up to confusion and boredom on the part of the reader. One sequence from a television camera was better able to catch the spirit of Viet-Nam in many cases. But the wire services argued that the roundup was what 90 per cent of the nation's newspapers and electronic media wanted—a few hundred words that could be ripped off a machine and quickly used without thought. Probably they were right. However, it was scarcely sufficient to keep turning out the same old prose in the same old way. Sometimes it seemed that a mere change in date and place would have made the roundups just as representative of the battles of 1944 or 1945 in the Pacific or of 1950 or 1951 in Korea.

There were, of course, the color stories and features that could be splashed across a page under a nice headline or mangled by a rich baritone over a microphone. And there were the daily "specials" in the newspapers, ranging from somewhat longer versions of wire-service roundups to analyses, interpretations, features in the Ernie Pyle manner, and occasional exclusives. But whether the correspondents worked for wire services or newspapers, they had to have a particular talent and an abiding toughness to break through the crust of such a tradition-bound system and bring this different kind of war home to America. For despite the brilliance of television and the universality of its appeal, it also took the more abiding magic of words on paper to give depth and meaning to what was going on in Viet-Nam. Fortunately, there were some who could write this story—each in his own way—and a few others who could tell it in a manner appropriate to the subject.

If there was any hope for the emergence of a more effective kind of journalism in Viet-Nam, it lay with those who had lived for a long time with the story. Whether older correspondents or new, most of them sensed the inadequacies of their presentation; often, in the few spare moments they had, it preoccupied their talk and their thinking. These were, for the most part, responsible people who could not abide the old methods of presenting the news in terms of whether the home team was winning or losing and giving figures of some kind to indicate a score.

Once, the chief of *Time's* Southeast Asia bureaus, Frank McCulloch, demanded on one of his frequent trips to Saigon, "What constitutes victory? How do you win a war of this kind? How do you impose your will on a billion people in Asia?" [92] He was not alone. Such things troubled any thoughtful correspondent long before he set foot in South Viet-Nam; the longer he remained, the more intense his doubts became. And in this he was scarcely different from the American diplomats and soldiers who came to this new battleground with any degree of concern over the shape of the future. For a majority of the correspondents' corps in Saigon, the pat answers of the State Department were not enough. They were not satisfied to be told, as they frequently were, that victory would consist of obliging Hanoi and Peking "to stop doing what they are doing" in South Viet-Nam. It took an enormously credulous person to believe that the answers were that simple in a land which had been ripped apart by a generation of revolution and which was now the center of a great power confrontation.

The attitudes of the correspondents had been shaped by the course of events in South Viet-Nam long before the escalation of the war. If there had been a turning point, it was the successful attack of the American Seventh Fleet against North Vietnamese gunboats in Tonkin Gulf on August 2 and 4, 1964. Up to that time, the coverage by the American press had been minimal: although Saigon had been the most-used international dateline for the preceding eighteen months to two years, even the news-agency staffs had been pitifully small. The correspondents who struggled to tell the story of Viet-Nam in those days were hardened by their experience. Almost inevitably, those who arrived after the Tonkin battle and the opening of air attacks on North Viet-Nam six months later would be affected, to some degree, by the attitudes of those who had preceded them. In any group of correspondents, such an interplay of ideas and opinions was important; in a crisis area, the correspondents' state of mind very often was a factor in the reporting of the news.

Since some of their reporting was bound to impinge on areas sensitive to both the American and South Vietnamese governments, and the military commands of both, it was inevitable that conflicts of interest would arise. The most violent clash, which became a factor in changing American policy toward the Diem regime, came before the escalation of the war. It was at this time that some correspondents adopted a fierce and sometimes unreasoning challenge to all information from official sources, a policy that was felt long afterward. Consequently, it appeared that the process of reporting the war might be better understood by examining the composition of the correspondents' corps as it existed immediately before the Tonkin Gulf incidents and inquiring into the prevalent attitudes at that time. As a result of a visit to South Viet-Nam during the course of this study in July, 1964, I had an opportunity to do this.[93]

Those who had known Viet-Nam the longest at that time were Robert Shaplen, of the *New Yorker,* and François Sully, of *Newsweek,* both seasoned veteran correspondents who had sojourned in Southeast Asia off and on for well-nigh two decades. Neither saw much hope then for an American-led stand against the Viet Cong and said so bluntly. It cost Sully, a French national, the confidence of many in American officialdom, but he never made a secret of his views.

Even more influential than these weekly correspondents, whose file had to be sporadic, were a daring trio in the AP office—Malcolm W. Browne, an American who was then thirty-three years old; his assistant,

Peter Gregg Arnett, a New Zealander who was four years younger; and the great West German combat photographer, Horst Faas, then thirty years old. All three were to win Pulitzer Prizes—Browne in 1964, Faas in 1965, and Arnett in 1966. While Browne left the AP, turned briefly to television work for A.B.C., and later free-lanced, Arnett and Faas on numerous occasions influenced both American and world opinion in the course of the Viet-Nam war with words and pictures. And since it was a losing war for the United States in 1964 and 1965, this was the story that was told—and illustrated—with skill and bravery by the AP's combat operations.

During those years, two younger men bore the primary responsibility for reporting the war for UPI—Mike Malloy and Ray Herndon, both less than thirty years old and relatively new to overseas service. Reuters had a single knowledgeable veteran, Nicholas Turner, and Agence France-Presse gave relatively minimal coverage except when there was a defeat for the United States. All four of the agencies depended, to a greater or lesser degree, on the services of local Vietnamese correspondents, whose contribution could not be overestimated. But whatever the nationality of the correspondents, not one of the regulars saw much hope for South Viet-Nam before Tonkin Gulf, and not many changed their views immediately afterward.

The coverage of even the greatest of newspapers was limited, also, by understaffing before Tonkin Gulf. Even the New York *Times* made do with a single correspondent, except for emergencies, for a considerable period. From 1961 on, Homer Bigart, David Halberstam, and Peter Grose each served in succession for about a year. It was only after Grose moved to Moscow and Charles Mohr succeeded him that the *Times* added two more combat correspondents.

Nor was the New York *Times* alone. In the summer of 1964, the Washington *Post* had one reporter, John Maffre, a Canadian, in Saigon, while the allied Los Angeles *Times*'s Ed Meagher moved around Southeast Asia. A year later, the *Post* took on Stan Karnow, and the Los Angeles newspaper sent in Jack Foisie as reinforcements. The New York *Herald Tribune* was represented, until its demise, by the young, capable, and handsome Beverly Deepe, who had come to Saigon on Valentine's Day, 1962, and stayed on as the only woman war correspondent in Viet-Nam until the escalation of the war.

Few other newspapers were represented before Tonkin Gulf with regulars who gave consistent coverage. The Chicago *Daily News* flew in its star, Keyes Beech, whenever necessary and assigned Albert Ravenholt from the Philippines at irregular intervals. The Minneapolis *Star-Tribune* was represented by Mr. and Mrs. Robert Hewett. The

New York *Daily News* picked up the most belligerent correspondent in Saigon, Joe Fried, and used him regularly; he also filed for a radio station. The Washington *Star* pulled in its New Delhi correspondent, Richard Critchfield, from time to time, and the *Wall Street Journal* assigned Norman Sklarewitz from Tokyo when it seemed necessary. The Baltimore *Sun* had no regular Saigon man until Ernest Furgurson, who had covered Moscow, was assigned in 1965.

The news magazines generally followed the same pattern, although both *Time* and *Newsweek* were accustomed to fly in reinforcements from Hong Kong and try to cover in some depth long before Tonkin Gulf. The *U.S. News & World Report* staff was probably the most seasoned of all, with one of the last of the old China hands, Robert P. ("Pepper") Martin, coming to Saigon from Tokyo, and a veteran correspondent in India, Sol Sanders, relieving him.

Television, covering its first war, was even more understaffed at the outset. Before Tonkin Gulf, the veteran Peter Kalischer carried on for C.B.S. for long periods without assistance and seemed to thrive on it. For N.B.C., the chores were divided between Jim Robinson and John Rich. And for A.B.C., Charles Arnot worked for weeks without relief.

Thus, in the summer of 1964, after three years of American involvement in the fighting in South Viet-Nam, the correspondents' corps was still small and often on the defensive. Generally, the atmosphere was poisonous at the regular daily briefings at USIS and MACV and, to a lesser extent, USOM. When these were combined under JUSPAO, there was little change for the better at the outset. Shouting matches between correspondents and senior officers were not uncommon. Challenges of official information were a matter of daily routine. A trip almost anywhere outside Saigon often would yield a discouraging story, obtained without trouble from younger American military and economic assistance people. It was possible to present a conflict between the Americans and the South Vietnamese by talking with the premier of the moment, if he could be found. And the Buddhists, always eager for publicity, put out threats and staged demonstrations with such lavishness that eventually they wore out their usefulness. But the basic information, like the attitude of most of the regular correspondents, accurately reflected the status of the war at the time.

While it is true some of the correspondents were young and untried, a check of fifteen of the regulars in a questionnaire showed that the age level was only a little lower than the general average for Asia. Eight, in the period immediately before Tonkin Gulf, were thirty years old or less; four were between thirty-one and forty; and three were over forty. Among them were thirteen American citizens, one Frenchman, and one New Zealander. Ten were college graduates, and of them six had master's degrees. They included a Pulitzer Prize-winner, three Nieman Fellows, and a C.B.S. Fellow.

All filed regularly to their news organizations; of the three who estimated the cost of their file each month, the estimates all were between $800 and $1,000 a month—and this was before the war escalated. As for estimated costs to employers, exclusive of filing charges, one correspondent placed his total expense including salary and office at $50,000 a year; one, at $30,000; three, at about $25,000; five, at between $10,000 and $15,000; and one at less than $10,000. Four did not reply. It was apparent that the average salary was somewhere between $7,000 and $9,000 a year, with a few earning up to $15,000 and perhaps one or two above that figure.

In evaluating assistance from the American embassy and its various branches, seven correspondents said it was good; one, fair; three, poor; three, variable; and one made no comment. The correspondents also registered their opinion of the credibility of American officials in Saigon. Five called news from such sources believable most of the time; eight, believable part of the time; one, seldom believable; and one made no reply. It was the lowest rating of any American government-agency complex in the study.

The correspondents' attitudes didn't change markedly in the year that followed. Within six months, Sol Sanders was writing, "My own feeling is that America is heading for catastrophe unless there is a revolutionary change in our approach to the whole area." [94] Beverly Deepe was saying, "They don't like me [at the embassy] because I won't say what they want me to say." [95] And a little later, after another flap, Frank McCulloch, of *Time*, was writing of the daily Saigon briefings conducted jointly by the American military and USIS representatives:

> Frequently, information provided has been found to be shaded. Often it is incomplete. Sometimes, although not as often as critics allege, it is deliberately misleading. This is an exasperating but thoroughly predictable practice. I think a reporter should expect the government to gold-plate what it tells him and assume it is his job to do what he can to temper it. . . . I think pointing the finger of blame at any of the exasperated parties in the press-military conflict is a serious mistake. No one is really at fault. It is just Vietnam. [96]

The ever critical Charles Mohr was not as charitable. Toward the end of 1965, he wrote in the New York *Times* that "a steady stream of misinformation about the war in Vietnam is reaching the American public." He blamed the military briefing officers in Saigon for issuing what he called fictitious figures of "enemy body counts," and for announcing that Americans had "readjusted their positions" when in fact they had retreated.[97]

Such combative attitudes were bound eventually to arouse criticism in turn from within the press corps itself. There had been inner rumblings for years, with correspondents complaining about each other in a way that was far different from previous wars in this century. A new correspondent Ward Just, of the Washington *Post,* observed that "this is an odd press corps covering an odd war." Early in 1966, he noted that the correspondents were divided and showed less camaraderie than in any other large foreign news center. "The impression persists," Just wrote, "that it is a not especially distinguished press corps doing a not especially distinguished job. . . . Making the trick even more difficult is the legacy of the past. Many reporters here have staked out positions over the years and are now defending them." [98]

Another visiting correspondent, Martin Gershen, of the Newark *Star-Ledger,* wrote that readers and viewers at home received so much one-sided reporting that they had no alternative but to assume "that the American war in Southeast Asia not only is against Communism, but against the entire U.S. military establishment." Edward P. Morgan, the television commentator, was quoted in support of this view, saying that some correspondents in South Viet-Nam were "trying to become the Ernie Pyles of this war by baiting military officials at press briefings." [99]

After several visits to Saigon, during which he also traveled widely to battle areas, Jack Raymond, then the New York *Times*'s Pentagon correspondent, concluded, "In a war that has engaged the United States for more than a decade, with ever-increasing casualties, both press and government face crises in credibility." He accused some reporters of distortions by concentrating on headline-making news and ignoring equally important political and economic developments. Like so many others, he commented unfavorably on the sometimes combative "briefings" for the press in Saigon, in which a single jittery reporter often cross-examined senior officers with a scattering of insulting remarks on the theory that the military should be "shaken up." "Pentagon news conferences, notorious for their waspish atmosphere, were mild compared with those held in Saigon," Raymond wrote.[100]

Some of the things that went on in these "briefings" had to be seen and heard to be believed; certainly, they would have been tolerated nowhere else either by a responsible briefing officer or a responsible press corps. It was one reason why the standing of the Saigon correspondents, as a group, suffered by comparison with those who had covered the Korean War or World War II. Many in the Saigon group not only fought their principal information sources; they also battled with each other.

Necessarily, the government's attitude toward the press remained critical. Ambassador Henry Cabot Lodge, who had shown forbearance under provocation, was heard to remark to a member of Vice President Humphrey's official party during a visit early in 1966 that it was important to bring in Washington reporters who were not "jaded and cynical" about the Vietnamese war.[101] Senator Thomas J. Dodd, a Connecticut Democrat, charged after a trip to Viet-Nam that the "fundamental realities . . . cannot be gleaned from a reading of the press." He added that he could cite instances "where the truth has been distorted by twisted or misplaced emphasis or where important truths are not known." When the press clamored in rebuttal, Senator Mike Mansfield, of Montana, the Democratic majority leader, concluded diplomatically, "The essence of the issue is that the press has its individual responsibility under the Constitution, even as the Senators have theirs. We may be criticized. We may be applauded. We may be ignored. But in the end we are answerable only to our consciences and to our constituencies. The press of the nation is in much the same boat." [102]

At just about the time when the always touchy press-government relationship in Saigon appeared to be taking a turn for the better, and Phil Newsom, of UPI, observed that the correspondents and the military were more inclined to trust each other, two of the worst flaps of the war occurred.[103]

The first was started by Eric Sevareid, in an article in *Look* magazine, with a disclosure that during the Presidential election of 1964 the United States had rejected an offer by North Viet-Nam to meet in Rangoon, Burma, and discuss terms for ending the war. Sevareid had the best of sources. The information had been given to him in London on August 12, 1965, by Adlai E. Stevenson, two days before the death of the American Ambassador to the United Nations. Moreover, the truce bid had been obtained by U Thant, Secretary General of the United Nations, who "was furious over the failure of his patient efforts, but said nothing publicly."

The State Department, after its usual denial, had no alternative but to confirm Sevareid. The patient Robert J. McCloskey explained that "all our indications were that there was no serious intent on the other side" to enter into peace talks. "We saw nothing to indicate," he went on, "that Hanoi was prepared for peace talks and the Secretary of State said he would recognize it when it came. His antenna is sensitive." [104]

No sooner had the excitement over this disclosure died down than the St. Louis *Post-Dispatch,* in a Washington story by Richard Dudman on December 17, reported: "The United States received a report of a new peace feeler from North Vietnam last week and already has rejected it." This was the tale of Giorgio La Pira, former mayor of Florence, Italy, who had visited Hanoi in November and talked with Ho Chi Minh. Amintore Fanfani, the Italian foreign minister and President of the U.N. General Assembly, had written a letter to President Johnson about the matter, and Secretary of State Rusk had replied. Annoyed by the disclosure as well as the erroneous report of the rejection, the correspondence was made public because, as Ambassador Arthur J. Goldberg said at the United Nations, "We had a problem of maintaining our credibility with our own people." To which Dudman replied, "I knew only a relatively small part of the story. My report was incomplete." [105]

The Los Angeles *Times*'s Jack Foisie, like Dudman a correspondent of good reputation, also ran afoul of the government. Because he filed a story about a Marine amphibious landing in Quang Ngai Province, in South Viet-Nam, two days after it had taken place, his accreditation was suspended for thirty days.[106] He conceded that he had filed before the official release of the information; however, no one could accuse him of having given aid and comfort to the enemy after so long a waiting period. A certain amount of official pettiness was discernible in the case.

With the roster of accredited correspondents standing at 500 in the fall of 1966, ten combat correspondents and photographers had been killed, and more than thirty had been wounded. As had been the case in Korea, those who covered the war took a higher proportion of losses than those who fought it. Five of the dead were American citizens, four were Vietnamese, and one was a citizen of Singapore of Indian extraction. The most prominent was Dickey Chapelle, a photographer-correspondent for the *National Observer,* who stepped on a land mine while covering a Marine operation near Chulai on November 4, 1965. Just a month before, two other photographers, Bernard Kolenberg and Huynh Thanh My, both of the AP, had been killed.[107]

Yet, the widening war continued to draw more correspondents into action, and with them photographers and television cameramen. During 1966, 126 American citizens and 67 Vietnamese held accreditations in Saigon, most of them representing some 45 American news organizations, while there were more than 300 of other nationalities, some of whom also worked for American agencies.

It was a testimonial to the skill and courage of the foreigners that three of the four Pulitzer Prizes awarded between 1964 and 1966 for coverage of the Viet-Nam war went to a New Zealander, Arnett of the AP; a West German, Faas of the AP; and a brave Japanese combat photographer, Kyoichi Sawada, on the staff of the UPI, winner of the 1966 photography award.

The British and Japanese both had large correspondents' corps in

South Viet-Nam, but nearly every other major nation in Europe and Asia was also represented. To handle this growing and contentious group, JUSPAO assigned more than 100 officials who were present wherever they were needed. Four press courier flights a day went from Saigon to Pleiku, Danang, Nhatrang, and Quinhon, taking correspondents and photographers on assignments. The AP and the UPI each had more than a dozen men on duty around the clock.[108]

There was no lack of war reporting now. It dominated the news periods on the nation's television screens and thus helped stimulate a greater amount of space in both the newspapers and the news magazines. The studied indifference of a large part of the American press to much of the Korean War and the early stages of the Viet-Nam conflict was now nowhere in evidence. If television had its shortcomings, and they were many, the stimulation of greater public interest in the war was its greatest triumph. By the mere fact that it reported the conflict in flashing, dramatic sequences, often obtained by its correspondents and cameramen at the risk of their lives, the war came out to Page 1 and stayed there. In the fall of 1966, it was impossible to pick up a newspaper, news or picture magazine, flip on the radio, or look at television without becoming steeped in combat reports from Viet-Nam.

Despite the continuing complaints against the correspondents' corps and the in-fighting, no one could say that these men and women were shirking their duty. Every day some of them were in combat, and others were actively seeking out trouble. Looked at objectively over a range of many months, their work for the press and the electronic media was far better than it seemed when judged merely from one day to the next. Their critics, all too often, were guilty of looking at them through the wrong end of a telescope instead of considering the whole broad pattern in all its intricacy. That pattern, as it developed during the escalation of the war, was a credit to American journalism. For even those who complained that too many correspondents were young, brash, and inexperienced had to concede that a majority of the Viet-Nam press corps showed devotion to duty, great courage under fire, and the ability to work for long periods with little sleep, bad food, and constant danger about them.[109]

This was part of the reporters' job in Viet-Nam. Theirs were the voices that were heard above the tumult of war. It was to them that the people of the United States inevitably turned for information and, very often, a true interpretation of the course of events. But for leadership, the nation still depended on Lyndon Baines Johnson.

VII

New Times in South Asia

1. THE END OF AN ERA

ON A GOLDEN MORNING in November, 1963, a flight of U.S. Air Force F-100 jets landed at Palam Airport outside New Delhi. They had flown directly from their American bases to participate in joint maneuvers with the Indian Air Force and supporting aircraft from the British Commonwealth. For Ambassador Chester Bowles and the leaders of the small American military mission to India, it was a proud occasion; for the first time since World War II, American and Indian armed forces were operating jointly.

A large and solemn Indian government official, standing beside a gaily decorated and beflagged canopy that had been erected for the brief welcome ceremony, remarked sagely as the American pilots scrambled out of their lean fighter aircraft: "The Chinese Communists will observe and they will take warning." There were, of course, no Chinese correspondents in India at the time, but the Western global agencies and Tass were covering the event, as were the few American specials who were permanently assigned to India. Peking would know as quickly as Moscow, London, and Washington.

Ambassador Bowles, confining himself to a modest 200-word welcome to the pilots, judiciously steered away from placing any stress on American air power that might have embarrassed the relatively small and outmoded Indian Air Force. When he had finished, he stepped away from the microphone in the expectation that the ranking Indian officer, Air Vice Marshal A. M. Engineer, later to become a marshal and the chief of the Indian Air Staff, would say a few words of greeting. But the Air Vice Marshal merely walked away with his aides, saying nothing.

The American correspondents hustled off to file the story of the snub. The large and solemn Indian government official cried out in dismay, "What's wrong? Why are they running?" Told that the correspondents were reporting the lack of an Indian welcome, he protested, "I shall never understand you Americans." An American general, meanwhile, had reproached the Air Vice Marshal. "Why couldn't you at least say, 'Good morning, glad to see you?'" To which the Indian replied stiffly, "I had my orders." It was late that afternoon before the government authorized a few lines of welcome in a mimeographed announcement.[1]

Such things were typical of Indian-American relations in the last days of Jawaharlal Nehru. The old Prime Minister, disillusioned by India's shattering defeat during the Chinese border incursion of 1962, no longer could maintain his country's northern defenses by trusting to the Communists in Peking. He had had to dispense with the services of his old and valued friend, V. K. Krishna Menon, the most rabid anti-American in the Indian cabinet, for failing to prepare India's armed forces during his term as defense minister. The policy of nonalignment (known with much bitter humor in Washington as "non-aligned against us") had failed. The vision of India as the moral arbiter of the world, the prime mover of disarmament, the great force for peace, had been dissolved. Yet, in the last year of his life, Nehru could not unbend toward the United States, although he had accepted $6 billion in economic aid from the American government, and though he had been betrayed by Peking. He still had the Soviet Union.

Americans in New Delhi had long observed that both the government and press of India often had taken American good will and assistance for granted, but had assiduously paid court to the Soviet Union. The reaction to the American F-100 flight therefore, was, part of a familiar pattern. Norman Isaacs, executive editor of the Louisville *Times* and *Courier-Journal,* had written at the conclusion of a study of the Indian press: "Mr. Nehru's general policies would seem to be almost automatically the policies of the editors . . . Where international politics are concerned, it is difficult to distinguish between the government and the press. Indian editors are strongly neutralist. Many resent the word 'neutral.' They borrow from Mr. Nehru [and] call themselves 'uncommitted.'"[2] As long as Nehru lived, that was very largely true.

It was a testimonial to the old Pandit's greatness that he never tried to seize absolute power in India. He believed in parliamentary democracy and the exercise of most of the familiar categories of democratic privileges, except for a nagging doubt about the manner in which a free press exercised its responsibilities. He, too, had the itch to control its utterances; but, like most liberals who were illiberal toward the press, he clothed his hard-fisted policy in fine, liberal phrasing. Often, he would say, "What is meant by freedom of the press? Is it freedom merely for the proprietor?" By which he meant to warn the proprietors to watch their step. They all received the message.

When the government of India subsequently issued a brochure six months after the Chinese invasion entitled "Guidance for the Press in the Present Emergency," it was not an empty gesture. The rules it laid down were based on Defense of India legislation, and it decreed self-censorship of a particularly strict nature. An additional warning, in italics, read: *"It should be ensured that no mention of any sort occurs in any publication of the contents of this pamphlet or of the Guidance Notes or of any confidential advice of a similar nature."* [3]

Some of the American correspondents, nettled because they believed that their mail had been opened and their telephones tapped, took this to be an overt challenge to their unrestricted right to report the news. They sent pieces to the United States about it, all of which got through without trouble. The Indian Ministry of Information and Broadcasting afterward had some of the Americans in to tea, denying any intention of censoring their work. But it was evident that the domestic press had been taken firmly in hand. To the end of Nehru's days, the most that ever happened to an American foreign correspondent was that he received a lecture if his work was deemed consistently "anti-Indian"; occasionally there was a mild threat. But that was all.

Undoubtedly, Nehru's nonalignment policy and his controversial treatment of the Soviet Union and the United States accounted in large measure for the relatively indifferent figure that India cut in the American press. While the violent and often bloody dispute with Pakistan over the occupation of Jammu and Kashmir by India's armed forces was the major nondomestic topic in the press of both countries from the time of their independence in 1947, the issue never made much of an impression on the American public until the threat of a real war grew in 1965. Even at the United Nations, where Indian and Pakistani representatives each were accustomed to make speeches several hours long whenever Kashmir was discussed, few correspondents outside the wire services, the New York *Times,* and the Indian and Pakistani papers paid much attention to it in the early days. The frequent American newspaper prejudice against India in such matters as Kashmir and the armed invasion of Goa stemmed primarily from Nehru's foreign policy as it affected the United States.

It was ironic that the United States should have shown less favor to so great a champion of parliamentary democracy than to the military regime of Pakistan's Field Marshal Mohammad Ayub Khan, who seized power on October 7, 1958, as the self-proclaimed Chief Martial Law Administrator and, later, as President. The two parts of the troubled Muslim nation of 100 million people, separated by 1,000 miles of Indian territory and forever fearful of fanatical Hindu nationalists, fell quietly under authoritarian rule. The free press no longer existed; it became a mere echo of government, showing itself to be the most vicious, cynical, and unprincipled press outside the Communist lands in all Asia.

Yet, General Ayub's stance as an uncomprising anti-Communist endeared him to both the American government and the American press. Pakistan, anxious to build a strong diplomatic and military position against India, had joined the Southeast Asia Treaty Organization (SEATO) in 1954 and the Middle East Treaty Organization (Baghdad Pact) in the following year. The Pakistani dictator maintained these commitments and, when the Baghdad Pact foundered, joined the new Central Treaty Organization, with which the United States was associated but was not a member. Out of these arrangements came $1.5 billion in American military assistance for Pakistan, which, added to nearly $2.5 billion in American economic aid, made a healthy addition to its general well-being. To General Ayub's credit, Pakistan used its foreign aid to better advantage than most other recipients. It all added up to Pakistan's becoming a favorite child of the American press, at least for those newspapers that paid attention to South Asian affairs.

India, naturally, resented American efforts to arm Pakistan. It led to an even more critical press reaction. If there had been doubts before about the wisdom of Nehru's nonalignment policy, they seemed to melt away in New Delhi. It was resoundingly correct, among those who influenced Indian public opinion, to maintain a middle ground between the West, which had inherited the ill will of Asians for its old colonialist policies, and the Soviet Union and Communist China, which were pictured as noble powers that sought only a better life for their peoples. Not even the rising quarrel between the two Communist giants seemed to shake the Indians out of their dreamlike torpor. Then, on October 20, 1962, the Chinese struck southward from the Himalayas, and the dream ended. Although the Communist armies withdrew, India was nearly prostrated by the sudden and unexpected military humiliation by an erstwhile friend.

Even so, Nehru still clung to nonalignment, and his friends apologized for him. "It was not non-alignment that was wrong," said a Cabinet minister to a correspondent. "It was not carried out right by Krishna [Menon] because he is so allergic to the West. Nehru listened to him too much. We were betrayed by the Chinese and the Russians. We did not pay enough attention to our friends." [4]

It was the Chinese attack that produced the first attempt to change the chilly atmosphere that had persisted in both Washington and New

Delhi, despite the massive foreign-aid transactions between them. A modest military-assistance program now was inaugurated, one which produced such small but significant changes as the flight of the USAF F-100's to Palam Airport in 1963. However, the transition to a different relationship was not smooth. After a prolonged controversy, Congressional opinion in the United States appeared to be going against a proposal to build a $1.5-billion steel mill for India at Bokaro, and the Indian Government withdrew its request for assistance in 1963. The job went to the Russians. At just about the same time, after a blistering attack in the *Times* of India, Prime Minister Nehru shelved an agreement he already had signed to give the United States authority to build a powerful radio transmitter in India to be used jointly by the Indian Government and the Voice of America.

However, the Pakistanis were also dissatisfied. Criticism of the United States suddenly increased in the controlled press, led by vituperative reports in a newspaper called *Dawn,* because of the flow of American military supplies to India. While General Ayub maintained his pro-Western, anti-Communist manner, his foreign minister, Zulfikar Ali Bhutto, began seeking new ties and new sources of support against India in the Communist world. Bhutto found a ready hearing in Djakarta and Peking, where a chance to separate Pakistan from the United States then was welcomed. Evidently, what Ayub sought to do was to maintain a steady flow of American military and economic assistance to Pakistan for as long as he could, while building up new sources of aid with those Communist nations that were likely to help him oppose India. Once again, Washington saw that the loudest professions of anti-Communism were meaningless if they conflicted with national self-interest.

The tension between India and Pakistan began rising in Kashmir once more. Toward the end of 1963, a relic that was claimed to be a hair of the Prophet Mohammed was stolen from a Srinagar mosque, resulting in fatal Hindu-Moslem rioting in East Pakistan and eastern India and an uproar in Kashmir. Pakistan brought up the Kashmir issue once again before the U.N. Security Council; India, for many reasons, was then in a weak political and military position.

Nehru, in consequence, decided on a calculated risk to restore calm to Kashmir and blunt Pakistan's diplomatic offensive. Early in April, 1964, he freed the fifty-eight-year-old "Lion of Kashmir," Sheik Mohammed Abdullah, after ten years' imprisonment for refusing to side with India. The Sheik had never agreed to the right of the Hindu Maharajah of Kashmir, Hari Singh, to sign an act of accession to India, on the basis of which 100,000 Indian troops were still occupying the lovely Vale of Kashmir, Jammu, and the northern district of Ladakh. He was hailed as a hero in these almost wholly Muslim areas as well as in the smaller and poorer part of Kashmir that was occupied by Pakistan before the U.N. cease-fire on January 1, 1949. What negotiations he planned to undertake with Nehru, and what fortune might have greeted his efforts, will never be known. At 2 P.M. on May 27, 1964, the Indian Steel Minister, Coimbatore Subramaniam, walked into the Parliament in New Delhi and announced simply, "The light is out." [5] Nehru had died of a heart attack at the age of seventy-four. He had used exactly the same words on January 30, 1948, to announce the assassination of Mahatma Gandhi.

Then, a tiny Indian in a white dhoti and a white Congress Party cap, an earnest-faced man of sixty with a placid smile and bright brown eyes and a voice that was gentle but determined sat in Nehru's chair and rested his small, childlike hands on the enormous desk in the Prime Minister's office in New Delhi. Not even the Indians knew too much about Lal Bahadur Shastri, who had been selected first by Nehru himself in his last illness and later by the discordant Indian political bosses at the insistence of the President of the Congress Party, Kumaraswami Kamaraj, of Madras. Their feeling about him was much like that of Americans who, after the death of Franklin Delano Roosevelt, saw that Harry S. Truman was their President and didn't quite know what to make of him.

Shastri, born into the family of a minor Indian official in a village in the state of Uttar Pradesh, was just as plain a man as Truman, but not as rash or outspoken. Yet, he had the credentials of a revolutionary, having spent nine years in British jails during the struggle for Indian independence. For those who were ready to give up on him—and on India—when he suffered a heart attack seventeen days after assuming office, he had a surprise. Soon, despite the most desperate food shortage since Indian independence and military actions against the increasingly aggressive Pakistanis in the Rann of Kutch and Kashmir, he was running India's affairs with a quiet confidence.

The United States came to the rescue in the food crisis, with nearly 7 million tons of food grains in 1964–65; and a good Indian harvest of 87 million tons in the latter year helped temporarily. But most important of all, Shastri himself was able to persuade India's warring party bosses to adopt rationing of wheat, rice, and sugar for the nation's sixteen states. Yet, he could do nothing about the nation's 220 million cows, held sacred by the vast majority of the people, and the countless swarms of monkeys that were permitted to make inroads into the grain that people so desperately needed.

The root of the problem was, of course, the staggering annual increase in population. With births estimated at forty-two per thousand

and deaths at twenty-three per thousand, the net gain of nineteen per thousand annually meant that India's population went up every year by about 10 million—more than the population of New York City. It was Shastri's responsibility, also, to help his Health Ministry stimulate the use of cheap birth-control devices, which were being produced in great quantities for pennies each.

Nothing was easily accomplished in India, with its estimated 480 million people crammed into an area one-third the size of the United States and subject to a fantastic variety of hardships and temperatures. The mere problem of communication was enormous in a land where the All-India Radio in the mid-1960's probably reached only about 15 million people.[6] The total press circulation was considerably less. With nearly 50 million children in school, there was measurable progress in public education, but the populace was still only 20 to 30 per cent literate (depending on whether one listened to university authorities or the government). Eighty per cent of all Indians lived in 550,000 villages, scattered from the Himalayas to tropical Cape Comorin, and from the desert of Rajasthan on the west to crowded Assam on the east. While the villages found out quickly about an increase in the price of rice or most other things that immediately affected their daily lives, their knowledge of outside events was hazy. A public-opinion test showed that the Chinese invasion had been only dimly perceived in distant areas of India.[7] In a test of twenty-seven villages near Jaipur, it was found that while everybody knew, within two hours, of Nehru's death, some still had never heard of Shastri.[8]

Even the language that the nation chose to speak could become the cause of a major political and social crisis. When the new Prime Minister sought early in 1965 to carry out the law that imposed Hindi upon the nation as the official language, dropping English and the various southern native tongues, the Tamil-speaking people of Madras began rioting, with fatal effect. The younger ones, in particular, feared that they would automatically be disqualified from holding government or school posts if Hindi became the only language in which tests could be taken. Shastri had to rescind the order for the time being, after two cabinet ministers resigned and then were persuaded to change their minds. English, the lingua franca of India, was retained as an associate official language, and the use of fourteen native tongues in addition to Hindi was continued on All-India Radio and elsewhere.

The trend toward Hindi, however, was only temporarily arrested. R. K. Narayan, India's leading novelist, conceded sadly that it would not be politically feasible to retain English as a long-term matter, although he doubted if Hindi could be imposed on the south in less than fifty years. "The teaching of English in our schools and universities is simply deplorable," he said. "I don't want to say, 'After me, the deluge,' but I am afraid that my generation is the last which will produce English writing of an international standard in India." [9]

Like almost every other goal in India, that of economic independence seemed almost beyond reach at the slow rate of progress in the mid-1960's.[10] The Indian had an average annual income of only $60 a year, and the rupee was falling prey to inflation. Although the official rate was 4.75 to the dollar, it went for about 6.50 to 7.50 on the free market. The price rise in India, particularly for food, was a matter of major concern to the government. Its confidence in socialism as a way of life was far from certain; the private sector of the economy—some of it run in the hard-fisted way of the 1890's in the United States—was still more important. Lack of housing, lack of jobs, lack of adequate health facilities, and a widespread and pernicious political corruption complicated every effort by the government to push India even a short distance along the road to progress. These things were discussed in the press at home but seldom abroad except in a few serious publications.

It was inevitable that Prime Minister Shastri would turn aside from Nehru's grandiose domestic program of showy public works and spectacular industrial developments in order to try to bring some immediate benefits to the average Indian. He did give priority to fast-maturing consumer-goods industries, but even that took time. As a result, India's foreign-exchange reserves remained dangerously low, and lack of capital goods and raw materials impeded the growth of heavy industry. Steel output remained static while some gains were shown in coal production, the generation of electricity, and oil-refining. The pressure was very great on Shastri to authorize a drive to develop atomic weapons in order to match the Chinese atomic bomb, but he refused, although Dr. Homi Bhabha, the Indian atomic expert, estimated just before his untimely death in an air crash that the job could be done in five years for $52 million.

As one of the most experienced of American journalists in India, Sol Sanders, wrote in *U.S. News & World Report,* "The problems in India —and to some extent in Pakistan—are so bad that I don't see how anybody can be optimistic." [11] So sensitive and sympathetic a correspondent as Selig S. Harrison of the Washington *Post* wrote in *Foreign Affairs* that the Chinese incursion of 1962 had set off a continuing "process of internal political deterioration" in India. "The old vision is gone," he went on, "and there are few signs pointing to the birth of a renewed spirit of common purpose to take its place. The mood is increasingly of every man for himself." [12]

All in all, it was a dark and gloomy portrait that the American specials drew, at the end of the Nehru era, of the India they had learned to live with, if not to admire. They detected very little of the enormous vitality, the spiritual strength, the constant movement, and the sheer will to be free that Gandhi had found in the Indian masses during the bright and challenging years of their struggle for independence. However, the governments of the United States and the Soviet Union were not giving up. The pragmatists of Washington and Moscow were well aware that the Indian masses, second in number only to China's, were likely sooner or later to have an impact on the power structure in Asia. To disregard them or to abandon them would mean, in effect, that primary influence over this turbulent continent would be handed to the grim old xenophobes of Peking.

This was not likely to happen. While it was a grievous error to consider that the United States and the Soviet Union were cooperating in any sense in a parallel effort to aid India—a favorite line of the Indian politicians and intellectuals—it was true that both were deeply involved in Indian commitments from which neither could easily extricate itself. The cold war here was being fought with different purposes. The Americans and Russians sought advantage over each other with the Indians, but both also were anxious to do everything possible to injure the Chinese. For New Delhi, this was nonalignment with a vengeance. And since Pakistan was turning to Peking while weakening its ties with Washington, the prospect was that the Soviet Union would eventually take more interest in the machinations at Rawalpindi, as well. The outburst of fighting over Kashmir in 1965 intensified this process.

In India, the Soviet commitments included more than $1 billion in economic aid, nearly $300 million in military assistance, and an undetermined amount in the future to help support such projects as new factories, steel mills, and plants for the construction of Russian MIG fighter aircraft. With Krishna Menon and his followers still active on the fringes of the Indian power structure, the Russians did not lack for friends. They were also believed to have fortified their propaganda position by channeling funds into at least forty different Indian publications of varying influence and gaining converts among younger journalists and the restless student groups. However, in the 120,000-member Indian Communist Party, the Russians had not done well. Despite the Chinese attack, the Indians who were attracted to Peking's policies won a majority of seats in the elections in the southern state of Kerala in 1965. Although the Indian government held the victors in prison and named a governor for the dissident state, the outcome was a clear warning to New Delhi that Moscow did not have all the answers.

The American stake in India was much greater than Russia's. Up to 1965, the United States had spent $160 million in three years on Indian military aid and in each of these three years there had been an additional $100 million in military assistance, half grant, half loan, more than half a billion dollars in all. But with India's decision to turn to Moscow for MIG fighters, the United States refused with good reason to place its newest and most sensitive aircraft at the disposal of the Indian Government. However, from 1965 on, grants for military aid were expected to total $300 million, plus an annual credit of $50 million for Indian military procurement. Moreover, the Americans were providing the crucial aid for the first Indian atomic power plant at Tarapur, north of Bombay.

All these things did not take into account the rapidly expanding American commercial interest in India. From a mere $23 million at the time of Indian independence, private American investment in India had risen to more than $300 million in the mid-1960's and was growing at the rate of $30 million a year. India was second only to Japan as an American customer in Asia, having absorbed $804 million in American exports in 1963. In the same year, India had sold $294 million as American imports, third after Japan and the Philippines. Nor did this mean a great profit for American business; by arrangement, much of the money for such things as grain sales did not leave India but was used there.

Not many American firms were doing business under license in India —fewer than fifty. But fifty-six Indian firms had American investments and seventy-four American companies were active in trade and services. With the relaxation of Indian tax laws and the long overdue modernization of the slow and cumbersome Indian administrative practices in foreign trade, few doubted that American private investment in the country could be doubled, provided there was some assurance of peace.

In a relatively short time, the Shastri regime had accomplished more to improve India's standing in Washington than the great Nehru was able to do. Of course, the ill-advised Pakistanis also contributed to the elevation of the Indians in American eyes through their precipitate rush to win friends in Peking and elsewhere in the Communist world. It was after General Ayub paid his respects in Moscow and Peking, and incidentally failed to support American aims in the Viet-Nam war, that President Johnson suddenly canceled the Pakistani leader's scheduled visit to Washington in the spring of 1965. The fact that a similar visit by Prime Minister Shastri was put off at the same time scarcely served to conceal Washington's growing displeasure with Pakistan.

Soon, Shastri was accusing Communist China of being too rigid in its Viet-Nam policy and of being unwilling to make moves toward world peace. While he denied that this represented a change in position, he observed that "at least the United States has shown some willingness to negotiate, even if it has imposed some very heavy conditions." He added, "I would like to see some sign from China that she is prepared to take steps toward peace there." [13]

Unfortunately, it was at this time that Pakistan, angered and frustrated over its failure after years of effort to force India out of Kashmir by diplomatic means, chose to try to settle the issue by force. On August 5, 1965, Pakistanis began to infiltrate Kashmir, using the guerrilla tactics made famous by Mao Tse-tung. The Indians at first made a limited attack within Kashmir to balk the infiltrators. After that had failed, the three-week war began on September 6, 1965. When the Pakistanis drove into Indian-held territory with American Patton and Sherman tanks, supported by American-supplied F-104 jet fighters and older but still effective F-86 aircraft, the Indians struck toward Lahore, in Pakistan, to try to force the invaders to halt. The Indians had mostly British aircraft, with some French jet fighters and a few Russian MIG's. There was a mélange of American and other military hardware for their ground forces. Consequently, from the outset, the Johnson Administration found itself in the middle, with both sides accusing each other of the misuse of American war matériel in violation of agreements with the United States.

While Communist China egged on Pakistan, with Foreign Minister Chen Yi praising the Pakistanis for "just action to repel Indian armed aggression," the United States and the Soviet Union joined in two unanimous U.N. Security Council votes for a cease-fire in Kashmir. Despite the valor of Pakistan's 250,000-man army and the far superior forces of the Indians, neither could keep fighting for very long; in the face of both American and Russian disapproval, the war ended almost as quickly as it had begun. It was ironic that the old foes of the cold war should find common ground in India. It was ironic, too, that anti-Communist Pakistan and nonaligned India should have come so close for a time to reversing their roles in American relations. India, as Max Frankel noted, had been "driven toward the West by China's hostility and thus to the top of the list of American interests in Asia." [14]

With the tacit approval of the United States, Marshal Ayub and Prime Minister Shastri agreed to Soviet mediation and on January 10, 1966, signed a nine-point declaration at Tashkent, in the U.S.S.R., under which they pledged speedy withdrawal of their forces in Kashmir to the positions held before August 5. In the early hours of the next morning, Shastri was fatally stricken with a heart attack in the villa that the Soviet government had set aside for his use in Tashkent. He died at the height of his brief but turbulent rule, a hero to his people. Eight days later, the moderates in the Congress Party, led by Kumaraswami Kamaraj, selected another Prime Minister. Indira Gandhi became the third Prime Minister of India, and the first woman in modern times to rule over a great Asian nation. At forty-eight years of age, Nehru's daughter, his disciple and confidante, took up the struggle to maintain democratic rule in India. As Shastri's Information Minister, she had attempted to modernize India's much-criticized radio, made a start on introducing television, and fought hard to make the foreign press give a more favorable account of news from India. Her success with the press had been limited as a Cabinet Minister; as Prime Minister, she could not afford to fail.

In the first months of her regime, crises abounded on all sides. It became certain that both economic aid and massive food shipments were urgently needed from the United States to combat a mounting food shortage that threatened disaster. Consequently, it was to Washington that Nehru's daughter first turned, with President Johnson welcoming her. As an initial effort to put their governmental relations on a better basis than before, the President proposed to establish a $300-million Indian-American Foundation to stimulate education in India. It was an imaginative use for the Indian currency that was held by the United States in Indian banks as payment for grain and other American products, but education on an empty stomach would have meant little. Consequently, Prime Minister Gandhi's main effort was to ensure the kind of relations with Washington that would mean a steady supply of food and funds for India.

In this, she succeeded brilliantly. The American President called upon the Congress for a $1-billion emergency famine-relief program which would include the shipment of 3.5 million tons of food grains to India during 1966 and the donation of 125 million pounds of milk powder and 150 million pounds of vegetable oils. He appealed, as well, to the "conscience of all nations that can render help."

However, the American and Indian heads of state could not fail to notice that halfway around the world, the Pakistanis at the same time were enthusiastically hailing a party of Communist leaders from Peking, headed by Chairman Liu Shao-chi and Foreign Minister Chen Yi. While President Ayub Khan's government was quick to protest that this was not to be interpreted as a change of policy toward the United States, it was clear that the effects of the Pakistani leader's own visit to Washington late in 1965 had worn off.[15] Meanwhile, also, India's own anti-American politicians succeeded in shelving the proposed Indian-American Foundation.

Great power rivalry in the vast Indian subcontinent was rising. New times, indeed, had come to South Asia.

2. ON UNDERSTANDING INDIA

When Bayard Taylor, of the New York *Tribune,* visited India in 1853, he was overcome by the beauty of the Taj Mahal, astonished that a Hindu minstrel could play "Oh, Susannah!" on his mandolin, and enraptured by the Ganges Canal, which was then being completed. He predicted, with a flourish, that the fabulous new waterway would "cover with perpetual harvests the great peninsula plain between the Ganges and the Jumna, and render famine impossible in the north of India." [16]

Like many another correspondent who followed him, the laureate of the Gilded Age was undone by his romantic involvement with India. More than a century later, the crowded and tortured land still could not produce enough food to sustain its vastly increased population. But curiously, much as the Indians were concerned with this agonizing problem, they were nearly as worried about the poor figure they cut before the world because of their misfortune. At a time when ships laden with American food grains were arriving in Bombay harbor at the rate of two a day to relieve the critical food shortage, a leading Indian journalist, Prem Bhatia, wrote: "India is getting an unfavorable press overseas with regard to the food crisis. Newspapers abroad have written sympathetically, if a little sensationally, about our difficulties, but many in the outside world cannot possibly think well of our capacity to plan our economic future." [17]

What the Americans, British, French, and Japanese thought of the Indians in this connection mattered far less than what the Indians thought of themselves. For the doubts that Bhatia and other responsible Indian editors detected abroad, although they created little stir among foreign publics, were also present in large and gloomy measure at home. It is an observable phenomenon that bad news feeds on itself and can, if permitted to grow, create a panic atmosphere. Nehru, with his sublime indifference, even contempt for the press, never worried about this aspect of his relations with the Indian people; to the end, he was sure that his words counted for more than the combined power of the Indian press. Manifestly, he was right.

But neither Lal Bahadur Shastri nor Indira Gandhi could afford to take so lordly an attitude, particularly in the face of India's developing food crisis. The Indian press's repetition of adverse foreign comment and the varied editorial reactions to it, ranging from despair to anger, scarcely improved the situation. Consequently, two successive Indian governments had to wrestle with public disturbances graver than any Nehru had faced in his long rule.

Early in his regime, Prime Minister Shastri had recognized that one of his main tasks was to restore India's shaken confidence in itself. While many cried out that he was no Nehru, which he was the first to recognize, and others shouted that India also needed an Ayub, which it did not, he went about his work without showing doubt or fear. His first task was to still panicky talk that India was on the verge of dissolution. His second was to persuade his people that the nation could survive without Nehru.

Yet, Shastri was no miracle worker. It was his particular virtue to appear to be a very ordinary man. He would stand before his people saying, "I am a man of peace." And, with a wan gesture indicating his 4-foot 8-inch stature, he would add, "What else can I be?" Frank Moraes, the large, self-assured editor of the *Indian Express,* thundered, "Leaders have no business being humble." But Shastri, despite his stature, had no Napoleonic illusions. People felt comfortable with him because he appeared to be humble and spoke in terms that they could understand.

From the outset, Nehru's successor made himself readily available to both the domestic press and to foreign correspondents, but he issued no inspiring messages and he seldom made news in the conventional sense. He was the very opposite kind of world leader to which India had grown accustomed. He had no genius for creating headlines. And if there was any charismatic aura about him, it was that of the schoolteacher who knew how to lead his class easily and with good humor through a difficult problem. Yet, in his constant references to Gandhi and Nehru one could detect a note of sadness because he seemed to believe himself so unworthy to succeed them. But he did not let his modesty paralyze him, and it was one of his most attractive traits.

Listening to him in the enormous office that had been Nehru's, a visitor could follow him and understand him with far greater ease than his illustrious predecessor. It was his view that India's problems were not new and that he had no novel solutions to offer. They were what they had been—and he ticked them off—poverty, unemployment, health, the problem of raising enough food to feed India's people, the problem of industrializing and of unifying the country. These had been the problems of India during the first seventeen years of independence, and before, and these also were the problems of the future.

But the most important of all, in his mind, and the one to which he gave top priority, was agriculture. Grateful as he was to the United States for its assistance, he deeply believed that India could not long continue to depend on outside help to feed its people. India's farming operations and methods had to be improved. It was his frequently expressed opinion that both the government and the cultivator had been at fault in failing to raise the level of production.

True, there had always been food shortages at certain times of the year in India, but a variety of causes had combined to make the 1964-66 crises more severe. Among these he listed the drought, the increased consumption of food grains, a rise in the consumption of wheat and rice by people who formerly had used only the coarser grains, and the lack of better means of distribution. But most of all, he seemed to place the blame on the high priority that had been given in the past to the development of the steel industry and other major projects.

If there was a Shastri program, it was that India had to change the direction of its efforts. In agriculture, for instance, there had been a concentration on big canals for irrigation purposes; he now wanted more attention paid to the small irrigation projects that he felt were more necessary and more meaningful. The essence of the changed direction, as India's second Prime Minister saw it, was that the cultivator must be provided with water quickly—otherwise there was no hope of better crops. Moreover, he intended to see to it that the cultivator had more fertilizer, better ploughs and implements, and sturdy bullocks.

And what of machines?

To such a question, Shastri permitted himself a small and rueful smile. It took time to teach people to operate machines. And in a country like India, where agriculture accounted for half the output while industry and mining accounted for only 20 per cent and services 30 per cent, there was no time to devote to increasing mechanization. Small machines, perhaps, were possible if they could be cheaply provided. But for the most part, Indian agriculture for the immediate future would have to get along with traditional methods. With greater efficiency and with more water and fertilizer, there could be an improvement. In a crop area of 325 million acres, about equal to that of the United States, India had been able to produce only one-quarter to one-third as much food as the United States for more than twice as many people.

It was difficult to divert the Prime Minister from his almost single-minded attention to agriculture, for the food shortage weighed heavily on him. But when he did venture some observations on foreign policy, which had so preoccupied his predecessor, it was mainly to point out that he could make no changes for the present. However, when he spoke of nonalignment, it was in a far different vein than Nehru or Krishna Menon or Indira Gandhi. Nonalignment seemed to him to be a policy, rather than a way of life, and policies could be changed. He did not believe in nonalignment as a means of playing one country off against another and profiting at the expense of both. It was, he felt, a moral position which enabled India to be friendly with the Commonwealth countries and the United States and others. But, he insisted, India did not want to join the Soviet bloc or any other power bloc.

As for China, and here his bright brown eyes fairly shone with challenge, he recognized that it might have some temporary successes in Southeast Asia and elsewhere, but over the long period the Chinese could not, he believed, profit by their aggression. He also was determined that China could never make India accept conditions that were not in India's interest.

While Shastri paid tribute to Nehru's genius, he conceded that there had, indeed, been a shift in emphasis. But that, as he so often said later, was no more than Gandhi would have done. For Gandhi, too, had always put domestic problems first and had tried to raise the condition of the common man as a matter of the first importance. The more Shastri talked of Gandhi, in simple and unadorned English, the more evident it was that there was something remarkably similar about them beyond their mere physical resemblance. For it was, certainly, the influence of Gandhi rather than Nehru that dominated India's second Prime Minister.[18]

His successor, Indira Gandhi, was quite different. She did not give the impression of forcefulness and power so often credited to her, being small, thin, and rather ascetic-looking, with a touch of gray in her black hair and a directness about her dark-eyed gaze that commanded respect. From childhood on, in her native Allahabad and later at Oxford, she had been trained to be a leader, and she looked the part. She was no martyr to widowhood (her husband was Feroze Gandhi, a lawyer [not related to the Mahatma]). Nor did she walk in her father's footsteps, despite her adoration for him. On her thirtieth birthday, he wrote to her: "What presents can I give you? They can only be of the air and the mind and spirit, such as a good fairy might have bestowed on you."

These were her gifts. During her father's lifetime, she did not run for public office, and she entered Shastri's Government only under pressure. A certain amount of American apprehension was evident when she became India's chief propagandist as the head of the Information and Broadcasting Ministry. Yet, regardless of her strength in the left wing of India's Congress Party, she dealt implacably with the domestic Communists in the state of Kerala. And on her various visits to the United States, she carried everything off, not even creating panic among the Daughters of the American Revolution. In her 1966 visit as Prime Minister, she excited comment among the women journalists with her colorful saris and her mink; as for the men, she often charmed them with her wit as well as her wisdom.

Like Shastri, she made herself constantly available to the press, although she remained highly critical of the domestic newspapers and was little impressed with the quality of foreign correspondence out of India. To visitors who called at her office in one of the massive red sandstone buildings of the government complex in New Delhi, she spoke in a low voice, often quite rapidly but always with crisp authority. Now and then she would finger a small chain of black beads about her throat, tap on the arms of her chair, or rearrange her sari. She seemed somehow to be in almost constant motion but gave the impression of great earnestness and sincerity. There was no light chitchat in her office. She was not the kind of woman who could be asked about who drank too much at last night's cocktail party.

While in the Communications Ministry, her problems, as she saw them, were threefold: to improve communication from the Indian Government to the people and from the people to the government, to modernize All-India Radio and provide the people with more sets, and to create a national television network. On the first point, she constantly sought new ideas. On the second, she was determined to increase the size of the listening audience far beyond the modest size that was indicated by the taxes paid on 3 million radio sets with an estimated five persons for each set. On the third, she was well aware that there was no industrial base for television in India, but she sought both help and ideas from abroad on how the newest and potentially the most powerful means of mass communication could be brought to India.

In the months before she succeeded to the Prime Ministry, she did her best to try to overcome public uncertainty about the course of the Shastri Government. At the time of her father's death, on May 27, 1964, she had learned vividly of the result of a lack of effective governmental communication with the public. After All-India Radio's first brief announcement of Nehru's death, mournful and dirgelike music had been played for almost two hours. During that time, Mrs. Gandhi's friends in Bombay told her, the most incredible rumors began circulating there of what was going on in New Delhi, all because of the vacuum in the information process. Belatedly, public uncertainty was banished when the news flow was resumed by the badly frightened All-India Radio officials. It was a lesson that the Prime Minister-to-be did not forget; on such things as grave food shortages, political corruption, and the ever-tense situation in Kashmir, there was no substitute for a steady flow of information to the public. Necessarily, it would take time to develop people who had the will, the courage, and the know-how to do the job.

Whatever happened in India, Indira Gandhi was convinced even before she came to power that her country would have to continue to be governed by what she called progressive policies. Her reasoning was clear enough. With 85 per cent of India's people at the poverty level, she could not understand how the government could afford to stand pat on any program, even though big business wanted it to do so.

She supported continued Indian arms purchases from the Soviet Union, particularly when sensitive items like new fighter aircraft were unavailable from the United States. India, she said, had nothing to fear from the Soviet Union and everything to fear from Communist China.

As for the foreign correspondents, she had a major complaint that she never hesitated to voice whether she was in London, Washington, or New Delhi. She agreed that much of the correspondence from India was basically truthful, but she argued that the correspondents usually didn't balance their stories of the woeful and never-ending procession of calamities by digging out a few good things that were happening in her country. It was, in short, the point of view to which she objected, not the substance of the accounts.[19]

Once, after she became Prime Minister, she learned to her horror that the state-controlled television system in Italy, stimulated by a public appeal from Pope Paul VI to relieve India's hunger and suffering, had raised more than $8.8 million in small contributions to send grain and milk to her country. Quickly, she used the press to send up signals, letting it be known that she was "deeply distressed at the exaggerated picture of a starving India being portrayed to the world." The Italians smoothly glossed over her displeasure, noting, as one commentator put it, that Indians "are an extremely proud people." [20]

In both the Shastri and the Gandhi regimes, the President of the Congress Party, Kumaraswami Kamaraj, was considered the most potent political figure in the nation. It was he who had assured Shastri's election as Prime Minister after Nehru's death with a firm rejection of the counterclaims of the leading rightist, Morarji Desai. During the succeeding party conference at Bangalore, the name of Kamaraj had dominated the proceedings to such an extent that he had been re-elected in 1965 to an unprecedented second term as its President. And when tragedy befell Shastri in Tashkent, it was Kamaraj once more who had swept aside the wrathful Desai and insisted on the election of Indira Gandhi.

Some of his foes called him a "political python" who ruthlessly crushed all opposition. Others saw him as the head of the "Syndicate" of Congress Party politicians—the inner ruling group that dominated its deliberations. Others in his own Madras State idealized him as the man who was really holding India together—"the man the people trust." He had served three times as chief minister of the state, its first non-Brahmin chief executive, and had been rewarded with a state-wide celebration on his sixty-third birthday in July, 1965.

To foreign correspondents who sought to learn what manner of man he was, Kamaraj often displayed an impish sense of humor. Many of them wrote that he understood no English, which wasn't true; while he could speak only the simplest sentences in English, he quickly caught any political reference spoken in English in his presence. At his small but comfortable villa on Ashoka Road, New Delhi, his door was always open to supplicants in the immemorial manner of old-line politicians the world over. There, he presided—a thick-set, bullet-headed, dark-faced Indian version of Jim Farley with a scrub of a mustache, shrewd dark eyes, and a deep rumbling laugh that made his big stomach shake. For foreign affairs, he had little patience: "We are friends to everybody," he would say, and chortle as if it were genuinely funny. But when the talk turned to domestic politics, he was all attention. That was his life.

During the Shastri and Gandhi regimes, he built up the power of the unwieldy Congress Party. Looking toward the 1967 elections, he could count 375 Congress seats in the Lok Sabha, the lower house of the Indian Parliament, compared with only 22 for its nearest rival, the con-servative Swatantra ("Freedom") Party. All states except Kerala were ruled by his associate leaders—and in Kerala the Communists had won at the ballot box even though they were in jail and couldn't rule. The state was governed from New Delhi.

It was Kamaraj's good fortune that his most powerful rivals were poor politicians. The outstanding opposition figure, Jayaprakash Nara-yan, the brilliant and attractive founder of the Socialist Party, had abandoned it and caused a split in its small membership. The Commu-nists were divided even more and under deep suspicion because of the Chinese Communist influence within their ranks. As for the leaders of India's 48 million Muslims, they were accounted fortunate to have rep-resentation within the Congress Party and, for all practical purposes, were looked upon as hostages to fortune.[21] Barring the breakup of the Congress Party—an unlikely possibility—it was almost a foregone con-clusion that it would return to power, for Kamaraj and his associates had been able to keep the opposition scattered. The only real threat was the ominous growth of the fanatical Jan Sangh organization of Hindu nationalists.

The passing of Nehru seemed to symbolize the passing of India from the center of the world stage as a moral force in international affairs. Nehru had run his own Foreign Office. India's first Minister of Ex-ternal Affairs, appointed during Shastri's regime, was Sardar Swaran Singh, a Sikh, an imposing white-clad figure, well over six feet, with an iron-gray beard, gold-rimmed glasses, a grandfatherly air, and the usual turban. Although he had been a domestic politician most of his life, his natural dignity and his habit of talking in ellipses made him appear to be a veteran of diplomacy. He had made several trips to the United States without creating much of a stir and seemed to have survived the attentions of both the American Government and the press.

It was a time when the usual barbed American inquiry about India's interest in Soviet arms did not bother the Indian Foreign Ministry. Swaran Singh even chuckled about it, but not very heartily. He usually replied that he would have been greatly concerned over a critical American press reaction to Soviet arms aid to India on earlier occasions, but not in the mid-1960's. In his view, despite the differences over the Viet-Nam war, there was less tension between the United States and the Soviet Union and a great deal more strain between the Soviet Union and Communist China. That philosophy served him reasonably well until the Kashmir war, the suspension of American aid, and the deepening Indian crisis over food shortages. Then, the strain of making new arrangements with Washington on the one hand and placating some of the violently anti-American politicians in the Lok Sabha on the other, would have tried the genius of even a Nehru. It was no wonder that Indira Gandhi, like her father, conducted her own mission to the United States.

Everybody in the government took the task of explaining India to the world with extreme seriousness. But the cause of international understanding was not substantially advanced in New Delhi any more than it was in Washington because of the highly complex and changing relationships that were involved. This was a matter for specialists, and few were available in the Indian capital. L. R. Nair, the principal information officer of the government, an active public relations man, constantly complained over the failure of India to achieve a more satisfactory status abroad. He was too shrewd to believe that he could either influence or control the foreign correspondents, but he did see to it that a copy of everything sent abroad was read at his office. He usually protested over what he considered to be "extreme views of India" in the dispatches, but disclaimed the opportunity for the occasional harassment of foreign correspondents. That was the responsibility of the Defense Ministry.[22]

It was with reason that the AP reported in 1966: "In India, censorship and interference with free news flow intensified because of the September, 1965, armed clash with Pakistan over Kashmir. A cease-fire brought little relaxation. India established a 'press adviser' to examine outgoing dispatches. News that might inspire communal rioting was banned." [23]

The India of the mid-1960's bore little resemblance to the dreamlike land of which Bayard Taylor had written to a delighted small-town America. It had outgrown the romancers and was far more difficult to understand. True, there were still a few old-fashioned correspondents who clung to the reliable old fare—the jeweled maharajahs and moonlit palaces, the snake charmers and fakirs who trod on hot coals, the holy men and perfumed maharanis and brave hunters who stalked the jungles for tigers and wild elephants. But such journalists were not taken seriously.

All was not well in the new India. There was hunger and misfortune. Caste discrimination, although outlawed, was still cruelly practiced against the untouchables and others. A new attitude of mind was needed, Frank Moraes said, to root out the practice of untouchability, with its concomitant of caste, for these beliefs were deeply imbedded in orthodox Hindu society.[24] The farmer still tilled the sunbaked soil much as he had for a thousand years. The destitute and the unwanted, by the hundreds of thousands, still lived and died on the streets of Calcutta and elsewhere.

There was also a sense of challenge and excitement in this ancient land that Taylor and Kipling and the rest of their kin had never perceived in their time. It could be felt in the spotless new city of Chandigarh that had been planned by Le Corbusier, with its square, soaring columns rising from the bare Punjab plain. It fairly radiated from the bustling business section of Bombay, crowded along the wide blue curve of a busy harbor. It could be seen in the changes that were coming—the 400-mile Rajasthan Canal, the great new atomic plant in the south of India, the Nagarjuna Sagar Dam, the oil refineries, steel mills, automobile factories and food-processing plants, and all the other symbols of the industrial age that rose across the land. For all of its ills, the new India that struggled to fulfill its destiny was far more compelling than the old. It had a will to survive.

3. AMERICANS IN INDIA

John Kenneth Galbraith, a Harvard economist, applied his manifold talents to the cultivation of American foreign correspondents of whom he approved during his two years as Ambassador to India. The regulars were few in number during the Galbraith years, 1961-63, consisting only of the two American news agencies, the New York *Times,* the Baltimore *Sun, Time,* N.B.C., *U.S. News & World Report,* and, toward the end, the Washington *Post.* To three, the Ambassador gave his highest accolade, dubbing them first-rate scholars—Henry Bradsher, of the AP; Paul Grimes, of the New York *Times;* and Selig S. Harrison, of the Washington *Post.* To another, Philip Potter, of the Baltimore *Sun,* he expressed his special gratitude for keeping him informed. The non-

Americans who worked for American news organizations, such as Sharokh Sabavala of the *Christian Science Monitor,* were seldom in his presence. As for the "fire brigade" of correspondents who rushed in and out of India in response to alarms, he had little use for most of them, assuming that few could be well-informed under the circumstances.[25]

As far as the Ambassador was concerned, he had a cozy relationship with the American regulars. He liked to think that he was able to promote a two-way flow of information—from the embassy to the correspondents and from the correspondents back to the embassy. At his weekly sessions with them, he hoped for "knowledge of what Indian officials were saying in their press conferences, background briefings or press leaks; for the rumors that were making the rounds of the parliament and press gallery; and for the knowledge of the stories that members of the press corps were going to play." [26]

Galbraith was not the first public official who had the bright idea of using the press corps as a private information service, nor was he the last. He did not seem to realize, however, that most first-rate correspondents genuinely dislike to convey the impression that they are trading information when they seek embassy reactions to pending developments of which American officials have not yet become aware. Consequently, it was a policy that was likely to result in diminishing returns and, eventually, some awkward situations, even embarrassment.

When Louis Rukeyser replaced Potter as the Baltimore *Sun*'s correspondent, he was not quite so ready to become a part of the inner circle, and the Ambassador's regard for the *Sun* apparently dwindled. At one time, he is reputed to have expressed a low opinion of the extent of the *Sun*'s readership and influence in Washington. The embassy at the time was trying its best to swing the American Government behind the proposed Indian steel mill at Bokharo, but many of the correspondents had their doubts. Sol Sanders of *U.S. News & World Report* wrote a blistering article criticizing the Bokharo project. Rukeyser also developed a great deal of information adverse to the embassy line and presented it effectively in the Baltimore *Sun*. While the correspondents were not solely responsible for the collapse of the Bokharo deal, their efforts probably contributed to the air of disillusionment in both the American Congress and the Indian Government, which finally withdrew its request for aid at Bokharo.[27] In any event, nothing more was heard about Ambassador Galbraith's estimate of the Baltimore *Sun*'s influence. And in the *Sun*'s office, a few ancient copyreaders might have been pardoned if they thought they heard a snort of delight from the editorial sanctum where H. L. Mencken had daubed acid on the foibles of the mighty and the "booboisie" for so many years.

When Chester Bowles returned to India for his second tour as Ambassador, and Galbraith went back to Harvard, an entirely different relationship grew up between the embassy and the correspondents. Some of the American regulars had been rotated to new assignments, while others had been dispatched to such widely separated points as Cyprus and Viet-Nam. Only the Washington *Star* and the Chicago *Daily News* had been added to the short list of news organizations that were represented in India by regularly assigned American correspondents, while N.B.C. had withdrawn.

Among those who remained, Bowles had remarkably few favorites, and he had the old professional's pride in reliance on his own methods for gathering information. It was no secret to the correspondents that the Ambassador believed that India was undercovered by all except a few American news organizations, that most of the correspondents assigned to India stayed too much in New Delhi, and that the net result was unsatisfactory. He also challenged the attitude of most correspondents, arguing, "You always say the pail is half empty. Why don't you say the pail is half full?" And, from time to time, he would bedevil editors at home to send correspondents to India, even if only for short periods, to increase both the amount and the diversity of information available to the American public.

Bowles was then sixty-three years old—a vigorous, gray-haired six-footer with a prize-fighter's face and a lantern jaw, a ready flow of talk for all occasions, and a calm, assured, confident manner. He often made his visitors feel more important than they perhaps were—the product of his long experience in advertising—and he was both courteous and encouraging by turn. Moreover, he was a shrewd man and a wise one, much shrewder and wiser than the correspondents gave him credit for being, and he was entirely unselfish in the promotion of American interests in India. He had undergone an operation for Parkinson's disease, which would have sent a less determined and a less motivated man into retirement.

No ambassador seeks to antagonize a press corps, and few have either the skill or the courage to joust with them on their own terms. Bowles had both, held his ground, and even managed to attain a slight advantage at times on issues that were in the news. But where he dealt with his own government, he was at a hopeless disadvantage on a few occasions because he was unable to control the news flow from India. On one occasion, he wanted to see Y. B. Chavan, the Indian Defense Minister, about India's interest in military supplies and had sent a memo about it to Washington. But before the meeting, in Washington's own inscrutable way, the news of the memo leaked to the press and was speedily reported in the Indian newspapers. Chavan, accordingly, read all about Bowles's intentions in the projected interview, which caused the Ambassador to cancel his talk for fear that the Indians would think he had inspired the leak. In India itself, he had better luck. While on tour with some of the American correspondents, they happened to stumble on a source of valuable information about the Chinese Communists, which might have been sealed up through premature disclosures. Bowles asked them not to write about the matter and they agreed to grant his request.

It was evident, however, that the familiar dichotomy between the interests of the press and government was often present among Americans in New Delhi in a particularly virulent form. Something about the atmosphere in India seemed to bring out the entirely human urge to be as argumentative, brutally frank, and even combative on occasion as some of the more pugnacious Indians. Among the ambassadors of recent years, only Ellsworth Bunker seemed to have escaped the scars of journalistic controversy in India. And among American officials who visited India, Arthur Goldberg, then a member of the Supreme Court, was one of the few to be gratefully remembered by the press for going out of his way to meet correspondents despite the effort of a foundation official to keep his presence a secret.

The abrasiveness among Americans in India sometimes created divisions in the embassy itself and in its USIS adjunct. During the second Bowles ambassadorship, the group immediately around him was known rather enviously as the "Chet set" by the embassy outsiders, who quickly communicated the designation to the correspondents. And during the Eisenhower Administration, Arthur Goodfriend, then a USIS official in New Delhi, caused an uproar within the agency with a memo that said in part:

> The vast majority of the materials placed by USIS in the Indian press is either flaccid, or feckless, or so far removed from the problems and realities of Indian life as to impel wonderment about the morality of an agency that dispenses such stuff in a country where newsprint sells at $200 a ton. . . . How is it possible, in an entire month, to avoid the placement of one single identifiable positive piece clearly contrived to dispel the Indian prejudice against the alleged crimes of American capitalism, racism, materialism, imperialism? To what degree, finally, may our successful intrusion in Indian news columns be considered a form of cultural imperialism —and of a debased culture at that?

This was, to USIS, a "proof of unwillingness to play on the team," and the offending Goodfriend, a capable official, was banished forthwith from India.[28]

One looks in vain in the excellent pamphlet "The American Ambassador," a study by the Jackson Subcommittee on Governmental Operations of the United States, for anything that bears even remotely on an ambassador's responsibility for the public dissemination of information about his country. The only reference to these duties is the following: "With respect to representation, it used to be that an Ambassador represented his sovereign at the court of the other sovereign. Now things are different. An Ambassador still has the tedious round of official parties and entertainment. He must still participate in the pomp and ceremony of official life. But he must also hold the hands of newsmen . . ."[29]

The concept of Bowles (and some other American ambassadors) as a professional hand-holder would have brought rueful smiles to many a foreign correspondent, had they known of it. In New Delhi, it was not possible thus simply to dismiss either the foreign correspondents, the officials in the Indian Government who were in contact with them, or those in the various embassies who had a direct interest in what was said about India (and themselves) abroad.

The controversy over the reporting of the Indian food shortages of 1964–66 was a case in point. The outburst of food riots in the summer of 1964, together with the publication of items in the Indian press about people eating grass in Rajasthan, led to the use of somewhat more material of the same general nature in the relatively few American and British publications that paid attention to news from India. Of the handful of correspondents who remained in New Delhi (others were on vacation, in Saigon, and one was in Cyprus), only one or two were able to keep out of the controversy that developed with Ambassador Bowles. Both he and officials of the Indian Government objected to what they called sensational reporting, but the correspondents insisted that they were only sticking to the facts.

For example, the New York *Herald Tribune,* which had no correspondent in India at the time, rewrote wire-service reports and published a 250-word item on Page 15 under the headline, "INDIA FACES FOOD CRISIS," which began as follows:

The Indian government started raiding wholesale food grain dealers and slapped price controls on the grain amid near-riots and a food price crisis characterized by Prime Minister Lal Bahadur Shastri as "the most formidable and urgent problem facing India today."

The crisis wasn't something that was about to happen. With millions on a near-starvation diet of 1,000 calories or less a day, it had happened. On Tuesday [July 28] the belly-pinched people of Hapur, north of New Delhi, were reported to have entered a storage center and helped themselves to some rice before police beat them off. Markets closed in panic. A returning CARE assistant mission chief said half-starved people in Calcutta have been raiding stores, stopping food trucks to shout: "We want rice." [30]

Sharokh Sabavala, of the *Christian Science Monitor*, graduate of Oxford, ex-captain in the British Indian army, ex-editor of the Bombay *Free Press Journal*, was one of the few who interpreted the problem for the American reader. As one who could not be accused of being either sensational or anti-Indian, he wrote an article in the *Monitor* entitled "Facets of Hunger," which aroused unusual interest at the American embassy:

I have heard many erudite, balanced and reasoned explanations as to why every so often India runs into the mesh of a lean year. But no one has even begun to explain why so many Indians who seem to know so much about the root causes of their difficulties do so little to fit their thinking and their habits to changing circumstances.

One explanation concerns the massive and steady shipment of food-grains from the United States. An Indian opinion section, while grateful for the sustained support, is veering to the belief that it is engendering unnecessary complacency, even lethargy. But suppose the United States stopped its imports. Would the Indian people, shedding the superstitions and dogma of centuries, rise up as one man to protect their crops from their friends—the cow and the monkey? Would they, as they often talk of doing, put their country on an emergency war footing with the single intention of growing more and more food until self-sufficiency is reached? Would they force their government to build silos and warehouses and fertilizer factories before steel mills and atomic powerhouses?

Sabavala went on to discuss the American decision to supply India with emergency shipments of wheat in 1964-65:

After 17 years of independence and planned effort, my personal reaction was not one of gratitude, but a feeling of humiliation over the seemingly endless chain of handsome presents. The general reaction, however, was different. Said more than one newsman: "The announcement is appropriate. It will further discourage the activities of hoarders and black marketeers." No one commented on the massive failure that it seemed, to me, to represent.[31]

The American correspondents were more restrained; however, at one point in the developing story, a group of them came to the American embassy in response to an invitation and received lectures from embassy economists on what they called "improvements in India's economic position." When this exercise was over, and the somewhat bewildered correspondents wondered what they were supposed to do with this nonnews, an embassy official said loudly, "Now let's get this food shortage story straightened out." No correspondent was willing to concede that any "straightening out" was necessary, however.

It was then that Ambassador Bowles made a considered decision to do his own reporting. Whether he feared an adverse Congressional reaction to further large-scale aid to India or an attack on all foreign aid during the then maturing Presidential campaign was not completely certain. But in any case, it seemed to some that these elements and a long-time interest in the well-being of the Indian people led him, as the master publicist he was, to take part in a skirmish with the correspondents.

First, he fired off a letter of protest, which appeared on Page 1 of the New York *Times* and was widely used elsewhere, too. It denied that there was starvation in India and ascribed the Indian food shortage to hoarding and the insistence of more Indians on eating more wheat and rice rather than their former diet of coarser food grains.[32] Next, he wrote an article for the Sunday magazine section of the New York *Times,* which was duly published under the heading, "Not Enough Food for Too Many People." With a tilt of his lance at the foreign correspondents, he observed that it was "not surprising that some reports have been alarmist," and pointed out that many of the food riots had been the work of Communists. This was his assessment:

> My appraisal would be that India is not facing anything approaching a famine. Food shortages do exist, however, and in a country which is accustomed to a high degree of price stability, prices have risen sharply. As a consequence, there is widespread, often bitter, criticism of the government, and until the fall harvest in October and November, the situation will remain critical. It may, indeed, get worse before it gets better . . .[33]

The Ambassador's final words were prophetic. In 1966, the worst drought of the century imperiled India; an expert, testifying before a House Agricultural subcommittee in Washington, predicted that "tens of millions will starve." It was much more extreme than any journalist's forecast, although certainly the threat of famine was rising. The United States already had begun rushing a new consignment of 4.5 million tons of grain to India, and made a new grant of $100 million for economic aid. Many other nations joined in the effort to help the people of the stricken subcontinent. *Time* magazine predicted with a grim flourish, "Until India's parched acres begin to flower, huge shipments of U.S.

food—perhaps as much as 15,000,000 tons a year—will be needed to help the subcontinent's masses fend off starvation . . ." [34]

In this extremity, not even masterful news management could make a bad situation look good, and not even the gallant Bowles tried. Yet his anxiety was understandable in terms of U.S. hopes for India and India's continued reliance on American foreign aid. India had been the beneficiary of American aid for years; of the $80 billion given away by the United States after World War II, the Indians had received nearly 8 per cent. Moreover, of the $2.3-million economic-aid budget of the Agency for International Development in fiscal year 1965, India was one of the top recipients—a situation that continued the following year.

Commenting on the uses of foreign aid, Bowles once wrote:

> With 75 per cent of Asia's industrial output, millions of skilled and potentially skilled workers and, in the case of India, ample natural resources, Japan and India constitute the only effective Asian industrial counterbalance to China. With her long religious and cultural heritage, . . . India is by far the most significant Asian spiritual and ideological counterbalance to China . . .
>
> American policy makers can never afford to forget that the strategic keys to the future of free Asia are India and Japan . . . Unless these two nations maintain both their independence and their progress, historians may some day describe what we now call "free Asia" as no more than a brief and passing phase in the upheaval that swept over all of Asia following World War II . . . [35]

The Ambassador and the correspondents thus looked at India with entirely different attitudes and objectives. In a time of drastic food shortage, the Ambassador was preoccupied with maintaining American confidence in India, particularly in Congress, as an urgent policy matter. The correspondents, however, could have no other immediate concern except their reportage—the complete story of India's food problem regardless of its political consequences. Both fulfilled their assignments.

The apparent rise of the United States in Indian esteem in the mid-1960's was particularly heartening to the American embassy. In the "prestige polls" that were shown to correspondents before the Kashmir war, the United States was depicted as a clear choice of the Indian public over the Soviet Union in every major population center except Calcutta. At a time when the United States was on the verge of overtaking the Soviet Union in the space race, the same polls showed that Indians accounted the United States to be the greatest military power, while the Soviet Union was given a lead in rocketry, space flights, and atomic energy.

The change in the image of the United States in India came at about the time of the Chinese Communist invasion of 1962, if the polls were correct. An India-wide survey just before the invasion, and another just afterward, indicated that the approximately 2,000 persons in the sample had markedly shifted their sympathies from Communist China and the Soviet Union to the United States and Great Britain. The United States had a 9 per cent rise when respondents were asked which countries India should cooperate with, while the Soviet Union suffered a 27 per cent drop. China, which had only a 3 per cent response before the invasion, lost all its adherents afterward. However, nonalignment continued to attract a large following.[36] With the Sino-Soviet split, the Soviet Union was able to detach itself in part from the anger directed against Peking.

It was a time when USIS stepped up its efforts to bring a greater awareness of the United States to the Indian public, a massive job which promised no marked change in sentiment for some years to come. The USIS program was directed primarily at special publics— government officials, Parliament, teachers, students, business and labor groups, scientists, and various other specialized groups. Some of the criticisms of the Goodfriend era had been absorbed; now, there was no monumental effort to persuade the Indian press to print odd bits and pieces of USIS releases. A study showed that while USIS remained a fairly important source of news for the vernacular press in India, the English-language newspapers used very little USIS material.[37]

The USIS staff of 68 Americans and 630 Indians, distributed through ten offices in India, including the four major ones in New Delhi, Bombay, Madras, and Calcutta, concentrated on the maintenance of libraries; the publication of book reprints, pamphlets, and magazines; a large film service; touring exhibits; and a well-developed lecture program. The usual press facilities were also maintained. As a total effort, the USIS budget for India exceeded $5 million annually in the mid-1960's and was likely to go higher.

Apart from the embassy, its adjuncts, and the mass media, one other aspect of American representation in India was of major importance— the activities of the private foundations. Such agencies as the Ford Foundation, the Rockefeller Foundation, and the Asia Foundation contributed in many facets of Indian life and were welcomed because they were nongovernmental organizations. Everything from urban development and family planning to rural progress and mass communications studies were of interest to them. While the government for the most part conducted the growing exchange-of-persons program, some of the foundations did a good deal of the same work on their own.

It often happened that a foundation expert on Indian economics or family planning had a better background in his field than government officers who had been more recently assigned to India. Such authorities, therefore, were sought out by knowledgeable correspondents and frequently became a not unimportant source of news. However, the last thing a foundation wanted in India was publicity for its efforts; the chance of arousing an adverse reaction from politically motivated and usually anti-American sources was too great. For the most part, the foundations' good works were seen but not extensively advertised.

Much the same feeling permeated the American business community in India. There was still an enormous amount of obstruction for both business and industry in India, particularly when it was conducted by a non-Indian concern. While a considerable part of the trouble was caused by maladministration and the Indian devotion to multiple inquiries and multiple forms for anything that pertained to government, a certain amount of anti-American feeling had to be taken into account. Consequently, the businessman kept his head down and hoped for the best. When correspondents sought him out, he generally preferred to say as little as possible for the record and kept everything he could on a background basis. The nationalist tide was running so strongly in the large cities of India that it didn't seem very practical to call attention to foreign operations.

And yet, the old Indian attitudes were changing. The Shastri and Gandhi governments did not pound at the United States for escalating the Viet-Nam war, as Nehru almost certainly would have. Nor was there more than a perfunctory protest in the Parliament against the presence of American naval power in the Indian Ocean. Privately, the Indian Government welcomed its presence as added insurance against the possibility of a new Chinese attack. In the power structure in New Delhi, there was a growing feeling of respect for the United States, aside from its sizable contributions for Indian military and economic aid, that had not existed to any great degree in Nehru's time. Even among the impatient young intellectuals, there was no longer so strong a disposition to dance to Moscow's tune. Had it not been for the differences with Pakistan over Kashmir, which aroused feeling against the United States in both New Delhi and Rawalpindi, the influence of the United States might have been much greater in South Asia than it actually was.

In spite of the fissiparous tendencies that threatened to overwhelm India—the terrors of communal strife, the differences over language, the shame of caste discrimination, and the disgrace of political corruption—there was an abiding faith among many of the more thoughtful Americans in India that the resources of the Indian spirit would surmount these threats and that India would remain unified.

4. INDIA'S NEIGHBORS

In the early days of the United Nations, India's representative, Sir Ramaswami Mudaliar, sometimes would try to call attention to his country's plight by exclaiming, "Look at India! She is surrounded by a wall of fire!" He did not make much of an impression on American opinion. Within a generation, however, large sections of India's borderlands either had been threatened or set aflame by conflicts with old foes. In some areas, an uncertain truce had been restored in one way or another; elsewhere, the fighting could not always be immediately contained, thus continuing to upset India's faltering economy.

To the north, Communist China mustered its forces behind the Himalayan ramparts. From Tibet, seized and subdued by the Chinese in 1957, there came only the silence of the grave. Frightened Nepal permitted Chinese roadbuilders to push a highway through toward Katmandu. And in the tiny Indian principality of Sikkim, a young king, Palden Thondup Namgyal, ruled with his youthful American bride, the former Hope Cooke of New York, knowing all the while that only the Indian army could preserve his throne.

To the east, Burma was effectively sealed off by the constant efforts of its dictator, General Ne Win, to placate the Chinese, and it had already begun driving out its Indian merchants. And on the border of East Pakistan, there was a brooding hostility, broken now and then by the most ferocious communal rioting. In the Naga Hills district of Assam, for nearly a decade, a bitter rebellion by the rebel tribesmen had at last been contained with the conclusion of a cease-fire, but it did not contribute greatly to the return of tranquility in eastern India. The tribal grievances were too deep-seated to be dissipated at once.

To the south, there had been at least a temporary break in the pressures on India with the defeat of the Communist-influenced regime of Mrs. Sirimavo Bandaranaike, the world's first woman prime minister, and the rise to power of a somewhat shaky conservative, pro-Western government. Yet, even as the new Cambridge-educated Prime Minister, Dudley Senanayake, took office on March 25, 1965, he was obliged to make a deferential bow to nonalignment because his United National Party had not achieved an absolute majority. He gave India some hope. He had, after all, committed himself to block what he charged was an agreement by his predecessor to permit China to use the Ceylonese port of Trincomalee as a military base against India.[38]

Had Communist influence continued unchecked in Ceylon, it could have been a very serious matter. For in the nearby Indian state of Kerala, the pro-Peking Communists in 1965 had been able to elect the largest single party bloc of candidates to the State Legislature, although most of them were obliged to campaign from jail. Of the forty Communists, twenty-nine remained in prison immediately after the election, and the badly defeated Congress Party combined with the Moslem League to try to govern under the direction of the national government. The arrests, coinciding with the seizure of nearly 1,000 others throughout India on December 30 and 31, 1964, had been justified by the Home Ministry on the ground that the "left Communist Party" had planned to "launch a violent revolutionary struggle, which they hope will coincide with a fresh Chinese thrust on our borders." [39]

It was in the west, however, that India had to fight off the most immediate threat to her stability when the always difficult relationship with Pakistan flared into war over Kashmir. The U.N. cease-fire ended the fighting, and the agreement at Tashkent led to the withdrawal of both sides to their previously held positions. But after eighteen years, the Kashmir crisis remained unsettled, and Pakistan and India continued their tense and uncertain relationship. Thus, Sir Ramaswami Mudaliar's image of a beleaguered India was verging uncomfortably on reality in the latter half of the decade.

One of the most unsettling factors in the subcontinent was the fluctuation of Pakistani policy between East and West and the effort of Rawalpindi to set up some kind of bargaining position between Peking and Washington. Along the road from the airport to the center of Karachi (Pakistan's largest city)—a fine new concrete highway built with American aid—a big billboard flashed a colorful advertisement for travel to Communist China. "See Canton and Shanghai via Pakistan International Airways" was the persuasive message. The new service, initiated in 1963, was so popular that the two weekly PIA flights to China (using Boing 707's) were soon crammed to capacity.

In Karachi, with its restless 2 million population, there were other signs of the divisive struggle that was going on in the fifth most populous nation on earth. Along a broad modern boulevard leading to the main section of the city was a magnificent new Intercontinental Hotel, as American as Park Avenue but nowhere near as expensive. The unmistakable stamp of American tourism shone from its glistening exterior, and every concession to mass American culture could be found inside, from bone-chilling air conditioning to red-jacketed waiters ceremoniously bearing a hamburger on a roll.

Yet, sad to relate, relatively few American tourists reveled in this Pakistani Valhalla, cast in the Hilton image. Its most prominent guests soon after its opening were clusters of dour Chinese diplomats from Peking. On one memorable occasion, a group of Chinese generals in loose, baggy uniforms ostentatiously paraded through the lobby, saluting smiling Pakistanis and one rather startled American, to a fleet of well-polished Ford Galaxies bearing small Chinese and Pakistani banners.

The cause of Pakistan's split personality in international affairs was due to its President, Field Marshal Mohammad Ayub Khan, who was at once the source of its foreign and domestic policies and of any public intelligence that could be obtained about them from within his country. His strength was his domestic success. It was under his regime, beginning in 1958, that Pakistan had been brought almost to the point of agricultural self-sufficiency with American help, producing nearly enough rice and wheat to feed the 40 million people of West Pakistan and the 60 million people of East Pakistan. His regime, too, had boosted the country's gross national product by 5.4 per cent a year for the first four years of the 1960's. As a result, despite a bumper population increase of 2.8 per cent a year, the per capita income had jumped from $67 in 1959-60 to $75 in 1963-64. Pakistan's first two Five Year Plans, largely financed by the United States with the help of a consortium, had come nearer to achieving their goals than most such projects in Asia.[40]

With such a record, it was no wonder that the Pakistanis had chosen to follow him, wherever he led. In 1965, he had run up a two-to-one victory over seventy-one-year-old Miss Fatima Jinnah, sister of the late founder of Pakistan, Mohammed Ali Jinnah, in a Presidential contest that was decided by 80,000 popularly chosen electors. Miss Jinnah had accused him of creating an "atmosphere laden with fear and reeking with corruption" and had called upon her people to follow her toward a more democratic government. However, the government belonged to Ayub, and Miss Jinnah had to accept her defeat in relative obscurity.[41]

Pakistan's ties with the West, based on its membership in SEATO and the Baghdad Pact, began to be loosened. Ayub made no secret of his belief that increased American military aid for India would eventually be used against Pakistan. After concluding a border agreement with Peking in 1963, he felt no hesitation about a trip to the Chinese capital in the spring of 1965 to confer with Foreign Minister Chen Yi. When he returned, he won the praise of his sycophantic press.

Shortly before, *Jang,* an Urdu newspaper with a 78,000 circulation, the largest in the country, had sounded an anti-American theme: "As long as the United States is allowed to remain in the area, she will continue to involve countries of the area in war. This is because the United States is out to encircle and destroy the People's Republic of China. But all countries of the area except India have friendly relations with China and are confident of her help in adverse circumstances." Peking did not disappoint its new friend. An interest-free $60-million loan was China's way of showing appreciation.[42]

Only the two American wire services and the New York *Times* regularly maintained correspondents in Karachi at that time, and the pressure on Americans for self-censorship was so great that it was all they could do merely to send the formal news. But a touring correspondent, Marquis W. Childs, of the St. Louis *Post-Dispatch,* took a relatively charitable view of the proceedings in Rawalpindi. Without any restraints on him, and with no necessity to appease the Pakistanis to keep himself from being ejected from their country, he wrote:

Understandably, the United States is not happy over the growing community of interest between Pakistan and China. The American line is that this is seduction and that sooner or later disillusionment will come as Peking replaces the carrot with the stick under the Chinese policy of divide and rule in all of Asia. But the Pakistanis insist they know just what they are doing and how far they can go. Certainly, no one could accuse this strongly individualistic Muslim people of being pro-Communist.[43]

Ayub's problem was to keep the unhappy and overcrowded East Pakistanis in union with their fellow nationals in the west, 1,000 miles away. The fighting in the Rann of Kutch and in Kashmir helped him create a feeling of common purpose, but at a tremendous and eventually unbearable cost. The Pakistani military machine found in Kashmir that it couldn't keep going merely on the fighting words from Peking against the combined efforts of the United States and the Soviet Union to force an end to the fighting. Thus, West Pakistan relapsed into an angry mood of such an unpredictable nature that the press was forbidden to publish the news of Pakistan's troop withdrawals after the agreement at Tashkent. However, if there was any wavering in East Pakistan about the benefits of so difficult a union with Rawalpindi, the fanatical Jan Sangh of India with its continual threats against Muslims kept the two parts of the severed nation together. Fear, too, was a powerful motive in the divided subcontinent.

During the initial period of friendship with Peking, the Pakistanis saw their few newspapers flop over from the West with bewildering rapidity. The Pakistan *Times,* for example, was quick to rate China's friendship as the "choicest fruit of Ayub's foreign policy." [44] As further evidence of change, UPI was forced to stop distributing news in Pakistan when it refused to channel its report through a government-controlled news agency under conditions of which it could not approve. It wasn't necessary to bar correspondents from the country, as Sukarno had done in Indonesia, because very few were regularly assigned to

Pakistan. Generally, the New Delhi correspondents also were responsible for East and West Pakistan, too.

Among the more sophisticated Pakistanis, there was a good deal of resentment because of the government's rigid imposition of controls on the domestic press and its attempts to harass the foreign correspondents. As early as March, 1962, all foreign news agencies were ordered to distribute their news exclusively through national Pakistani agencies. There were two—the Associated Press of Pakistan and the Pakistan Press Association, both heavily subsidized and both government-controlled. For a while, there was procrastination; then, in late November, 1963, the order to the foreign agencies was enforced.

The domestic press curbs were tightened at about the same time. The *Civil and Military Gazette* closed, presumably at the publisher's own decision to avoid further financial loss, but probably some government pressure was also involved. The Press Information Department ordered all reporters, including foreign correspondents, to file answers to a government questionnaire. An accreditation committee in Rawalpindi then denied further accreditation to a number of Pakistani reporters, in effect depriving them of their livelihood as journalists.

Because commercial advertising was almost nonexistent in Pakistan, the nearly 100 daily newspapers in the country were virtually dependent for their existence on government support. It was widely believed, since the total press circulation was less than 500,000, that there eventually would be only one English-language and one vernacular newspaper published in Pakistan's major cities. This was, however, merely a surmise, but it kept rebellious journalists in line. It was also likely that the two national agencies would be merged. In 1966, the Associated Press of Pakistan still was distributing Reuters and the AP, while the Pakistan Press Association was putting out Agence France-Presse and the Deutsche Press Agentur. Of course, the copy was closely edited. The New China News Agency was often used, while Tass was almost as unpopular as the American services.

These and the Indians were the principal news organizations represented in Karachi; others had stringers. When there was fighting, as in the Rann of Kutch or Kashmir, the "fire brigade" arrived to do its hasty job.

During the long dull periods, Pakistan was not a particularly pleasant place for the few American correspondents who had to stay there. If a correspondent sent a dispatch abroad that was not pleasing to the regime, he could expect to be denounced by the Pakistani press. If he happened by chance to write something favorable to Pakistan in any dispute involving the Indians, he could just as readily expect to be quoted with approval. But any favorable mention of the Indians in dispatches was regarded as something akin to treason.

Pakistan could be a nightmare. A correspondent could be harassed in many petty ways, even dragged into court on trumped-up charges. Then, too, dispatches that were inconvenient could be delayed until they had lost their timeliness. All these things happened to American journalists in Pakistan at one time or another.

As one correspondent said:

> It became an endurance contest merely to stay on the job in Pakistan. A correspondent had to work hard if only to keep his mind from reeling. There was astonishingly little to read. Pakistani officials merely shrugged or laughed off requests for information. They had nothing to worry about. A correspondent was almost alone. Therefore, they paid little attention to him. All in all, after working in Pakistan, it was a pleasure to be assigned to New Delhi.

In a country with a literacy problem as great as Pakistan's (some estimates placed literacy at only 19 per cent in the mid-1960's), Radio Pakistan was a more important channel than the press for placing the government's daily version of events before the citizenry. Just how far the state radio's influence extended over its people, particularly in distant East Pakistan, was problematical. There were only an estimated 850,000 radio receivers in the whole country in 1964, by no means enough to cover the population.[45] For the semiliterate and illiterate villagers, life went on pretty much as it always had. What news there was usually came by word of mouth. The outside world was seldom perceived, except in the most confused terms.

Consequently, it lay within Ayub's power to eradicate quickly the image of a beneficent United States that had existed in his country for much of the time since its independence. Although it was difficult to imagine this Sandhurst-educated general maintaining friendship with Peking, after pursuing for so long a policy of cooperation with the West, this was the position he adopted before the Kashmir war. Ayub's Government had in fact become desperate. It wanted a counterweight to growing Indian power, and, receiving no satisfaction from Washington, in consequence turned to Peking. In the aftermath of the three-week war, it became evident that all powers concerned had lost except the Chinese Communists.

Why could the Kashmir issue not have been settled through compromise between India and Pakistan? Were both governments and their peoples locked into such a rigid position that unrest and suspicion had to be a way of life for the unfortunate people located on the border and in Kashmir? Frank Moraes, the editor of the *Indian Express,* was one of the very few leaders of opinion on the subcontinent who did not think so in the dangerous time of the mid-1960's. He publicly proposed the partition of Kashmir in the critical summer of 1964. It was his belief that the largely non-Muslim areas of Jammu and Ladakh should go to India and the heart of the area, the beautiful and wonderfully productive Vale of Kashmir, should go to Pakistan, because it was as Muslim as "Azad" ("Free") Kashmir, which the Pakistanis already occupied. His plan, he wrote, would "free India of an incubus which has weighed heavily and profitlessly on us in terms of money, lives, continuous harassment, drain of administrative ability and loss of international good will and prestige."

Moraes called Kashmir nothing more than a sieve that was absorbing tremendous Indian effort. With partition, he argued, a new and far stronger frontier state could be created out of Jammu and the Himachal Pradesh, straddling the northern Kangra area of the Punjab. "This state, with the hard cushion of a resolute Punjab beside it, would strengthen the protective defense screen on our Western frontier, provide gainful employment and insure productive returns for the benefit of the whole country," he concluded. "We would no longer be haunted or distracted by the expensive, elusive ghost of the Valley of Kashmir . . ." [46]

Moraes was not the only journalist who urged a reasonable settlement of the Kashmir issue. The editor of the *Hindustan Times,* Shri Mulgaokar, also urged some form of settlement, although he did not go quite as far as his distinguished colleague. With these exceptions, it was conventional for both the Pakistani and the Indian press to drop all thought of responsibility in both the reporting and commentary on Kashmir. All the Pakistani press had become a mere propaganda machine; on Kashmir, a very large part of the Indian press was in almost as bad a situation. The leadership of Moraes and Mulgaokar in urging India to consider an equitable solution was, therefore, a noteworthy development in the history of the Indian press—one that had been seldom emulated in Asia.

But Kashmir, through the hot-headed utterances of a generation of Hindu and Muslim patriots, had become a holy cause. The faltering Nehru, in the last months of his life, was still mystically drawn to the concept of an all-India Kashmir, the home of his forebears. It was he who had said after independence in 1947 that "there should be no forced marriage between Kashmir and Pakistan." It was he, too, who had accepted the instrument of accession to India, signed by the frightened Maharajah of the Princely State of Jammu and Kashmir as Pakistani tribesmen swept over his borders. Indian armies had seized most of the territory, with a 4.5 million population that was predominantly Muslim in an area about the same size as Idaho's. Despite everything the weaker Pakistani forces could do at the time, the Indians had held on and confirmed the reality of their occupation with the agreement on a U.N. cease-fire on January 1, 1949.

That was the way matters had remained. The United Nations had called for a plebiscite to enable the people of Kashmir to choose whether they wanted to accede to India or Pakistan. Pakistan had eagerly agreed. India had rejected such a vote, arguing that the Maharajah's instrument of accession was a sufficient proof that this was Indian territory. The proposed plebiscite also had the support of the "Lion of Kashmir," Sheik Mohammed Abdullah, who resumed his campaign for an independent Kashmir after his release from an Indian prison in 1964. Just before his death, Nehru vaguely inquired into the possibility of a confederation between India, Pakistan, and Kashmir, but Ayub rejected it. Various other schemes had been proposed—a condominium, with India and Pakistan jointly responsible for Kashmir's defense; a U.N. trusteeship for five or ten years, followed by a plebiscite; and a moratorium for two years on any moves whatever in Kashmir.[47] Nothing came of any of them.

There was a momentary hope when the Shastri Administration began making a new examination of the Indian position on Kashmir. But even though the new Prime Minister went to Karachi in October, 1964, to discuss the matter with Ayub Khan, nothing came of it. "I made our position very plain," Shastri said later. "I told him that my people felt just as strongly about the Kashmir issue as his people did. I told him that India wasn't going to change its position on Kashmir and that, if we wanted to improve relations between our two countries, we ought to tackle other problems one by one. I thought we agreed on that, but I guess President Ayub wasn't satisfied to do it that way." [48]

A considerable number of the people of Kashmir turned in this extremity to Sheik Abdullah. He was a commanding figure, this broad-shouldered, bearlike six-footer, who strode about Srinagar, New Delhi, and Karachi with an astrakhan cap perched on his balding head. As a result of his efforts to solve the Kashmir problem, he had spent ten years in Indian prisons. In India, he had attracted a certain amount of sympathy because of his devotion to his cause and his affinity with the many journalists who constantly sought him out. He was easy enough to find. Miss Mridula Sarabhai, daughter of a Hindu industralist and friend of Nehru, had given him the shelter of her home in New Delhi off the Rajdoot Marg.

There was no doubt that he was a hero to his followers in Kashmir.

It was a moving experience to see thousands of people cluster about him upon his arrival at the Srinagar Airport and, at a single movement of his hands, sit obediently in a circle about him and listen to him speak. When he departed, his joyous people decked him with garlands, pelted him with flowers, and called him their savior.

Yet, for all his crusading activity, Sheik Abdullah was a realist. He often expressed great doubt that anything could be accomplished to help unravel the tragic complications over Kashmir until after the Indian elections of 1967. He pointed out that both the ferociously nationalistic Jan Sangh Party, on the far right in India, and the Menonites, followers of Krishna Menon, and their Communist allies on the far left, were against any concessions to Pakistan on Kashmir. While the Shastri government had made timid moves toward eventual conciliation in the period before the three-week war, the conflict ended any immediate prospect of negotiations. It was almost symbolic that the Sheik and all other prominent leaders of the Kashmir self-determination movement were thrust back into Indian prisons. Even Miss Sarabhai, a tiny spinster in her fifties, was not spared; under Defense of India rules, she was ordered into confinement at her home in her native city of Ahmedabad.

Both Moraes and Mulgaokar had played important roles in persuading Nehru to release the Sheik from prison, although they scarcely favored his point of view. Together with a few foreign correspondents, they and a small circle of other Indian journalists gave publicity to his ideas in order to try to unfreeze the Indian position in Kashmir. It was a public-spirited exercise of the journalist's function—which was exceedingly rare in Asia. Political leaders in India and Pakistan might well have been bold enough to try to emulate it. Because they did not, any possibility of solving the problem through reason vanished, and both nations made their futile resort to arms. Thereafter, neither Shastri and Ayub at Tashkent, nor Indira Gandhi and Ayub on their separate visits to Washington, made any real progress toward a settlement of the Kashmir issue.[49]

In retrospect, there could be only a melancholy contemplation of what might have been if Frank Moraes' proposed solution of the Kashmir problem had been submitted to negotiation. It was ironic, indeed, that a journalist—and not a diplomat—should have acted in the role of a disinterested statesman.

There were, however, few such prophets in journalism. In the difficult and demanding job of maintaining an even flow of significant information about the nations of Asia, there was often too much guessing and too little knowledge, too much effort to pander to the prejudices of large masses of readers and too little public-spirited determination to tell them some of the unpleasant truths that they did not want to hear. In the smaller Asian nations, this was also one of the failings of foreign correspondents.

Newsweek, for example, made this prophecy when Mrs. Bandaranaike submitted her Communist-supported government to the test of a free election in Ceylon in 1965, hoping to be re-elected to the prime ministership she had inherited from her assassinated husband:

> The victory . . . will go to the candidate who can garner the biggest share of the Buddhist vote, which makes up 64 per cent of the Ceylonese electorate. It was because of active support from Buddhist monks that Mrs. Bandaranaike's husband originally came to power. . . . No one knows for sure how strong their influence will be, but expectations are that it will not be strong enough to prevent Mrs. Bandaranaike from squeaking back to power.[50]

A week later, *Newsweek* overlooked its pre-election piece and reported what had actually happened:

> Ceylon's powerful Communists licked their wounds last week after a stunning electoral defeat. . . . The new Prime Minister, Dudley Senanayake, 53, who has held the post twice before, will have to rule with coalition partners like his predecessor. . . . Senanayake, who is personally pro-Western, has guaranteed a better deal for private enterprise and foreign investment . . .[51]

Newsweek's embarrassing experience was, of course, not unusual as election forecasts go. If it is often difficult to pick a winner in an American election, it was to be expected that the odds were against a right assessment being made in so distant and little-known a land as Ceylon. *Newsweek,* like the few other American news organizations that bothered to take notice of Ceylon, had only a stringer in Colombo and rarely sent in a staff man. Yet, in accordance with American journalistic practice, any election anywhere seemed to call for a forecast, reliable or not, even if many American readers couldn't readily locate Ceylon.

The island republic, which lies only thirty-one miles off the southern tip of India, is more important than its journalistic treatment indicates. It dominates the approach to the Indian Ocean. For many years, it supported a British naval base. Certainly, the Indians and the Chinese both recognized its strategic value. And with 10 million people—fourteen times the population of the Hawaiian Islands in four times their area—Ceylon needed foreign aid badly.

Almost from the time it turned itself from a British dominion into a republic tied to the Commonwealth in 1956, its troubles began. While its tea, rice, and tobacco crops were important, it could supply only half the food necessary to feed its people. It sought to raise their standard of living and, in the process, nationalized both British and American oil companies in 1962. Inflation was a result. The loss of $4 million a year in American economic assistance was another. Foreign-exchange reserves fell to their lowest point since 1941.[52] To add to all the rest of Ceylon's troubles, tensions increased between the majority Singhalese peoples and the Tamil minority, which had torn into each other in serious riots in 1958.

There had been a struggle for many years between the government and the eight daily newspapers in Ceylon. While their total circulation was estimated at only 350,000, their readership was put at more than 1 million in a land with 70 per cent literacy and a per capita income of $122 a year. The two English-language morning papers were read by the more influential people in and out of government; although the Singhalese papers were the most popular, more attention was probably paid to the Tamil ones. All except one of the papers was owned by two family newspaper chains, but for a long period they were able to maintain their independence.

A qualified American observer said of the Ceylon *Observer* during the period when A. G. T. ("Tarzie") Vittachi was its editor: "The *Observer* has more guts than any other newspaper in Ceylon. . . . Its editor is probably the most influential newspaperman here, the man most feared by government. His paper is a real watchdog of government and is a real friend of the West." [53]

After Vittachi relinquished his editorship and became the director of the Asian program of the International Press Institute, he examined the relationship between press and government in his native land and came to this unflattering conclusion:

The Ceylon government has apparently discovered that the Sword of Damocles can be used very effectively in place of the censor's scissors. In three years, seven different bills to nationalize or otherwise control the "dissemination of all news and views" have been passed by the cabinet whenever the press became critical of the cost of living or of the growing corruption in public life. These measures were never actually enacted— apparently on the rather canny reasoning that if the press can be threatened into conformity, why undertake the financial burden of running nationalized newspapers which, like most other state undertakings in Ceylon, is likely to be a business failure? [54]

In Ceylon's struggle for stability against the continued Communist efforts to foment racial and political strife, the press had a crucial role to play. But it could not operate with the heavy hand of government upon it. A restoration of the Ceylonese press to the vitality of Vittachi's time was even more essential than renewed millions in American foreign aid and the friendly support of India's Government. It was also not too much to expect that leading American news organizations would send a competent staff correspondent to Ceylon periodically to report on the continuing battle for the strategic island.

Ceylon could not be taken for granted. It was not foreordained to remain a part of the Western defense system, a sentinel guarding India's exposed southern flank.

Despite the uncertainties that clouded the future of Ceylon, as well as India's other neighbors, it remained within India's power to erect an atomic barrier formidable enough to give pause to any foe. But the government of Jawaharlal Nehru scornfully rejected atomic protection, either its own or from America, and the governments of Lal Bahadur Shastri and Indira Gandhi hesitated over an unenviable choice. Nehru, perhaps, may have thought that he had said the last word, shortly before his death in the spring of 1964, when he protested in the Indian Parliament against the presence of American surface warships armed with nuclear weapons in the Indian Ocean.

However, the Pandit's death and the explosion of the Chinese atomic bomb that October changed the minds of many in India about the desirability of an American nuclear presence in the Indian Ocean. By the end of the year, a U.S. Polaris submarine, capable of firing nuclear-tipped intermediate-range ballistic missiles, was stationed in Asian waters, and nobody in the Indian Government made a to-do about it.[55]

In an effort to stave off the rising demand in India for the manufacture of an Indian atomic bomb, which would have diverted precious funds from national development, Prime Minister Shastri even went so far as to propose that India and other nonnuclear nations receive a "guaranteed immunity against nuclear attack by China." It was clear that the United States was envisioned as one source of such a guarantee, which infuriated the bitterly anti-American editor of the *Times* of India, N. J. Nanporia. He wrote: "Does this mean that even without Soviet participation, a nuclear umbrella exclusively sponsored by the Western powers will be acceptable to New Delhi?" He went on with an effort to link the government with a proposal for a Western nuclear umbrella that had been advanced by Minoo R. Masani, secretary of the conservative (for India) Swatantra Party.[56]

Masani lost no time in striking back at Nanporia, "whose political line is well-known," saying:

Of course Mr. Nanporia would not like us to have that umbrella. He evidently wants to give the Soviet Union a veto . . . on our foreign policy. He wants to give the Soviet Union a veto on our security. He wants to give the Soviet Union a veto on our very survival. And this is really the issue. Is the guarantee good enough only if Soviet Russia joins in it? . . . I am sure it would be agreed that we cannot tolerate a Soviet veto when our very existence is at stake.[57]

In Nehru's time, the notion that India could not be nonaligned unless both the United States and the Soviet Union joined in providing atomic protection against China would have received a certain amount of approval. But the Shastri Government laid down no such qualification. Instead, even as Indira Gandhi came to power, the debate widened in India over the desirability of producing an Indian atomic bomb. The reality of vast and hostile Chinese armies on India's northern frontiers, backed up by nuclear power, had begun to shake some of the cobwebs out of the thinking on India's foreign policy.

The alternative to an Indian atomic bomb or to Indian dependence on guarantees against nuclear attack was Nehru's moral position of working for disarmament through the United Nations and somehow persuading Communist China to participate. But even the faithful B. K. Nehru, who had been the Pandit's secretary general of the Ministry for Foreign Affairs, conceded that it was now a risky policy. He added, "It is a legitimate risk, and it is a risk that has been taken in the interests of the world community." [58]

The Indian press joined in the debate with greater vigor. It echoed in the Lok Sabha, where eighty-six members representing all political parties submitted a demand to the government late in 1965 for approval of an Indian atomic bomb. The letter said: "India's survival both as a nation and a democracy, in the face of collusion between China and Pakistan, casts a clear and imperative duty on the government to make an immediate decision to develop our nuclear weapons."

It was a measure of the profound change in India that only a little more than a year before, in this same Lok Sabha, the old Pandit had professed shock at the very notion of American nuclear power in the Indian Ocean. There was a great deal more realism now. Nobody except the pro-Peking rabble rousers in India were inclined to ridicule President Johnson's pledge of "strong support" and his reaffirmation of American defense commitments in Asia. In this different India, there was favorable comment on the American guarantee, but it was not regarded as sufficient. The pressure rose on the government to go ahead with an Indian atomic bomb.[59] It was, sadly, a world in which there was no place for neutrals.

5. THE PRESS: FREE AND NOT SO FREE

For more than a century, there has been a certain amount of difficulty in bringing the news to the Indian subcontinent and almost as much, from time to time, in getting it out. Obstacles, natural and man-made, have cropped up with dismaying regularity. Whatever a correspondent may have thought of his term of service in India, he has seldom been bored. And if his clients have usually been quicker to criticize the incoming file than to praise it, that is the time-honored way of editors.

There was trouble from the beginning, when twenty-two-year-old Henry Michael Collins arrived in Bombay in 1866 as chief Far Eastern agent for Reuters and opened its service from London. The cable to India had not then been laid and Collins had to use overland lines through Persia and Russia to bring in the news. Persian nomads would take the wire down to reinforce primitive weapons. Whole tribes would use telegraph poles for target practice. Snow in the Caucasus snapped lines at inconvenient places during the winter. And on one celebrated occasion, after a cable was laid in the Persian Gulf, a whale promptly became entangled in it. But eventually, with the completion of the 1,800-mile cable across the Indian Ocean, the news got through regularly. It was a proud day for Collins when he flashed the result of the English Derby to his clients four minutes after the race had been run.[60] From that moment on, Reuters—to borrow an appropriate term—had the inside track in India.

It took years, however, for British correspondents to learn to deal with the best and the worst of India—to get the news in and to send it out. Among the most illustrious were the roving correspondent for the *Pioneer* of Allahabad, Rudyard Kipling, and the soldier-correspondent of the London *Morning Post* with the Malakand Field Force, Winston Churchill. But it was the workaday people of Reuters, like Henry Collins, who, by their example, taught the Indian press the value of foreign news. It was more important for him to bring the price of cotton to India from the great English centers in two minutes or less than it was for Kipling to chant of the white man's burden.

The United States took its news of India mainly from Reuters during the long reign of the grand cartel of news agencies, finally broken by the independence of the UP under Roy Howard and the abrogation by the AP of its agreement with Reuters and Havas in 1934. But until that time, and for some years thereafter, the Americans who went to India on journalistic missions were either news correspondents on limited assignments or letter writers in the grand tradition of Bayard Taylor. In the view of most American editors, India simply had no relevance for the United States unless it was engulfed by catastrophe, revolution, or war. Besides, it "belonged" to Reuters.

Webb Miller, the veteran UP war correspondent, was one of the first to cover a major assignment in India at the time that the cartel agreement was beginning to break up. It was the strength of his organization that it had never been party to such a restrictive compact; therefore, when he ventured into Reuters territory, he was violating no agreements. However, the British took a dim view of his presence and placed all manner of difficulties in his path, for he was bringing a non-British view of Gandhi's civil-disobedience campaign to the United States and the world at large.

It was at the time of the Mahatma's march to the sea to extract salt from sea water, his dramatic protest against the imposition of a British salt tax that discriminated against the poor. After many adventures, Miller finally joined the demonstrators 150 miles north of Bombay. Almost at once, he was caught in a police attack on thousands of Gandhi's followers, who, true to their beliefs, offered no resistance although 2 of them were killed and 320 others injured.

Miller had to travel many miles to find a telegraph office at a provincial railway station. With the prescience of the seasoned foreign correspondent, he filed five messages of 100 words each, conveying the same news, hoping that one would escape the notice of British officials who were watching everything that went through the Bombay cable office to London. Then, on the train to Bombay, he wrote a 2,000-word report on the attack; upon his arrival, he entered into the most vigorous argument with the British authorities, who did not want to let it through and also were under the impression that they had stopped all his other messages. Fortunately for him, three of his five short dispatches had reached London and were on UP's wires everywhere. Grudgingly, the British let the rest through.[61]

The Gandhi assignment attracted more Americans from time to time, but it was never covered as thoroughly as it was by Reuters or by the British specials. The story had particular relevance for British and Indian readers; for the Americans, there was always a certain amount of detachment. Not until the coming of World War II did the AP send Preston Grover to India to open its first bureau in 1942 in New Delhi. Shortly thereafter, the UP followed.

The AP used New Delhi as its base for the coverage of the war in the China-Burma-India theater, with nine to twelve correspondents moving in and out, and others permanently stationed in Chungking, Rangoon, Calcutta, and elsewhere.[62] It was the first time any American agency had tried to do so extensive a job in South Asia. With smaller reservoirs of manpower, UP and INS, the other American agencies, and a small group of specials brought an entirely new concept of India to the United States. To Americans beset with the single-minded notion of winning the war, an India that took advantage of a time of great peril to the Anglo-American alliance to seek independence did not deserve much support. Consequently, American editorial opinion of India was largely negative in tone during the war.[63]

The views of some 250,000 American soldiers who moved through India at the same period did not improve matters. It was the first real encounter between the American and Indian peoples. The effects of that initial meeting required years to repair.

Harold Isaacs, a World War II correspondent in the China-Burma-India theater, wrote of the American soldiers:

> Perhaps as many as half of these remained in India for periods ranging from three months to three years. For the great mass of these young Americans, this was an ordeal. The war-time conditions, the tea patches and jungles of Assam, and the fetid slums of Calcutta were no breeding places for educational or elevating experiences. All the stereotypes of glamor that might have been brought to India by these men were swiftly enveloped by squalid reality. The Indians were the *wogs* (a term applied by Englishmen to nonwhites from North Africa to India), recognizably human only to the rare GI. [India was] a country they were desirous only of leaving.[64]

Nor was the educated Indian's view of the GI any more flattering. In retrospect, many of them conceded that their first jarring notion of what the United States was actually like came from the soldiers—a boisterous and arrogant lot, in Indian opinion, who quickly manifested the worst kind of color prejudice. It was, perhaps, the soldiers' notion of American superiority and their comments on Indian life that alienated most of the Indians who had anything to do with them. With rare exceptions, the Americans not only knew nothing of India; they didn't want to know. And their dislike of the people who were their involuntary wartime hosts was repaid in kind. At the time of India's independence two years after the end of the war, Nehru's disposition to equate the United States with British colonialism on the basis of guilt by association was widely emulated among Indian intellectuals.[65]

It followed that, for some time after India's independence, the United States continued to occupy a secondary position in the calculations of the small and rather tightly knit Indian power structure. It was one of the reasons for the failure of the AP and its American rivals to make a dent in Reuters' dominant position as the prime supplier of news for the Indian market. Beginning in 1949, with the formation of India's own wire service, the Press Trust of India (PTI), pressures rose to oblige all foreign agencies to distribute their file in India through the PTI. Reuters completed such an agreement in 1952, thus making the PTI in effect its Indian agent. As a cooperative enterprise owned by the Indian press, but also remarkably sensitive to the wishes of government, PTI in the early 1960's offered three services to English-language newspapers at rates of approximately $720, $480, and $250 a month each, with a 50 per cent concession on these rates to Indian-language papers. It was estimated that Reuters received more than $100,000 a year in India, and a substantial amount extra from its Comtelburo clients.

The American agencies continued, for a short time, to supply individual Indian newspapers. At different periods, they sold news to the *Times* of India which, besides maintaining a few correspondents abroad, also had subsidiary services. But in 1954, India decided it was time to halt all foreign news entering India unless it was filtered through an Indian agency. In 1956, UP had to stop its distribution within India, although it continued, of course, to maintain a bureau for the reporting of news of India to the world. The AP continued to distribute its file within India until 1958, then was obliged to discontinue it. For a few months in 1960, an organization called the Indian News Service distributed the merged UPI service, but it didn't last long. With the exception of pictures, special services, and syndicated columns, the Americans were in effect squeezed out of India as distributors of foreign news and opinion, with considerable loss to the agencies directly concerned. UPI even had a tax suit filed against it in Bombay, which dragged on for years.

With its American rivals squelched for the time being, Reuters was still the prime supplier of foreign news in India in the early 1960's. Its relationship with PTI was excellent. To perpetuate the myth that the Indian press had access to more than one foreign agency file, the British giant grudgingly yielded a small share of the PTI report to Agence France-Presse (AFP). AFP came cheap, and it provided even less competition in India than the few PTI foreign correspondents, most of whom used the mails. With the growth of France's association with Communist China, AFP became even less popular, and at least one of its correspondents had to be withdrawn from India.

But as is so frequently the case in journalism where a new organization has no competition, PTI grew stodgy and slow. Its most important members complained about the service. In 1961, several of the leading members of the PTI organization formed a rival service, the United News of India (UNI), to provide themselves with an alternative source of foreign news.* For three years, UNI struggled along without making any progress. Even the founders didn't pay too much attention to it, and they certainly didn't support it with much money. The Indian press as a whole was prosperous because it had low costs, paid low salaries, and was just beginning to develop its advertising revenues; moreover, each of the big chains was dominated by industrial interests that could well afford to invest more money in the coverage of national and international news.

Then Kuldip Nayar, former information officer for Prime Minister Shastri, became general manager for UNI, and things began to happen. Nayar was a hard-hitting, American-trained journalist with an enormous amount of enthusiasm and ambition, a 1951 graduate of the Medill School of Journalism at Northwestern University, a former member of the USIS–India staff, and one of the best of the Indian Government's Public Information Bureau staff. He towered well over six feet and was in his mid-thirties, lean and broad-shouldered, with the look of a beneficent Nasser about him. Within ten weeks he shook up UNI, boosting its total clients to more than fifty, and in the process gave PTI the jitters. By 1966, UNI was beginning to move, and Nayar occupied an important place in Indian journalism.

Nayar offered a combination of AP and Deutsche Press Agentur (DPA) service to his clients at the outset, but he was anxious to add others. Soon after he took over, his budget was running to about $40,000 a year, of which he paid $25,000 a year to the AP and $5,000 more to DPI. It didn't leave him much to pay his small staff in New Delhi and Bombay and his stringers all over India, so he pressed his clients hard for more funds. It was a struggle all the way, and the wonder was that he didn't tire of the effort. The AP, having lost considerable money in India before, was ready enough with technical advice from its New Delhi bureau but cautious about committing substantial funds in view of its status as a cooperative. It was ironic, therefore, that talk should have circulated in New Delhi that Nayar was being subsidized by the Americans to give AP an opening in India. He could have used a subsidy at the time.

His situation was such, however, that he had to turn to DPA for fifty-five German Siemens teletype machines, which cost him $2,000 a month until paid for. With the growth in his list of clients, he could have used

* They were the *Times* of India; Hindustan *Times,* and its Indian-language paper, *Hindustan; Amrita Bazar Patrika* and its Bengali daily, *Jugantar;* the Bengali daily, *Ananda Bazar Patrika,* part of the *Hindustan Standard* group; *Indian Nation; Araja Varta* of Patna; *Hindu; Deccan Herald;* and *Prajavani* of Bangalore.

fifty more machines immediately, but he couldn't afford them then. The Indian communications equipment also left something to be desired, for it had difficulty picking up the Tangier signal and UNI often lost 25 to 40 per cent of the AP file. When that happened, Nayar simply pieced together his report from DPA, since reception from West Germany frequently was better.

It would be pleasant to report that the Indian press subscribed to UNI and increased the use of its service because of its AP report from the United States and elsewhere. But that was, apparently, not the major factor in the growth of UNI. Nayar's strength was his own ability to generate news through his intimate acquaintance with the leaders of India's government. He endeavored to develop one exclusive story a day of either political or economic consequence—an impossible job, but one that was bound to make a difference in the attitude of editors. When the competition had a UNI exclusive and it stood up, the PTI began to receive complaints. Just how far Nayar would be able to go was problematical, unless he received major support from his clients. But while he was able to maintain his pace, he did more than any other young man in India to shake up the complacency of most of its newspaper editors.

In the charged atmosphere, there was a good deal of haggling back and forth over the prospect of a return to India by the UPI. But Nayar wanted only one American service and looked over Japanese, Yugoslav, and other services because he didn't want to be accused of running a pro-American service. Even when AP became available in some volume, there was no concerted rush to use its file. Reuters, PTI, and the Indian foreign correspondents in the United States together constituted the most frequently used sources of American news. (In November, 1966, UPI completed new contracts to service both the Associated Press of Pakistan and PTI, the latter at a reported fee of $1,500 to $2,000 a month. Thus, both American wire services again were available to the press of South Asia.)

Yet, over the course of a few years, there was a decided change in the foreign news content and tone of the Indian press. In 1958, Norman Isaacs was deeply disturbed by the pro-Russian, anti-American content of the Indian newspapers, their ill-concealed bias against the American Government, and the distortions he noted in their coverage of the United States. He wrote:

Almost all Americans in India are restive about the Indian press. To American eyes, the daily papers are preoccupied with news of nuclear testing, possible poisoning of the atmosphere, Russian pronouncements (which Americans see as propaganda), American evasions, the struggle of rebellious groups everywhere with the United States seemingly allied against those seeking freedom . . .

Are Indian editors conscious that their papers carry far more Russian-oriented material than American? Yes and no. It depends on which editor. Take one who has traveled widely and you are apt to have a man critical of what is being printed in this [Indian] nation's press. Take one, however, in a smaller city, worrying about finances and the coverage of his area, he is likely to shrug, or defend stoutly what is being printed as "completely objective." [66]

Four years later, ending with the week of the Chinese attack on India, a USIS study of the Indian press found things had improved. In the period studied, 7 per cent of the average English-language papers' news space in India was devoted to American news, and the vernacular press ran 3.4 per cent. "Most of the news published about the United States originates with Reuters, a British news service," said the USIS report. "Reuters' news judgment appears to be more in tune with Indian interests than AP's. Unlike AP, Reuters gives roughly the same emphasis to different types of news about the U.S. as the Indian news agencies do."

One of the reasons for the lively interest in American affairs at this period, of course, was the Cuban missile crisis and the confrontation between the United States and Russia. In its diplomatic way, the USIS study reported that the Indian press was "following closely the developing situation between the U.S. and Cuba prior to the actual October 20 crisis. After that date this topic became the single most important U.S. news topic in the Indian press." [67] There was no comment on the orientation of the Indian press during the struggle.

Two years later, during the period of the passage of the Civil Rights Act of 1964, the Presidential nominating conventions, and the battles in Tonkin Gulf that began the escalation of the Viet-Nam war, the tone of much of the Indian press had perceptibly changed. With one or two exceptions, the English-language newspapers did a great deal more straight news reporting of American events, and the editorial comment, while not exactly friendly, seemed to be a bit more disposed to be fair. The irritating tendency to glorify the Russians and take the Americans for granted, which Isaacs had noted, was still present in some newspapers, but not to as marked a degree. A respectful notice was taken of the passage of the Civil Rights Act. As for the racial disorders that were an almost regular part of American news of the time, the play was usually proportionate to the day's run of news, and Indian editors, as a whole, tended to discuss them in a sensible and sophisticated manner.

On the 1964 Presidential campaign, the Indian English-language press, like all the rest in East, Southeast, and South Asia, received the news of Barry Goldwater's nomination for President on the Republican ticket with scathing comment. The Tonkin Gulf incidents found the Indian press as a whole in so bewildered a mood that it couldn't seem to make up its mind whether to boo or cheer.

The foreign news content of the English-language press was still running at about 20 to 25 per cent of its total news space, and the American news content, if the Viet-Nam war was included, was about what the USIS survey had noted. But purely domestic events, with the exception of foreign-aid legislation and racial disorders, usually received short shrift. All of which led Eric da Costa, director of the Indian Institute of Public Opinion, to observe that he doubted if Indians knew as much about the United States as Americans knew about India.[68] He made the point that Indians as a whole are much more inclined to show interest only in matters of immediate concern close to home than the peoples of the more developed countries. An examination of the vernacular press —the press of the future in India—showed that it tended to publish very little foreign news and the barest minimum from the United States. One of the most prominent editors of Indian-language newspapers made it a deliberate practice to concentrate on local news—in the American manner—and reported joyfully that his circulation had gone up by 25 per cent in a single year.

It was a time of change in Indian foreign policy, with new ministers, many of them just out of the hurly-burly of domestic politics, trying to find their bearings. While most of the Indian newspapers seemed as uncertain as the government over exactly how the "new nonalignment" should be developed, there was a certain amount of relief—politely expressed—that the press no longer had to fear the hypercritical Nehru. Prem Bhatia wrote in the *Indian Express:*

For those who, like newspapermen, deal with public opinion, the most significant change is a greater degree of government responsiveness. There is a conscious effort . . . to keep in touch with what the country thinks and says. . . .

This is no small change from the past when not only Jawaharlal Nehru but much smaller people by comparison conveyed the impression of indifference. Newspaper opinion was then not regarded as "public opinion." It was the voice of the "monopolies," of the "vested interests," of "personal bias." In disregarding what the press said about the government or the then leadership, those concerned reflected a bias of their own and perhaps they lost in the bargain.[69]

The seeming determination to take a more vigorous and independent line with the new government was everywhere in evidence in the Indian press. It was almost as if a mordant fear had been removed. Few if any editors would have dared write so trenchantly of Nehru at the height of his power, or to have waged an all-out battle against his policies, however much his underlings may have been belabored. Shastri had almost no honeymoon period with the press; but as the depth of his governmental crisis evolved, the same sense of national purpose that had rallied the press so often to Nehru's side began to act to the benefit of his successor. At the time of the Pakistani fighting in 1965, the press was as united behind the government as it ever had been.

The Indian Government's enduring concern about the growth of the newspaper chains and the tightening of what it feared was a press monopoly continued to be in evidence. The *Annual Report* of the Registrar of Newspapers for India, 1964, expressed the government's view that "monopolistic trends continue to exist." The report added:

This growing trend would have been higher and the rate of growth much faster had it not been for the inevitable curbs which had to be placed on the allocation of newsprint to the newspaper combines who have, during the past 18 months, from time to time, approached the government for additional quota to bring out new publications. . . . It is, therefore, the shortage of foreign exchange which is retarding the growth of these combines . . .[70]

The total circulation of the 345 daily newspapers in all languages in India in 1963, the latest year for which figures are available, was only 5,579,000—less than that of the combined morning and evening circulations of any one of the Japanese big three dailies. But the small size of the Indian daily press reflected neither its influence nor its comparative affluence; for better or worse, its leaders were the principal medium, next to Parliament, for the exposure of government to the limited force of public opinion. Because the press was so much more subject to government pressures in India than it was in either the United States or Great Britain, the wonder was that it displayed so great a measure of independence and fought as hard as it did to maintain its position. It was remarkable, despite the limitations of newsprint and other government-imposed restrictions, that the Indian press was able to show a gain in daily circulation of nearly 200,000 in a single year between 1962 and 1963. For the average Indian, whose hourly wage sometimes was less than the price of a newspaper, the press was a luxury.

The 47 English-language newspapers, with 1,452,000 circulation, were the largest of the various language groupings and had the largest circulation gain over 1962—78,000. The Hindi daily newspapers were second, with 764,000 circulation, and a gain of 59,000 over the previous year. But, unfortunately for those hundred-percenters who were eager to have Hindi as India's national language, the other Indian-language dailies together had a circulation of 3,363,000, and some of them showed larger proportionate gains than the Hindi press. The Tamil daily press was the third largest, with 688,000; followed by Malayalam, with 613,-000; Marathi, with 536,000; Gujerati, with 441,000; and Bengali, with 303,000; with a smaller number for each of the other principal languages —Kannada, Telugu, Urdu, Oriya, and Assamese. For the 4,570 newspapers of all kinds surveyed by the government, the rate of increase for the English-language press was 10.5 per cent; for the Bengali press, 5.5 per cent; and for the Hindi press, 4.3 per cent. In the periodical field, the combined circulation of the English-language weeklies in 1963 was 1,248,000, with Hindi close behind at 1,154,000. It was apparent, despite its prosperity and its leadership, that the English-language press could scarcely be considered to be dominant. In each of the great chains, the major English-language daily newspaper was matched by one or more Indian-language dailies, weeklies, or magazines. All publishers had concluded for years that there would be an inevitable rise in the fortunes of the Indian-language press and a consequent decline in the English-language dailies.

The nature of the press in India in the mid-1960's was best illustrated by an examination of its leaders' positions. Of the 47 English-language dailies, 36 were controlled by chains, groups, and other multiple units. Because some of the prominent shareholders in some of the chains were identified with the jute industry, the derogatory term "jute press" was applied to much of the group by its critics. The heart of the English-language press consisted of 9 dailies with almost 76 per cent of the combined English-language press daily circulation in 1963, as follows:

Indian Express (Bombay, Delhi, and four other cities)	294,949
Times (Bombay and Delhi)	180,344
Hindu (Madras)	133,210
Statesman (Calcutta and Delhi)	127,219
Hindustan Times	106,709
Amrita Bazar Patrika	94,451
Free Press Journal (Bombay)	86,453
Hindustan Standard	47,802
Indian Nation	29,890
	1,101,027

The two leading newspaper chains were the Express Newspapers (consisting of 10 publications), with 11.5 per cent of the total circulation of all dailies in 1963, and the Times of India Publications (numbering 14), with 7.3 per cent. Other important publications were the multiple units represented by *Thanthi,* a Tamil daily with 232,926 circulation, or 4.2 per cent of the total; the *Hindustan Times* and allied publications, with 4.1 per cent; the *Amrita Bazar Patrika* and its Bengali daily, *Jugantar,* with 3.9 per cent; the Bengali daily *Ananda Bazar Patrika,* with 146,819 circulation, which was a part of the *Hindustan Standard* group; and the *Hindu,* which, alone among the leaders, was dominated by family interests with a long history of journalistic affiliation.[71]

The influences at work behind the scenes in the Indian press were extremely complicated, as was illustrated by the shift of Frank Moraes from the editorship of the *Times* of India to the *Indian Express.* In 1957, when a representative of the *Times* announced that Moraes's three-year contract was not being renewed, he issued a statement pointing out that Jai Chand Jain, a principal *Times* stockholder, had informed *Blitz,* the leftist Bombay magazine, that this meant "the removal of the American bloc from the *Times* of India." Moraes added, "If I am pro-American, it is because I am pro-Indian and sincerely believe my country's best interests lie in closer association with the West." The actual basis for his departure, he went on, was the issue of editorial independence.[72] Following his assumption of the editorial direction of the *Indian Express,* its circulation soon passed that of the *Times,* and he was twice asked to return, but refused.

The *Times* of India had troubles. Seth Ramakrishna Dalmia, once the dominating influence in Bennett Coleman and Co., Ltd., the owners of the *Times* chain, was arrested in 1955, accused of embezzlement. A *Times* official announced that Dalmia had disposed of his newspaper holdings four months before his arrest. The case involved the alleged misappropriation of funds, beginning in 1946, from one of Dalmia's many companies to float a bond issue for an airways company. Following a prolonged hearing before the Vivian Bose Commission beginning in 1956, the financier was convicted in 1959. His offer of restitution was refused, and he was sentenced to a jail term. However, the case dragged on for years, involving past and then current officials of the *Times.*[73] The newspaper was closely watched to determine if it seemed to be bending toward the government line or showed other signs of undue influence. But if there was any feature that distinguished the work of its editor, N. J. Nanporia, it was his hostility to the United States. He was credited very largely with having influenced the government to cancel the deal with the United States for the installation of a powerful transmitter that would have been jointly used by All-India Radio and the Voice of America. M. R. Masani protested in the Lok Sabha: "We wanted the transmitter to combat enemy propaganda on our borders. Because of the noise made by a few Communists and fellow-travelers, the agreement has been dismissed by those who entered into it. I am quite sure that if the government had stood by the agreement and said it was in the national interest, nothing would have happened." [74]

Nanporia's attitude toward the United States was not generally shared by some of the other executives of the *Times,* notably P. K. Roy and Joe D'Souza, the general manager and business manager, respectively. Both had thought enough of American ways to attend the American Press Institute with the assent of their superiors. But the American influence on the paper, if any, did not extend to the editorial page in Nanporia's time.

The spectrum of attitudes on the *Times* toward the United States also included the correspondence of H. R. Vohra from Washington. While he took a critical stance, it was usually as fair as could be expected under the circumstances. It would have been difficult, if not impossible, for anyone not familiar with the background of the *Times* to make much sense out of the differing attitudes of its editor, its Washington correspondent, its managers, and its owners. Most readers seemed not to pay much attention to it, taking it all as a part of the ins and outs of Indian journalism.

There was, however, a good deal more substance to the *Indian Express,* under Frank Moraes's direction, and the *Hindustan Times,* with Shri Mulgaokar as editor. Neither was particularly impressed with the wisdom of American policies in Southeast Asia, but there was never a disposition to attack a position merely because it came from Washington. Both were thoroughly familiar with both the American process of decision-making and with some of its puzzling by-products; as critics, they were probably more moderate than some of the Americans who attacked President Johnson's foreign policy. But certainly, their position as Indian editors was thoroughly understandable.

As for the *Statesman,* British to the core for many years during the long reign of Evan Charlton as editor, it was changing slowly with the acquisition of control by Indian interests headed by the Tata industrial empire. Its most brilliant younger editor, Pran Chopra, who was in charge of its Delhi edition, was widely read. Like his older colleagues, Moraes and Mulgaokar, he had a thorough knowledge of, and few illusions about, the United States. Consequently, when he addressed himself to the interests of India at a time when American foreign policy was in a state of change, his writing was required reading for those in New Delhi who were particularly concerned with such matters.

The hope of Indian journalism was in such editors of the rising generation as Chopra and the wise and observant Krishnamachari Balaraman of the *Hindu* of Madras, a U.N. correspondent for many years before he was called home to assume higher responsibilities. With such men, the future of independent Indian journalism was in good hands; they knew it was worth fighting for, and they knew how to wage their battle for public support when it proved necessary. The Indian press was fortunate, too, in its managers. Such men as Roy and D'Souza, of the *Times;* T. S. Krishnan, of the *Indian Express;* G. Kasturi, of the *Hindu;* and K. M. Mathew, of the *Malayala Manorama,* were thoroughly conversant with modern newspaper operations. With relief from newsprint shortages and with greater flexibility in the use of foreign exchange, the prospect of a major expansion for the Indian press was no dream. These managers had learned how to make do with a little; they would not fail to take advantage of their new opportunities, once they developed.

Both managers and editors, however, fully realized that they had to make changes in the Indian journalist's wages—through the Press Commission—at the earliest possible time if any progress was to be achieved. An average basic wage of $25 a month and less for India's 5,200 journalists was not adequate. The nine leading English-language newspapers were the largest employers, with 723 journalists, with the Delhi edition of the *Times* alone employing 330.[75] Not all Indian journalists, of course, were poorly paid. The big newspapers paid $7,000 to $10,000 a year in salaries to first-rate foreign correspondents and estimated that it cost $15,000 to $18,000 to keep a man in Washington.

Referring to the low basic salaries recommended by the Industry's Wage Committee at the outset, one Indian authority wrote:

> This was an absurdity which brought on its own nemesis. For no newspaper that comes into existence these days can hope to secure competent men on these salaries, and no newspaper with the huge investment the enterprise involves will think of working with incompetent and inexperienced staffs. . . . The journalist of today has gained little by the changes in the profession initiated by the Press Commission or by the publicity attendant on them.[76]

It was not surprising that a cabinet minister reported to Parliament in the 1960's that the Communist Party ran "a number of dailies, weeklies and monthlies all over the country." [77] The independence of a newspaper, in India as elsewhere, depended on something more than solvency for the proprietor. If he could not adequately reward his people and allow them to take pride in their work, he could not expect very much in return. It was true that many Indian journalists needed a better education and better training for their work. But most of all, they needed a living wage.

6. FOREIGN CORRESPONDENTS IN INDIA

Neville Maxwell, the correspondent of the *Times* of London, addressed Indira Gandhi at a Foreign Correspondents' Association tea at the Claridge in New Delhi in this manner:

We know that Mrs. Gandhi doesn't think we report enough of the good things that happen in India. But I'm sure, Madame Minister, that you will find most of us in agreement that it is scarcely the business of a foreign correspondent to pick and choose those events that please governments. The correspondent, I daresay, more often sends the bad things that happen because they are what interest people. Your professional correspondent is bound to have a critical attitude toward whatever country he covers, whether it is the United States, Great Britain, Russia or India.[78]

Madame Minister pursed her thin lips, gave an angry hitch to her white cotton sari, and proceeded to lecture the hardy little group of foreign correspondents. None of it was new to them. Such strictures were a part of the job in India. There were as many views of what should be done to—or for—the foreign correspondents as there were readers. Some, like Indira Gandhi, viewed them with suspicion on general principle. Others, like Chanchal Sarkar of the Press Institute of India, accused them of seeking special privileges, living like maharajahs, and acting the part. Still others, like Frank Moraes of the *Indian Express,* felt that they were rather poorly treated on the whole. But common to all these views was the feeling that the foreign correspondent, in greater or lesser degree, bore some responsibility for the comparatively shabby figure which India now cut in the world press.

Mrs. Gandhi, while Minister for Information and Broadcasting, and later as Prime Minister, seldom let an opportunity slip to emphasize that foreign correspondents should tell the good as well as the bad about India. She acknowledged the essential truth of what was reported about India. But she was more deeply concerned with the point of view —a feeling that correspondents somehow should always dig up something nice to report from India along with their usual negative accounts. This was also the journalistic gospel according to Chester Bowles.

Mr. Sarkar's view was more waspish. As the man in charge of an effort to form a training school for young Indian journalists, he was inevitably concerned with what the foreign correspondents said and thought of his country. He, too, lectured them:

> In reporting a country over a considerable stretch of time, I feel that the correspondent should approach it with some basic sympathy or liking, or else voluntarily give up his assignment if he can. In the long run, the draining away of sympathy is bound to warp one's reporting. . . . A correspondent must be able to appreciate points of view which run contrary to the interests of his *own* country and, above all, he must always be interested, deeply and enduringly interested, in the countries he reports.[79]

This was the kind of special pleading that most Indians do very well, thinking, of course, only of their own circumstances and their own country. But when the point of view was applied to an Indian correspondent in, say, Pakistan or Communist China, it didn't seem to fit quite as well.

It remained for Moraes, the old pro of the Indian press, to define the responsibilities of the foreign correspondent in terms that were, at least, understandable to members of the fraternity. He equated the duties of the foreign correspondent with those of the foreign diplomat in projecting the image of India abroad, even though they operated independently and on different levels, and expressed disappointment over the manner in which both generally were treated in India:

> In the majority of cases when they are summoned to appear before the Establishment, it is either to be obliquely dressed down or more often than not to be crudely advised or persuaded. Yet, both the diplomat and the foreign correspondent represent media of communication which, if honestly and adroitly handled, could be invaluable in promoting and consolidating good relations with their individual countries, thereby reinforcing or repairing [as the case may be] the good work or damage done by our own diplomats and correspondents abroad.

Mr. Moraes's prescription for the treatment of the foreign correspondent in India concluded:

> It is axiomatic that in order to do business the customer should feel relaxed. A man with a problem on his mind rarely reaches out for his purse. Foreign journalists should be conceded special facilities in importing cars and other equipment necessary for their work such as typewriters, cameras, films, etc. Correspondents posted here, particularly those with families, are entitled to consideration in securing suitable accommodation.

The habit of various official and officious underlings to patronize foreign journalists and in dealing with perfectly reasonable requests behave as if they were conferring some ethereal favor or honor on mundane individuals beneath their lordly notice is reprehensible and cannot be too strongly condemned. A severe example should be made of one or two such habitual offenders, and order will be quickly restored.

Excessive demands by foreign correspondents are equally reprehensible, but, to this writer's knowledge, they are happily the rare exception rather than the rule. Since confidence begets confidence, there is no reason why ministers or officials should be persuaded to treat foreign correspondents as highly suspicious characters. As a rule, the foreign correspondent does not want to be mollycoddled, but equally he does not want to be mauled unnecessarily.[80]

What of the foreign correspondents themselves? In the days before the Chinese border incursions of 1962, most of the Americans who served in India were genuinely pleased to be there. Some of them called it one of the great experiences of their lives. To correspondents of such a turn of mind, the notion that one of their number could be "mauled," as Moraes so indelicately put it, was well-nigh heresy. Those with happier experiences were therefore unprepared for the grimmer atmosphere of war and famine that pervaded wide areas of India in the mid-1960's. Once, an editor who had enjoyed being a correspondent in India was heard to mutter after reading the work of a valued colleague: "What's the matter with that guy? Why doesn't he like India?"

There were numerous reasons for "not liking India" that had nothing to do with the difficulties of living there or the failure of most correspondents to live as well as, say, Japanese or Indian correspondents in the United States. One of the strongest factors shaping the attitudes of foreign correspondents was that they found it difficult to persuade editors at home to pay attention to news from India when there was no war or other catastrophe. At least three Americans assigned by major news organizations requested and received transfers out of New Delhi for this reason alone in the mid-1960's.

Next to the death of Nehru and the Kashmir war, the biggest continuing story from India was the food shortage, but it attracted minimal attention outside major U.S. and British centers. Indira Gandhi's election as Prime Minister was widely reported because she was the world's second woman Prime Minister and because she was Nehru's daughter. But one looked in vain for much reportage on India's progress against its monumental problems. And during the Kashmir war, the correspondence from the Indian side was disappointing, primarily because Indian authorities stopped the reporters from going to the front.

There were other handicaps. Few Americans left India without being ill themselves or nursing their families over a bad spell. A foreign editor with a large staff of correspondents summed up such family problems as follows: "Fifty per cent of my troubles are caused by correspondents' wives."

For the younger and less experienced among the American group, there was also the constant worry about making both ends meet on comparatively small salaries, some as low as $5,200 a year, in a land where even Indian families paid $300 a month rent in New Delhi. The average American correspondent did somewhat better—a range of $9,000 to $16,000 a year for the regulars. Only one, perhaps, may have received a bit more. No television salaries were paid in India because C.B.S. had moved out long before, and N.B.C., discouraged by being forced to put up $60,000 bond for its equipment when it sought to make two documentaries about India, followed in 1963. Both, of course, summoned the fire brigade when the fighting broke out.

The unwelcome attentions of unskilled Indian government gumshoes, which dated from the time of the Chinese incursions of 1962, helped liven things up for some of the correspondents. While Louis Kraar was in India for *Time* magazine, he was telephoning on one occasion to a native stringer when a voice broke in to warn the Indian: "Don't sell out your country!" Another time, Kraar's piece on one of the communal riots, addressed to his home office through Montreal, was lifted bodily for publication in some of the Indian press and attributed to the correspondent of *Time* in Montreal. Others reported acts of surveillance that sometimes reached ludicrous depths. Once, a correspondent found one of his incoming letters carelessly torn open and just as carelessly patched together. When he wrote a note of protest to the government, he received a polite reply that an effort would be made henceforth to open his letters with greater care. When the correspondent indignantly displayed his correspondence before the official he believed responsible, the government agent roared with laughter. "The bloody fools," he said. "They don't even know what they're doing." Louis Rukeyser recorded his own mail and telephone surveillance by writing an article about it for the Baltimore *Sun,* much to the annoyance of the Indian authorities.[81] The piece attracted the melancholy attention of his editor, Price Day, one of the authentic "old India" hands, who had won a Pulitzer Prize for his correspondence.

The British, on the whole, were much more composed about such matters. There were only a few of them, usually less than six. The best-adjusted, and the most important, were Peter and Adrienne Jackson, the Reuters correspondents, who ran an efficient, twenty-four-hour-a-day operation with a capable Indian assistant in an office attached to their home. Adrienne Farrell had come to New Delhi in 1951 for Reuters, and Peter Jackson had arrived in Karachi the following year to work for the agency. In 1953, after he covered the ascent of Mount Everest, Reuters' staff on the subcontinent joined forces and were married. In 1966, they were still on the job and found time to look after their four children, as well.

Reuters was the first to use the Indian Government's telex circuit to London for direct teleprinter service, but it was too expensive for their regular file. They averaged about 800 to 1,000 words a day to London at the regular penny-a-word Commonwealth rate. Generally, they filed about 60 per cent of the news on Reuters' wires from India, the rest coming directly from the Press Trust of India via Bombay. With stringers in Ceylon, Afghanistan, Nepal, and Kashmir and a man in Karachi, they were better staffed than anybody else, and they also knew a great deal more about the country. In emergencies, Reuters could send in reinforcements within a matter of hours.

Under the circumstances, some of the lengths to which Americans went to circumvent Reuters were amusing. When Phillips Talbot came to India in 1964, the American embassy arranged a background briefing for the Americans and another for the Indians. Reuters, however, was invited to neither, but received a quick fill-in on both from friendly correspondents. With such experienced people watching Reuters' interests in India, it was understandable that the British still dominated the news out of India much of the time and maintained their supremacy over their rivals on the incoming wire.

Most of the other British correspondents—the representatives of the London *Daily Telegraph*, London *Observer*, and London *Daily Mail*—were generally on roving assignments. While Neville Maxwell covered for the London *Times*, he traveled infrequently although there was but one other *Times* man regularly assigned in all of East Asia, a correspondent in Tokyo. Only one British correspondent reported having had his mail opened—correspondence with the Reverend Michael Scott, the Naga rebels' representative—and he roared that he was "damn mad about it." Even those Indians who were anti-Western generally turned out to be pro-British, which made India rather pleasant for the British correspondents on the whole. They seemed to have almost a preferred status.

Usually, during the mid-1960's, about a dozen Americans were assigned to India, but not all of them stayed there day in, day out. The AP had the most manpower with two Americans and a veteran Indian correspondent. The UPI had an American and the usual Indian local. Otherwise, only the New York *Times*, the Washington *Post*, the Baltimore *Sun*, the *Christian Science Monitor*, and *Time* magazine were covered at all times by staff people or their capable Indian assistants. *Newsweek* had an Indian stringer. The Washington *Star,* Chicago *Daily News,* and *U.S. News & World Report* used their correspondents to handle all wars, insurrections, and other disorders within quick flying distance.

Some of the basic attitudes and problems involved in the coverage of India were quite apparent in a questionnaire filled out in the summer of 1964 by eleven of the correspondents for American news organizations who were permanently assigned to New Delhi. Nine of them were Americans and two were Indians. All except one had completed his college education. Of the Americans, only one spoke Hindustani (popularized Hindu) and Urdu. Four of them had been in India for less than a year, four others for less than two years. Only one had three or more years of service, and he departed soon afterward. Neither India nor Pakistan were long-term assignments for any American. But as it turned out, none of those in the group were youngsters, the junior man being twenty-nine. The rest were in their thirties and forties.

While most of the salaries were moderate to low, the American newspaper and news-magazine specials were well paid and estimated that it cost their organizations about $35,000 a year or more to maintain them in India, without including filing charges. This is the way one correspondent analyzed his costs: salary, $16,000; cost of living allowance, $3,000 annually; educational allowance, $500 per child, or half the cost; travel costs, office rent, auto operation, cost of a local assistant, $10,500, for a total of $30,000 annually. The correspondent paid $350 for the rental of a comfortable house in a good section of New Delhi. His medical expenses were not large, although he had had hepatitis and amoebic dysentery, and he paid the doctor although his office had offered to meet the bill for him.

Of the correspondents in the group, five represented newspapers; three, wire services; and three, news magazines. For those who estimated the cost of their file per month, the bill averaged about $400.

They were satisfied, in the main, with the press services of the American embassy although few of them depended on such sources as a main channel of news. One called the embassy's assistance excellent; five, good; one, poor; two, variable; and two had no comment. They were not quite as complimentary about the assistance given by the Indian Government. One rated it as excellent; three, good; two, fair; three, poor; and two made no comment. The American embassy made a high score for credibility, two correspondents saying its news was "always believable," while six others called it "believable most of the time." There were three skeptics, who believed the embassy "part of the time."

Six of the correspondents cited suspicion and mistrust as the principal obstacles that separated them from their sources. They apparently were not impressed with the Indian newspapers. The nine Americans divided, five saying that the Indian press gave "fair" coverage to American events, while four rated it as "poor." Nobody called it either excellent or good. However, six correspondents felt that the coverage of the United States was improving.

Primarily, they attributed the indifferent coverage of American news to the political orientation of the Indian press and its lack of interest in American domestic news generally. Three correspondents attributed the distortions and gaps in the American coverage to the partisan approach of the Indian press, while two felt there was too much Washington reporting and too little elsewhere in the country. Only one correspondent felt that the Indian press distorted the reporting of American racial problems. Asked whether they believed the Indian press was generally favorable to the United States, only one American said yes, four others gave a qualified affirmative response, and three said no. Most of them had found India to be a friendly country, but expensive for Americans. They reported no discrimination in the usual sense, but two complained that they had been taken advantage of by landlords and shopkeepers because they were foreigners.

Nearly all the correspondents, both in their general remarks in the questionnaires and later in depth interviews, had profound reactions to their stay in India. They were either enormously attracted to the land and its problems, its people, and the sweeping panoramas through which they moved, or they were thoroughly repelled. There did not seem to be any in-between. Regardless of the turn of mind, none could be indifferent to India.

One correspondent said:

The South Asian continent, which I cover, might some weeks fall into the Indian Ocean for all the attention it gets in the United States. The country, after all, has been less dramatic for a long time than Southeast Asia or Korea, where American interests were in direct conflict with Communist China's. But this area, for many reasons, is far more important and interesting than American editors think.

Another correspondent commented:

When I was asked if I wanted to go to India, I said at once, "Yes!" I thought it would be a glamorous, challenging, exciting assignment. I did not find it so. The reasons are very difficult for me to determine, but I believe it is a very discouraging assignment, in the main, because so much of it is a record of failure, and sometimes I lose hope that anything at all can be accomplished. It so happens that I have not been spied on, but even if I had been, it wouldn't matter to me. These things have no real influence on a correspondent, or should not have. The magnitude of the Indians' problems and the manner of the Indian response have both changed my mind, I think. The Indians have done so little to help themselves.

One of the few correspondents in all Asia who was able to maintain a reasonably balanced personal point of view in the face of so many difficulties was Selig S. Harrison, who covered India for the Washington *Post* for several years until he was replaced in 1965 by Warren Unna. Harrison, thirty-seven-years-old, was a bright, energetic, and highly articulate reporter who was extraordinarily well prepared. He had an A.B. from Harvard, had been a Nieman Fellow, an AP correspondent for a period of seven years in India, Pakistan, Nepal, Ceylon, and Afghanistan from 1951 on, and twice since had been in India on study tours. On his return to Washington, he had become an associate editor of the *New Republic* and later had joined the Washington *Post* staff as its New Delhi correspondent.

There was nothing particularly mysterious about the regularity with which Harrison's news essays appeared in the *Post* and elsewhere in the syndicate network that was built up through partnership with the Los Angeles *Times*. A considered decision to cover India and publish the results had been made at the *Post,* and it was taken seriously. Harrison's only instructions when he left were to write for the uninformed reader who wanted to know something about India and not to duplicate the agencies on ordinary stories. (By contrast, a colleague was told by his editor: "Write every story about India for your Aunt Minnie in the Bronx. And remember this, the minute you go native, you're going to get pulled back into the office.")

The years in India had not been easy for Harrison, although he had lived comfortably in a big house in the Friends Colony district of New Delhi. Perhaps the critical Sarkar had had him in mind when he referred to correspondents living like maharajahs. But it was an unkind and altogether inaccurate assessment of the manner of life that was led by a correspondent of Harrison's caliber. He worked steadily during most of his waking moments at the trying business of finding out what was happening in India and assessing its importance. He had been ill repeatedly with debilitating ailments; moreover, in the hot weather, he carried on alone and sent his family away to the cooler hill stations in the old British manner. In common with other correspondents, he had been subject to petty harassments by Indian officialdom but he hadn't let it bother him. He had been told, at times, that his work was not friendly to Indian interests; usually, such sentiments were conveyed by a pompous official when he had written with a certain degree of sympathy about the Muslims. But he realized that the Indians were trying very hard to insure a favorable press for their country and often tended to become overzealous in trying to impress correspondents with the supposed obligation of being nice to India.

It is the business of a first-rate correspondent to know the past of the area to which he is assigned, to write with clarity and meaning of the present, and to have an awareness of the future. Toward the end of 1963, more than eighteen months before Pakistan's desperate gamble to take power over Kashmir, Harrison had this to say:

> Pakistan now finds diplomatic avenues to a Kashmir settlement rapidly closing up . . . and this has prompted a search for new ways to keep the issue alive. Guerrilla warfare requires long preparation and a spirit of commitment yet to be activated in Pakistan-subsidized Azad [Free] Kashmir. Still, the prospect has to be kept in mind if only because it offers Pakistan's last chance. The risks of limited incursions would be relatively low and the stakes high in Indian discomfiture.[82]

What Harrison foresaw came to pass; and when it happened, American editors suddenly rose up in their wrath—as they always do at such times—and demanded, "Why weren't we told about all this?" They had been told at great length, just as they had been told before the outbreak of the Korean war. The correspondents had done their job. But because too many editors were bored with places like Korea and India, they weren't listening. And that, essentially, was the most trying part of a correspondent's job in Asia.

7. THE TRUTH IN SOUTH ASIA

When an American traveler returns from India exhilarated by his experience, he is generally viewed with suspicion. "But how can anybody *like* India?" he is often asked. If he then rashly proceeds to enlarge on the enormous potential of this awesome land, and the virtues of its people, he is challenged with the inevitable question: "But what about the terrible poverty in India? How can you have any hope when they take care of their cows and their monkeys and let hundreds of thousands of people starve in the streets?"

Such was the image of India that was most frequently encountered in rich and comfortable America. It was almost as if a libertarian lord of the manor had looked from his window with pity at the ragged farmers in the neighboring fields, seeing only their poverty and not the bitterness and the unrest that welled up inside them. For the tragedy of India—and, indeed, all of South Asia—was that few in the outside world had the slightest conception of the tremendous forces that were building up in the Indian subcontinent for an explosion which, if it occurred, would shake the earth. Every schoolchild in America had been taught what Napoleon had said and what Lenin had not said about the power of China to change the world, but India had remained a sleepy lotus land in the American mind for too many years.

There was a sense of shock in the United States when independence from Great Britain in 1947 plunged the subcontinent into the excesses of communal rioting, endangering the Muslim communities in India as well as the 8 to 10 million Hindus in Pakistan. But afterward, the world turned aside, and America, in particular, was only too ready to forget. The wire services kept sending their items from India and Pakistan, and occasionally, a correspondent would break through the wall of indifference. But until fighting erupted over Kashmir once again in 1965, the United States plucked up momentary interest in India when Jacqueline Kennedy rode an elephant there and thought of Pakistan only when the then Vice President Johnson brought a Pakistani camel driver to the United States. One could learn more from an occasional Indian film, a product of one of the greatest cinema industries in the world, than from 95 per cent of the daily American press, about the discontent on the subcontinent. But even here the Indians hurt themselves, for they never developed a strong documentary film product that might have been of interest to a U.S. television audience that was starved for substance.[83] As for the Pakistanis, their repressive press policies choked off what sympathy might have developed for their cause.

But the truth about South Asia was many-sided and could scarcely be summed up by the hostility of Muslim power against India; at worst, that was but a tremor compared to the upheaval of Indian life during the great Muslim conquests between the eleventh and the sixteenth centuries. For behind the Pakistani attacks to the West and the anti-Indian rioting in Indonesia to the East lay Communist China. Frank Moraes once wrote: "China does not confront India merely across 2,000 miles of mountainous frontier, for Sino-Indian rivalry and competition run like a jagged spine throughout South Asia."[84]

The question was not whether India and Pakistan could coexist. Despite their manifold differences, they had been able to do so for most of the first two decades of their independence. The real problem was whether China and India could coexist in Asia without a war that could, if it spread, engulf much of the earth. The neoisolationists who cried out in America that there were no vital American interests in

South Asia had forgotten the terrible lesson of World War I and World War II—that peace was indivisible. This was the American stake in the Indian subcontinent. It was not the truth that people in the United States wanted to hear, but it was the truth, nevertheless, that drew them against their will to the edge of the precipice.

VIII

Confrontation: America and Asia

1. PORTENTS AND PROSPECTS

IT IS MORE THAN a century since Bayard Taylor trod the decks of the U.S.S. "Susquehanna" off Shanghai and expressed his horror at the degradation of human life in Imperial China. The view from the Whangpoo had shocked him. "Welcome be the thunder storm which shall scatter and break up, though by means of fire and blood, this terrible stagnation," wrote the New York *Tribune*'s poet-correspondent. Like so many others who were to see Asia only in terms of an isolated, small-town America, however, he had no comprehension of what would happen when the gathering storm finally burst over China. He confessed to a "powerful aversion to the Chinese race" and solemnly admonished his countrymen: "Their touch is pollution, and, harsh as the opinion may seem, justice to our own race demands that they should not be allowed to settle on our soil." [1]

Such were the dominant American sentiments about the Orient in 1853. It is, of course, impossible to say what part Taylor may have played in propagating them across the land. But certainly, as the most popular lecturer of his time, he was not without influence, and he was not a man who easily concealed his feelings. He sought the "broader and higher human culture" for America, but in it he could find no place either for the Chinese or other Asians. [2] Four years after his death in 1878, the authors of the Chinese Exclusion Act of 1882 solidified the American feelings, which he had expressed, into an American law. That statute, with its subsequent modifications and the national-origins quota system imbedded in American immigration law from 1924 on, combined to turn Asians of talent and good will away from the United States for eighty-three years. It was not until the 1965 Immigration Act, which placed the peoples of all nations on an equal footing in applying for 170,000 annual admissions, that American policy at last moved away from the palsied hand of the past.

Mythologies of race do not color the feelings of today's Western journalists in Asia, by and large; nor do they infect much of the reportage of Asians in general from the United States, Great Britain, or Europe. If some of the modern journalists have a failing of the spirit, it is manifested in their inclination to panic over bad news, of which there is an unlimited quantity in Asia. Their weakness for "scare" stories, in particular almost anything that deals with Chinese Communist military might, is a case in point. Another is their tendency to continue to pander to old-fashioned editors' notions of Asia with outdated little gems about the quaint, exotic East. A stand has to be made somewhere against this kind of reportage; it must begin with the correspondent, because he is the only one who can stop it.

Yet, it would be a mistake to believe that the power of the correspondent, particularly those serving American media, is as great as it was in the past. Actually, it is not. His efforts to get at the truth all too often are unavailing against the vast engines of government publicity; for, especially in the liberal-minded West, the bureaucrat has learned all too quickly how to compete on better-than-equal terms with the independent reporter. Moreover, the pattern of the mass media in the West today is so intricate and their interests are so diverse that the relatively few correspondents in Asia (outside war zones) find it difficult to compete for attention against sensational news at home, burgeoning women's pages, sports, and all the other trappings of daily journalism. It takes the blundering of a Diem to cause the press to focus, even for a short time, on a single objective or cause.

It is still true, as it was in Bayard Taylor's time, that the primary decision about whether to publish news of Asia in any volume or degree of expertness rests not with the correspondent, but with the editor and publisher. If they believe it to be important, they will see that it gets into their newspaper (provided they have a correspondent who knows his job) and do their utmost to attract public attention to it. Should they be dissatisfied for any reason with the increasingly large wire-service file that passes between the United States and Asian countries, they may decide to use either the rapidly expanding syndicates or engage a trained specialist in Asian affairs. While the unskilled, untrained, unreliable correspondent still exists in various parts of Asia, and sometimes achieves temporary prominence, editors of even moderate discernment now realize that such a reporter can cause more trouble than no correspondent at all.

During too many years between Bayard Taylor's time and our own, despite a few brilliant exceptions, American editors and publishers for the most part neglected their responsibilities to present news of Asia in a manner that would be understandable to the informed reader, let alone the average man. The years of World War II and, to some extent, the Korean War, were exceptions, but only for news of military actions. Editors didn't seem to be interested in anything else.

Virtually all the stresses and strains of shaken economies and changing social patterns were ignored by the bulk of the American press. The rise of Communist China, therefore, came as a shock; its intervention in the Korean War, a stunning surprise. To a lesser extent, the destruction of the British, French, and Dutch colonial empires in the wake of Japanese conquests also caught the American public unprepared.

It was the Viet-Nam war, plus the three-week India-Pakistan war over Kashmir in the summer of 1965 and Chinese actions on their borders that brought Asian affairs forcibly to the forefront of American attention for the third time in a quarter-century. At the outset, the gloom of the American correspondents was monumental; had it not been for the good sense of their editors and a certain amount of blissful ignorance of what was being published, the American public might have been persuaded that the enormous American power in the South Pacific was on the point of being forced back to Hawaii by a comparatively small guerrilla army. Some of the academic authorities, notably Bernard Fall, made no secret of their feeling that the U.S. military position in South Viet-Nam was so bad as to be almost irretrievable.

The panic subsided, in any event, as more than 300,000 American troops established themselves along the coast of Viet-Nam while American air power began pounding North Viet-Nam as well as the guerrilla strongholds in South Viet-Nam. Even the gloomiest correspondents saw that things weren't quite as hopeless as they had seemed. And Fall, who had been called the "No. 1 pessimist," was persuaded to think somewhat better of American military strength.[3]

The turn of events in the Viet-Nam war demonstrated the power of the government over public opinion in the short term. The Johnson Administration displayed more resolution in South Viet-Nam and knew more about successfully applying American military strength than was evident from many dispatches during the escalation period of the conflict. When American forces quickly achieved stabilized positions along the coast and even took up posts in the highlands, the American public was pleasantly surprised. In the sudden flush of optimism, the tendency arose once more to overlook the basic weakness of the American intervention—the probability, admitted by the South Vietnamese Government, that the Communists came closer, at least in mid-1965, to representing the desires of more people than did Saigon.[4]

The publicizing of noble intentions for land reform and for an end to graft and profiteering in South Viet-Nam were not in themselves sufficient to allay all doubts, and the restiveness of the Buddhists in 1966 increased them.

Yet, it was evident from the conduct of the American intervention in Viet-Nam that the authority of the Presidency could tip the balance in many a struggle between press and government for the support of the public. While the record is replete with instances of the ability of a good newspaper to arouse and lead public opinion in a constructive manner, it is a rare newspaper that can successfully challenge a President of the United States. In the mid-1960's, few editors were disposed to try. One, who edited a prominent state-wide newspaper, even insisted that he could not hope to attract public attention to news of Asia unless the President himself attached importance to it in a public statement. Such an attitude was a tacit admission that a determined President could dominate the press in making a decisive impact on public opinion. It was certainly true of Lyndon Baines Johnson in his crusade for public support of his Viet-Nam policy. The stimulus that he exerted on the flow of news between the nations of Asia and the United States often took precedence over the desires of editors and publishers on what they should print. President Johnson, like Franklin Delano Roosevelt whom he so often tried to emulate, proved that he could dominate Page 1 as well as radio and television whenever he believed it sufficiently important to do so.

Another factor in the Asian-American news flow was the competence of the correspondents, their distribution, and the readiness of editors to accept what they sent. In most of Asia, outside war zones, both the shortage of American correspondents in key areas and the increasing use of local correspondents created a great deal of concern. In 1959, Coleman A. Harwell, then editor of the Nashville *Tennessean,* came home from a State Department lecturing program that took him to Afghanistan, Ceylon, and Indonesia with misgivings on both counts. While he recognized the excellence of many local correspondents and would not argue for sending more Americans to Asia than a news organization's earnings could justify, he said:

It seems obviously impractical to station a reporter in every country. But I feel that our news services should not only have men available for "action," they should develop men as area specialists and maintain close and regular tab on events in every country. It is good to know that a trend in this direction is already developing. It is to be hoped that the editors of America will take note of this coverage, insist that it be extended, and use it! [5]

Six years later, as a few more editors were using Asian copy other than war news, the wire services, the news syndicates, and even television began paying more attention to Asia, although the press as a whole did not do so. The growing awareness was an undoubted by-product of the rise of Communist China; for, just as Fidel Castro at one time constituted a threat to countries in Latin America, so Peking helped direct attention in the United States to countries in Asia that otherwise might have escaped notice.

It was also true that the very volume and viciousness of Communist China's propaganda against the United States did not always have quite the intended effect. The Chinese were not greatly beloved by the Asian nations around their perimeter, and the extent of their ill will sometimes served to raise doubts among the very people Peking wanted most to influence.

Necessarily, one of the most damaging blows that Chinese propaganda could strike at the United States was to question the basis for American intervention in Asian affairs. This was precisely the most sensitive area for American propaganda, for both American and Asian journalists frequently wrote that few people in Asia really understood what the United States wanted. The theme of such pieces was that people in South Viet-Nam, for example, could scarcely believe that American armed force and wealth were being used in lavish degree solely to save them from Communism and preserve their independence as a nation. Yet, a captured Viet Cong prisoner quite readily said that he understood that the United States and China were enemies, and the United States couldn't afford to let its ally South Viet-Nam be conquered by the pro-Peking forces of North Viet-Nam. It was an oversimplified view, but the unflagging hostility of Peking toward the United States had made the American presence understandable to an unlettered peasant. His views were found to be fairly representative among the Viet Cong who either defected or were captured.

By contrast with the slenderness of the coverage elsewhere in Asia, the large number of correspondents, photographers, and television newsmen who flocked to Saigon was impressive. Yet, once again, the end product was an illustration of the journalistic truth that the size of a correspondents' corps, although an indicator of the importance of the subject, did not in itself insure broader coverage of the news. The great necessity for making Asia understandable to the American people was an enlargement in the number of news organizations and syndicates that were willing to place well-trained, well-qualified correspondents in all key areas, regardless of whether wars were imminent or not. More correspondents like this were being trained at Far Eastern study centers in the great American universities, but their opportunities for employment were still limited. If it was encouraging to note the enlargement of the newspaper-syndicate field and the improvement in news-agency coverage of Asia in the 1960's, it was still difficult to persuade large numbers of editors to print the product. One wire-service series on the Japanese economy, for example, was generally ignored in the United States but published at length in the Manchester *Guardian*. There were, happily, instances to the contrary that led wire-service editors to continue to offer such material.

It was a great temptation for a young newspaper special, venturing into Asia for the first time, to make certain his stuff was played on Page 1 by concentrating on the menace of Red China, the imminence of an American defeat somewhere in Asia, the blundering inefficiency of foreign-aid administrators, the rapacious graft among Asian politicians who sided with the United States, and the amusing reactions of "funny little Asians" upon being exposed to such blessings of Western culture as the transistor radio, the frug, and the Beatles. This was what many editors had been led to expect from Asia and it was, unfortunately, a relatively simple matter to provide them with such heavily angled copy. Inevitably, some newcomers succumbed. In any large group of correspondents, it was also possible to find a young ex-GI who was only too happy to be given a chance to work off his grudges against the brass and a television reporter who would improve on the miseries of life by thoughtfully stage-directing scenes for his cameraman, although such operators were in the minority.

The press itself continually refused to deal with the far more important problems of trying to restrict mass coverage in places that either were dangerous or open to only limited coverage for other reasons. The correspondents left it to the officials of Asian governments or the American embassy, and sometimes both, to decide which correspondents should be accredited and which others were a part of the rag-bag assortment of foot-loose adventurers and stringers who flocked to every center of world interest.

In South Viet-Nam, for example, the refusal of both the correspondents and their editors for years to form any kind of working organization left the entire burden of administration to the American Government. Except for routine accreditation procedures, the South Vietnamese were not equipped to handle a large and diverse group. It ill became the press, therefore, to preach responsibility to the hard-pressed officials of JUSPAO when the correspondents showed so little trust in each other that they refused for a long time to form an organization to represent themselves and work with the governments concerned on problems of mutual interest.

Under the circumstances, it was remarkable that field censorship was not clapped on at once. Despite continual threats from the military to do so, however, the voluntary agreement of the correspondents to abide by the rules was not often violated and the penalties imposed were not too onerous, at least, not at the beginning.

After a year in Saigon, Barry Zorthian concluded on behalf of the American embassy:

> I think by and large that the press is doing a conscientious job in a very difficult, complicated situation. They are observing ground rules based on military security, and they are trying to provide the American people with a full picture of what is happening. The difficulties come about through the competitive nature of the news business, the difficulty of achieving balance in a tremendously complex situation, and the tendency of American readers to be interested primarily in the military aspects of the effort and, particularly, in the American involvement.[6]

It was, finally, the willingness of the American public to accept more news of Asian countries in the press and the electronic media that led to whatever improvements were possible in achieving a better understanding of Asians by Americans. This, the most basic principle governing the flow of news, was indispensable to the operation of the rest. That it happened at all was a tribute first of all to the expanding interests of the American educational system. It was to be expected that the war in Viet-Nam would quicken public awareness of the importance of the American commitment in Southeast Asia and elsewhere on that continent. The problem of both government and press in a democratic society was to sustain this greater public interest in Asia beyond the conclusion of the Viet-Nam war and the damping of the fires of conflict in adjacent areas.

2. PROBLEMS OF GOVERNMENT

Just before President Johnson's trip to Southeast Asia in 1961, while he was still Vice President, he welcomed an old friend from the Interior Department, Arthur ("Tex") Goldschmidt, who had become a U.N. official. During a quick lunch of hamburgers at the Vice President's desk, Goldschmidt spoke enthusiastically of the Mekong Valley development project, which was then in its planning stage. Rice production alone, he said, would be increased five- or six-fold and the completion of dam-building would, he added, "make TVA look like a minor operation."

Johnson became deeply interested in the Mekong Valley program during his visit. By chance, he came across another familiar face, Cesar Ortiz, who had been one of his pupils in a Texas high school and who was then the U.N. information officer attached to the Mekong development office. Although Ortiz put out press releases on the Vice President's visit and otherwise attempted to call attention to the importance of the Mekong project, there wasn't the slightest interest in the United States.

Just before President Johnson's speech at Johns Hopkins on April 7, 1965, when he was drafting his proposal for a billion-dollar American investment in the development of Southeast Asia, including the Mekong Valley, he had his office search the press for items bearing on his 1961 visit and found only a casual mention of it. What he finally had to do to get a record of what he had said was to send to the headquarters of the U.N. Economic Commission for Asia and the Far East for Cesar Ortiz's press release of May 17, 1961. There, he was on record as having said that he could "think of nothing that would help Thailand, Laos, Cambodia and Vietnam more than working together" on the Mekong project, which, he predicted, would "bring prosperity to millions in the region." [7]

For four years thereafter, whatever American public interest there was in Southeast Asia remained focused on the growing American military commitment. It was a part of the tacit understanding between most foreign correspondents and their editors that such vast projects as the Mekong, despite their importance, had no relevance to the United States, and few paid any attention to them. Yet, in the aftermath of President Johnson's speech at Johns Hopkins, when the plaudits came from Asia and Europe for this imaginative approach to Southeast Asia's most basic needs, it became clear that, once the war subsided, the Mekong program was the best hope for a durable peace.

C. V. Narasimhan, the Indian civil servant who had become chief of cabinet to the U.N. Secretary General, pointed out that, until the President made his proposal for the Mekong Valley, there had been little public understanding of what it really meant to the 20 million people of the lower river area. Even afterward, a substantial body of American opinion entertained the notion that the Mekong project was something new, made possible only by the United States, although nearly a score of nations had already given material and technical aid. Moreover, the political and military conflicts in the area had never been permitted to interfere with the joint planning meetings of the four riparian states—Cambodia, Laos, South Viet-Nam, and Thailand. [8]

The incident illustrated one of the basic difficulties of the American Government in projecting its Asian policies to its own public, let alone to the publics of Southeast Asia. It was, primarily, a human problem—

the essential interest in the drama of war and the boredom with the
long and intricate discussions that were necessary for resolving conflicts
and in the search for a more durable peace. The power of the Presidency itself had to be invoked, in conjunction with the pledging of a
billion dollars, to awaken public interest even momentarily in the Mekong program. In Southeast Asia and elsewhere, many worthy American contributions were overlooked because of the greater interest in war
news; and it became extremely difficult to make even well-disposed
Asians understand that the American interests in Asia were often identical with those of many underdeveloped countries of the area.

It fell to a relatively small number of American officials in Washington—a handful of top people in the White House, State Department,
and Pentagon—to explain American policy in Asia to those correspondents, columnists, commentators, and editors who were willing to listen.
It was often suggested by the unknowing that lower-echelon officials
could do this kind of briefing. However, few except the youngest and
least experienced journalists were disposed to accept information from
officials who had no hand in decision-making. The more important the
journalist, the more disposed he was to go to the top. Since there were
so few decision-makers at the top, and since they were already working
seven days a week on the problems developed by various Asian conflicts, a decreasing amount of time remained for publicizing foreign
policy properly. It continued to be the business of the President of the
United States, the Secretary of State, and a few officials around them to
do much of this work themselves in talks with individual journalists or
small groups of correspondents and editors. Some ambassadors in Asia
were equally in demand by the Asian press leadership.

A few powerful figures in the American Government thus had the
almost impossible job of funneling what they could tell into a fantasti-
cally complicated communications network serving hundreds of millions
of people. Even a whisper bearing on the development and promotion
of American policy in Asia, when fed into so powerful an engine of
publicity, could be amplified into a thunderclap. Under the system as it
existed in the mid-1960's, it is a wonder that American support for
policies that were only partly understood, at best, could have remained
so great and so steadfast. As for the Asians, it was remarkable that there
was as much sympathy and understanding for the basic American position as was evidenced in at least a part of their press. In short, because
of the limitations of the decision-making process in Washington, too
few Americans were trying to do too many things to persuade too
many people. The President's exhausting Asian trip in 1966 was a case
in point.

If there was any doubt about the importance of the newspaper in this communications process, it was allayed by the third of a series of surveys conducted at four-year intervals by the American Institute of Public Opinion. The 1965 study, conducted by Dr. George Gallup, showed that 71 per cent of 3,205 respondents in the United States read a daily newspaper as compared to 58 per cent who listened to radio news and 55 per cent to television news. The Gallup report said:

> Analysis of the figures by groups reveals even greater advantages in terms of actual coverage of the newspaper in reaching the better educated and higher income groups. Whereas 85 per cent of those persons who have a college education reported having read a daily newspaper yesterday, only 72 per cent report having heard radio news yesterday and only 61 per cent report having looked at TV news yesterday.
>
> In the lowest education level the differences are much less marked. A total of 57 per cent of those who did not go beyond grade school report having read a daily newspaper yesterday, 46 per cent report having listened to radio news yesterday and 48 per cent looked at news on TV.[9]

This estimate of the communications process served to emphasize the conclusions of Secretary of State Rusk about reporting on developments in Asia. These were his comments in an interview:

> It is the responsibility of the press to get at the news and publish it or broadcast it. The functions of the press and of the public official are in a sense conflicting in some areas of foreign policy and it is a good thing in a democratic society that they are.
>
> While the press must make every effort to get at the news, it is scarcely the function of the press to make foreign policy, whatever it may do with its independent right to comment and criticize. However worthy an editor or a columnist may be, and however profound his knowledge, he has not been elected to the government and does not therefore have the responsibility for the conduct of foreign policy.
>
> There are certain clear lines of foreign policy that have led down a broad highway ever since the beginning of the post-war era. It is interesting to see how, when a government has tended to swerve over to the soft shoulders, either to the right or the left, the pressure of public opinion has been exerted to bring it back to the center of the road. Certainly, there is an interaction between government and public opinion in foreign policy that is readily observable.
>
> It is, therefore, the function of the Department of State in this area to provide maximum access to the knowable, and this we do to the fullest extent of our ability. Only a fraction of one per cent of what is knowable is withheld for one reason or another. We strive to be accurate and to be

complete in presenting the facts. The one thing that cannot be tolerated in the Department under any circumstances is to lie to the public. We may not be able to say anything on a developing issue but what we do say must always be truthful.

I think the American public is the best informed in the world. It is important to us that this educational process be continued and enlarged. But there are, of course, limits to what the public can absorb, and we are aware of that as much as any editor is.

There is only a certain amount of time that even the most interested citizen can devote to foreign affairs and the mounting volume of information that is available to him—in the newspapers, the news magazines, on TV, the radio, in current books. People have their own interests, their business and social activities, the affairs of their own neighborhood and community. They can't give a great deal of time to the tremendous amount of new material that is made available daily. I doubt, for instance, that many editors, except for those primarily responsible, ever get through the complete daily wire service file on foreign developments.

I give the press high marks for publishing so much material bearing on foreign affairs. There may be differences of view in interpretation, emphasis and selection of what is reported, in one matter or another, but there is no doubt whatever that on the hard news of events, the press does an excellent job.

The policy-makers in the American Government had learned long since to live with the imperfections of the free press, considering the benefits that it extended to them as well as to the public at large. But few who had any teaching experience in American universities were content with the manner in which the press discharged its educational function—an area in which old-line editors denied they had any responsibility. Secretary Rusk, for example, was concerned at one time with the tendency of columnists, editorialists, and radio-TV commentators to try to peer into the future instead of attempting with equal facility to explore the past. He said:

With the increasing activity of the electronic media in making available the hard news almost as it happens, many of our leading newspapers are turning more and more to comment. In the 19 years since I first came to the Department of State, for instance, there has been a tremendous increase in the popularity of the signed column and, consequently, in its availability and influence.

The focus of interpretive material, however, is seldom on the knowable, on the past and the present, but rather on the unknowable future—what will happen next in Southeast Asia? In Europe? In Latin America and

Africa? We are in such a rush to meet the future and deal with it that we sometimes hasten the present and disregard the lessons of the past. And yet, we can only understand foreign policy in terms of what has already happened. The events that have occurred in Southeast Asia can be explained only in terms of what happened there in 1954 and 1962—and this kind of background information is seldom published in any great volume except by particularly perceptive editorial writers and commentators.

I think we would all be better off if we took the time and made the effort to know the lessons of the past before we tried to peer into the unknowable future to judge our foreign policies.

In a nation in which 40 per cent of all the people were under twenty years of age and 54 million were going to school, it was inevitable that there would be talk about addressing information about foreign policy primarily to an intellectual elite. It was greatly to the credit of the decision-makers in Washington that such authoritarian notions fell on deaf ears. Elitism was not regarded as a solution for the flaws either in the communications system or in the natural lag between policy formulation and public understanding of it. Secretary Rusk said on this score:

It is a part of the governmental process in a democratic society for the press both to report the news fully and fairly and to take a hard, questioning look at all governmental policy. Without an able press, the whole character of an open society would be in danger. We are well aware of our own responsibilities and, now and in the future, intend to improve our information facilities [in the Department of State] so far as it is possible for us to do so.[10]

Despite the government's difficulties in explaining its policies, the press maintained its traditional posture with relatively few exceptions. Even in the midst of the Viet-Nam war, it was considered impossible to introduce so mild a cooperative measure as the British D-Note [D for Defense] system, informally requesting editors not to publish certain matters bearing on national defense. When publication tended to interfere with military security, the most the government could do was to threaten to impose censorship, but nobody in authority wanted to go through with it except in the unlikely event of some life-and-death emergency. In a press that was animated by a kind of philosophical anarchism, the best that could be expected was a degree of self-imposed restraint and regulation. The only program that existed for trying to close the communications gap on Asian-American affairs was to muddle through.

3. CORRESPONDENTS IN ASIA: A SUMMARY *

In the summer and fall of 1965, several hundred correspondents for American news organizations were hard at work in Asia. They covered the intensified war in Viet-Nam, the three-week war between India and Pakistan over Kashmir and its consequences, the overturn in Indonesia, the separation of Singapore from Malaysia and the provocative Communist Chinese border incidents. Japan and the Philippines were of interest primarily as communications centers, and little was heard of Taiwan, Thailand, Burma, and other areas.

Despite all adverse factors, it was fair to say in one sense that the flow of news between the principal nations of Asia and the United States was greater than at any time since World War II, that the corps of correspondents was better than it had been since the Korean war, and that the American public was the best-informed in the world on Asian affairs. Yet, it was equally true that the news exchanges, the work of the correspondents, and the degree of public understanding of Asian affairs in the United States left much to be desired. Comparisons could be very misleading when there were few correspondents in Asia other than those of American organizations, Reuters, and the Japanese press, when the flow of news was based primarily on war coverage, and when the American public was the least poorly informed, rather than the most knowledgeable. It all depended on how the case was put.

The wire services were still the work horses. The AP and the UPI provided the vast majority of the American press and the electronic media with Asian news. In lively rivalry with Reuters and, to a lesser extent, AFP, the Deutsche Press Agentur, and Kyodo, the Japanese agency, they also brought a large volume of American and world news to Asia. Of the newspapers, the New York *Times* still had the largest number of correspondents in Asia and the most impressive coverage, although the Washington Post-Los Angeles Times alliance was stepping up its coverage and the old Chicago *Daily News* syndicate was trying hard to improve its limited file. Of the individual newspapers with more than a lone representative in Asia, the Baltimore *Sun, Christian Science Monitor,* and *Wall Street Journal* covered certain areas in depth, and such newcomers as the Copley Press were getting established. In both numbers and enterprise, the Time-Life service was the leader among the weeklies; but *Newsweek* did outstanding and sometimes distinguished work, and *U.S. News & World Report,* with only a few correspondents, could provide meaningful interpretations of events. McGraw-Hill and Fairchild gave specialized business and financial

* See Appendix I.

coverage of Asian news. As for television, the individual worth of the few regularly assigned correspondents contrasted strikingly with the helter-skelter use to which they were put. The television war reporters and photographers in South Viet-Nam soon proved that they could do first-rate work if they were left on an assignment for any length of time. Theirs was a heartening example of what television could do if it really tried.

Occasionally, a waspish intellectual would challenge the quality of American coverage in Asia, which was obviously not above serious criticism. The charge was made on more than one occasion that the *Times* of London, the *Guardian* of Manchester, the *Economist, Le Monde, Figaro,* the *Neue Zürcher Zeitung,* and some lesser known publications gave better coverage of Asian news than the American papers. The only trouble with such a charge was that few of these papers could afford to keep enough permanent correspondents in Asia to give reasonably consistent and complete coverage. While not all American correspondents could stand up to the best of the foreigners, the outstanding ones were their equals if not superiors. For one thing, they had the experience; for another, they had the support of wealthy and powerful news-gathering organizations. The New York *Times,* the Washington *Post,* the Los Angeles *Times,* the Baltimore *Sun,* and the *Christian Science Monitor* often came off with honors in a comparison with foreign competition. Those newspapers that subscribed to the best of the American news syndicates usually could have confidence that the service offered to them from Asia was as good as any abroad, and often better, although that did not mean that correspondents in Asia as a whole could approach the expertness of their colleagues who served in Europe. The correspondents stationed in Europe, London, and Washington, for many reasons, were more highly regarded, some because they were better known, others because of long years of service in a single capital.

The decline of both British and European interest in Asian affairs coincided with the liquidation of the colonial empires in Asia. Reuters, AFP, and the American wires services delivered most of the Asian news in Great Britain and Europe. In a typical year, such as 1964, one could travel from Japan to New Delhi and find few Western newspaper correspondents other than the Americans. There were a handful of British, an occasional Frenchman, one or two Swiss, Dutch, and West Germans. As for the Asians, the Japanese appeared in strength whenever their national interests were involved. The Indians tried, within their smaller means, to staff key points. Here and there, one could find an occasional Korean or Filipino working for publications at home. With these exceptions, and the local stringers, Asia generally was not covered by Asian newspapers, and in not too great depth by most Europeans. A few British publications like the London *Daily Telegraph*, the *Times*, the *Guardian*, the *Observer*, and the *Express*, continued to make a serious effort, with minimal staffing, to report from key points in Asia. So did *Le Monde* and *Figaro* in Paris.

Consequently, the American news organizations, despite their shortcomings, merited the more detailed study which has been undertaken in these pages, and which now is to be summarized. In all, ninety-one representatives of American news organizations who seemed to meet the definition of a foreign correspondent answered detailed questionnaires during the summer of 1964. About a dozen others between Tokyo and New Delhi were on the list for questionnaires and depth interviews but were not included because they were on home leave or otherwise not available.

This was not a census of foreign correspondents in the area, although it came close to the total of permanently assigned Americans, their foreign counterparts who worked for American news organizations, permanent stringers or other replacements for full-timers on leave, and locals with major responsibilities. The only omissions were locals with technical jobs and those who did not want to answer a questionnaire or be interviewed for their own reasons.

Those who participated in the questionnaire analysis of their work included 75 Americans; 3 each from Japan and Korea; 2 each from the Philippines and India; and 1 each from Great Britain, New Zealand, Australia, France, Lebanon, and Nationalist China. Their average age was 38.5 years. They had served in the area for an average of 20.3 months in the post they held at the time of the survey. Except for 9 correspondents who were either locals in fixed positions or permanent stringers, the rest had put in an average of 7.8 years overseas. They had been journalists for an average of about 15 years. They represented 15 American newspapers or newspaper groups, 3 weekly news magazines, 2 business-news organizations, 2 magazines of general circulation, 2 American wire services, 3 radio networks, and 2 other radio services. Four regional chiefs and numerous bureau chiefs were included, although many of the latter ran a bureau with 1 local or perhaps 2 at most. There were also 2 photographic area managers who acted as correspondents when they were in the field.

While all except 9 correspondents claimed an acquaintance with one language other than English, there were relatively few accomplished linguists in the group except for those who had been born abroad. European languages predominated. Not many Americans had been able to become proficient in Japanese, Chinese, or Russian, and only 1 had a nodding acquaintance with Hindi and Urdu. The linguistic talent among the correspondents was centered largely in the Asian correspondents who worked for the American news organizations represented in the survey. As one American explained it, "We are shifted around too frequently to make a serious effort to learn a language for which we will have little use later. No American news organization is going to take the trouble to train us in languages for an assignment of only short duration. Only the government would have the money to support such a project."

Of the 39 newspaper and wire-service correspondents who estimated the average size of their dispatches, not all filed daily; however, the average length of their dispatches came to 600 to 690 words. Of the 6 radio-TV correspondents who estimated what their daily file was, 5 said they normally transmitted 45-second voicecasts daily and one normally transmitted a 90-second voicecast. Of 10 correspondents for news weeklies who estimated the average size of their dispatches, the average came to 1,120 to 1,540 words in a normal week. For a cover story, of course, the wordage could go up to 10,000 words or more. Of the 18 correspondents who were willing to estimate the cost of their file per month in cable or radioteletype tolls, the average came to $627.50. However, this varied widely with the story. Some files in Saigon during a major period of activity could run to $2,500 a month or more for a single newspaper special. In the sample, the highest estimates were $1,500 and $1,800, respectively, for newspaper specials.

It was rather interesting that the correspondents were, on the whole, lower in estimating their costs to their employers, exclusive of filing charges, than were the employers in figuring what their correspondents cost them on the same basis. In the following tabulation, salary, cost-of-living bonus, housing allowances, travel, etc., are a part of the correspondents' estimates:

Category	Range of Estimated Annual Costs	Average
5 radio-TV correspondents	$10,000–$50,000	$30,000
16 magazine correspondents	$ 7,500–$50,000	$27,780
17 newspaper specials	$ 7,500–$45,000	$27,000
7 regional and bureau chiefs	$12,000–$45,000	$18,714
9 wire-service and deskmen correspondents	$ 4,800–$15,000	$ 9,935
8 stringers	$ 600–$ 9,000	$ 4,675

AVERAGE COST PER CORRESPONDENT IN SURVEY, BASED ON ABOVE $20,184

These estimates of costs, of course, reflected the actual salaries in only a few cases. For example, in Asia, a stringer could be paid as little as $25 to $50 a month and a wire-service correspondent might be given $4,800 a year and sometimes less. Experienced wire-service men earned from $8,000 to $9,000 a year. Among newspaper specials, the going rates ranged from $12,000 to $16,000 a year, and an old-time star could go higher. The news magazines paid from $8,000 to $10,000 for younger men to around $18,000 to $20,000 for their top people, and one or two probably received more. The radio-TV correspondents who flew all over Asia with little rest were the top earners in the group, with one exception, their rates going to $25,000 a year, plus bonuses. The top man was in the $45,000 to $50,000 range.

While it was difficult for correspondents to say precisely what their travels had been for a twelve-month period preceding July–August, 1964, this was their best recollection:

Eight correspondents had six to ten months' travel away from their base, ranging from 75,000 to 100,000 miles or more.

Eighteen correspondents had three to six months' travel away from their base, ranging from 25,000 to 75,000 miles.

Forty-five correspondents had at least three months' travel away from their base, up to about 25,000 miles.

Ten traveled within the country to which they had been assigned. Ten others reported no travel.

The 91 correspondents appeared reasonably well satisfied, for the most part, by the assistance that was given them by American embassies. In response to a question, 16 rated embassy assistance as excellent; 31, good; 15, fair; 8, poor; 11, variable; and 10 made no comment. They were less pleased with assistance given them by host governments, the response in this question being 7, excellent; 26, good; 17, fair; 15, poor; 16, variable; and 10, no comment, Seventy of the correspondents said news was generally not difficult to obtain in Asia; but most of them qualified their responses, based on their experiences in trying to go below the surface of events. Nineteen others said news was difficult to obtain, particularly in places like South Viet-Nam, Indonesia, Pakistan, and Burma. One correspondent summed it up this way: "Substantive news not contained in official announcements is always difficult to get in Asia."

On the question of the credibility of news from official U.S. sources, the correspondents divided as follows: always believable, 2; believable most of the time, 55; believable part of the time, 26; seldom believable, 1; varies, 4; and no reply, 3. The correspondents appeared to be more generous in their evaluation of American official credibility in the questionnaire than they were in their in-depth interviews, where individual gripes more often came to the surface.

In an analysis of obstacles that separated correspondents from their sources in Asia, the respondents named the following: language barrier, 22; suspicion and mistrust, 17; local customs (meaning the Japanese press clubs), 7; geography, 4; communications, 4; other causes, 13 (including 10 who protested their inability to visit Communist China). Ten made no reply and 14 reported they had found no obstacles. Only 1 correspondent charged that U.S. embassy personnel had blocked him off from news sources.

The correspondents leaned heavily to spot news as their primary interest in Asia, for it was listed by 43 out of the 91. Of the rest, 33 specialized in analysis, 5 in features, and 10 were interested in general news of all kinds. Their primary subjects were as follows: politics, 24; military (the Viet-Nam war), 18; Communist China, 17; the cold war in general, 7; business and finance, 7; general subjects, 4; news of dominant leaders and cultural news, 1 each; and no choice, 12. As second choices, there was little change, so that in a summary of both first and second choices it was not surprising that the three top interests of the 91 correspondents in Asia were political affairs, the Viet-Nam war, and Communist China.

When asked to estimate how much of their material was published or broadcast, most of the correspondents seemed satisfied. Their estimates were:

Per Cent Used		*Number of Responses*
90–100	24,	mainly newspaper specials
75–90	11 ⎱	mainly radio-TV, plus a few other
50–75	5 ⎰	newspaper specials
50 or less	14,	mainly news magazine men; as little as 25 per cent is used at times
Used in Asia more than in U.S.	33,	wire services, excepting Saigon copy (which is more widely used than any other dateline in the U.S.)
Nothing	1,	a magazine special who had run into bad luck and seen nothing used for an entire year
No estimates given	3	

While 36 correspondents had no suggestions for improving the use made of their file, others thought that editors should pay more attention to news of Asia, give more space to foreign news generally, make a greater effort to publish or broadcast news analyses, and do less rewriting of dispatches. Four hard-shelled correspondents suggested that better informed editors would help. Among miscellaneous suggestions were the following: more editors should visit Asia; shorter dispatches; brighter writing; a daily TV show based on news in perspective; less accumulation of stories to avoid having them mashed together in one roundup for the Sunday paper; a larger magazine section; and less second-guessing by editors.

The 91 correspondents saw considerable room for improvement on the coverage of the United States in the Asian press. In response to a question about the adequacy with which the United States was reported in the press of their host country: 11 said it was excellent; 18, good; 38, fair; 14, poor, and 10 made no comment. Thirty-four correspondents thought the coverage of the United States was improving in the Asian press; 10 others didn't; 18 detected no change and 29 had no comment. The principal reasons given for a relatively poor American image in the Asian press were lack of interest in the United States, lack of knowledge about the United States, the political orientation of the Asian press, sensationalism, lack of professional competence among some Asians, lack of space, and the anti-American policy of some governments. Those who had noted that the United States had a relatively good press in certain countries (Japan, the Philippines, and Malaysia) attributed it to the strength of American ties in those lands and the professional competence of the press.

In answer to a question which asked them to specify the reasons why and the general areas in which there were distortions or gaps in the reporting of the United States in the Asian press, the correspondents listed the following: reporting of U.S. racial tensions, 11; partisan approach, 10; inability to understand the American political and social system, 9; too much reporting from Washington and too little from elsewhere, 6; poor quality of the Asian press, 5; and lack of knowledge of the United States, 3. In spite of all their objections, however, the correspondents concluded that the press (all media) in their host countries was generally favorable to the United States. In the responses, 40 said yes, 21 said yes with qualifications, only 7 said no, and 23 made no comment.

The respondents were asked to name the outstanding specialists in their area and were free to name academic authorities or journalists. Thirty-one of the 91 correspondents either declined to answer or said there were no specialists they cared to name.

Of the academic authorities who were mentioned by five or more correspondents, this was the standing: Ambassador Edwin O. Reischauer (on Japan), 13; Professor A. Doak Barnett (on China), 8; Professor John K. Fairbank (on China), 5; and Professor Bernard Fall (on Viet-Nam), 5.

There were scattered votes for General Maxwell Taylor, the late Sir George Sansom, James Morley, Donald Keene, P. J. Honey, Shintaro Ryu, and Tom McHale, of the Ford Foundation.

Of the journalists who were mentioned five times or more, this was the standing: Keyes Beech, Chicago *Daily News;* Robert P. Martin, *U.S. News & World Report;* and John Roderick, AP.

These following were mentioned three or more times: Selig Harrison, Washington *Post,* on India; Dennis Bloodworth, London *Observer,* on Southeast Asia; Tillman Durdin, New York *Times,* on China; Loren Fessler, *Time,* on China; Stan Karnow, Washington *Post,* on Southeast Asia; Sol Sanders, *U.S. News & World Report,* on India; and John Randolph, formerly AP, on Japan. There were scattered votes for many others including A. M. Rosenthal, who left Tokyo in 1962 to become the New York *Times's* metropolitan editor.

Most of the correspondents reported that they had found friendly attitudes in the countries to which they had been assigned, for only 5 complained of unfriendly receptions, and 9 made no comment. Sixty-two found their assignments expensive, whereas 20 did not. Of the total, 58 said they had visited frequently in the homes of citizens in their host country, 16 reported they seldom were invited, and only 8 said they had never been asked out. While most correspondents talked about the deteriorating position of the "white man" in Asia, 48 of them reported that they had experienced no discrimination in any form and only 2 complained of racial discrimination. Curiously, both cases arose from marriages to Asian girls. Eleven of the correspondents said they had felt discrimination against them because they were foreigners; 7, because they were foreign journalists who were barred from Japanese correspondents' clubs; 7, because of unduly high rents and high prices; 4, because they had been barred from Japanese inns and bars; and 2, because they were Americans. Given their own free choice, 51 of the correspondents said they would return to the countries to which they were assigned at the time of the survey; 5 said they might; and 20 said they wouldn't; while 15 made no reply. As an illustration of the rapidity with which assignments shift in Asia, more than 50 per cent of the participants of the survey were in different posts or working for different organizations two years after its completion.

If the survey established anything at all, it was that the correspondents for the most part liked their work and wanted to continue to report from Asia. Moreover, it appeared that many of them displayed a considerable difference in their personal and professional attitudes toward Asia and the Asians. Personally, many were charmed; professionally, they concentrated on the adverse trends in war and politics on the Asian mainland that had become almost standard fare for the American newspapers that were interested in news from Asia.

The result was far from perfect. But it was the best that could be obtained, under the circumstances, by a group of independent correspondents of less than battalion strength, in military terms, who strove under the greatest difficulties to report the struggles of the larger part of the underprivileged of mankind to their more fortunate brethren.

4. THE USES OF FOREIGN NEWS *

Tension was rising all over Asia in the summer of 1964. The war in Southeast Asia had reached a critical point in both Viet-Nam and Laos despite American intervention, with the Viet Cong and the Pathet Lao holding the advantage in their respective countries. In Tokyo, the Philippines tried unsuccessfully to mediate between its feuding neighbors, giant Indonesia and tiny Malaysia; following the collapse of summit talks, small Indonesian commando landings began along the exposed Malaysian coast. The United States was shipping arms to Thailand. And in India, gripped by its worst food shortage since independence, there was renewed concern over hostile Pakistani moves in the Kashmir area. From the Himalayan ramparts, where Chinese Communist soldiers threatened the vast Indian subcontinent, to the cities of Korea, where student rioters strove in vain to overthrow the government of the Republic of Korea, peace seemed a far-off prospect and peoples everywhere in the area waited to see what the United States intended to do.

A survey of the news published during that period between June 15–21, July 13–19, and August 17–23, inclusive, showed that the New York *Times* devoted a daily average of 4.2 columns to Asian affairs, out of its daily average of 18.3 columns given over entirely to cabled or radioed foreign news. The Los Angeles *Times,* for the same three-week test period, published 3.3 columns of Asian news on the average, out of its daily average foreign news space of 9.4 columns. The *Christian Science Monitor*'s averages were 2 columns of Asian news out of a daily total of 10.1 columns for foreign news; the Washington *Post,* 1.8 columns out of 7; the St. Louis *Post-Dispatch,* 1.3 columns out of 3.7; the Chicago *Daily News,* 0.95 of a column out of 3.8; the Philadelphia *Inquirer,* 0.9 of a column out of 3.5 columns.

These newspapers were selected as representative of the internationally minded sector of the American press in its coverage of Asian affairs. The period, chosen in advance for the survey, was admittedly

* See Appendix III.

one in which all foreign news, including news of Asia, was less likely to attract maximum attention than some other time of the year. It was, in fact, probably the slowest time of the year for the publication of Asian news because of the passage of the Civil Rights Bill during the June week of the test period, the Presidential nomination of Barry Goldwater by the Republicans during the July week, and the preoccupation with preparations for the nomination of President Johnson by the Democrats during the August week. It was hoped that these events would evince a livelier appreciation of the value of American news in the Asian press than was usual. For the American press, it was worth noting that a basic minimum of the news of Asia did get in despite the heavy run of domestic news that summer, traditionally a time for slack advertising and tight newspapers. That was the best that could be said for the performance.

An expression of the results in terms of percentages gave an even clearer indication of the priorities for Asian news among some of the American press leaders. The New York *Times,* for example, devoted 22 per cent of its live news space (excluding financial, sports, women's, amusements, etc.) to foreign news during the test period and 20 per cent of that to Asian news. The Los Angeles *Times* averages were 15 per cent of its live news space for foreign news, and 35 per cent of that for Asian news; the Washington *Post,* 12 and 25 per cent; the *Christian Science Monitor,* 37 and 19 per cent; the Chicago *Daily News,* 10 and 25 per cent; the St. Louis *Post-Dispatch,* 9 and 34 per cent; and the Philadelphia *Inquirer,* 8 and 26 per cent.

All except two of the American newspapers used their own foreign correspondents as the major source of their foreign news, including news of Asia. The New York *Times* filled 85 per cent of its foreign news space with the work of its own correspondents, the *Christian Science Monitor,* 77 per cent; the Chicago *Daily News,* 55 per cent; the Los Angeles *Times,* 47 per cent; the Washington *Post,* 31 per cent. The St. Louis *Post-Dispatch* and the Philadelphia *Inquirer,* without regular foreign staffs of their own, used only 8 per cent and 2 per cent, respectively, of foreign news from their staff people. The next largest source of foreign news, on the average, was the AP running as high as 43 per cent of the foreign news space of the St. Louis *Post-Dispatch.* UPI, Reuters, and the syndicates of the newspapers with foreign news staffs followed.

If there was anything at all remarkable about the American performance, it was the extent to which the Los Angeles *Times,* a newcomer to the field of foreign news reporting by staff correspondents, had devoted its efforts to improving its coverage of the world in general and of Asia in particular. The Washington *Post,* similarly, had made considerable progress in improving its foreign service, which was run as a part of its cooperative venture with the Los Angeles *Times*. There were, of course, other newspapers with enduring interests in foreign news coverage and small staffs of correspondents, but none with as much scope as the leaders and such specialized newspapers as the *Christian Science Monitor*. From the performance of other first-rate newspapers without foreign staffs of their own, there was reason to suspect that the American press was not overly excited about Asian news at that particular time. In any event, nobody was within reach of the New York *Times*, even if it was publishing less foreign news than it had a decade before.

No direct comparison, of course, could be made between the American press and the far smaller newspapers published in Asian countries. While the largest Japanese newspapers had three times the circulation of the largest American newspaper, the Japanese reader had to absorb his news from far fewer pages. For the 1964 test period, the live news space of the Japanese "Big Three" was roughly the same as that of the *Christian Science Monitor*. The leading newspapers of Southeast Asia and India were slightly larger as far as space for live news was concerned. But all the Asian papers were edited far more closely than most of the leading American papers. They were as watchful of space as, for example, the New York *Daily News*, probably the most tightly edited paper in the United States.

The results of the study of the Japanese press leaders indicated that Japanese newspapers featured domestic affairs just as heavily as American newspapers in 1964 and seemed relatively unexcited by the big domestic news from the United States. It was a period when the U.N. Trade Conference was under way in Geneva; when the marathon disarmament conference was still dragging along; and when Japan was preparing for the Olympic Games, watching for a new approach to Communist China, and absorbing the shock of the Niigata earthquake.

The morning editions of *Asahi Shimbun* ran 21.6 columns a day of live news, on the average, during the test period, with 5.6 columns devoted to foreign news and 2 columns of that given over to news of the United States. The morning editions of *Mainichi Shimbun* averaged 25.4 columns of live news space, with 4.3 columns of foreign news and 0.95 of a column of U.S. news. The morning editions of *Yomiuri Shimbun* averaged 24.2 columns of live news space, with 2.9 columns of foreign news and 0.6 of a column of U.S. news.* In both *Mainichi* and *Yomiuri* there was more news of Europe and Asia, respectively, than there was of the United States—and the American dispatches included both foreign and domestic news.

* Japanese columns have been expressed here in terms of New York *Times*-sized columns. See appendix for calculation.

Asahi devoted 26 per cent of its live news space to foreign news and divided this as follows: U.S. news, 37 per cent; Asian, 26 per cent; European, 30 per cent. *Mainichi* gave only 17 per cent of its live news space to foreign news, divided as follows: U.S. news, 21 per cent; Asian news, 25 per cent; European news, 46 per cent. *Yomiuri* devoted 22 per cent of its live news space to foreign news, divided as follows: U.S. news, 19 per cent; Asian news, 34 per cent; European news, 39 per cent. The dominant morning editions referred to here set the pattern for the rest of the Japanese press.

Just as was the case with the leading American newspapers, the Japanese took most of their foreign news from their own correspondents, with the AP being the next largest source (except for *Mainichi Shimbun*). The morning editions of *Asahi Shimbun* carried 60 per cent of its foreign news from its own correspondents, 11 per cent from the AP. The spread was even greater on the morning editions of *Mainichi Shimbun,* with 71 per cent of the foreign news coming from its own correspondents and only 10 per cent from UPI. For the morning editions of *Yomiuri Shimbun,* almost 55 per cent of the foreign news came from its own correspondents and 18 per cent from the AP.

Regardless of whether the Japanese correspondents in Washington took their news from American newspapers and wire services or dug it up on their own, the survey established their primacy as major sources of intelligence about the United States. What they said was prominently published and carried great weight, not only with their editors but with their enormous reading public. The relative obscurity in which they worked in such capitals as Washington, London, and Paris was a testimonial to the blindness of most Western policy-makers, who devoted more time to the Dutch or the Danes than they did to the Japanese and then complained over the difficulties of reaching the Japanese public.

The press of Southeast Asia, which had no correspondents in the United States or Europe except when there were visits of heads of state, naturally depended on the wire services for most foreign news. In the Philippines, it was to be expected that the AP would supply much of the news of the United States, along with UPI, the New York *Times* Foreign Service, and other syndicates. For the most part, this was what happened. But a newspaper that was critical of American policy, such as the powerful Manila *Times* or the Manila *Chronicle,* resorted, now and then, to the use of the AFP for a more astringent view of the United States. Even though the AP still topped the AFP by three-to-one or more, the needling process was worth watching.

Outside the Philippines, in Hong Kong and Malaysia, the press leaders divided rather sharply between those with a British or an American orientation. Thus, the South China *Morning Post,* in Hong Kong, and the Straits *Times,* in Kuala Lumpur, both used more Reuters than anything else, while the Hong Kong *Tiger Standard* leaned heavily on both the AP and UPI, as well as pages of American comics. A paper like the *Tiger Standard* devoted 44 per cent of its live news space to foreign news and gave 20 per cent of that over to American news. Probably the largest volume of American news in the Far East, on a percentage basis, was published by the Philippines *Herald,* which gave 24 per cent of its live news space to foreign news and loaded that with 46 per cent of news from the United States.

In India, the United States was seen very largely through the eyes of the few Indian correspondents in Washington, followed by Reuters correspondents. The AP received barely minimal use on some papers, and was not printed at all by others. But this did not mean that the Indian press received a generally unfriendly interpretation of American events; in 1964, for the most part, the special correspondence was relatively favorable. If an Indian editor wanted to load his news columns with an anti-American slant, he could thumb through the AFP file that was made available to him or, failing that, rewrite his own version of events. For in Washington, even the AFP correspondents were generally unwilling to write sharply angled copy.

The Indian press, from its record in the survey, gave its readers a much broader view of the world than they had any right to expect from newspapers so handicapped by lack of space and funds for foreign coverage. The Indian *Express,* for example, published 31.5 columns of live news daily on the average, gave 5.7 columns to foreign affairs and 1.2 columns of that total to American news. The *Hindustan Times* and the *Statesman,* with less live news space, gave almost as much to foreign news and allotted one column each day on the average to news of the United States. The *Times* of India, with an average live news total of 32.6 columns daily, published 6.7 columns of foreign news and devoted 1.3 columns of that to U.S. news. It was in the Indian-language press that the bottom dropped out of both United States news in particular and foreign news in general. The large Bengali daily, *Ananda Bazar Patrika,* for example, gave its readers an average of 1.4 columns of foreign news a day and 0.13 of a column a day of American news, which is just about the kind of performance one would expect of a purely local American daily. It was scant wonder that the readers of such a press, either in India or the United States, had the dimmest notion of what was going on in the world. If anything, the Americans had a distinct advantage, for they could turn to the well-edited news magazines or flip on radio or television if the newspapers failed them. The Indians had no recourse but to twiddle their thumbs. There was no five-minute newscast on the hour over All-India Radio. The Indian radio experts didn't believe in it.

Thus, from Japan to India, the individual foreign correspondents appeared to be the strongest forces for explaining the United States and its policies to the public at large. While they had comparatively little space in which to work, their impact was probably greater than that of their more numerous American colleagues. But with very few exceptions, neither the American nor the Asian correspondents could hope to develop a broad-gauged assessment of the country to which they were assigned; except for the events of the day, newspaper space was too limited for lengthy expositions. The magazines of news and comment had an undoubted advantage over the daily press in developing meaningful interpretations of foreign affairs, but they were seldom willing to exercise it. As for television, potentially the most influential of all, it did not seem to realize its own strength.

5. FACING THE FUTURE

American commitments in Asia are widening. It seems unlikely, in the foreseeable future, that they will diminish, regardless of the American public's fervent desire to be free of them in order to be able to concentrate on the Great Society. Short of an act of national suicide, there is no way for the United States to withdraw from its responsibilities toward the nations which it has pledged itself to protect in East, Southeast, and South Asia. The dreams of the neoisolationists will not change that hard reality.

If American foreign policy is to be effective, then the requisite first step which the government must undertake is to restore faith in its intentions in Asia. The valor and self-sacrifice of the American fighting man in South Viet-Nam, admirable though they are, will not be sufficient. His government must do something to make his deeds add up to gaining something more than a temporary advantage in a strange land. It cannot permit its credibility to be undermined, with a reckless disregard of the consequences.

It is tragically simple to document the great American weakness today. It began with the U-2 incident in the Eisenhower administration. It continued with the Bay of Pigs disaster during the Kennedy Administration, and reached its climax in the era in South Viet-Nam immediately before the overthrow of the Diem regime. It has cropped up with dismaying regularity ever since on a variety of occasions in which responsible officials, doubtless out of the highest of motives, failed to deal truthfully and forthrightly with the publics at home and abroad.

Such conduct does damage not only to the government, the most important single source of news in the nation, but also does damage to the credibility of the news media that seek to report the affairs of the nation in good faith. Today, more than at any time in the recent past, there is a greater element of doubt attached to official governmental announcements than veteran journalists can remember. The trust that links the American Government and the American people has worn dangerously thin.

The government, to be sure, is by no means entirely to blame. There is an element of irresponsibility, too, in the conduct of the mass media in large areas of the country where not even the bare bones of foreign news are made available to the public. Such self-executing censorship cannot be justified except by the small weekly, operating in communities where decently edited daily newspapers are available. Despite the yearning of a substantial part of the American press to concentrate on local news, higher circulation, and more advertising contracts, the obligation to develop a more meaningful daily report on foreign affairs for an enlarged public cannot be escaped. In such a report, Asian affairs of necessity should have a fair share.

This is an equally important part of the responsibility of television. A few leading newspapers, the wire services, the magazines of news and comment, and a handful of first-rate TV commentators alone cannot carry the burden of informing the nation on Asian problems that have brought American armies to Asian shores three times in twenty-five years. It may be less difficult for the news weeklies to splurge on cover stories on Asian affairs; their foreign coverage, on the whole, has been made profitable by their international editions. But out of its enormous domestic revenues, television surely can plow back enough in money and time to do more to fulfill its obligations. An uninformed public can sometimes become an unstable public; and instability, in a democratic society, can become a formidable threat to public order.

The greatest single objective of the two worlds represented by Asia and America is peace. Yet, that prospect is far off today. And because this is so, the turmoil in Asia deeply affects the rest of the world, in which the United States has tried to assert its leadership. Today the center of turbulence is Southeast Asia; tomorrow it may be India; the day after, Communist China. The revolutionary storm that began sweeping over the Asian continent in the wake of World War II will not blow itself out for the rest of this century, and probably, for much of the succeeding one as well.

In a single generation, that storm has wrecked the old colonial power structures of two centuries or more, torn up much of a complex society by its roots, and turned tens of millions of suffering peoples into helpless victims of brutal and continuing strife. The Asian Communists, seeking primacy over the Soviet Union, have profited enormously by the virtual disappearance of the old order, but they have not, as yet, been able to organize a new society in their own image in the key area of Southeast Asia. Long-suppressed peoples, once having caught a brief and tantalizing glimpse of what life would be like if they were their own masters, will not easily submit to a new conqueror. Nor are they likely to do so over the long stretch of history, whatever may happen in the immediate future.

This is the struggle into which the United States has been drawn, very largely against the will of its people. The problem of bringing peace to Viet-Nam and Laos, and to India and Pakistan, is one that will tax the best efforts of the international community. Beyond that lies the even greater task of restoring order in both Southeast Asia and South Asia as a whole, and creating an atmosphere in which established and emerging nations may be able to work out their own destinies without fear of aggression. This is the basic commitment of the United States.

The role of the mass media in such a national effort was explained more than 125 years ago by Alexis de Tocqueville in terms of the responsibility of the newspaper in a democratic society:

When men are no longer united among themselves by firm and lasting ties, it is impossible to obtain the cooperation of any great number of them unless you can persuade every man whose help you require that his private interest obliges him voluntarily to unite his exertions to the exertions of all the others. This can be habitually and conveniently effected only by means of a newspaper; nothing but a newspaper can drop the same thought into a thousand minds at the same moment. A newspaper is an adviser that does not require to be sought, but that comes of its own accord and talks to you briefly every day of the common weal, without distracting you from your private affairs.

Newspapers therefore become more necessary in proportion as men become more equal and individualism more to be feared. To suppose that they only serve to protect freedom would be to diminish their importance; they maintain civilization. I shall not deny that in democratic countries newspapers frequently lead the citizens to launch together into very ill-digested schemes; but if there were no newspapers there would be no common activity. The evil which they produce is therefore much less than that which they cure.[11]

It is scarcely worth while, however, for editors merely to publish whatever news from Asia they choose from the wire services, the foreign news syndicates, or their own correspondents and hope for the best. If the public will not read it—and the available evidence indicates a low rate of public absorption of foreign problems that are complex—both the effort and the newspaper space are wasted. Neither the urge to fight Communism nor the attraction of reading about Americans in combat, or viewing them on television, has yet produced an overwhelming demand for more news on Asia aside from war reports. A realization that their private interests are tied up with the affairs of some of the principal nations of Asia first has to come to the American public. However slowly it is emerging, its development is an observable phenomenon in the United States, particularly among younger people whose lives already have been affected by the growing pressures of the confrontation between the two continents.

The most pressing need, therefore, is to develop many more communicators—correspondents, commentators, editors, teachers, civic leaders, government officials, and others—with a better-rounded knowledge of Asian affairs together with vastly expanded sources of current and background information for the public at large. There is no conflict in this area of essential public education between a democratic government and an independent press, including television, for both have the same obligation to inform the people despite their differing interests. Such "teach-ins" would be welcome.

The first difficulty that will have to be overcome is the lack of available centers, outside Washington and a few other places, where essential materials may be easily obtained by the public. It is simply not possible for the greatest of newspapers, news magazines, or television networks to keep repeating the background material that the public must have if there is to be any understanding of American policy in Asia. Provided the Congress grants sufficient funds, the government is in a position to prepare and distribute essential documents, decent maps, and other factual materials to additional public libraries, university centers, and other places that consent to maintain special shelves on current foreign developments.

Some newspapers already are conducting such educational programs on their own, with salutary results, the most important being the Minneapolis *Star*'s weekly background studies in foreign affairs, which are widely used throughout the Midwest. The Kansas City *Star* and the Philadelphia *Inquirer,* too, have embarked on such broad educational programs, while the *Christian Science Monitor* has published a map series that drew grateful appreciation from a large public.

In a further effort to stimulate public interest, the government has taken to television by placing leading officials before the teleprompter to make statements that are, for the most part, mere repetitions of policy pronouncements. Except when the President speaks, such efforts do not often attract a large public. But personal appearances by young American servicemen, AID officials, and others who have come home from South Viet-Nam to tell of their experiences have been eagerly welcomed. The same reaction has been reported by foreign correspondents. It would appear, therefore, that the government, on its part, and the mass media, acting separately, could make more of these attractive personalities available to audiences across the nation that have a special interest in Asian affairs.

The increase of exchange programs of journalists, teachers, and other communicators between the United States and Asian nations is, of course, another essential part of the educational process, as are undergraduate and graduate programs for foreign study, and the production of a series of cheap paperback books discussing various aspects of Asian-American affairs. The enlargement of the audience for Asian news is dependent to some extent, too, on the activities of those nongovernmental agencies and foundations that are primarily interested in American problems in Asia.

It will take a considerable time to expand the interest as well as the size of the currently rather limited public that makes a particular point of being informed on Asian affairs. In the interim, it will be possible also to examine practical methods of creating more openings in Asia for permanently assigned correspondents for American news organizations and providing better-trained journalists to fill them. As an important first step, the highly profitable television industry has a public obligation to permanently station more correspondents in Asia, whether or not they are able to produce usable film footage and interesting stories every day.

Walter Cronkite, the highly competent wire-service war correspondent who became the star C.B.S. news commentator in his later years, recognized television's broad commitment to improve its news programs in these words: "I'm afraid that the public is getting brainwashed into a belief that they're getting all that they need to know from television. And this is not so. They needed to know a great deal more than we can communicate to them. Somehow or other, we have to teach the American people to seek more information, to be a little more discriminating, perhaps. And when they do, they'll get even better news programs on television." David Brinkley, of N.B.C., concurred, saying, "When it comes to covering the news in any kind of detailed way, we are just almost not in the ball game." [12]

It is clear that better correspondents, stationed in major world capitals, including those in Asia, will help stimulate a public desire both to seek and to receive more information. The duty of television is plain enough. The first-rate television newsmen and commentators are too few in number and usually too rushed to do a consistently effective job of news coverage, particularly in Asia. A larger and better-trained corps of electronic correspondents is needed—and they deserve more time on the air and far more attention than they get.

One of them, Bernard Kalb of C.B.S., illuminated the processes of thought by which a capable correspondent is able to interest a large audience in an unfamiliar aspect of world affairs—the crux of all good reporting. Out of his experience as a New York *Times* correspondent, as well as his more recent role as a television reporter, he wrote:

> Now that I look back on those first traumatic experiences in India—I was to spend the next nine years or so in Asia—I must confess that they were among my most dangerous moments in the Far East. Asia over the years did erupt with epidemics, violence and war—but so did non-Asia. Asia, in fact, turned out to be the friendliest of places and peoples, a part of the world that has a way of insisting that you be on a first-name basis with her. . . .
>
> The very differences of Asia, compounded by Asia's around-the-clock rush hour crowds and ragged poverty, Asia's values and contradictions, compounded, too, by antique, caricatured images of an Orient of secret societies, opium and orgies—all this can add up to a kind of assault on the senses that at once produces distortions and jolts common sense.[13]

It is this kind of reporter who is needed in Asia in increasing numbers for all American media—the correspondent who is not afraid of a personal involvement with his story but who can not be knocked off balance by its impact. In addition to television, the news magazines, and the wire services, there are great newspapers in the United States of prestige and affluence that also have an obligation to establish their own flow of correspondence from Asia. Too few now do so. Despite the multiplication of their influence through the distribution of their material by the syndicates, the limited number of correspondents do not provide the diversity of information and variety of viewpoint that is essential in order to maintain a meaningful public discussion of the American role in Asian affairs.

If the basic commitment of the American mass media in Asia continues to be as small as it has been in the immediate past, there will be little public support for the long campaign to get American correspondents into Communist China. For if only a few Americans are assigned permanently to India and Pakistan to report on nearly 600 million people, what kind of correspondence can be expected from China after the first rush of self-promotion is over? Despite the willingness of the State Department to grant permission to American correspondents to visit Communist China, provided they can get a visa from Peking, one cannot help but sympathize with those officials who now wonder what good purpose would be served by it all. Compared to the coming assignment in Peking, the early days in Moscow will seem no more difficult than a report from the Leipzig fair.

For too many years, the mass media in the United States have assumed that correspondents properly trained for such responsibilities in Asia and elsewhere will come beating a path to their door. The support, financial and otherwise, of universities and other educational institutions, has not been a notable feature of the broad mass of American journalism to date; mostly, the newspapers and magazines and the electronic media have been disposed to take what they could get and give little in return. The Pulitzers and the Niemans have been rare. It is only in recent years that such journalistic representatives as the Noble, Newhouse, Annenberg, and other interests have made major contributions to American education. The Ford, Rockefeller, Sloan, and Carnegie foundations, among others, have had to carry a disproportionate share of the burden of training journalists for special responsibilities. Most of the profession, with a few generous exceptions, has concentrated on organizations of immediate benefit such as the American Press Institute, a notable development in itself.

Nevertheless, a new era is approaching in which the mass media may have to find some more adequate approach to the universities in devising better methods of personnel selection and training for the responsibilities in the reporting and editing of national and international affairs. More fellowships are needed to widen the areas now covered by the Nieman fellowships at Harvard, the Ford, Sloan-Rockefeller, and Pulitzer fellowships at Columbia, and the various government and private grants. Some effort will have to be made to arrive at a better understanding of the requirements of correspondents by the government, and of government officials by the press, possibly by opening the National War College and the Foreign Service Institute to correspondents of established merit or by having seminars for government policy-makers at an organization like the American Press Institute. Nothing should slacken the rivalry between government and press to serve the public interest; yet, national policy scarcely requires the two to participate in a continual dogfight before a wondering public.

Outside Washington the government, on its part, has often made little effort to discuss some of the intricacies of American policy in Asia either with the press or the public at large. The Department of State has experimented with sending small teams of officials into the Georgia backwoods and elsewhere to talk about the Viet-Nam war and has drafted a program for regional press briefings. But these are minimal steps, for the most part, and they require far more precious manpower, time and funds than the Department can spare. The Congress, moreover, has always been suspicious of regional activities by the Department and has kept its information budget considerably lower than that of the Department of Defense. If the Department of State is therefore to enter realistically upon regional information activities, it will take a great deal more support than the mass media has evidenced so far in order to overcome the fundamental mistrust of a reluctant Congress. There have been times when Congressional committees have disapproved the printing of explanatory booklets dealing with foreign policy. It will be very difficult to reverse the trend. Certainly, the Department of State by itself will not be able to make Congress change old habits of thought overnight.

It is to be expected that the American Government will continue to do what it can to stimulate travel by American and Asian journalists, oppose censorship in all its forms, and arrange for more assistance for Asian journalists in this country. On the key problem of lower rates for press messages from various parts of Asia, the British-subsidized penny-a-word Commonwealth rate is still the main recourse of all foreign correspondents, including the Americans. With the coming of more sophisticated systems of transmission at far greater speeds, it may be in the American interest for the government, in cooperation with the mass media, to make a new approach to the whole matter of international communications rates. Some reductions have been made, but more are needed. The sheer expense of maintaining a steady daily file is keeping smaller news organizations out of Asia and limiting the amount of cabled or radioed correspondence sent to nations with foreign-exchange troubles, like India. No matter how it is done, the maintenance of a foreign correspondent is an added expense that only the most prosperous news organizations now can bear.

For a long time to come, there will be no substitute for the daily wire-service file between Asia and the United States for the bulk of the mass media. If doubt existed about their speed and efficiency, it was offset to some extent by a compliment from a totally unexpected source—*Kommunist,* the ideological journal of the Communist Party of the Soviet Union. In the queer upside-down language of world Communism, the paper reported:

> We have to admit that bourgeois news agencies have achieved a high degree of speed in reacting immediately to all that happens in the world while we are sometimes late. It means that a false version is spread around the world more rapidly than the true and correct one. It is the first pronouncement that sometimes produces the greatest impression.[14]

Despite the mendacious form of the compliment, the wire services are scarcely perfect, and their work could well undergo a more thorough periodic examination by their own managers as well as their subscribers. If they have a major fault, it is their terrifying sensitivity to the slightest breath of outside criticism. Yet, even an unpracticed eye, scanning the regional file that comes into Asian publications, can see whole successions of items that are of dubious use to the entire region. Far more than the main trunk wires of the domestic services, the Asian wires seem frequently to be loaded with trivia. In place of the material stuffed into the daily thirty-minute radiocasts from remote places in Asia, a single backgrounder—researched over a week's time—would be more useful. Some of it is done now. More could be developed, but it would take patient editors and better reporters.

One of the other criticisms of wire-service work in general is the enormous amount of rewriting that goes into the daily file. On some of the major stories out of Asia, it is not unusual for both the AP and the UPI to have a rewrite battery in New York beefing up the dispatches of correspondents who are on the spot. There is, of course, a competitive necessity for this arrangement; the agency with the sharpest lead and the most dramatic account of a breaking story anywhere in the world generally takes the national play. In New York, the top editors have a sensitive electronic watchtower to check on the usage of their own material and that of the opposition. The correspondent in the field, so the argument runs, never knows what is happening on his story in other parts of the world. Consequently, the mass-produced news that is so characteristic of the news magazines on a weekly basis is an intrinsic part of the daily work of the wire services as well. Except for star performers, the individual is submerged.

The issue of hiring more and more locals and giving them major responsibility in Asia is one that has perplexed a number of American editors. To any one who has watched such talented and devoted people on the job, there cannot help but be sympathy for the practice of training Asians to tell the story of Asian countries at home and abroad. The AP, for example, has begun to bring outstanding Asian newsmen in its overseas bureaus to headquarters in New York for training periods of six months to a year.

The mere matter of saving money by hiring Asians instead of Americans is by no means the whole story, and in some cases there is no appreciable difference between the rates paid to two persons of equal ability. The news agency obtains a linguist it could not afford to train, one with an expert knowledge of the country, its leaders, and its people. But, of course, the danger is that there may come a time—and for some it has already arrived—when Asian governments put the pressure on their own nationals to conform to the policies of their own countries. The wire services recognize the threat, but for many reasons the policy of using locals will continue. It would seem to be prudent, at the very least, to place an American in charge of any bureau where a local would be at a disadvantage with his own government, particularly in Asia. Even in the Asian countries that are not ruled by dictators, the theory of a free press is often brushed aside when it becomes inconvenient.

The fact is that the frontiers of press freedom in Asia are shrinking fast. "Many Asian governments are beginning to take a hostile attitude toward the press and tend to reject the concept of the freedom of the press as an outmoded product of 19th century Western liberalism which has no validity in the modern world, least of all in the Asia (or Africa) of the 1960s," writes Tarzie Vittachi. He believes only Japan and the Philippines permit the press to exist without government pressure and points out that the Indian press is still subject to wartime security regulations. "The picture is even grimmer elsewhere in Asia," he continues. "There is, by definition, no question of a free press in Red China. Pakistan, Burma, Indonesia, Taiwan, Korea, and Thailand have dictators at the head of their governments and it is axiomatic that where there is autocracy, press freedom—or any other human freedom—is only permissive if it exists at all." [15]

It is a harsh judgment, but it is shared by Macario T. Vicencio, of the Philippines, who writes:

> Freedom of the press often appears a luxury for many a developing country involved in consolidating its new-found independence and eradicating its age-old ills. Thus Asian strong men have easily found support for their argument that an unrestricted press under present conditions is a threat to national unity and security; that press freedom, like other civil liberties, must wait a more relaxed future. The most casual survey of the state of the press in Asia would reveal restrictions of one kind or another even in some of the countries which are not part of the frankly totalitarian bloc.[16]

There is little doubt that the Asian press will labor under more restrictions rather than fewer ones even in the more advanced countries as the pressures for revolutionary change intensify. And yet, it is essential that the lingering Asian belief in a free press be maintained, regardless of practical difficulties. Without a tradition of popular, representative government in Asia, it is perfectly true that there is constant danger that national leaders will turn to totalitarian methods. The few freedoms that are permitted, including freedom of the press, could be impatiently swept aside in the countries where they still exist. Any investment to try to shore up the independent press is, with only a few exceptions, a precarious undertaking. But it is necessary.

A show of support for the professionally competent section of the Asian press is required in these hard and dangerous times. While no editor or publisher of independent mind and strong convictions seeks charity, there are a number of good ones who need help. Many could use technical advice, better equipment, more competent staffing, and some financing, as well, to keep pace with the needs of an expanding readership.

The establishment of press institutes such as those that already exist in India, the Philippines, and Iran will be of considerable assistance in training better journalists. Study programs for foreign journalists at American universities will also help. The availability of technical experts through the International Press Institute and other organizations will fill a particular need in the Asian mass media. But without recourse to an international agency for financing—an agency which is geared to risk-taking on a limited scale—a section of the Asian press that has so far escaped government control is likely to fall under the influence either of private industrial power or devious foreign interests. It is worth the trouble of international financial agencies to consider the predicament of the press as well as the people who look to it hopefully to tell the truth.

Many years ago, Joseph Pulitzer wrote:

Our Republic and its press will rise or fall together. An able, disinterested, public-spirited press, with trained intelligence to know the right and courage to do it, can preserve that public virtue without which popular government is a sham and a mockery. A cynical, mercenary, demagogic, corrupt press will produce in time a people as base as itself. The power to mold the future of the Republic will be in the hands of the journalists of future generations.[17]

The idea of the Republic, as Pulitzer conceived it, is remote in Asia. Few people understand it, even fewer believe in it. There is little sign of popular government in the American sense, for it does not fit the needs of Asian lands. And as for public virtue, that, too, is in short supply. But there is a press—an Asian press, put together with Asian brains and Asian hands—that is struggling against enormous odds to maintain a semblance of freedom. And there are editors who have gone to prison defiantly for their beliefs. It is a story that is little known in the United States. But, in many ways, it is more important than the tales of war that come clattering over the teletypes each day in thousands of American newsrooms. For the editor who dares to display his independence in print is a rare and precious being in much of Asia today.

It is irritating to many Americans that the nations of Asia do not aspire to be made over in the image of the United States. And yet, both Americans and Asians outside the circle of Chinese power are committed to a future which was envisioned many years ago in a prayer written in the form of a poem by Rabindranath Tagore:

> Where the mind is without fear and the head is held high;
> Where knowledge is free;
> Where the world has not been broken up into fragments by
> narrow domestic walls;
> Where words come out from the depth of truth;
> Where tireless striving stretches its arms towards perfection;
> Where the clear stream of reason has not lost its way into
> the dreary desert sand of dead habit;
> Where the mind is led forward by thee into ever-widening
> thought and action—
> Into that heaven of freedom, my Father, let my country
> awake.[18]

For all their frustrations and their differences, the independent-minded Asians can share with Americans the vision of such a goal. It is the shape of the future as both would have it—a future far different from the mindless procession of the blue ants of China in their endless demonstrations and their endless toil. If it can be achieved one day, it will truly represent a new order for the ages, which poets and singers, novelists and historians will celebrate.

The vision passes, the realities remain. For today and tomorrow and the dark days yet to come, it will be the hard lot of the journalist to tell a different story—the struggle of mankind to be free of the sodden morass of ages past. In his words will be cast the fall of nations and the rise of new ones, the death of old heroes and the coming of young leaders, the tragedies of defeat in battle and the stubborn hope for a better future. It is a task of few rewards and many disappointments, but for the journalist there is no easy role in a world of gathering shadows. He must try, as best he can, to convey understanding between Asia and America. It is the most challenging assignment he has ever faced. May he be worthy of it.

Notes

INTRODUCTION

1. Dean Acheson kindly consented to write his now celebrated statement to James Reston. It was included in a letter to the author, dated April 6, 1965.
2. James Reston, New York *Times,* May 10, 1961.

I. THE SPINNING OF THE WEB

1. "AMERICA . . . AMERICA . . ."

1. Douglas MacArthur, *Reminiscences* (New York: McGraw-Hill, 1964), p. 277.
2. Meyer Berger, *The Story of the New York Times* (New York: Simon and Schuster, 1951), p. 533; editorial dated March 2, 1945.
3. *Ibid.;* editorial dated March 4, 1945.
4. Joe Alex Morris, *Deadline Every Minute: The Story of the United Press* (Garden City, N. Y.: Doubleday, 1957), pp. 295–96.
5. Herbert Feis, *The China Tangle* (Princeton, N. J.: Princeton University Press, 1953), pp. 360–61.
6. Bernard B. Fall, *The Two Viet-Nams* (New York: Frederick A. Praeger, 1963), pp. 62–63; see also Fall, *Street Without Joy* (rev. ed.; Harrisburg, Pa.: Stackpole, 1964), p. 26.
7. Elliott Roosevelt, *As He Saw It* (New York: Duell, Sloane & Pearce, 1945), p. 251.
8. Robert J. Donovan, *Eisenhower, The Inside Story* (New York: Harper & Bros., 1956), p. 263.
9. Robert Leckie, *Conflict: The History of the Korean War* (New York: Putnam's, 1962), pp. 31–32.
10. *Ibid.,* pp. 33–34.
11. M. S. Venkataramani and B. K. Shrivastava, "The U. S. and the 'Quit India' Demand," *India Quarterly,* XX, No. 2 (April–June, 1964), 135–39.

437

12. Berger, *op. cit.*, p. 534.
13. Matthew B. Ridgway, as told to Harold H. Martin, *Soldier* (New York: Harper & Bros., 1956), p. 157.
14. Harry S. Truman, *Memoirs* (New York: Doubleday, 1955), I, 506–10.
15. Louis L. Snyder, *The War, A Concise History, 1939–45* (New York: Messner, 1960), p. 505.
16. Harold Isaacs, *Scratches on Our Minds* (New York: John Day, 1958), p. 37.
17. I am indebted to a distinguished member of the U.S. Mission to the United Nations in 1946 for this charming anecdote.
18. Robert Trumbull, *The Scrutable East* (New York: David McKay, 1964), p. 7.

2. RETURN TO JAPAN

19. MacArthur, *op. cit.*, pp. 282–83.
20. See discussion in William J. Coughlin, *Conquered Press: The MacArthur Era in Japanese Journalism* (Stanford, Calif.: Stanford University Press, 1952).
21. Susumu Ejiri, deputy secretary general, Nihon Shinbun Kyokai (N.S.K. [Japanese Editors and Publishers Association]), a paper entitled "The Survival and Death of Newspapers in Japan," read before the International Press Institute in Istanbul in 1964.
22. *World Communications, 1964* (New York: UNESCO Communications Center, 1964), pp. 226–27. The Japanese Government's support for the Kyodo and Jiji news agencies is commonly known among journalists in Tokyo.
23. Morris, *op. cit.*, p. 297.
24. Harry Emerson Wildes, *The Press and Social Currents in Japan* (Chicago: University of Chicago Press, 1927), pp. 33–35.
25. All unattributed material concerning salaries, agencies' earnings, estimates, and similar data come from present and former correspondents, Japanese editors, and others who are familiar with the details of such closely held information. It has been gathered, at considerable effort and with some risk of inaccuracy, because it is deemed an important influence affecting the flow of news between Asian nations and the United States. Every figure has been checked with responsible sources in an attempt to ensure a reasonably accurate presentation.
26. James A. Michener, "America's Greatest Writer," *Newsday* (Garden City, N. Y.), February 23, 1952.
27. Earnest Hoberecht, *Asia Is My Beat* (Rutland, Vt. and Tokyo: Charles E. Tuttle, 1961), pp. 192–93.

3. EXODUS FROM CHINA

28. Hollington K. Tong, *Dateline: China* (New York: Rockport Press, 1950), p. 239.
29. *Ibid.*, p. 256.
30. O. Edmund Clubb, *Twentieth-Century China* (New York: Columbia University Press, 1964), pp. 289–91. See also Hollington K. Tong, *Chiang Kai-shek* (Taipei: China Publishing Co., 1953), pp. 428–30.

31. Joseph and Stewart Alsop, *The Reporter's Trade* (New York: Reynal, 1959), pp. 131–33 (a column by Stewart Alsop originally published May 13, 1949, in the New York *Herald Tribune*).
32. Tong, *Chiang Kai-shek*, pp. 453–54.
33. Mark Gayn, Toronto *Star* series on Communist China, the first article of which was published in the New York *Times*, June 17, 1965, p. 1.

4. THE RIVALS

34. The 1964 budget for UPI is from *Editor & Publisher*, April 24, 1965, p. 112. The later figure is from the New York *Times*, April 24, 1966, p. 82. Figures on personnel for both AP and UPI were checked on a name-by-name basis for editorials with responsible Tokyo bureau officials of each agency, and then cross-checked. The result is believed to be as accurate as competitive conditions and an on-the-spot census can produce.
35. AP membership figures from *Editor & Publisher*, April 30, 1964, p. 97. UPI American newspaper and broadcast subscribers for 1965 listed in a letter from UPI to the author dated July 9, 1965. UPI total global subscribers for 1966 from annual report, in New York *Times*, April 24, 1966, p. 82. In the latter, there was no breakdown for American newspaper and broadcast subscribers, but it is presumed they increased slightly because of the claim of a net gain of 201 global subscribers in the previous year.
36. The 1966 projected annual expenditures of the AP were reported to the author from the office of AP General Manager Wes Gallagher.
37. The estimates of AP and UPI gross profits in Japan are from responsible agency and Japanese officials. The AP staff was calculated as described in note 34, above. The six leading American newspapers, checked from April 8–14, 1966, by the author's Foreign Correspondence Seminar, at the Columbia Graduate School of Journalism, were: the New York *Times*, Los Angeles *Times*, *Christian Science Monitor*, St. Louis *Post-Dispatch*, Washington *Post*, and Chicago *Tribune*. The 1964 American newspaper survey will be found in Appendix III.
38. Reuters annual report for 1963, dated May 13, 1964, an estimate by an agency official.
39. These figures are from Japanese editors and agency people, and were cross-checked.
40. *World Communications, 1964*, p. 282.
41. AFP document is Law No. 57-32, January 10, 1957, *Journal Officiel* (Paris), January 11, 1957.
42. These figures may be found in *Projet de Loi de Finances pour 1965, Annexe, Services Votes Mesures Nouvelles, Services du Premier Ministre, II, Information* (Paris: Imprimerie Nationale, 1964). The data are on p. 29 under Titre IV, Interventions Publiques, Sections 01, 01-7, 01-7-08.
43. Data from an agency official.
44. *Statistical Abstract of the United States, 1965*, p. 392, table 523.

5. STORM OVER SOUTHEAST ASIA

45. Robert Shaplen, "Letter from Saigon" dated June 30, 1964, in *The New Yorker*, July 11, 1964, p. 37.

46. Relman Morin, *East Wind Rising* (New York: Knopf, 1960), pp. 357-58.

47. Richard Tregaskis, *Vietnam Diary* (New York: Holt, Rinehart & Winston, 1963), p. 2.

48. Fall, *The Two Viet-Nams*, p. 72.

49. *Ibid.*, pp. 73-111 *passim*.

50. For the number of correspondents covering the Korean War, see John Hohenberg, *Foreign Correspondence: The Great Reporters and Their Times* (New York: Columbia University Press, 1964), p. 391. For U.S. assistance to Viet-Nam, see Fall, *The Two Viet-Nams*, pp. 219-20.

51. David Halberstam, *The Making of a Quagmire* (New York: Random House, 1965), p. 309. James MacGregor Burns, *John Kennedy: A Political Profile* (New York: Harcourt, Brace, 1959), p. 83.

52. Fall, *The Two Viet-Nams*, p. 122.

53. George F. Kennan, *Russia and the West Under Lenin and Stalin* (Boston: Little, Brown, 1960), p. 26.

54. Alsop, *op. cit.*, pp. 48-49.

55. Dwight D. Eisenhower, *Mandate for Change* (Garden City, N. Y.: Doubleday, 1963), pp. 348-51.

56. Fall, *The Two Viet-Nams*, pp. 227-28. Citations by the author are from the *Congressional Record*, April 6 and 14, 1954, pp. 4402-4977 *passim*.

57. Truman, *Memoirs*, II, 519.

58. Keyes Beech, *Tokyo and Points East* (Garden City, N. Y.: Doubleday, 1954), p. 252.

59. From an AFP official.

60. St. Louis *Post-Dispatch*, May 8, 1954.

61. John Mecklin, *Mission In Torment* (Garden City, N. Y.: Doubleday, 1965), pp. 31-32.

62. For the general summation, I am indebted to material published by Fall, Mecklin, and Halberstam, and to correspondents still in Viet-Nam in 1964 who had witnessed earlier events.

63. Mecklin, *op. cit.*, p. 105.

64. *Ibid.*, p. 106. See also Stan Karnow, "The Newsman's War in Vietnam," *Nieman Reports*, December, 1963, p. 4.

65. Anonymous author, "Behind the Vietnam Story," *Columbia Journalism Review*, Winter, 1965, pp. 17-18.

66. Admiral Felt's remark is relayed to the visitor almost as soon as he arrives at the airport at Saigon.

67. Joseph J. Mathews, *Reporting the Wars* (Minneapolis, Minn.: University of Minnesota Press, 1957), p. 86.

68. Based on my own inquiry in Saigon, in the summer of 1964.

69. Mecklin, *op. cit.*, pp. 49-51.

70. Malcolm W. Browne, *The New Face of War* (Indianapolis, Ind.: Bobbs-Merrill, 1965), pp. 175-82. Mecklin supports Browne's account of the Hué

incident, pp. 153–55, but Fr. Patrick O'Connor disputes both accounts in *America,* July 3, 1965, pp. 11–17.

71. Browne, *Columbia Journalism Review,* Fall, 1964, pp. 6–7; Mecklin, *op. cit.,* pp. 172–74. Fr. O'Connor (*op. cit.*) charged some correspondents favored the Buddhists by inflating the figures. In September, 1965, a private survey arrived at a figure of 40 per cent as the "correct" proportion of Buddhists in South Viet-Nam.

72. Mecklin, *op. cit.,* pp. 174–78 *passim;* Halberstam, *op. cit.,* pp. 236–43 *passim.*

73. *Time,* September 20, 1963, p. 44.

74. *Ibid.,* October 11, 1963, p. 65; *Newsweek,* October 7, 1963, pp. 44–45.

75. Letter from Arthur Ochs Sulzberger to author, dated January 19, 1965. The incident is related in Halberstam, *op. cit.,* p. 268.

76. Of all the newspapers that permitted their correspondents to take a junket in 1964 paid for by the Defense Department, I was told that only the *Christian Science Monitor* returned the $1,000 cost of the trip.

6. THE LESSONS OF TWENTY YEARS

77. The *Times Literary Supplement,* June 3, 1965, in a page 1 article on "News of the World from Our Own Correspondent."

78. Walter Lippmann, text of address "On the Profession of Journalism," before International Press Institute in London, May 27, 1965. Published in *Editor & Publisher,* May 29, 1965, p. 64.

79. Wilbur Schramm, *Mass Media and National Development* (Stanford, Calif.: Stanford University Press, 1964), p. 61.

II. AT THE CENTER OF POWER

1. THE NEWS MANAGERS

1. New York *Herald Tribune,* April 25, 1965, p. 1.

2. New York *Times,* April 25, 1965, p. 1. Copyright 1965 by the New York Times Company. Reprinted by permission.

3. Arthur Krock, New York *Times,* April 27, 1965, p. 36.

4. Ben H. Bagdikian, *Columbia Journalism Review,* Winter, 1963, p. 8. See also Jack Raymond, *Power at the Pentagon* (New York: Harper & Row, 1964), pp. 327–28.

5. "McNamara Calls Hanoi Aggression More Flagrant," New York *Times,* April 27, 1965, p. 1.

6. Krock, New York *Times,* April 27, 1965, p. 36.

7. Richard C. Wald, "The Two-Handed Approach to U.S. Military Strategy," New York *Herald Tribune,* May 10, 1965.

8. W. E. Leuchtenberg, *Franklin D. Roosevelt and the Coming of the New Deal* (Chicago: University of Chicago Press, 1963), pp. 330–31.

9. J. R. Wiggins, *Freedom or Secrecy* (rev. ed.; London and New York: Oxford University Press, 1964), pp. 100–101.

10. David Wise and Thomas B. Ross, *The U-2 Affair* (New York: Random House, 1960), pp. 95–119 *passim*.
11. *Newsweek*, September 22, 1958, p. 78.
12. Bagdikian, *op. cit.*, pp. 5–11. See also James Reston, New York *Times*, May 10, 1961.
13. Marquis Childs, St. Louis *Post-Dispatch*, November 18, 1962.
14. Wiggins, *op. cit.*, pp. 234–35.
15. "Sylvester Says He Was Rude But Right," *Editor & Publisher*, December 15, 1962, p. 14. See also New York *Times* report on his testimony, September 1, 1966, p. 7.
16. Tom Wicker, New York *Times Book Review*, February 7, 1965. See also "The Jenkins Case," *Bulletin of the American Society of Newspaper Editors*, December 1, 1964.
17. Price Day, lead editorial in Baltimore *Sun*, November 22, 1962.
18. Reston, New York *Times*, June 20, 1965, p. E10.

2. THE VIEW FROM FOGGY BOTTOM

19. Chart following p. 73, illustrating article by Karl E. Meyer, "The Washington Press Establishment," *Esquire*, April, 1964.
20. *Editor & Publisher International Year Book, 1965*, list beginning on p. 568.
21. These figures were checked informally against U.S. State Department records.
22. List issued by U.S. Mission to the United Nations, December 31, 1964.
23. Edward W. Barrett helped with this section. See also Leo C. Rosten, *The Washington Correspondents* (New York: Harcourt, Brace, 1937), p. 102.
24. See articles by Henry M. Wriston and John S. Dickey in Don K. Price (ed.), *The Secretary of State* (Englewood Cliffs, N. J.: Prentice-Hall, 1960), pp. 101 and 148–49, respectively.
25. *Statistical Abstract of the United States, 1965*, p. 391, tables 521 and p. 406, 542; and letter from James L. Greenfield, dated April 22, 1965.
26. Dickey, in Price (ed.), *op. cit.*, p. 149, says in 1940, the salary and budget for news and public events totaled about $200,000 for seventy people.
27. Wise and Ross, *op. cit.*, pp. 93, 106–7.
28. Arthur Sylvester, quoted in *Editor & Publisher*, December 15, 1962, p. 14.
29. Caryl Rivers, *Editor & Publisher*, February 1, 1964, p. 15. Also *Statistical Abstract of the United States, 1965*, p. 856, tables 1213, and p. 407, 542.
30. New York *Times*, June 6, 1965, p. 21.
31. *Newsweek*, June 7, 1965, pp. 16–17.
32. *Editor & Publisher*, February 1, 1964, p. 15; and *Time*, August 13, 1965, p. 60.
33. New York *Times*, July 29, 1965, p. 1, and in the President's transcript, p. 12; also *Time*, August 6, 1965, p. 52.
34. New York *Times*, February 16, 1966, p. 1.

3. THROUGH ASIAN EYES

35. All material in this section was based on the author's reporting, and additional data from the questionnaires completed by the panel of ten Asian newsmen in the United States.

4. AMERICAN MEDLEY

36. AP file, March 22, 1965; AP log, March 17–24, 1965; "The Great Gas Flap," *Time,* April 2, 1965, pp. 19–21; New York *Times* editorial, September 11, 1965.

37. John Hightower, "Goodbye to the Scoop Artist in a Trenchcoat," *Dateline,* VIII, No. 1 (published by the Overseas Press Club), 14.

38. Watson Sims, AP *World,* Spring, 1965, p. 13.

39. *Ibid.* See also Ben Bassett, "AP Foreign Correspondents," AP *World,* Spring, 1965, p. 5.

40. Estimates made by various wire-service editors.

41. "Providing Readers with 'Plus' Coverage," *Bulletin of the American Society of Newspaper Editors,* September 1, 1964, p. 4; *Time,* January 14, 1966, p. 58; New York *Times,* March 13, 1966, p. 34.

42. TV Profits from New York *Times,* August 7, 1965; N.B.C. figures, letter dated October 27, 1964, signed by James A. Jurist, Director of Business Affairs, N.B.C. News; C.B.S. figures, *Newsweek,* February 22, 1965, pp. 60–61; estimates of 1964 performance based on author's on-the-spot observations.

5. THE INFLUENCE OF THE NEW YORK *Times*

43. Hanson Baldwin, New York *Times,* December 11, 1964, p. 4.

44. The Tchepone protest story was obtained from a well-qualified source.

45. Baldwin's military survey in New York *Times,* February 21, 1966, p. 1; McNamara's rebuttal, New York *Times,* March 3, 1966, p. 1, and March 31, 1966, p. 9.

46. Bagdikian, *Columbia Journalism Review,* Fall, 1962, p. 26.

47. New York *Times, Annual Report, 1965,* published April 1, 1966, p. 54. See previous A.B.C. statements for six-month periods ending March, 1964, and March, 1965.

48. New York *Times,* April 25, 1966, p. 26.

49. New York *Times,* April 1, 1966, p. 54.

50. I.P.I., *The Flow of the News,* p. 22. A careful reading of the entire report is recommended.

6. PRESS AND GOVERNMENT: A DIALOGUE

51. New York *Daily News,* September 2, 1965, p. 1; New York *Times,* August 31, 1965, p. 5, and September 2, 1965, p. 1.

52. New York *Times,* April 25, 1966, p. 1.

53. Allen Dulles, *The Craft of Intelligence* (New York: Harper & Row, 1963), pp. 5–6.

54. David Wise and Thomas Ross, *The Invisible Government* (New York: Random House, 1964), pp. 136–37; see also Seymour Topping, New York *Times,* September 2, 1965, p. 5.

55. John Kenneth Galbraith, *Nieman Reports,* March, 1964, p. 17.

56. Oscar Hammerstein II, lyric from *The King and I,* reprinted by permission.

57. Carver incident reported in New York *Times*, April 30, 1966, p. 10; conclusion on CIA in New York *Times*, April 29, 1966, p. 18.
58. Louis M. Starr, *Bohemian Brigade*, p. 170.
59. David Halberstam, *The Making of a Quagmire*, p. 316. The reference was to an article by Charles Mohr in the New York *Times*.
60. *Editor & Publisher*, October 7, 1961, p. 11.
61. Robert J. Manning, speech before Massachusetts Joint Bar-Press Symposium, Boston, May 5, 1964.
62. *Editor & Publisher*, November 14, 1964, p. 80.
63. T. V. Parasuram, *Nieman Reports*, March, 1964, p. 9.
64. Reston, speech at International House, New York, March 23, 1964.
65. *Editor & Publisher*, March 5, 1966, p. 56; see also publishers' report, New York *Times*, April 24, 1966, p. 72.
66. Earl J. Johnson, UPI *Reporter*, February 22, 1962.
67. From one of the participants in the survey.

III. THE RESTLESS JAPANESE

I. IMAGES AND REALITIES

1. New York *Times*, November 9, 1964, p. 4.
2. Lawrence Olson, "Japan's Relations With China: Some Recent Developments." *American Universities Field Staff Reports* [hereafter cited as *AUFS Reports*] ("East Asia Series," XI, No. 4 [June, 1964]), 13.
3. Shigeki Toyama, *Journal of Social and Political Ideas in Japan*, II, No. 1 (April, 1964), 112.
4. A. M. Rosenthal, "The New Japan," New York *Times*, June 24, 1963, p. 1.
5. New York *Times*, June 23, 1965, p. 1.
6. *Wall Street Journal*, June 30, 1965, p. 1.
7. *The Japan of Today* (published by the Japanese Ministry of Foreign Affairs), p. 27.
8. Daniel Wolfstone, "Asian Commentary," *Far Eastern Economic Review*, XLV, No. 2 (July 9, 1964), 47.
9. *Editor & Publisher*, October 3, 1964, p. 59.
10. Kazuo Takita, *Far Eastern Economic Review*, XLV, No. 2 (July 9, 1964), 63. See also *Economic Development of Post-War Japan* (Japanese Committee for Economic Development, 1963), p. 12; Lawrence Olson, "A Note on Japan," *AUFS Reports* ("East Asia Series," XII, No. 4 [July, 1965]), 11–12. See also New York *Times*, January 24, 1966, p. 37 and February 12, 1966, sec. 3.
11. Robert Trumbull, New York *Times*, July 2, 1965, p. 37.
12. *The Japan of Today*, pp. 32–55 *passim*. See also A. M. Rosenthal, New York *Times*, June 24, 1963, p. 12; *Newsweek*, December 20, 1965, p. 46.
13. New York *Times*, March 29, 1966, p. 25.
14. Arthur Koestler, *Life*, September 11, 1964, p. 79.
15. The editor asked not to be identified.
16. Takita, *op. cit.*, pp. 61–63.

17. *The Japan of Today*, p. 31.
18. *Ibid.*, p. 39.
19. *Statistical Abstract of the United States, 1965*, p. 861, table 1216.
20. Emerson Chapin, New York *Times*, January 18, 1965, p. C42.
21. The examples are borrowed from Edwin O. Reischauer, *The United States and Japan* (Cambridge, Mass.: Harvard University Press, 1961), pp. 15–16.
22. *The Japan of Today*, pp. 59–60.
23. Emerson Chapin, "Militant Japanese Buddhist Group Forms Party," New York *Times*, November 18, 1964. See also Lawrence Olson, "The Value Creation Society," *AUFS Reports*, Vol. XI, No. 6. The 1965 elections were reported in the New York *Times*, July 5–7, 1965, and are the basis for the standing of the political parties. The Upper Chamber of the Diet in 1965 was composed of 139 Liberal Democrats, a loss of 5; 73 Socialists, a gain of 8; 20 Komeito, a gain of 5; 5 Communists, a gain of 1; 7 Democratic Socialists, a loss of 1; and 4 independents; with 2 vacancies (Robert Trumbull, New York *Times*, July 6, 1965, p. 5). The Tokyo elections were covered in the New York *Times*, July 25, 1965, p. 3; and the *Asahi* poll, on August 22, 1965, p. 7.
24. Masaru Ogawa "Thunder on the Right," reprinted from *Asia Magazine*, in *Atlas*, September, 1964, pp. 105–6.
25. Lafcadio Hearn, quoted in Elizabeth Stevenson, *Lafcadio Hearn* (New York: Macmillan, 1961), p. 200.

2. THE JAPANESE PRESS

26. Japanese editors are often modest about their opinion-forming role. Many of them contend they are "impartial" and have no effect on public opinion because their papers generally do no more than report the news. Such attitudes are not uncommon in journalism. In the United States, the most famous instance of journalistic dissembling is the insistence of most New York drama critics that they have nothing to do with the success or failure of a new Broadway show, despite considerable evidence to the contrary.
27. Susumu Ejiri, deputy secretary general, Nihon Shinbun Kyokai (N.S.K. [Japan Newspaper Publishers and Editors Association]). "Characteristics of Japanese Newspapers," paper delivered before the International Press Institute, Ninth Asian Seminar, Tokyo, April 13, 1964. Because of the N.S.K.'s insistence on giving figures mainly for its own members, the totals for the Japanese press in 1964 were arrived at as follows: there are 102 members of the N.S.K. who publish daily, according to the N.S.K. volume *The Japanese Press* (Tokyo, 1964), p. 119. In a paper entitled "The Survival and Death of Newspapers in Japan," that Ejiri delivered in 1964 before the International Press Institute in Istanbul, he quoted a nationwide survey made in March, 1964, which showed that there were 174 daily newspapers not affiliated with N.S.K.; hence, the 1964 total of 276 for the daily Japanese newspapers. In addition, Ejiri said there were 1,570 newspapers "not coming out every day" which are not N.S.K. members, but which are small local journals of a few thousand circulation each. In his own estimation, the 5 national dailies and

90 (approximate) provincial newspapers covered 95 per cent of the total Japanese daily newspaper circulation.

28. According to *The Japanese Press,* the figures for the five national daily circulations were: *Asahi Shimbun,* 4,919,390 (A.M.), 3,475,459 (P.M.); *Mainichi Shimbun,* 3,692,647 (A.M.), 2,232,650 (P.M.); *Yomiuri Shimbun,* 3,873,310 (A.M.), 2,548,892 (P.M.); *Sankei Shimbun,* 2,012,708 (A.M.), 1,059,089 (P.M.); *Nihon Keizai,* 918,315 (A.M.), 584,610 (P.M.).

29. "This Is Japan," 10th Anniversary Special Issue, *Asahi Shimbun,* pp. 26–29 *passim.*

30. Richmond Croom Beatty, *Bayard Taylor* (Norman, Okla.: University of Oklahoma Press, 1936), pp. 142–43.

31. Kanesada Hanazono, *The Development of the Japanese Press* (Osaka: Mainichi, 1924), p. 6. See also Harry Emerson Wildes, *The Press and Social Currents in Japan* (Chicago: University of Chicago Press, 1927), pp. 12–13.

32. *Yomiuri,* June 21, 1964, p. 3.

33. Wildes, *op. cit.,* pp. 14–15.

34. Hanazono, *op. cit.,* p. 26.

35. Wildes, *op. cit.,* pp. 18–19.

36. Hanazono, *op. cit.,* p. 24.

37. Wildes, *op. cit.,* pp. 40–41; Hanazono, *op. cit.,* pp. 33–35.

38. Wildes, *op. cit.,* pp. 42–43.

39. *This Is Japan,* pp. 26–27.

40. Hanazono, *op. cit.,* pp. 50–51.

41. John Hohenberg, *Foreign Correspondence,* pp. 178–80.

42. Hanazono, *op. cit.,* pp. 51–52; see also *This Is Japan,* pp. 27–28.

43. Wildes, *op. cit.,* pp. 39–40.

44. *Ibid.,* pp. 105–7, see also *This Is Japan,* p. 29.

45. Russell Brines, *MacArthur's Japan* (Philadelphia: Lippincott, 1948), p. 246.

46. *Ibid.,* pp. 248–49.

47. Ralph E. Lapp, *The Voyage of the Lucky Dragon* (New York: Harper & Bros., 1957), p. 72.

48. *Ibid.,* pp. 77–78.

49. *Ibid.,* pp. 126–28. On March 2, 1954, the official announcement from Washington, D.C., was: "Lewis L. Strauss, chairman of the U.S. Atomic Energy Commission, announced today that Joint Task Force Seven has detonated an atomic device at the AEC's proving grounds in the Marshall Islands. This detonation was the first in a series of events." The Bikini bomb was an H-bomb with power more than a thousand times greater than the Hiroshima bomb. Ambassador John M. Allison called Aikichi Kuboyama, the only member of the *Lucky Dragon's* crew to die, an "innocent victim." According to the Japanese Ministry of Health and Welfare, a total of 683 tuna boats had contaminated fish in their holds, and some 457 tons of tuna fish had to be discarded.

50. *Ibid.,* pp. 175, 183–84.

3. THE "BROKEN DIALOGUE"

51. Sannosuke Matsumoto, *Journal of Social and Political Ideas in Japan,* I, No. 2 (August, 1963), 8.
52. Edwin O. Reischauer, *Foreign Affairs,* October, 1960, pp. 11-26.
53. Yoshihiko Seki, *Journal of Social and Political Ideas in Japan,* I, No. 1 (April, 1963), 3.
54. First session on Foreign Assistance Program, hearing before Senate Committee on Foreign Relations, 89th Cong., April 7, 1965.
55. Transcript of Robert J. McCloskey's press conference, Department of State, April 29, 1965.
56. Transcript of McCloskey's press conference, Department of State, April 30, 1965.
57. Record of Under Secretary Ball's conversation with Konishi, made available by the Department of State, May 1, 1965.
58. Seki, *op. cit.,* p. 6.
59. Brines, *op. cit.,* p. 256.
60. W. J. Coughlin, *The Conquered Press* (Palo Alto, Calif.: Pacific Books, 1952).
61. Edward P. Whittemore, *The Press in Japan Today: A Case Study* (Columbia, S.C.: University of South Carolina Press, 1961), p. 16.
62. Lawrence Olson, "Shimizu Alters Course," *AUFS Reports* ("East Asia Series," XI, No. 1 [February, 1964]).
63. Seki, *op. cit.,* pp. 2-3.
64. *Ibid.,* pp. 8-9.
65. *Peking Review,* May 13, 1958; *People's Daily,* November 1, 1958, quoted in Whittemore, *op. cit.,* pp. 3-4.
66. Seki, *op. cit.,* pp. 9-10.
67. Department of State *Bulletin,* XLII (February 8, 1960), 180. Text of treaty and related documents, pp. 184-201.
68. Whittemore, *op. cit.,* pp. 17-18.
69. *Asahi Shimbun,* May 20, 1960. Translated in Whittemore, *op. cit.,* pp. 88-90.
70. Reischauer, *Foreign Affairs,* October, 1960; see also Whittemore, *op. cit.,* pp. 56-76 *passim.*
71. Whittemore, *op. cit.,* pp. 65-66.
72. Seki, *op. cit.,* p. 10.
73. Olson, "Shimizu Alters Course," pp. 10-11. Shimizu's article in *Chuo Koron* was "Toward a New View of History," published in December, 1963.
74. Olson, "Shimizu Alters Course," p. 1.
75. Yuzuru Okada, *Journal of Social and Political Ideas in Japan,* II, No. 1 (April, 1964), 6-7.
76. Matsumoto, *op. cit.,* pp. 7-8.
77. Seki, *op. cit.,* p. 4.
78. Yasumasa Oshima, *Journal of Social and Political Ideas in Japan,* I, No. 3, 9-10.

4. JAPAN'S AMERICA

79. Koji Mori, "TV Industry of Japan," *Mainichi Daily News,* September 6, 1963, p. 7.
80. Survey of average of forty-four stations as of January–March, 1963, by the N.S.K., *Asahi Evening News,* January 20, 1964, p. B-1.
81. Interview with Matsutaro Shoriki, July 31, 1963.
82. Most Japanese surveys of television give highly pleasing figures for the fields of education and culture. The figures here, and the viewer ratings of foreign imports, are from Kiyoshi Hara, " 'Threat' of Culture and Education," a TV and radio summary published in the *Asahi,* 10th Anniversary Special Issue, 1963, pp. 41–42. An N.S.K. survey for the following year published a jump to 40 per cent for culture and education and 49 per cent for entertainment, without explanation and without accounting for a drop in news coverage. The N.H.K. *Handbook* (Tokyo, 1964), p. 28, claimed its general television network devoted 25 per cent to entertainment, 37.9 per cent to culture, 9.2 per cent to education, 22.2 per cent to news, and 5.7 per cent to sports.
83. Mori, *op. cit.,* p. 7.
84. *The Japanese Press,* pp. 46–47.
85. Interviews with Japanese experts familiar with N.H.K. operations.
86. An independent survey of Radio Japan newscasts for June 15–21, 1964.
87. Interviews with Japanese experts familiar with N.H.K. operations.
88. Interview with Ryugen Hosokawa, June 27, 1964. Information on ratings came from qualified Japanese sources.
89. John R. Morris, "Cable Congestion at Guam Delays News Sent to Japan," *Editor & Publisher,* December 17, 1921, p. 13.
90. N.H.K. *Handbook,* pp. 134–35. See also Naoyoshi Horikawa, "Rapid Strides in Television Expansion," *Asahi Evening News,* January 20, 1964, 2d sec., p. 12.
91. "Japan-America Direct Voice Contacts," *Mainichi Daily News,* June 19, 1964, p. 12.
92. This is generally known. Although the United States did not use Syncom 3 telecasts (possibly with one exception), they were picked up and used by Eurovision in some parts of Europe.
93. *The Japanese Press,* pp. 133–45 *passim. Shipping & Trade News* circulation in *Editor & Publisher International Year Book, 1965.*
94. Clyde McGregor (pseudonym of correspondent living in Japan), "A Look at Japan's English Language Newspapers," *Asahi Evening News,* January 20, 1964, p. B-5.
95. A.B.C. figures for six months ending December 31, 1964.
96. Composition of foreign staffs listed in each magazine in summer, 1965. These are permanently assigned foreign correspondents. Each magazine has a number of stringers, usually not listed.
97. McGregor, *op. cit.*
98. Interview with Shintaro Fukushima, June 29, 1964.
99. Susumu Ejiri, "Public Relations Activities of the Japanese Press," paper read before the FIEJ, Montecatini, 1964.

100. Ejiri, "Characteristics of Japanese Newspapers."
101. Emerson Chapin, "Japan's Biggest Paper Is At Stake," New York *Times,* May 17, 1964, p. 3; "The Founder's Daughter," *Time,* July 3, 1964, p. 48; "It Gives Us Light," *Newsweek,* July 6, 1964, pp. 38–39. Other details from various executives of *Asahi* and other knowledgeable persons.
102. I am indebted to *Asahi Shimbun* for the most recent information.
103. Based on interviews with a number of Japanese editors and foreign editors.
104. New York *Times,* March 20, 1966, p. 16.
105. Ejiri, "Characteristics of Japanese Newpapers."
106. *The Japanese Press,* pp. 92–93.
107. Interview with Masayoshi Ohira when he was Foreign Minister, June 23, 1964.

5. AMERICAN CORRESPONDENTS IN JAPAN

108. "Hot Water," *Time,* May 7, 1965, p. 47.
109. "Farming Under Wraps," *Newsweek,* June 28, 1965, p. 3.
110. "Gone for Broke," *Newsweek,* June 7, 1965, p. 72.
111. "The Sockeye That Swims Too Far," *Time,* June 11, 1964, p. 86; "Bluebird on Wheels," same issue, p. 91.
112. "Merry Bonenkai," *Time,* December 31, 1965, p. 18; *Newsweek* also had an article celebrating the Ginza's girls, May 17, 1965, p. 80.
113. New York *Times,* July 11, 1965, sec. 11.
114. Membership list of Foreign Correspondents Club of Japan in 1964.
115. Chicago *Daily News,* June 4, 1964, p. 1.
116. As of November 1, 1963, the *Asahi Shimbun* scale was as follows for college graduates on the news staff:

Years of Service	Average Age	Average Monthly Base Pay [a]	Average Monthly Gross Pay [b]
Starting	22	$ 70	$140
5	27	$ 90	$186
10	32	$120	$260
15	37	$180	$360
20	42	$240	$470

SOURCE: Mimeographed publication of *Asahi* made available to the author.

[a] Base pay might vary as much as 15 per cent above or below the average base pay, depending on individual circumstances.

[b] Average overtime and average monthly bonus plus average base pay were added to give the average monthly gross pay.

117. Salary estimates are reasonably accurate since in most cases they come from the correspondents themselves; in the higher brackets, it was more difficult to persuade correspondents to discuss their wages.

6. COVERING JAPAN: A SURVEY

118. See also Appendix I.

7. THE EMERGING PATTERN

119. Norman Sklarewitz, "None of Your Business," *Wall Street Journal,* June 9, 1964. Other correspondents talked of this in interviews.
120. Edwin O. Reischauer, "The Broken Dialogue With Japan," *Foreign Affairs,* October, 1960, pp. 11–12.
121. Ralph C. Powell, "China's Bomb," *Foreign Affairs,* July, 1965, p. 621.
122. This was a recurrent theme among Japanese journalists in Japan. When the author held up *Asahi* as an example of a newspaper that had earned wide respect among journalists throughout the world, the vast majority—including members of *Asahi*'s own staff—demurred that it was not in the same class as the New York *Times* and the *Times* of London.

IV. ALONG THE ASIAN PERIMETER

1. THE "INITIAL RELIANCE"

1. John Hohenberg, *Foreign Correspondence,* pp. 76, 133.
2. W. W. Rostow, *The United States in the World Arena* (New York: Harper & Row, 1960), p. 235, for complete Acheson quotation. Richard W. Leopold, *The Growth of American Foreign Policy* (New York: Knopf, 1962), p. 679, for summary of background. General MacArthur on March 1, 1949, told a British correspondent that Korea was not a part of the American defense perimeter. Robert H. Leckie, *Conflict: The History of the Korean War,* pp. 36–37, gives only the partial quotation from Acheson and leans toward the interpretation that it encouraged the Communists.
3. The results of the private State Department poll are from a qualified source.
4. *Community Relations Summary* (Pacific Air Force, USAF), Vol. III, No. 2, (2d quarter, 1963).
5. Theodor Mommsen, *The History of Rome* (New York: Dutton, 1932), IV, 142.
6. Pyong Choon Hahm, "Korea's 'Mendicant Mentality'?," *Foreign Affairs* XLIII, No. 1 (October, 1964), 168.

2. KOREA: THE FORGOTTEN FRONT

7. "South Korea: Deadly Choice," *Newsweek,* International Edition, June 15, 1964, p. 38.
8. Letter from Professor Floyd G. Arpan to Osborn Elliott, editor, *Newsweek,* dated Seoul, June 14, 1964.
9. Letter from Mrs. Marie Nagorski to Peter Kalischer, dated Seoul, August 26, 1963.
10. Letter from Charles Collingwood to Mrs. Nagorski, dated New York, September 17, 1963.
11. Gunnar Myrdal, "With What Little Wisdom the World Is Ruled," New York *Times Magazine,* July 18, 1965, p. 21.
12. Address at Harvard Law Institute, quoted in the New York *Herald Tribune,* May 26, 1962.

13. Emerson Chapin, New York *Times,* June 26, 1965, p. 4. Copyright by the New York Times Company. Reprinted by permission.

14. Pyong Choon Hahm, *op. cit.,* p. 166. Later figures in New York *Times,* January 24, 1966, p. 39, and James McC. Truitt, *Newsweek,* February 7, 1966, pp. 36–37.

15. Earl H. Voss, Washington *Evening Star,* May 22, 1960. See also Bin Min Yung (ed.), *The April Heroes: A Report on Korea's Freedom Revolution.* (Seoul: In Shin Sa, 1960), a compilation of news articles. For background, Pyun Yung-tai, *Korea, My Country* (Seoul: Council on Korean Affairs, 1962).

16. Soon Il Hong, "On Current Political Phenomena," *Korean Affairs,* II, No. 1 (1963), 95–104; *Time,* International Edition, October 25, 1963, p. 30; and "South Korea: Tired of Turmoil," *Newsweek,* December 9, 1963, p. 43.

17. Robert Eunson, two-part series on Korea offered to AP members in late June, 1964.

18. Memo from Eunson to author, giving full text of the Park quotation, dated Tokyo, June 29, 1964.

19. Ki Uk Hahn, spokesman for Ministry of Information, Republic of Korea, at Seminar for College Newspaper Editors, American Embassy Club, Seoul, June 12, 1964.

20. Kyu Whan Kim "The Past and Present of Journalism in Korea," *Korean Affairs,* I, No. 3 (1962), 261–66.

21. *World Communications, 1964,* p. 231.

22. *Editor & Publisher International Year Book, 1965,* pp. 559–60.

23. AP report, January 1, 1966; New York *Times,* January 2, 1966, p. 17.

24. *World Communications, 1964,* p. 231. Also, mimeographed document of Department of State, entitled "Communications Fact Book, South Korea."

25. "Communications Fact Book, South Korea."

26. Eunson articles on Korea, June, 1964.

27. Hyo Chai Lee, "The Koreans' Understanding of Democracy," *Korean Affairs,* II, No. 1 (1963), 17. An article based on a study project sponsored by the Korean Christian Institute for Social Concern.

28. *Ibid.,* p. 19.

29. Chi Ho Lew, "Seminar in American Studies Sponsored by the Fulbright Commission for Korea," Seoul, February 6, 1964; record of proceedings available at the American Embassy.

30. Ki Uk Hahn, spokesman for Ministry of Information, Republic of Korea, appearing at conference for college editors in Seoul on June 12, 1964.

31. The author did the interviewing for the material on the local correspondents. Necessarily, identifications must be safeguarded.

32. On the Japan–South Korea treaty, see New York *Times,* August 15, 1965, p. 7; December 12, 1965, p. 8; and December 22, 1965.

33. There is a broad range of material on Korean industrial progress. Among the materials consulted were: Han Nae Bok, "South Korea: Changes in Aid," *Far Eastern Economic Review,* annual survey on America and Asia, XLV, No. 2 (July 9, 1964), 73–74; "South Korea: The Striking Parallel," *Time,* May 21, 1965, pp. 35–36; K. C. Cho, "Korea Struggling on an Uphill Road," New York *Times,* January 18, 1965, p. C49; Emerson Chapin, "Pusan Strug-

gles To Untangle Its Urban Snarl," New York *Times*, July 18, 1965, p. 3; and "Korea Is Planning a 'Pittsburgh' at Rural Center," New York *Times*, July 19, 1965, p. 4; New York *Times*, January 24, 1966, p. 39; and *Newsweek*, February 7, 1966, p. 36.

3. OKINAWA: THE BILLION-DOLLAR BASE

34. Rafael Steinberg, "Our Unhappy Asian Bastion," Washington *Post*, May 3–7, 1964.
35. Robert Eunson, AP file, April 23, 1964, under date line Naha, Okinawa.
36. Rafael Steinberg, Washington *Post*, May 3, 1964.
37. *Ibid.*
38. Emerson Chapin, New York *Times*, March 29, 1964, p. 12.
39. Rafael Steinberg, Washington *Post*, May 7, 1964, p. A26.
40. Eunson, AP file, April 23, 1964, under date line Naha, Okinawa.
41. Based on interviews with Norman Sklarewitz, *Wall Street Journal*, in the summers of 1963 and 1964 in Tokyo, and with Robert Eunson, AP, in Seoul and Tokyo in the summer of 1964.
42. Eunson, AP file, April 23, 1964, under date line Naha, Okinawa.
43. *World Communications, 1964*, p. 250.
44. Shoichi Kobayashi, Japan *Times*, June 28, 1964, p. 8.
45. "Okinawa and Autonomy," *Mainichi Daily News*, June 19, 1964, page 1 editorial.
46. George F. Kennan, *Foreign Affairs*, XLIII, No. 1 (October, 1964), 24.
47. New York *Times*, November 1, 1964, p. 8; March 24, 1966, p. 6.
48. New York *Times*, October 11, 1964, p. 25; August 21, 1965, p. 3; August 25, 1965, p. 8; March 27, 1966, p. 32.

4. THE CHANGING PHILIPPINES

49. Philippines *Herald*, October 29, 1963, p. 1; editorial, p. 10.
50. Carlos P. Romulo, typescript, "Asia: World War and Revolution," p. 10.
51. New York *Times*, January 26, 1965, p. 1.
52. *U.S. News & World Report*, January 11, 1965, p. 59.
53. Macario T. Vicencio, "Asia's 'Free' Press," *Atlas*, April, 1964, p. 229, reprinted from *Asia Magazine*.
54. Manila *Bulletin* editorial, June 17, 1964.
55. J. V. Cruz, Manila *Times*, June 27, 1964, p. 5A.
56. Nestor Mata, Philippines *Herald*, July 14, 1964, p. 11.
57. Vicencio, *op. cit.*, p. 228.
58. *World Communications, 1964*, pp. 246–47. Circulation figures from *Editor & Publisher International Year Book*, 1965, p. 558.
59. Interview with Joaquin P. Roces, July 16, 1964, in the Manila *Times*.
60. New York *Times*, December 31, 1964, carried obituary of Andres Soriano, Sr.
61. State Department background document on the Philippines, October, 1962. Salaries and similar material from correspondents and editors.
62. P. K. Macker, address, "Growth of Asia Advertising Media, Print," before

sixth session of the fourth Asian Advertising Congress, Hong Kong, November 5, 1964.

63. Cynthia Lowry, AP, published in Philippines *Herald*, June 21, 1964, p. 15.

64. Ramon Mabuto, Philippines *Herald*, July 14, 1964.

65. Maximo V. Soliven, Manila *Times*, July 16, 1964, p. 5A.

66. Robert Trumbull, "Red Filipino Terrorists Employ Vietcong Tactics," New York *Times*, January 10, 1965.

67. Soliven, New York *Times*, January 18, 1965, p. 57C.

68. Bernardino Ronquillo, "Philippines: Seeking New Patterns," *Far Eastern Economic Review*, annual survey on America and Asia, XLV, No. 2 (July 9, 1964), 75.

69. "Poor English: A Growing Problem of Filipino Students," *Manila Chronicle Magazine*, July 18, 1964, pp. 14–15.

70. Romulo, "American Literature and the Modern Sensibility," inaugural lecture at the University of the Philippines, January 13, 1965.

71. "Philippine-American Cultural Foundation Grant Expires," USIS press release, July 29, 1964. See also Benito F. Legarda, "Answer to Stevenson," Manila *Chronicle*, June 15, 1964, p. 5.

72. Moved on UPI report, February 26, 1964, in Manila, published in Philippines *Herald*, February 27, 1964, and denied by the President on the following day. On Macapagal's policy, see Philippines *Herald Magazine*, July 18, 1964, p. 15.

73. On Marcos' policy, see Seymour Topping series, New York *Times*, November 21, 1965; for Marcos' election result and sketch, the New York *Times*, November 13, 1965, p. 2; for Marcos' policies, *Time*, January 27, 1966, p. 26; *Newsweek*, February 14, 1966, pp. 44–45; and New York *Times*, January 24, 1966, p. 44C; for new U.S. military aid, New York *Times*, March 27, 1966, p. 1.

74. UPI file in Manila, July 15, 1964.

75. Albert Ravenholt, A. V. H. Hartendorp, *AUFS Reports* ("Southeast Asia Series," XII, No. 13 [December, 1964]).

76. The reference to the Indonesian matter is to a time between 1962 and 1964. Necessarily, officials concerned cannot be identified.

77. Interview with Foreign Secretary Mendez at the Padre Faura, Manila, July 15, 1964. He died January 1, 1966.

78. DPA and Kyodo both were offering their service on a trial basis without charge, after which a relatively small fee was asked. Editors said AFP was charging between $100 and $200 a month for its service in the Philippines. Antara, a propaganda service, was being offered to anybody who wanted to use it, but had very few takers.

79. Some of Ravenholt's subjects were individual Filipinos and their work: "J. V. Garcia Homecrafts," *AUFS Reports* ("Southeast Asia Series," Vol. XII, No. 14); "Broilers for Manila's Housewives," *ibid.*, No. 9; and "Scissors from Tabaco," *ibid.*, No. 8.

80. Report of the Philippine–American Assembly, Davao, R. P., February 23–26, 1966, p. 6.

5. THE VOICES OF TAIWAN

81. Robert J. Donovan, *Eisenhower: The Inside Story,* p. 300.
82. Harry S. Truman, *Memoirs,* II, 430.
83. Donovan, *op. cit.,* p. 302.
84. *Statistical Abstract of the United States, 1965,* p. 24, table 19.
85. *The American Public's View of U.S. Policy Toward China.* A report prepared for the Council on Foreign Relations by the Survey Research Center, University of Michigan. Released December 15, 1964, p. 10. Samuel Lubell in the *Columbia Journalism Review,* Spring, 1966, questioned the validity of the findings, saying that it rested on one "gimmicky question."
86. AP file, January 2, 1965, published in the New York *Times,* January 3, 1965.
87. Article 32, Publications Law, Republic of China, revised in 1958. Quoted in James Shen, "Press Freedom vs. Responsibility," pamphlet published by Government Information Office, Republic of China, Taipei, 1962, p. 3.
88. UPI file, Asian service, May 3, May 29, and May 31, 1963. Also, press release of the Taiwan Garrison Command dated December 3, 1963.
89. Max Frankel, New York *Times,* July 1, 1965, p. 1.
90. New York *Times,* March 8, 1964, p. 24.
91. New York *Times,* July 21, 1965, p. 3; July 22, 1965, p. 21.
92. *World Communications, 1964.* Some figures are from qualified American sources.
93. Observation by author.
94. *Catalogue of Books,* Autumn, 1963, Literature House, 143 Chungking Rd., S Sec. 1, Taipei, P.O. Box 1151, Taipei.
95. The following is an example of the lengths to which the policy was carried. It was written in longhand for a visitor in 1963 by an American official who has since finished his regular tour of duty and moved to another post.

Out of a total population of 11 million, about 2 million are mainlanders, *i.e.,* Chinese, mostly Mandarin-speaking, who came here in 1949–50. The other 9 million are equally Chinese, originally residents of Fukien province. . . .

There is no significant conflict between these two groups—the Taiwanese have profited greatly from the 1952–54 land reform and the subsequent economic development, and they are fully represented in the Taiwan Provincial Assembly and various municipal and county councils and farmers' associations.

This does not mean, however, that the Taiwanese are not proud of their own history and their particular province's part of the Chinese cultural heritage.

It is good manners—accepted and practiced by those born in Taiwan as well as those who came from the mainland—to refer to the place as the Republic of China and to its citizens as Chinese, whatever their province of origin.

The mainlanders are found all over the island, especially in positions of some importance—although they do not monopolize these—in the government, police, military, education, etc. The mainlanders are, however, concentrated in Taipei. The proportion of Taiwan-born Chinese in influential places, including newspapers, is much higher in the center and south than in Taipei.

96. A. Doak Barnett, *Communist China and Asia,* pp. 396–97.
97. Wolf Ladejinsky, "Land Reform In Asia," *Foreign Affairs,* XLIII, No. 3 (April, 1964), 449.
98. Leon M. S. Slawecki, in "The Two Chinas in Africa," (*Foreign Affairs,* Vol. XLI, No. 2 [January, 1963]), gives a rather optimistic evaluation of Nationalist China's efforts in Africa. For the situation two years later, I am indebted to N. K. Aggarwala for the material in his unpublished, "Red China and the U.N." (Master's thesis; Columbia Graduate School of Journalism, 1965).
99. "Chiang Succession Plans," in New York *Times,* March 22, 1966, p. 8; see also New York *Times,* March 25, 1966, p. 6.

6. THE HALF-FORMED IMAGE

100. "57 Varieties," *Newsweek,* September 14, 1964, p. 63. For Korean tourists, see New York *Times,* March 20, 1966, p. 8.
101. Kyoko Baba, "The Sad Lot of Japan's Korean Residents," Japan *Times,* June 18, 1964, p. 5. Tarzie Vittachi, "We Have Our Own Color Bar," *Asia Magazine,* June 28, 1964, p. 6.

V. IN RED CHINA'S SHADOW

1. OUTSIDE THE BAMBOO CURTAIN

1. For an attractive layout, see New York *Times* travel section, June 27, 1965, p. 37.
2. "Mao Speaks," *Newsweek,* February 22, 1965, p. 36.
3. Michael Cope, "Red China's Changing Face," a series distributed in November, 1964, through the Toronto *Globe & Mail,* and published November 23–28, 1964, in the Cleveland *Press.*
4. Mark Gayn, Toronto *Star,* published in the New York *Times,* June 7–12, 1965.
5. San Francisco *Examiner* series began June 20, 1965. Background reported in *Editor & Publisher,* June 19, 1965, p. 15, and *Newsweek,* June 28, 1965, p. 50.
6. "Red China News Visa Bids Urged," *Editor & Publisher,* January 23, 1965, p. 14.
7. New York *Times,* May 2, 1957. Letter to Arthur Hays Sulzberger.
8. Edgar Snow, *The Other Side of the River,* p. 9.
9. Jacques Marcuse, "How To Talk To the Chinese in Peking," New York *Times Magazine,* May 23, 1965, p. 82.
10. Marvin Kalb, "China, the Greatest Story Never Told," in *Dateline,* 1965, p. 26.
11. John Roderick interview in Tokyo, June 17, 1964.

2. THE HONG KONG BEAT

12. Sources for the description of Hong Kong's economy and related journalistic materials, in addition to interviews, included *Asia Magazine,* Special Issue on Hong Kong, Vol. IV, No. 28 (July 12, 1964); *Far Eastern Economic Review,* Vol. XLV, No. 2 (July 9, 1964), presenting annual review of America and Asia and Frederic Kaplan, "Hong Kong: Magnet for Visitors," pp. 57–61; "Hong Kong Trade and Investing Swell Peking Exchange Income," New York *Times,* May 30, 1965, p. 14; "Hong Kong Boom Ignores Politics," New York *Times,* January 18, 1965, p. C48; "Hong Kong: Another Kind of Crisis," *Time,* February 19, 1965, p. 96.

13. Most of the journalistic data in this section are from qualified American sources. While the Hong Kong press circulation figures are published in the *Editor & Publisher International Year Book, 1965,* some of them are open to doubt and have been checked as far as possible. A number of correspondents, American and British, contributed to the material on sources.

3. THE CHINA-WATCHERS

14. Letter from Takashi Oka, dated July 10, 1964. Despite his modesty, Oka's Chinese sources were regarded as excellent and he knew how to use them discreetly.

15. Much of the personal information on correspondents was derived from interviews. The author wishes to acknowledge, with thanks, the use of an unpublished piece by Robert K. McCabe, of *Newsweek,* about his colleagues.

16. Hong Kong correspondents' reference list, May 15, 1964, made available by USIS, Hong Kong.

17. From answers to questionnaires and interviews.

4. THE PROPAGANDA WAR

18. "Marcuse Quits Peking; 'Mutual Disagreement,'" *Editor & Publisher,* December 26, 1964, p. 40.

19. Quoted in Frederick T. C. Yu, "Communications and Politics in Communist China," in Lucian W. Pye (ed.), *Communications and Political Development,* p. 274.

20. *World Communications, 1965* (New York: UNESCO Communications Center, 1965), pp. 209–10; *Editor & Publisher International Year Book, 1965,* p. 549.

21. *Editor & Publisher International Year Book, 1965,* pp. 549–50.

22. Robert Guillain, *600 Million Chinese* (New York: Criterion, 1957), p. 137.

23. S. Chandrasekhar, "Red China Today," written for the AP and published in the Boston *Globe,* February 16, 1959.

24. Mark Gayn, New York *Times,* June 7, 1965, p. 3.

25. A. Doak Barnett, "The United States and Communist China," in Willard L. Thorp (ed.), *The United States and the Far East* (2d ed.; Englewood Cliffs, N. J.: Prentice-Hall, 1962), pp. 120–21.

26. Information from correspondents.

27. S. Richard Hughes, "Peking's 'Indispensable' Front Man," New York *Times*

Magazine, October 4, 1964, p. 16; Jacques Marcuse, "It Doesn't Matter Who Succeeds Mao," New York *Times Magazine,* July 11, 1965, p. 8; Seymour Topping, " 'Long Live Chairman Mao! Long Live Lin Piao!' " New York *Times Magazine,* July 17, 1966, pp. 18-19, 38-40.

28. Richard Dudman, St. Louis *Post-Dispatch,* February 13, 1963, p. 1C.

29. Ray Vicker, *Wall Street Journal,* December 21, 1964, p. 1.

30. Norman Sklarewitz, *Wall Street Journal,* September 2, 1964, p. 1; Peter Grose, New York *Times,* March 16, 1966, p. 8; see also Harrison Salisbury's page 1 series of his tour of the Chinese border, New York *Times,* August 15-19, 1966.

31. Takashi Oka, *Christian Science Monitor,* February 14, 1964; New York *Times,* March 20, 1960, p. 18; March 24, 1966, p. 8.

32. Samuel B. Griffith, "Communist China's Capacity To Make War," *Foreign Affairs,* XLIII, No. 2 (January, 1965), 217. His testimony before the Senate Foreign Relations Committee was reported in the New York *Times,* March 19, 1966, p. 2.

33. Hanson Baldwin, New York *Times,* October 26, 1964.

34. Donald S. Zagoria, New York *Times Magazine,* October 18, 1964, p. 115.

35. New York *Times,* October 18, 1964, p. 1.

36. "China's Power Mania," *New Age* (New Delhi), reprinted in *Atlas,* December, 1964, p. 311.

37. *Mainichi,* May 15, 1965.

38. Ralph L. Powell, "China's Bomb: Exploitation and Reaction," *Foreign Affairs,* XLIII, No. 4 (July, 1965), 619.

39. Edward Crankshaw, "Cold War of the Communisms," New York *Times Magazine,* May 26, 1963, p. 25.

40. Merle Fainsod, *Problems of Communism,* Special Supplement (published by USIA), X, No. 6 (December, 1961), iv.

41. *Ibid.,* p. xi.

42. Philip E. Mosely, "Khrushchev's Party Congress," *Foreign Affairs,* LXI, No. 1 (January, 1962), 183.

43. John Hightower, AP file, November 22, 1962.

44. Philip E. Mosely, "The China-Soviet Rift: Origins and Portents," *Foreign Affairs,* XLII, No. 1 (October, 1963), 17-18. See also A. Doak Barnett, *Communist China and Asia,* pp. 337-83.

45. Chinese letter in New York *Times,* March 24, 1966, p. 14.

46. George F. Kennan, "A Fresh Look At Our China Policy," New York *Times Magazine,* November 22, 1964, p. 27 ff.; Roger Hilsman, text of address before Council on World Affairs of Northern California and Columbia University and Barnard Alumni, in San Francisco, November 18, 1964.

47. UPI file, June 17, 1964; published in Japan *Times,* June 18, 1964, p. 1.

48. New York *Times,* June 28-29, 1965.

49. Chinese propaganda text excerpts, New York *Times,* September 4, 1965, p. 2; warning to British over Hong Kong, New York *Times,* September 7, 1965, p. 3; Senate Foreign Relations Committee hearings reported in New York *Times,* March 11-19, 1966; Vice-President Humphrey on "Meet the Press," March 13, 1966; Peking's reply, New York *Times,* March 15, 1966; Rusk policy statement, New York *Times,* April 17, 1966, p. 34.

50. General Assembly vote on China admission, New York *Times*, November 18, 1965, p. 1; Rowe's accusation, New York *Times*, March 29, 1966, p. 4.

5. OVERTURN IN INDONESIA

51. John Hughes, "U.S. Influence Hangs by a Thread," *Christian Science Monitor*, December 7, 1964. The incident occurred on December 4, 1964. Report of burning of Chinese school in New York *Times*, October 16, 1965, p. 1.
52. Seth S. King, New York *Times*, October 23, 1965, p. 4. Also New York *Times*, November 25, 1965, p. 28; John Hughes, *Christian Science Monitor*, November 19, 1965; New York *Times*, January 10, 1966, p. 4.
53. Bernard Krisher, "A Talk with Sukarno," *Newsweek*, October 5, 1964, p. 84.
54. Willard A. Hanna, introduction to *The Formation of Malaysia* (New York: American Universities Field Service, 1964), p. 5.
55. John Hughes, *Christian Science Monitor*, December 22, 1964; "Sukarno, Headman to a Nation," *Newsweek*, February 15, 1965, p. 40.
56. John Hughes, "No A-Arms in Sight for Indonesia—Yet," *Christian Science Monitor*, December 19, 1964; "Sukarno Asserts Indonesia Will Build Atomic Bomb Soon," New York *Times*, August 4, 1965, p. 2.
57. "Indonesian Press Loses Its Freedom," *Editor & Publisher*, March 6, 1965, p. 37.
58. Rohan Rivett, "Corruption Denounced From a Prison Cell," IPI Report, June, 1963.
59. Neil Sheehan, New York *Times*, July 18, 1965, p. 5.
60. Paul Nielsen, Public Affairs Officer at American embassy in 1964, checked the guests at a USIS party in Djakarta.
61. AP file, January 2, 1965.
62. Seth S. King, New York *Times*, March 29, 1964, p. 1.
63. New York *Times*, August 1, 1965; *Time*, August 6, 1965, p. 30.
64. *Time*, August 6, 1965, p. 27. See also Sheehan, New York *Times Magazine*, August 15, 1965, p. 9; and Frank N. Trager, New York *Times Magazine*, August 29, 1965, p. 26; *Newsweek*, February 15, 1964, p. 44; John Hughes, "How Reds Gain in Indonesia," *Christian Science Monitor*, December 31, 1964; Neil Sheehan, "Sukarno Pushes Toward Break With U.S.," New York *Times*, August 1, 1965, p. E4.
65. Seth S. King, New York *Times*, October 17, 1965, p. 1; October 31, 1965, p. E3; "Sukarno Losing Fight Over Press," New York *Times*, November 19, 1965, p. 9; "Now, No U.S. Reporters in Indonesia," *Editor & Publisher*, January 23, 1965, p. 11; "Latter-Day Children's Crusade: Reds Ousted by Djakarta Youths," AP, Djakarta, March 26, 1966, published in New York *Times*, March 27, 1966, p. 24; King, "Few From China Left in Djakarta," New York *Times*, March 27, 1966, p. 25; other details reported by *Times* correspondents throughout April and May. Of particular significance was C. L. Sulzberger's dispatch published April 10, 1966, p. E8 and his report on Lubis, April 17, 1966, p. 3; "Indonesia," *Time*, July 15, 1966; Seymour Topping, New York *Times*, series on Indonesia, August 22–25, 1966.

6. THE DOMINOES

66. Robert J. Donovan, *Eisenhower*, p. 261.
67. Crosby Noyes, "Vietnam: The Domino Theory," Washington *Star*, February 15, 1965, p. A12.
68. Interview with Ronald Stead, Singapore, August 7, 1964.
69. John Hughes, "Indonesia Flexes Might," *Christian Science Monitor*, December 28, 1964.
70. Hanna, *op. cit.*, p. 2.
71. Robert Trumbull, *The Scrutable East*, p. 82.
72. Robert K. McCabe, "Malaysia: Endurance Contest," *Newsweek*, February 15, 1965, pp. 44–46.
73. For AP estimate, see Tony Escoda, "Spotlight on Asia Series," Issue 31B, AP, July 25, 1964; also Hanna, *op. cit.*, p. 10.
74. *Time*, International Edition, July 31, 1964, p. 29.
75. Escoda, *op. cit.*
76. *Editor & Publisher International Year Book, 1965*, p. 549.
77. The source is one of the highest officials in Malaysia. The interview was for background use.
78. Some totals are from G. Williams Skinner, "Overseas Chinese in Southeast Asia," *The Annals*, January, 1959, cited in Barnett, *Communist China and Asia*, p. 176. There are also figures for Cambodia and the Philippines in 1965, based on Skinner's estimates, and used through the courtesy of Professor L. E. Williams, of Brown University. Other figures are in Robert S. Elegant, *The Dragon's Seed* (New York: St. Martin's, 1959). Few estimates on the overseas Chinese seem to be more than educated guesses.
79. "Communism Today, A Refresher Course," *Time*, August 6, 1965, p. 27; *Time*, International Edition, July 31, 1964, p. 29.
80. Seymour Topping, New York *Times Magazine*, October 31, 1965, p. 67; Hanna, *AUFS Reports* (Jeamia Series), Vol. XIII, No. 21 (September, 1965).
81. Reuters dispatch, New York *Times*, August 9, 1965, p. 1; see also New York *Times*, August 10–14, 1965.
82. New York *Times*, January 18, 1965, p. C51.
83. *Editor & Publisher International Year Book, 1965*, p. 560.
84. *Atlas*, X, No. 2 (August, 1965), 72–73; see also Oden Meeker, *The Little World of Laos* (New York: Scribner's, 1959), p. 121.
85. Seth S. King, New York *Times* News Service, published in Philippines *Herald* (Manila), July 16, 1964, p. 9; also see AP consorship report, January 2, 1965.
86. *Newsweek*, August 6, 1965, p. 41, was one example. There were many others of a similar nature.
87. The *Nation* (Rangoon), January 25, 1958.
88. *Time*, March 5, 1965, p. 28. *Time* pointed out that despite U Thant's contention, the United States in 1958 had agreed to sell Burma $8.8 million worth of military equipment ranging from jeeps to patrol boats under the terms of a forty-year, 3.5 per cent loan.
89. The *Nation* (Rangoon), March 25, 1960. For a description of the Burmese

press before Ne Win, see Milton Hollstein, "The Press in Burma," *Journalism Quarterly* (Spring, 1961).

90. *Statistical Abstract of the United States, 1965*, p. 861, table 1216.

91. S. C. Banerji, "Burma: No More Roadbuilding," *Far Eastern Economic Review*, XLV, No. 2 (July 9, 1964), 86. See also Dennis Bloodworth, London *Observer*, in the *Straits Times*, June 15, 1964, p. 10.

92. I am indebted to Miss Lourdes Jaramilla for some of the information about Law Yone, which was included in "Three Asian Newspapermen" (Master's thesis, Columbia Graduate School of Journalism, 1965). I am also grateful to an IPI *Report* for its detailed documentation on the issues of August, 1963; October, 1963; July, 1964; and July–August, 1965.

93. From my correspondence.

94. The estimate of Ne Win's position is from a diplomatic source. Harrison Salisbury's Burmese adventure was in New York *Times*, June 20, 1966, p. 1. President Johnson's welcome was reported in New York *Times*, September 9, 1966.

95. Keyes Beech, Chicago *Daily News*, November 18, 1964.

96. *Newsweek*, April 5, 1965, pp. 46–47. Copyright 1965 by Newsweek, Inc. Reprinted by permission.

97. New York *Times*, April 27, 1965, p. 1.

98. New York *Times*, May 4, 1965, p. 1.

99. *Newsweek*, May 24, 1965, pp. 2–8.

100. New York *Times*, May 6, 1965, p. 38. Copyright 1965 by the New York Times Company. Reprinted by permission.

101. New York *Times*, June 4, 1965, pp. 34–35.

102. The diplomat gave his views to the author under a pledge that his identity would not be disclosed.

103. Based on talks with a number of correspondents.

104. Jack Langguth, New York *Times*, January 18, 1965, p. C50.

105. *Atlas*, August, 1965, p. 97, translated from *Réalités Cambodgiennes* (Phnom Penh); Seymour Topping, "Sihanouk Bid to U.S.," New York *Times*, October 13, 1965, p. 1; "Moscow Snub," New York *Times*, October 18, 1965, p. 1.

106. Willard A. Hanna, H. R. H. Norodom Sihanouk of Cambodia," *AUFS Reports* ("Southeast Asia Series," XII, No. 2, [February, 1964]), 2.

107. Jacques Champagne, IPI *Report*, XII, No. 7 (November, 1963), 3.

108. Views of correspondents based on interviews. Report about road from Seth S. King, New York *Times*, July 25, 1965, p. 3. See also "Laos," *Time*, June 26, 1964, p. 16.

109. Meeker, *op. cit.*, p. 106.

110. Champagne, *op. cit.*, pp. 2, 4.

111. *Far Eastern Economic Review*, XLV, No. 2 (July 9, 1964), 86.

112. Seth S. King, New York *Times*, July 25, 1965, p. 3.

113. Trumbull, *op. cit.*, p. 159.

114. Eric Pace, "Laos: Continuing Crisis," *Foreign Affairs*, XLIII, No. 1 (October, 1964), 64.

115. Rusk press conference, August 2, 1965, reported in New York *Times*, August 3, 1965, p. 1.

116. Pace, *op. cit.*, p. 65.

117. Various correspondents contributed to these experiences. Piece by Tammy Arbuckle in New York *Times*, January 18, 1965, p. C52.

118. Seymour Topping's protest was made May 24, 1964, in Vientiane. Various correspondents contributed information for this part of the chapter.

119. James Reston, New York *Times*, August 15, 1965, p. E8.

VI. THE WAR IN VIET-NAM

I. THE PRESIDENT AS NEWSMAKER

1. Quoted in Ray Stannard Baker, *Woodrow Wilson, Life and Letters* (8 vols.; Garden City, N.Y.: Doubleday, 1927–39), VI, 506–7.

2. Ray Stannard Baker and William E. Dodd (eds.), *The Public Papers of Woodrow Wilson* (6 vols.; New York, 1925–27), I, 6–16.

3. The *Nation*, CVII (November 30, 1918), 638.

4. Text of President Johnson's news conference, New York *Times*, July 29, 1965, p. 12.

5. *Ibid.*

6. See news reports in New York *Times*, July 29, 1965 and February 1, 2, 6, 7, and March 3, 1966.

7. *Time*, February 18, 1966, pp. 26–31; *Newsweek*, February 21, 1966, pp. 21–25; Charles Mohr, New York *Times*, February 7, 1966, p. 6; James Reston, New York *Times*, August 22, 1965, p. E10; Bernard B. Fall, New York *Times Magazine*, March 6, 1966, p. 67. Troop strength from General William C. Westmoreland, New York *Times*, August 16, 1966, p. 4.

8. *Time*, February 18, 1966, p. 19.

9. Myron Kandel, New York *Herald Tribune*, August 12, 1965, p. 2. See also Lester Markel, "Public Opinion and the War in Vietnam," New York *Times Magazine*, August 8, 1965, p. 9, 68 ff.

10. *Time*, August 6, 1965, p. 20.

11. *Time*, July 23, 1965, p. 60; *Time*, July 30, 1965, p. 5. Letter by John B. Oakes.

12. *Time*, March 11, 1966, p. 64.

13. New York *Times*, August 11, 1965, p. 1.

14. New York *Times*, August 13, 1965, p. 1.

15. New York *Times*, August 13, 1965, p. 28; New York *Herald Tribune*, December 29, 1964, p. 18.

16. *Newsweek*, August 6, 1965, pp. 52–57.

17. Murrey Marder, Washington *Post*, August 23, 1964, p. A–27.

18. New York *Times*, August 6, 1965, p. 1; *Time*, August 6, 1965, p. 20.

19. Peter V. Curl (ed.), *Documents on American Foreign Relations, 1954* (New York: Harper & Bros., 1955), p. 366.

20. *Time*, August 6, 1965, pp. 21–22; *Newsweek*, August 2, 1965, p. 18.

21. New York *Times*, July 30, 1965, p. 1; *Time*, August 6, 1965, p. 22.

22. New York *Times*, March 10, 1966, p. 8; March 15, 1966, p. 6.

23. *Newsweek*, August 2, 1965, p. 19.
24. Ben H. Bagdikian, "The President's Brand of Press Agentry," *Columbia Journalism Review*, Summer, 1965, p. 13.
25. Henry F. Graff, "How Johnson Makes Foreign Policy," New York *Times Magazine*, July 4, 1965, p. 17.
26. *Time*, August 6, 1965, p. 20.
27. Private correspondence.
28. Bagdikian, *op. cit.*, p. 13.
29. James Reston, New York *Times*, January 7, 1966, p. 28; Dorothy McCardle, Washington *Post*, February 22, 1966, p. B-1.

2. THE ROLE OF THE U.S. EMBASSY

30. New York *Times*, September 15, 1965. Copyright 1965 by the New York Times Company. Reprinted by permission.
31. Homer Bigart, New York *Times*, February 25, 1962, p. E3.
32. John Mecklin, *Mission in Torment*, p. 180.
33. *Ibid.*, p. 286.
34. New York *Times*, June 30, 1964.
35. *U.S. Government Organization Manual, 1964–1965*, p. 506.
36. Claude Witze, *Air Force–Space Digest*, August, 1964, p. 16.
37. *Ibid.*
38. *Newsweek*, September 4, 1964. Copyright 1965 by Newsweek, Inc. Reprinted by permission.
39. "U.S. Aide Warns Vietnam Critics," New York *Times*, August 20, 1965, p. 2.
40. New York *Herald Tribune*, December 27, 1964, p. 4.
41. Beverly Deepe, New York *Herald Tribune*, December 23, 1964, p. 1.
42. John W. Finney, New York *Times*, December 23, 1964, p. 1.
43. Beverly Deepe, New York *Herald Tribune*, December 25, 1964, p. 1.

3. THE BIG CHANGE

44. New York *Times*, January 27, 1965, p. 1; New York *Herald Tribune*, January 28, 1965, p. 2.
45. Seymour Topping, New York *Times*, January 29, 1965, p. 1.
46. Private correspondence.
47. Murrey Marder, Washington *Post*, April 14, 1965, p. A-14; President Johnson's estimate, New York *Times*, July 10, 1965.
48. Richard Critchfield, Washington *Star*, April 14, 1965, p. A-8.
49. George A. Carver, Jr., "The Real Revolution in South Vietnam," *Foreign Affairs*, XLIII, No. 3 (April, 1965), 388–408 *passim*.
50. New York *Times*, June 13–15, 1965.
51. IPI *Report*, July–August, 1965.
52. New York *Herald Tribune*, August 7, 1965, p. 2.
53. Mecklin, *op. cit.*, p. 220.
54. *Newsweek*, August 23, 1965, p. 30; New York *Herald Tribune*, August 21, 1965, p. 2; Marshal Ky's views in article by R. W. Apple, Jr., New York

Times, November 15, 1965, p. 6; New York *Times,* March 14, 1966, p. 2.

55. Mecklin, *op. cit.,* pp. 251–79 *passim.*
56. Edward G. Lansdale, New York *Times,* August 19, 1965, p. 2, and August 21, 1965, p. 3. See also Lansdale, "Vietnam: Do We Understand Revolution?," *Foreign Affairs,* XLIII, No. 1 (October, 1964), 75–86.

4. BATTLEGROUND

57. Neil Sheehan, New York *Times,* August 22, 1965, p. 2.
58. Letter, August 4, 1965.
59. Charles Mohr, New York *Times,* August 10, 1965, p. 2.
60. Charles Mohr, New York *Times,* August 4, 1965, p. 1.
61. Vietnam Press dispatch, Saigon *Post,* July 20, 1964, p. 5.
62. Arnold Beichman, "As the Cookie Crumbles in Vietnam," *Columbia University Forum,* Spring, 1965, p. 10.
63. S. L. A. Marshall, "The Hardening Process," Bangkok *World,* May 28, 1962.
64. David Halberstam, *The Making of a Quagmire,* pp. 154–55.
65. Bill Mauldin, Chicago *Sun-Times,* February 9, 1965.
66. Jack Langguth, New York *Times,* August 12, 1965, p. 1; *Time,* August 20, 1965, p. 24.
67. Neil Sheehan, New York *Times,* August 23, 1965, p. 1.
68. Charles Mohr, New York *Times,* August 19, 1965, p. 1; August 15, 1965, p. 1.
69. New York *Times,* December 8, 1965, p. 15.
70. New York *Times,* September 16, 1966, p. 2.
71. Neil Sheehan, New York *Times,* February 24, 1966, p. 1.
72. Bernard Fall, New York *Times Magazine,* March 6, 1966, p. 21.
73. Hanson W. Baldwin, "The Cost of Vietnam," New York *Times,* August 6, 1965, p. 2; see also New York *Times,* March 23, 1966, p. 13; figures on U.S. aid from unclassified fourteen-page State Department mimeographed document on Viet-Nam; the 1967 budget, New York *Times,* January 25, 1966, p. 18; "Doubled Aid to Saigon," New York *Times,* January 13, 1966, p. 1; "Increase in South Korean Troops," New York *Times,* March 1, 1966, p. 7.
74. State Department document on Viet-Nam. See also R. W. Apple, Jr., New York *Times,* January 24, 1966, p. L37.
75. *Newsweek,* August 23, 1965, p. 30; *Time,* August 6, 1965, pp. 29–30; New York *Times,* January 19, 1965, p. G52.
76. New York *Times,* quoting C.B.S., August 4, 1965, p. 2.
77. "Nitze Supports Burning of Huts," AP, Washington, in New York *Times,* August 15, 1965, p. 2.
78. Charles Mohr, New York *Times,* August 9, 1965, p. 1.
79. Jack Raymond, New York *Times,* August 7, 1965, p. 3.
80. Max Frankel, New York *Times,* August 22, 1965, p. 3; James Reston, New York *Times Magazine,* September 12, 1965, p. 116.
81. "War Censorship Discussed by U.S.," New York *Times,* August 16, 1965, p. 3.
82. Edwin Q. White, *Editor & Publisher,* July 24, 1965, p. 9.
83. Jean Greenwald, *Editor & Publisher,* July 24, 1965, p. 36.
84. "Strange War Perplexes Hal Boyle," *Editor & Publisher,* July 24, 1965, p. 40.

85. *Time*, July 23, 1965, p. 16; Max Frankel, New York *Times*, October 11, 1964, p. E6.
86. Jack Raymond, "When GI Joe Meets Ol' Charlie," New York *Times Magazine*, July 25, 1965, p. 4.
87. *Time*, August 6, 1965, p. 28.
88. "Top Aides Tell U.S. Truce Stand," New York *Times*, August 24, 1965, p. 1. Reports of peace demonstration of November 27, 1965, Communist reaction, and Seymour Topping commentary in New York *Times*, November 28, 1965, p. 1. Copyright 1965 by the New York Times Company. Reprinted by permission. Sketch of Le Duan, *Newsweek*, January 31, 1966, p. 34.

5. THE VIET-NAM CORRESPONDENTS

89. Received by the author from a correspondent.
90. Private correspondence.
91. Ben Bassett, address before New York State Society of Newspaper Editors, Cooperstown, N.Y., August 9, 1965. Quoted in *The Bulletin*, Gannet Newspapers, August 13, 1965.
92. Letter, January 7, 1965.
93. Comments of correspondents and questionnaires were recived on a confidential basis.
94. Sol Sanders, "Can the U.S. Win in Vietnam?," *U.S. News & World Report*, January 11, 1965, pp. 44–52.
95. *Time*, January 8, 1965, p. 38.
96. *Time*, May 7, 1965, pp. 62–63.
97. New York *Times*, November 26, 1965, p. 2.
98. Ward Just, Washington *Post*, February 23, 1966, p. 1.
99. Martin Gershen, *Columbia Journalism Review*, Winter, 1966, p. 62.
100. Jack Raymond, "It's A Dirty War for Correspondents, Too," New York *Times Magazine*, February 13, 1966, p. 32.
101. Tom Wicker, New York *Times*, February 14, 1966, p. 4.
102. Senator Thomas J. Dodd, speech in U.S. Senate, June 10, 1965, and letter to Senator Mike Mansfield dated same day; Mansfield's speech in the Senate, also June 10, 1965. See reply in UPI *Report*, July 1, 1965, by Roger Tatarian.
103. Newsom, quoted in UPI *Report*, October 14, 1965.
104. Sevareid article in *Look*, November 15, 1965. McCloskey confirmation in New York *Times*, November 16, 1965, p. 1; see comment in New York *Times* by Arthur Krock, November 18, 1965, and James Reston, November 21, 1965.
105. Richard Dudman, St. Louis *Post-Dispatch*, December 17, 1965, p. 1; AP Log, December 15–21, 1965; *Newsweek*, January 3, 1966, p. 53.
106. *Editor & Publisher*, February 5, 1966, p. 14.
107. Beverly Deepe, *Overseas Press Bulletin*, Vol. XXI, No. 9 (March 5, 1966); see also *Newsweek*, August 30, 1965, p. 32; AP Log, June 10–16, July 7–13, September 29–October 5, and October 6–12, 1965.
108. Statistics on correspondents from the Department of Defense, document dated January 14, 1966.
109. James Reston, New York *Times*, August 26, 1965. For other views, see Jimmy

Breslin, quoted in *Newsweek,* September 6, 1965, pp. 49–50; and Walter Lippmann, New York *Herald Tribune,* September 9, 1965, p. 18.

VII. NEW TIMES IN SOUTH ASIA

1. THE END OF AN ERA

1. The incident occurred at Palam Airport, November 6, 1963. The author obtained details from trustworthy sources.
2. Norman Isaacs, "The Press of India," *The American Editor,* II, No. 3 (October, 1958), 7.
3. "Guidance for the Press in the Present Emergency," booklet issued under the authority of the Government of India, Ministry of Information and Broadcasting, 1963, p. 3.
4. A. M. Rosenthal, "Awakening for India—And the Non-Aligned," New York *Times Magazine,* November 18, 1962, p. 122.
5. New York *Times,* May 28, 1964, p. 1. See also Rosenthal, "His Life Was India's," *ibid.,* p. 17.
6. Estimate by Eric da Costa, Indian Institute of Public Opinion.
7. Study by Hadley Cantril.
8. Reported by Dr. Lakshman Rao, mass communications specialist who studied at the University of Minnesota, interviewed August 12, 1964, in New Delhi.
9. J. Anthony Lukas, New York *Times,* August 1, 1965, p. 9. See also New York *Times,* February 17, 1965, p. 6; Washington *Post,* February 17, 1965, p. A-11.
10. Sources for material on India's economy, military statistics, and associated data include *India, A Reference Annual, 1964,* compiled by the Research and Reference Division, Ministry for Information and Broadcasting, Government of India; mimeographed material made available by the American embassy, New Delhi; *Far Eastern Economic Review,* annual survey of America and Asia, Vol. XLV, No. 2 (July 9, 1964); "Review of Economic Development in Asia," New York *Times,* January 18, 1965, p. C37; "India Without Nehru," *Time,* August 13, 1965, pp. 18–27; Selig Harrison, "Troubled India and Her Neighbors," *Foreign Affairs,* XLIII, No. 2 (January, 1965), 312–330; Marquis Childs, St. Louis *Post-Dispatch,* November 21, 27, 28, December 5, 12, 1964; Sharokh Sabavala, *Christian Science Monitor,* April 28, 29, June 1, July 2, October 16, 27, 1964; Harrison, Washington *Post,* November 9, 23, December 15, 29, 1963; and *Statistical Abstract of the United States, 1965,* statistics on foreign aid and foreign trade. For much of the diplomatic background, the author is indebted to Alexander de Conde, *A History of American Foreign Policy* (New York: Scribner's, 1963). Some material was also developed from interviews with various correspondents and government officials. While every effort was made to check the accuracy of statistical data, it should be stressed that almost any figures that relate to India are subject to variation, depending on the sources.
11. *U.S. News & World Report,* January 11, 1965, p. 51.
12. "Troubled India and Her Neighbors," *Foreign Affairs,* XLIII, No. 2 (January, 1965), 314.

13. J. Anthony Lukas, New York *Times,* August 22, 1965, p. 4.
14. Max Frankel, New York *Times,* August 30, 1965, p. 1.
15. For news of the Tashkent agreement, Shastri's death, Mrs. Nehru's accession, and her visit to Washington, see the New York *Times* for January 11, 12, 20, 21, and March 27–April 1, 1966; Chinese leaders' visit to Pakistan, in New York *Times,* March 27, 1966, p. 2.

2. ON UNDERSTANDING INDIA

16. Richmond Croom Beatty, *Bayard Taylor,* pp. 135–36.
17. Prem Bhatia, *Indian Express,* August 12, 1964, p. 6.
18. Based on a conversation with Prime Minister Shastri in his office, August 27, 1964.
19. Indira Gandhi interview, August 26, 1964, in New Delhi.
20. Jack Gould, New York *Times,* March 4, 1966, p. 67.
21. "India Party Chief Soaring to Fame," New York *Times,* August 1, 1965, p. 11; *Time,* August 13, 1965, p. 26; "Political Python of India," New York *Times Magazine,* February 20, 1966, p. 27; also based on my own interview with K. Kamaraj in New Delhi, August 27, 1964.
22. Interview with Swaran Singh in New Delhi, August 17, 1964; interviews with L. R. Nair there, August 16, 1964.
23. AP report, New York *Times,* January 2, 1966, p. 17.
24. Frank Moraes, *India Today* (New York: Macmillan, 1960), p. 6.

3. AMERICANS IN INDIA

25. Three years later, the resident American correspondents in New Delhi were Conrad Fink, AP; John Barton, UPI; James Keat, Baltimore *Sun;* Paul Hurmuses, Chicago *Daily News;* Joseph Lelyreld, New York *Times;* Warren Unna, Washington *Post;* and Marvin Zim, Time-Life. It was still a very small group.
26. John Kenneth Galbraith, *Nieman Reports,* March, 1964, p. 16.
27. Based on interviews with correspondents. See also Louis Rukeyser, "Beyond the Indus," Baltimore *Sun,* June 20, 1963.
28. Arthur Goodfriend, *The Twisted Image* (New York: St. Martin's Press, 1963), pp. 217–18.
29. "The American Ambassador," a study submitted by the Subcommittee on National Security Staffing and Operations to the Senate Committee on Government Operations, 88th Cong., 2d Sess. (Washington: Government Printing Office, 1964), p. 1–2. Released June 22, 1964.
30. New York *Herald Tribune,* July 30, 1964, p. 15.
31. "Facets of Hunger," *Christian Science Monitor,* August 18, 1964.
32. Felix Belair, Jr., New York *Times,* August 19, 1964, p. 1.
33. Chester Bowles, New York *Times,* September 6, 1964, p. 7. Copyright 1964 by the New York Times Company. Reprinted by permission.
34. *Time,* February 25, 1966, p. 33.
35. Chester Bowles, *The New Dimensions of Peace* (New York: Harper & Bros., 1955), pp. 364–65; 367–68.

36. These private polls were circulated among correspondents in New Delhi in 1964.

37. "Flow of U.S. News to India, a Summary" (USIA, Research and Reference Service, R–55–64), May 7, 1964.

4. INDIA'S NEIGHBORS

38. New York *Times,* March 26, 1965, p. 3.

39. New York *Times,* February 19, 1965, p. 12; March 10, 1965, p. 5.

40. New York *Times,* January 18, 1965, p. C54.

41. New York *Times,* January 3, 1965, p. 1, and November 8, 1964, p. 124.

42. Quoted by Marquis Childs, St. Louis *Post-Dispatch,* December 5, 1964.

43. *Ibid.*

44. *Ibid.,* December 12, 1964.

45. *World Communications, 1964,* pp. 244–45. Also, Henry Bradsher, AP summary, in Bangkok *Post,* November 2, 1963.

46. Frank Moraes, "Alternatives in Kashmir," *Indian Express,* July 13, 1964.

47. *Ibid.*

48. J. Anthony Lukas, New York *Times,* August 22, 1965, p. 4.

49. Abdullah interview, August 22, 1964, in New Delhi; visit to Kashmir, on which these observations are based, came thereafter; Kashmir group's arrest, New York *Times,* November 7, 1965, p. 6.

50. *Newsweek,* March 29, 1965, p. 44. Copyright 1965 by Newsweek, Inc. Reprinted by permission.

51. *Newsweek,* April 5, 1965, p. 44. Copyright 1965 by Newsweek, Inc. Reprinted by permission.

52. Thomas F. Brady, New York *Times,* March 29, 1964, p. 10.

53. Kenneth F. Olson, *Editor & Publisher,* May 16, 1959, pp. 66–68.

54. A. G. T. Vittachi, "Asia Faces a Newspaper Revolution," *Nieman Reports,* September, 1963, p. 26.

55. AP dispatch from New Delhi, January 7, headed: "Indians Now Approve of Polaris Off Asia"; New York *Times,* January 8, 1965.

56. N. J. Nanporia, *Times* of India, December 14, 1964.

57. M. R. Masani, lecture before Indian Council of World Affairs, December 17, 1964, published in *India Quarterly,* XXI, No. 1 (January–March, 1965), 27.

58. R. K. Nehru, lecture before Indian Council of World Affairs, December 8, 1964, published in *India Quarterly,* XXI, No. 1 (January–March, 1965), 14.

59. New York *Times,* October 20, 1965, p. 1; see also Ralph L. Powell, "China's Bomb—Exploitation and Reactions," *Foreign Affairs,* XLIII, No. 4 (July, 1965), 623.

5. THE PRESS: FREE AND NOT SO FREE

60. Henry M. Collins, *From Pigeon Post to Wireless* (London: Hodder & Stoughton, 1925), pp. 18–20, 57–92 *passim.*

61. J. Alex Morris, pp. 162–64.

62. Preston Grover interviewed in New Delhi, August 17, 1964.

63. M. S. Venkataramani and B. K. Shrivastava, "The U.S. and the 'Quit India' Demand," *India Quarterly*, XX, No. 2 (April–June, 1964), 101–34.
64. Harold Isaacs, *Scratches on Our Minds*, p. 317.
65. Based on conversations with a number of Indians in 1963 and 1964.
66. Norman Isaacs, *The American Editor*, October, 1958, pp. 8–11 *passim*.
67. "Flow of U.S. News to India."
68. Eric da Costa interviewed in New Delhi, August 16, 1964.
69. Prem Bhatia, *Indian Express*, August 15, 1964, p. 1.
70. Registrar of Newspapers for India, *Annual Report, 1964*, issued by Ministry of Information and Broadcasting, Government of India, Part I, p. 59.
71. *Ibid.*, pp. 58–90.
72. New York *Times*, November 2, 1957.
73. There is a long record on this case. Reference is made to these partial sources: New York *Times*, September 26, 1955; Indian Government Public Information Bureau announcement dated November 28, 1955; *Time*, October 10, 1955; New York *Times*, June 2, 1959; *Indian Express*, May 5, 6, 21, 1964; *Financial Express* of India, July 3 and August 3, 1964.
74. M. R. Masani, speech in the Lok Sabha, August 19, 1963, reprinted in a booklet entitled, "Time for a Change."
75. Data on basic wage from S. Natarajan, *History of the Press in India* (New York: Asia Publishing House, 1962), p. 314; totals of journalists and other figures from Registrar of Newspapers for India, *Annual Report, 1964*, Part I, pp. 128–29.
76. Natarajan, *op. cit.*, pp. 314–15.
77. *Ibid.*, pp. 318–19.

6. FOREIGN CORRESPONDENTS IN INDIA

78. Indira Gandhi reception at the Claridge, New Delhi, August 31, 1964.
79. Chanchal Sarkar, *Nieman Reports,* June, 1964, p. 18. This view was elaborated on in subsequent conversations in New Delhi.
80. Moraes, *Indian Express*, August 3, 1964, p. 4.
81. Based on talks with correspondents. See also Louis Rukeyser, "Beyond the Indus," Baltimore *Sun*, April 26, 1964.
82. Selig S. Harrison, Washington *Post*, November 23, 1963.

7. THE TRUTH IN SOUTH ASIA

83. Erik Barnouw and S. Krishnaswamy, *Indian Film* (New York: Columbia University Press, 1963), p. 271.
84. Moraes, *India Today*, p. 214.

VIII. CONFRONTATION: AMERICA AND ASIA

I. PORTENTS AND PROSPECTS

1. Beatty, *Bayard Taylor*, pp. 139–40.
2. *Ibid.*, p. 360.

3. James Reston, New York *Times,* September 12, 1965, p. 43.
4. *Newsweek,* September 27, 1965, p. 19, quoted Bernard Fall. James Reston, New York *Times,* September 1, 1965, p. 36, reported Premier Ky as saying the "Communists were closer to the people's yearnings for social justice and an independent national life than his own government."
5. C. A. Harwell, "Grave Lack of U.S. Reporters," ASNE *Bulletin,* July 1, 1959, p. 1.
6. Barry Zorthian, letter to author, September 5, 1965, from Saigon.

2. PROBLEMS OF GOVERNMENT

7. Press Release ECAFE/88, May 17, 1961, U.N. Press Services, Office of Public Information.
8. New York *Times,* April 8, 1965, for text of Johnson speech; New York *Times,* April 9, 1965, p. 13, for U.N. reaction.
9. *Editor & Publisher,* August 28, 1965, pp. 9, 52. It should be pointed out that a Roper survey put TV news ahead by 58 per cent, giving it as their first source of news.
10. Interview by author with Secretary of State Rusk at the Department of State, February 18, 1965, authorized for publication.

Sections 3 and 4 are documented in Appendixes.

5. FACING THE FUTURE

11. Alexis de Tocqueville, *Democracy in America* (2 vols.; New York: Random House, 1954), II, 119.
12. *Time,* February 26, 1965, p. 52; *Newsweek,* November 29, 1965, p. 56.
13. Bernard Kalb, "Asia: A Measure and a Memoir," *Saturday Review,* September 18, 1965, p. 36.
14. *Editor & Publisher,* July 17, 1965, p. 6.
15. A. G. T. Vittachi, *Nieman Reports,* September, 1963, p. 26.
16. Macario T. Vicencio, *Atlas,* April, 1964, p. 228.
17. *North American Review,* May, 1904.
18. Quoted in Jawaharlal Nehru, *Glimpses of World History* (New York: John Day, 1942), p. 953.

Appendix I

Between June 3 and September 3, 1964, the following correspondents for American news organizations in Asia completed detailed questionnaires for a survey that I conducted. Most of them, as well as a number of correspondents for both American and non-American news organizations, were interviewed in depth. All of them were assured that their answers and observations were confidential; wherever any disclosure has been made either of interview or questionnaire material with acknowledgment of the source, it has been done with the knowledge and permission of the correspondent. In the table beginning on the following page, the numbers beside the names of the correspondents are assigned at random and serve merely to facilitate the reading of the table.

BASE OF OPERATIONS: TOKYO

Name	Age	Na- tionality	Organization	Education	Language (In Addition to English)	Years in Post	Years Over- seas	Years of News- paper Ex- peri- ence	Post One (and Two) Years Later
1. Samuel Jameson	27	U.S.	Chicago *Tribune*	Northwestern, B.S, M.S.	Japanese	1	1	5	Same
2. A. M. Adams	39	U.S.	San Francisco *Chronicle*	Missouri, A.B, B.J.; North Carolina, M.S.	Spanish	3	3	10	Same
3. James MacC. Truitt	43	U.S.	*Newsweek* (chief)	Virginia, A.B.	None	¼	¼	20	Same
4. Bernard Krisher	32	U.S.	*Newsweek*	Queens (N.Y.C.), A.B.; Ford Fellow, Columbia	French, German, Japanese	1½	1½	9	Same
5. Richard Halloran	34	U.S.	*Business Week* (chief)	Dartmouth, A.B.; Michigan, M.A.; Ford Fellow, Columbia	French, Japanese	2½	2½	7	Washington *Post*—Tokyo
6. Robert P. Martin	50	U.S.	*U.S. News & World Report* (chief)	Washington, A.B.; Columbia, M.S; Nieman Fellow	Chinese, French	10	25	28	Washington assignment

	Age	Nationality	Organization	College	Languages				Washington assignment
7. Lea Martin	48	U.S.	U.S. News & World Report	Washington, A.B.	Japanese, Danish	10	19	28	
8. Lee Griggs	36	U.S.	Time (chief)	Yale, A.B.	French	2	5	12	Beirut
9. Peter Kalischer	49	U.S.	C.B.S. (chief)	No college	French	7	7	19	Same (Paris)
10. John Rich	46	U.S.	N.B.C. (chief)	Bowdoin, A.B.; Fellow, Council on Foreign Relations	Japanese, French	2	18	25	Same
11. Jack Fern	48	U.S.	N.B.C. (Producer)	Ohio, B.S.; Missouri, B.J.	German	1	5	25	Same (changed)
12. J. W. ("Buddy") Cohn	53	U.S.	Fairchild (chief)	Pennsylvania, A.B.	French	2	17	30	Same
13. Keyes Beech	50	U.S.	Chicago Dailys News (chief)	Nieman Fellow	None	17	17	35	Same
14. Emerson Chapin	43	U.S.	New York Times	Rochester, A.B.; Columbia, M.S.	Japanese	1	3	12	Same (New York)
15. Robert Morse	42	U.S.	Life	Oregon State, A.B.; Northwestern, M.S.	French, Russian	1	9	16	Hong Kong
16. Norman Sklarewitz	40	U.S.	Wall Street Journal	Indiana, A.B.	French	2	8	14	Same
17. Donald Neff	33	U.S.	Los Angeles Times	New York University	None	½	½	9	Changed (changed)
18. Jun Ofusa	56	Japanese	New York Times	Attended college	Japanese	34	34	34	Same
19. John Flager	42	U.S.	New Yorker	Michigan, A.B.	Japanese	1	1	18	New York
20. Robert Eunson	51	U.S.	AP (Regional chief)	Arizona State, A.B.	Japanese	8	15	26	New York

473

Name	Age	Nationality	Organization	Education	Language (In Addition to English)	Years in Post	Years Overseas	Years of Newspaper Experience	Post One (and Two) Years Later
21. Robert Liu	26	U.S.	AP	City College of San Francisco, A.B.	Russian, Chinese	½	½	4	Same (changed)
22. Forrest Edwards	49	U.S.	AP (Bureau chief)	Minnesota, A.B.	None	5	13	28	Hong Kong
23. Ken Ishii	39	Japanese	AP	California, A.B.	Japanese	5	—	17	Same
24. John Roderick	49	U.S.	AP	Colby, A.B.	French, Chinese, Japanese	5	19	29	Same
25. John Randolph	45	U.S.	Seattle *Times* (ex-AP chief)	No college	French, Japanese	14	14	27	Same
26. Tak Ishii	55	Japanese	AP	Attended college	Japanese	18	—	28	Same
27. G. F. Simmel	34	U.S.	UPI	Princeton, A.B.	German, French	2	7	13	Same
28. Earnest Hoberecht	46	U.S.	UPI (vice president for Asia)	Oklahoma, A.B.	Spanish	19	22	30	Same (resigned)
29. Don Brydon	42	U.S.	UPI (bureau chief)	Missouri, B.J.	Spanish	2	2	17	Texas (In charge in North Asia)

	Age	Nat.	Organization	Education	Languages				Status
30. Kim Willenson	27	U.S.	UPI	Wisconsin, B.S.; Columbia, M.S.; Pulitzer Fellow	French	1	1	5	Same
31. Al Kaff	44	U.S.	UPI	Colorado, A.B.	None	½	½	12	Same
32. Dan Southerland	27	U.S.	UPI	North Carolina, A.B.; Harvard, M.A.; Columbia, M.S.	Russian, Japanese, Chinese	1	1	1	Same (Saigon)
33. Robert Crabbe	39	U.S.	UPI	San Jose, A.B.	Japanese	3	3	14	Same
34. Glenn Troelstrup	34	U.S.	U.S. News & World Report	Missouri, B.J.	Japanese, German	7	10	14	Same
BASE OF OPERATIONS: SEOUL									
35. Sam Kim	37	Korean	UPI	Seoul National University	Korean, Japanese	10	—	12	New York Times
36. K. C. Cho	36	Korean	New York Times	Seoul National University	Korean, Japanese	3	—	14	Deceased
37. C. S. Chin	35	Korean	AP	Seoul National University	Korean, Japanese	6	—	11	Same (No report)
BASE OF OPERATIONS: HONG KONG									
38. Takashi Oka	39	U.S.	Christian Science Monitor	Principia, A.B.; Harvard, M.A.	Japanese, Chinese, French	5	5	10	Saigon
39. Guy Searls	40	U.S.	Radio free lance (ex-C.B.S.)	Washington, A.B.; C.B.S. Fellow, Columbia	Chinese	12	12	22	Same

Name	Age	Nationality	Organization	Education	Language (In Addition to English)	Years in Post	Years Overseas	Years of Newspaper Experience	Post One (and Two) Years Later
40. Stanley Rich	40	U.S.	A.B.C.	Harvard, A.B.; Columbia, M.S.	French	6	20	20	Same
41. Sidney Liu	44	Chinese	Newsweek	Chiao Tung University, Shanghai; API seminar	Chinese	1	21	21	Same
42. Robert K. MacCabe	34	U.S.	Newsweek (chief)	Dartmouth, A.B.	French, German, Chinese	2	6	13	Same (New York)
43. Roy Essoyan	44	U.S.	AP (chief)	No college	Russian, Chinese	5	19	26	Cairo
44. Ed Neilan	32	U.S.	Copley News Service	California, A.B.	None	2	7	12	Same
45. Seymour Topping	42	U.S.	New York Times	Missouri, B.J.	German, Russian	7	17	18	Same (New York)
46. Jim Robinson	42	U.S.	N.B.C.	Washington State, A.B.	None	12	14	14	New York
47. David J. Roads	42	U.S.	Business Week	Denver, B.J.	Chinese	3	15	15	Same
48. Frank McCulloch	44	U.S.	Time (chief)	Nevada, A.B.	French, Spanish	½	½	25	Same

Name	Age	Nat.	Publication	College	Languages				Location
49. John Shaw	33	British	*Time*	Attended college	French, Italian	4	7	12	Same
50. Loren W. Fessler	41	U.S.	*Time*	Harvard, A.B.	Chinese	5	9	9	Same
51. Charles Smith	34	U.S.	UPI (chief)	Missouri, B.J.	Spanish	1	7	8	Same (London)
52. Robert Hewett	50	U.S.	Minneapolis *Star-Tribune*	Attended college	French	8	19	30	Same
53. Walter Friedenberg	35	U.S.	Scripps-Howard	Wake Forest, A.B.; Harvard, M.A.	German, Chinese	3	6	7	Roving assignment

BASE OF OPERATIONS: SAIGON

Name	Age	Nat.	Publication	College	Languages				Location
54. Charles P. Arnot	47	U.S.	A.B.C.	Attended college	German, Arabic	1	17	29	Same (Bangkok)
55. Beverly Deepe	29	U.S.	New York *Herald Tribune*	Nebraska, A.B.; Columbia, M.S.	French, Vietnamese	1	4	6	Same
56. Stan Karnow	39	U.S.	*Saturday Evening Post*	Harvard, A.B.; Nieman Fellow	French	5	14	14	Washington *Post*
57. Ray Herndon	27	U.S.	UPI	Attended college	French	1	2	2	Same (Singapore)
58. Mike Malloy	28	U.S.	UPI (chief)	Attended college	French	1/4	5	9	Same (New York)
59. John Sharkey	34	U.S.	N.B.C.	Holy Cross, A.B.	French	2	6	6	Same
60. Jerry Rose	30	U.S.	*Saturday Evening Post*	Johns Hopkins, A.B.; Iowa, M.A.	French	3	3	3	Same (deceased)
61. Arnold Beichman	51	U.S.	New York *Herald Tribune* (special)	Columbia, A.B.	French	Roving			New York

Name	Age	Nationality	Organization	Education	Language (In Addition to English)	Years in Post	Years Overseas	Years of Newspaper Experience	Post One (and Two) Years Later
62. Peter Grose	29	U.S.	New York *Times*	Yale, A.B.; Oxford, M.A.	French, German	1	5	5	Moscow
63. David Horowitz	27	U.S.	N.B.C.	Bradley, A.B.; Northwestern, M.A.	Spanish	½	½	9	New York
64. Peter Arnett	29	N.Z.	AP	Attended college	French	2	6	12	Same
65. Malcolm Browne	33	U.S.	AP (chief)		Vietnamese	3	5	8	A.B.C., Saigon (New York)
66. François Sully	37	French	*Newsweek* (chief)	Nieman Fellow	French, Vietnamese	2	11	11	Same
67. Robert Shaplen	47	U.S.	*New Yorker*	Wisconsin, A.B.; Columbia, M.S.; Nieman Fellow	French, German	—	8	30	New York
68. Garrick Utley	24	U.S.	N.B.C.	Carleton, A.B.	German, Russian	1 mo.	1	1	Same
BASE OF OPERATIONS: MANILA									
69. Don Becker	30	U.S.	UPI (chief)	San Jose, A.B.	None	2	4	7	Same
70. Henry Hartzenbusch	41	U.S.	AP (chief)	German College, Tsingtao (China)	German, Chinese	3	17	20	Tokyo

478

	Age	Nationality	Organization	Education	Languages				
71. Carl H. Zimmerman	32	U.S.	AP	Lehigh, A.B.; Michigan, M.A.	German	4	4	10	Same
72. Maximo Soliven	34	Philippine	New York *Times*	Ateneo, Manila, A.B.; Fordham, M.F.A.	Tagalog, Spanish	3	—	13	Same
73. Albert Ravenholt	44	U.S.	Chicago *Daily News*	Attended college	Chinese, Danish	15	22	22	Same
BASE OF OPERATIONS: KUALA LUMPUR									
74. John Wheeler	33	U.S.	AP	Missouri, A.B.	French	2	2	7	Saigon
75. Tony Escoda	34	Philippine	AP	Yale, A.B.; Columbia, M.S.; Pulitzer Fellow	Tagalog, Spanish	4	4	11	Same
76. Pat Killen	35	U.S.	UPI (chief)	Colorado College, A.B.; U.C.L.A., M.S.	None	2	6	8	Same (changed)
77. Seth S. King	44	U.S.	New York *Times*	Oklahoma, A.B.	French	1	7	7	Same (New York)
BASE OF OPERATIONS: VIENTIANE									
78. Martin Stewart Fox	25	Australian	UPI	Queensland, Australia	None	1	1	1	Saigon
BASE OF OPERATIONS: DJAKARTA									
79. Roberta Roth (Mrs. Tony Yared)	23	U.S.	UPI (chief)	Barnard, A.B.	Chinese, Indonesian	1	1	2	Same (changed)

Name	Age	Nationality	Organization	Education	Language (In Addition to English)	Years in Post	Years Overseas	Years of Newspaper Experience	Post One (and Two) Years Later
80. Tony Yared	39	Lebanese	AP (chief)	Attended college	French, Arabic	1 mo.	4	15	Same (changed)

BASE OF OPERATIONS: NEW DELHI*

Name	Age	Nationality	Organization	Education	Language (In Addition to English)	Years in Post	Years Overseas	Years of Newspaper Experience	Post One (and Two) Years Later
81. Sharokh Sabavala	46	Indian	*Christian Science Monitor*	Oxford, B.A.	Hindi, French	7	—	19	Same
82. Conrad Fink	31	U.S.	AP (chief)	Wisconsin, B.J.	Japanese	7 mos.	3	8	Same
83. Dan Coggin	29	U.S.	AP	Huntingdon, A.B.	Japanese	6 wks.	6 wks.	10	Same (left AP, changed)
84. Selig S. Harrison	37	U.S.	Washington *Post*	Harvard, A.B.	None	19 mos.	5	16	Bangkok
85. John Barton	32	U.S.	UPI (chief)	Michigan State, A.B.	French	1 mo.	3	5	Same
86. Louis Rukeyser	31	U.S.	Baltimore *Sun*	Princeton, A.B.	French	1½	6	10	Paris
87. Thomas Brady	48	U.S.	New York *Times*	U.C.L.A., A.B.	French	22 mos.	12	26	Beirut
88. Louis Kraar	30	U.S.	*Time*	North Carolina, A.B.	Spanish	1	1	9	Changed
89. Richard Critchfield	33	U.S.	Washington *Star*	Washington, A.B.; Columbia, M.S.	Urdu, Hindi	2	2	5	Same (changed)

480

90. Sol Sanders	38	U.S.	U.S. News & World Report	Missouri, B.J.	Japanese, German	3	11	18	Bangkok
91. R. Ramasujam	49	Indian	Newsweek	Madras, A.B.	Tamil, Telegu	5	—	22	Same

481

* Some of those listed are also responsible for Pakistan.

SUMMARY

MEDIA REPRESENTATION IN SURVEY

Post	Newspapers	Radio-TV	Magazines	Wire Services
Tokyo	8	3	10	13
Seoul	1			2
Hong Kong	5	3	6	2
Saigon	3	4	4	4
Manila	2			3
Kuala Lumpur, Djakarta, Vientiane	1			6
New Delhi, Karachi	5		3	3
	25	10	23	33

This includes four regional chiefs and numerous bureau chiefs, some of whom run a one-man bureau or a bureau with one local in addition to themselves.

SERVICE AND DURATION OF ASSIGNMENTS

Of the 91 correspondents, 38 were either roving correspondents or locals permanently assigned to a particular place. The remaining 53 had served in their posts up to August, 1964; the following tabulation shows the distribution in detail:

Less than 1 year	11	3–4 years	6
1–2 years	17	4 years	1
2–3 years	16	5 years	2

Except for 9 correspondents who are either locals in fixed positions, stringers, or substitutes for permanent people who were out due to illness, the correspondents in the survey had the following periods of service overseas, for an over-all average of 7 years and 10 months:

Less than 1 year	6	15–19 years	13
1–4 years	26	20–24 years	4
5–9 years	22	25 years or more	1
10–14 years	10		

For 90 correspondents in the survey, this is the record of total years of service as a journalist, averaging almost 15 years:

1–4 years	7	15–19 years	11
5–9 years	22	20–24 years	7
10–14 years	24	25 years or more	19

In October, 1965, a little more than a year after the completion of the survey, a check showed the following shifts to other parts of the world:

Post	Total	Shifted	Post	Total	Shifted
Tokyo	34	10(17)	Manila	5	1
Seoul	3	1*	Kuala Lumpur	4	1(3)
Hong Kong†	16	4(7)	Laos	1	1
Saigon†	15	6(10)*	Djakarta	2	0(2)
			New Delhi†	11	5(7)
			Total	91	29(49)

* One correspondent died.
† Enormous influx of temporary correspondents.

Appendix II

Interviews with the following persons, in addition to American correspondents, greatly assisted the development of this study (titles or affiliations are those at time of interviews):

Officials of the U.S. Government: Secretary of State Dean Rusk, Assistant Secretary of State James Greenfield, Assistant Secretary of Defense Arthur Sylvester; Ambassadors Edwin O. Reischauer, Samuel Berger, William Stevenson, Jerrauld Wright, Maxwell D. Taylor, and Chester Bowles; Ministers Charles B. Fahs and Frank Galbraith; Public Affairs Officers Barry Zorthian, William Phipps, Paul Neilson, William Weathersby, and John H. Esterline; General William C. Westmoreland; Consul General E. E. Rice; and many of their principal assistants.

Officials of the governments of Asian nations: Mrs. Indira Gandhi, then Minister of Information and Broadcasting and now Prime Minister of India; the late Prime Minister of India, Lal Bahadur Shastri; Foreign Minister Sardar Swaran Singh of India; K. Kamaraj, President of the Congress Party of India; Foreign Ministers Mauro Mendez of the Philippines, Masayoshi Ohira of Japan, and Subandrio of Indonesia; Tun Razak, Deputy Prime Minister of Malaysia; Ambassador Salvador Lopez of the Philippines; and many of the members of their staffs. One of the most helpful was the President of the University of the Philippines, Carlos P. Romulo.

Asian journalists: Isamu Suzukawa, managing editor, *Asahi;* Minoru Omori, foreign editor, *Mainichi;* Minoru Okuhata, foreign editor, *Yomiuri;* Shintaro Fukushima, publisher, Japan *Times;* Kasushige Hirasawa, editor, Japan *Times;* Roy S. Otake, Kyodo News Agency; Susumu Ejiri, Nihon Shimbun Kyokai; Professor Yujiro Chiba; Shigeharu Matsumoto, now director of International House; Joaquin P. Roces, publisher, Manila *Times;* P. K. Macker, publisher, Philippines *Herald;* Eugenio Lopez, Jr., general manager, Manila *Chronicle;* Juan Mercado, director, Philippine Press Institute; Osmundo Santos, director, Philippine News Service; Aw Sian (Sally Aw), publisher, Hong Kong *Tiger Standard* and other papers; Dato Leslie

Hoffman, editor, *Straits Times,* Kuala Lumpur; P. K. Roy, general manager, *Times* of India; Joe D'Souza, business manager, *Times* of India; N. J. Nanporia, editor, *Times* of India; T. S. Krishnan, general manager, *Indian Express;* Frank Moraes, editor, *Indian Express;* D. R. Mankekar, managing editor, *Indian Express;* Shri Mulgaokar, editor, *Hindustan Times;* Pran Chopra, Delhi editor, *Statesman;* Krishnamachari Balaraman, associate editor, the *Hindu;* K. Subramaniam, Press Trust of India; Tarzie Vittachi, former Asian director, International Press Institute; Amitava Chowdhury, Asian director, International Press Institute; Chanchal Sarkar, director, Press Institute of India; L. R. Nair, Principal Information Officer, Government of India; G. K. Reddy, political editor, *Times* of India; Kuldip Nayar, manager, United News of India.

Reuters officials: Gerald Long, director; Doon Campbell, editor; Monhin Ali, diplomatic correspondent; David Chipp, Asian director; Jimmy Hahn, manager for Southeast Asia; Kevin Garry, manager for Japan; Peter and Adrienne Jackson, correspondents, New Delhi; Ian MacCrone, correspondent, Hong Kong; Bill Gasson, correspondent, Djakarta.

AFP officials: Fernand Moulier, editor; Pierre Leveque, chief of foreign services; Roger Pierard, chief, English-language services; Leon Prou, correspondent, Tokyo; Jean Louis Arnaud, correspondent, New Delhi; M. K. Menon, correspondent, Singapore; Yves Causse, correspondent, Hong Kong; G. Unny, correspondent, Djakarta.

Foreign correspondents: Neville Maxwell, London *Times,* New Delhi; Victor Anant, Manchester *Guardian,* New Delhi; Cyril Dunn, London *Observer,* New Delhi; Pran Sabarwal, Baltimore *Sun,* New Delhi; Hessell Tiltman, Tokyo; Richard Hughes, London *Sunday Times,* Hong Kong; Nestor Mata, columnist, Philippines (Manila) *Herald;* Vic Nyagam, *Straits Times* (Kuala Lumpur).

There were many others, including Sheik Mohammed Abdullah, the "Lion of Kashmir"; Eric da Costa, Director, Indian Institute of Public Opinion; Dr. Lakshman Rao, sociologist; Sydney Brooks, of the International Public Relations Co., Tokyo; Genzaburo Yoshino, Iwanami Publishing Co., Tokyo; James L. Stewart, Japan representative, Asia Foundation; Raymond V. Johnson, Manila representative, Asia Foundation; Bert Johnson, Ford Foundation, New Delhi; Minoo R. Masani and Morarji Desai, members of the Lok Sabha; and Nguyen Thai, a former Nieman Fellow, in Saigon.

Appendix III

The Flow of the News Between the United States and Asia

The basis for this compilation was a study of the news published in representative newspapers of the United States and some of the principal cities of Asia between June 15–21, July 13–19, and August 17–23, 1964, inclusive. These periods were selected well in advance, with knowledge that one of the two major parties in the United States would be holding a Presidential nominating convention during the July test week. With this exception, it was assumed that the summer, generally a time for tight newspapers in the United States, would tend to show more use of American news in the Asian press and less use of Asian news in the American press. These figures, therefore, should not be considered to be a reflection of average performance; in no sense can they be considered to be maximums. Moreover, although the fifteen-column Japanese-language press and some others with five column pages have been adjusted to American column sizes in the tables, it would be unwise to accept these as comparative figures. There are some slight but essential differences that would make comparisons misleading. Finally, no exact comparison can be made between the figures in this study and those used in the IPI's *Flow of the News* study of 1953 because different criteria were used. For example, in this study, the total news hole (everything except advertising) was not used as a measurement; instead, the top measurement was of total *live news* space, that is, the material in the main news section, excluding cartoons, columns, pictures, and comment. Instead of considering the average news hole of 295 columns for the New York *Times,* an average of about 80 columns a day—the *live news*—was used to calculate the percentage of foreign news against total live news. The same standard was used throughout. Necessarily, this called for a subjective judgment on what constitutes *live news*—and such judgments were exercised throughout with every effort being made to be impartial.

TABLE I

ASIAN NEWS IN SELECTED U.S. NEWSPAPERS

Newspaper	Live News for 3 Weeks, Total Number of Columns	Daily Average Live News, Number of Columns	Per Cent Foreign News	Per Cent Asian News	From Own Correspondents	Sources of Foreign News (In per cent)				
						AP	UPI	Reuters†	Other
New York Times	1,697	80.8	22	20	85	8	2.5	3	1.5
Los Angeles Times	1,307	62.2	15	35	47	34	9	1	9
Washington Post	1,219	58	12	25	31	18	18	13	20
Philadelphia Inquirer	944	45	8	26	2	27.4	14	2	54.6
St. Louis Post-Dispatch	833	40	9	34	8	43	12		37
Chicago Daily News*	673	37.2	10	25	55	32	12		1
Christian Science Monitor*	486	27	37	19	77	11		11	1

* No Sunday edition.

† While Reuters has many non-newspaper clients in North America, the actual number of Reuter newspapers at the end of 1966 was less than 35.

TABLE 2

News in Selected Japanese Newspapers

(A Japanese-language newspaper averages 15 columns, each 1.35 inches wide and 15.3 inches long. Measurements were first taken in column inches for the data that follows. This was then computed in terms of New York *Times*-size columns, measuring 1.687 inches wide by 21 inches long. For example, the *Mainichi Shimbun* morning edition had a live news space for the three-week test period of 13,983 column inches. This was multiplied by a factor of 0.0381 [1.35/1.687 divided by 21], resulting in 532.75 columns of New York *Times* size.)

Newspaper	Live News for 3 Weeks, Total Number of Columns	Daily Average Live News, Number of Columns	Per Cent Foreign News	Percentages of the Foreign News Report				
				U.S.	Asia	Europe	U.N. and Other	
Asahi Shimbun (A.M.)	453.2	21.6	26	37	26	30	7	
Asahi Shimbun (P.M.)	295.8	14	24	35	16	33.5	15.5	
Mainichi Shimbun (A.M.)	532.75	25.37	17	21	25	46	8	
Mainichi Shimbun (P.M.)	280.75	13.37	19	35	14	39	12	
Yomiuri Shimbun (A.M.)	507.34	24.16	11	19	34	39	8	
Yomiuri Shimbun (P.M.)	285	13.6	22	38	18	35	9	
Nihon Keizai Shimbun (A.M.)	336	16	14	30	31	31	8	
Nihon Keizai Shimbun (P.M.)	291	13.8	18	31	14	43	12	
Japan Times	434	20.7	46	34	32	25	9	

TABLE 3

SOURCES OF FOREIGN NEWS IN SELECTED JAPANESE NEWSPAPERS

(In per cent)

Newspaper	Own Correspondents	AP	UPI	Reuters	Kyodo	AFP	Other
Asahi Shimbun (A.M.)	60	11	3	4	0.4	4	17.6
Asahi Shimbun (P.M.)	64	10	4	10	4	4	4
Mainichi Shimbun (A.M.)	71	3	10	2	2	4	8
Mainichi Shimbun (P.M.)	70	6	10	4	2	7	1
Yomiuri Shimbun (A.M.)	65	18	6	3	2	1	5
Yomiuri Shimbun (P.M.)	52	22	4	4	6	8	4
Nihon Keizai Shimbun (A.M.)	59	12	8	5	5	3	8
Nihon Keizai Shimbun (P.M.)	43	13	13	13	11	2	5
Japan Times	6	43	40	8.1	2		0.9

TABLE 4

U.S. News in Selected Southeast Asia Newspapers

Newspaper	Live News for 3 Weeks, Total Number of Columns	Daily Average Live News, Number of Columns	Per Cent Foreign News	Per Cent U.S. News	Sources of Foreign News (In per cent)					
					From Own Correspondents	AP	UPI	Reuters	AFP	Other
Manila Times	744	35.4	17.2	32.4	23.2	64.4			7	5.4
Philippines Herald*	655	31	24.4	46	15	24	16			45
Manila Chronicle	798	37	22.5	40.8	9.6	65			21	4.4
Straits Times (KL)	891	42.4	23.2	22.2	18	11.4	11.4	30		29.2
Hong Kong Tiger Standard	667.5	31.8	44	20		31	31	19	4	15
South China Morning Post	599	28.5	38	13	5.9	17	17	29	9.5	21.6

* A 5-column paper—its space has been computed in terms of an 8-column paper the size of the Manila *Times*.

489

TABLE 5

U.S. News in Selected Indian Newspapers

Newspaper	Live News for 3 Weeks, Total Number of Columns	Daily Average Live News, Number of Columns	Per cent Foreign News	Per cent U.S. News	Sources of Foreign News (In per cent)						
					From Own Corre-spondents	AP	Reuters	AFP	PTI	UNI	Other
Indian Express	663	31.5	18	21	35.8		24.6	6	21.7		11.9
Hindustan Times	559	26.6	20	19	37	13	16	7.1	12	0.4	14.5
Statesman	528.5	25.5	22	18	35	14	23.5	4.5	10.8	0.6	11.6
Times	685	32.6	20	19	35	6	15	2.1	11	0.5	30.4
Ananda Bazar Patrika (Bengali)	392.6	18.7	10	7	18	7	25	3	17	0.5	29.5
Malayala Mamorama*	585	28	6.6	40			31.6	6.3	17		45.1

* Percentage of the foreign report applies to U.S. news only.

Index

COUNCIL ON FOREIGN RELATIONS

PUBLICATIONS

FOREIGN AFFAIRS (quarterly), edited by Hamilton Fish Armstrong.

THE UNITED STATES IN WORLD AFFAIRS (annual). Volumes for 1931, 1932 and 1933, by Walter Lippmann and William O. Scroggs; for 1934-1935, 1936, 1937, 1938, 1939 and 1940, by Whitney H. Shephardson and William O. Scroggs; for 1945-1947, 1947-1948 and 1948-1949, by John C. Campbell; for 1949, 1950, 1951, 1952, 1953 and 1954, by Richard P. Stebbins; for 1955, by Hollis W. Barber; for 1956, 1957, 1958, 1959, 1960, 1961, 1962 and 1963, by Richard P. Stebbins; for 1964, by Jules Davids; for 1965, by Richard P. Stebbins.

DOCUMENTS ON AMERICAN FOREIGN RELATIONS (annual). Volume for 1952 edited by Clarence W. Baier and Richard P. Stebbins; for 1953 and 1954, edited by Peter V. Curl; for 1955, 1956, 1957, 1958 and 1959, edited by Paul E. Zinner; for 1960, 1961, 1962 and 1963, edited by Richard P. Stebbins; for 1964, by Jules Davids; for 1965, by Richard P. Stebbins.

THE CONSCIENCE OF THE RICH NATIONS: The Development Assistance Committee and the Common Aid Effort, by Seymour Rubin (1966).

ATLANTIC AGRICULTURAL UNITY: Is it Possible?, by John O. Coppock (1966).

POLITICAL HANDBOOK AND ATLAS OF THE WORLD (annual), edited by Walter H. Mallory.

COMMUNIST CHINA'S ECONOMIC GROWTH AND FOREIGN TRADE, by Alexander Eckstein (1966).

TEST BAN AND DISARMAMENT: The Path of Negotiation, by Arthur H. Dean (1966).

THE AMERICAN PEOPLE AND CHINA, by A. T. Steele (1966).

POLICIES TOWARD CHINA: Views from Six Continents, by A. M. Halpern (1966).

INTERNATIONAL POLITICAL COMMUNICATION, by W. Phillips Davison (1965).

MONETARY REFORM FOR THE WORLD ECONOMY, by Robert V. Roosa (1965).

AFRICAN BATTLELINE: American Policy Choices in Southern Africa, by Waldemar A. Nielsen (1965).

NATO IN TRANSITION: The Future of the Atlantic Alliance, by Timothy W. Stanley (1965).

ALTERNATIVE TO PARTITION: For a Broader Conception of America's Role in Europe, by Zbigniew Brzezinski (1965).

THE TROUBLED PARTNERSHIP: A Re-Appraisal of the Atlantic Alliance, by Henry A. Kissinger (1965).

REMNANTS OF EMPIRE: The United Nations and the End of Colonialism, by David W. Wainhouse (1965).

THE EUROPEAN COMMUNITY AND AMERICAN TRADE: A Study in Atlantic Economics and Policy, by Randall Hinshaw (1964).

THE FOURTH DIMENSION OF FOREIGN POLICY: Educational and Cultural Affairs, by Philip H. Coombs (1964).

AMERICAN AGENCIES INTERESTED IN INTERNATIONAL AFFAIRS (Fifth Edition), compiled by Donald Wasson (1964).

JAPAN AND THE UNITED STATES IN WORLD TRADE, by Warren S. Hunsberger (1964) .

FOREIGN AFFAIRS BIBLIOGRAPHY, 1952-1962, by Henry L. Roberts (1964).

THE DOLLAR IN WORLD AFFAIRS: An Essay in International Financial Policy, by Henry G. Aubrey (1964).

ON DEALING WITH THE COMMUNIST WORLD, by George F. Kennan (1964).

FOREIGN AID AND FOREIGN POLICY, by Edward S. Mason (1964).

THE SCIENTIFIC REVOLUTION AND WORLD POLITICS, by Caryl P. Haskins (1964).

AFRICA: A Foreign Affairs Reader, edited by Philip W. Quigg (1964).

THE PHILIPPINES AND THE UNITED STATES: Problems of Partnership, by George E. Taylor (1964).

SOUTHEAST ASIA IN UNITED STATES POLICY, by Russell H. Fifield (1963).

UNESCO: ASSESSMENT AND PROMISE, by George N. Shuster (1963).

THE PEACEFUL ATOM IN FOREIGN POLICY, by Arnold Kramish (1963).

THE ARABS AND THE WORLD: Nasser's Arab Nationalist Policy, by Charles D. Cremeans (1963).

TOWARD AN ATLANTIC COMMUNITY, by Christian A. Herter (1963).

THE SOVIET UNION, 1922-1962: A Foreign Affairs Reader, edited by Philip E. Mosely (1963).

THE POLITICS OF FOREIGN AID: American Experience in Southeast Asia, by John D. Montgomery (1962).

SPEARHEADS OF DEMOCRACY: Labor in the Developing Countries, by George C. Lodge (1962).

LATIN AMERICA: Diplomacy and Reality, by Adolf A. Berle (1962).

THE ORGANIZATION OF AMERICAN STATES AND THE HEMISPHERE CRISIS, by John C. Dreier (1962).

THE UNITED NATIONS: Structure for Peace, by Ernest A. Gross (1962).

THE LONG POLAR WATCH: Canada and the Defense of North America, by Melvin Conant (1962).

ARMS AND POLITICS IN LATIN AMERICA (Revised Edition), by Edwin Lieuwen (1961).

THE FUTURE OF UNDERDEVELOPED COUNTRIES: Political Implications of Economic Development (Revised Edition), by Eugene Staley (1961).

SPAIN AND DEFENSE OF THE WEST: Ally and Liability, by Arthur P. Whitaker (1961).

SOCIAL CHANGE IN LATIN AMERICA TODAY: Its Implications for United States Policy, by Richard N. Adams, John P. Gillin, Allan R. Holmberg, Oscar Lewis, Richard W. Patch, and Charles W. Wagley (1961).

FOREIGN POLICY: THE NEXT PHASE: The 1960s (Revised Edition), by Thomas K. Finletter (1960).

DEFENSE OF THE MIDDLE EAST: Problems of American Policy (Revised Edition), by John C. Campbell (1960).

COMMUNIST CHINA AND ASIA: Challenge to American Policy, by A. Doak Barnett (1960).

FRANCE, TROUBLED ALLY: De Gaulle's Heritage and Prospects, by Edgar S. Furniss, Jr. (1960).

THE SCHUMAN PLAN: A Study in Economic Cooperation, 1950-1959, by William Diebold, Jr. (1959).

SOVIET ECONOMIC AID: The New Aid and Trade Policy in Underdeveloped Countries, by Joseph S. Berliner (1958).

RAW MATERIALS: A Study of American Policy, by Percy W. Bidwell (1958).

NATO AND THE FUTURE OF EUROPE, by Ben T. Moore (1958).

AFRICAN ECONOMIC DEVELOPMENT, by William Hance (1958).

INDIA AND AMERICA: A Study of Their Relations, by Phillips Talbot and S. L. Poplai (1958).

NUCLEAR WEAPONS AND FOREIGN POLICY, by Henry A. Kissinger (1957).

MOSCOW-PEKING AXIS: Strength and Strains, by Howard L. Boorman, Alexander Eckstein, Philip E. Mosely and Benjamin Schwartz (1957).

RUSSIA AND AMERICA: Dangers and Prospects, by Henry L. Roberts (1956).

DATE DUE

MAY 21 1968		
JAN 30 1974 JE 30 '74		
FE 8 '78		